Identity in Formation

THE WILDER HOUSE SERIES
IN POLITICS, HISTORY,
AND CULTURE

The Wilder House Series is published in association with the Wilder House Board of Editors and the University of Chicago.

A complete list of titles appears at the end of this book.

Identity in Formation

The Russian-Speaking Populations in the Near Abroad

DAVID D. LAITIN

Cornell University Press ITHACA AND LONDON

First published 1998 by Cornell University Press
First printing, Cornell Paperbacks, 1998

Printed in the United States of America

Library of Congress Cataloging-in-Publication Data

Laitin, David D.
Identity in formation : the Russian-speaking populations in the near abroad / David D. Laitin.
p. cm. — (The Wilder House series in politics, history, and culture)
Includes index.
ISBN 0-8014-3495-5 (Cornell University Press : cloth : alk. paper). — ISBN 0-8014-8495-2 (Cornell Paperbacks : pbl. : alk. paper)
1. Russian language—Political aspects—Former Soviet republics. 2. Nationalism—Former Soviet republics. 3. Former Soviet republics—Ethnic relations. I. Title. II. Series.
PG2074.73.L35 1998
491.7—dc21 97-48670

Cornell University Press strives to use environmentally responsible suppliers and materials to the fullest extent possible in the publishing of its books. Such materials include vegetable-based, low-VOC inks and acid-free papers that are also either recycled, totally chlorine-free, or partly composed of nonwood fibers.

Cloth printing 10 9 8 7 6 5 4 3 2 1

Paperback printing 10 9 8 7 6 5 4 3 2 1

To the memory of my maternal grandmother,
Anna Ruback Blumenkranz

Born in Kremenchug, downstream on the Dnieper from Kiev, she aspired to become Russian. (She told me so, though I never heard her speak a word of Russian.) About her Jewish identity she could only say (in Yiddish), "Feh!" which I glossed as "Yuck!" In fear of pogroms, her father took her out of gymnasium and brought his family to the United States. There she worked in a sweatshop, married, and taught herself to read English, yet still dreamed of Russia and her childhood aspiration. But her daughters were overwhelmed by the need to conform to the local scene, and they humiliated her into becoming an American.

Whatever insight there is in this volume on the pains and payoffs to assimilation I owe to my Grandma Anna.

Contents

Preface

This book provides a description of the nationality question involving the Russian-speaking populations living in four of the republics of the former Soviet Union: Kazakhstan, Estonia, Latvia, and Ukraine. With the collapse of the Soviet Union, effective sovereignty fell into the hands of the titular nationalities—that is, the nationality groups after which the republics were named. As a consequence, Russian-speakers in all fourteen non-Russian Union republics experienced a cataclysm that has but few analogies; perhaps the Palestinians after the recognition of Israel's statehood; perhaps the *pieds noirs* after Algerian independence; perhaps the English settlers after the transformation of Rhodesia into Zimbabwe. Things fell apart for Russian-speakers in these republics because their center did not hold.

The Russian-speakers in the post-Soviet republics are facing a radical crisis of identity. Daily they face a set of questions about who they are and what they may become. Are they a people in diaspora, even if it was not they but their country that moved? Would they "return" to a homeland many of them had never seen? Would they join forces to fight politically for Russian rights in these republics, or even militarily for the right to reunite with the Russian Federation? Would they become loyal citizens of the new republics but maintain a Russian identity? If they remained as loyal citizens, would ethnic conflict between them and the titulars become a permanent feature of social life? Would a new identity form, not quite Russian, but not titular either? Would these Russians move along a path that leads, for their children if not for them, to assimilation with the titular nationality? This book outlines early trends toward resolution of these questions.

Exploring these questions helps me address two more general questions concerning all nation-building projects. First, what will be the relationship of nation to state in the republics of the former Soviet Union? Second, to the degree that national heterogeneity persists, what are the prospects for peace between the nationalities, and how might it break down?

The post-Soviet republics have been independent states for a very short time. It would be the height of folly to make predictions about their future on the basis of early trends. Present outcomes are too unstable. It is enough, at this stage, to give a comprehensive portrait of the early years of independence and of the choices that Russian-speakers have made in the wake of the cataclysm they faced. This is why I claim to have provided only a descriptive account.

But the description here is unique in its range. First, my colleagues and I conducted a large survey of both titular and Russian respondents in each of the republics. The survey tells us about the degrees of nationality intermixing and the attitudes of both Russians and titulars toward assimilation, toward mobilizing for group rights, and toward the possibility of the Russians' return to their homeland.

Further, I report on four complementary ethnographies, one in each republic. My collaborators and I compiled extensive biographies of a half-dozen Russian-speaking families in each republic and engaged in participant observation of these Russians in their daily lives. From this fieldwork we know the degree to which they understand the titular language and their orientations toward learning it. Ethnographies of this sort, if taken in isolation, could hardly be thought of as representative. But in conjunction with large surveys, they enable us to know whether our informants are typical or not. These ethnographies, when put into a social context, provide a shockingly clear portrait of the nationality scene in the post-Soviet world.

As the project developed, it became increasingly clear that the resolution of an identity crisis for the Russian-speaking population was immensely influenced by signals coming from the nationalizing governments and the titular societies of the four republics. Within each republic, therefore, my colleagues and I gathered data from interviews, from state documents, and from the press on government policies on nationality questions. Whether the government, its leaders, and viable opposition groups envisioned their republic as a future France (with a single nationality), a Belgium (with divided cultural zones), or a United States (with conglomerate identities within an assimilationist framework) had a lot to do with how Russian-speakers framed their identity choices.

Finally, through a large collection of articles published in each republic's press—and about each republic published in the Russian press—I conducted an analysis of Russian-language discourse concerning the present and future identities of Russians living in the "near abroad." This discourse analysis reveals that, along with movement toward assimilation to the titular culture, at least in the Baltics, a new category of identity, the "Russian-speaking population," has emerged in all four republics. This conglomerate identity includes Russians, Belarusans, Ukrainians, Poles, and Jews, all of whom speak Russian as their first language in republics outside their putative national homelands. The Russian-speaking population is not a "nationality," but there is reason to believe it will take on the feel of a nationality, just as the Palestinians in the Middle East and the Hispanics in the United States, both conglomerate groups that formed under special political conditions, have done. The emergence of such new "identity formations"—with distinct features in each of the republics—has implications for the kinds of national states that are likely to form in the post-Soviet world. It has implications as well for understanding the sources of inter-nationality conflict.

No one person could have carried out a large survey, a comprehensive local ethnography, an analysis of postindependence nationality policies of the government and contenders for power, and a discourse analysis of the local press in four separate republics, all with their own state languages. Indeed, my own principal work has been on issues of politics and culture in Africa, and when I jumped into this project I was just consolidating a study of Catalonia and the revival of the Catalan language in Spain.

Yet I was inexorably lured into Soviet studies because the issues of language and nationalism, on which I have concentrated throughout my career, moved to center stage in the former Soviet republics and demanded theoretical and empirical analysis. In 1988, prodded by an offer from Alexander Motyl to address issues of Soviet nationalities from an Africanist's perspective, and by an invitation from Jerry Hough to give a theoretical presentation at Duke University on Soviet inter-nationality issues, I began reading about the Soviet Union in a systematic way.[1] I quickly realized that my theories about Catalonia could be tested with the enormous number of cases of linguistic revival that were wide open for study in the glasnost period of political flowering in the USSR, when language legislation in the republics reflected a newfound freedom. In particular, Estonia made for a theoretically interesting comparison with Catalonia, and I visited Estonia twice in the Soviet period.[2] At that time I ceased my Catalan language studies and began to study Russian. Thus began the trek that led to this book.

A newcomer to Soviet studies, I could not have accomplished the research that went into this book alone. Jerry Hough became my godfather. Through a grant from the Carnegie Foundation, he brought Priit Jarve, of the Estonian Academy of Science, to Duke University and gave me the chance to consult with him. That grant also paid for my first trip to Estonia, and Jarve was my host in Tallinn. He facilitated several early and important contacts. My connection with the research team of Aksel Kirch, Marika Kirch, and Tarmo Tuisk at the Academy of Science enabled me to keep regular scholarly contact in Estonia. Hough later became co-principal investigator for the National Science Foundation grant that financed most of the work for this project.[3] He directed the large-*n* surveys, although I wrote the questions having to do with language and nationalism. For that research, Hough introduced me to the distinguished sociolinguist Michael Guboglo and his wife, Tat'iana, a data analyst, who were the principal subcontractors for a number of the

[1] For results of these early speculations, see David Laitin, Roger Petersen, and John Slocum, "Language and the State: Russia and the Soviet Union in Comparative Perspective," in Alexander Motyl, ed., *Thinking Theoretically about Soviet Nationalities* (New York: Columbia University Press, 1992), pp. 129–68; David Laitin, "The Four Nationality Games and Soviet Politics," *Journal of Soviet Nationalities* 2, no. 1 (1991): 1–37; and my review essay "The National Uprisings in the Soviet Union," *World Politics* 44, no. 1 (1991): 139–77, written as a result of much reading of the secondary literature in preparation for the first two articles.

[2] For the results of the controlled comparison, see David Laitin, "Language Normalization in Estonia and Catalonia," *Journal of Baltic Studies* 23, no. 2 (1992): 149–66.

[3] Financial support was provided from the NSF, Grant POLS/SES 92125768.

surveys and became my closest contacts in Russia. The NSF grant also enabled me to fund three young political scientists to carry out fieldwork in the three other republics while I was in Estonia. Hough also integrated me into a research team with Timothy Colton, Susan Lehmann, and Ralph Clem, where I imbibed their accumulated expertise in Russian studies. Colton introduced me to his graduate students—most significant among them Dmitri Gorenburgov, who began working on some of the data I collected—and from them I gained greater area sensitivity.

On the fieldwork side of the project, Dominique Arel (Ukraine), Bhavna Dave (Kazakhstan), and Vello Pettai (Latvia and Estonia) proved to be my mentors rather than my research assistants. They all speak at least three languages: English, Russian, and the titular language of the republic in which each conducted field research. As any reader of this book will see, their field notes were a gold mine of insights. We presented our fieldwork together at the American Association for the Advancement of Slavic Studies in a panel creatively organized by Ellen Gordon, herself an excellent fieldworker. The presentations were selected for a special volume of *Post-Soviet Affairs*,[4] and working with the editor of that journal, George Breslauer, was a professional treat. His impressive area wisdom enriched our analyses and indirectly enriched this book.

My own field research in Narva, Estonia, where I lived for about seven months, mostly with a Russian-speaking family, enabled me to understand the real, on-the-ground situation of the Russians in the near abroad. Narva stands right across a narrow river from Ivangorod, in Russia's Leningrad oblast. My hosts, Pavel and Liuba Grigor'ev, with their children, Natalia, Andreu, and Roma, became my family. Without their interest in my safety, in the success of my project, and in me, this project would have lost its rootedness in people's lives.[5]

At the University of Chicago, whose Division of Social Science generously supplemented my resources for carrying out this project, I had great intellectual support as well. John Slocum and Roger Petersen provided initial research assistance. Olga Beloded tutored me regularly in Russian. Elise Giuliano provided research assistance, especially on the sociolinguistic testing (where she was aided by Joshua Fruhlinger) and in the discourse analysis. I am indebted to Matthew Light, Eleanor Gilburd, and Alexander Belomoin for their diligent work on the compilation of the discourse data. Eytan Meyers, Andrew Kydd, Ari Zentner, Merri Rolfe, and Matthew Kocher guided me through much of the statistical work on the survey. Sheila Fitzpatrick, Terry Martin, and Ronald Suny—all colleagues at the University of Chicago—helped me in numerous ways to hide (and occasionally to overcome) my ignorance of the Soviet past. Throughout this period, by virtue of an asymmetric collaboration with James D. Fearon—of which I was the overall net beneficiary—I developed more systematically than I thought possible a theory of identity and interethnic conflict. My career owes a great deal to his teaching.[6]

[4] George W. Breslauer, Special Issue, *Post-Soviet Affairs* 12 (January–March 1996): 1.

[5] I therefore introduce the principal themes of this book through a portrait of the Grigor'ev family in Chapter 1.

[6] For the first fruit of our collaboration, see James D. Fearon and David D. Laitin, "Explaining Interethnic Cooperation," *American Political Science Review* 90, no. 4 (1996): 715–35.

Early formulations of my theses found willing ears and critical comments in universities and research institutes throughout the world. At the University of California, Berkeley (Ned Walker, George Breslauer, and Robert Price) and Santa Barbara (Cynthia Kaplan), Harvard University (Timothy Colton and Robert Bates), MIT (Steven Van Evera), University of Wisconsin (M. Crawford Young and Mark Beissinger), University of Connecticut (Henry Krisch), Estonian Academy of Science (Aksel and Marika Kirch, with support from IREX), Institute of Ethnography at the Russian Academy of Sciences (Michael Guboglo), School of Oriental and African Studies, University of London (Donal Cruise O'Brien), All Souls College at Oxford (Diego Gambetta), Central European University (John Hall), Rutgers University (Robert Kaufman), University of Michigan (Michael Kennedy), and UCLA (Rogers Brubaker and Barbara Geddes) I was stimulated to continue developing the ideas that emerged from my fieldwork. I owe my hosts and the audiences they provided a great debt for their interest.[7]

With more data than I ever dreamed of having, and writing on a topic of immense contemporary importance, I desperately needed, immediately, a year of uninterrupted writing. A fellowship from the John Simon Guggenheim Foundation—along with supplemental financial support from the University of Chicago—gave me the academic year 1995–96 to write a draft of this book. First draft completed, I received telling and demanding commentaries from Dominique Arel, Meskerem Brhane, Sheila Fitzpatrick, Peter Gourevitch, Michael Guboglo, Elise Giuliano, Roger Haydon, Jerry Hough, Peter Katzenstein, Jeremy King, Pål Kolstø, Isabelle Kreindler, Tracy Strong, and Ronald Suny. The Rockefeller Foundation kindly capped the year by hosting me at the Bellagio Study and Conference Center on Lake Como, in Italy, to address those commentaries and to put the penultimate touches on the manuscript. A post-Bellagio presentation of the manuscript—this time before the Wilder House editorial board, where I had to take the very medicine that I myself had administered to many of the authors of previous works in this series—compelled me to return to the theoretical drawing board. Because of the stimulating environment, where being director and series co-editor get me no intellectual deference, I am proud that this volume is part of the Wilder House Series in Politics, History, and Culture.

David D. Laitin

Chicago, Illinois

[7] Those early papers have found their way into the journal literature. See David Laitin, "Identity in Formation," *Archives européennes de sociologie* 36, no. 2 (1995): 281–316; "Nationalism and Language: A Post-Soviet Perspective," in John Hall, ed., *Ernest Gellner and the Theory of Nationalism* (Oxford: Oxford University Press, in press); and "The Cultural Elements of Ethnically Mixed States: Nationality Re-formation in the Soviet Successor States," in George Steinmetz, ed., *State/Culture* (Ithaca: Cornell University Press, in press).

A Note on Transliteration and Terms

I rely on the United States Library of Congress system of transliteration,[1] but with a few exceptions: (1) Names well known in the West (e.g., Tolstoy) retain their popular Western transliterations.[2] (2) The authors and titles of published books and articles that have been transliterated in a way inconsistent with the Library of Congress standard are cited as they are printed. (3) Direct quotations from other sources retain the transliteration of those sources. (4) Place and group names have changed in conventional representations. I have not altered spellings in direct quotations, but I have standardized some uses. I refer to residents and citizens of Kazakhstan as Kazakhstanis, but to ethnic Kazakhs as Kazakhs. For the pre-1991 era, I use Byelorussia. After 1991, it is Belarus', and its inhabitants are Belarusans. I use the currently preferred renderings of the Turkic names of republics (except, of course, in direct quotations or citations).

Throughout the book, I refer to the nationality group after which the republic was named as "titulars." When used in connection with events before 1991, the word is something of an anachronism, as the Soviet literature referred to the "rooted" nationality. I have been reluctant to use the term "rooted" lest I appear to agree with a social theory that nontitular people who may have lived in a republic for four or five generations do not have roots there. After 1991, titulars are often referred to as the "republican" nationalities. I have been reluctant to use the term "republican," as monarchist voices are audible among the titular nationality in Estonia. Technically, therefore, they cannot be called republicans. "Titular" is neutral, and easy to remember (certainly better than "eponymous," which I used earlier), even if tainted by a touch of anachronism.

[1] The principal difference between the Library of Congress system and the systems used in Europe and the American popular press lies in the last letter of the Cyrillic alphabet, which the Library of Congress system renders as "ia" rather than the more familiar "ya."

[2] This strategy leads to some difficult judgment calls, which may not stand the test of time. Thus we get Yeltsin (not El'tsin) but Iavlinskii (not Yavlinsky). The noted philosopher Nikolai Berdyayev loses stature in these pages by being transliterated as Berdiaev.

PART ONE

INTRODUCTION

I

A Theory of Political Identities

On April 25, 1994, the Estonian state-run bus service dropped me off, after a four-and-a-half-hour trip from the capital city of Tallinn, in the historic Hanseatic city of Narva. This was my fifth journey to this city of 80,000 people, 95 percent of whom speak Russian as their primary language. The city is only a stone's throw across the Narva River, from Russia. For centuries, the river represented a civilizational divide. A leading Estonian sociologist, Marika Kirch, puts it in stark terms. "If one supposes hesitatingly," she writes,

> that the civilizational border between Estonia and Russia is anachronistic or negligible, one need only stand on the bridge over the Narva river . . . and witness carefully the "overt civilizational confrontation" of two cultures: on the Estonian side there is an historic fortress built by the Swedes, Danes and Germans in accordance with the cultural traditions of Western Europe; on the other [in Ivangorod], a primeval fortress as an exponent of Slavic-Orthodox cultural traditions.[1]

But the Second World War altered this boundary. The Soviets shelled Narva heavily when they occupied Estonia, and either killed, captured, or drove off virtually the entire population. After the war the town was rebuilt, largely by demobilized Russian soldiers, most of whom believed, and still believe, that they helped save the Estonians from fascism and merit honor for rebuilding the city, which their own army had destroyed. From the early 1950s up until 1991, Narva and Ivangorod formed a single Russian-speaking metropolitan area.

On my first visit to Narva, in July 1992, I met with a parliamentarian, Pavel Grigor'ev, who had been quoted in the *New York Times* as a Russian activist standing up against the nationalizing tendencies of the new Estonian state. After the interview, he invited me to his home in the seaside village of Narva Jõesuu, just a few kilometers north of Narva, and the home of many Soviet writers and intellectuals who had

[1] Marika Kirch, ed., *Changing Identities in Estonia: Sociological Facts and Commentaries* (Tallinn: Estonian Science Foundation, 1994), p. 12.

been rewarded by the state with private homes in peaceful communities. The kilometers-long beach at Narva Jõesuu made it quite attractive to many Russians, especially to well-connected Leningradians seeking restful summer dachas.

Grigor'ev lived there, not as a reward for artistic achievement but because he was a long-time machinist in the nearby October fishing kolkhoz. He was born in Kingisepp (near Narva, but in Leningrad region) in 1941 and started his career working in Murmansk, an industrial fishing city, which he and his wife found depressingly dark. He found an opening at the October kolkhoz in 1966 and lived in a one-room flat with wife and son on the Ivangorod bank of the river. Two years later they moved into a lovely three-room flat in a three-story building constructed for the kolkhoz on the Estonian side of the border, where they still live today. Articulate, open-minded, and uncannily able to get people of a variety of persuasions to believe that they share his vision, Grigor'ev moved up the political ladder and was eventually elected to the Supreme Soviet of the Estonian Republic.

In my second trip to Narva, in December 1992, I took Grigor'ev and his wife out to dinner, and he graciously responded by helping me with my research. I returned for a two-week visit in April 1993, and this time he invited me to live in his home while I tried (desperately, but with little to show for it) to develop facility in Russian, a language I had been studying for a few years but without great success. I got to know better his wife, Liuba, who pretended, as they used to say, to work in a sanatorium while the government pretended to pay her. On my first trip to Narva, I had brought packaged herbs and spices. She was appreciative and (being a superb cook) used them with great ingenuity. From then on, I was always a welcome guest at their dinner table, and I eventually taught her to cook on a wok, and in the Mexican style as well. I met their oldest child, Andreu, who had been decommissioned from the Soviet army, much to his chagrin, when his country (the USSR) disappeared. I also met their daughter Natasha, who had an excellent ear for languages, had excelled since her early grades (so her elementary school teacher in Estonian, who herself was a native speaker of Estonian, told me the following year), and was training at the Tallinn Pedagogical Institute to become a teacher of Estonian in Russian schools. Finally, I met their youngest, Roma, then in the sixth grade, whose goal then was to become a hockey player of note.

In the spring of 1993, Grigor'ev was a lame-duck parliamentarian. Because he was not an Estonian citizen, he could not run for reelection to the Riigikogu, the Estonian parliament. But the Estonian political establishment considered him a moderate, a man with whom they could do business. A little-known (and rarely publicized) provision of the Estonian Constitution allowed the prime minister to recommend citizenship to residents of Estonia for "service to the state." Grigor'ev was told that if he applied for citizenship, even though he understood hardly a word of Estonian, he would be granted it. Indeed, he received citizenship, and Roma, who was under twelve at the time, received it as well. Roma was studying Estonian at school for a few hours each week, and his closest friend and next-door neighbor was Estonian, but he could hardly utter a grammatical sentence in that language himself. His English, though primitive, was far better. And so Pavel and Roma were Estonian citizens, but Liuba, Andreu, and Natasha remained "Soviet" citizens, or citizens without a country.

During my visit in April 1993, I told the family that I planned to do a year of field research in Narva beginning the following fall. Pavel and Liuba worried about my safety and sanity and urged me to live with them, in Andreu's room, since Andreu was about to get married and move into his own place. Despite many rules of anthropological thumb against becoming associated with any one side of a community conflict, I consented, and moved in that September. The next month Grigor'ev ran successfully for chairman of the Narva Jõesuu city council, something he could not have done had he not become an Estonian citizen. Russian-speaking candidates could run successful campaigns in these local elections, because all adult residents were eligible voters in these, but not in general elections, where citizenship was necessary in order to vote. Since citizenship for service to the state was granted only to the moderates among the Russian politicians, the Estonian prime ministers, who had discretion on this matter, could assure their constituents that only a moderate group of Russian-speaking politicians would get office in the initial years of the new republic. (To be sure, the Estonians were not unified on this issue. Prime Minister Tiit Vähi gave the gift of citizenship to people with whom he had good bargaining relations, much to the chagrin of the opposition. But when the opposition leader Mart Laar came to power, he sought to cultivate "his" Russians in the same manner, and Vähi, then out of office, criticized Laar for abusing the practice. Nonetheless, neither Vähi nor Laar gave citizenship to potential fifth columnists.)

During the fall of 1993, I enrolled in a class in Estonian for Russian-speakers at the Narva Language Center and began writing the family biographies, one of which is the basis for this vignette. I returned home to Chicago for a few months in the winter and returned to Narva, as I began this story, in April 1994.

Liuba was waiting for me at the bus stop. She was extremely agitated, and as we waited for nearly two hours for Pavel's official car (a late-model Lincoln Town Car, with a chauffeur!) to take us to Narva Jõesuu, I learned that it wasn't the extraordinary inflation that was bothering her the most. Indeed, the bus fare to Narva Jõesuu was 90 cents (100 cents to the kroon; about 13 kroons to the dollar) when I left in December and had increased to 3 kroons that April. Rent for their apartment had jumped to 650 kroons a month from 330 a few months earlier. This inflation was harsh but not threatening. Her principal concerns were deportation and the possible forced dispersal of her family.

Her strategy for avoiding deportation was to become a full-time student of Estonian. She had just paid 650 kroons for the course designed to provide citizenship-level competence in Estonian. Her rush to learn Estonian was induced by a new requirement that noncitizens had to register for temporary residency permits; a permanent residency permit might or might not be issued later. Noncitizens who failed to register by July would be deported. Liuba was worried. Rumors abounded that political criteria would be applied in the granting of permanent residency status. Unwanted Russians would be deported. In Tallinn the minister of nationalities, Peter Olesk, was already being called, in a bitter pun (*vyselenniia* for *natseleniia*), the minister for deportation. Liuba accepted the local notion (among Russians) that there was a small window of opportunity: if she passed the citizenship language test by June, she would not need to register. Her application for citizenship would serve as her *propusk* (permit), giving her all the rights of a permanent resident. The situation for Russians, she emphasized, was very uncertain. The right of foreign travel, among other things, was in the arbitrary hands of the Estonian authorities. Up till recently you could get an empty Soviet foreign passport and have it issued by Estonian authorities for foreign travel. But the Estonian government had run out of such passports and had no access to others, or at least that was what Russians applying for such passports in Narva were being told. So Russian residents of Estonia who wanted to travel abroad could not get papers without special intervention. Even members of sports teams and other Russians with institutional ties to Estonian organizations were having problems. To get the right to foreign travel, Estonia's Russians theoretically could get "Russian citizen" stamped in their Soviet internal passports—and indeed many did so—but that strategy (despite official denials) was felt to prejudice future applications for Estonian citizenship.

Liuba was near catatonic. Estonian is a Finno-Ugric language, with virtually no cognates in Russian. She found its structure impenetrable. She was convinced that there was no way she could reach the citizenship level in the time remaining. Indeed, the Narva Language Center has calculated that to reach level B, enabling one to qualify for a job requiring only a low level of language skill, 70 hours of instruction is necessary. Another 50 hours is required to reach level C, qualifying one for most clerk and administrative jobs. Level D, for professional use, requires 120 additional hours. The citizenship level requires 60 more hours in the classroom. Each of these courses involves considerable homework and additional computer-assisted grammatical drills (an extra fee is charged for computer time). Liuba, before her course began, could get through a basic greeting in Estonian, and she had named her cat Lumi, Estonian for "snow," in a demonstration of cultural accommodation to the country in which she lived. After that, as far as Estonian was concerned, she was mute.

Liuba might have responded to the new language regime earlier. Indeed, a language law passed in January 1989 sought to institute real bilingualism in the society and induce Russians to learn Estonian. But the law had little bite, since under Soviet hegemony, the Estonians had lacked the authority to enforce it. But after independence, the project of "naturalizing" some 500,000 mostly Russian noncitizens (a large number of whom had been born in Estonia or had lived there for decades) provided an opportunity to impose sanctions on Russians who had not learned Estonian.

As the precise terms of the naturalization process were laid down, the language test (as Liuba herself experienced) became the most challenging of the hoops to be jumped through. In a new citizenship law passed in January 1995, the Estonians added another civics examination to the naturalization procedure for Soviet-era immigrants. Many noncitizens viewed this new requirement as an attempt to slow the naturalization process, and their belief was reinforced when the government delayed more than three months in issuing specific information on the new examination.

Moreover, the Estonians interpreted the noncitizens' status to mean that all of their Soviet-era residency documents would have to be reprocessed. The Aliens Law passed in July 1993 caused a major political crisis. Its administration was a bureaucratic nightmare. Many observers interpreted these regulations and the slow processing of applications for citizenship as clear signals that the titulars wanted Russians to leave rather than integrate. Although many Estonian nationalists openly voiced that wish, the reality was that the great majority would remain in Estonia, and they would have to come to terms with Estonian authority.

So Liuba studied Estonian in all her free moments, and even practiced pronunciation from her word lists with her Estonian neighbor, who came over regularly to gossip (in Russian). Liuba all but abandoned TV for study, though occasionally she sat with her word lists to watch the American soap opera *Santa Barbara* on Ostankino, the most popular Russian TV station. Even young Roma's interest was sparked by his mother's obsession, and he began to study with her, even engaging in Estonian small talk when they sat down together in the kitchen after he returned home from school. Once I showed off to the family that I had the latest Estonian grammatical exercise program on my laptop computer. I conjugated a verb perfectly, and the program rewarded me with an electronic version of "Merrily We Roll Along." Liuba often borrowed my computer late in the evenings when I was through working, and I'd be awakened in the wee hours of the morning to the tinkling strains of "Merrily . . . " Liuba was possessed.

She was strategic as well. On my first morning back, she phoned an old buddy of Pavel's, whom I had met when he was on border guard duty the previous fall, to see if he could help her get her citizenship application forms without waiting in a long line in an office that was open only a few hours a week. All this strategic activity took place in an atmosphere of considerable uncertainty. The highly nationalistic government then in power—the Isamaa or "Fatherland" coalition—was ambivalent about Russians' learning the Estonian language. On the one hand, Isamaa leaders insisted that race or civilization had nothing to do with citizenship. It was only natural for a country to require immigrants to learn the language of the country before they could receive citizenship. Indeed, as Pavel sardonically observed, "race" could not possibly be a criterion for the Estonian national chauvinists. After all, he pointed out, his roots are in Ingerland, whose inhabitants are closer to the indigenous Ugrics than most Estonians, who have much "foreign" (German, Swedish, Danish) blood. On the other hand, many leading Estonian nationalists claimed that the percentage of Russians in Estonia was so high that they would never assimilate. If two-thirds of them were to "return" to Russia (though many of them had been born in Estonia), these nationalists claimed, Estonian culture could survive. This ambivalence led to a program with contradictions. Language centers were indeed created, but barely funded, and therefore tuition was high. (The Swedish and U.S. embassies took the initiative to provide funds for these centers, which the Estonian government was not pleased to accept but could not decline.)

Russian speakers who passed the language exam complained that their citizenship applications were languishing (or disappearing) in the bureaucratic mill. One of my informants told me that three times over the course of a year he had been told that crucial official documents were "missing" from his file, although he knew he had submitted them. Each time he had to reapply for citizenship. Natasha, Pavel and Liuba's daughter, faced the same Kafkesque nightmare. Pavel told me that she passed the Estonian language exam without difficulty in Tallinn, where standards are higher than in Narva, where informal dispensations are made, given the extreme difficulty of learning Estonian in a city where hardly anyone speaks it, and where Estonian radio and TV reception is poor. Yet two years later Natasha was still waiting for her citizenship papers. The Estonian government, he reckoned, worked with an unannounced citizenship quota that violated international human rights agreements.

Pavel is a realist. He told me that if he had the choice, he would vote for the secession of northeast Estonia and for reintegrating it with Russia. But this would not be possible without bloodshed, and he emphasized to me, and to conferees at a diplomatic panel in Tallinn, that a bad peace is far better than a good war. Moreover, his desire to rejoin Russia would not involve emigration, even though his mother lives in the Russian town of Kingisepp. His dacha keeps him in Estonia. In a former swamp just south of the Baltic coast, thousands of Russian families have built lovely summer homes from materials appropriated from the state, and in their gardens grow fruits and vegetables that last most families for the entire year. Many men, including Pavel and Andreu, spent all their free hours for years constructing those dachas. In fact, Pavel secured a special visa for his mother, and she spends the entire summer managing the garden at the dacha. (I once asked her if she spoke any Estonian, and she looked at me with astonishment, as if I had asked her whether she had even been to Disneyland.) Property keeps Pavel a loyal Estonian.

Pavel's realism is combined with a complete lack of prejudice. I have heard him make insinuations about colleagues and public officials, but I have never heard him make an ethnic slur. Pavel used to spend hours talking politics with his next-door neighbor, an Estonian, who died of a heart attack a year before I first came to Narva. Pavel's electoral "ticket" for the Narva Jõesuu city council, when he successfully ran for chairman in October 1994, was ethnically mixed, without tokens from either the Russian or Estonian communities. He had even named his youngest son after the Estonian who founded his kolkhoz. A true Soviet man, he really did not see the world in ethnic terms. In this way, he was quite open-minded about Estonian sovereignty.

On language, however, Pavel was less open-minded, although still more in tune with the times than his mother. Pavel's monolingualism was as natural to him as it is to nearly all third-generation Americans. He had traveled as far east as Samarkand, as far south as Sukumi, as far north as Murmansk, and could communicate with anyone in Russian. For Pavel it was as if the whole world spoke Russian; what need did he have for a second language? This attitude infuriated Mart Rannut, first head of Estonia's State Language Office, who once complained that Estonia might cave in to international pressure and extend citizenship to Russian-speakers who had only reached, in Rannut's phrase "dog level" proficiency in Estonian—in other words, the ability to respond to a small set of commands. When I repeated this to Grigor'ev, he laughed uproariously. That much he knew he could do. Pavel would often greet others with *tere*, the standard Estonian greeting, to show his socialist internationalism; but that was just about the limit of his proficiency. Seven time zones, he was fond of pointing out, and all you need is Russian. Sometimes he would stare, eyes glazed, at an Estonian text, making believe he was giving it a gloss, but he rarely caught a word. To be sure, the cataclysm of the Soviet collapse in 1991 had opened his eyes, and he was adjusting quite rapidly to the new order. He took Roma out of the local school and enrolled him in Narva, where the principal had given the school an international flavor, specializing in foreign languages. The school, because it offered foreign language training, was quickly becoming more popular among parents than the prestigious baccalaureate school. In his school, Roma was getting adequate English and a touch of Estonian, but far more than he was receiving in Narva Jõesuu. Pavel, like his wife, believes that Russian-speakers in Estonia should speak Estonian, but unlike Liuba, he is not learning it himself. Still, he is making sure his children are equipped linguistically for the new reality.

Andreu, like his father, had no yearning to learn Estonian. He remained more Soviet than his parents and often accused Gorbachev of having destroyed the Soviet Union on behalf of U.S. intelligence. In his long period of semi-unemployment after his demobilization from the army—during which he had small jobs at the local TV station and elsewhere—he attained a level B proficiency in Estonian, which qualified him for white-collar jobs. But when he landed a job as a senior technician in a new insurance firm and had to reach level C, he copied the grammar program from my hard drive and installed it on his own computer in the insurance office. He too began to study assiduously.

Natasha's proficiency in Estonian was legendary. Her primary school teacher in Estonian, who became an official at the Narva Language Center in the 1990s, often used Natasha as the example of the possibility for linguistic assimilation. In 1994, Natasha was living in Tallinn, studying education in order to teach Estonian in a Russian-speaking school. She keeps her hair short—and I think bleached—to make herself physically indistinguishable from her Estonian counterparts. This was the situation as I left the field in June 1994.

The news of the Grigor'ev family in the Christmas letter that Liuba sent me in December 1994 was joyous. Liuba had passed her language examination at level D and at the citizenship level as well, and now had only a year's wait for her official papers. Natasha had received her citizenship passport from Estonia. Andreu would one day catch up.

It would be a mistake to see in this story the assimilation of the Grigor'ev family from "Soviet" to "Estonian." They see themselves as Russians who have from practical necessity added a few Estonian cultural practices to their own Russian repertoire. Yet cultural assimilation is like religious conversion, and as the literature on religious conversion makes clear, what one generation considers simple pragmatism the next considers natural. Thus children who are brought up in a religious community will—egged on by religious authorities—castigate their parents for what they see as their hypocrisy.[2] What we see with the Grigor'evs, then, is the beginning of assimilation, not its end. Their experiences and those of their compatriots

[2] The intergenerational aspect of conversion is developed in the classic work of A. D. Nock, *Conversion* (London: Oxford University Press, 1933).

throughout the detritus of the Soviet Union give us a glimpse of what it means to have "identities in formation."

The Question of Identities

Stalin's ideas on national identity continue to have a profound influence on the national identity question throughout the former Soviet Union. For him, nations were the result of a common culture, a common language, a common economic life, and a common territory. Scientific investigation could determine true nations from mere ethnic or religious groups. Children are born into national communities, and their national identification can be fixed, as it were, on the fifth line of a passport.[3] Even after the collapse of the Soviet Union, and especially in light of the outbreaks of grotesque nationalist violence in postcommunist lands, this Stalinesque view of nationality marks quite strongly the understanding of nationality issues in postcommunist countries and throughout the world. Analyses of ethnic conflict point to nationality groups as if they were eternal actors on the stage of warfare. Books on the so-called new Russian diaspora worry whether they will become a fifth column, return to Russia in a horde, or become loyal citizens of their new republics. But the notion that they might assimilate or develop an identity other than "Russian" is rarely even considered.[4] Reflecting this rather rigid view of national identity, Anatoly Khazanov writes that he "was personally acquainted with Ukrainian, Belorussian, Daghestanian, Tatar, Kazakh, Kalmyk, Buryat, Yakut, and Tuvinian scholars, including anthropologists, who cannot speak their native language." These people, he judges, were "doomed to acculturation."[5] The notion that for a Ukrainian, Ukrainian is "his" language suggests that he is not fulfilled as a person until he recognizes his "real" identity and is doomed as an individual unless he develops the language skills to become his real self. Even Robert Kaiser, who wrote a book sensitive to the Soviet construction of nationality groups, writes that "the more expansive perception of homeland in evidence among Russians [in the post-Soviet world] enhances the probability that international conflicts will arise in border republics such as Kazakhstan, Ukraine, Belarus', and the Baltics, where Russians live in concentrated settlements and where a Russian sense of homeland has developed over time."[6] He doesn't even raise the issue that if changed boundaries could affect national identifications among Tajiks or Ukrainians in an earlier period, the

[3] Joseph Stalin, *Marxism and the National Question* (New York: International Publishers, 1942). Stalin was an assimilated Georgian whose published views and political programs denied the possibility of nationality shift. See also Iu. I. Semenov, *Sekrety klio: Szhatoe vvedenie v filosofiiu istorii* (Moskow: Moskovskii fiziki-mekhanicheskii institut, 1996), p. 60.

[4] See Vladimir Shlapentokh et al., *The New Russian Diaspora* (Armonk, N.Y.: M. E. Sharpe, 1994), and Paul Kolstoe, *Russians in the Former Soviet Republics* (Bloomington: Indiana University Press, 1995). But also see Pål Kolstø, "The New Russian Diaspora—An Identity of Its Own?" *Ethnic and Racial Studies* 19, no. 3 (1996): 609–39, for an open-ended approach to Russian identity shift. This paper helped inspire the approach I take in this book.

[5] Anatoly M. Khazanov, *After the USSR* (Madison: University of Wisconsin Press, 1995), pp. 15, 7.

[6] Robert J. Kaiser, *The Geography of Nationalism in Russia and the USSR* (Princeton: Princeton University Press, 1994), p. 372.

changed boundaries of the post-Soviet world might have similar effects on today's "Russians." The reversal of the tides in Estonia, manifesting itself in a shift in the identity of the Grigor'ev family—from "Russian" to an inchoate conception that includes an Estonian cultural component—all in the space of a few years, belies the notion that the boundaries and social meaning of the Russian nationality are fixed.

What we need, if we are to place the study of Russian nationalism and identity into a plausible theoretical framework, is a notion of "identity" and how it might be studied comparatively that does not require us to consider people like the Grigor'evs to be anomalous. The definition of identity I use is the one provided by the Freudian psychologist Erik H. Erikson a generation ago. I build on Erikson's definition of identity in order to formulate a microtheory of identity shift, which also relies on the "tipping" model developed by Thomas Schelling. This theory can account for both the depth of feeling and the capacity for change associated with identity politics. It allows us to analyze the different types of identities that populations construct, such as conglomerate, diasporic, transnational, and multiple—all within a simple framework.

Identity in Social Theory

There is a growing consensus among academic observers of identity politics that identities are not inherited like skin color—which is the Stalinist view; its academic variant is called "primordialism"[7]—but constructed like an art object. People, as they go through their youth, are exposed to family, community, and national histories; they are brought up with a particular repertoire of languages and speech styles; they may be given training in certain religious rituals. Within their wider societies, others have adopted a variety of other social categories, local, national, religious, linguistic. Usually people's identities change with the level of aggregation: within their community, they may identify themselves on the basis of socioeconomic background; within their country, outside of their community, they may identify themselves with a brand of politics; and outside their country, they may identify themselves with their nation. All societies—perhaps especially today—have cultural entrepreneurs who offer new identity categories (racial, sexual, regional), hoping to find "buyers." If their product sells, these entrepreneurs become leaders of newly formed ethnic, cultural, religious, or other forms of identity groups. As individuals grow up they consequently feel pressure, in the phrase of Rom Harré, to organize "identity projects"; that is to say, to choose the category that exemplifies them as individuals and ties them to a social group. These identity projects carry with them, whether in religious texts or social practices of past members, sets of "beliefs, principles and commitments."[8] Although the choice of an identity may have had little to do with those beliefs, principles, and commitments, by attaching oneself to such an identity project, one is expected by others hold to them, and perhaps is motivated

[7] For this view, see Edward Shils, "Primordial, Personal, Sacred, and Civil Ties," *British Journal of Sociology* 8 (June 1957): 130–45; and Clifford Geertz, "The Integrative Revolution," in his *Interpretation of Cultures* (New York: Basic Books, 1973), chap. 7.

[8] Rom Harré, *Personal Being: A Theory for Individual Psychology* (Cambridge: Harvard University Press, 1984). The quotation is from John D. Greenwood, "A Sense of Identity: Prolegomena to a Social Theory of Personal Identity," *Journal for the Theory of Social Behavior* 24, no. 1 (1994): 28.

to do so by virtue of one's own identification. Construction and choice, rather than blood and inheritance, is now the standard story line about identities.

This notion of constructing an identity is modern. Although the ancients raised identity issues, it was not until the nineteenth century, with Nietzsche and Hegel, that social theorists began considering the transformation of identities and the emergence of new identity categories. Walt Whitman articulated the revolutionary idea that each individual has within him- or herself a nearly infinite set of identity possibilities. George Kateb suggests that this idea is quintessential to the democratic age.[9]

Yet twentieth-century political figures, from Woodrow Wilson to Adolf Hitler and Joseph Stalin, continued to assume that social identities were primordially given. A school of anthropology gave academic credence to such views. Indeed, some scholars still hold to the biological analogy of identities and assume that they are like inherited characteristics. A 1993 study on ethnic identity among Hispanics, relying on psychological theories of cognitive development, sought to find the bases on which Hispanic youth brought up in the United States would have "correct ethnic labels" and "more ethnic knowledge."[10] In another psychologically based analysis, George De Vos saw constructed identities as deviant. In his terms, "excessive instrumental expediency . . . betokens inner maladjustment." This "Zelig phenomenon," he suggests, "occurs in what Durkheim termed *anomic* social conditions," and its presence forecloses strong emotional ties.[11]

Nonetheless, prevailing social science research demonstrates that while there are many constraints against the Zelig phenomenon, normal people do in fact engage in the construction of "identity projects." The motivating question in these studies is how to assess the sources of constraint. In political sociology, the formative tradition on identity shift focused on previous societal shifts in communication patterns. According to Karl W. Deutsch, the pathbreaker in this tradition, there cannot be effective nationality shifts unless the probability of interacting with a person from a different nationality is equal to that of interacting with a co-national. We are, in this tradition, prisoners of our communications net.[12] The search for the social background conditions for identity shift has continued with vigor. A post-collapse study of the "Yugoslav" identity found that in the years after World War II, demographic

[9] See Tracy B. Strong, ed., *The Self and the Political Order* (New York: New York University Press, 1992), for a series of essays that cumulatively lead to a social history of identity. The reference to Whitman is from George Kateb's essay in that volume, "Walt Whitman and the Culture of Democracy," pp. 208–29.

[10] George P. Knight et al., "Family Socialization and Mexican American Identity and Behavior," in Martha E. Bernal and George P. Knight, eds., *Ethnic Identity: Formation and Transmission among Hispanics and Other Minorities* (Albany: SUNY Press, 1993), p. 123.

[11] George A. De Vos, "A Psychocultural Approach to Ethnic Interaction in Contemporary Research," in Bernal and Knight, *Ethnic Identity Formation*, pp. 235–68. Zelig is the character in Woody Allen's film of the same name, who, chameleon-like, can change his personality and physiognomy to fit unobtrusively in different social environments.

[12] Karl W. Deutsch et al., *Political Community and the North Atlantic Area* (Princeton: Princeton University Press, 1957). For a sympathetic critique of the "caught in the net" determinism of this model, see William Foltz, "Modernization and Nation Building: The Social Mobilization Model Reconsidered," in Richard L. Merritt and Bruce M. Russett, eds., *From National Development to Global Community* (Boston: Allen & Unwin, 1981), pp. 25–45.

conditions, urbanization, participation in the Partisan war effort, and minority status within the separate republics all "predicted" the declaration of oneself as "Yugoslav" in the state census. Even though the percentages who identified themselves as Yugoslav were never large, the study did demonstrate the influence of social conditions on changes in self-perception of national identity. The authors were humbled, however, by the complete collapse of the Yugoslav identity project and remain uncertain about the persistence of newly constructed identities.[13]

Proposing an alternative to the focus on social background conditions, several scholars began to examine the role of the state (or state institutions) in manipulating the range of identities available either by subsidizing or recognizing certain group identities and ignoring others.[14] Others focused on the cultural material and economic resources of the entrepreneurs seeking to empower a newly formed identity category.[15] Still others focused on how strategies of exclusion and inclusion by dominant cultural groups in a society tend to foster reactive identities.[16] A compelling research tradition focused on historical legacies argued that the burdens of our ancestors weigh heavily on who we are and who we can become.[17] Yet another research program focused on how social networks—marriage ties, business dealings, neighborhood proximity—limit but by no means preclude identity shift.[18] For all the focus on constraints, there is a shared understanding, as Bhikhu Parekh puts it, that if identities are the products of history, they can be remade by history."[19] All of these studies promote a "constructivist" as opposed to a "primordialist" paradigm, but they differ on the causes, constraints, and effects of that constructing.

Contemporary Understandings of Identity

For all the debate between constructivists and primordialists, there is little agreement on what constitutes "identity."[20] A tried-and-true first cut at an answer to such

[13] Dusko Sekulic, Garth Massey, and Randy Hodson, "Who Were the Yugoslavs? Failed Sources of a Common Identity in the Former Yugoslavia," *American Sociological Review* 59 (February 1994): 83–97.

[14] Ernst B. Haas, *The Uniting of Europe* (Stanford: Stanford University Press, 1958); David Laitin, *Hegemony and Culture* (Chicago: University of Chicago Press, 1986); Melissa Nobles, "Responding with Good Sense: The Politics of Race and Censuses in Contemporary Brazil" (Ph.D. diss., Yale University, 1995).

[15] Yen Espiritu, *Asian American Panethnicity* (Philadelphia: Temple University Press, 1992); Joane Nagel, "Constructing Ethnicity: Creating and Recreating Ethnic Identity and Culture," *Social Problems* 41, no. 1 (1994): 152–76; Ran Greenstein, "Racial Formation: Towards a Comparative Study of Collective Identities in South Africa and the United States," *Social Dynamics* 19, no. 2 (1993): 1–29.

[16] Espiritu, *Asian American Panethnicity*.

[17] Greenstein, "Racial Formation"; Ian Buruma, *The Wages of Guilt: Memories of War in Germany and Japan* (New York: Farrar, Straus & Giroux, 1994).

[18] The landmark work in this tradition is Harrison White, *Identity and Control: A Structural Theory of Social Action* (Princeton: Princeton University Press, 1992). Also see Craig Calhoun, "The Problem of Identity in Collective Action," in Joan Huber, ed., *Macro-Micro Linkages in Sociology* (Beverly Hills, Calif.: Sage, 1991), pp. 51–75.

[19] Bhikhu Parekh, "Discourses on National Identity," *Political Studies* 42 (1994): 503–4.

[20] This section owes a great deal to long discussions with my colleague James D. Fearon. He shared with me his lecture notes on the concept of identity for his course "Nationalism and International Conflict," and the formulations herein owe much to his subtle analysis of the issue.

a question is to observe how the term is used in popular discourse. A survey of reports from the English-language press from around the world helps us sort out these academic arguments and gives us a clearer notion of what we mean by identity.[21] In the popular press, there is one realm in which writers insist that our identities are primordial. Indeed, there is a clear notion of a personal identity (in the *OED* sense of "the condition of being the same as a person or thing described or claimed") in which "identity projects" are either criminal or bizarre. These discussions about personal identities—usually arising in legal discourse—are in a different discourse realm from that of social identities, in which constructivist identity projects are considered permissible, though not always successful. The resulting social identities are built on cultural materials coming from the family, the community, and the nation, but they are not totally determined by these background conditions. Since social identities are seen as constructed, they are always subject to reconstruction. Following from this constructed nature of identity is a popularly accepted notion of a "crisis of identity" when a person fails to fit easily or comfortably into any social category. A short digression into the language of the popular press on "identity" questions should make this distinction between primordial personal and constructed social identities clear.

Personal Identities

Personal identities are firmly entrenched in a primordial or genetic discourse realm. A person who is *x* today will surely be *x* tomorrow. My name, my gender, the fact that I am the father of two children, and my credit history have a DNA-like continuity to them.[22] While I (say, through a sex-change operation) or others (say, by posing as David Laitin) may tamper with my personal identity, such acts are considered bizarre or criminal. Indeed, press accounts of "stolen" identities have all the appeal of the bizarre, like reports of sightings of space aliens.

"A titanic network of shared information gives each of us a credit identity but it has a major flaw," reports the *Tampa Tribune* (August 7, 1995). "A crook can steal your identity and swamp you in so many bad debts that it could take months or even years to clear your record." The *Chicago Tribune* (June 20, 1995) reports in the

[21] My teacher Hanna Pitkin introduced me to the possibilities of ordinary language analysis. Frederic Schaffer, another student of Pitkin's, gave me the idea of using the Lexis-Nexis database for such analysis. Schaffer also directed me away from some misguided distinctions I made in an earlier draft of this chapter. In the Lexis-Nexis database for 1994–95, I retrieved 904 stories that had at least seven uses of the term "identity" or "identities." This section is based on the first 100 of these stories (all from June–August 1995).

[22] That there is currently an articulate social movement in the United States to move gender from the primordial to the constructivist discourse realm is confirmation that the distinction proposed here is indeed part of popular understanding. That the stakes are high is seen in an article on the front page of the March 14, 1997, *New York Times*, "Sexual Identity Not Pliable After All, Report Says," by Natalie Angier. Angier reports the outcome of a famous case in which a child born with superficially ambiguous genitalia was raised as a girl. It had been expected that socialization as a girl would in fact produce a girl, but the child had always preferred "boyish" activities, and as an adult opted for a masculine identity. That gender perhaps really is primordial is first-page news for this politically correct newspaper.

same vein: "Authorities have charged Janetzke, 40, of Streamwood with what amounts to the theft of another person's identity. Police say he used the name and credit history of a 35-year-old truck driver from Wood Dale . . . and even took out a telephone number in his name. 'He just took away my husband's identity,' the truck driver's wife said. 'It's just a big mess.' " This practice can take on Gogolian proportions. *USA Today* (July 13, 1995) reports that a Kenneth John took on the identities of forty-five dead souls, using them to kite checks. "The growing crisis," Cheryl Phillips writes, "costs the living billions of dollars—and the dead their identities."

Legal discourse is replete with references to the genetic aspect of personal identity. The *New Jersey Lawyer* (June 26, 1995) reports on the continued requirement of federal courts that the public and the defendant "know the identity of the parties in public court proceedings in a civil case for money damages." The *St. Petersburg Times* (August 7, 1995) assures readers that "authorities usually can enter it into a computer network and quickly learn the person's true identity. But if the alias has not been used, the only way to confirm identity is by comparing fingerprints." Furthermore, "Even though criminals sometimes move in and out of the court system without their true identities being discovered, law enforcement officials think suspects . . . under different names" eventually will get found out. On questions of immigration, the *Federal News Service* (June 30, 1995) reports that "without documents, there is no place to begin an inquiry into the true identity and the true purpose of an applicant for admission. . . . Every recent terrorist act perpetrated by aliens was committed by an alien who intentionally misrepresented his true intention for coming to the United States or attempted to conceal some aspect of his identity, using a claim of asylum." The same problem occurs in Canada; the *Ottawa Citizen* (August 13, 1995) reported that thousands of Somali refugees "cannot become landed immigrants because they have no documents proving their identity." On the issue of adoption as well, contemporary discourse accepts personal identities as primordial. A program reported in the *New York Times* (June 18, 1995) allows donor-inseminated offspring, when they are eighteen years old, to find out the names of their real fathers. This is called the "identity-release" policy. This program is for young adults who want to know who they "really" are, as opposed to what they have socially become.

Everyday speech (as reported in newspapers and magazines) helps resolve a debate that consumes the attention of social scientists. Identities are inalienable, at least when we are talking about personal identities. Identities are also constructed, when we are talking about social membership. To be sure, the languages of these realms are not totally distinct. We understand when Nader Mousavizadeh means when he writes in the *New Republic* (June 19, 1995) that for the Germans and Japanese, the "memories of war and defeat have been internalized as burdens of identity." In a sense, no German (of the postwar generation) can ignore that burden and remain a German. We can say, hardly requiring metaphor, that the subsequent generation of Germans (an identity constructed through history) inherited that burden. So the two realms of discourse, personal and social, at times overlap.

But this is not to deny a distinct realm for the legal notion of personal identity (which assumes a primordial quality). In a widely reprinted essay (see the *Bergen*

Record, July 5, 1995, for one of its printings), Thomas Sowell pointed out that "nothing polarizes the political left and right like the idea of a national identity card." But the objection to an identity card is not that constructed, fictitious, or possibly reconstructed identities will be exposed. The objection (which has also been raised in the United Kingdom) is that the government will know all too much about who we really are. In this debate, as in other legal realms, identities are not in formation; they are absolutely real.

Constructed Social Identities

Social identities are labels that people assign to themselves (or that others assign to them) when they claim membership (or are assigned membership) in a social category that they (and others, whether members of that category or not) see as plausibly connected to their history and present set of behaviors.[23] It is further implied that this assignment has powerful emotional appeal, both to its holder and to others in the society.

Social identities are distinct from personal identities, and they are built from available categories that both divide and unite people in a society. People have inter alia national identities, racial identities, religious identities, and hometown identities. Yet issues of social identity become part of public discourse only when the categories themselves become fuzzy. Self-appointed boundary-keepers arise to redefine these categories so that rules of inclusion and exclusion, as well as the behavioral implications of belonging to this or that category, can be clarified.

One of the main reasons there is so much talk of identity in the press in our times is that the boundaries and behavioral implications of many of our social categories are being contested. Gerald Poyo reports for the *Houston Chronicle* (August 2, 1995) that recent immigration laws are forcing "immigrants to conform to a mythical and narrow notion of American identity." Digby Anderson, writing for the *Sunday Telegraph* (July 23, 1995), sticks needles into the chief executive of the United Kingdom School Curriculum and Assessment Authority for a similar reason:

> He is undoubtedly right in worrying that the children may be learning a wishy-washy multiculturalism, a sort of cocktail identity. But he is wrong in suggesting Britishness classes. For the true identity of most of our children is not Britishness at all. It is Englishness. Indeed, Britishness is almost as artificial and newfangled an imposition as multi-culturalism. The vast majority of the British are English . . . not British. Scottish people tell me they think of themselves first as Scottish and only second as British. English people just do not go about thinking of themselves in this explicit sort of way. . . . Englishmen travel, it is the same. An hour from ar-

[23] Plausibility is a key requirement in conventional understandings of group attachment. The discovery in Australia that two whites, one a novelist and one a painter, had taken Aboriginal pseudonyms to increase the market for their artistic works was met with outrage. That these assumptions of Aboriginal identity were implausible (once the truth was revealed) subjected the claimants to the charge of "fabrication" and the threat of legal action. Conventional opinion had it that they had no "right" to assign themselves Aboriginal identities. See Clyde H. Farnsworth, "Two Exposed Artists, Neither Aboriginal (Nor Original) After All," *New York Times*, April 2, 1997.

> rival at Kennedy Airport, as the passengers scratch their dried-up ballpoints over their crumpled immigration forms, the attentive British Airways staff have to tell countless of them their identity lest they get it wrong: "No, no, it's not England. You have to put UK." Who on earth thinks of themselves as a UKer? There is no such thing as a British village. So, if any identity is to be taught in the schools, at least in English schools, it is not Britishness but Englishness. To teach Britishness would take about 10 minutes, for all there is of it. What does Englishness consist of? . . . If the aim is to educate, to inculcate manners and identity—the manners and identity of England—then it must be cricket: and old-fashioned cricket at that.

But Mike Marqusee, in an earlier article in the *Guardian* (July 4, 1995), on the implications of a Canadian playing on the English tennis team, had trouble finding even Englishness. He reveals that "the truth is that the 'English' national identity was problematic long before immigrants from the West Indies and South Asia began arriving in the fifties." In fact, he admits, "Outside war zones, sporting teams are today the main visible bearers of national identity." Capturing an "English" identity is like grasping a wet bar of soap. High levels of immigration lead education authorities and other officials to feel the need to grasp that bar. Correspondents, who feel rather more secure than the officials, are freer to report on these issues with a smirk.

In Eastern Europe, of course, talk about national identity does not have this ironic tone. In an article about Serbs and Croats, Michael Ignatieff in the *Ottawa Citizen* (July 2, 1995) frets that "nationalism is a fiction of identity, because it contradicts the multiple reality of belonging. It insists on the primacy of one of these belongings over all the others. So how does this fiction of the primacy of national identity displace other identities? How does it begin to convince? Here we begin to reach for theory." He writes, "Globalism brings us closer together, makes us all neighbors; it destroys boundaries of identity and frontiers between states. We react by insisting ever more assiduously on the margins of difference that remain."

For secure communities—such as the English in Britain—identity talk has an ironic tone. Like East European minorities, however, race and gender groups in North America and Western Europe take their identity projects with resolute seriousness. The *St. Louis Post-Dispatch* (June 18, 1995) had a headline, "A Respectful History of Gays and Lesbians," and the article reflects on the 100-year history since the first articulation of a "homosexual identity." *Newsweek* (July 17, 1995) reported that in the 1990s bisexuals are "now claiming their own identity." The Bisexual Resource Guide, the magazine reports, lists 1,400 groups throughout the world, including "Bi Women of Color." In a sense, a choice of identity is not, Zelig-like, completely free (it would be outrageous, at least in some circles, for a homosexual white man to claim he is a bi woman of color); but in another sense, identities are constructed (it is hard to imagine anyone claiming the identity of bi woman of color before 1980).

Crises of Identity

Because social identities are constructed from the available repertoire of social categories, misfits are inevitable. Some people cannot find a label that adequately represents their identities. Or they may not like the identity they have chosen or were compelled to go by. Consider the case of Maria Maggenti, who in the *Village Voice* (June 27, 1995) reported that throughout her "adult life, I have called myself a lesbian. A dyke, sapphist, muff diver, lover of women. In this identity, I found a home for my desire, my politics, my upside-down sense of humor." But to her horror, she fell into a heterosexual relationship. She was in shock: "To me, calling myself a bisexual versus claiming a lesbian identity is the difference between Muzak and Mahler." She is facing, in our everyday language, an identity crisis.

The *Houston Chronicle* (August 2, 1995) diagnoses incidences of this sort as "gender identity disorder." The newspaper reports that "gay and lesbian teen-agers often find society unsympathetic to their situation, and this can provoke psychological problems, many of which are also symptoms of gender identity disorder: depression, attempted suicide, alienation and what psychiatry calls 'borderline personality disorder.' " Readers were assured that at least in California, such people would not be hospitalized, since "insurance companies just wouldn't pay for it."

Ambiguity of identity indeed represents a "problem," or more commonly a "crisis." In the United States, *Newsday* (July 13, 1995) asks whether black children raised by white parents develop a positive sense of self and a strong racial identity. The *Orlando Sentinel* (July 9, 1995) reports an initiative by the U.S. Census Bureau to include a "multiracial" category in order to "help children of biracial marriages with their self-identity." To go back to the sardonic article about British identity (*Sunday Telegraph*, July 23, 1995), Digby Anderson further remarks that "crises of identity are for people who haven't got one, like the Belgians, or who have got too many, such as the Italians."

This notion that lack of a clear identity can lead to a "crisis" is strongly contested. In Britain it pits conservatives against liberals. In one formulation (reported in the *Guardian*, July 20, 1995), "The liberal believes that a man, once stripped of his national and cultural identity, will become Everyman—citizen of the world. The conservative knows that, in fact, he will become bewildered, schizophrenic, unhappy and lonely." Liberal thinking remains strong in the United States. An editorial in the *San Francisco Chronicle* (June 29, 1995) argues that "racism requires the destruction of an individual's confidence in his own mind. Such an individual then anxiously seeks a sense of identity by clinging to some group, abandoning his autonomy and his rights, allowing his ethnic group to tell him what to believe." And an article in the *Village Voice* (June 20, 1995) reported that Georgia O'Keeffe "detested being considered a woman artist. Identity-related adjectives attached to the noun 'artist' always demean." These protests, in support of the rights of individuals against outsiders' attempts to label them, demonstrate the power of these identity categories to subsume and even colonize individuals. In a sense, the protests demonstrate the power of identity categories in spite of their arbitrariness and constructed nature.

Intellectuals who understand that identity categories are constructed yet wish to fight for opportunities for people with whom they identify face a problem the reverse of O'Keeffe's. How can they purposefully reify categories, giving people with complex pasts a single dominant label, when they know those categories are constructed? Anthony Appiah addressed this problem with great sensitivity while advocating the politicization of an African American identity. Gayatri Spivak articulated the concept of "strategic essentialism" to address this issue. As Lisa Lowe puts it, Spivak argues that "it is possible to utilize specific signifiers of ethnic identity, such as Asian-American, for the purpose of contesting and disrupting the discourses that exclude Asian-Americans, while simultaneously revealing the internal contradictions and slippages of Asian-American so as to insure that such essentialisms will not be reproduced and proliferated by the very apparatuses we seek to disempower."[24] On the one hand, identities such as African or Asian American can mobilize thousands of adherents; on the other hand, these identities, when careful archaeological work is done, are revealed as fabrications.

Both academic and popular analyses of the concept of identity (and especially national identity) are thus "both awed by its power and dumbfounded by its weakness."[25] By emphasizing the constructed character of identities, they tend to underrate the power of identity attachments to guide behavior, to drive people into incredible acts of heroism and terror. But when these acts of heroism and terror are reported, suddenly the language of primordialism (the Stalinesque categories of membership) is revived. Thus reports of the Croatian and Bosnian ethnic wars in the wake of the Yugoslav collapse often refer to "ancient hatreds," hatreds that for some reason did not stand in the way of the high levels of intermarriage in previous generations between the combatants of the mid-1990s. These analyses elide the historical facts of constructedness and change. Clearly we need a better understanding that accounts for both the constructed nature of social identities (the current conventional wisdom) and the power of these identities to seem natural to those who hold them. The search for this better understanding takes me beyond everyday discourse and on to approaches developed in psychoanalysis and game theory.

A Definition of Identity

The popular notion of a "crisis of identity" comes from the pioneering psychoanalytic work of Erik H. Erikson. A reading of his work sheds new light on these debates on identity and helps us address the problem of explaining both the constructedness and the power of social identity categories. Erikson attributes his focus on identity to a cryptic autobiographical passage in Freud's corpus, when he spoke about his "consciousness of [his] inner [i.e., Jewish] identity." Erikson went far beyond the master in developing a psychoanalytic notion of identity, even seeking to explain the sources of the Protestant Reformation in one man's identity crisis.[26]

[24] Kwame Anthony Appiah, *In My Father's House* (New York: Oxford University Press, 1992); Gayatri Spivak, *In Other Worlds* (New York: Routledge, 1987), p. 205; Lisa Lowe, "Heterogeneity, Hybridity, Multiplicity: Marking Asian American Differences," *Diaspora: A Journal of Transnational Studies* 1, no. 1 (1991): 24–44.

[25] David Laitin, "The Game Theory of Language Regimes," *International Political Science Review* 14, no. 3 (1993): 228.

[26] On the references to Freud, see Erik H. Erikson, *Identity: Youth and Crisis* (New York: Norton, 1968), pp. 20–21. On the Reformation, see Erikson, *Young Man Luther* (New York: Norton, 1958).

For Erikson, here relying on William James, identity is "a voice inside which speaks and says: 'This is the real me.' " Finding that identity is often a lifetime quest, and failure to find it (as Erikson suggests was the case with Hitler) can have a damaging impact on oneself and others. In light of this quest, which is both personal and social, Erikson sees "identity formation [as] a process . . . by which the individual judges himself in the light of what he perceives to be the way in which others judge him in comparison to themselves and to a typology significant to them; while he judges their way of judging him in the light of how he perceives himself in comparison to them and to types that have become relevant to him."[27]

This formulation elegantly captures what I have elsewhere called the "Janus-facedness of culture."[28] One face of culture reveals identities to be real and given, to be something that can be searched for and discovered. Theories of culture that rely on primordialist imagery see only this face of identity. Social solidarities are built on real foundations. While we may lose our bearings, our true identities are there for each of us to find.

But the second face of culture—and here I focus on the quest rather than the goal, the "real me"—is not primordial but instrumental. This face of culture reveals identities as constructed and reconstructed as social opportunities change. Ernesto Laclau is discussing this face of culture when he argues that "once the obviousness of social identities was put into question," it was no longer possible to imagine people "discovering or recognizing their own identity." Rather, the problem today is to think about "constructing" an identity with the "explicit assertion of a lack at the root of any identity."[29] Gustave Flaubert understood this face of culture well. L'Heureux, the clever draper, he wrote in *Madame Bovary*, was "born in Gascony, but a Norman by adoption." In this way he could marry his southern verbosity with a northerners' cunning. Identities from this point of view are adopted, or constructed, according to how well they serve individual purposes and reconstructed to take advantage of new opportunities.

It is here that Erikson is so useful. Primordialists and constructivists live in their separate intellectual universes, each deriding the blindness of the other. Neither side comprehends that each is looking at only one face of Janus. But Erikson positioned himself to see both faces. He understood, with the primordialists, that not any identity will do. People are limited in their senses of self by their families, their communities, the prevalent typologies of identity that surround them, and what he called the "identity possibilities of an age."[30] In this sense, identity is given. Yet individuals also seek to adjust their identities to the judgments of relevant others and tend not to settle on an identity for much of their youth. In this period of search,

[27] Erikson, *Identity*, pp. 19, 22–23.

[28] In my *Hegemony and Culture* (Chicago: University of Chicago Press, 1986) I discuss the primordialist approach associated with Clifford Geertz and the instrumentalist critique associated with Abner Cohen. See Geertz, "The Integrative Revolution," in his *Interpretation of Cultures*, and Cohen, *Two-Dimensional Man* (Berkeley: University of California Press, 1974).

[29] Ernesto Laclau, ed., "Introduction," in *The Making of Political Identities* (London: Verso, 1994).

[30] Erikson, *Identity*, p. 36.

individuals look to themselves and others, trying out new identities to see how they feel, both to themselves and to others judging them, before adopting one permanently. In this sense, for Erikson (and for Whitman's democratic citizen), identity is constructed.

Identities are therefore categories of membership that are based on all sorts of typologies—gender, race, class, personality, caste. People are limited by, but they are not prisoners of, their genes, their physiognomies, and their histories in settling on their own identities. And if powerful social forces motivate identity exploration—as they seem to do in our age—it is the constructivist face of identity that seems the more real.

How Identities Change

A compelling model of identity must not only define the concept in a coherent way—as I believe Erikson has done—but also be able to account for both the impressive power of identity groups to give their adherents a sense of natural membership and the equally impressive power of individuals to reconstruct their social identities. Relying on a model developed by Thomas Schelling, I propose to interpret identity shift in terms of a "tip" or "cascade."[31] Tips and cascades are common features of social life. Consider the case of one or two African Americans who buy homes in a stable "white" neighborhood. Suddenly the white families, fearing that they will be the last whites in the neighborhood, all seek to sell out at the same time. But only African Americans are willing to buy. Very quickly the neighborhood "tips" from stable white to stable African American.

In the late 1980s, protest cascaded across Eastern Europe in a similar way. Societies in which street protesting was nonexistent experienced sporadic demonstrations that were not quickly put down. Suddenly, protest grew to literally revolutionary levels. Thoroughly hopeless and demobilized societies suddenly became highly mobilized and active. In 1988 political protest seemed impossible; in 1989 it was normal.[32]

Such cascades occur because people's choices about their actions are based on what they think others are going to do. If I think none of my neighbors will sell his house if a few African American families move close by, I have no incentive to sell mine. But if I think many others will—or better, if I think many others will think that many others will—then I have an interest in selling my house before those others do, that is to say, before property values plummet. Or in the case of protesting: if I think that no one will be out picketing in the streets, I know I will be an easy target for the police. But if I think that others will be out—or if I believe that many others will be sure that many others will be out—suddenly prudence no longer dictates that I remain at home.

[31] Thomas Schelling, *Micromotives and Macrobehavior* (New York: Norton, 1978).

[32] Timur Kuran, "Now out of Never: The Role of Surprise in the East European Revolution of 1989," *World Politics* 44, no. 1 (1991): 7–48; Susan Lohmann, "Dynamics of Informational Cascades," *World Politics* 47, no. 1 (1994): 42–101.

Both of these situations have two stable equilibrium outcomes: an all-"white" or all–"African American" neighborhood; and streets with no protesters or streets filled with protesters.

Identity shift can also cascade. In order to keep the discussion and the model focused, I limit my remarks to one aspect of identity—one's language community.[33] Like almost all social identities, one's language community (or mother tongue, as it is popularly understood) often has a near mystical quality conferring membership in a category of similarly endowed people. Yet language repertoires, like social identities, are subject to rapid intergenerational shift. Therefore, we hear stories of language retention despite all efforts by a state to erase a language,[34] and stories as well—for example, of Lutheran children in nineteenth-century Ohio mocking their ministers who insisted on speaking German—in which mother tongues get lost within a generation. Both story lines are accurate. When my grandparents came to New York in the late nineteenth century, they knew that other children of Yiddish speakers would be learning English, and it would be irrational for them to seek to maintain the intergenerational transmission of Yiddish. Meanwhile, when Russians moved into the "virgin" lands of Kazakhstan at that very time, they fully expected other Russians to maintain the linguistic repertoires they had in the Russian heartland. Here we have examples of opposite and extreme equilibria. In New York after a generation, hardly any monolingual Yiddish speakers were left. In Kazakhstan after a generation, very few descendants of Russian immigrants were even bilingual in Russian and Kazakh.

The tipping model can account for both the constructed nature (to those who study it) and the naturalness (to those who live it) of social identities. At any equilibrium, it appears to actors that the world is completely stable. In this situation, identities are not under question. There is (by the definition of equilibrium) no incentive for anyone to explore new identities. It is obvious to people who in fact they are. A point of coordination, in which there is a tacit understanding among all people in a community that this is an aspect of their identity (for example, that Russians address all others living in Kazakhstan in Russian), is an example of what Thomas Schelling calls a focal point.[35] Cultural and political elites of a group in equilibrium, by giving meaning to the equilibrium—that is, by providing it with the "beliefs, principles and constraints" that Harré identified—make it into a focal point. In this way they expand their authority and gain the legitimacy to speak on "their" group's behalf. In Max Weber's terms, these elites will seek to ascribe ultimate value to the focal point identity—that is, give it "value rationality"—in order to defend it against all pragmatic considerations.[36]

[33] For more on my preoccupation in this book with language, which I acknowledge to be only one element of a person's complex social identity, please see the appendix.

[34] This is a principal theme of Toivo Raun's *Estonia and the Estonians* (Stanford: Hoover Institution Press, 1987). He cites the nineteenth-century poem of Jaak Peterson—"May not the language of this land / On winds of song and / Rising to the heavens / Seek eternity?"—to show how commitment to a Finno-Ugric identity could overcome historically powerful Germanic and Russian efforts to stamp it out.

[35] Thomas Schelling, *The Strategy of Conflict* (Cambridge: Harvard University Press, 1960).

[36] I owe this last point to Martin Riesebrodt.

Exogenous events (such as the independence of Kazakhstan), however, can nonetheless bring some instability, with certain people exploring new identities (such as Russian-Kazakhstani). At such times, cultural entrepreneurs of the once-stable identity emerge and try to stem any tide away from the old equilibrium, and seek to naturalize, or essentialize, the status quo ante. Those claims will appear compelling, for the very fact that there was coordination at a particular equilibrium over generations does, indeed, make that equilibrium look like a law of nature. Other cultural entrepreneurs, more forward-looking, will seek to induce a cascade toward a new equilibrium, and if they are successful, the change will be thought of as natural, or inevitable. The tipping game therefore shows why identities are powerful "focal points" of coordination, yet are also subject to change.

One might argue that adopting a new language does not automatically mean one has adopted a new identity. Yet if Liuba Grigor'ev had felt like a traitor or a fool for taking Estonian language lessons, her motivation would have been sapped. Her identity was becoming "a Russian who has accommodated to the realities of Estonian sovereignty." This was the real "Liuba." But these microadjustments in identity—a nuance Erikson did not consider—alter the identity possibilities of a following age. In this sense, Liuba's quest to keep her family intact lays the foundation for a constructed Estonian identity for her grandchildren. In Schelling's terms, she is in her microactivities moving her family, and the Russian-speaking community of Narva, toward an identity tip.

One might also object that the tipping game, with its emphasis on binary choices, does not capture the fact that multiple identities are common in social life. Many people, for example, want to be Catalans, Spaniards, and Europeans all at the same time. Some, I am sure, see themselves as lesbians, workers, Catholics, and Hispanics and alter the emphasis to fit the context. A resident of Harlem might identify himself as a black in the context of New York politics but as an American in the context of international affairs. People's "identity projects" are clearly more nuanced than making either/or choices between matched pairs of identity alternatives.

Multiple identities, however, can coexist within a person only insofar as choice is not necessary. Yet when the actions or behaviors consistent with one identity conflict with those of another identity held by the same person, as they do when the two identities represent antagonistic groups on the political stage, people are compelled to give priority to one identity over the other. A person who sees herself as both a "Russian" and an "Estonian" may one day have to choose—say, if there were a border war—which identity is dominant. In this case, the tipping game is a powerful analytic tool, as surely one's choice is affected by the number of people (of like multiple identities) who have given priority to their "Russian" or their "Estonian" identities.[37]

Consider the rise of a politicized homosexual identity in the United States and its implications for an African American whose sexual preference was heretofore a private matter. Perhaps his partner or some of his past partners have been mobilized

[37] Roger Petersen, in "Rationality, Ethnicity, and Military Enlistment," *Social Science Information* 28, no. 3 (1989): 563–98, relied on the tipping game to do just this, using the case of Japanese-Americans' enlistment behavior during World War II.

into action as homosexuals. Now they are in daily political alliance with whites and Hispanics, and their former political identity group, the African American community, becomes less prominent as a basis for their political information and mobilization. It is useful to model this man's choice situation and do an accounting of the payoffs for "coming out" politically as a homosexual based on how many other black homosexuals have chosen to come out, and the social benefits and costs of either decision, again depending on the percentage of African American homosexuals who have reoriented their political activity. This is not to deny that this person's identity is multiple; rather it is to emphasize that the everyday reality of identity politics forces us to weigh alternative presentations of self, keeping in mind how others, like ourselves, are representing themselves. This is a basic dynamic in identity shift.

A final objection to the tipping motif has to do with the rational choice framework itself. How can one calculate the costs and benefits of identity shift, especially under conditions of trauma and uncertainty?

In response to this skepticism about rational choice models, I should like to offer two preliminary counters. First, it is correct that a variety of identity projects can be offered to a population in crisis. In this book we will observe two of them, toward a titular and toward a conglomerate identity. Before people can strategize, they need to know what the choices are. Much of the "work" of identity choice, in consequence, precedes the tipping dynamic.[38] In times of crisis, then, people may be playing more than one game at a time. Nonetheless, the tipping model neatly encapsulates people's strategic dilemmas once the game has begun. In this sense, the tipping game is but a partial rendition of the overall cultural dynamic.

Within the tipping game, however, and somewhat counterintuitively, it is not the case that trauma and uncertainty undermine rational calculation. Despite the powerful arguments of Ann Swidler to the contrary, in unsettled times, people—at least those families with whom I and my fellow field researchers interacted—feel compelled to calculate and coordinate their calculations with others. In this sense—as the ethnographies in this book make clear—uncertainty is the breeding ground for coordination dynamics such as those evident in the tipping game.[39]

National Identities

National identities, like social and neighborhood identities, have cascade qualities. National projects—such as Catalan, Flemish, or Mayan—may seem quixotic and antiquarian at one point in time, yet suddenly burst onto the historical stage as if by spontaneous combustion. In the modern age, national projects have usually involved the reinsertion of a folk language as part of the core identity of people who

[38] I owe this point to Prasenjit Duara.

[39] Ann Swidler, "Culture in Action: Symbols and Strategies," *American Sociological Review* 51 (April 1986): 273–86. I develop more fully the notion that uncertainty breeds rationality in "Identity Choice under Conditions of Uncertainty" (paper presented at the faculty seminar of the Department of Political Science, University of Michigan, Ann Arbor, November 1996).

are descendants of speakers of that language, most of whom rely principally on a more cosmopolitan state language. Language movements, with the goal of restoring languages in desuetude as a tool to create modern nations, have been a constant source of identity politics in the modern age.

Nationalist politics involve two interrelated identity issues. First is the issue of a "national revival" in a relatively homogeneous region in a culturally heterogeneous state. Consider Estonia in its period as a Union republic of the Soviet state. Estonians who wished specialized higher education and occupational mobility found the inclusion of Russian in their language repertoires to be of great value. Within a generation, it became normal to rely on Russian in a variety of professional and political domains. This is why families such as the Grigor'evs had no need to learn Estonian. In the late 1980s, radical Estonian nationalists, fearful that the massive immigration of Russians into their republic had set in motion a long-term threat to the viability of the Estonian nation, pressed for the elimination of Soviet-period immigrants from Estonian political life. This move would make possible the sole use of Estonian in all political, educational, and administrative domains. From their point of view, such policies would forestall a tip toward Russian-language dominance in Estonia.[40] These nationalists were seeking to undermine a Soviet-inspired identity project that emphasized the merging of nations. Nationalists in other Union republics, where Russian was beginning to replace the titular languages in many social domains, were also seeking to reverse a linguistic tide. The key for regional nationalists, whether stemming or reversing a tide, is to induce their followers to abjure the central language. An important element for success is to get people from the regional culture to believe that all their fellow regionals are already beginning to switch to a regional-dominant language repertoire. To the extent to which people who identify ethnically as members of the regional culture rely principally on the regional language for family, work, and cultural affairs, we can say that the nationalists have successfully induced a tip in the national-revival game.

A second issue in nationalist politics involves the "assimilation" of members of minority groups, or immigrants, into the new national culture. To the extent that the Estonian national revival is a success, for example, people such as the Grigor'evs, who relied principally on Russian, must work to add Estonian to their repertoires and to seek education for their children in Estonian. They will, of course, keep a careful eye on the choices made by fellow Russian-speakers. If all Russian-speakers feel that all others will remain monolingual in Russian, they will see little need to learn Estonian. But if they fear that many others are already adjusting to the new language regime by learning Estonian, they will feel pressure to join the cascade.

In both national revivals and assimilation cascades, there are political pressures to alter one's "identity project." I shall now explicate these two processes more formally from the perspective of the tipping game.

[40] Raun, *Estonia and the Estonians*, p. 210, cites three documents from the early 1980s in which Estonian intellectuals expressed "the fear . . . that the Estonian language and culture were in danger of losing their leading role in Estonia as Russian increasingly became the language of administration and was emphasized in education."

National Revival

In his explication of the problem of consolidating a national revival, Ernest Gellner referred to the revivalist region as "Ruritania" and the central state as "Megalomania."[41] He assumed that the political leaders of Ruritania are fully bilingual in both the language of state power and the language of the region. As Megalomania consolidated power, he explains, the great mass of the regional population became at least partially assimilated as well. But there was resentment, and Ruritanian leaders sought sovereignty for their cultural group in a national revival.[42]

Most portrayals of political movements that are dedicated to a region's political, economic, or cultural autonomy focus primarily on the conflict of interest between the power at the center and the united national movement at the periphery. What these portrayals often miss is the conflict of interest that exists *within* the regional nationality population. The major problem for regional revivalists is to induce a tip within their own constituencies.

Let us suppose that in Megalomania, of which Ruritania was a part, access to wealth and power required fluency in the language of the state. In fact, residents of any distinct region would be able to communicate with residents from any other distinct region only through the state language. Usually, under these conditions, people who live in culturally distinct regions become "diglossic."[43] This is a special form of bilingualism, where the state language is used mostly for "high" functions (such as trade, high culture, and contacts with state authorities) and the regional language is used for "low" functions (for intimacy, and for celebrations of folk culture).

If Ruritania, whose population is diglossic, is to achieve a national revival, its leaders must reverse the functional domains of the two languages. Many people who consider themselves Ruritanians will feel uncomfortable using what they see as a folk language in domains of high culture or technology. They are likely to believe the myth that "their" language is not capable of expressing complex or modern thoughts. Those Ruritanians who are members of the local bureaucracy—those whose jobs and advancement required facility in Megalomanian—will have an interest in maintaining the linguistic status quo.

The national revival tipping game—displayed in Figure 1.1—illustrates these constraints. Here, for illustrative purposes, I leave Gellner's fantasy world of Megalomanians and Ruritanians for the actual world of the republics of the former Soviet Union. On the *x* axis I have plotted the percentage of the regional nationality (whom I shall call here, with the Soviet case in mind, titulars) in full compliance with the laws and principles of the nationalizing movement (the function TT) and the percentage of the regional nationality continuing to rely on the language of the former center (the function RR). On the *y* axis is the payoff an individual receives for his or her linguistic choice. The payoff for an individual linguistic choice depends on how many other individuals made the same choice.

[41] Ernest Gellner, *Nations and Nationalism* (Ithaca: Cornell University Press, 1983). In Chapter 9, I elaborate on, criticize, and extend Gellner's theory.

[42] Ernest Gellner, *Thought and Change* (Chicago: University of Chicago Press, 1964).

[43] Charles Ferguson, "Diglossia," *Word* 15 (1959): 325–40.

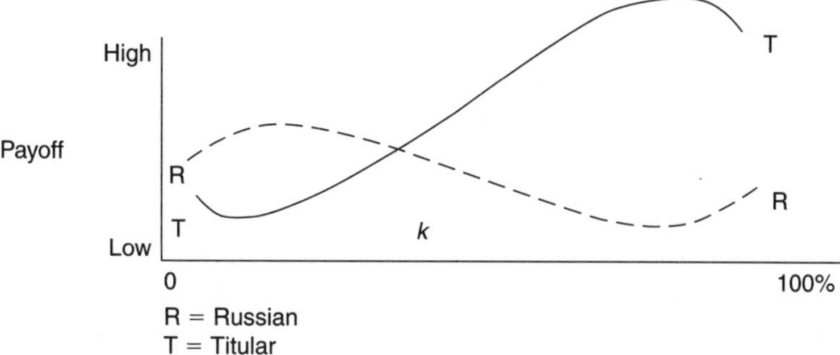

Figure 1.1. National revival game: Percentage of titulars who comply fully with nationalist language laws

The dilemma portrayed in this diagram reflects practical decisions that real people face. Those school principals, directors of industrial plants, newspaper publishers, retailers, and professionals who operated in environments where Russian was the dominant language need to decide whether to comply with new state laws requiring the monopoly of official use for the newly legislated national language. Parents (of the titular nationality) need to decide whether to send their children to titular-language schools. If the children have already been attending Russian-language schools, the cost of change will clearly be high, and the change will be worth it only if other enterprises (or parents) adopt it as well. Therefore, no organization (or parent) has an incentive to move first, even if all agree that the payoffs for all would be higher at 100 percent indigenous than they are at, say, 20 percent indigenous, which is the point at which many revival movements begin. This is why many titulars will vote for a nationalizing program, believing in it theoretically, but then subvert it in their own private and professional lives.[44] When people personally subvert the goals of the very movement they have given their elected leaders a mandate to promote, that movement will fail. It will fail not only because of the nefarious interference of the declining center (although the revivalists will want to blame their failure on the center's lust for reintegration) but also because of the rational linguistic strategies of already partially assimilated members of the nationality group in whose name the revival is being promoted. Cultural entrepreneurs directing a national revival movement must somehow induce a language tip, and they can do so by convincing key members of the titular population that other key members are already in the process of changing their linguistic practices. The success of this effort cannot be predicted from the size of the vote in favor of new nationalizing language laws.

With such heavy constraints facing regional revivals, how do their leaders push societies toward the desired equilibrium state? This is clearly the question regional

[44] In Laitin, "The Game Theory of Language Regimes," *International Political Science Review* 14, no. 3 (1993): 233, I call this the "private subversion of a public good." This strategy is similar to that caricatured by Will Rogers when he said that Oklahomans would continue to vote for prohibition as long as they could stagger to the polls.

revivalists everywhere face. As we shall see, historical patterns in the way regions have been incorporated into centralized states tell us a good deal about the possibilities for success of regional revivals. Furthermore, the degree of success of regional revivals is an important clue to the power of competitive assimilation, the second crucial game in the drama of nationality politics.

Competitive Assimilation

Let us now consider the situation of the members of an immigrant nationality (let us, following Gellner, call them Ruritanians) in a state (Megalomania) in which the dominant language is different from their own. Let us further suppose that this immigration was economically, not culturally, motivated. These Ruritanians very much want to maintain their language and culture and to pass it on to their children, who will, they hope, subsequently pass it on to their children. If the entire Ruritanian community thinks more or less in this way, they will be able to demand from Megalomania a certain degree of cultural autonomy, such as the right to maintain Ruritanian-language schools, and to have local administration and legal proceedings conducted in Ruritanian.

Suppose, however, that at the time these people immigrated there were no schools, no local services, and no entry-level middle-class jobs in which Ruritanian was used. Further suppose that those who wanted those jobs would need to be literate in Megalomanian. It would then be rational for an immigrant to send her child to a school that ensured rapid training in Megalomanian. A Ruritanian child attending such a school would have a competitive advantage in the upwardly mobile job market. But if it is rational for any parent to do this, then all parents will think that other parents will probably do it, and that therefore they should get their children competent in the language of their new society (i.e., move toward linguistic assimilation) before the middle-class job market is saturated.

Under these conditions, which are more or less what immigrants to America have faced for over a century, we get rapid assimilation into the national language even if all parents agree that it would be better if all immigrant families held together and nurtured their home culture in the new environment. In the case of the Russians in the titular republics, however, as represented in Figure 1.2, the rate of change may be slow at first until the number of people who switch begins to increase. As more Russians learn the titular language, others will perceive the trend and calculate that the payoffs for not speaking the titular language will, before too long, be lower than those for learning it. As this process unfolds, and the feeling spreads that the direction of change is toward the language of the national state, the rate of change will rapidly increase.

When are such cascades most likely to begin? Because this book focuses on the plight of the Russian immigrants in the near abroad, this game gets special attention. As a preliminary matter, it should be clear from a perusal of Figure 1.2 that at the far left of the x axis, it is still irrational for Russians to study the titular language. Something must occur to change the payoffs for at least a few pioneers. From a macro point of view, changes in world trade patterns, interstate relations, immigra-

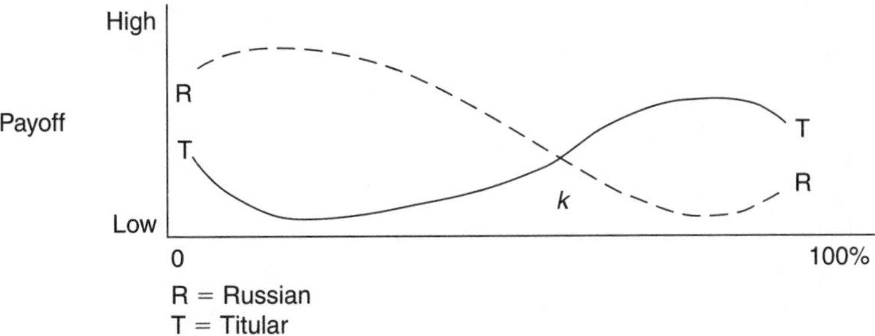

Figure 1.2. Competitive assimilation game: Percentage of Russians who speak titular language

tion possibilities, and state policies on education and administration have discernible effects on individual incentives and can certainly induce a few Russians to shift their linguistic repertoires. A micro perspective focuses on how such changes actually happen, and under what conditions the tipping point (*k*) will be reached. From this micro perspective, several (un)favorable conditions can be enumerated as initial hypotheses. First, assimilation cascades are likely to occur when the expected lifetime earnings of a young person are substantially greater when that person is fluent in the language of the state in which the family now resides. Second, assimilation cascades are likely to occur when the immigrant community is itself divided and puts few constraints on its members to remain a tight-knit community. Put another way, assimilation cascades can be halted if cultural entrepreneurs within the immigrant community can raise the status of people who refuse to give up their cultures, or lower the status of those who mimic the practices of the majority culture. Third, assimilation cascades are likely to occur when members of the majority culture accept as one of their own (on the marriage market, in social affairs) those immigrants who have attempted to assimilate. I call these three factors expected economic returns, in-group status, and out-group status. Calculations about these returns, I hypothesize, will have implications for the likelihood of a linguistic tip, with a concomitant change in the Russian population's social identity; perhaps after the tip they will see themselves as "Bilingual Russian-Titulars."

Assimilation, Diasporas, and Conglomerate Identities

Throughout this book, I refer to the Russian population living in the states of the former Soviet Union as a diaspora—although, since they acquired that status because the borders of the Soviet Union receded, rather than because they dispersed from their homeland, it is perhaps better to think of them as a beached diaspora. Yet we should not forget that these Russians are being pressed not only to assimilate but also to consolidate as part of a conglomerate identity group. Calling them a diaspora tempts one to forget about the social pressures for assimilation. Calling them a conglomerate identity group tempts one to place them in the same category as Hispanics or Asian Americans in the United States and appeal to the literature on reactive identity formation. The naming, as it were, presupposes the category of analysis.[45] One of the advantages of the tipping model I propose is that it allows us to analyze the identity situation faced by Russians without presupposing the genre of group they have become.

In the social science literature, many attempts have been made to distinguish assimilation from other forms of cultural and political incorporation into dominant society.[46] But the tipping model allows us to cut through many of those distinctions, and to talk simply about rates of assimilation in a variety of contexts. For our purposes, assimilation can be defined as "the process of adoption of the ever changing cultural practices of dominant society with the goal of crossing a fluid cultural boundary separating [minorities] from dominant society."[47] From the point of view of the tipping game, assimilation can be thought of as a successful switch, in a variety of cultural realms, to the practices of dominant society. To the extent that in a range of these cultural realms the minority population crosses the tipping threshold, we can say that societal (as opposed to individual) assimilation has occurred. Note well that even with apparently complete assimilation, there will always be those "half-forgotten poets and lonely philologists" whose expected returns for holding on to languages and rituals in desuetude are larger than the returns for assimilating.[48] These cultural elites will always be ready, in the hope that social conditions will someday allow a tip back to the status quo ante. In this sense, assimilation, according to the tipping game, is never completely settled.

What, then, is a "diaspora"? In the contemporary literature, the attempt to distinguish "diasporas" from immigrants, expatriates, refugees, guest workers, exile communities, overseas communities, and ethnic communities has led to a plethora of distinctions that make little difference.[49] William Safran recognized that originally "diaspora" referred only to Jews, and it was therefore somewhat redundant to theorize about diasporas as a category of communities. Defining it merely as a "segment of people living outside the homeland" (as Walker Connor does), however, dilutes it of all its meaning, as it would then include all immigrant communities. Safran therefore suggests the following criteria,

[45] Rafael compares nicely across categories. His comparison of Filipinos living under Japanese colonial rule with diasporic populations is extremely productive, but his approach does not lead to a genuine comparative analysis. He cannot offer a general calculus, for example, on the relative probability of assimilation in different settings. See Vicente L. Rafael, "Anticipating Nationhood: Collaboration and Rumor in the Japanese Occupation of Manila," *Diaspora: A Journal of Transnational Studies* 1, no. 1 (1991): 67–82.

[46] The most sophisticated in this genre, where "integration," "acculturation," and "assimilation" are shown to be distinct, is that of R. A. Schermerhorn, *Comparative Ethnic Relations* (Chicago: University of Chicago Press, 1970). See also, John W. Berry, "Ethnic Identity in Plural Societies," in Bernal and Knight, *Ethnic Identity Formation*, pp. 271–96.

[47] David Laitin, "Marginality: A Microperspective," *Rationality and Society* 7, no. 1 (1995): 35.

[48] David Laitin, "Language Games," *Comparative Politics* 20 (1988): 289–302.

[49] This is the point of Kachig Tölölyan, "The Nation-State and Its Others: In Lieu of a Preface," *Diaspora: A Journal of Transnational Studies* 1, no. 1 (1991): 4, writing as the founding editor of the journal.

> 1) they, or their ancestors, have been dispersed from a specific original "center" to two or more "peripheral," or foreign, regions; 2) they retain a collective memory, vision, or myth about their original homeland—its physical location, history, and achievements; 3) they believe that they are not—and perhaps cannot be—fully accepted by their host society and therefore feel partly alienated and insulated from it; 4) they regard their ancestral homeland as their true, ideal home and as the place to which they or their descendants would (or should) eventually return—when conditions are appropriate; 5) they believe that they should, collectively, be committed to the maintenance or restoration of their original homeland and to its safety and prosperity; and 6) they continue to relate, personally or vicariously, to that homeland in one way or another, and their ethnocommunal consciousness and solidarity are importantly defined by the existence of such a relationship.[50]

Jews remain the paradigmatic case, but Armenians, Turks, Maghrebis, Palestinians, Cubans, Greeks, and maybe the Chinese meet at least some of these criteria.

From the perspective of the tipping game, no such subtle distinctions, or criteria of inclusion, are necessary. A diaspora is a population living in a society distant from the homeland that its leaders claim as their own, and to which they expect one day to return. By emphasizing the group's diasporic qualities, identity entrepreneurs seek to raise the probability in the minds of their constituencies of a successful return to that homeland. To the extent that they are successful—by inculcating a sense of nostalgia among people who have never lived there, for example[51]—they will be able to stem the tide of complete assimilation, for the members of their identity group will want to cultivate intergenerationally the linguistic skills, cultural knowledge, distinct names, or at least a sharp memory of ancestral belonging that would become essential if they or their descendants were in fact to return. This is a form of in-group policing, giving social status to people who invest in the possibility of a future return.

A "conglomerate" identity is a category of membership that is a common denominator among a set of identity groups that share some characteristics that are distinct from those in the dominant society in which they live. One must not think of conglomerate identities as false by definition; after all, most of today's nationalities—note the earlier discussion of Britishness—are conglomerates of historically separable elements. Conglomerate identities often form when members of dominant society refer to a set of distinct groups in a common way (as South African Boers would talk about "kaffirs"); but conglomerate identity groups can also arise when the social boundaries separating a set of related groups all living on a foreign soil (as is the case of Ukrainians and Russians now living in Kazakhstan) are relatively weak. Under conditions of a "conglomerate identity" group, there is often no credible traditional elite to protect the group's boundaries or to punish defectors who seek to reidentify themselves as members of the dominant society. Conglomerate identity groups may

[50] William Safran, "Diasporas in Modern Societies: Myths of Homeland and Return," *Diaspora: A Journal of Transnational Studies* 1, no. 1 (1991): 83–84.

[51] This point is nicely developed by Hamid Naficy, "The Poetics and Practice of Iranian Nostalgia in Exile," *Diaspora: A Journal of Transnational Studies* 1, no. 3 (1991): 285–302.

therefore be demographically large but politically weak. Lisa Lowe recognizes this in her analysis of an Asian American identity. "As with other diasporas in the United States," she reasons, "the Asian immigrant collectivity is unstable and changeable, with its cohesion complicated by intergenerationality, by various degrees of identification and relation to a 'homeland,' and by different extents of assimilation to and distinction from 'majority culture' in the United States."[52] Theoretically it makes no difference whether Asian Americans (or Hispanics) are diasporas or not; the important point is that by lumping Japanese and Chinese within the same identity group, or Cubans and Mexicans—as a conglomerate identity—the forces of dominant society easily overrun attempts by Asian American or Hispanic activists to protect the integrity (or separateness) of constructed Asian American or Hispanic cultures.

What, then, *are* the Russians in the near abroad? Are they a diaspora like the Palestinians, forming a bomb about to detonate? Or are they the forgotten people in the drama of decolonization, like the *pieds noirs*, likely to be evacuated from their republics and ignored in their supposed homeland? Maybe the analogous case is the English Rhodesians, a settler community that will continue to maintain its privileges, even though they will never develop a true Zimbabwean identity. Still again, as the Russians, Ukrainians, Belarusans, Poles, and Jews develop a sense of a common plight, as a "Russian-speaking population," the analogous case may be the Asian Americans or Hispanics, in the development of a docile conglomerate identity.

My answer to this question is that the analogy should not precede the analysis, but rather should follow from it. No category—neither settler, diaspora, nor conglomerate group—precisely fits the situation. The real question is the extent to which cultural entrepreneurs in the former Union republics will be able, like the leaders of the Palestinian Liberation Organization, to lay cogent claim to a lost homeland that will one day be returned to them. To the extent that this move succeeds, the analogy of diaspora will be self-fulfilling. To the extent that Russian leaders feel compelled to categorize themselves as part of a larger group, involving non-Russian Russian-speakers, they will have a more difficult time making claims about a common religious identity, or a common homeland that one day will be returned to them. I do not seek to fit Russians living in the near abroad into a particular category. My purpose is rather to understand the dynamics of identity shift and the implications for the kinds of states they will be living in, and for the degree of conflict they are likely to experience in their relations with the titular populations.

Preliminary Statement of Findings

This book provides a coherent explanation of why Liuba Grigor'ev has already made some major cultural adjustments in the direction of assimilation. It does so in

[52] Lowe, "Heterogeneity, Hybridity, Multiplicity," p. 27. On the growing political weakness of the Cuban diaspora in the United States as the Cubans become part of a "fluid diaspora of twenty-five million" Latinos, or Hispanics, see Román de la Campa, "The Latino Diaspora in the United States: Sojourns from a Cuban Past," *Public Culture* 6 (1994): 293–317.

a way that differentiates her from Russian-speakers in Ukraine and Kazakhstan, who face different pressures and have different opportunities. This book takes several hefty jumps into the rarefied atmosphere of theory—especially as the tipping game is developed—but it does so in a way that is grounded in the lives of real people.

More specifically, this book shows that each of the titular republics was incorporated into the Russian and Soviet states in one of three ways (Chapter 3). The key to distinguishing these three macro patterns of state incorporation of peripheral territories is the degree to which elites in the incorporated peripheries had mobility prospects in the political center. To the extent that they were treated as equal to the elites in the center—and Ukraine is the exemplar—the mode of incorporation was what I refer to as "most favored lord." To the extent that mobility prospects were virtually blocked—and Kazakhstan is the exemplar in this study—the mode of incorporation was "colonial." To the extent that mobility prospects were partially blocked but rather rapid within the republic—Estonia and Latvia fit this picture—I shall refer to this as "integral" incorporation. These macro patterns help us understand the setup of the linguistic tipping games that were unleashed with the breakup of the Soviet Union.

The micro data presented in this book suggest two fundamental trends concerning identity shift in the republics of the former Soviet Union. The principal finding (reached in Chapter 9) concerns the prospects for assimilation by Russians into the national cultures of the states in which they were beached. I shall show why the prospects for Russians' assimilation into the titular society (despite cultural distance and anti-Russian policies and practices by the titulars) is greater in the Baltic states than in Ukraine or Kazakhstan. Furthermore, I shall show that the prospects for Russians' assimilation are greater in Latvia than in Estonia, despite the higher expected economic returns for learning Estonian. From both ethnographic and survey data, I shall also show why Russians' assimilation is more problematic in culturally proximate Ukraine than in the culturally distant Baltic states.

A secondary movement in the former Union republics is acting alongside and against the pressure to shift from Russian to titular (elaborated in Chapter 10). Most of those people who fall outside (by virtue of language) the nationalizing projects of the republican governments in the states of the near abroad have begun to form (or be formed into) a single identity group. They have begun to see themselves—in conglomerate terms—as a "Russian-speaking population." A major finding of this book is that the development of such a conglomerate identity—although its membership is quite different in the different republics—is the principal countertrend to assimilation.

With these two trends identified—that of assimilation and that of the creation of a conglomerate identity—I shall (in Part 5) analyze the implications of these findings to address two outstanding questions on the post-Soviet agenda. First is the question whether violent conflict is likely between the Russian inhabitants and the titular nationalities of the nationalizing states. Some analysts, such as my collaborator Marika Kirch, rely on Samuel Huntington's notion of a "clash of civilizations" to suggest that a Russian/titular divide is inevitable, no matter how fluid the actual cultural scene. My response is that a micro theory of identity shift, such as the tipping game, reveals conflicts *within* civilizations which diminish the cogency of a model that focuses principally on claims to broad cultural difference as the fountainhead of post–Cold War conflict.

Other analysts, relying on models of interstate conflict, study the issue of ethnic conflict as if it were a game between a team of Russians and a team of titulars. Ignoring civilizational divides, these analysts portray ethnic conflict as purely an issue of the security dilemma. My response (provided in Chapter 12) is that there is a crucial difference between internationality and interstate conflict. In the former, the boundaries of group membership are always subject to redefinition. Political leaders of ethnic groups must constantly worry about defections from their own group, as people move into other identity groups. This situation, I argue, puts great pressure on self-appointed representatives of nationality groups to rely on coercion to assure group solidarity. The sources of a significant part of interethnic violence, I contend, are to be found in the intragroup politics of internal policing and boundary protection. The politics of identity itself—of cultural elites seeking to protect the boundaries of the groups they purport to represent—creates even more incentives for violence than the tensions between identity groups do.

Second, there is the debate about whether the "nationalizing states"[53] of the former Soviet Union will become nation-states (on the order of France, Germany, and the United States) or retain their multinational character (on the model of Belgium, Switzerland, and the Soviet Union). Elsewhere I have shown that both international conditions and the nature of state-building itself in the present era make the construction of nation-states quite unlikely today, even if there are significant pressures for assimilation of minorities.[54] In accord with this perspective, I shall show (in Chapter 13) the considerable constraints that leaders in the republics of the former Soviet Union face in fashioning nation-states. Yet, in contrast to my projections in *Language Repertoires*, I show how Soviet rule helped to undermine those constraints, leaving the road open for successful nationalizing projects in the Baltics and Kazakhstan (but not in Ukraine).

I do not return to the theses concerning violence and the nation-state until Part 5, in the final two chapters of this book. In the remaining two chapters of Part 1, I provide a macrohistorical framework for understanding the nationality situation that Russians faced as the republics they lived in consolidated their nationalizing programs. In Part 2 I then provide an extensive ethnographic description of the identity scene among Russians in the former Union republics after the collapse of the Soviet Union. These chapters provide the flesh and blood that past renditions of the rather skeletal tipping game lacked. In Part 3 I introduce survey data and a sociolinguistic experiment to probe further the question whether Russians can become titulars. In Part 4 I address the question whether Russians in diaspora may develop a new conglomerate identity, neither titular nor "Russian." I ask repeatedly throughout: Who

[53] For a sensitive definition of what "nationalizing state" means in practice, see Rogers Brubaker, "National Minorities, Nationalizing States, and External National Homelands in the New Europe," *Daedalus* 124, no. 2 (1995): 107–32.

[54] David D. Laitin, *Language Repertoires and State Construction in Africa* (New York: Cambridge University Press, 1992).

were the Russians and what are they becoming? The answer to this simple question—with data from Kazakhstan, Estonia, Latvia, and Ukraine—consumes my attention for the bulk of this book and helps provide a coherent yet novel set of answers to the questions concerning what type of state and what sort of ethnic violence we can expect in the post-Soviet world.

2

Why the Peripheral Peoples Did Not Become Russians

In the nineteenth century Alexis de Tocqueville accurately foresaw the clashes of civilization that would mark Russian society for a century and a half:

> There are, at the present time, two great nations in the world, which seem to tend towards the same end. . . . I allude to the Russians and the Americans. Both of them have grown up unnoticed; and whilst the attention of mankind was directed elsewhere, they have suddenly assumed a most prominent place amongst the nations. . . . All other nations seem to have nearly reached their natural limits, and only to be charged with the maintenance of their power; but these are still in the act of growth. . . . The American struggles against the natural obstacles which oppose him; the adversaries of the Russian are men; the former combats the wilderness and savage life; the latter, civilization with all its weapons and its arts: the conquests of the one are therefore gained by the ploughshare; those of the other, by the sword. The Anglo-American relies upon personal interest to accomplish his ends, and gives free scope to the unguided exertions and common sense of the citizens; the Russian centres all the authority of society in a single arm: the principal instrument of the former is freedom; of the latter, servitude. Their starting-point is different . . . yet each of them seems to be marked out by the will of Heaven to sway the destinies of half the globe.[1]

Manifest destiny, Russian style, did not foster the construction of a new continent-wide identity (such as "American"). To be sure, attempts to construct an inclusive "Russian" identity in the nineteenth century, and a "Soviet" identity in the twentieth, had some success. But within the boundaries of the Russian empire (and the

[1] Alexis de Tocqueville, *Democracy in America*, trans. Henry Reeve (1835; New York: Schocken Books, 1961), 1:521–22.

Soviet Union), linguistic diversity in particular and national diversity more generally remained and even prospered.

The incomplete rationalization of language and culture within the boundaries of the Russian empire provides the historical context for this book. But this chapter—in going over well-trodden historical fields—seeks as well to demonstrate the contingency of this outcome. I seek to show how Russian (and Soviet) rationalization was possible but unsuccessful. The subsequent rationalization projects of four of the former Union republics resulted (or have as yet failed to result in) a strategic turning of the cultural tide rather than the inevitable (in the Hegelian sense) fulfillment of four national dreams. We cannot assume that all states will become nation-states by historical necessity, a myth that underlies many of the post-Soviet national projects—but with historical perspective it will be possible to analyze the likelihood that these four will.

Russian Expansion to the Continental Peripheries

From the end of the fifteenth century, with Ivan the Terrible's conquest of Kazan and Astrakhan, through the end of the nineteenth, with the conquest of the khanates of Kokand, Bokhara, and Khiva and the annexation of the Transcaspian region, the Russian empire expanded at a rate of some fifty square miles per day.[2] Eastern Ukraine (the left bank of the Dnieper) came under tsarist protection in 1654. In the early eighteenth century after victory over Sweden, Peter the Great took the territory that is today's Estonia and Latvia. Throughout the eighteenth century, Russian trade and state control moved into what is most of today's northern Kazakhstan and annexed it.

Like the Habsburgs in Spain and the Bourbons in France, the Romanovs did not make formal distinctions between their governance in what Pipes calls "Russia proper" and in its "imperial hinterlands."[3] To be sure, the western end of empire was marked by "boundaries" (*rubezhy*, or *granitsy*), while the east was marked by a frontier (*mezha*). These terms were used conventionally and represented a clear distinction in imperial expansion. In the east, expansion was through peace treaties (*shert'*, a Turkic word), which were conceived of by Moscow as pledges of allegiance of "eternal slavery to the grand tsar." The main mechanisms of rule were through hostages. Tribute in furs was expected; the tsar made exchange through gifts (*gosudareevo zhalovan'e*, or sovereign's compensation).[4] Despite these different vocabularies of rule, tsarist lands east and west were divided into provinces (*gubernii*), which were ruled by governors general or viceregents. All rules were equally valid throughout

[2] Richard Pipes, *The Formation of the Soviet Union: Communism and Nationalism, 1917–1923* (Cambridge: Harvard University Press, 1957), p. 1, calculation attributed to A. Brückner, *Die Europäisierung Russlands* (Gotha, 1888).

[3] Pipes, *Formation of the Soviet Union*, pp. 6–7.

[4] Michael Khodarkovsky, "From Frontier to Empire: The Concept of the Frontier in Russia, 16th–18th Centuries," *Russian History* 19 (1992): 115–28.

the empire, were written in Russian, and were administered in a unified bureaucratic system of classified offices. Furthermore, nobles from non-Russian lines were given rights similar to those of the Russian nobility, and russified foreigners were quickly recruited into state service.[5]

Russian-speakers emigrated to the new tsarist territories in waves. From the earliest period of territorial incorporation, the state recruited a quasi-independent military caste, the Cossacks, and entrusted them with the task of protecting Russian settlements in the borderlands, and with protecting the boundaries of the empire from foreign predators. For this, after twenty years of service, they were given land to till, and they became moderately wealthy landowners. By the beginning of the twentieth century, 4.4 million people living outside Russia proper traced their origins to Cossack settlement. Peasant migrations from Russia and Ukraine to the south and west were a second major source of settlement into imperial territories. The lust for the black earth, especially by freed serfs who were unable to cover their redemption payments, led at first to temporary migrations to the cities to earn cash, and after 1906 (when redemption payments were canceled, railroad transportation was available, and formal travel restrictions had been removed), to the rapid prerevolutionary colonization of Central Asia and the eastern steppes.[6] Traders, artisans, and skilled workers moved inexorably to the frontier through much of the second half of the nineteenth and the early twentieth centuries. By the 1897 census, those characterized as Russians constituted 8.5 percent of the population (and over a quarter of the urbanites) outside the boundaries of what was to become the Russian Federation.[7]

State and Nation-Building in Russian History

This tale of expansion appears no different from that of France into Languedoc or England into Wales.[8] Those expansions are without question thought of as examples of early state building. Yet today (with the knowledge of the Soviet collapse in 1991), we think not of France (vis-à-vis Languedoc) or England (vis-à-vis Wales) as the proper framework for understanding Russian expansion, but rather of the Ottomans and the Austrian Habsburgs (where the states shed their separate national components). It is true that in comparison with the expansions of England and France, Russia's cultural impact on the indigenous populations was quite limited. Linguistically, Welsh and Languedocians by the end of the nineteenth century were assimilated into the dominant state language; meanwhile Balts, Kazakhs, and even Ukrainians relied principally on the language of their forefathers; very few had developed fluency in Russian.

[5] Roman Levita and Mikhail Loiberg, "The Empire and the Russians: Historical Aspects," in Vladimir Shlapentokh, Munir Sendich, and Emil Payin, eds., *The New Russian Diaspora* (Armonk, N.Y.: M. E. Sharpe, 1994), p. 5.

[6] Robert Kaiser, *The Geography of Nationalism in Russia and the USSR* (Princeton: Princeton University Press, 1994), pp. 47–50.

[7] Robert A. Lewis et al., *Nationality and Population Change in Russia and the USSR* (New York: Praeger, 1976), p. 149.

[8] See James Given, *State and Society in Medieval Europe* (Ithaca: Cornell University Press, 1990).

What explains the incomplete incorporation of peripheral subjects into the Russian state-building project? Russian state building was not all that unlike its Western counterparts. In fact, Russian tsars since Catherine II saw rationalization of the Russian language—that is, its standardized use in all official and quasi-official domains—throughout their empire as an important ingredient of state building.[9] This is not simply a function of "Great Russian chauvinism." Catherine II, after all, was a German princess. And for generations, the Russian nobility communicated with one another in French. Rather it was a part of a program "to extend [the legal] administrative system into the countryside."[10] Catherine II wrote (in 1764) that Ukraine, the Baltic provinces, and Smolensk should russify "and cease to look like wolves in the forest," implying that russification would lower the chances of political subversion. Surely this is why she promoted Russian most actively in the Polish provinces, where loyalty was of the greatest concern.

The nineteenth century is a story of toleration for language diversity (under Alexander I) mixed with periods of promotion of an "official nationality" (under Nicholas I). Yet the logic of rationalization—especially in response to foreign threat—regularly appeared on the tsarist agendas. Nicholas's response to the Polish rebellion (1830–31) was to demand a fusion of the languages spoken in the Polish-influenced areas of the empire—a mix of dialects that were much later formalized as Byelorussian and Ukrainian—with Russian.[11] Alexander II put down a rebellion in Poland and Lithuania in 1863 and subsequently sought to limit the use of Polish and Lithuanian. In the face of Polish aristocrats' courting of Ukrainians peasants with an eye to possible incorporation of western Ukraine into a restored Poland, Alexander II issued the Ems Ukaz (1876) prohibiting inter alia the import of Ukrainian-language books and the teaching of the Ukrainian language.

Rationalization continued under Alexander III and Nicholas II. Alexander III reversed earlier efforts by Catherine II to rule the eastern provinces through a unified Turkic tongue. In the eighteenth century, Catherine induced the Tatars to settle in the steppe area of today's Kazakhstan, and Tatar became the official language of imperial administration. When a Kazakh became a clerk, he had to write in Tatar, which was of the same family but a distinct language nonetheless. By the mid-nineteenth century, egged on by Nikolai Il'minskii, a Russian Orthodox lay missionary (and linguist), who feared that the Tatars represented a threat to Orthodox rule of Central Asia, Alexander III ordered instruction in the schools to be conducted in Russian, effectively banning the Tatars from teaching in the school system.[12] Later, Nicholas II promoted Russian in the administration of Finland, fearing that the

[9] This notion of rationalization relies on Max Weber's "formal rationality," that is, the use of standardized procedure rather than "substantive rationality," which concerns the content of the law. See Weber, *Economy and Society* (Berkeley: University of California Press, 1968), pp. 809–38.

[10] George L. Yaney, *The Systemization of Russian Government: Social Evolution in the Domestic Administration of Imperial Russia, 1711–1905* (Urbana: University of Illinois Press, 1973), pp. 75–76.

[11] Hugh Seton-Watson, *The Russian Empire, 1801–1917* (Oxford: Oxford University Press, 1967), p. 269.

[12] Martha Brill Olcott, "The Politics of Language Reform in Kazakhstan," in Isabelle T. Kreindler, ed., *Sociolinguistic Perspectives on Soviet National Languages: Their Past, Present, Future* (Berlin: Mouton de Gruyter, 1985), p. 188.

continued use of Finnish would make their administrative incorporation into Russia less secure.[13]

To be sure, the tsars were not entirely successful in their russification program. But the point here is that they perceived an administrative and security advantage in having a single official language and sought to change the language repertoires of officials in incorporated territories so that Russian would become predominant for official uses. While they often faced counterpressures, there is little doubt that except for Alexander I, the tsars tried to enhance the role of Russian whenever they had the chance.

Perhaps (as Tocqueville implies) the elites in the Russian periphery were more resistant to russification than the lords ruling over the incorporated regions of Western European states? One reason might be that the lords in the periphery of the Russian empire could seek the protection of the rulers of other states. Georgian elites, for example, wavered between the tsars and the rulers of Iran and Turkey.[14] But the lords of Catalonia, Toulouse, and Alsace had options to negotiate with more than one central leader, and did so. Once a state establishes effective administrative rule, as was the case in France and Spain, peripheral elites might hope for systemic breakdown, but they cannot bargain their way out of the central state. The situation for lords in Russia's periphery was therefore similar to that faced by lords in other states' peripheries.

Historical evidence suggests that Russian rulers paid a higher cost for compliance with language-rationalization legislation than the rulers of other multinational societies did. But the outcomes were not wholly different. Evidence from the Baltics, Georgia, and Kazakhstan demonstrates the considerable pressure that regional elites faced to pay the transactions costs in communicating with the center by learning Russian. In the Baltics, despite the attractions of German for ambitious Estonians and Latvians, the rising classes (in the mid–nineteenth century), as well as the German nobles (in the late nineteenth century), began making concerted efforts to learn Russian. Edward Thaden reports that the Baltic representatives in the first two dumas (mostly Baltic peoples) and the second two dumas (mostly from the German nobility) all spoke Russian fluently.[15] Ronald Suny has similar findings in his work on the Georgian nationalist intelligentsia in the mid–nineteenth century. Dmitrii Kipiani, one of its luminaries, wrote primarily in Russian, including his memoirs.[16] By the end of the century, 91 percent of the schools in the Caucasus relied on Russian as the sole medium of instruction. Both the intelligentsia and those co-opted by the Russian state apparatus had become fluent in Russian.[17] Martha

[13] Edward C. Thaden, "The Russian Government," in Edward C. Thaden, ed., *Russification in the Baltic Provinces and Finland, 1855–1914* (Princeton: Princeton University Press, 1981), p. 82; Baron von der Osten-Sacken, *The Legal Position of the Grand-Duchy of Finland in the Russian Empire* (London: Lamely, 1912), p. 154.

[14] Ronald Suny, *The Making of the Georgian Nation* (Bloomington: Indiana University Press, 1988), chap. 3.

[15] Thaden, *Russification*, p. 75.

[16] Ronald Suny, personal communication.

[17] Suny, *Making of the Georgian Nation*, pp. 70, 351.

Olcott's history of the Kazakhs tells a similar story. After 1870, aristocrats and elders sent their children to Russian schools "in order better to represent their people upon assuming their fathers' positions." That generation wrote exclusively in Russian.[18] The regional elites in the Russian empire, this evidence demonstrates, had a strong incentive to invest in Russian-language competence.

If language rationalization occurred on the peripheries of the Russian empire as it did in the continental peripheries of Western European states, a major difference between the cases is that the broader societal ramifications of rationalization were different. Although France, Spain, and England would face language-revival movements in their peripheries in the 1970s, it is fair to say that a dominant language had achieved quasi-hegemony by World War I. But Russia could only be described as an aggregation of nationalities where co-opted elites and a small intelligentsia in various provinces had facility in Russian. Why was the expansion of Russian so limited, and why did the ultimate success of rationalization among the elites not motivate successively lower strata of the populations to learn Russian?[19] Scholars point to two crucial factors to account for these differences in outcome.

First is the geography of the open steppe.[20] The Russian countryside was always open to marauding bands of conquerors. One consequence, it is sometimes pointed out, is a far greater cultural heterogeneity than in the West. A second consequence was that the Muslim hordes brought such fear to the Russian settlers that cultural intermingling rarely took place. Muslims were considered to live on the other side of a divide that was unbridgeable for Europeans. A third consequence of the open steppe—and this adumbrated by Anthony Smith[21]—is that unlike the state builders of Western Europe, whose expansionary appetites were constrained by natural barriers, the Russian tsars could continue to expand without limit. Their ability to assimilate such a gargantuan space would be beyond even a Napoleon. Although the expanse and heterogeneity of the empire cannot be denied, I am reluctant to rely too heavily on this explanation. First, Eastern expansionary appetites are probably exaggerated in Western historiography. Second, cultural differences among peoples in today's successfully consolidated nation-states would have been emphasized more strongly, had their national projects failed.

A second reason why rationalization in language did not quickly penetrate to the lower strata is that state rationalization occurred later than it did in Western

[18] Martha Brill Olcott, *The Kazakhs* (Stanford, Calif.: Hoover Institution Press, 1987), pp. 104–5.

[19] This dichotomy between a bilingual elite and monolingual lower strata is exaggerated. Itinerant merchants and artisans (such as the Chuvash) picked up Russian; Muslim elites, however, tended to ignore the imperial language. Yet compared with other states where language rationalization occurred, in Russia there was far less of a cascade through all levels of society toward monolingualism in the state language. This is the outcome that I seek to explain.

[20] John A. Armstrong, "Toward a Framework for Understanding Nationalism in Eastern Europe," *East European Politics and Societies* 2 (1988): 280–305. Reinhard Bendix, *Kings or People* (Berkeley: University of California Press, 1978), as I discuss in Chapter 11, emphasizes this same phenomenon to explain the persistence of Russian patrimonialism.

[21] Anthony D. Smith, "Ethnic Identity and Territorial Nationalism in Comparative Perspective," in Alexander J. Motyl, ed., *Thinking Theoretically about Soviet Nationalities* (New York: Columbia University Press, 1992), p. 54.

Europe, which put new constraints on leadership.[22] The early state rationalization laws in France were in place by the early sixteenth century; in Tudor England rationalization of language was in full development in the late sixteenth century. In Spain, the essential decrees were passed in the early eighteenth century, but the pressure on lords to learn Spanish occurred much earlier.[23] Comparable legislation did not occur in Russia until the mid–nineteenth century, in a world-historical period of mass literacy, which was itself a factor inducing language-revival movements among incorporated nationalities throughout the world. Under these circumstances, newly instituted mass education policies relying on the language of state rationalization more easily engendered popular resistance. The spread of a state language, under novel historical circumstances, faced new and powerful popular obstacles.

We get a clear sense of language politics for late developers by examining the career of Il'minskii, whose activities in mid-nineteenth-century Kazan coincided ideologically with Nicholas I's promotion in 1833 of "official nationality." Just like his French and English "colleagues" in Africa, Il'minskii was faced with the problem of teaching "natives" basic literacy. He found that it is easier to fulfill educational goals (and to reach students' souls) in the mother tongues of the students, and therefore helped develop written forms for a variety of Asian tongues.

To be sure, as already mentioned, Il'minskii's work had russifying elements. He relied on the Cyrillic alphabet as a means of promoting Orthodox values, and to wean Asians away from the Arabic script with its links to Islam. Also, in his schools, while the local languages were taught as subjects, the language of instruction after the second year of primary education was Russian.[24]

Yet we see in Il'minskii's career a problem for nineteenth-century state builders. Since mass literacy was becoming an essential aspect of the "state function," by virtue of the needs of increasingly bureaucratized business firms and the state itself (soldiers, clerks, and others needed to send and receive written messages), virtually all states had Ministries of Education with mandates to provide trained personnel to fulfill these new functions. As these ministries sought to widen the scope of educational activities, the issue of the language of instruction in the mass public school became relevant for the first time.[25]

There remained, however, pressures and counterpressures in the educational establishment. On the one hand, the lessons of the missionaries had considerable influence in state educational circles. As early as 1879, the Russian Ministry of Education issued regulations authorizing "elementary schools with Volga languages as

[22] David Laitin, Roger Petersen, and John Slocum, "Language and the State," in Motyl, *Thinking Theoretically about Soviet Nationalities*, pp. 129–68.

[23] I show this quantitatively in David D. Laitin, Stathis Kalyvas, and Carlota Solé, "Language and the Construction of States: The Case of Catalonia in Spain," *Politics and Society* 22 (1994): 5–29.

[24] Isabelle T. Kreindler, "Nikolai Il'minski and Language Planning in Nineteenth- Century Russia," *International Journal of the Sociology of Language* 22 (1979): 5–26; see also her article "The Non-Russian Languages and the Challenge of Russian," in Kreindler, ed., *Sociolinguistic Perspectives on Soviet National Languages* (Berlin: Mouton, 1985), pp. 345–67.

[25] Abram de Swaan, *In Care of the State* (Oxford: Oxford University Press, 1989).

media of instruction."[26] On the other hand, in the 1880s, I. D. Delianov, the minister of education, strongly favored russification; and his successor, D. A. Tolstoi (who had earlier russified the Polish educational system), fought to get the Baltic educational system out of Lutheran (with German as the medium of instruction) hands through the promotion of Russian. Yet Tolstoi also supported Il'minskii's efforts to promote native-language education in the east, suggesting that the Ministry remained cross-pressured on this issue.

Economic planners also began to speak, albeit haltingly, for the recognition of peripheral languages. N. Bunge, minister of finance in the 1880s, supported tolerance of the Baltic languages in order to permit economic growth without provoking nationalist disturbances; and Count Witte in the 1890s supported German education in the Baltics in order to get competent and loyal economic managers.[27]

When mass education and government economic management arrived in states that had consolidated in earlier eras, there was already an elite stratum among nearly all language groups—children of state functionaries or commercial bourgeois families seeking "national" markets—that was capable of teaching in and interested in spreading the language of the central state. In Russia, the historical fact of starting late changed the context of language rationalization. Built into the state apparatus was a core institution (the Ministry of Education) that was in the business of standardization and development of languages of the periphery. Also, with the state interested in the management of industrial firms, its functionaries perceived (especially in the regions designated as growth nodes) language rationalization as a threat to development.

In light of these two variables—the special geographical context of Russian state expansion and the fact that Russia did not begin building a consolidated state until so late in its history that state interest in linguistic rationalization conflicted with state interest in mass literacy and economic growth—we see that at the time of the Revolution, despite successful language rationalization among peripheral elites, the Russian language was not a core part of the language repertoires of many social strata in the periphery. Whereas in the final third of the nineteenth century, peasants had already become Frenchmen,[28] in Russia, although peripheral nationality groups had many elites who were capable Russian-speakers (fulfilling the rationalization program), their peasants (and members of other strata as well) had not become Russian.

Russification in the Soviet Period

The legacy of limited language rationalization was not substantially altered during the seventy-four years of Soviet rule, in spite of unremitting state centralization.

[26] Isabelle T. Kreindler, "The Mordvinian Languages: A Survival Saga," in Kreindler, *Sociolinguistic Perspectives*, p. 241.

[27] Thaden, "Russian Government," pp. 48–49, 54–55, 70–71.

[28] Eugen Weber, *Peasants into Frenchmen* (Stanford: Stanford University Press, 1976).

The startling fact among the nationalities of the Soviet Union was that "unassimilated bilingualism" remained the widespread and stable language repertoire.[29]

To be sure, there were exceptions. In eastern Ukraine, Belarus', and in a number of industrial cities outside of Russia, there were unambiguous trends toward full assimilation. Meanwhile, in rural Central Asia, there are large rural pockets where parochialism remains the linguistic norm. Data collected by Martha Olcott and William Fierman suggest that in the Asian republics, vast numbers of youth have no functional knowledge of Russian. Finally, in some areas such as in Armenia and in the Baltics there has been a deliberate deemphasis of Russian, even to the extent of (based on census figures) intergenerational loss of proficiency. From a Russian or Soviet specialist's point of view, these exceptions carry great weight. From a comparative perspective, however, the variations are small compared to the general outcome of stable "unassimilated bilingualism."

Brian Silver's analyses of Soviet census data suggest that the level of intergroup contact was sufficient to explain variation in the move from parochialism to unassimilated bilingualism.[30] The Muslim/Orthodox variable and the degree of urbanization, however, had little explanatory power. Silver suggests from this that the acquisition of Russian as a second language is almost entirely a matter of economic and practical consideration, with the ethnic significance of this language step playing only a minor role.[31]

As for the switch from unassimilated bilingualism to assimilation, Silver's data show a clear difference by cultural group. With high levels of contact with Russians, non-Russian but Orthodox nationalities (which include the ambiguous case of the Ukrainians) move in a monotonic way toward assimilation. For the Muslim, Arme-

[29] This term is Brian Silver's. He distinguishes parochialism (knowing only the language of the locality), unassimilated bilingualism (knowing as well the language of the center, but using it in limited domains, and with great difficulty), assimilated bilingualism (relying principally on the central language, but maintaining some facility in the local language), and assimilation (becoming monolingual in the central language). Brian Silver, "Methods of Deriving Data on Bilingualism from the 1970 Soviet Census," *Soviet Studies* 27 (October 1975): 574–97.

[30] Soviet census data are not fully to be trusted. Respondents gave subjective accounts of their language abilities, but the accuracy of these self-assessments was not tested. Also, respondents often denied competence in Russian to voice opposition to the regime. There is also evidence of political tampering with the data. William Fierman reports, for example, that the first secretary of the Uzbekistan Communist Party, a promoter of the Russian language, delivered a census report in 1979 that showed a 34.8 percent rise in the use of Russian over a period of nine years. See William Fierman, "Language Development in Soviet Uzbekistan," in Kreindler, *Sociolinguistic Perspectives*, pp. 220–21. This is highly unlikely from a sociolinguistic point of view. The 1989 census data show that knowledge of Russian among Uzbeks dropped from approximately 53 percent in 1979 to about 22 percent in 1989, confirming that the reported 34.8 percent rise of the previous decade was most likely fraudulent. On these 1989 data, see Barbara A. Anderson and Brian D. Silver, "Demographic Sources of the Changing Ethnic Composition of the Soviet Union," *Population and Development Review* 15, no. 4 (1989): 644–46. For an excellent study of verbal self-identification in the Soviet census, see Rasma Karklins, "A Note on 'Nationality' and 'Native Tongue' as Census Categories in 1979," *Soviet Studies* 32, no. 3 (1980): 415–22.

[31] Brian Silver, "Language Policy and the Linguistic Russification of Soviet Nationalities," in Jeremy Azrael, ed., *Soviet Nationality Policies and Practices* (New York: Praeger, 1978), pp. 282–86, and "Bilingualism and Maintenance of the Mother Tongue in Soviet Central Asia," *Slavic Review* 35, no. 3 (1976): 414.

nians, and Baltic nationalities, both contact and high levels of urbanization are necessary for a full switch, and even in those cases the level of switch is very low. More precisely, Silver found that the switch from original language to Russian was higher than predictions based solely on contact and urbanization in 14 of the 17 Orthodox ethnic groups, lower than expected in 22 of 23 Muslim groups, and lower for the three Baltic groups.[32]

Marginal differences in region aside, the overwhelmingly clear outcome (based on data from the 1970 and 1979 Soviet censuses and ignoring the more nationally charged environment of the 1989 census; see Table 2.1) is that of stable unassimilated bilingualism, especially among the "titular nationalities," those language groups that gained control over Soviet republics.[33] As E. Glyn Lewis puts it, perhaps too forcefully, the data on retention of national languages, "make nonsense of the claim that . . . it is possible in the foreseeable future to envisage a merging of languages or the creation of a common language."[34]

An explanation for the maintenance of unassimilated bilingualism in the Soviet peripheries needs to account for how the titular national elites successfully consolidated local power through a linguistic regime under their control.[35] To be sure, nationality policy in the early Soviet years focused on the linguistic rights of the individual, not the territorial republic of settlement. In many areas, this policy continued to define the Soviet educational mission. By 1938–39 I. T. Kreindler points out that Uzbekistan offered instruction in twenty-two languages; Ukraine in seventeen, and Dagestan in twenty.[36]

But a very different policy arose from seeds planted in the People's Commissariat for Nationalities, the Treaty with Union Soviet Republics (December 1922), and the first constitution of the USSR (1924), where the political relations between nations were organized along strictly territorial principles, and within each republic, political advantages accrued to the titular nationalities at the expense of minorities. These decisions had far-reaching effects. As Lewis puts it:[37]

[32] See Brian Silver, "Social Mobilization and the Russification of Soviet Nationalities," *American Political Science Review* 68, no. 1 (1974): 59; similar findings are reported in Ronald Wixman, *Language Aspects of Ethnic Patterns and Processes in the North Caucasus*, Research paper no. 191, University of Chicago, 1980, for the North Caucasus and Central Asia; Olcott, "Politics of Language Reform," for Kazakhstan; and George B. Hewitt, "Georgian: A Noble Past, a Secure Future," in Kreindler, *Sociolinguistic Perspectives*, pp. 163–79, for Georgia.

[33] These data are from titular nationalities of only the highest level of republic, known as union republics. Below that level are the autonomous soviet socialist republics (ASSRs), which received, as I shall analyze later, far fewer resources for cultural autonomy. In Table 2.1, I ignore 1989 census data, since it is highly likely that in 1989 respondents were declaring ignorance of Russian to make a political point, at least in several republics.

[34] E. Glyn Lewis, *Multilingualism in the Soviet Union: Aspects of Language Policy and its Implementation* (The Hague: Mouton, 1972), pp. 134–35.

[35] B. A. Anderson and B. D. Silver, "Some Factors in the Linguistic and Ethnic Russification of Soviet Nationalities: Is Everyone Becoming Russian?" in Lubomyr Hajda and Mark Beissinger, eds., *The Nationalities Factor in Soviet Politics and Society* (Boulder, Colo.: Westview Press, 1990), pp. 95–130.

[36] I. T. Kreindler, "The Changing Status of Russian in the Soviet Union," Research paper no. 37, Soviet and East European Center, Hebrew University of Jerusalem, 1979, pp. 4–5.

[37] Lewis, "Multilingualism," pp. 58–59. But, as Edward A. Allworth, *The Modern Uzbeks: From the Fourteenth Century to the Present, A Cultural History* (Stanford, Calif.: Hoover Institution Press, 1990),

Table 2.1. Unassimilated and assimilated bilingualism of titular nationalities, 1970–1979

	Percent claiming Russian as second language		Percent switching native language to Russian	
	1970	1979	1970	1979
Turkmen	15.4	25.4	1.1	1.3
Kirghiz	19.1	29.4	1.2	2.1
Uzbek	14.5	49.3	1.4	1.5
Tajik	15.4	29.6	1.5	2.2
Georgian	21.3	26.7	1.6	1.7
Azerbaijan	16.6	29.5	1.8	2.1
Kazakh	41.8	52.3	2.0	2.5
Lithuanian	35.9	52.1	2.1	2.1
Estonian	29.0	24.2	4.5	4.7
Latvian	45.2	56.7	4.8	5.0
Moldovan	36.1	47.4	5.0	6.8
Armenian	30.1	38.6	8.6	9.3
Ukrainian	36.3	49.8	14.3	17.2
Byelorussian	49.0	57.0	19.4	25.8

Note: These data include members of each nationality living outside their republic and therefore overstate the switch to Russian for titulars living in "their" republics.

Source: Tsentral'noye Statisticheskoye Upravleniye pri Sovete Ministrov, SSSR, *Itogi vsesoyusnoy perepisi naseleniia 1970 goda* (Moscow: Statistika, 1973), 4:20–319, and *Chislennost' i sostav naseleniia SSSR: Po dannym vsesoiuznoi perepisi 1979 goda* (Moscow: Finansy i Statistika, 1984), pp. 71–137.

> In consequence, whereas before this decision 66.5% of the total Uzbek population of Central Asia lived within the Turkestan ASSR, 22.2% and 11.3% within the Republics of Bukhara and Khorezm respectively, after the delimitation of 1925 over 82% of all Uzbeks in Central Asia were concentrated in Uzbekistan. The Turkmen population were originally even more dispersed, only 43% living within the Turkestan Republic, 27% and 29.8% in the Bukhara and Khorezm Republics respectively. After delimitation of territories over 94% of all Turkmen were brought together. . . . Naturally the concentration helped to ensure . . . the greater linguistic homogeneity of the various republics. The Uzbeks came to constitute nearly 75% of the population of the Republic, Turkmen over 70% of the population of the Turkmen SSR, and in the case of Tajikstan and Kirgistan the national group in each constituted over 74% and 66% respectively. Such unification and increased homogeneity made the task of providing vernacular education and literature much easier, and so promoted the non-Russian national languages.

Thus began a system, originally sold as a policy of *korenizatsiia* (nativization). Its origins were in the Twelfth Party Congress in 1923, when Great Russian chauvinism

---

perceptively insists, it is anachronistic to think of this as the movement of peoples to "their" republics. More probably, people identified themselves (or were compelled to identify themselves) with the titulars and made the (often slight) cultural adjustments to fit in with their newly adopted group.

was declared a greater danger than local nationalism. The campaign, lasting more than a decade, not only gave special rights to minorities within both Russian and non-Russian regions through the creation of "national soviets" (a policy that had no long-term legacy), but also (and with a profound legacy) gave considerable leeway for national elites controlling titular republics to promote their national cultures. In one interpretation, *korenizatsiia* "provided opportunities for nationalities representing over 93% of the non-Russian population to create ethnically distinct stratification subsystems within Union or autonomous republics."[38]

Within the distribution politics of each republic, based in part on access to linguistic capital, the titular nationals used their positions to assure their ethnic brethren the more visible jobs of power and patronage;[39] they were (in the Asian republics especially) the beneficiaries of affirmative action programs for educational placement and technical jobs;[40] they had subsidized publications in their languages;[41] and they used the lack of language competence to deny minorities within their republics access to educational and job opportunities.[42] In light of these policies, children of mixed Russian/titular marriages, when living in the titular republic, often declared themselves as members of the titular nationality.[43] And, after decades of russianization (that is, the migration of Russians into the titular republics), the titular elites were by the 1980s able to reverse the tide. In the late Soviet period, therefore, there was significant migration of nontitulars out of the republics, and of titulars from outside back into their "home" republics.[44] The titular elites took responsibility for managing ethnic relations within their republics in order to retain control of a vast "neotraditional" patronage system.[45] To be sure,

[38] On *korenizatsiia* see William Fierman, *Language Planning and National Development: The Uzbek Experience* (Berlin: Mouton de Gruyter, 1991), and George Liber, *The Urban Harvest: Ethnic Policy, Legitimization, and the Unintended Consequences of Social Change in the Ukrainian SSR, 1923–1933* (London: Cambridge University Press, 1992). The quotation is from Philip G. Roeder, "Soviet Federalism and Ethnic Mobilization," *World Politics* 43 (1991): 204. He exaggerates the level of opportunity for non-Russians, because he counts members of nationality groups living outside their titular republics as being advantaged by the system when they were not. According to Kaiser, *Geography of Nationalism*, p. 155, in 1926 only 79.5 percent of the members of the eleven titular nationalities lived within their titular republic.

[39] Rasma Karklins, *Ethnic Relations in the USSR* (Boston: Allen & Unwin, 1986), pp. 80–81; Suny, *Making of the Georgian Nation*, p. 290.

[40] Nancy Lubin, "Assimilation and Retention of Ethnic Identity in Uzbekistan," *Asian Affairs* 12 (1981): 227–85.

[41] Lewis, *Multilingualism*, p. 177.

[42] Soviet ethnographers confirm the linguistic advantages that have accrued to members of titular nationalities. See M. Guboglo et al., "Etnolingvisticheskie protsessy," in I. V. Bromlei, ed., *Sovremennye etnicheskie protsessy v SSSR* (Moscow: Nauka, 1975), pp. 259–313; table 12, p. 301. For example, between 1926 and 1970, the correspondence between nationality and native language increased for ten out of fifteen titular nationalities, but decreased for seventeen out of nineteen nationalities having a lower form of autonomy. See also Roeder, "Soviet Federalism and Ethnic Mobilization," p. 204, and Karklins, *Ethnic Relations*.

[43] Karklins, *Ethnic Relations*, p. 38.

[44] G. I. Litvinova and B. Ts. Urlanis, "Demograficheskaia politika Sovetskogo Soiuza," *Sovetskoe gosudarvstvo i pravo* 3 (1982): 45, quoted in Karklins, *Ethnic Relations*, p. 94; see also Anderson and Silver, "Demographic Sources."

[45] Andrew G. Walder, *Communist Neo-Traditionalism: Work and Authority in Chinese Industry* (Berkeley: University of California Press, 1986).

not all titular nationals were pleased; there is some evidence that many titular nationality parents wanted more Russian education than "their" elites were willing to provide.[46] Yet as long as the titular leaders could assure Moscow that there would be peace in the republic, they were, for decades, able to sustain neotraditional political structures.

This system permitted the Soviet elites to promote "primordialism" but to severely limit its mobilization into direct confrontations with Soviet power.[47] Primordialism, in the Soviet context, could be promoted by allowing nationalities to use their "own" languages, just so long as they did not make political demands on the basis of nationality on the central state. But with titular languages used not only for cultural expression but for republic-level administration as well, titular nationals had an incentive to remain unassimilated bilinguals. Their languages represented capital for jobs and opportunities. The question that remains puzzling is why would a regime that was so centralized support and even protect titular languages?

Some might suggest that the Leninist ideology of national self-determination became enshrined in the organization of language zones controlled by titular nationals. But Lenin's writings on language and nationality give equal and contradictory regard to the goals of national self-determination and proletarian internationalism. If either of these themes is emphasized at the expense of the other, Lenin's pronouncements can be invoked in support of a wide continuum of language and nationality policies. Lenin is widely known for his support for the national self-determination of peoples. Yet he can also be cited for his ultimate goal of the "complete Russification of non-Russian nationalities."[48] In fact, Lenin's followers used his name to give greater autonomy to the titular nationalities *and* to make special opportunities available for native-language primary education to the members of nontitular nationalities. Lenin's writings on nationality could have been used to support both the rationalization of Russian and the promotion of regional languages.

There is a macrohistorical as well as a micro-incentive alternative to the explanation based on Leninist ideology. The macro dimension concerns the pacification efforts of the new Soviet state in the period immediately following the civil war, both to preempt pan-Turkism and pan-Islamicism and to expand the revolution westward. Both of these strategies had the consequence of giving republican elites

[46] Karklins, *Ethnic Relations*, p. 105, interprets her data to emphasize the considerable majorities of the titular nationals who wanted *more* education in their language. But the data can also be read to show that there were significant minorities that wanted more Russian. The Soviet state attempted at various times to respond to the felt demand for Russian as a medium of instruction in the union republics. Khrushchev's policy of 1958 to allow for parental choice in regard to medium of instruction was severely criticized by the titulars, since they feared that their own people would choose Russian. This policy did not have a major impact on educational reality within most republics. See Lewis *Multilingualism*, pp. 67–80. In the 1970s, the Ministry of Education proposed that in Georgia, technical material in higher education should be in Russian. Concomitant attempts to delete Georgian from its official status in Georgia induced the titular elites to argue vociferously against these efforts. See Suny, *Making of the Georgian Nation*, p. 301.

[47] Roeder, "Soviet Federalism and Ethnic Mobilization," pp. 196–232.

[48] This quotation is Anatoly Khazanov's gloss. See Khazanov, *After the USSR* (Madison: University of Wisconsin Press, 1995), p. 12.

far more linguistic autonomy than an overall strategy of russification would have permitted. The micro dimension brings us to the tipping game, introduced in Chapter 1, to explain why there was no cascade toward Russian after accommodating elites attained power helped by their knowledge of Russian.

Overcoming Pan-Turkism

The awesome power of nationalism shocked Lenin in 1917, and again during the civil war.[49] The territorial integrity of Russia was immediately threatened. In Central Asia, the revolutionaries faced a credible pan-Turkic threat. Pan-Turkism had been crystallized in 1882 when Ismail bey Gaspraly developed a Turkic *koine* for his newspaper, *Terjuman* (The Interpreter), that was easily understood through much of Russian-controlled Central Asia. In 1904–5, a political organization, Ittifaq al-Muslimin, advocated pan-Turkic social and linguistic but not political goals.[50] By 1917, at the Pan-Russian Conference of Muslims, delegates assumed—surely ignoring the existence of quite separate Tatar, Azeri, and Kazakh literary languages—that there was in Russia a single Muslim nation with one tongue. The Soviet regime was compelled, for lack of other allies, to deal with these Pan-Turkic ideologues. For example, Najmuddin Efendiev-Samurskii, leader of the Communist Party of Daghestan, published a book in 1924 advocating education in a common Turkic language. Sultan Galiev, the highest-ranking Muslim official in the communist hierarchy, was also a strong advocate of pan-Turkism. These "national communists" found themselves in a good bargaining position, mediating between local cultures and the weak Soviet state, whose leaders thoroughly distrusted their Asian allies. The Bolsheviks probably overestimated the possibility of a mobilized secession from a united Turkic movement. Nonetheless, this fear explains their primary goal to weaken these elites' claims for a common Turkic culture. The Communist Party's "divide and rule" policy "involved breaking up the large mass of Muslim and Turkic populace into fragments and then putting the pieces together into the required number of units, each of them having an exact territorial demarcation."[51] This was not a difficult task, given the dialect, tribal, and social differences that already existed, and the fears of some Central Asian peoples that they might face Volga Tatar domination in the name of pan-Turkic unity.[52] The regime named and subsidized publications in

[49] This section is borrowed from Laitin, Petersen, and Slocum, "Language and the State." In that article, we portray this conflict as a formal game in which the equilibrium outcome is the promotion of the local variants of Turkic. Here I summarize the argument without the game model. In that article, we portrayed the outcome of this conflict as the motor for *korenizatsiia* throughout the Soviet Union. Since the publication of that article, Terry Martin has convinced me, as reflected in the next section, that there was a more powerful motor driving *korenizatsiia* in the west.

[50] Alexandre Bennigsen, "Panturkism and Panislamism in History and Today," *Central Asian Survey* 3, no. 3 (1985): 41–43.

[51] Alexandre Bennigsen and Chantal Lemercier-Quelquejay, *Islam in the Soviet Union* (New York: Praeger, 1967), p. 126.

[52] Allworth, *Modern Uzbeks*.

new languages and worked to distinguish them from their dialectical cousins. Examples of dividing close speech forms and calling them separate languages, as was done with Tatar and Bashkir, with Kazakh and Kirgiz, and with Balkar and Karachai, have been well documented.

Lenin, whose father was a colleague of Il'minskii, and (perhaps because of that) was very sensitive to the nationality issue, felt that it was important not to alienate the Turkic peoples. Turning them into active supporters of the regime would need to be delayed. He therefore pressed Stalin and others to respond positively to nationalist demands and to challenge "Great Russian chauvinism."[53] In Central Asia the development of loyalty was especially crucial, given the nature of the Muslim communist elite. In the period of communist consolidation, this elite was still composed of "unreliable" class elements heavily tainted with nationalism; they were tolerated only because of the weakness of the Soviet state. The central party foresaw that long-term stability would depend on replacing this old elite with a new set of cadres from the general population, especially workers. Forcing the Russian language on this population would no doubt alienate the future base of recruitment to an extent that the Bolsheviks could not afford.[54]

The politics of orthography in Central Asia nicely illustrates the desire first to block pan-Turkism, and only later to seek loyalty to the Soviet regime. In the 1920s, the Latin alphabet became the new script for the Turkic languages to replace the Arabic script, which might have helped foster a pan-Muslim identity. The Latin script, richer in vowel representation than Arabic, also helped to differentiate dialects that looked the same with Arabic spellings.[55] It was not until the late 1930s, after the First Five-Year Plan had utterly destroyed the so-called Turkish feudal elite, when loyalty to the Soviet regime was no longer a pressing problem, that the conversion to Cyrillic (done through a central dictate, without any linguistic preparation) was made. The Cyrillic script, along with the introduction of Russian root words for key concepts dealing with political and technical areas, helped the project of blending the languages, a precursor, in Soviet thinking, to linguistic rationalization.[56] Thus the primary goal to prevent pan-Turkism was met first by eliminating the Arabic script; the secondary goal of procuring loyalty (or at least not engendering anti-Russian feelings) was met by abjuring the Cyrillic script; the tertiary goal of language rationalization was delayed a decade.

By the late 1930s, circumstances had changed; full rationalization was both feasible and desirable. With the pacification of Central Asia, cyrillicization would be possible. At this time, international security issues might have been decisive. Perhaps reflecting the need for Russian-speaking conscripts in the face of the growing secu-

[53] I. T. Kreindler, "A Neglected Source of Lenin's Nationality Policy," *Slavic Review* 36 (1977): 86–100, and "The Non-Russian Languages and the Challenge of Russian: The Eastern Versus the Western Tradition," in *Sociolinguistic Perspectives*, p. 348.

[54] See Olcott, *Kazakhs*, p. 206.

[55] Michael Kirkwood, "Language Planning: Some Methodological Preliminaries," in M. Kirkwood, ed., *Language Planning in the Soviet Union* (New York: St. Martin's Press, 1990), p. 32.

[56] Simon Crisp, "Soviet Language Planning, 1917–53," in Kirkwood, *Language Planning*, pp. 29–30.

rity threat from Germany, the Soviet state in 1938 required the teaching of Russian in all non-Russian schools.[57] In the following year, again with the probable linking of state security to rationalization, the Latin script for Central Asian languages was officially replaced by Cyrillic. This would facilitate bilingualism in Russian among Turkic speakers.

Turkic elites had their own agenda. At the Pan-Russian Congress of Muslims in May 1917, "the delegates [including traditionalists and radical communists such as Sultan Galiev] expressed near unanimity on the fundamental concern of all factions—that the destiny of the Muslim peoples must be made separate and distinct from that of Russians."[58] This desire for a separate destiny was held equally strongly by the Muslim National Communists in the period following the October Revolution. They had replaced the traditionalists who dominated the 1917 congress but shared their goals in regard to language.[59] The primary goal was indeed to nurture a Pan-Turkic language. But if this goal could not be reached, they saw a necessity to prevent Russian from overrunning their language(s), and would have accepted separate development of their local languages rather than russification. Given the Soviet fear of pan-Turkism, the Turkic elites saw room for a compromise that would serve their interests. If the representatives of Central Asia were willing to accept the promotion of local languages, they speculated, Soviet authorities would grab the opportunity.

Indeed this compromise depicts what transpired in language politics during the period following 1923: the center opted for promotion of local languages while the Muslim elites held on to the pan-Turkic alternative. Alexandre Bennigsen and S. Enders Wimbush describe the historical dynamics in the following terms:[60]

> The Muslim national communists['] . . . opposition to the linguistic division of the Soviet Turkic world after 1923 was especially pronounced. Seeking at first to have Kazan Tatar declared as the lingua franca of all Turkic territories of the Soviet Union . . . in 1926 [they] fell back to a three-region linguistic strategy. Under this plan Kazan Tatar would become the language of the European part of the Soviet Union, Azeri would be the language of the Caucasus, and Chagatay would serve all Central Asia. They also opposed the introduction of Latin and later of Cyrillic alphabets, arguing instead for the universal use of the Arabic alphabet.

From 1923 on, the regime sought to reduce the power of the pan-Turkic elite. By 1928, as Stalin consolidated his power, a massive purge severely reduced the leadership

[57] Terry Martin, "The Soviet Nationalities Policy, 1923–1938" (Ph.D. diss., University of Chicago, 1996), p. 919, reports that Stalin's speeches in 1935 offer a *military* justification for linguistic rationalization (knowing enough Russian to obey orders), without any implications of assimilation.

[58] Alexandre A. Bennigsen and S. Enders Wimbush, *Muslim National Communism in the Soviet Union: A Revolutionary Strategy for the Colonial World* (Chicago: University of Chicago Press, 1979), p. 20.

[59] Although there were some among this new communist elite who believed the best way to avoid Russian domination was to more fully develop local cultures, the pan-Turks who stressed Central Asian regional unity in politics and culture were the more significant group, especially in the maneuverings concerning language development of the 1920s.

[60] Bennigsen and Wimbush, *Muslim National Communism*, p. 88.

ranks of the already weakened pan-Turks. Sultan Galiev was imprisoned and later executed, and anyone suggesting a pan-Turkic agenda was accused of "Sultangalievism" and suffered a similar fate.[61] The purge effectively eliminated the pan-Turkic (or even the three-region) option, but there was still a local alternative to russification. The Muslim elite, recognizing the fact that the Party could now insist, without opposition, on the local variants of Turkic, accepted this as certainly better than russification. Galimdzhan Ibragimov, an influential Muslim communist, argued along these lines. His widely publicized essay in 1927 *Which Way Will Tatar Culture Go?* advocated the spread of his local Tatar language, which in his statistical semantics, was growing in importance and use. Unconnected to the "Sultangalievist" circle, his controversial statements gave legitimacy to the local option.[62] Stalin's *korenizatsiia* campaign, which lasted in Central Asia through 1933, and in many places up till 1938, reflects this agreement.

The Piedmont Principle

Soviet pacification of Ukraine had a very different plot but an outcome similar to that of Central Asia—the promotion of the republican language at the expense of russification.[63] When the leaders of the Ukrainian Communist Party felt pressured to russify after the civil war, an article in the newspaper of the Central Committee observed: "There was a time when Galicia served as the 'Piedmont' for Ukrainian culture. Now, when Ukrainian culture is suffocating in 'cultured,' 'European' Poland, its center has naturally shifted to the Ukrainian SSR."

The image of Piedmont—the magnet to draw in all of Italy—suggested the idea, in Terry Martin's account, "that Soviet Ukraine would likewise first culturally and then politically unify the divided Ukrainian populations of Poland, Czechoslovakia and Romania . . . [since] cross-border ethnic ties could be exploited to foment national discontent in neighboring states."

This Piedmont perspective helps explain a good deal of the nativization that took place in the western republics. It is certainly true, as was the case in Central Asia, that the Bolsheviks lacked support in the countryside and did not want further to provoke the populace with a russification drive. Yet in the west, the Bolsheviks had a grander vision supporting nativization policies. Ukraine's communists pressed for minority national soviets within each republic, as this would humiliate Poland, which was being criticized by the League of Nations for its national minority policies. Similarly, the Soviets created the Moldavian ASSR, in the hope of using that

[61] The question of Sultan Galiev's loyalty to the Soviet regime has been reopened in "Who Is Sultangaliev," published in 1989 in the Tatar journal *Kazan Ultari*. See Azade-Ayse Rorlich, "The Disappearance of an Old Taboo: Is Sultangaliev Becoming *Persona Grata*?" *Report on the USSR*, September 29, 1989, pp. 16–17.

[62] Azade-Ayse Rorlich, "Which Way Will Tatar Culture Go? A Controversial Essay by Galimdzhan Ibragimov," *Cahiers du monde russe et soviétique* 15, no. 2 (1974): 363–71.

[63] This section relies heavily on Martin, "Soviet Nationalities Policy." Although references to "Piedmont" abound in contemporary accounts, the term "Piedmont principle" in this context is Martin's invention.

territory as a Piedmont to attract Bessarabia, which Romania had annexed to the chagrin of the Soviets. Again, in late 1923, the Politburo of the Soviet Union agreed to extend the boundaries of Byelorussia by transferring sixteen *uezdy* from the RFSFR (the Russian Federation), in order to make it a strong and attractive republic. This would help, in the eyes of Soviet authorities, to foment rebellion by White Russians against Polish rule in Polish Belorussia. The Soviet chairman of the border dispute commission insisted that for this policy to succeed, it was necessary to derussify the population. The apotheosis of the Piedmont principle took place in the late 1920s in Kuban, where Cossacks were able to ukrainize all districts in which they were the majority in this area of the RFSFR. A bureaucratic cascade ensued, in which even the fully russified Ukrainian peasants in Kazakhstan were compelled to ukrainize. In accordance with Piedmont strategy, Ukraine sent teachers, books, theatrical productions, and radio programs to all areas in which Ukrainians lived within the Soviet boundaries. By 1932, after a brutal collectivization effort had nearly caused a counterrevolution in the Kuban, and after Moscow had adopted a less missionary foreign policy orientation, the Piedmont principle was drastically modified. Ukraine would have no more cultural influence outside its republican boundaries. Although Ukrainian schools would continue to educate virtually all Ukrainians, there was to be full russification of Slavs within the RSFSR.

Stalin continued his assault on the titular languages through the decade. In 1933 a decree abolished the right of the constituent republics to grant orders of distinction. In this era, Frederick Barghoorn writes,

> Writers such as [Mykola] Khvylovi, who proclaimed an "Asiatic Renaissance," in which a Western-oriented Ukraine, not Moscow, was to be the leader of socialism, statesmen such as education Commissar [O.] Shumski, economists like [N.] Volobuev, who in 1928 denounced Moscow's "colonialism," leaders like [G. I.] Petrovski, who as early as 1926 attacked the habitual use of the Russian language at Ukrainian Party meetings, were imprisoned or shot, committed suicide, or simply disappeared.

By World War II, Stalin was unrestrained in his substitution of Russian nationalism for Soviet patriotism. In November 1941, in an oft-quoted speech, Stalin declared that the fascists "have the impudence to demand the destruction of the Great Russian nation, the nation of Plekhavov and Lenin, of Belinski and Chernyshevski, of Pushkin and Tolstoi, of Glinka and Chaikovski, of Gorki and Chekhov, of Sechenov and Pavlov, of Repin and Surikov, or [and now, Stalin lists two tsarist generals] Suvorov and Kutuzov."[64]

After Stalin's death in 1953, the Soviet government continued what was tantamount to a policy of russification. Khrushchev's educational reforms of 1958, for

[64] Frederick C. Barghoorn, *Soviet Russian Nationalism* (New York: Oxford University Press, 1956), pp. 16, 37, 39. Jerry F. Hough, in chapter 6 of his *Democratization and Revolution in the USSR: 1985–91* (Washington, D.C.: The Brookings Institution, 1997) takes the counter view. By his recruitment of non-Russians into the Party, and by reifying nationality on the passport in 1934, Stalin, because "he remained a Georgian at heart," actually promoted non-Russian identities.

example, promoted parental free choice for educational medium of instruction in schools throughout the Union. Many national elites saw this as a code word for russification. Talk about the "merging" of nations (that is, the russification of the Soviet Union) as a historically inevitable process was a leitmotif in the Khrushchev years. But under Brezhnev, the notion of "merging" was quietly dropped. The historical legacies of the Piedmont principle and the effort to destroy pan-Turkism through the promotion of distinct Turkic languages had an enduring legacy in the Soviet Union. Both policies, although repealed, helped to perpetuate the unassimilated bilingual outcome throughout the Soviet Union through the greater part of the twentieth century.

The Failure to Tip to Russian

Macrohistorical factors, having to do with the state-building efforts of Russian tsars and commissars, explain why language rationalization did not spread through all social strata as it did in Western European states. Yet a microanalyst will ask: what prevented ordinary people, despite interests by local elites to prevent them, from assimilating into the dominant culture (and becoming fluent in the dominant language) of the ruling state? To answer this question, the microfoundations of Russian language rationalization must be examined. Before I provide those foundations, I shall specify more fully than I did in Chapter 1 how payoffs can be assigned in a tipping model.

Consider a state-building tipping game, as portrayed in Figure 2.1 but identical in structure to the national-revival game portrayed in Figure 1.1. In this game, the principal players are people living in the periphery of a heterogeneous state who must decide whether to adopt, or equip their children to adopt, the state language. An examination of Figure 2.1 shows that the overall payoff for speaking the central state language (Lc) as opposed to the regional language (Lr) is largely determined by whether other members of their community (speakers of Lr) are adopting Lc. Thus people, by the logic of the model, are pushed into an intergenerational coordination game with their conationals.

As with all coordination efforts, strategic problems arise. What incentive was there for the first Kazakh to learn Russian, or to send his child to a Russian-language school? Was he excoriated by his own community for having done so? Did the Russians praise assimilators in general but discriminate against them in particular because of other cultural differences? Would it have been wiser to wait for a significant Russian-speaking community of Kazakhs to develop? If so, suppose every speaker of Lr decided to wait until 40 percent of the Kazakhs had learned Russian, or a significant number of Kazakh children had completed a Russian-language school? The macroresult of this microprocess would have been the nonassimilation of Russian by the Kazakh speech community.

It follows from this strategic situation that it is individually irrational for a speaker of Lr to switch to Lc (or prepare her children to do so) if virtually no one in the speech community has made the switch. If this is the case, and we accept ratio-

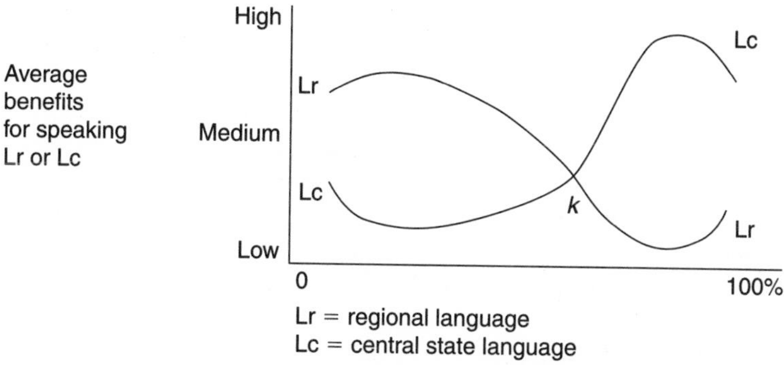

Figure 2.1. State-building tipping game: Percentage of population that speaks central state language

nality assumptions, how could intergenerational assimilation ever occur? There are a number of possibilities. For one, an individual's payoff for switching may be higher than the average, for example if he learns language easily or if he falls in love with a speaker of Lc. Also, states often coerce individuals into assimilation—by putting them in labor camps or in the army, for example. In the Soviet army, there were units with Russian majorities and units with mixed minorities, but no units of a majority of any one minority. The mixed minority units were usually stationed in Russian-speaking zones. This strategy evidently worked well in catalyzing the widespread understanding of Russian in all social strata.[65] When soldiers returned home, they automatically raised the percentage of Lr members who spoke Lc.

Several intricacies of the model might be raised now. First, if it is irrational at first to assimilate, at the tipping point *k*, it becomes irrational to refuse to switch. The tipping model should therefore enable us to calculate the rates of language shift depending on the number of Lr speakers who have already made the shift. Second, on both payoff functions (Lc–Lc and Lr–Lr) the curves reverse direction at the extremes. I explain the phenomenon that this represents—the high returns for being one of the very few members of your group with an unusual language repertoire—in Chapter 9. Here it is best to focus on the central aspect of tipping—that great social shifts seem impossible at one point but inevitable at another.

If rational-choice theory is to be applied to issues of cultural identity, as I indicated in Chapter 1, it must go beyond material calculations. If it were the case that the only rationality is that of material benefit, then rational models would quickly

[65] Robert Cullen reports that the Soviet comedian Evgenii Petrosian earned hilarious laughter in Rostov-on-Don when a punch line mentioned that in an army base of thousands of soldiers, "none of them speak Russian." *New Yorker*, June 12, 1989. M. B. Olcott and William Fierman, "Soviet Youth and the Military" (U.S. Department of State, contract no. 1724-620124, Washington, D.C.), report that this image of incompetence in Russian among non-Russian army recruits is reflected in many stories in the regional newspapers. But once in mixed minority units, we can surmise, with Karklins, *Ethnic Relations*, p. 101, that most soldiers achieve some facility in Russian. In my discussions with Estonians who had served in the Soviet army, I found that they developed a rudimentary understanding of Russian and a rich and eloquent mastery of Russian *mat'* (profanity).

find themselves ill-equipped to deal with issues of culture. But I do not believe that the only form of rational calculation is that of material benefit. In fact, a good first cut into the utility functions Lr–Lr and Lc–Lc is to think about three separate calculations. First, and this concerns material benefits, a potential assimilant needs to calculate the expected economic returns for adding a language to her child's repertoire (less the opportunity costs for learning it). But after this calculation, we enter the world of honor and status. Second, a potential assimilant will want to assess whether members of the in-group will punish potential assimilants as cultural apostates. This value I call *in-group scorn*. Third, the potential assimilant will want to consider the degree to which members of the out-group (who speak the language her child might be assimilating) will accept an assimilant as one of their own, for example, as a potential marriage partner for a member of their family, or as a member in a private club. This factor I call *out-group acceptance*.

Applying the tipping model to the Soviet Union makes it possible to analyze the largely successful tip from parochialism to unassimilated bilingualism.[66] The economic benefits for bilingualism were moderately high, and the first learners of Russian did not face any significant in-group scorn. Though out-group acceptance was not great outside the Slavic republics in the west, in the move toward unassimilated bilingualism, out-group acceptance (outside of gaining rewards for linguistic mediation) was not consequential. Most regions of the Soviet Union, as I showed, passed the tipping point toward unassimilated bilingualism. As long as the Union was holding, an increasing number of non-Russian Soviet citizens were developing competence in Russian as a second language.

The Soviets, at least by the 1930s, were not satisfied with unassimilated bilingualism. Their hope was basically to attain assimilated bilingualism.[67] But this was in most republics not very successful. Consider first economic returns. Given the patronage power of titular elites who favored speakers of Lr, the added economic returns for assimilation into Russian were low through much of the country. Perhaps only in regions economically behind central Russia, and especially in ASSRs and lesser units where the patronage for speakers of the titular language was paltry, were

[66] Readers might still object—as have scores of seminar participants who have heard me present this model—that this is not a realistic portrayal of how people really think about cultural matters, even if I abandon a pure materialist choice perspective. I urge the reader to suspend disbelief, until Chapter 5, where I use extensive ethnographic data to demonstrate the real-world calculus of cultural identity.

[67] There is no consensus on this point. Frederick Barghoorn, "Russian Nationalism and Soviet Politics: Official and Unofficial Perspectives," in Robert Conquest, ed., *The Last Empire: Nationality and the Soviet Future* (Stanford, Calif.: Hoover Institution Press, 1986), p. 32, refers to "Stalin's policy of maximum feasible Russification." Most Soviet commentators, e.g. Iu. Bromlei, in *Natsional'nye protsessy v SSSR: V poiskakh novykh podkhodov* (Moscow: Nauka, 1988), emphasized the goal of the flowering of all nations. Although the Soviet policy was not graced by consistency in this matter, it is fair to say that in Soviet eyes, an ideal patriot was, in an earlier statement by Frederick Barghoorn, in *Soviet Russian Nationalism*, p. 11, "a complex of the highest values and loyalties of Soviet citizens, with loyalty to the particular culture of one's own nation in the second order of priority and loyalty to international communism on the third level." This sense of priority is consistent with the goal of assimilated bilingualism.

these payoffs (less learning and in-group scorn costs) for assimilated bilingualism positive. A Tatar—in Tatarstan, an ASSR—who knew Russian better than Tatar, one study found, had over a 50 percent chance to improve his or her job training while a Tatar who still knew the Tatar language better than Russian had only a 10 percent chance of improvement.[68] But in regions that were economically more advanced or not dependent on Russia, such as the Baltic republics, Georgia, and Armenia, people throughout the Soviet era saw little economic advantage in making Russian their primary language, though learning Russian as a second language was considered useful.

Concerning in-group status, there was some variation across republics, and over time. In regions that are culturally similar to Russia (the Slavic republics of Ukraine and Byelorussia), early assimilators faced little in-group scorn. In Ukraine of the 1970s, for example, with arrests still being made of Ukrainian cultural figures, it was imprudent for self-appointed patriots to sanction their brethren for not upholding national traditions.[69] In other republics, assimilators were held in much deeper suspicion by their fellow nationals. Many sold out indeed, but they paid an in-group cost for so doing. As time went on, however, in-group status took on greater importance in titular calculations. This was due to the perception, beginning in the Brezhnev period but accentuated in the Gorbachev years, of imperial decline. If, for example, Georgians believe that Georgia is likely to become an independent country in the next generation, they will worry far more about in-group status and will begin to discount heavily the expected economic returns for learning Russian. To the extent that people believe that one's children will be living in a sovereign state of Armenia, Georgia, Estonia, Kirghizia, they will worry about what fellow nationals will think about their having assimilated into the culture of the former center. Especially for those groups that had tasted sovereignty in the recent historical past (Baltics, Georgia, west Ukraine), and those whose linguistic brethren have sovereignty across an international border (Moldovans and Tajiks), the in-group status costs of Russian dominance in one's linguistic repertoire increase.

Concerning out-group status, despite the propaganda supporting the "merging" of all peoples, the rewards for assimilation were hardly impressive. Ability to penetrate all-Union party circles was clearly related to whether the non-Russians were Orthodox in religion and Slavic in culture, and even then the widespread belief that all power positions were reserved for Great Russians lowered the potential status rewards for assimilation. A Ukrainian who spoke Russian may not have been considered a complete outsider; but a Kazakh who spoke perfect Russian continued to experience residual prejudice and suspicion as a possible fifth columnist. So religious and cultural similarity raised the probability of out-group acceptance, but they never raised it very high.

[68] Peter Shearman, "Language, Sovietization and Ethnic Integration in the USSR," *Journal of Social, Political, and Economic Studies* 8, no. 3 (1983): 243–44.

[69] Alexander Motyl, *Will the Non-Russians Rebel?* (Ithaca: Cornell University Press, 1987), chap. 6.

Despite the seventy-seven years of "Moscow Center" in Soviet rule, the expected returns for the intergenerational move toward assimilated bilingualism—from unassimilated bilingualism—were not impressive for the titular nationalities of the Union republics. The microanalysis of individual choice complements the macro-historical account in helping to explain the maintenance of unassimilated bilingual repertoires in the Soviet period.

3

Three Patterns of Peripheral Incorporation

Alain Besançon portrayed the Russian empire as having three faces.[1] It expanded into Siberia like the United States, incorporated Central Asia like Great Britain, and controlled Ukraine and the Baltics like Austria-Hungary. Yet, as Besançon points out, central leaders, ultimately to their chagrin, denied these differences. In the previous chapter, I emphasized the broad historical similarities of Russian expansion into the peripheries. In this chapter, while not replicating Besançon's categorization precisely, I illustrate three different patterns of Russian state control that spanned the tsarist and Soviet periods: a most-favored-lord pattern exemplified by Ukraine, a colonial model exemplified by Kazakhstan, and an integralist model exemplified by the Baltic states. I also show the effects of the heroic, if ultimately unsuccessful, attempts by Moscow center to deny, or even defy, those differences.

This chapter will therefore set the stage for an examination of the national revivals in the Union republics that began in the late 1980s. The cultural revivalists in Ukraine, Estonia, Latvia, and Kazakhstan faced a common problem, that of dismantling the centralized Soviet structures. Because of their different legacies of political incorporation, however, the revivalists had quite different levels of resources and their populations were linguistically russified to different degrees. The historical legacy of political incorporation influences three key outcomes: first, the degree to which Russians assimilate into the titular cultures now that independence has been achieved; second, the threat of interethnic conflict in the newly independent states; and third, the degree to which the newly independent states will become rationalized as classic nation-states.

[1] Alain Besançon, "The Russian Past and the Soviet Present" (1974), summarized in Paul Goble, "Three Faces of Nationalism in the Former Soviet Union," in Charles A. Kupchan, ed., *Nationalism and Nationalities in the New Europe* (Ithaca: Cornell University Press, 1995), pp. 134–35. My differentiation relies more heavily on John Armstrong's classic statement, "The Ethnic Scene in the Soviet Union: The View of the Dictatorship," in Erich Goldhagen, ed., *Ethnic Minorities in the Soviet Union* (New York: Praeger, 1968), pp. 3–49.

The Elite-Incorporation Model of State Expansion

The elite-incorporation model of state expansion focuses on the role of elites in the periphery at the time their territory was first incorporated into a centralizing or expanding state.[2] If the newly incorporated elites can join high society at the political center, at more or less the same rank and standing they had in their own territories, they are said to enjoy a status of "most favored lord." By this I mean that elites in the incorporated region of a state have rights and privileges equal to those of elites of similar status and education in the political center.[3] These concerns might be thought of as the historical or macro basis for the "out-group status" calculation that drives the tipping game.

Under most-favored-lord conditions, there are strong incentives for many of the elites in an incorporated territory to allow themselves to be co-opted into the power establishment at the center. Some elites in the incorporated territory do not take advantage of this opportunity, in large part because of the social pulls of their community. They seek instead to build a future in their own region. But intergenerationally, if increasing numbers of the upper strata of the regional society identify culturally with the central elites, the regional language and culture begin to be seen as backward and poor. Over generations, mass education and military conscription provide inducements to lower strata to assimilate into the dominant culture.[4] When this process reaches fruition, the imperial state is transformed into a national state—or, in Eugen Weber's oft-repainted image, "peasants become Frenchmen."[5]

The construction of a nation-state from the variety of nationalities within a territory need not be permanent. Regional cultures, attended to by poets and philologists, help preserve (or even create) the memories of national glory. These memories can be mobilized, Peter Gourevitch argues, when the regional bourgeoisie in industrialized capitalist societies exhibits economic dynamism while the political center experiences economic decline.[6] Under these conditions, the bourgeoisie will want

[2] David D. Laitin, "The National Uprisings in the Soviet Union," *World Politics* 44, no. 1 (1991): 139–77. This key variable was recognized by Rupert Emerson; see his *From Empire to Nation* (Cambridge: Harvard University Press, 1967), pp. 44–47. The variable is embedded in a model that relies on the dynamic approach toward nations developed by Karl Deutsch—see his *Nationalism and Social Communication* (Cambridge: MIT Press, 1953)—but is more sensitive to the expected utility of elites and their choices. Ernest Gellner also used a variant of this model in his *Nations and Nationalism* (Ithaca: Cornell University Press, 1983). I compare his model with mine in Chapter 9. Gary B. Miles relies heavily on a model of elite expected utility in his "Roman and Modern Imperialism: A Reassessment," *Comparative Studies in Society and History* 32, no. 4 (1990): 638–40.

[3] My concept of most favored lord is borrowed from the notion of most favored nation in international trade negotiations. Many of the states given most-favored-nation status are not themselves nations; similarly, many of the incorporated elites were not lords.

[4] The most sophisticated elaboration of this pattern, without the focus on "most-favored-lord" being a necessary condition for success, is in Abram de Swaan, *In Care of the State* (Oxford: Oxford University Press, 1988), chap. 3.

[5] Eugen Weber, *Peasants into Frenchmen* (Stanford: Stanford University Press, 1976).

[6] Peter Gourevitch, *Paris and the Provinces* (Berkeley: University of California Press, 1980), chap. 10. Before a peripheral nationalist movement can mobilize, the people of its region must see

rapid changes in tariff policies, capital markets, and corporate laws—changes that will not strike a responsive chord at the center. The regional bourgeoisie will patronize and promote the national poets and philologists, as their symbols will help mobilize the rural folk, who, in seeing a new recognition of folk culture, will suddenly find themselves having common ground with the bourgeoisie. Although the rural populations will not be concerned about capital markets, they will see regional independence as a way to protect their communities from "foreign" encroachment.[7] Nationalism is an ideology—infused as it is with symbols of language and religion, and reinforced through common folk rituals—that can forge a peasant and bourgeois alliance. From such an alliance may spring national revivals in economically dynamic but politically peripheral regions. Leaders of such movements often dream of national separation from the consolidated state.

Political movements seeking regional sovereignty in the most-favored-lord peripheral regions of modern states have achieved considerable successes in our democratic age. Canada, Belgium, Spain, and even France have yielded autonomy to their regions in several policy domains. The willingness of the political center to be responsive to the appeals from the regions has, however, exposed deep tensions within the elites of the newly revived nations. Those members of the peripheral elites who fully assimilated into the culture and society of the center—that is, those who took advantage of their most-favored-lord status—saw the nationalist symbols of the revival as antiquated and provincial. Unable to compete in the language of their own ancestors, they feared the consequences of the full realization of their national dream. Symbolic nationalism would have sufficed for them. The most bitter tensions of national revival under conditions of previous incorporation through most-favored-lord status have thus been the tensions *within* the new national elites.[8] In the cases of revival politics in Western democracies in the 1970s, the apparently rapid movement toward full independence was slowed, not so much by central resistance, as by the conflict of interest within each of the national elites.[9]

---

themselves as having a distinct identity. Gourevitch does not speculate on how ethnic identities are seen to be distinct. Without independent criteria of ethnic difference (very difficult to establish, given the multiple possibilities of ethnic reidentification), Gourevitch's theory tends toward tautology. In Laitin, "National Uprisings," I suggest a way to avoid this move.

[7] Rural populations in Catalonia, for example, blamed Madrid for extortionate taxes and for forcing them to billet troops. When "Spain" was in trouble in the seventeenth century and in need of new taxes, rural folk in the peripheries saw local nobles as potentially more benign than those at the center. J. H. Elliott, *The Revolt of the Catalans* (Cambridge: Cambridge University Press, 1963). The Catalan national revivals in the 1920s and 1970s also relied on an alliance between the rural folk and the rising bourgeoisie.

[8] This is the argument in my study of the Catalan revival in Spain: see Laitin, "Linguistic Revival: Politics and Culture in Catalonia," *Comparative Studies in Society and History* 31, no. 2 (1989): 297–317.

[9] Hudson Meadwell, "A Rational Choice Approach to Political Regionalism," *Comparative Politics* 23, no. 4 (1991): 401–21. His discussion of national revival politics in Brittany is a sophisticated analysis of the internal dynamics of nationalism among elites from the periphery. I do not wish to imply that these tensions are invariably unresolvable. Note the division of the Jura into two cantons, one French and one German, in Switzerland, or the velvet divorce in Czechoslovakia. I only suggest that the internal conflicts of separating groups are often neglected in analyses of regional movements.

This situation of ethnic difference crossed with economic dynamism is not, as Gourevitch recognizes, the only route to national revival.[10] Suppose, for example, that in the period of political incorporation, elites from the region do not receive most-favored-lord status, as was the fate of Indian and African royalty during the era of European expansion. This is the standard "colonial" model of expansion. Control from the center requires mediators from the elite strata of the "titular" nationality. Native elites serving as mediators between the center and their own masses garner rich payoffs. Many will be co-opted for sure; but even so they will not be able to translate their economic rewards into social status at the center. Suppose those elites who learn the language of the political center, and even convert to its religion, still face status deprivation and are not accepted as elites with a status similar to those who trace their ancestry to the culture of the ruling classes. Under these conditions, the most ambitious and powerful members of the periphery will operate with an eye to their homeland, rather than to the state that controls it. Economic dynamism is constrained under these conditions because indigenous elites tend to suppress the activities of entrepreneurs whose economic successes might challenge their status in society. And without economic dynamism, the logic of Gourevitch's model will not hold.

National independence movements have a distinct development path when they arise in the wake of political incorporation that has been achieved without granting elites most-favored-lord status. In these cases, younger generations of subject nationalities, educated in the schools built by the political center, face many barriers to mobility: the ruling native elites have no incentive to turn over power across generations; and by definition the opportunities at the center are equally constrained. The idea of full political independence becomes attractive to these "new men," who feel blocked by the center and by their fathers' generation as well. Independence, however, would give them access to all sensitive jobs currently held by nationals from the center, and this would benefit both the older and the younger generation. The strategy for seeking sovereignty has a political twist—it places the co-opted native elites in a bind. On the one hand, the status quo protects their welfare; on the other hand, they cannot let themselves be seen as opponents of independence—that would cost them their credibility as the "natural" leaders of the region. They are therefore compelled to support, albeit unenthusiastically, a national-independence coalition with the "new men," with the goal of full national sovereignty.

Pressure by the "new men" is not the only possible motor that will propel a movement for national sovereignty in a subject territory. The lower strata of these societies pay heavily for having to rely on their elites for any communication with the political center: they will have uncountable grievances about the corruption of their leadership and their own inability to communicate directly with political authority. Furthermore, they will surely take note of neighboring regions or countries

[10] Gourevitch, *Paris and the Provinces*, pp. 209–10, points to Ireland as the principal exception to his model for Western Europe but provides a rather ad hoc account for this exception. The elite-incorporation model proposed here (see Laitin, "National Uprisings," for a fuller statement) provides a theoretical account of cases such as Ireland.

that are mobilized into national action: nationalism is "contagious" in this situation. And once the lower strata are mobilized, the titular rulers, in fear of being supplanted by the new men, find themselves leading the movement for national sovereignty.

Whichever the motor, the new men or contagion—the ensuing national independence movement will follow a script different from that of the national uprisings in areas where elites "enjoyed" most-favored-lord status. Here, the alliance between the established titular elites and the new men (or the mobilized lower strata) must rely on notions of cultural distance from the center, a belief that they represent (in Michael Doyle's words, setting the criterion for imperialist as opposed to state-building expansion) "another political society."[11] This alliance will muzzle the antagonisms between social strata within the periphery for the duration of the struggle. (These will reappear after independence, though.)

There is a concomitant conflict associated with nationalist movements of this type: that between the "authentic" nationals of the periphery and minority populations. An exclusivist nationalist ideology will be attractive to the new men and the lower strata of the dominant nationality group in the periphery—in the Soviet world, all those who were called titulars. The potentially oppressed minority peoples will likely see continued rule by the center as their only chance for a better life. Since the national cause is built on the indignities suffered by the authentic cultural group, nonmembers who live within its designated boundaries become forgotten people—or worse, they will face discrimination. Since non-most-favored-lord situations offer few incentives for minority groups within the territory to assimilate into the larger groups, central rulers, in an attempt to co-opt minorities, often appoint them to subaltern positions. For this reason, peripheral regions tend to remain multiethnic. The titular groups, especially the new men seeking social mobility, will have an incentive to exclude minorities from government jobs. The hidden struggle for independence in regions that were incorporated without receiving most-favored-lord status is therefore the one between the titular nationals and minority peoples.

Three Contexts of State Expansion

At the twilight of tsarist rule, considerable demographic differences between Ukraine, the Baltics, and Kazakhstan were apparent. Consider Table 3.1, culled from material in Robert J. Kaiser's *Geography of Nationalism in Russia and the USSR*.[12] On indicators of literacy, education, concentration of titulars, and Russian settlement, three distinct patterns are clear. In 1897, literacy rates in the Baltics were on the order of three times that of Russia. Meanwhile literacy in Russia was about three-and-a-half times that of Kazakhstan. Literacy in the Russian heartland

[11] Michael Doyle, *Empires* (Ithaca: Cornell University Press, 1986).

[12] Robert J. Kaiser, *The Geography of Nationalism in Russia and the USSR* (Princeton: Princeton University Press, 1994).

Table 3.1. Demographic differences across republics (percent)

	Kazakhstan	Estonia	Latvia	Ukraine	Russia
Literacy in 1897	8.1	96.2	79.7	27.9	29.6
Russians in republic, 1917	20.5	2.8	6.7	9.9	
Number of students per 1,000 aged 10–19, 1911	104.3[a]	390.8[b]	390.8[c]	232.1[d]	290.2[e]
Concentration of titulars in their republic, 1959	77.2	90.3	92.7	86.3	

[a] Data from the north only.

[b] Data generalized for the three Baltic republics.

[c] Data generalized for the three Baltic republics.

[d] Data represent the mean value of separate figures provided for Novorossiia, Left Bank and Right Bank.

[e] Data from central industrial region only.

Source: Robert J. Kaiser, *The Geography of Nationalism in Russia and the USSR* (Princeton: Princeton University Press, 1994), tables 3.6, 3.2, 2.9, and 4.1.

and Ukraine were about the same. As for education, now in 1911, the Baltic states had far greater percentage of the school-aged population enrolled in school than Russia did. North Kazakhstan (and here we are mainly talking about the colonists; the figure would be far less if all of Kazakhstan were counted, or if only Kazakhs had been counted) had far less. The figure for Ukraine is again comparable with that of Russia. On the issue of Russian settlers in the imperial periphery, the percentages are quite low in the Baltics, very high in Kazakhstan, and near the mean in Ukraine.

Ukraine represents the classic most-favored-lord model. In Ukraine ambitious titular elites were able, with minimal transition costs, to cultivate career ambitions in both Ukraine and Russia. In 1785 the tsar's "Charter to the Nobility" exempted Ukrainian nobles from all government and military service. The Cossack ruling body, the Hetmanate, invented a noble tradition and created ex nihilo a Society of Notable Military Fellows. Thousands of Ukrainian petty officers and wealthier Cossacks took advantage of a period of uncertainty and their ability to forge documents to claim and be awarded noble status. Consequently, as most favored lords, members of the Ukrainian elite obtained posts not only in the imperial administration of the former Hetmanate, but also in the recently acquired Crimean lands and even in Georgia. In this period, many Ukrainian nobles abandoned their colorful Cossack dress, began to speak Russian and French, and accepted the Russian church hierarchy.

The Soviet period, albeit with one long relapse, told a similar story for Ukraine. In the *korenizatsiia* period, Ukrainians flourished in an era of expanding opportunities, both in Ukraine and elsewhere in the Soviet Union. But this closed up in the famine and repression of the 1930s, and after 1938, there were no Ukrainians in the Politburo. Yet by 1954, with the 300th anniversary of the Russian-Ukrainian reunion, Ukrainians were elevated to "junior elder brothers" in relationship to the lesser nationalities, and data from Seweryn Bialer show that they received more top jobs at the Soviet center than any other non-Russian nationality group.[13]

The incorporation of Ukraine on equal terms with the center was an easy political task. Not only are the languages quite similar, but the level of social development, as we saw in Table 3.1, was similar as well. A strategy of co-opting Ukrainians into central organs of power would not be threatening to Russian bureaucrats. Furthermore, a policy of co-optation would be attractive to many educated Ukrainians, especially those in the east. If they developed literacy in the hegemonic Slavic language, they could be core members of a vast state apparatus. As Soviet ethnologist Iu. V. Bromlei has pointed out in regard to the Soviet era, it was quite expensive to prepare "national cadres" to lead development outside Russia and Ukraine.[14] With 7.9 million Ukrainians living in the Russian republic (according to the 1926 census) who were largely russified in language, and many millions of Ukrainians in the east of their republic treating the Ukrainian language as a "hick" dialect of Russian (locally called *khokhol*, a term of derision, evidently used by russified Ukrainians), co-optation had very low costs. Furthermore, as waves of rural Ukrainians urbanized in the late-nineteenth and early-twentieth centuries, their children abandoned the peasant dialects spoken at home, and most became "Russian" in language.[15] Rather than see Ukraine as Besançon did, as analogous to a province in the Austrian empire, I see it as the exemplary case of most favored lord and therefore closer to the model of Languedoc and France.

Kazakhstan represents the classic "colonial" model, where elite ambitions could only be fulfilled as subalterns under Russian surveillance within the titular republic. In the subaltern pattern, the ladder of ambition can only be realistically climbed within the republic, and even there at substantial cost. To achieve high positions within the republic required learning the language and bureaucratic norms of the center. The benefits, however, were greater still, since the prospects of mobility in colonial society were extremely high compared to that of nomadic life in Kazakhstan. Mediating between Russian authority and Kazakh society brought rewards

[13] See Seweryn Bialer's data on Ukrainians holding high all-Union positions in the 1970s, in *Stalin's Successors* (Cambridge: Cambridge University Press, 1980), pp. 219, 223–24. The classic study of the recruitment of Ukrainians in Soviet political structures is that of John Armstrong, *The Soviet Bureaucratic Elite* (New York: Praeger, 1959). This discussion also relies on material from Frederick Barghoorn, *Soviet Russian Nationalism* (New York: Oxford University Press, 1956), pp. 52–57. He cites John S. Reshetar Jr., "National Deviation in the Soviet Union," *American Slavic and East European Review* 12 (April 1953): 173. Kolstø, in a personal communication, suggests that western Ukraine (where I did not collect data) did not experience any sort of most-favored-lord advantage under Soviet rule. It was ruled in "integral" style, very much like the Baltics. I address some of the implications of this regional difference in Chapter 13. For the best study on regional differences, see Dominique Arel, "Language and the Politics of Ethnicity: The Case of Ukraine" (Ph.D. diss., University of Illinois, Urbana-Champaign, 1994).

[14] Iu. V. Bromlei, *Natsional'nye protsessy v SSSR: v poiskakh novykh podkhodov* (Moscow: Nauka, 1988), p. 60

[15] George Liber, *The Urban Harvest: Ethnic Policy, Legitimization, and the Unintended Consequences of Social Change in the Ukrainian SSR, 1923–33* (London: Cambridge University Press, 1992), provides data on early rural-urban migration and its social consequences as background for this period.

for incorporated Kazakh elites; but their prospects for positions in Moscow in tsarist times were negligible. In the Soviet period, rewards for co-optation were perhaps higher than in tsarist times, in part because it was not the case that Kazakh subalterns were submissive agents of Russian principals. Kazakh leaders such as D. A. Kunaev—as first secretary of the Party and member of the Politburo—attained great autonomy to take care of his own horde in Kazakhstan (while ruling with impunity over the competing hordes) and not inconsiderable power at the center as well. When Gorbachev tried to replace him with a Russian in 1986, there were riots in Almaty, and Gorbachev quickly abandoned his policy of the "interrepublic exchange of cadres." Within three years a Kazakh, Nursultan Nazarbaev, was appointed first secretary, and he achieved great power and wealth. Despite the great benefits for becoming subalterns, Kazakh elites were not really taken seriously in Moscow circles. Perhaps the most telling evidence of this is the fact that in the wake of the Soviet collapse, Russian president Yeltsin did not even invite Nazarbaev to the founding meeting of the Commonwealth of Independent States (CIS). Leading Kazakhs had considerable distributive authority within their republic but remained outside the corridors of Soviet power.

Thus the incorporation of Kazakhstan was very different from that of Ukraine. Few Kazakhs had the education qualifying them for positions of central authority. And the cultural differences between Russians and Kazakhs raised considerably the costs of accepting Kazakhs as equals in Moscow ministries. Here Besançon's analogy with the British empire is apt, but given the developmental differences and high rates of colonial settlement (a variety of non-Muslim nationalities including Russians, Belarusans, Ukrainians, and Jews settling in a Muslim area), perhaps France and Algeria (with French, Portuguese, Greeks, and Jews as colonists) is closer to the mark. Kazakhstan's incorporation followed, in the terms of the elite-incorporation model, the "colonial" pattern of state expansion.

Estonia and Latvia represent a unique historical form, not recognized in Besançon's categories. In the early eighteenth century Russia ruled those states indirectly through a German aristocratic elite. While in the nineteenth century small segments of the Estonian and Latvian population converted to Orthodoxy and learned Russian in the hope of displacing their German overlords in service to the tsar, it was generally the case that the Balts converted to Lutheranism and learned German in order to achieve social mobility.[16] Social intercourse between Russians and Balts in the imperial period was therefore minimal. In the interwar period, with independence, full social mobility was possible for Balts without any need to learn a foreign language or convert to a foreign religion. After the war, now under Soviet rule, but legally recognized in the West as independent states, Baltic titular elites (except in those rare cases of Russian-born Balts who participated in the Revolution) had little need for Russia. Their levels of education and literacy were far higher than those in Russia itself. One can see the results of this in Table 3.1. Few titulars could be induced to move elsewhere in the Union. Bureaucratic practice was largely institutionalized

[16] Edward C. Thaden, "The Russian Government," in Edward C. Thaden, ed., *Russification in the Baltic Provinces and Finland, 1855–1914* (Princeton: Princeton University Press, 1981), p. 75.

in the titular languages. The Russian rulers of the Baltic periphery had to adapt to the peripheral culture rather than the other way around. Not only were Estonian and Latvian elites fully capable of running their own republics; because those who experienced freedom in the independent republics were never trusted by Soviet elites, they could not aspire to high appointments in the *nomenklatura*. Victor Zaslavsky, relying on a theoretical notion developed by Raymond Breton, claims that under Soviet rule, the Baltics achieved "institutional completeness." By this he means that each of the Baltic republics developed parallel set of institutions for indigenous and Russian speakers with little communication across the language divide. It was fully possible for Balts to experience a complete cultural, professional, and social life without entering into the Russian (or Soviet) world.[17] This notion of institutional completeness parallels what I have called the integralist model of political incorporation. Or to put it differently, the expanding state was unable to undermine the cultural integrity of its conquered people on its periphery. If Languedoc is the model for Ukraine and Algeria that for Kazakhstan, then perhaps Germany into Alsace is a reasonable analogy for the Baltics. While Alsatians certainly have had a long-standing claim for cultural autonomy, they considered German rule to be culturally demeaning; identification (as with the Balts to Germany or Scandinavia) with the West (i.e., France for most Alsatians) was more suitable.

Soviet Nationality Policies

Soviet nationality policies were deeply contradictory. On the one hand, reflecting a centralizing—difference denying—mentality,[18] the ultimate in political *hubris*, all Union republics were treated as if they were the same. On the other hand, Soviet cadre policy reified and extended the three patterns of incorporation that I just identified.

The Denial of Difference

In three crucial respects, Soviet policy sought to incorporate all Union republics on the same terms. First, as I indicated in Chapter 2, Bolshevik authorities after the civil war began to reject the goal of full assimilation of any nationality, and all non-Russians were to be returned to, or nurtured by, their roots, in a policy that came to be called *korenizatsiia*. The "Piedmont principle" and the fear of pan-Turkism led in this period to the near total rejection by Soviet authorities of the right to assimilate.

[17] Victor Zaslavsky, "The Evolution of Separatism in Soviet Society under Gorbachev," in Gail W. Lapidus et al., eds., *From Union to Commonwealth: Nationalism and Separatism in the Soviet Republics* (New York: Cambridge University Press, 1992), p. 73. See also Raymond Breton, "Institutional Completeness of Ethnic Communities and the Personal Relations of Immigrants," *American Journal of Sociology* 70 (1964): 193–205.

[18] The literature on the history of Soviet nationalities policy is vast. In my judgment, the research of Terry Martin, "The Soviet Nationalities Policy, 1923–1938" (Ph.D. diss., University of Chicago, 1996), based on recently opened archives, is now the authoritative source.

The wishes of the populations in these territories, should they have aspired to assimilation, were ignored. This policy, serving a foreign policy interest to the west, and an internal security interest in the Turkic regions, came to be generalized for the entire Union. Every nationality would have its own "Piedmont." Stalin waxed about this opportunity in his "Marxism and the National Question" as a "flowering" of nations. The results were impressive: Ukrainians living in Kazakhstan, who had been going to "European" schools (with Russian as the medium of instruction) would now be educated in Ukrainian by people who had voluntarily left Ukraine to support the flowering program. In the Mari Autonomous Oblast, 20 percent of the population who lived in the mountains spoke a different dialect from the meadow Maris. In 1932 central Soviet authorities, to the shock of the Mari oblast leadership, declared the mountain Mari to be a new nation, deserving its own national *raion* (district). Central authorities, now to the deep chagrin of Georgian leadership, sought (but this time unsuccessfully) to declare the Mingrelians a separate nation, though Georgian permission was required for the publication of educational material in that language.[19] In these first two decades of Soviet rule, assimilation was impermissible, and all nationalities merited recognition. The nationality scene in the Soviet Union altered substantially later; but the antipathy toward assimilation has left an enduring imprint.

In a second general pattern in Soviet nationalities policies, even after the collapse of *korenizatsiia* in the mid-1930s, national cultures were subsidized not according to their social, demographic, or economic situations but rather according to their place on the territorial hierarchy. Thus all Union republic titular nationalities were to be treated similarly. Data on party membership in 1970 show the percentage of party members of the five titular nationality groups analyzed in this book (Russians, Kazakhs, Estonians, Latvians, and Ukrainians) as a percentage of high-school graduates ranges from nineteen to twenty-six, reflecting Herculean efforts to give every Union republic nationality group equal representation in formal party structures.[20] Following also from this principle, titulars in Union republics had greater national rights than those in autonomous republics (ASSRs), who themselves had greater rights than those in autonomous oblasts (AOs), who had greater rights than those in autonomous okrugs (ADs), who had greater rights than recognized indigenous nationalities without territorial recognition. For example, Anderson and Silver looked at the average highest grade with the titular language used as a subject of study in 1981–85. At the Union republic level it was 10.0; at the ASSR level it was 8.9; at the AO level it was 7.4; at the AD level it was 1.9; and for the nonterritorialized nations, it was 0.4.[21] The hierarchy is reproduced in almost all domains of social, economic, and political life. Given these data, it is not surprising that sover-

[19] Martin, "Soviet Nationalities Policy," chap. 4.

[20] Jerry F. Hough and Merle Fainsod, *How the Soviet Union Is Governed* (Cambridge: Harvard University Press, 1979), p. 352.

[21] Barbara A. Anderson and Brian D. Silver, "Some Factors in the Linguistic and Ethnic Russification of Soviet Nationalities: Is Everyone Becoming Russian?" in Lubomyr Hajda and Mark Beissinger, eds., *The Nationalities Factor in Soviet Politics and Society* (Boulder, Colo.: Westview, 1990), p. 105.

eignty was won in the post-Soviet collapse only by the Union republics, and for all of them. Furthermore, this centralized hierarchalization of national rights meant that Estonia and Latvia, even though they were not part of the Soviet Union during the *korenizatsiia* period, shared the same rights, resources, and privileges as did Ukraine and Kazakhstan, since all were Union republics.

Third, and crucial for this book's concerns, Russians outside of the RSFSR were protected from coming to terms with their "minority" status. After the retreat from *korenizatsiia*, Soviet authorities worked unremittingly to cultivate a Russian cultural presence in all the Union republics. No titular nationality had the right to speak in the name of its people who were living in another Soviet republic. But the Soviet Union could speak for Russians outside the RSFSR. Russians in other republics beyond the RSFSR would no longer be called "minorities" as they had been during the *korenizatsiia* period when they were classified with all nontitulars, each having rights to connect with their cultural roots.[22] In consequence, the RSFSR could never represent the Russian nation, and unlike all other republics, there was never an RSFSR Communist Party. Only the Soviet Union could speak in the name of a Russian national interest. Tatars in Bashkortostan, Ossetians in Georgia, and Ukrainians in Kazakhstan all knew themselves to be, in an important sense, minorities. But for Russians in non-RSFSR republics, minority status was unnecessary; they were a plurality in the Soviet Union. These Russsians, as we shall see, were the quintessential new Soviet men and women.

The totalitarian ambitions of Soviet rule therefore provided an impressively similar climate for all Russians living in the Union republics. A Russian manager in Kazakhstan who was transferred to Estonia would have available to her a flat with perhaps the exact room layout as the one she left. The radio station would be on the same frequency. The educational curriculum for her child would be the same. The costlessness of transferring schools is truly impressive: an Estonian who had traveled to many places in the Soviet Union said he could find the office of the director in every technical college with his eyes closed. All such schools shared the same architectural design.

Survey results demonstrate that Russians in all republics were able to and in fact did live in separate enclaves.[23] In these post-Soviet surveys, Russian respondents in the four republics reported on the level of cultural mixing with the titular nationalities (see Table 3.2 for the similarities). The five rows represent distinct indexes on internationality mixing. These indexes reflect the degree of mixing in friendship, in marriage, and in language use.[24] As can be seen from the table, the scores on cosmopolitanism, Russian-titular mixing, and language mixing are quite low, reflecting

[22] Martin, "Soviet Nationalities Policy," pp. 921–22, writes that in 1926 Russians were treated as "national minorities" in Central Asia, but after 1933, the term was not often used, and in 1937 it disappeared, along with "Russian national soviets," as these organizations were not sufficiently dignified. Russians, according to contemporary Soviet records, should "no longer feel like minorities anywhere in the Soviet Union."

[23] These surveys were conducted in collaboration with Jerry Hough. Subsequently, they will be referred to as the "Laitin/Hough surveys." Details about the surveys and information on access to the data for purposes of replication are available in the Methodological Appendix.

[24] For the full specification of the indexes, see the Methodological Appendix.

Table 3.2. Common situation of Russians in the four republics

Index	Kazakhstan	Estonia	Latvia	Ukraine
Cosmopolitanism (probability that close family and friends are of different nationality from respondent)	.169	.150	.234	.278
Russian-titular mix (probability that close family and friends are of the titular nationality)	.036	.048	.094	.253
Language-use homogeneity (probability that respondent speaks his or her native language with family members, at work, and with best friend)	.881	.850	.786	.893
Language mixing (probability that respondent mixes language with close family and friends)	.019	.065	.094	.036
Linguistic homogeneity of family (probability that respondent's family all have same first language)	.863	.847	.786	.832

Note: All figures are mean scores for respondents who claimed Russian nationality in the Laitin/Hough surveys. All indices are scaled from 0 to 1. For rows 1, 2, and 4, a 0 reflects absolute Russian homogeneity; for rows 3 and 5, a 1 represents absolute homogeneity.

low levels of internationality mixing, whereas the scores on language homogeneity, within family and for general use, are quite high. Only in Ukraine do the scores suggest moderate degrees of mixing; but it should be emphasized that these data represent only two cities, one in eastern, the other in central Ukraine, neither having an insular Ukrainian-speaking population. But since all the data are from urban areas, where mixing might be considered most likely, it is reasonable to conclude from these data that in the four republics, Russians and titulars lived in separate social worlds, with no significant differences based upon mode of elite incorporation.

Differing Recruitment Practices

The impressive similarity of situation of Russians throughout the four former Union republics, despite the vast differences in the imperial challenges, needs to be kept firmly in mind. Nonetheless, the realities of difference—levels of social and economic development, degrees of cultural similarity with Russians, degree of rootedness of the Russian settlers, and previous experiences of sovereignty in the Baltics and western Ukraine—had a discernible impact on the experience of Russians and titulars in the Union republics. Here, the elite-incorporation perspective helps delineate those differences, and we can see clearly the impact of the three patterns of elite incorporation even under centralizing Soviet rule.

Both the most-favored-lord and the colonial models, in contrast to the integralist model, gave high incentives for ambitious titulars to adopt many aspects of Soviet culture. In Ukraine, one motivation for titulars to learn Russian (a major element of Soviet culture) was to become Soviet officials, transferable to any region within a vast state apparatus. The Soviets eliminated virtually all opportunities in east and central Ukraine for education in Ukrainian; yet there is little indication of hostility against this policy among Ukrainians. Furthermore, learning Russian for a Ukrainian, especially an east Ukrainian, was inexpensive, since the languages are similar and the territories are contiguous. Low cost and moderate rewards assured high rates of assimilation. For Kazakhs, the motivation to learn Russian was to become, in Abram de Swaan's formulation, "monopoly mediators" standing between Russian rule at the center and Kazakh society in the periphery.[25] Those who learned Russian and developed other forms of cultural capital enabling them to earn the trust of Soviet officials were not only able to get higher education (unavailable in Kazakh) but were also able to advance to positions of local or regional authority. They were rewarded for their efforts at indirect rule—that is, assuring compliance and political quiescence among "their" people, while following guidelines set by (Russian, or sometimes Ukrainian) second secretaries, who themselves had direct access to all-Union hierarchies in Moscow. With ambitious titulars in Ukraine and Kazakhstan rushing to invest in cultural capital as Russians, there was little incentive for Russians working in these republics to accommodate at all to local mores. Assimilation into republican society was seen as either unnecessary (in Ukraine) or absurd (in Kazakhstan).

In the integral regions, by contrast, ambitious titulars had fewer incentives to accommodate themselves to Russian culture and norms. To be sure, as in the case with Kazakhstan, second secretaries in Estonia and Latvia were at first monolingual Russian speakers; however, nearly all of them were russianized Balts—that is to say, Balts born in Russia who had not lived under sovereign republican rule during the interwar years, and who had participated in or shown sympathy with the Revolution. These russianized Balts, over the course of the 1950s, assiduously studied the languages of their ancestors and maneuvered within the Leninist framework to indigenize administrative and managerial practice. The result of widespread indigenization of political authority was that in both Estonia and Latvia, higher education, government directives, intraregional memoranda, and high party gossip all relied far more on the indigenous language than was the case in Kazakhstan and Ukraine. The indigenization of high officialdom in the Baltics helped close titular networks from any incentives to develop social ties with Russians. Meanwhile, at least relative to the titulars (and more so in styles of living than language) the Russians in the Baltic states made greater efforts to adapt to local culture than they made in other republics.

Data on elite recruitment support this claim that despite the centralizing goals of the Soviet state, there were clear republican differences in practice. Consider the data (published in Kolstoe) in Table 3.3. Ukrainians captured the highest percentage of all-Soviet positions in their republic, with the Kazakhs capturing the fewest. The Baltic republics come very close to Ukraine, and although they had fewer members in the Central Committee Secretariat, they had full control over the position of the Capital Gorkom secretary. Estonia also did better than Ukraine in getting positions

[25] Abram de Swaan, *In Care of the State* (Oxford: Oxford University Press, 1988), chap. 3.

Table 3.3. Russian occupancy of leading positions in four Union republics, 1955–1977

Position	Kazakhstan	Estonia	Latvia	Ukraine
Central Committee Secretariat	29.5	79.2	91.7	100
First secretary	33*	100	100	100
Organizational secretary	0	75	50	100
Agricultural secretary	40	0	100	67
Capital gorkom secretary	0	100	100	50
Trade union chairman	100	100	100	100
Komsomol first secretary	67	100	100	100
KGB chairman	25	50	50	100
Member of Presidium, Council of Ministers	48.8	94.4	75.7	86.7
Chairman, Council of Ministers	100	100	100	100

*In Kazakhstan two Russians served as first secretary for a total of about five years, and the one Kazakh for the remaining seventeen. It is therefore not very useful to think of this figure as far lower than the comparable figures for the other republics. Jerry Hough provided me with this insight.

Source: Paul Kolstoe, *Russians in the Former Soviet Republics* (Bloomington: Indiana University Press, 1994), p. 94.

on the Presidium's Council of Ministers. In general, Ukrainian communists were the most-favored-republican-lords in the four republics, while Kazakhs were the least-favored. The Baltic titular communists were in an intermediate position. Other data presented by Paul Kolstoe show that Russians in the Baltics did far better than Russians in Ukraine or Kazakhstan in getting jobs in administrative and production sectors; but the Baltic Russians did far worse than their counterparts in Ukraine and Kazakhstan in getting positions in the sciences and the arts.[26] Control over intellectual life (and loss of it in administrative control) captures some of what I have meant by integralist incorporation. In the Baltics, the Russians were never the accepted *intelligentsiia*.

Data from the Soviet period on cadres moving into important roles outside their republics—the real incentive for the most-favored-lord model—also support the three-part elite-incorporation model. It should be emphasized at the outset, however, that movement from republican to all-Union circles throughout the Soviet period was quite low, and a leading student of quantitative measures of cadre selection, Grey Hodnett, did not even quantify movement from republican positions to all-Union ones, since the phenomenon was so rare. Rather, he relied on providing the few outstanding examples.[27] On data concerning transfers from the republics to positions in RSFSR (which were assumed to be promotions, often involving moves to Moscow) and to ambassadorships, less than ten percent of all transfers were to positions in another republic or abroad. Hodnett concludes from this that "there are no . . . career based incentives for republic leaders to concern themselves with the interest of several national republics."[28] This implies that the logic of "most

[26] Paul Kolstoe, *Russians in the Former Soviet Republics* (Bloomington: Indiana University Press, 1995), p. 96.

[27] Grey Hodnett, *Leadership in the Soviet National Republics* (Oakville, Ont.: Mosaic Press, 1978), pp. 5 and 49–50n.

[28] Ibid., p. 306.

favored lord" doesn't carry all that much weight in the career planning of republican cadres. Yet, as the data show, to the extent there were incentives for career planning, they are consistent with the three models of elite incorporation that I have outlined.

Table 3.4 provides the data on elite positions in the Center that went to republican elites, and elite positions in the republics that went to nationals. The first two rows show the considerable number of Ukrainian elites who held key positions in the Soviet Politburo; on this dimension, Kazakhstan comes in second place. Estonians and Latvians played almost no role at this level of great symbolic importance, though Latvians did get some representation.[29] We can surmise, from data on the third row, that the Kazakh presence on the Politburo was largely symbolic. Here, I took Hodnett's data on all transfers out of the republic (that is, of the 9.8 percent of all transfers that went outside the republic) and subtracted the percentage of native cadres from non-native cadres. A high negative number reflects the much greater probability of natives getting promoted out of the republic than non-natives. Again, Ukraine is the "most-favored" republic. Here the position of the Baltics and Kazakhstan is reversed. Kazakhs, it seems, can be put into high symbolic positions, but hard-nosed administrative positions (which Hodnett's data capture) elude them. For the Baltics, natives do about as well as non-natives among the low number of transfers.

The data on rows 4 and 5, showing the percentage of natives in all leading jobs within each republic, and then on jobs concerned with personnel (which Hodnett says requires a very high level of trust), again show the supremacy of Ukraine. The Baltics are a close second on this dimension, after Ukraine. Kazakhstan is a distant fourth, a reflection of its near-colonial status within the Soviet regime. The final two rows, which reflect a degree of autonomy within the republics, give an indication of why I refer to the Baltic relationship with the USSR as "integral." The Balts have almost complete control over their scientific apparatuses, with Ukraine in third place and Kazakhstan once again a distant fourth.

The data on Table 3.4 show that Ukrainians in the Soviet period had comparatively good access to positions in Russian and Soviet structures.[30] Ukraine is therefore best categorized as a most-favored-lord republic. Kazakhstan received strong symbolic representation in the Soviet system, but its cadres played virtually no role in mid-level structural jobs in the RSFSR; nor did they play much of a role in technical and scientific roles in their own republic. Kazakhstan reflects a typical colonial

[29] For Latvians born in Russia who served key roles in the Latvian Communist Party (LKP), central roles in Moscow were not out of the question. Boris Pugo became head of the Party Control Commission in Moscow. Arvīds Pelše joined the CPSU Politburo. Augusts Voss became chair of the Committee of Nationalities of the USSR's Supreme Soviet. But I know of no Latvians born in Latvia who in Soviet times became "favored lords." See Andrejs Plakans, *The Latvians* (Stanford, Calif.: Hoover Institution Press, 1995), chaps. 8–9. Jerry Hough, in a personal communication, suggests that in the Brezhnev era, young Latvians were beginning to secure prized all-Union positions. In Estonia, elite mobility into Russian circles in Russia was apparently even rarer.

[30] Seweryn Bialer, *Stalin's Successors* (New York: Cambridge University Press, 1980), pp. 223–24, gives abundant examples in support of this claim. John Armstrong, *The Soviet Bureaucratic Elite* (New York: Praeger, 1959), pp. 91–92, notes that nationality has little effect on the career prospects of newspaper editors.

Table 3.4. Most favored lord: Evidence from the Soviet period

	Ukraine	Estonia	Latvia	Kazakhstan
Full members of Politburo	37	0	0	14
Candidate members of Politburo	47	0	3	6
Percentage of native cadres subtracted from percentage of non-native cadres transferred to administrative positions outside the republic	−8.8	−3.4	3.0	9.3
Native occupancy, all leading jobs, 1955–72 (percent)	85.3	83.7	81.5	46.6
Native occupancy, jobs related to personnel, 1955–72 (percent)	83.5	37.5	60.5	6.7
Non-Russian scientific workers, 1960 (percent)	48.3	78.9	65.4	21.4
Non-Russian scientific workers, 1973 (percent)	50.6	85.3	56.1	29.8

Sources: Donna Bahry, *Outside Moscow* (New York: Columbia University Press, 1987), p. 28; Grey Hodnett, *Leadership in the Soviet National Republics* (Oakville, Ont.: Mosaic Press, 1978), pp. 309, 103, 108; Seweryn Bialer, *Stalin's Successors* (New York: Cambridge University Press, 1980), p. 216.

model. The Baltics lie somewhere in between. They had virtually no role in Soviet affairs (although Latvia had some key actors on the high-visibility Soviet political stage); but their dominance within their region, in technical positions and in the scientific establishment, suggest that in the nonpolitical technical fields, they were nearly autonomous republics within a gigantic heterogeneous state. This is why I code them as "integral" republics. Despite, then, heroic attempts at centralization of rule and homogenization of bureaucratic practice, the Soviet regime replicated the pattern of elite incorporation that they inherited from the ancien régime. These differences had vital implications for Russian-titular social relations within each of the republics.

Elite Incorporation and Social Relations in the Four Republics

Most-Favored-Lord and Colonial Models versus the Integralist Model

The elite-incorporation model makes some similar predictions for the most-favored-lord and colonial republics. For both types, we should expect high incentives for titulars to develop cosmopolitan cultural practices—in the most-favored-lord case, in order to achieve mobility at the center, and in the colonial case, in order to serve as mediators between central rulers and their people. Meanwhile, in the integral republics, it would be the Russians who would have the greater incentive to develop cosmopolitan practices, since the titulars have sufficient autonomy to run their republics in their own cultural mode. This expected pattern, differentiating the most-favored-lord and colonial models from the integral model of incorporation, shows up on five indexes, most of which rely on language use as a proxy for national identification. Each of the indexes is a conglomerate of responses to the Laitin/

Hough mass urban survey. The first two indexes reflect patterns that go back into the Soviet period. Consider first Figure 3.1, "Linguistic Homogeneity of the Family," described earlier. Kazakhstan and Ukraine stand apart from the Baltics. In Kazakhstan and Ukraine, it is the Russian respondents who are relatively more linguistically homogeneous in their family networks. In the Baltics, on the other hand, the titular respondents were more likely to emphasize linguistic homogeneity at home than were the Russian respondents. Thus in the integralist model of state expansion in the Baltics, in the few cases of intermarriage, the titulars are more likely to report an all-titular linguistic home than the Russians are likely to report an all-Russian linguistic home. In Kazakhstan and Ukraine it is the Russians who are (slightly) more likely to emphasize linguistic homogeneity at home.

The second index provides data on bilingualism, and is reported on Figure 3.2. This index picks up on a five-point scale on reported fluency (I think in it; I speak it freely; I speak it with some difficulty; I speak it with great difficulty; I don't speak it at all) in the titular language for Russian respondents and Russian for the titular respondents. Because reported fluency is a very weak measure of actual fluency, on this index we add value to those respondents who have used the language as a medium of instruction in school, or who buy newspapers, watch TV, or read literature in the other language. A score of 1 is normalized to reflect the maximum level of bilingual ability possible; a score of 0 is normalized to reflect the minimum. The results here are extremely robust for the pattern elucidated in this section. In Kazakhstan and Ukraine, the titulars have higher bilingualism scores than do the Russians; in the Baltics the levels of bilingualism are more symmetric between the two nationalities.

The third index moves us to issues of language use and language-use homogeneity. The pattern reflected in the data on intermarriage and bilingualism holds. The results are portrayed on Figure 3.3. A score of 0 reflects using a language other than the one respondent declared as his or her native language for all reported relationships; a score of 1 reflects total use of one's native language in all dyadic relations to

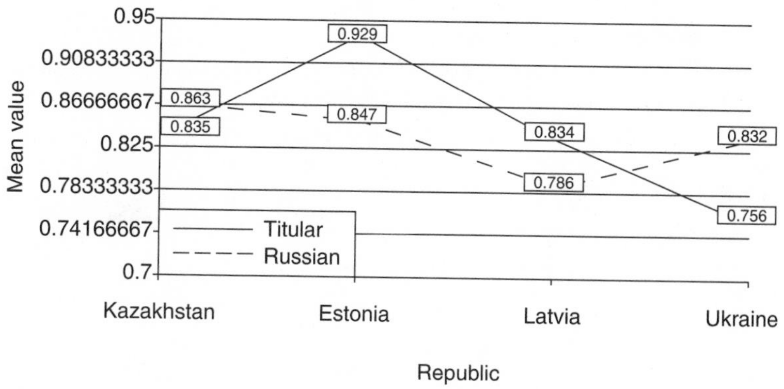

Figure 3.1. Linguistic homogeneity of titular and Russian families in the four republics: Probabilities that respondent's mother, father, and first spouse have the same first language as the respondent

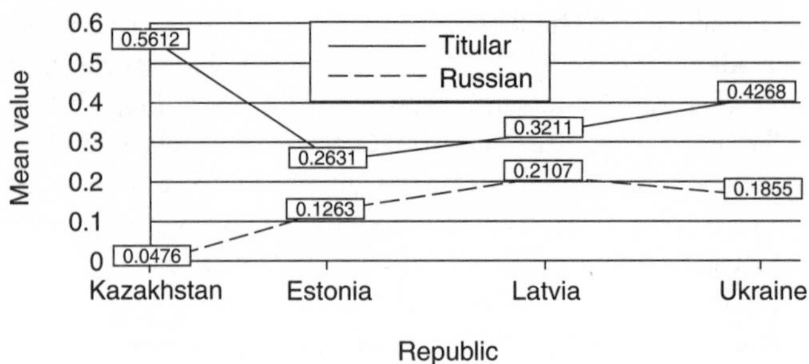

Figure 3.2. Bilingualism of titulars and Russians in the four republics: Mean bilingualism scores, from 0 (completely monolingual) to 1 (fully Russian-titular bilingual).

which the respondent gave an answer. As the data show, the titulars in Kazakhstan and Ukraine are the least homogeneous in their language use of any group. Meanwhile, the titulars in the Baltics are far more homogeneous than the titulars in Ukraine or Kazakhstan, though less so than the Russians in the Baltics, although these scores are quite close.

The fourth index reflecting this same pattern is that of "Language-Use Mixing," also described earlier. In Kazakhstan and Ukraine, titular respondents were far more mixed in their language use across relationships than were the Russians. In contrast, in the Baltics, while both groups were far less prone to mix than were the titulars in Ukraine and Kazakhstan, it was the Russian respondents who reported mixed use of language at higher rates than did the titulars. The comparative data on language mixing are presented on Figure 3.4.

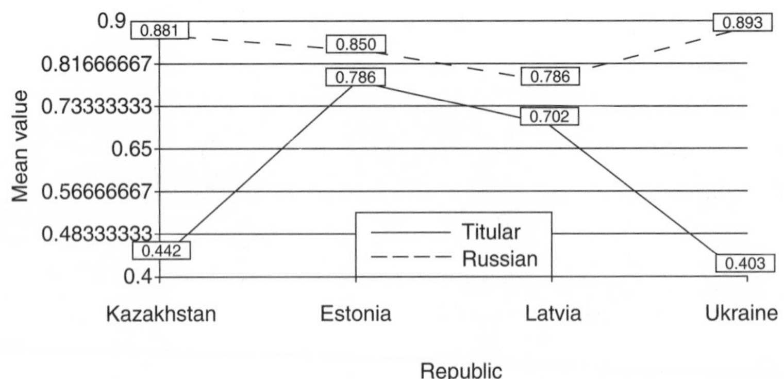

Figure 3.3. Homogeneity of language use by titulars and Russians in the four republics: Mean scores (from 0 to 1) on the probability of using one's native language in a variety of home and work settings

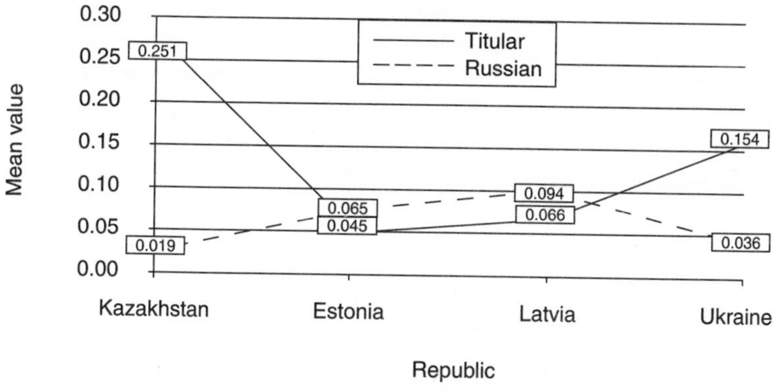

Figure 3.4. Mixed use of language by titulars and Russians in the four republics: Probabilities (from 0 to 1) of mixing Russian and titular in normal conversations at home and at work

The final index, "Language and National Accommodation," takes us to attitudes about who should accommodate to whom in situations of societal multilingualism. Here we asked respondents about the language of street signs, controlled for degree of bilingualism of the respondent and the percentage of the respondent's nationality group in the locale of the interview. As we can see from Figure 3.5, Russians and titulars in both Kazakhstan and Ukraine were more or less equally accommodating to the needs of the other group. Meanwhile, in the Baltics, Russian respondents were far more accommodating linguistically than were their titular counterparts, who compared with the titulars in Ukraine and Kazakhstan, were remarkably unaccommodating linguistically.

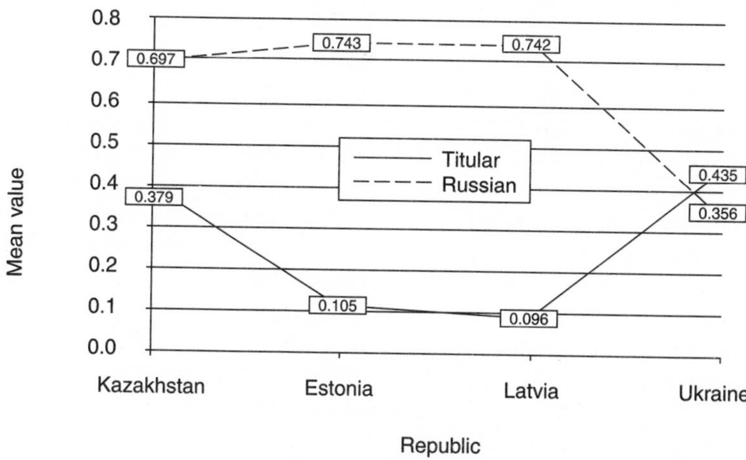

Figure 3.5. Language and national accommodation of titulars and Russians in the four republics: Accommodative attitudes (normalized from 0 to 1) in regard to the appropriateness of street signs in the other language, controlling for the population mix of the city in which the interview took place

The elite-incorporation model predicts that in the most-favored-lord (Ukraine) and colonial (Kazakhstan) republics, titulars would be far more cosmopolitan and live in far more mixed cultural environments than would the Russians. Meanwhile, in the integralist (the Baltics) republics, the titulars would remain insular, and the dominant Russians would show greater cosmopolitanism than their compatriots in Ukraine and Kazakhstan. The survey data reported in this section confirm these expectations.

Most-Favored-Lord and Colonial Models Differentiated

The curvilinear relationship portrayed in Figures 3.1–3.5 is based on a claim that there are three distinct patterns based on rates of elite incorporation into positions of authority in the Soviet period: high in Ukraine, moderate in the Baltics, and low in Kazakhstan. The data on relative internationality accommodation are consistent with the hypothesis that the relationship between the rate of incorporation and the pattern of internationality accommodation is curvilinear. Titulars are relatively more accommodating than Russians at low and high levels of elite incorporation; while Russians are more accommodating than titulars at medium levels of elite incorporation. My reason for this, stated earlier, is that titulars in most-favored-lord republics and colonial republics have different incentives to learn Russian and accommodate to Russian rule—one for social mobility at the center, the other for mediation in the periphery. But an equally plausible interpretation is that the data reveal only two patterns, with some underlying variable differentiating Ukraine and Kazakhstan from Estonia and Lativa. This interpretation, however, is inconsistent with other data collected in the survey which show that relatively high titular accommodation in Ukraine and Kazakhstan occurs for different reasons, a conclusion that is in accord with the expectations of the elite-incorporation model.

Perhaps it is best to begin with a revealing similarity and difference between Ukraine and Kazakhstan on intergenerational shifts in the media of instruction at the kindergarten and elementary levels in the four republics. We asked respondents what the medium of instruction was for themselves at each level up the educational ladder, and the same question in regard to their first child. Standard accounts of Soviet education policy suggest that a generation ago (when most respondents were in kindergarten and elementary school) residues from the policy of *korenizatsiia* guided most students into schools where their native language was the medium of instruction; however, the 1958 Khrushchev educational reforms, which allowed for more parental "choice" in the language of instruction, signaled to many analysts that an inexorable shift toward Russian as the medium of instruction was about to begin. Given that the average respondent began secondary school in 1959, the theory of inexorable russification of education predicted that Russian respondents and their children would not report an intergenerational shift in the language of instruction but that titular respondents and their children would.

The data, portrayed on Table 3.5, reveal that intergenerational shift from the titular language to Russian among titulars was significant in both Kazakhstan and Ukraine, but inconsequential in the two Baltic countries. This reflects the initial

Table 3.5. Intergenerational shift in medium of instruction

	Kazakhstan	Estonia	Latvia	Ukraine
Kindergarten (titular)				
From titular to Russian	11.0	1.2	3.7	27.0
From Russian to titular	15.2	2.1	4.5	6.5
Kindergarten (Russian)				
From titular to Russian	0.2	1.8	2.0	1.3
From Russian to titular	0.6	7.5	5.6	5.5
Elementary (titular)				
From titular to Russian	14.7	2.4	2.4	32.8
From Russian to titular	11.1	2.0	0.8	5.2
Elementary (Russian)				
From titular to Russian	0.1	0.4	1.7	3.0
From Russian to titular	0.6	3.1	4.6	2.5

Note: Figures represent percentages of respondents whose medium of instruction at various levels was different from that of their first child. These were all urban samples.

Source: Laitin/Hough surveys.

pattern, that in both the most-favored-lord and the colonial republics, especially long after Khrushchev permitted "free choice," titular children moved into the Russian language stream. Meanwhile, in the integralist republics, the titulars continued to be educated in their own language.

Yet the data also reveal significant countertrends among titulars in Kazakhstan and Ukraine, from Russian to the titular language in the past generation. While the countertrends in Ukraine are rather small, the countertrend in Kazakhstan is higher than the trend itself at the kindergarten level and somewhat smaller than the assimilationist trend at the elementary level. These data suggest that under the colonial model, there were pressures by state authorities to expand the indigenous language stream, most probably (as our ethnography will suggest) to create a class of workers literate enough for low-status jobs but insufficiently "worldly" to seek jobs at the all-Union level. This "colonial" educational strategy (used by the British in India and Africa) served as an unintended investment in a separatist future, one that gave a generation of workers an interest in an exclusively Kazakh-language mobility structure. Assimilationist trends, therefore, were discernible in both the most-favored-lord and colonial situations (as opposed to the lack of such trends in the integralist situation); but only in the colonial situation do we see, at least in the intergenerational shifts in medium of instruction, a strong anti-assimilationist interest.

With intergenerational shifts in medium of instruction as background, we can now consider the attitudes, first of the titulars, and then the Russians, about the national rights of the other group. In both of these cases, we will see strong differences in inter-nationality assimilationist attitudes between Ukraine and Kazakhstan. Consider first the index of "National Exclusiveness" reflected in Figure 3.6, which captures titular attitudes. For this index, we asked four questions that tapped into

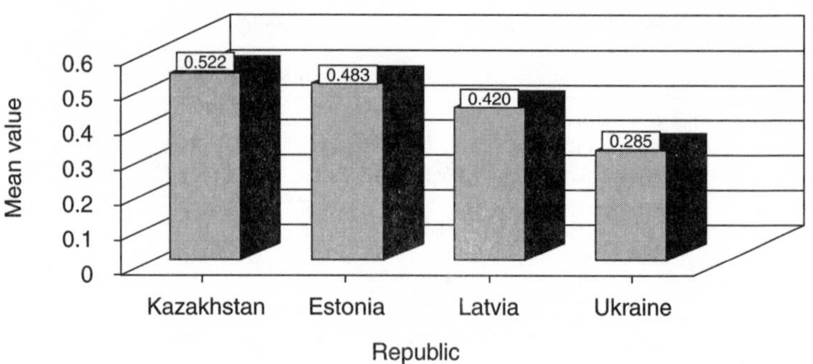

Figure 3.6. National exclusiveness of titular groups in the four republics: Index of titular respondents, normalized from 0 (open) to 1 (closed) on the degree to which they were closed to nontitulars in their families and in their republics

titular values about assimilation that were divorced from the strategic learning of Russian for purposes of occupational mobility. We asked how they felt about small entrepreneurs operating freely in their republic. This, in the late Soviet context, is often a proxy for feelings about foreigners coming to live in the titular republic. We also asked how they felt about their son, and their daughter, marrying outside the nationality. On this chart, the Kazakh respondents, who are by far the most exclusive, diverge in a polar manner from the Ukrainians, who are the least exclusive. Learning Russian and accepting the political reality of high Russian linguistic status, as we saw in the previous section, are attitudes prevalent in most-favored-lord *and* colonial settings; but seeing that strategy as part of a more assimilatory cultural framework occurs only in the most-favored-lord environment. In the colonial pattern, language learning has a far more instrumental quality, with the expectation that even learning the language of the central state would not give the titular full acceptance in the society of that state. This leads to a greater cultural solidarity among the colonized.

The differences among the three patterns show up not only on the mass survey but on census data as well. Consider Table 3.6, derived from Robert Kaiser's *Geography of Nationalism in Russia and the USSR.*[31] First, the situations of Estonia and Latvia are distinguished from those of Ukraine and Kazakhstan by the rates of titulars who are directors of enterprises or organizations and titular-language publications compared with the percentage of Russians in the republics. In 1989, enterprise directors in the Baltic states were far more likely to be titulars than Russians. The greater relative presence of titulars in the corridors of industrial power allowed for the regional languages to remain languages of upward mobility. The data on publications of books, journals, and newspapers again distinguish the Baltic states, where

[31] Robert J. Kaiser, *The Geography of Nationalism in Russia and the USSR* (Princeton: Princeton University Press, 1994), chap. 3.

Table 3.6. National differences in the Union republics

	Kazakhstan	Estonia	Latvia	Ukraine
Indigenous directors, 1989[a]	100	134	121	109
Publications in indigenous language, 1988[b]				
Books	72.7	102.7	96.4	29.4
Journals	83.1	108.9	110.4	65.6
Newspapers	94.5	112.6	114.4	96.8
Russians who speak titular language, 1989 (percent)	0.09	13.7	21.1	32.8
Change in composition of urban population from 1959 to 1989 (percent)				
Titulars	10	−11	−8	4
Russians	−7	8	7	−1

[a] The figures in this row reflect the percentage of titular directors divided by the percentage of titulars in the republic multiplied by 100.

[b] The figures in this row reflect the percentage of total publications in the indigenous language, indexed to the titular percentage of the republic's population. For example, the figures for book publications in Ukraine equal the Ukrainian-language percentage of the titles published in Ukraine divided by the Ukrainian percentage of the total population in Ukraine multiplied by 100.

Source: Robert J. Kaiser, *The Geography of Nationalism in Russia and the USSR* (Princeton: Princeton University Press, 1994), tables 5.14, 6.3, 6.9, and 5.6; p. 259.

in 1988, the rate of titular-language publications was higher than the percentage of titulars in the republic. On both of these measures, Ukraine and Kazakhstan have discernibly lower rates than the Baltics do. Finally, the change in the national composition of Union republic cities from 1959 to 89 shows a corresponding pattern. Kazakh and Ukrainian cities, in the period of massive industrialization, were able to draw on their own rural peripheries, leading to greater rates of indigenization. But the two Baltic states were already highly urbanized with their indigenous bourgeoisies, and the post–World War II industrialization drew mainly on demobilized or otherwise geographically mobile Russians. Here again the integral model stands opposite that of both the colonial and most-favored-lord models.

But the differences between the most-favored-lord and colonial models show up in these data as well. The fact of widespread (as opposed to a few monopoly mediators) Ukrainian facility in Russian explains the extremely low rates of Ukrainian book and journal publications in 1988. Most Ukrainians, unlike Kazakhs, were taking full assimilation as a practical (if unwanted) reality.[32] If Ukrainians were comfortable reading in Russian, the third row of Table 3.6 shows that Russians were at ease in developing facility in Ukrainian, as 34.4 percent claimed to have in the 1979

[32] "Unwanted" may be an understatement. With the crackdown on the Ukrainian intelligentsia in the Shcherbit'skyi period, Russian was imposed in many elite milieus. Still, this reaction succeeded only because Ukrainian elites were already fluent in Russian.

census.[33] Meanwhile, less than one percent of Russians in Kazakh claimed facility in the Kazakh language. This asymmetry in language facility reflects a colonial, rather than a most-favored-lord pattern of incorporation. On this measure, Russians in the Baltics were less linguistically accommodating than in Ukraine. But the greater difficulty for Russians in learning either Estonian or Latvian, as compared with Ukrainian, needs to be factored in. And even still, the survey data (those reported earlier and the data that will be presented in Part III) show that in the Baltics Russians have been relatively more accommodative to local culture than Russian residents have been in Ukraine.

THE data in this chapter show that in both the tsarist and Soviet periods, the incorporation of elites from the peripheral republics had three distinct patterns: the most favored lord, the colonial, and the integral. Furthermore, despite Soviet territorial policies seeking to treat all Union republics similarly, the three distinct strategies of elite incorporation have had discernable implications for interethnic accommodation. For the cases of low (Kazakhstan) and for high (Ukraine) incorporation of elites into central hierarchies, there were strong incentives for titulars to learn sufficient Russian as a language of work and knowledge; meanwhile, for cases of medium incorporation in the Baltics, there were weaker incentives for titulars to rely on Russian, and greater relative incentive for Russians (especially the russianized Balts who were born in Russia and returned to the Baltics as rulers) to accommodate themselves to, and even begin to assimilate into, titular culture. Yet the cases of low and high incorporation yield strong differences in regard to internationality relations. In the case of low incorporation (Kazakhstan), there are higher levels of titular separation from Russian culture (where language learning is instrumental, and not a basis for a more complete cultural shift) and therefore greater attempts to invest in a separatist future than was the case of high elite incorporation (Ukraine), where linguistic assimilation coincided with other forms of cultural blending, and where there were fewer attempts by parents in the Soviet era to invest in a separatist future.

These findings from the elite-incorporation model—the macro complement of the tipping game—play an important role in understanding the response by Russians to titular sovereignty when the political tides turned, leaving Russian-speakers beached in the newly independent Union republics.

[33] This figure should be discounted somewhat because it is likely that a significant number of russified Ukrainians claimed to be Russian to the census takers and claimed facility in Ukrainian as a second language.

PART TWO

AN ETHNOGRAPHY OF THE DOUBLE CATACLYSM

4

The Double Cataclysm

Nearly all titular populations equated *Soviet* rule with *Russian* rule. The spokesmen for the titular populations each saw their own nationality as especially oppressed by Soviet rule, in the starvation of their populations in the 1930s, in the exile of so many in their parents' generation, in the russianization of the population, in the russification of local culture, and in the blatant disregard of their liberal rights as citizens.[1] With the small opening afforded by Mikhail Gorbachev in the 1980s, titular elites, often with the massive support of their populations, pressed for national autonomy. Nationalists in the republics—driven either by a desire for revenge or a longing to live in a republic truly representative of the titular population—began to demand that the Russians go "back home" or adopt the titular culture.

In 1989 and 1991 the Russian-speaking populations of the Union republics were struck by a double cataclysm that turned their world upside-down. The first blow was the passage of the republican language laws in 1989, which threatened their security in speaking only the Soviet language of "internationality communication." It was as if, at least to many of them, New Yorkers were suddenly faced with the prospect of learning Iroquois or being deported to England. The second punch was the collapse of the Soviet Union itself. While this cataclysm was devastating to many in the Russian Federation, it had special consequences and worries for the

[1] Several of the volumes of *Studies of Nationalities in the USSR*, edited by Wayne S. Vucinich and published by the Hoover Institution Press, sound this tone. See my review of the series, Laitin, "The National Uprisings in the Soviet Union," *World Politics* 44, no. 1 (1991): 139–77. For sources on the national revivals in the four republics treated in this volume see Orest Subtelny, *Ukraine: A History* (Toronto: University of Toronto Press, 1988); Andrejs Plakans, *The Latvians* (Stanford, Calif.: Hoover Institution Press, 1995); Toivo Raun, *Estonia and the Estonians*, 2d ed. (Stanford, Calif.: Hoover Institution Press, 1991); Rein Taagepera, *Estonia: Return to Independence* (Boulder, Colo.: Westview, 1993); and Martha Brill Olcott, *The Kazakhs*, 2d ed. (Stanford, Calif.: Hoover Institution Press, 1995). Two excellent edited volumes have chapters covering all republics: Lubomyr Hajda and Mark Beissinger, eds., *The Nationalities Factor in Soviet Politics and Society* (Boulder, Colo.: Westview, 1990), and Ian Bremmer and Ray Taras, eds., *Nations and Politics in the Soviet Successor States* (Cambridge: Cambridge University Press, 1993).

Russian-speakers in the countries that would be referred to as the "near abroad." These Russian-speakers suddenly found their citizenship, their homeland, and their very identities in question. If Iurii Afanas'ev could write in 1988 that there was already an "identity crisis" throughout the Soviet Union, caused by the "systematic destruction of collective memory," the one-two punches of 1989 and 1991 compounded that crisis for Russian-speakers in the near abroad many times over.[2]

The growing ethnic unrest in Nagorno-Karabakh, Tajikistan, and Transdniester gave Russian-speakers in the near abroad real cause to fear for their very physical safety. Even where violence was not on the horizon, Russians who migrated back to the Russian Federation reported incidents of *bytovoi natsionalizm* (everyday nationalism)—insults on public transport, in stores, and so on—that only began in the late 1980s.[3] This sense of loss, insult, and uncertainty pervaded everyday life for the Russian-speaking populations in the newly independent post-Soviet republics. Yet under those very conditions, with paltry information and much confusion, people had momentous life decisions to make. Should they learn the titular language; should they apply for citizenship in their new countries; how were they to go about constructing a new social and political identity?

The Four Republics in the Gorbachev Era

Gorbachev's call for *glasnost'* (openness) and *perestroika* (rebuilding) brought him allies stronger than he could have ever imagined. Although I agree with Jerry Hough that it was Yeltsin's brilliant use of Russian nationalism (rather than the nationalist ferment in the Union republics) that brought down the Soviet Union,[4] it is nonetheless true that the freedoms allowed by Gorbachev's policies, first in the Baltics, and much later in Kazakhstan and Ukraine, encouraged national revivals in all the Soviet republics, including Russia. It is the effects of these national revivals on the Russian-speaking populations in the near abroad that will concern us throughout Part II.

The problem for the newly elected nationalist governments, as Table 4.1 demonstrates, was that Russians constituted a significant minority population in each of the four republics under study, and one that could not be ignored. While a considerable number of these Russians were recent immigrants, by 1989 (especially in Estonia) a substantial percentage were in their second generation. In Latvia, Kazakhstan, and Ukraine, many had roots that went far deeper. Indeed, it is fair to say that during the final years of the Soviet Union, when nationalizing elites were seeking to create national republics, these four republics were solidly binational.

[2] Iurii Afanas'ev, "Restructuring and Historical Knowledge," *Literaturnaia Rossiia*, June 17, 1988.

[3] E. I. Filippova, "Novaia russkaia diaspora," in M. Iu. Martynova, ed., *Novy slavianskie diaspory* (Moscow: RAN, 1996), p. 69.

[4] Jerry F. Hough, *Democracy and Revolution in the USSR, 1985–1991* (Washington, D.C.: Brookings Institution, 1997), chap. 6.

Table 4.1. Demographics of Russians in the four republics

	Kazakhstan	Estonia	Latvia	Ukraine
Population of republic in 1989 (in thousands)	16,476	1,567	2,664	51,384
Russians in republic in 1989 (in thousands)	6,228	475	906	11,356
Russians as percentage of total population in 1989	37.8	30.3	34.0	22.1
Russians as percentage of population in capital city in 1989	59	42	47	21
Russians claiming fluency in titular language (1989 census, percent)	0.8	14.9	22.0	34.0
Percentage of Russians in 1979 who were immigrants to the republic	59.7	66.9	63.4	59.1
Percentage of Russians in 1989 who were immigrants to the republic	53.2	34.9	58.4	57.7

Sources: *Natsional'nyi sostav naseleniia SSSR* (Moscow: Finansy i statistika, 1991); Iu. V. Arutiunian, ed., *Russkie, etnosotsiologischeskie ocherki* (Moscow: Nauka, 1992), pp. 25, 52.

The Double Cataclysm

The 1989 Language Laws

The Russian-speaking populations in the Union republics had a charmed linguistic existence. As my portrayal of the Grigor'evs in Chapter 1 illustrated, they could—and did, on the cheap—travel through seven time zones without needing any language other than Russian. Vacations in Samarkand, Bukhara, Crimea, Odessa, Batumi, Kazan, and Arkhangel'sk were all possible, and since Russian was the language of internationality communication, the tourist could negotiate his or her way through the local society in Russian. In the republics in which they lived, even though the titular nationalities had rights of their own, Russian-speakers sent their children to Russian schools, watched TV and listened to radio in Russian, had full access to the Soviet and republican presses in Russian, and spoke to government officials, doctors, merchants, bus drivers, and coworkers in Russian as well. Street signs were usually in the titular language but with a Russian translation. It was this world, a world that privileged those who had grown up speaking a language of a great power, that was deeply threatened by the republican language laws of 1989.

Out of political context, these laws do not seem threatening. They all guaranteed to citizens the right to choice of language, and none regulated the use of language for private conversations. But in all the Union republics, the titular language was named as the "state language." The republican government was required to guarantee that language's predominance in official proceedings, the media, and in universities. Many of the language laws were so harsh toward Russian in their original forms that Soviet authorities had been obliged to intervene to soften the final versions.[5] The intentions of the titulars were revealed by those draft laws, to the chagrin of the Russian-speakers who lived in the Union republics. Furthermore, as the actual laws got down to specifics (Table 4.2 summarizes the basic differences in the laws faced by the Russian-speaking populations in Estonia, Latvia, Kazakhstan, and Ukraine), Russian-speakers realized that the era of easy monolingualism was over. At the very least (and including even the Kazakh law, which was most accommodating to the Russian language), Russians holding jobs in state enterprises, especially those that entailed contact with the public, would need to learn the titular language. This was an indignity in itself. But the unequivocal tone of all the laws, that the state language was the titular tongue, sent shivers down the spine of most Russians.

The degree of nationalizing pressures in these laws accords with the patterns outlined in Chapter 3. Lawrence R. Robertson has coded these language laws according to their "secessionist strength" as determined by five indicators: (1) the timing of the laws; (2) the degree to which the titular language would be required for economic exchange; (3) the role in the republic foreseen for the Russian language; (4) the extent to which knowing the titular language would become mandatory in the republic; and (5) the timetable for the full implementation of the law's provisions.[6] Based on these criteria, with a "5" representing the strongest secessionist threat, Robertson comes up with the values indicated on Table 4.3. Here Ukraine and Kazakhstan have relatively low scores; Estonia and Latvia somewhat higher ones. But in all the cases, these laws, even in their milder forms, were dark clouds for monolingual Russian-speakers whose linguistic repertoires had never been challenged before.

The Collapse of the Soviet Union

"The idea of a new man," writes Andrei Sinyavsky with bitter irony, "is the cornerstone of Soviet civilization." Roman Szporluk adopts the same sardonic tone. "The 'Soviet people,'" and here he is giving the official line, "is a new historical community embracing the Russians and the non-Russians in an entity that is not ethnic per se, though it has certain ethnic features, for example, the Russian language as a medium of 'internationality communication.'" Nevertheless, Szporluk points out, "the concept of the Soviet people as now elucidated has all the marks of

[5] See, for example, A. Pigolkin and M. Studenikina, "Legal Interpretations of the Draft Law on Language from Estonia," *Izvestiia*, January 7, 1989, and translated in *Current Digest of the Soviet Press*, February 2, 1989. See the special issue of *Nationalities Papers* 23, no. 3 (1995), "Implementing Language Laws: Perestroika and Its Legacy in Five Republics," ed. William Fierman. See especially Toivo U. Raun, "The Estonian SSR Language Law (1989): Background and Implementation," pp. 515–34. The social and administrative realities made implementation of language shift a much more difficult process than the drafters of the original laws had foreseen. My purpose here is not to chronicle implementation but to demonstrate the psychological affect of the passage of these laws on the Russian-speaking inhabitants of the Union republics.

[6] Lawrence Rutherford Robertson, "The Political Economy of Ethnonationalism: Separatism and Secession from the Soviet Union and the Russian Federation" (Ph.D. diss., Department of Political Science, UCLA, 1995), pp. 106–9.

Table 4.2. A summary of the republican language laws of 1989

Topics by republic	Specific provisions
Date of adoption	
Kazakhstan	September 22
Estonia	January 18
Latvia	May 5
Ukraine	October 28
Object of law	
Kazakhstan	"Languages"
Estonia	"Language"
Latvia	"Languages"
Ukraine	"Languages"
Official role of Russian[a]	
Kazakhstan	"Knowledge of the Russian language by members of all nationalities answers their fundamental interests." (Art. 2)
Estonia	Treated only as "proceeding from the needs of all-Union communication" and as "the language that, after Estonian, is used most often as a native language." (Preamble)
Latvia	Recognizes Russian as the language of the Supreme Soviet of the USSR, border guards, army, and railroad police stationed in Latvia. (Art. 3) "Russian, after Latvian, is the second most widely used language in Latvia, and one for internationality communication." (Preamble). Mention of state support for Latvian, but no mention of support for Russian. (Preamble)
Ukraine	Need "to create the necessary conditions for the development and use of the Russian language." (Art. 2)
Language of republican laws and acts[b]	
Kazakhstan	"Acts of the republican government and administrative organs are adopted in the Kazakh and Russian languages." (Art. 9)
Estonia	"Acts of organs of state power and government . . . are to be adopted and published in Estonian, and for a temporary period, in Russian." (Art. 8) In local institutions (except for the Tallinn area), where Estonian is not spoken, Russian can be used, and the introduction of Estonian can be delayed. (Art. 36)
Latvia	Acts of organs of state power and government . . . are to be adopted and published in Latvian. They are to be published in Russian translation as well "in cases defined by legislation." (Art. 6)
Ukraine	"Acts of the republican ministries and departments, as well as of local governments and administrative organs, are adopted and published in the Ukrainian language, and in case of necessity, are also published in another language." (Pt. II, Art. 10)
Language requirements for jobs[c]	
Kazakhstan	Officials in government, social security, communications, and transport are to be "proficient in the Kazakh and Russian languages—and in another language as well in places where other national groups live in a compact territory—at a level necessary for the fulfillment of their official duties." (Art. 16)
Estonia	State language, Russian and other languages (if needed for the job) for all official posts, in state enterprises, and for a variety of professions, including journalists, doctors, merchants. (Art. 4) Those already having such positions are granted four years to learn the state language. (Art. 37)

Table 4.2. A summary of the republican language laws of 1989, *continued*

Topics by republic	Specific provisions
Language requirements for jobs[c]	
Latvia	State language, Russian, and other languages, as necessary to fulfill professional duties, for workers in government and state institutions, and those institutions which are in contact with citizens [unspecified]. (Art. 4)
	Three years to learn the state language. (From accompanying decree on activating the law, para. 1)
Ukraine	For most jobs, both the state language and Russian is required. Officials must "in cases of necessity" know another language besides Ukrainian and Russian at a level adequate to their official obligations, and are granted a 3- to 5-year grace period to meet this requirement. (Art. 6)
Language on public signs[d]	
Kazakhstan	No direct mention of signs, but official graphic displays are to be "in Kazakh and Russian, and in localities with compact settlements of other nationalities, in their native language." (Art. 29)
Estonia	In Estonian, except when based on historical or historical-cultural factors. (Art. 27)
Latvia	Local soviet decides whether it is necessary to translate names in a language other than Latvian. (Art. 16)
Ukraine	Signs are to be in Ukrainian, and can also be in the national language of the majority of the population of the locality. (Art. 38)
Language of instruction[e]	
Kazakhstan	Promises material guarantees to implement the right to free choice of language of instruction. Entrance examinations for higher education schools can be in Russian, Kazakh, or any of the national languages.
Estonia	Guarantees education in the Estonian language anywhere on its territory. The non-Estonian population has only an equal right to receive a general education in its native language. No guidelines for the teaching of Russian in schools where it is not the medium of instruction.
Latvia	Absolute right for education in Latvian or Russian; also rights for citizens of other nationalities to have education in their native languages. Russian is not an obligatory subject where another language is the medium of instruction.
Ukraine	Guarantee for the study of Russian, but only where Russians or citizens of other nationalities constitute a majority of the population. For specialized schools, students can take entrance exams in Russian only if they were taught in educational institutions with instruction in Russian.

Note: All laws recognized the role of Russian as the language of all-Union communication.

[a] Pigolkin and Studenikina, "Republican Language Laws," pp. 46–52.

[b] Ibid., pp. 52–54.

[c] Ibid., pp. 55–61.

[d] Ibid., pp. 67–68.

[e] Ibid., pp. 68–73.

Source: The organization of material for this table is based on the analysis of Albert S. Pigolkin and Marina S. Studenikina, "Republican Language Laws in the USSR: A Comparative Analysis," *Journal of Soviet Nationalities* 2, no. 1 (1991): 38–76. The language laws of 1989 are usefully collected in M. N. Guboglo, *Perelomnye gody*, vol. 2, *Iazykovaia reforma—1989: Dokumenty i materialy* (Moscow: Rossiiskaia Akademiia Nauk, 1994).

Table 4.3. The secessionist strength of the republican language laws

Indicators of secessionist strength	Kazakhstan	Estonia	Latvia	Ukraine
Timing	3	5	5	2
Economic role	2	5	3	1
Role of Russian	2	4	3	3
Mandatory use in speech	4	5	4	2
Implementation	2	5	1	2
Aggregate score	13	24	16	10

a synthetic, artificial device and is treated with the utmost suspicion by the non-Russians. They suspect, with good reason, that behind the talk of a Soviet people . . . lies a much less noble design—the desire to transform the peoples of the USSR into a Russian political nation . . . to realize a goal that eluded earlier Russian nationalists." Hélène Carrère d'Encausse, without the bitterness, arrived at a similar conclusion. Khrushchev's vision of a merging (*sliianie*) of peoples into a single nation was "negated" by the hard facts (of retained national consciousness) reflected in the 1970 census.[7] With this consensus about the failure of the "Soviet" cultural project, the universal approval among titulars that greeted Yeltsin's call to the republics that they should "take all the independence [they] can handle" should have come as no surprise.[8]

Our commentators, I believe, have dismissed the cultural residue of the new Soviet man all too quickly. As Sinyavsky acknowledges in his prefatory remarks: "Soviet civilization is a singular and formidable power of the twentieth century. . . . Soviet civilization is so novel and extraordinary that at times even those who grew up within it, who are its children, see it as a sort of monstrosity or alien environment—one, however, in which they belong."[9] This too is written in an ironic tone. Yet among the twenty-five million Russian-speakers who were living in Union republics outside of the Russian Federation, the idea of a Soviet civilization that was international, that was helping to merge the nations, was no monstrosity. It was the hegemonic project that defined their cultural space.

In interviews that my ethnographic research team and I conducted with ordinary Russian-speaking families in four of the former Union republics, we heard again and again the seriousness of the Russian-speakers' attachment to a Soviet identity. Olga, a Russian from Kiev told Arel that she has no attraction to "Russia," but she used to identify solely with the Soviet Union: "We lived in the Soviet Union, we

[7] Andrei Sinyavsky, *Soviet Civilization: A Cultural History*, trans. Joanne Turnbull (New York: Arcade, 1990), p. 114; Roman Szporluk, "The Ukraine and Russia," in Robert Conquest, ed., *The Last Empire* (Stanford, Calif.: Hoover Institution Press, 1986), pp. 168, 170; Hélène Carrère d'Encausse, "Determinants and Parameters of Soviet Nationality Policy," in Jeremy R. Azrael, ed., *Soviet Nationality Policies and Practices* (New York: Praeger, 1978).

[8] John B. Dunlop, *The Rise of Russia and the Fall of the Soviet Empire* (Princeton: Princeton University Press, 1993), pp. 59–65.

[9] Sinyavsky, *Soviet Civilization*, p. xi.

did not feel that we lived in Ukraine. As in the popular Soviet song, my address was the Soviet Union." Jelena Berotsova, on Latvian TV, was wistful watching the Latvians resurrect their traditions. "We [Russians] are many and we have lost all of this," she told Pettai. "We have no heroes. We were Soviet; now who are we? Russia is still far away."

Their powerful memories of Soviet culture make them feel that there is now something missing from their lives. An extremely sophisticated politician and educator in Estonia (who speaks fluent Estonian), Sergei Sovetnikov's fondest memories (which were recorded in photographs he exultantly showed me) were in the relay runs he helped organize through the Soviet Union, with the runners carrying the Olympic Torch. The Soviet team had meaning for him. He does not consider either the Russian or Estonian team a satisfactory substitute. For Olga Guzhvina, in Tallinn, as explained to Pettai, it was the Amateur Singing Clubs (*Klub samodeiatel'nogo peniia*) and the annual Soviet-wide organization of these clubs, bringing together some 60,000 people along the banks of the Volga River. For Natal'ia Berezhkova, also of Tallinn, the Pioneer and Komsomol activities at the school are her most powerful Soviet memories. The parties, outings, volunteer assistance to the elderly, with the children waving their Soviet flags, were special to her. "Now, the kids have nothing to do," she lamented to Pettai. For Liuba Grigor'ev, in whose house I lived for seven months, it was the music and the Soviet holidays. One morning, as we were eating breakfast, there was a (rare) Russian (Soviet) patriotic song on the Russian-language Estonian state radio, and Liuba sang along with it in some quiet joy. Then she lamented that it was a shame that such songs are almost never played anymore, and maybe even more important, there weren't any more holidays where great events or people or whatever are celebrated. It makes life less interesting and provides fewer times for family to gather in festivity.

These feelings are not merely nostalgic; they are powerful identity markers. Take Leonid, Arel's chauffeur, who is a passport Ukrainian, born in Kiev. His father is from Russia, from a small town in Saratov Oblast, along the Volga. His father's parents came to Ukraine before or during the Second World War. The grandfather was serving in the military and was probably dispatched to Ukraine for work. He died during the war. The grandmother remarried an ethnic Russian from Kiev. On his mother's side, the grandfather was Jewish and the grandmother Polish-Ukrainian. None of Leonid's four grandparents were Ukrainian. When Arel asked him point blank, in December 1995, whether he would vote for a reunification of Ukraine with Russia, he said he would all the way. His longing appears to be less, if at all, for a greater Slavic cultural-political world, than for a world (the Soviet Union) when things used to be more orderly, when "everything used to be linked."

When the Soviet Union collapsed, Andreu Grigor'ev, Liuba's older son, born in Narva, was in the Soviet Army. He could hardly believe that the country he was serving no longer existed. For him, it was easy to return to Estonia, though he thought of it then as his *republic* but not his *homeland*. For many others, the route back home was administratively more complex, but the feelings of loss were just as strong. Unlike the Russians in Russia, or the titulars in their own republics, the Russian-speakers in the titular republics had an interest in the Soviet civilizational project. It gave them the right to be monolingual, and to travel back and forth from Russia to their republics without crossing an international border. They could take full advantage of a vast employment market without losing access to their TV programs, or the ability to send their children to Russian-medium schools. The Russian-speaking population in the Union republics were the quintessential new Soviet men. Therefore, the collapse of the Soviet Union, raising the specter of being deprived of a homeland, holding a passport for a country (their country!) which no longer existed, was for them deeply traumatic.

Compounding the Trauma

The double trauma was compounded by two not-so-subtle factors. First, the official and semi-official discourse of the nationalizing state—especially that coming from those radicals who had most fervently pressed for independence and who had played key roles in the transition—was deeply offensive to Russian ears. Second, Russia seemed, in its public rhetoric, to be abandoning its "compatriots" in the near abroad.

The Policies and Discourse of the Nationalizing State

The new nationalizing states played to diverse audiences. To international organizations, they had to show their civic face; but to their mobilized supporters (at home and in diaspora) they had to exhibit a more nationalistic visage. Sometimes government policies were benign and bureaucratic but were advertised in a way to impress nationalists and thereby to offend Russians. Sometimes policies and practices themselves were discriminatory but were presented to international audiences as inconsequential. Russian-speakers in the republics saw both of these faces, but the Russian-language press tended to translate only the most nationalistic and anti-Russian orations of titulars (some of them intended to fight intratitular policy battles). As a result the Russian-language press was filled with a cacophony of anti-Russian nationalist rhetoric. This "spin" on nationalistic policies was deeply troubling and offensive to the Russian-speaking populations in those republics. Under conditions of cataclysm, many Russians accepted as obvious that the anti-Russian epithets and insensitive nationalizing policies represented the "real" titular face.

In the Baltics, a Kafkaesque "Trial"

The leaders of the restored Estonian and Latvian republics were unequivocal nationalizers. They were willing to accord internationally recognized human rights to nontitulars, but they had no intention of allowing them to play key roles in the rebuilding of the cultural foundation of the restored nation-states. In an interview between his two terms as prime minister, Tiit Vähi made clear that his goal was to make Estonia a country for Estonians. When asked whether the Belgian model (with each cultural pillar having autonomy) or the French (nationally homogeneous) model was more appropriate for Estonia, he responded:

> Still I would propose for Estonia the French model. I am sure that for this is needed to create conditions and this doesn't take place in a few months, but in some years. . . . [But, I ask, will the Russians integrate as Estonians?] I think, that my opinion is less important than their opinion. The question is, that very many Estonians have before and after the war happened to live in US, Canada, and Sweden. They have learned the language and all of them have remained Estonians, but their grandchildren already very conditionally. I see the Estonian state as a model for such a nation state, where the dominant nationality is Estonian, the state language is Estonian, where non-Estonians have been granted human rights, and also economic rights. And, at the same time, the processes have to take place peacefully. . . . The integration of non-Estonians with Estonia, Estonian culture and language—I think is very important. (DL, interview, October 21, 1993)

I posed the same question to Juris Baldunčiks, then a member of the Latvian Academy of Science. He insisted that the Latvians would never accept a "pillared" society. The Russians must assimilate! In the jargon of the late 1980s, Estonia and Latvia were "velvet" nationalizing states.

From the Russian point of view, the policies did not appear at all velvet. The Estonian Popular Front government under Edgar Savisaar, which came to power during the perestroika period, depended on electoral support from Russians and therefore did not press the French model very strongly. The government fell in January 1992, in part because many Estonians resented visible presence of Russians in its coalition. A citizenship law, passed by the new provisional government under Tiit Vähi, was quite harsh on the Russian-speaking population. Immigrants and their families who had entered Estonia in the Soviet period were not automatically granted citizenship in the new state, on the grounds that Soviet rule had been illegal, and therefore any immigration that occurred under Soviet auspices was "occupation." The citizenship law required noncitizens to pass an examination in Estonian. Noncitizens who could not pass such an examination would have to establish ten years of "legal" residence before applying for citizenship. There was no accompanying legislation to provide for language teaching; and it wasn't until the government was presented with (not unconditionally desired) foreign aid from Sweden, Germany, and the United States that the language programs got basic funding. Because they were no longer citizens, the great majority of Estonia's Russian-speaking population could not participate in the national elections of September 1992.

With most Russian-speakers unable to vote, a vehemently nationalist coalition called Isamaa (Fatherland) was able to win that national election. And Isamaa continued the trend of high internationality confrontation. Its education law, for example, implied that state subsidy for Russian-language schools would be discontinued. The coup de grace was a law passed by the Riigikogu (parliament) in the summer of 1993, called the "Law on Aliens," which required noncitizens (many of whom had lived their entire lives in Estonia) to register with the state or to face deportation. While registering aliens is a common state function, many Russians were shocked by this new identifying label. Worse, the government ruled that after registration, noncitizens were eligible only for temporary residence permits; Russians therefore feared that deportation would occur even if they complied with the law. The city councils of two towns (Narva and Sillamäe) rode a wave of public indignation and declared referenda to decide whether these cities should have "national territorial autonomy." The Estonian government declared these referenda to be invalid since the constitution (a document which was written virtually without the participation of the Russian-speaking population) declared Estonia to be a unitary state.

In Latvia, the Popular Front alliance between titulars and the Russian-speaking population was not merely tactical. In the parliamentary election of March 1990, Neil Melvin reports,

> The ethnic distribution of the deputies indicates that far more Russian-speakers voted for the ethnic Latvian candidates of the Popular Front than for the ethnic Russian candidates put up by Equal Rights. In the new parliament 74% of deputies were ethnic Latvians; the Russian-speakers had clearly voted for independence and trusted ethnic Latvians to represent their interests better than other Russian-speakers. . . . Two-thirds of Latvia's Russian residents indicated support for the Latvian Supreme Soviet and Council of Ministers in a poll taken two days before the Soviet crackdown in Riga in January 1991. The same poll indicated declining support among the Russians for the Soviet-inspired Interfront and the All-Latvian Salvation Committee. In January 1991, many non-Letts were reported to be on the barricades in Riga when the Soviet internal security forces launched their attacks.[10]

But this alliance did not persist once independence became a fact. Before the Soviet collapse, Latvian leaders of the Popular Front stated that all permanent residents of Latvia would be citizens. But by October 1991, a new consensus had emerged, one which would require most Russians to naturalize, with a parliamentary guideline that set a sixteen-year period before they could even apply for citizenship. This requirement would hold for those who were not themselves or direct descendants of persons who held Latvian passports during the interwar republic. This law was never officially ratified, but the long delay before a more moderate bill was passed in 1994 hampered naturalization and made life more worrisome for noncitizens. Later discussion of a naturalization law raised the specter of "quotas," suggesting that even people who qualified for citizenship would not necessarily be able to receive it. A policy known as the "window process," which limited by age sets eligible applicants for citizenship, went into effect. The way it was administered, furthermore, opened the window primarily to those age groups with the least propensity to apply. In 1996 the Latvian parliament granted citizenship to four hockey players and the chief physician of the Talsi Regional Environmental Health Center, much to the chagrin of the nationalists, who pointed to the language deficiencies of the candidates. In 1997

[10] Neil Melvin, *Russians beyond Russia* (London: Royal Institute of International Affairs, 1995), pp. 35–36.

President Guntis Ulmanis urged ending of the window policy, but the parliament, still nervous over the hockey players, refused to do so.[11]

Not only was access to citizenship severely restricted. The rights of noncitizens were restricted as well. In December 1991, the Supreme Council reserved a number of rights for citizens, including that of owning land, the right to travel back and forth from Latvia, the right to state office, and the right to vote, even in local elections. Job restrictions were so broad that *Rossiiskaia gazeta* published a sardonic article reporting that noncitizens were granted an "indulgence"—in the form of an amendment to the law prohibiting noncitizens to occupy state office—permitting them to work as volunteer firemen, so "noncitizens can now put on the fireman's helmet and risk their lives for the sake of saving from fire the possessions of the Latvian Republic."[12] And the Latvian government, even less accommodating than the Estonian, through 1994 had no provisions for noncitizen residents to vote in local elections.[13] Therefore, delay in passing a citizenship law prejudiced many Russian-speakers in direct ways.

To be sure, Baltic postindependence policies were largely in accord with international human rights norms. Unlike the other Union republics, the Baltic states had been illegally occupied by the Soviet Union; throughout the postwar period, the governments of the interwar republics were recognized by the West as the only legal representatives of the Baltic countries. Technically, then, immigrants during the Soviet era were indeed "occupiers." Therefore, a legal process of naturalization was called for.

Furthermore, and again showing legal correctness, when the Aliens' Law was first presented to Estonian president Meri, he asked to have it "cleared" by a board of European juridical experts. Those experts found technical violations of international human rights, inducing Meri to send the law back to the Parliament for redrafting. Both Estonia and Latvia have welcomed missions from the Conference for Security and Cooperation in Europe (CSCE; renamed OSCE in 1995), which has monitored the human rights situation. While the Baltic states remained in technical compliance with international standards, their laws and regulations did not have the soft feel of velvet.

If the policies had a threatening edge, the surrounding governmental or semi-official rhetoric was often threatening through and through. In confidential interviews, officials of the Isamaa government confided to me that the anti-Russian government rhetoric played a crucial economic role. With it, there was an electoral coalition of urban business (which wanted economic reform) and rural folk (farmers and pensioners) which was willing to accept the harsh realities of economic reform as long as the Russian population was being threatened. Without the chau-

[11] Andres Kahar, "Ulmanis Puts Citizenship on Front Burner," *Baltic Times*, April 10, 1997; Andres Kahar, "The Pitfalls of Selling Latvian Citizenship," ibid., May 29, 1997; Andres Kahar, "Opening the Floodgates of Citizenship," ibid., January 9, 1997; and ibid., November 21, 1996.

[12] *Rossiiskaia gazeta*, "Dali 'poblazhku' negrazhdanam," January 24, 1997. On the original "indulgence," see the *Baltic Times*, October 17, 1996, which reports that on October 10, 1996, the Latvian parliament amended the law to permit four hundred government officials who were noncitizens to retain their posts.

[13] Melvin, *Russians Beyond Russia*, p. 44.

vinism, I was told, a coalition of Russians and the rural elements would have defeated reform. Furthermore, the policies to allow the industrial base in the Russian-dominated northeast to wither, leading to 40 percent employment there, was not only to administer shock therapy. Isamaa officials feared that an economically vibrant northeast would attract massive immigration from northwestern Russia, thereby further threatening an Estonian majority in Estonia. Russian leaders in Estonia were not deaf to these themes and understood the "game" the nationalizing elites were playing. They felt that the Estonian government was trying to squeeze the Russians out of the republic that Estonians considered their own.[14]

Much of the radical nationalist language of Baltic leaders flooded into the Russian press. In an interview with *Molodezh' Estonii*, the then minister of nationality and immigration, Peter Olesk, was quoted as saying, "I consider that people without definite citizenship are dangerous from the point of view of the Estonian state." More inflammatory views worked their way into the Russian press. *Estoniia* had a regular column of translations from the Estonian press and had a knack for finding those most obnoxious to its readers. On September 18, 1993, its editor (disingenuously) prefaced that edition's translated articles from the Estonian-language press by saying, "For a long time we tried to find in the Estonian-language press even one good word about the Representative Assembly of the Russian-speaking Population. Alas! The tone of most of the articles and commentaries in the recent past . . . is aggravating." In one of them, in the highly nationalist *Hommikuleht*, there was an analysis by Andres Michaels, a member of the Estonian National Independence Party (and part of the Isamaa coalition), called "The Representative Assembly: A Wolf Hiding from the Sheep." He argued that as noncitizens, the potential members of the Representative Assembly did not have the constitutional right to political representation of any sort. Another example came from the *Narvskaia gazeta*, which translated an article of I. Tungal from the state-owned (but rented to the editorial board at the time) *Päevaleht*, with the following polemic: "Estonia cannot be free and independent, since 40 percent of its people are made up of newly arrived eastern colonists, since foreigners [*inorodtsy*] have usurped Narva, Kohtla-Järve . . . and especially that foreigners have overtaken, with half the residents, the capital. . . . The only way out is through active decolonization."[15]

The Russian-language press in Latvia was equally quick to pick up on inflammatory rhetoric coming from Latvians in government circles. In November 1991 Visvaldis Lacis, head of the Latvian National Independence Movement, declared that Russians are not even "second-class" citizens; they are "nobodies" having rights no greater than he would have, were he to travel in Sweden. This was sensationalized in the Russian press.[16]

[14] But see Thomas Endel McConnon, "Ethnic Competition and Post-Socialist Economic Reform in Estonia: A Qualitative and Quantitative Analysis" (B.A. essay, Harvard College, Department of Government, 1996), where cogent data are presented showing that the Isamaa government did not take economic advantage of the Russian population.

[15] *Molodezh' Estonii*, April 21, 1994; *Estoniia*, September 18, 1993; *Narvskaia gazeta*, January 29, 1994.

[16] *Sovetskaia molodezh'*, September 11, 1991; quoted in Paul Kolstoe, *Russians in the Former Soviet Republics* (Bloomington: Indiana University Press, 1995), p. 123.

Estonia and Latvia's strict legality and formal accord with international norms is chillingly reminiscent of the formal legality of the Habsburg bureaucracy in Franz Kafka's morbid imagination. The Russian-speaking populations of these two republics were being asked to walk through labyrinths—justifying themselves for crimes that remained unspecified—as did Joseph K. in *The Trial*.

Kazakhstan: "Will you still need me, when I'm 64"

Unlike in the Baltics, all legal residents of the Kazakh Soviet Socialist Republic had the automatic right to citizenship in independent Kazakhstan. The battle there was not over citizenship, but rather over dual citizenship, something the Kazakhstani state was unwilling to give to Russians but implicitly gave to Kazakh nationals in Afghanistan and China. Symbolic attacks, however, often had more power than legal ones. On the language question, the 1993 constitution reaffirmed the 1989 law, with Russian specified as the "language of internationality communication." And the president of Kazakhstan has sought to promote "a peculiar synthesis of the national sovereignty of the Kazakhs and the sovereignty of the people of Kazakhstan in general as an ethnopolitical community."[17] Yet the synthesis was symbolically quite revolutionary compared to the dominance of Russian in the Soviet period. In a similar vein, in my colleague Bhavna Dave's field reports, the Kazakhstani law that most disoriented the Russian population among her informants was the one creating a Kazakh national currency. Somehow Asian faces on their currency disturbed the Russians deeply, and they foresaw from it the impending disruption of trade ties between Russia and Kazakhstan.

Accommodating laws and pronouncements, however, were often countered by anti-Russian policies and claims by zealous officials. The National Council on State Policy, which works directly under the president, prepared a project on the sociocultural development of the republic. While it recognized that other national cultures of Kazakhstan had their own rediscovering to do, it posited that "the unquestioned priority should be given to Kazakh culture, that is, to the culture of people who have given their historical name to this state. The reason for this is that it is only in Kazakhstan, and nowhere else in the world, that this culture can undergo a genuine rebirth and essential development." To be sure, the internal wars among the nationalists in government, one faction dominating the State Committee on Languages and another the Ministry of Printing and Mass Communication, has held back the fulfillment of the project of the National Council.[18] Yet the message heard by Russians in Kazakhstan is somewhat more threatening than President Nazarbaev's speeches, which are oriented more toward international oil investors than his own electorate.

[17] Reported in *Kazakhstanskaia pravda*, November 28, 1992; quoted in Kolstoe, *Russians in the Former Soviet Republics*, pp. 248–49.

[18] For the National Council, see *Ekspress*, December 14, 1993, p. 4; for the bureaucratic battle, see Aleksandra Molchanova, "I dostalas' Komitetu po iazykam dyrka ot bublika," *Kazakhstanskaia pravda*, December 14, 1993, p. 3.

A closer examination at the workings of the independent state reinforces the view that Nazarbaev's secular internationalism is largely a show for a foreign audience. Data from 1993 published by Boris Giller and Viktor Shatskikh reveal that of the five state advisers to the president, there isn't a single non-Kazakh (*nekorennoe*) representative. Among vice-premiers, there is one non-Kazakh and six Kazakhs. In the presidential apparatus, the ratio is 1:6; in the Ministry of Education, 1:6; in the Ministry of Finance, 3:5; in the Ministry of Transport, 2:4; in the Ministry of Information and the Press, 1:4; in the Ministry of the Economy, 1:7; in the Ministry of Justice, 1:4; and in the State Television and Radio Committee, 0:5. The authors ironically ask in conclusion, "Shall we conclude from these that in recent years there has occurred a significant erosion in the intellectual potential and professional aptitudes among Russians, Ukrainians, Tatars, Koreans, Uighurs, Jews, and Germans living in Kazakhstan?"[19] Other data reported by I. A. Subbotina show that in the 1994 elections Kazakhs had 41 percent of the votes and were rewarded with 60 percent of the seats; meanwhile Russians had 40 percent of the votes and procured only 27.8 percent of the seats.[20]

Kazakh policy since independence in regard to Russians is one of formal protection, with a *sotto voce* message that there can be no future for Russians in Kazakh political life. Anatoly Khazanov reports the whispers he heard in his trips to Kazakhstan: "We bid farewell to Germans [voluntarily emigrating to Germany] and shake hands with them: we turn Russians out by kicking their backs."[21] Enormous need of Russian technical skill and the bureaucratic incapacity to administer a nationalizing program (for example, to staff schools with Kazakh-speaking teachers) will clearly stem the tide of progressive, inexorable kazakhization of the republic. But if Russians feel they are needed now (when the republic is young), what about the future? Will all job categories in the future have the same nationality ratios as those in officialdom today? To quote the Beatles, each Russian in Kazakhstan is asking, "Will you still need me when I'm sixty-four?"

Ukraine: Dr. Jekyll and Mr. Hyde

The unequivocal word from two presidents is that Ukraine is a country for Ukrainians of all nationalities. President Leonid Kuchma made this clear in his inaugural address:

> We have to understand that Ukraine is a multinational state. Any attempt to ignore this fact threatens to profoundly split society and to ruin the idea of Ukrainian statehood. Ukraine is the motherland for all citizens, irrespective of their nationality, religion, and mother tongue. In the short term I have the intention to propose

[19] Boris Giller and Viktor Shatskikh, "Opredelenie berega: russkoiazychnyie v Kazakhstane," *Karavan*, December 12, 1993.

[20] I. A. Subbotina, "Kazakhstan," in V. Tishkov, ed., *Migratsii i novye diaspory v postsovetskikh gosudarstvakh* (Moscow: Institut etnologii i antropologii, 1996), p. 211.

[21] Anatoly M. Khazanov, "Ethnic Strife in Contemporary Kazakhstan," working paper, National Council for Soviet and East European Research, Washington, D.C., 1994, p. 15.

a change in the current legislation in order to give Russian the status of a second official language while preserving Ukrainian as a state language.

Earlier, during the electoral campaign, he promised that in Ukraine there would be one state language (for diplomacy and legislation) and two official languages (for all other spheres).[22] This is as close to a "pillared" state as in any of the post-Soviet republics considered here.

But the civic face of Ukraine is only half the story. The conflict over what kind of nation Ukraine will become is not settled. In the parliament, debates on the constitution have brought to the fore the great divide on the national issue. After the first draft was presented to the parliament, nationalist deputies were offended at the references to the "people of Ukraine" (*narod Ukrainy*). They made more than eighty proposals to change this to "the Ukrainian people" (*Ukrainskii narod*), which connotes a nationality criterion for membership. The conflict between those trying to build a national state and those seeking a broader notion of membership remains strong.[23]

In some realms, the nationalizers have had the upper hand. In L'viv, Iryna Kalynets, the director of the bureau of public education, took the initiative to close all Russian-language schools, irrespective of parents' wishes.[24] And Ukrainian nationalists from Galicia traveled in large numbers to Crimea to demonstrate resistance to the Russian autonomy movement there. Under conditions of confrontation, state authorities had little choice but to stand up for their sovereign right to rule the peninsula. In a threatening statement, the Ukrainian National Assembly declared that Crimea would either be Ukrainian or depopulated.[25] Autonomy for Russians in Ukraine would have clear limits, at the risk of war.

Ominous clouds therefore remain on the Ukrainian nationalist horizon, and they can appear dark indeed. Although I discuss this issue in greater depth in Chapter 6, some of its elements need to be introduced here. The rhetoric that sometimes gets inserted into the mainstream nationalist press has a forbidding tone. At a congress of the ultranationalist Derzhavna samostiinist' Ukrainy (State Independence of Ukraine, or DSU), its chairman, Roman Koval' (from Donbass), was reported to have said: "Next year the DSU must not report on newspapers, pamphlets and meetings, but on the number of eliminated [*unichtozhennykh*] enemies." He then called for a switch from the educational slogan "Beware Russians" to the final slogan "Death to the occupiers!" Another DSU ideologue, Shcherbatiuk, called for the "sanitizing" (*sanatsiia*) and the purging (*vydalennia*) from Ukrainian society of

[22] On the inaugural address, see "Leonid Kuchma prines prisiagu na vernost' ukrainskomu narodu," *Holos Ukrainy*, July 21, 1994; on the promise, see *Kievskie vedomosti* (in Russian), April 8, 1994. Kuchma never followed up on this promise with actual legislation.

[23] Anatolii Zaiets' and Nina Tanatar, "Zi spal't hazet—do proektu. Za materialam obhovorennia proektu novuiu Konstitutsii Ukrainy u presi," *Holos ukrainy* (in Ukrainian), June 5, 1993; and Oleksandr Yemets', "Shchob zhyty v krashchykh umovakh," *Vysokyi zamok* (in Ukrainian), January 1995.

[24] Vitalii Panov, " 'Reformy' pani Kalinets," *Rossiia*, July 29–August 4, 1992; quoted in Kolstoe, *Russians in the Former Soviet Republics*, p. 182.

[25] *Jane's Intelligence Review Europe*, December 1992, p. 541; quoted in Kolstoe, *Russians in the Former Soviet Republics*, p. 195.

these parasitic elements (here meaning Russians, Jews, and so on) which prevent it from breathing fully, from being healthy and powerful.[26]

In the west, anti-Russian threats are of course quite strong. On July 25, 1993, during the celebration for the forty-ninth anniversary of the liberation of Ivano-Frankovsk from German aggressors, armed bands (*boeviki*) of fascist-sympathizing nationalist organizations—in broad daylight in the center of town—attacked a parade (*pokhod*) of veterans which had been sanctioned by the authorities. Two dozen people needed medical help. The author of the Russian-language article reporting on this incident suggested that there had been a cover-up by the government, since no formal charges were ever filed.[27] In 1997, the Russian press reported on a "moral terror" against Russians in Galicia, with reports of a "pogrom" against the Russian cultural center in L'viv, an attack on war veterans who were putting wreaths on the memorial to dead soldiers, and talk of a "St. Bartholomew's night for Russians" after the Russian-Ukrainian agreement on the Black Sea Fleet was signed, followed by vandalism directed at Russian schools, which was organized by the National Socialist Party of Ukraine.[28]

The Ukrainian-language press often prints nationalist threats against Russian-speakers. "An open policy of russianization [*rosiishchenniia*] of Ukraine," one author wrote, "can cause not only a split [*rozkol*] of Ukraine, but could lead to a possible all-European conflict." Another wrote that "the granting of official status to Russian in the Ukrainian state, showing contempt for the people of Ukraine, means civil war in Ukraine, insecurity in Europe, millions and millions of victims for whom nobody, as before, will answer." A third writer asks, while totally exaggerating the percentage of the population that is Ukrainian: "Do you think that the 37.4 million ethnic Ukrainians (84.7% of the population) would allow an attempt on the life of their mother Ukrainian tongue? Be sure that hundreds of thousands would rise for the defense of their language and culture. And this would mean—civil war, blood, death, grief, chaos."[29]

In the international press, the radical nationalists from western Ukraine are not taken as representative of the political center. But even the centrist Rukh engages in this xenophobic provocation. Consider the following from Ivan Drach, the first leader of Rukh:[30]

[26] The Koval' quotation is from "Obzor tekushchikh sobytii," *Kommunist* (in Russian), November 1994. This article is part of an exposé to demonstrate the danger of the rabid nationalists. "Unichtozhennykh" is a Russian gloss; Koval' himself, Arel pointed out to me in a private communication, would not have been using Russian in public. Viktor Desiatnykov, "Zahony Sanatsi vyrushaiut," *Demokratychna Ukraina* (in Ukrainian), December 11, 1993. The DSU has far more success in getting inflammatory articles published in the mainstream nationalist press than in getting votes from mainstream voters. It remains a fringe party, on the margins of the political debate. I use this material to demonstrate that the dark face of Ukrainian nationalism appears in daylight.

[27] Aleksandr Volkov, "Snova glas vopiiushchego?" *Tovarishch*, October 1994.

[28] See Iana Amelina, "Russkie v Galitsii," *Nezavisimaia gazeta*, April 4, 1997.

[29] Pavlo Movchan, "Ostannii rubizh," *Literaturna Ukraina* (in Ukrainian), October 6, 1994; "Zvernennia," *Visnyk prosvity* (in Ukrainian), no. 1, 1994; Vasyl' Zakharchenko, "Dvi derzhavni movy—tse nebezpechno!" *Literaturna Ukraina* (in Ukrainian), March 17, 1994.

[30] Ivan Drach, "Ukraina i Rossiia: perspektivy vzaimootnoshenii," *Nezavisimaia gazeta* (Moscow, in Russian), February 3, 1994.

> Russians, unfortunately, practically do not know the Ukrainian soul. . . . It is possible that we ourselves do not yet know fully who we are. Still it is useful from time to time to inform the Russians that Ukrainians will never accept the myth of the "one thousand years" of Russian statehood . . . that St. Sophia Cathedral belongs to the Russian Church, that our 700-year struggle for the restoration of our own state is a whim of nationalists. . . . Only in the Soviet period half of the Ukrainian nation was physically exterminated. . . . Ukrainians from Russia and other CIS states suffered a terrible, relatively recent horrific *deukrainizatsiia*. . . . The elements of apartheid and national segregation among them were usual daily occurrences.

Ukraine presents to the world a civic agenda; but just below the surface seethes anger against, even hatred of, Russians. The West sees the civic face of Dr. Jekyll; the Russians are beginning to see the enraged one, Mr. Hyde. Which half of the double personality will prevail is a question that is deeply worrisome to Russians now living in Ukraine.

The Abandonment by Russia

The Russian Federation has had anything but a consistent policy toward the so-called diaspora of the near abroad. In Chapter 12, I analyze the policy from the point of view of whether Russia's equivocation adds to or lessens the probability of internationality violence. For present purposes, I will examine Russia's policies from the point of view of the beached diaspora.[31]

A good indicator of Russia's ambiguous situation is that its diaspora lacks an accepted identity label. The conventional term for Russia in the eyes of its diaspora is *istoricheskaia rodina* (historical motherland). But there is no easy way for those in the historical motherland to refer to the Russians abroad. As Andrei Edemsky and Paul Kolstoe put it, "For several reasons . . . Russian journalists and politicians, especially in the liberal camp, often try to avoid the term 'Russians' when discussing Russia's relationship towards them. The reason for this seems to be that they want to take cognisance of the fact that Russia is a multinational state, and her diasporic populations are multinational also." They use alternate terms such as *grazhdaniny* (citizens), although they recognize how inappropriate that is, given that few Russians in the near abroad have taken Russian citizenship. An alternate term is *sootechestvenniky* (fellow countrymen). But this term *also* refers to, for example, Tatars in Central Asia or Ossetians in Georgia, as well as Russians in Western Europe so it doesn't adequately encompass the Russian-speaking populations in the near abroad. *Rossiiane*, meaning "citizens of Russia," is sometime used, even though this supposedly means only those living territorially in Russia. Thus, the development of the term *russkoyazychnye* (Russian-speakers), which "brings home the fact that for

[31] The following discussion of the Russian Federation's policy on the near abroad is based on the analysis of Andrei Edemsky and Paul Kolstoe, "Russia's Policy towards the Diaspora," chap. 10 of Kolstoe, *Russians in the Former Soviet Republics*. The quotations are taken from that chapter.

many russified Ukrainians, Belorussians . . . the only link to their ethnic homelands—Ukraine, Belarus' . . .—is the fifth point in their passport. Culturally they orient themselves towards Russia, even though they do not belong to one of the autochthonous ethnic groups of the Russian Federation." This term is not entirely appropriate, as we shall see in Chapter 10, because many people of the titular nationality, especially in Kazakhstan and Ukraine, are themselves "Russian-speaking" yet not part of the diaspora. Yet, and this will become a principal theme of this book, it is a term that has gained wide currency. Still, given the lack of a generally accepted category set of people for whom Russia might want to take responsibility, it is hard for Russia to develop a coherent policy.

Russian president Yeltsin's policy toward the near abroad just after the collapse of the Soviet Union was contained in the creation of a Community of Independent States (the CIS). It was seen by many in the diaspora to be a protection of their minority rights. In the Minsk meeting of January 1993, a CIS court to arbitrate interstate and interethnic conflict was agreed to, but as of 1996, it has not been established. With Latvia and Estonia outside the CIS, and the breakdown of the ruble zone in Ukraine and Kazakhstan, there is not much to the CIS but a series of protocols that have little effect—perhaps excluding the guarantee of the right of interstate travel—on daily life.

Andrei Kozyrev, Yeltsin's first foreign minister, strongly advocated negotiated political solutions to problems faced by Russians in the near abroad but with no direct aid to those Russians by the Russian Federation, which would be seen by other countries as a provocative act. He appealed first to international organizations to address issues of protection of rights for Russians living in these republics; and when this failed to put sufficient pressure on states that were violating, in the Foreign Ministry's judgment, human rights, he threatened economic sanctions. Yet, increasingly, these policies were seen, from the standpoint of nationalist Russians, as weak. Kozyrev blamed the problem on staffing problems. The Foreign Ministry, he wrote, had difficulty in getting a budget to fund permanent staffs in its new embassies in the near abroad, and to staff offices at which russophones could turn if they were in trouble. The Ministry made plans to send fourteen delegations to study the plight of Russian-speakers in the Soviet successor states, but it had trouble financing them. Yet it was more probably Kozyrev's ambivalence on the issue of the Russians in the near abroad, rather than his budget problems, that explains policies that were perceived by many—especially the Russian-speakers in the near abroad—as weak.

In June 1992, Defense Minister Pavel Grachev, perhaps trying to find a justification for a military budget, took a far more activist stand than the Foreign Ministry and declared that only the army was in a position to defend Russian-speakers in the CIS. In the 1993 Russian parliamentary elections Vladimir Zhirinovskii picked up on these themes and intimated that Russia should protect its "fellow countrymen" wherever they lived in the former Soviet Union. His impressive electoral support began to undermine Kozyrev's moderate position. In reaction Kozyrev began to articulate increasingly militant positions, though Yeltsin often voiced displeasure with the results. After the Yeltsin debacle of December 1994, when opposition forces dominated the parliamentary election, Kozyrev was dismissed, and under Foreign Minister Primakov, a more interventionist policy was promised.

President Yeltsin in 1990, it is to be remembered, advised the titular republics to take all the sovereignty they could handle. Although commentators insist, inasmuch as that speech was delivered in Kazan, that he was referring only to the ASSRs in the context of the Russian Federation, titular leaders in the Union republics took those remarks to mean that Yeltsin favored their complete independence. Russian-speakers in the Union republics made the same inference, and they were shocked. In his trip to Estonia in January 1991, Yeltsin faced pickets by Russians in Tallinn, since he forthrightly refused to make any contacts with the Russian nationality in Estonia.[32] On March 13, 1994, there was a demonstration in Latvia bringing about five hundred, mostly elderly protesters to the 1905 Revolution monument just outside downtown Riga, organized by the Association of Independent Trade Unions. Pettai asked Evgenii Kliuchnikov, a sixty-two-year-old pensioner and former night watchman whether there might come some support from Yeltsin. "Yeltsin has already betrayed us," he retorted angrily. "Yeltsin came to Latvia in 1990 and did not meet with the people here." He continued: "As long as Yeltsin and his clique are in power, there will be nothing to expect from them. Russia has the same kind of government as here." Kliuchnikov was half right. On the hot issues of citizenship in the Baltic states, and the right of autonomy for the Crimea within Ukraine, Yeltsin has sent at best ambiguous signals. While Russians in the near abroad can rest assured that Russian would protect them if they faced the mass violence that awaited the Serbs in Croatia, they sense clearly that their rights could be inexorably eroded while Russia consumes itself with its own internal problems.

THIS chapter has provided the political context in which our team of researchers entered the field. We lived with and regularly visited Russian-speaking families who were trying to come to terms with the double cataclysm. The trauma was compounded both by the policies and rhetoric of their nationalizing states, turning them into either foreigners or unwanted "minorities" and by the apparent indifference of Russia to their plight.

[32] *Narvskaia gazeta*, January 24, 1991.

5

Family Strategies in Response to the Cataclysm

A nationalizing state, one in which the titular nation claims "ownership" of that state, is an unsettling notion for those settled populations who are not owners.[1] The language of the nationalizing states that suddenly flourished in the former republics of the Soviet Union not only frightened the Russian-speaking population of the near abroad; it humiliated them as well. What they faced, rather immediately, was a sense of dread, of indignity, and uncertainty. This chapter, relying principally on data collected from anthropological observation, will reveal the general pattern of trauma among the Russian-speaking populations of the four republics under study. The choice model of identity presented in Chapter 1 can help us get a grip on the differential degrees to which the Russian-speaking populations sought linguistic assimilation into their new "homelands." The data presented in this chapter are consistent with the patterns of the elite-incorporation model identified in Chapter 3; they reveal strong assimilationist incentives in the Baltics, and weak ones in Kazakhstan. In Ukraine, a tip in either direction remains possible.

Dread, Indignity, and Uncertainty

The Russian-speakers living in the titular republics were well aware of the biting nationalist rhetoric that surrounded them. Russians in Latvia told Pettai, "I was insulted" ("Ia obidelsia"), or "I was helpless" ("Ia byl bezpomoshnyi"). Pettai met Lena, a Russian, born in Ukraine, married to a Pole, who studied nursing in Riga

[1] On the apparent unlikelihood up to the very end of the Soviet Union that the national idea would ever be fulfilled, see Alexander Motyl, *Will the Non-Russians Rebel?* (Ithaca: Cornell University Press, 1987); on the criteria of a "nationalizing state" and the idea of "ownership," see Rogers Brubaker, "National Minorities, Nationalizing States, and the External National Homelands in the New Europe," *Daedalus* 124, no. 2 (1995): 107–32.

and settled there. She understands, but does not speak, Latvian. When visiting some Latvian friends, she exclaimed to Pettai with great sarcasm: "I am the occupier, the immigrant, the enemy of the Latvian people." A Russian-speaking Latvian student, who had only good feelings about Latvian independence, suddenly feared, after hearing nationalist rhetoric, for his university education. "Up till now, I didn't think anything bad about the Latvian government . . . but now it seems they've suddenly begun to push us toward confrontation." Zheniia is a sixty-one-year-old factory worker. She favored Latvian independence and had no illusions about Soviet rule. She speaks Latvian and can pass for one. She was forcibly resettled from Novgorod to Latvia by the Nazis to work in factories. When she was denied citizenship, she said she was "insulted."

In Estonia, I heard the same complaint. Sergei Sovetnikov, in an article written for his constituents in Narva, quotes from a bitter letter he sent to the parliament of the Estonian Republic in January 1992. It says, "In the past years in the Estonian Republic Parliament it is expressed that the Russian-speaking population appear as occupiers in Estonia, and therefore they made laws that the Russian-speaking population was illegally residing in the Estonian Republic. For such cause, I consider myself [having been born in Estonia, with Russian nationality] a prisoner in Estonia." He asks for compensation for his "forty years of imprisonment." In May 1994, Pavel Grigor'ev took me to a morning of poetry reading and singing at the Narva-Jõesuu sanatorium, bringing together the cultural crowd of Narva, Sillamäe, and Narva-Jõesuu. They call their itinerant gathering "The Vagrant Dog Café." The singing was classical, peppered with old love songs, and the poetry was self-consciously deep. Afterward, Pavel said to me, with a burst of pride mixed with sarcasm, "and they call us occupiers." And his wife helped make this line a mantra. After explaining to me in October 1993 her hardships in getting an apartment in Narva-Jõesuu, in working to build up a fishing cooperative there, and in raising a young family in a cold-water flat, she exclaimed, "and for this move they [the Estonian government] call us occupiers!"

The rhetoric of the Estonian authorities fed this feeling of anger and distrust. Once on Estonian radio I sat with Liuba Grigor'ev listening to the transcript of a speech from a member of the Estonian parliament (May 10, 1994, in Russian, for broadcast in the northeast). The speaker demanded that the test of loyalty for citizenship ought to be a sworn pledge that they had always been and remain today committed to the full independence of Estonia. Liuba's anger was unconstrained.

Russians in Kazakhstan were just as angry, fearful, and uncertain. A third-generation Kazakhstani Russian told Dave that he was livid that "they" (the Kazakhs) now want to take over everything. He was trying to get his mother resettled from Siberia to Kazakhstan, but he was having tremendous difficulties in getting the proper permission. "I am already being thrown around like a football, bring this paper, or that paper," he told Dave. "They simply don't want any Russians to come here. . . . Of course for all those Kazakhs who want to come back from Turkey and Afghanistan, it is quick. After all, it is their country, as they say." The following incident is an ominous sign that the worst is yet to come. Dave was told of a Russian pupil being beaten up by a group of Kazakh students with the teacher egging them on, in a school that once was Russian but now has sections for each nationality. Evidently, the Russian student had crossed the boundary between the two sections. Repeated inquiries by the student's parents were met with a stonewalling reaction: "Don't try to raise the national question." On a more symbolic plane, the Kazakh State University, which had been named after Kirov, took on the name of Al-Farabi shortly after independence. Along with that change, the monument to Kirov was vandalized. Its ears and nose smashed, it was neither removed nor repaired for three years. It stood, for many, as the signal of the future when the *nekul'turnye* (the uncultured ones) take over the state. Polls conducted in the first year of independence also reflect the growing sense of Russian insecurity that Dave's family interviews portrayed. A survey conducted in August 1992 found that 57 percent of Russian residents say they feel "more insecure and fearful" as a result of the breakup of the Soviet Union and the shift of power to Kazakhstan, compared to only 13 percent who said they felt more secure.[2] Under these conditions, it is little wonder, as Boris Giller and Viktor Shatskikh report, "The prices of apartments are rapidly falling in Almaty as well as in other cities of Kazakhstan, supply of apartments exceeds demand, every day there are hundreds of 3–5 ton containers labeled 'to Russia' leaving the capital of Kazakhstan. In all 'Russian-speaking' kitchens, without any exaggerations, conversations center on who has already left, who's settled where, who's selling apartments, how much he settled for, and so on."[3]

In central Ukraine, where Arel conducted family interviews, there was not much fear among Russians that their very lifestyles as Russians were threatened. To be sure, on the language issue, there was a sense of absurdity. Marina Diatlova, an official of "Tovaristvo Rus'," which is monitoring the rapid ukrainization of Kiev schools, noted that in world literature classes in secondary schools, students are reading translations of Pushkin into Ukrainian. Besides the painful notion of seeing Pushkin in Ukrainian, Diatlova told Arel and me that acts of this sort are a "threat to Russian culture" in Ukraine.

In all the republics, the ethnic violence in Transdniester (and reports of violence against Russians in Tajikistan, Abkhazia, and Baku) fueled fears that the physical safety of the Russian-speaking population was no longer secure. In July 1993, when City Council chairman Vladimir Chuikin sponsored a referendum for the territorial autonomy of Narva, the Estonian government sought to stop any such electoral choice in its tracks. Chuikin denied Estonian government claims that he harbored "recidivist imperial ideas" and warned that the policies enacted at Toompea Castle (the seat of government) were pushing people into a new Transdniester.[4] And at the fourteenth session of the Odessa City Council, in spring 1993, a vote was taken twice on whether to discuss the issue of bilingualism. Although it was finally passed, the local leader of the Ukrainian nationalist party Rukh, V. Tsymbaliuk, said during the debate: "In the five years of its existence in Odessa, Rukh never raised the language problem. We are against a referendum or any discussion on this question. It would

[2] Robert Kaiser and Jeff Chinn, "Russian-Kazakh Relations in Kazakhstan," *Post-Soviet Geography* 36, no. 5 (1995): 268.

[3] Boris Giller and Viktor Shatskikh, "Opredelenie berega: russkoiazychnyie v Kazakhstane," *Karavan*, December 12, 1993, pp. 1–3.

[4] *Narvskaia gazeta*, July 18, 1993.

not lead to a solution, but to an acute polarization of opinions in the Council and in the streets. The experience of our neighbor Transdniester attests to that."[5] The regular evening portrayals of the killing fields of Moldova and other hot spots made these threats—however incredible from a local standpoint—poignant ones.

In Estonia one morning, over coffee at the Grigor'evs', I heard on the radio the announcement of yet another regulation concerning the crossing of the border to Russia. Liuba shook her head and complained that now she feels like a small child. Every day she must learn new ways to cope, since all the old strategies for getting through the day became obsolete in 1991. She doesn't know who she is or what country she is from. While times were difficult for everyone attempting to make the transition from a state socialist to a market economy, the Russians in the near abroad, especially those with only Soviet citizenship, had no real sense of security left.

Russians throughout the "near abroad" have had to ask themselves basic questions about their nationality. Were they "Russians," or were they denationalized residents of newly independent states? Our informants wavered on such identity issues, in part because the cataclysm was so sharp that they had little preparation to reposition themselves ethnically. They wavered as well because, like many Americans, their histories were too complex to be captured by a single hyphen.

Consider Militina Mikhailovna, who tried to remain calm about Kazakh nationalizing. She frequently insisted to Dave, when Dave questioned her about her language repertoire, that if it had been necessary to learn Kazakh "before," she and her family would have, but that for her it is too late to learn it now. She said someone like her belongs neither in Kazakhstan nor in Russia. Her last name is Brazgulis—a Lithuanian name, because her husband was Lithuanian. They divorced just a couple of years after her marriage. Lithuanians consider her Russian, because her passport nationality is Russian. Russians question her on her last name and suspect she is Jewish. She would like to go back to her maiden name, but it would be too difficult to change at this stage.

On the other hand there is the case of Galina Poma, the English teacher in School No. 1 in Narva, who began her career in Russia's far north. She applied to Narva, where the climate was better, and received an offer in 1977. With the Estonian language regulations, she was required to get a level C in Estonian, but at first wasn't worried about being fired, as English teachers were scarce and "in the future, I'll be communicating with Estonians in English." Her daughter speaks no Estonian and doesn't worry about herself. "I don't mind being called an immigrant and after ten years from 1991, I'll be a citizen with or without the Estonian language. I can wait." Here is someone who was perfectly content with Estonian citizenship and Russian nationality, who decided to take the pejorative "immigrant" and turn it into a simple description.[6]

[5] Leonid Zaslavskii, "Priz za iazykatost' poluchit Odesskii gorsovet," *Nezavisimost'* (in Russian), May 28, 1993.

[6] The distinguished political scientist Rein Taagepera of the University of California is an ethnic Estonian who ran credibly for president in Estonia's first free post-Soviet election. He reminded Russian-speakers in Estonia that "colonist" was not an epithet, merely a description. He knew. His family were *colons* in Morocco in the 1940s and 1950s. On the campaign trail, he won much favor

Shedding negative identities—occupier, immigrant, colonialist—attributed to them by titulars was only half of the identity work that Russians felt needed to be done. They needed as well to portray themselves in a positive light. Some rode the wave of religious revival and cultivated Orthodox identities. For example, in Latvia there is a Baltic-Slav Society, which publishes a monthly paper called *Russkaia gazeta* with the subtitle *Tserkov' i mir* ("The Church and the World"), filled with religious imagery. Pettai met a young Russian whose family had moved to Latvia from Novosibirsk in Russia only a few years previously. She did not get Latvian citizenship; nor did she worry. As she took Pettai to the Orthodox church for Easter service, she seemed secure in her Orthodox identity, which would not be challenged by Latvian authorities. I, too, found high school students from Narva attending the Orthodox church ceremonies quite regularly. Yet none of us who engaged in participant observations in the field noted that there was anything close to a popular religious revival. As our survey data make clear, most Russians in the near abroad remain quite secular. But for some, an Orthodox identity seems secure and serious, and religious identification was untouched by the nationality battles that were taking place on the political front.

The typical response to questions about identity among our informants was like that of Leonid, Arel's chauffeur, who, as I mentioned in Chapter 4, can make claims to being Ukrainian, Russian, Polish, or Jewish. Arel asked him how best to define the concept of nationality (*natsional'nost'*)? "Territory, perhaps, since I lived in Ukraine all my life. Also the nationality of my parents: my mother registered as a Ukrainian [*mats ukrainskoi zapisana*]." He reflects: "It would have been better had it been written Jewish. I would have lived in Israel." But he is exasperated by these types of questions ("Oi, kakie voprosy!"). Times were better for Leonid, as was the case for so many nontitulars (or people with mixed background) in the former Union republics, when they didn't have to answer such questions.

The Challenge of Linguistic Assimilation

A market model of identities in general, or of language in particular, would seem at first blush to be inappropriate for a situation in which the modeled actors are outraged, indignant, and uncertain. It seems intuitive that Russians, living in the detritus of the Soviet Union, suddenly finding themselves without a homeland, fearing violence, deportation, and split families, would lash back at titulars, or state authorities, like "bent twigs."[7]

Consider Igor. He is from a mixed background (Ukrainian, Belorusan, Tatar—"Who knows?" he asks!). His paternal grandfather came to Kazakhstan in the early part of this century from Kharkhov, Ukraine. He is married to a Kazakh woman.

---

with Russians by empathizing with them about the fate of being a colonizer. See his touching portrayal in *Estonia: Return to Independence* (Boulder, Colo.: Westview, 1993), pp. 218–19.

[7] Sir Isaiah Berlin develops Friedrich von Schiller's metaphor to illustrate the nonrationalistic source of nationalism in "Bent Twig: A Note on Nationalism," *Foreign Affairs* 51 (October 1972): 11–30.

When Dave asked him whether now that Kazakhstan is independent, he should learn Kazakh, he responded:

> I don't want to learn Kazakh now, for they are forcing me. Do I need it to talk to my wife and her relatives? Do I need it at work [where all speak Russian]? I don't want to be the president of this country, nor the head of the cabinet of ministers [the two positions that require the knowledge of Kazakh, as written in the constitution]. Besides, I just can't get over that resentful attitude to the Kazakh language. I remember it from school years, the most unpleasant teacher was the Kazakh language teacher.

Although in this case both anger and calculation would lead to the same result, the memory of the insensitive Kazakh language teacher, rather than a cool reckoning, seemed to be driving Igor's answer.

The fundamental question, however, that immediately faced Russian-speaking families in the countries of the near abroad was hardly about the adults—Igor would probably learn enough Kazakh to permit him to fill out official forms—but rather about the children. Parents suddenly had to ask themselves whether their children's life chances would be better if they were exposed to the titular language. In most parents' judgments, enrollment in kindergarten was the core decision—whether to matriculate their children in titular- or Russian-medium kindergartens. Because the choice of medium of instruction for your next child who reaches kindergarten age is dichotomous, it is easily modeled using the tipping game. The question is whether a choice model is appropriate under conditions of great uncertainty, when parents could not answer questions about even what the name of their "homeland" is with any surety.

In real political and social life, choices of this sort are often an illusion—or for economists, perhaps a delusion. In our interview with Marina Diatlova, the official of "Tovaristvo Rus'," she pointed out to Arel and me that the Ministry of Education was organizing local committees, district by district, to have parents "vote" for the medium of instruction in all the districts' schools. In these meetings, where strong pressure is put on parents to support the nationalizing program of the state, and where voting is not by secret ballot, parents who are opposed to ukrainization are made to feel unwanted, and they keep away from these meetings. Once the district switches to Ukrainian, a switch in the medium for all schools begins in the first grade and goes up a grade every year. Nearly all districts, she noted, are now moving year by year to a total ukrainization of the medium of instruction in Kiev's public education. It would be folly to suggest that this coercive logic represents the strategic outcome of individual decisions.

Indeed, to many parents who spoke to us about schools for their children, the "choice" of language medium had been made for them, and no strategic thinking was required. In Latvia, Svetlana Kovalchuk, a Russian who speaks Latvian and has Latvian citizenship, angrily rejected a choice model. She reported to Pettai that she was being forced to put her child in a Latvian school because the opportunities for Russian-language secondary and higher education were being cut back. Nikolai Iugantsev in Tallinn echoed these thoughts. "Even if I am a citizen," he protested, "I still can't offer my child Russian-language education or Russian culture."

These observations led Pettai, based on his research in both Latvia and Estonia to note in his field observations that hardly any Russian-speaking families have *strategically* sent their children to a titular-medium school, although he admits that newspaper accounts do note an increase in such enrollments. The cause of all this change may have nothing to do with strategy, as we saw in the previous examples. One of his informants in Estonia, an Estonian citizen from an "old Russian" family whose descendants had immigrated to the Lake Peipsi area centuries ago after a schism in the Orthodox Church, had just enrolled her daughter in an Estonian-medium school. But the key to her husband's finally accepting this "choice" was the construction of a new elementary school, located right behind their apartment house, with an impressive glass atrium and small greenhouse at its entrance, and thus a palm tree growing in –20° weather. The child's mother rejected the notion that she was investing in her child's life chances in Estonia; but she did say that she felt her child should know Estonian and Russian and the Russian schools do not teach Estonian very well.

The more common response to the question of whether they will send their children to Estonian-medium schools, especially in areas where the parents do not speak Estonian at all, is incredulity at the very thought of an intergenerational linguistic shift. Natal'ia Berezhkova lives in a Russian-dominated neighborhood in Tallinn. She has studied Estonian and is working hard to pass the citizenship exam. She works as an activities coordinator at a Russian-language secondary school. When asked what would happen to the Russian-medium schools if most parents chose to enroll their children in Estonian-medium institutions, Natal'ia had a look of disbelief: "It is not possible," she answered.

Yet when people feel themselves coerced into changing their language repertoires, they are really reacting to new (dis)incentives, and feel angry that a new logic is "forcing" them to alter the language repertoire they had initially expected to provide for their children. In a series of articles in *Estoniia* based upon several seminars sponsored by the Estonian Ministry for Culture and Education, Liudmila Poliakova philosophized on this dilemma for the Russian community in Estonia:[8]

> Our times are cruel also because each person is faced with a choice: either/or, and there's no going around it. Each school and its personnel also face a choice. Either to please the political authorities, each school adopts a course in its work toward the assimilation of Russian pupils, their faceless dissolution into Estonian society. Or each school takes on the difficult problems of integrating Russian pupils [as Russians] into Estonian society. Each school must decide for itself and take on the responsibility.

In an important way, this "choice" is merely a reversal of processes that affected the titular nationality's parents since Khrushchev's educational "reforms" of the late

[8] "Kto my?" *Estoniia*, May 26, 1994.

1950s, where parental choice (i.e., to move from titular to Russian-medium instruction) was encouraged by Soviet authorities. Pettai interviewed Inna Kustavus, whose father was a russianized Estonian and mother a Russian from Tver', and who was brought up in Estonia. When Inna's brother was born in 1952, "the logical step was to send him to a Russian-language school." But the parents felt a loss, and the child was sent to Tartu to live with his paternal grandparents and go to an Estonian school in the third grade. Inna was strongly supportive. She held that "whatever language you learn in, that will be your main language," and therefore put great stock in parental choice. The point she implicitly made was that even if large structures "determined" one's choice, individual ingenuity could often overcome those structures, in this case through sending the child to his grandparents' home.

The Russian-speaking family I lived with in Estonia faced the cruel reality of choice with some aplomb, and ingenuity as well. The Grigor'evs talked to each other about future opportunities for the next generation. They determined that while engineering was the skill of the Soviet period, language was the skill of the new market. They transferred Roma, their youngest child, to a school an hour away by bus that specializes in language instruction, both in English and Estonian.

Older students themselves feel this new choice framework like a closing vise. On Latvian TV, a Russian reporter interviewed Russian high school students in Riga, who were mourning lost opportunities for higher education. "Why not go to St. Petersburg?" asked the reporter. One student responded, "If I were to go, I would have to pay and pay even more than if I wanted to study here. . . . If they get rid of the Russian-language sections [in higher education], then they'll sink us for good. Then it will depend on how each person takes care of himself, how they survive and find for themselves some kind of niche."

Data provided by Natal'ia Lapikova for Estonia demonstrate an aging professorate in the school system and a wide range of future opportunities for teachers who are trained in the titular language, whether they will teach in titular-medium or in Russian-medium schools.[9] This social fact creates new opportunities for Russians who equip themselves as teachers of the titular language. Indeed, Natasha, the daughter in the Grigor'ev family, was doing just that. Upon graduation from the Tallinn Pedagogical Institute, she will be able to procure a salary higher than the average qualified teacher, given her credentials enabling her to teach Estonian to Russian-speaking students. If a titular-speaking professorate emerges because of these opportunities, it will reflect personal strategies to learn the titular language that go against heavy structural constraints. In turn, the strategic choices of university age students will have an impact on the costs and possibilities for parents making choices for the next generation of students.

The rapid emergence of illegal markets in language materials and certifications provides further evidence that a "choice" or "market" model is extremely appropriate for analyzing moves in post-Soviet space. In the early period of language revival, the Estonian government printed up language primers to help Russian-speakers

[9] The Russian-language newspaper *Estoniia* published a series of articles based on seminars run by the Estonian Ministry of Culture and Education. This information is from an interview published on March 25, 1994, with Lapikova.

learn the new state language and sold them through kiosks at 60 to 80 Estonian cents (100 cents to a kroon) per volume. Speculators bought out all the kiosks, and sold them for 30 to 35 kroons (13 kroons to the U.S. dollar), a fifty-fold markup.[10] Later on, when clear criteria for citizenship-level Estonian were set, an open market in language certificates quickly emerged. In Narva, a certificate of citizenship-level knowledge of Estonian was 2000 kroons; for level "D" (which qualifies a person for jobs that require significant knowledge of Estonian) it was 1,000 kroons. In Latvia there is a vibrant market in language certificates as well. The street price for a citizenship-level Latvian certificate in April 1994 was 162 lats (0.54 lats to the U.S. dollar). Since the common practice is to learn the language sufficiently well to pass the exam and then to "forget" it, as A. Kursitis, a language inspector from central Latvia wrote to the editor of *Diena*,[11] it is very difficult later to differentiate the illegal purchasers of certificates from those who merely lost their competence after passing the exam. In light of the market in language books and certificates that has emerged since independence, perhaps a rational choice model of language acquisition is especially appropriate in our times!

The market for language, especially in Estonia, has even gone above ground. In an examination of the classified section of a leading Tallinn Russian-language paper (*Molodezh' Estonii*) I found eleven firms (one of which had three separate notices) advertising private instruction in Estonian, with opening lines such as "Cheap courses by experienced teacher," "Diamella—classes using psychological means in Estonian," and "Estonian for Workers in Trade, 350 kroons/800 words." In the *Narvskaia gazeta*, I came across an advertisement paid for by the Narva Language Center for a variety of language products: language courses by videocassette, called *Tere Eestimaa* ("Hello Estonia"), for 300 kroons; an IBM-compatible grammar on diskette for 980 kroons; and an audiocasette for the E-level examination for 50 kroons.[12] The "market" for the state language has obviously matured.

In line with this perspective, it is fair to say that language "choices," at least for Russian-speakers, have only become strategic issues in the post-Soviet world. In the Soviet period, few Russian-speakers were confronted with dichotomous choices over the language of instruction for their children. Consider the situation of Olga, an ethnic Russian, born in 1961 in Irkutsk oblast. At the age of one, however, she moved to Ukraine, along with her mother, to the mining town of Pervomaisk, Dnipropetrovsk Oblast (eastern Ukraine). She has lived in Ukraine ever since. Her father remained in Siberia and she never saw him. Her mother remarried in Ukraine, to a Ukrainian from Pavlograd, Dnipropetrovsk oblast, whose family had been living there for generations. She has a sister, Larisa, five years younger, and a brother, Sergei, twelve years younger. Born in Ukraine of a Ukrainian father, they became Ukrainian by passport nationality, while Olga remains Russian.

Ironically, however, it is Olga who speaks the best Ukrainian in the family. Her brother studies in Russia at a mining institute. Her sister graduated from an institute in Ukraine and married a Belorusan, who grew up in Dnipropetrovsk oblast.

[10] David Laitin, interview with Sergei Gorokhov, Narva, December 1992.

[11] "Latviesu valoda nelatviesiem ir jaiemacas," *Diena*, April 16, 1994.

[12] *Molodezh' Estonii*, September 31, 1992; *Narvskaia gazeta*, March 26, 1994.

They live in Dnipro Oblast. He affectionately calls her *khokhlushka* (one who speaks the "peasant" tongue). She calls him *bilbash* (presumably the Belorussian equivalent of *khokhol*). According to Olga, the fact that her brother and sister are Ukrainians, and yet speak Russian, means absolutely nothing to them. They consider themselves Ukrainian because they were born there. In terms of language, there was never any problem.

This whole language issue, for Olga, is contrived. Whether we are speaking Ukrainian or Russian, she says, we understand each other perfectly. (As she pointed out below, however, very few people actually spoke Ukrainian.) Despite the fact that they studied Ukrainian in school, her siblings can only speak minimal kitchen-level Ukrainian, "and to attempt to do so would be funny," sounding like *surzhik* (the low-prestige mélange of Russian and Ukrainian). Asked whether she found it strange to have Ukrainian siblings, while she is Russian, Olga answered that it is only now, at this very moment, that she paid any attention to the difference in nationalities.

Pervomaisk, where Olga grew up, is a quintessential mining town. It is really not much more than a big village and actually had the status of a village until 1956. Since the town is built literally on top of the mines, the buildings cannot be higher than five stories. The miners came from all over the Soviet Union. In each mine, there were representatives from eighty to ninety nationalities. According to Olga, the concept *natsional'nost'* (nationality) in this town did not exist. All were equal. No one ever raised the issue of ethnic background. Maybe now, in light of all these processes, someone may remember that he is Armenian, or Korean, or Greek. But before, she believes, no one thought that way. In her class, at school, there were so many nationalities—for some reason, she says, she remembers it now—and her girlfriend was Greek. Yet she adds that "we children had no notion of what nationality meant."

The point here is that under the present conditions of uncertainty, and the sudden salience of nationality and language as issues, the choice model for languages is extremely relevant. The tipping game may not help analyze situations in which the equilibrium is not threatened, but it gives a useful handle on the social reality presently existing in the nationalizing states of the former Soviet Union. It is for this reason that we can examine more closely, in the following section, the payoff function for language choice in the countries of the near abroad. From our interviews and participant observations in the field, we were able to determine, in many cases, how payoff functions were internalized in parent and student choices. The tripartite preference function (economic returns, in-group scorn, and out-group acceptance) introduced in Chapters 1 and 2, we shall see, needs to be expanded.

Calculations about Language Repertoires

Economic Payoffs

To the extent that occupational mobility requires knowledge of the titular language, the expected utility of learning it, or sending your child to a school where he or she will learn it, rises. Our observations in the field confirm that Russian-speakers assessed the future value of knowing only Russian, and their assessments affected their decisions whether to invest in titular-language facility, either for themselves or for their children.

The link between language and future opportunity becomes of great concern to students seeking higher education. In my conversations with secondary school students in the only Narva school (number 11) that has a baccalaureate certification (and thus a university-linked curriculum), students by spring of 1994 had lost interest in studying in St. Petersburg. Their teachers (almost all of whom had received their degrees there) had cleverly arranged for them to be accepted blindly as Russian citizens, negating any pressures to find tuition money. But Russia to their students was a foreign land, and they desperately wanted to remain in Estonia. The problem was that in many departments, the Estonian university at Tartu was said to prefer students who had been educated in Estonian. The students therefore made private arrangements, for example, by living with an Estonian farm family for the summer, to acquire fluency in Estonian. One student, Pavel, told me that he found a Estonian girlfriend for just this reason. In Riga, Pettai interviewed a few young Russians who enrolled in the Russian Technical University primarily because it was one of the few that did not require Latvian, and they would not survive in a Latvian university curriculum. They recognized the RTU was second-rate, but this was the best they could do. The language laws also brought into public consciousness the link between language facility and jobs. In Estonia, in the immediate post-Soviet period, this was not the case, in large part because there was no Estonian bourgeoisie that saw the large educated Russian-speaking labor force as an asset for industrial growth. Many Estonian nationalists wished that these qualified workers, laid off from defunct all-Union factories, would just disappear. Soviet People's Deputy Endel Lippmaa, a distinguished chemist in the Academy of Science, said as much when I interviewed him in December 1992. "The labor force [in the northeast]," he declared, "is not necessary for Estonia." But in subsequent months, when it became clear that the Russians were not packing their suitcases, the connection between learning the titular language and social mobility became especially strong. This was not merely a question of having sufficient capability in the titular language to meet certain job requirements. There are also many jobs open only to citizens, and for most Russian-speakers, citizenship required developing considerable facility in Estonian. In an article by a government official originally for the Estonian press but translated into Russian, the author listed jobs such as airline pilot, captain of an Estonian registered ship, worker in a customs' house, member of the police force, representative of a city council, president of the Republic, and president of the Bank of Estonia that were constitutionally reserved for citizens. And a government minister emphasized in her trip to Narva that the Estonianization of the country would yield a "single labor market," and the key to its penetration would be competence in Estonian.[13]

[13] Merle Krigul', "Na kakikh dolzhnostiakh imeiut pravo rabotat' grazhdane Estonii?" originally in *Riigi teataja*, and translated in *Severnoe poberezh'e*, October 15, 1993; Andrei Ivanen, "Vzgliad na bezrabotitsu s tochki zreniia Ministerstva," *Severnoe poberezh'e*, October 29, 1993. The minister is Marju Lauristin.

This message was picked up by the Russian-speaking population in the high unemployment zone of northeast Estonia. N. Kampus, head of the Union of Unemployed Narvans, who was busily studying Estonian herself so that she could read basic documents coming from Tallinn, told me that it was necessary to speak Estonian to get off the dole. She had urged the government to help the senior workers pay for their language courses. "The next generation will need an education to adapt," she told me, "but the present adults need help."

In my first Estonian lessons at the Narva Language Center, I sat in with a group of young bankers who worked at the Estonian state bank, which was paying for the course. Throughout the course, there was hardly an absent student. The pressure to learn was high. To be sure, the economic returns for learning the language were not sufficient to capture this group's attention. The bank did dock the pay of those who missed classes. How much this encouraged actual learning and how much it only encouraged attendance is an open question. One day in the cloakroom before class, I watched the men surreptitiously copying the homework from the women. Yet the students accepted as normal the notion that a banking career in Estonia required professional knowledge of Estonian.

The belief that Estonian is necessary for many professions has filtered through Narva. Natasha Schmidt, who comes from a German-Russian background, told me that she will shortly begin classes in Estonian, "since it will be necessary for the next generation to speak it for any sort of job." At a Narva post office, a clerk cheerfully reported to me that to retain her job, she needed to reach level C. No problem, she said, "of course I will learn it, it is necessary." I interviewed an engineer in Baltic Energy, who by order of the factory, had to study Estonian to reach level C. There were sixteen technical personnel in his class, and he estimated five other groups were in operation. The goal was to enable them to fill in Estonian documents. His children are not getting any serious education in Estonian and will therefore need, he surmised, to learn it as adults. When faced with the prospect of closed labor markets, monolingual Russians have changed their minds about learning Estonian.

Not only will there be barriers to job entry for Russian monolinguals, but the nationalizing state will provide a whole new category of remunerative jobs for those who speak the state language well. This is even the case in Estonia. Even if at first the Estonian government was reluctant to fund Estonian-language instruction for non-Estonians, the logic of government policy led school authorities to create a new class of jobs. The rector of the Narva Teachers' Training Center, Nina Sepp, told me that "all the Russian schools are applying at the Education Employment Centers for specialists in the teaching of Estonian in Russian schools." She has been able to attract Swedish, Danish, and American aid to provide stipends for her students, and she attracts many ambitious applicants for her school. The Estonian Ministry of Education adds to this incentive by providing higher salaries for teachers of Estonian in Russian schools than they provide for teachers of other subjects. The motivation of this program was to induce Estonians to settle in Russian-dominated towns; but it is mostly Russians who are taking advantage of these salary opportunities.

I heard from Liuba Grigor'ev rumors of the "fat" salaries received by the teachers at the Narva Language Center and the opportunities those teachers have for giving private lessons. She was quite pleased that her daughter, who speaks good Estonian, was then at the Tallinn Pedagogical Institute, preparing herself for a chance to jump onto this gravy train.

Galina Puma, who told me in 1993 that she wouldn't bother learning Estonian, since she would get citizenship eventually, had changed her tune by 1994. She was unhappy with the slow speed at the Language Center and contracted the best teacher there to give a course privately at her neighborhood House of Culture. The reason for this, she admitted, is that she needs a third language to get to the next pay scale for her specialty. And since Estonian would be useful anyway, she chose it for her professional advancement.

In Latvia, a twenty-five-year-old Russian whom Pettai met at a dance party echoed these themes. The conversation was morbid about their futures, but no one mentioned leaving. "What can we do?" he asked Pettai. "Everyone has to work, but there are few jobs around. Without education and language you can't get ahead." As in Estonia, in Latvia, certain political offices require facility in the titular language. Once there was a reported shortage of candidates in some Russian-speaking districts. There was a news item in *Labrit*, a Latvian newspaper, which reported a surge in the study of Latvian by people who see elective office as a new career opportunity.[14]

In Ukraine, Arel heard similar calculations, but nowhere as powerfully as what Pettai and I picked up in Estonia and Latvia. In Kiev, Arel often spoke with Iaroslav, an ethnic Russian from Samara (formerly Kuibyshev), in the Volga region of Russia. When Iaroslav realized that he needed Ukrainian to get a good job, he learned it quickly and well. When Arel asked him, during the Christmas break of 1995, whether he would send his young son Stiopka to a Russian or a Ukrainian school, he unhesitatingly answered: Ukrainian. He said he does not worry that Stiopka will speak Russian badly because Russian will remain the language of home life, although he would like to find a school where Russian, as a second language, is well taught. The bottom line is that he does not want to limit his son's educational or career opportunities.

Less convincing is the claim that Kazakh is needed for future job opportunities. One of the editors of *Kazakhstanskaia pravda* explained to Dave:

> I tell my daughter, "Learn English." Of course she is studying Kazakh in the university as well. But the way the language is taught, there is hardly any progress. However, I tell her to learn Kazakh too—the economy of the country requires that she know Kazakh. Earlier it wasn't necessary. I remember in schools, we would study Kazakh for a week in the semester, then three weeks there was no teacher, and no one seemed to notice it. It was often the last class, and we would simply go home early. If only they start teaching the language in a proper way, if only they worked out a good methodology, why wouldn't the Russians not learn to speak Kazakh?

[14] "Velesanas mudina macities valsts valodu," *Labrit*, April 11, 1994. The data that I present in Chapters 7–9 show that Russians in Latvia see very little economic point to learning Latvian. This view did not come through in our ethnographic fieldwork.

There are no clear signals that jobs depend on knowing Kazakh. As Slava Kozlov, a young Russian engineer who himself planned to learn Kazakh, told Dave and me: "The only way to get a good job is breaking through family networks. No one," he said, "will lose his job because he doesn't know Kazakh. But on the other hand," he insisted, "no one will get a good job just for learning Kazakh."

In the Baltics the situation is clear: under post-Soviet conditions, learning the titular language provides better opportunities for higher education, qualification for a larger set of professional jobs, citizenship (which opens up the possibility for more jobs), and opportunities in a new sector of the economy. In Ukraine the trend is less pronounced. In Kazakhstan, these considerations play very little role in popular accounting. It is clear that despite the high levels of uncertainty, our Russian-speaking informants calculated the expected job returns of learning the titular language.

Expected Returns Less Cost

An expected-utility calculus requires that the discounted value of returns to an investment in a foreign language be greater than the up-front costs of learning the language. Costs are no doubt difficult to measure for social scientists; but our informants were highly aware of costs, and their behavior was significantly determined by the results of calculations of those costs. Our informants based their cost estimates on the answers to three basic questions. First, there was the question of language distance, that is, how different from Russian was the titular language. Second, there was the question of who was to pay for the instruction. Third, there was the question of whether the language, once acquired, could be retained in the social environment in which our informants lived.

Concerning language distance, Russian-speakers in Ukraine had apparently the least costly investment, given that Ukrainian and Russian are closely related languages. Consider Iaroslav, Arel's friend originally from Samara. He was sent by the Soviet Army to Zhytomyr in 1988 to perform his military service and has been in Ukraine ever since. Iaroslav did not learn Ukrainian at all, since the army functioned entirely in Russian and the town seemed thoroughly russified. But then, after his tour of duty, he decided to stay and enrolled in the pedagogical institute. Following the 1989 language law, the authorities decided to conduct all instruction at the institute in Ukrainian. Iaroslav found it hard, at first, to connect with Ukrainian terms, especially at the philosophical and scientific levels. But after a month or two, he adapted. After he graduated from Zhytomyr, he enrolled at the International School of International Studies in Kiev in the summer of 1992. Except for the somewhat artificial classroom atmosphere in Zhytomyr, this was the first time in his life that Iaroslav found himself in a totally Ukrainian-speaking environment. He learned fast and now says that he has no problem at all speaking Ukrainian. Similarly, at the newly ukrainized Kiev-Mohyla Academy, our host (and here Arel, Dave, and I were together) Oleksiy Haran told us that despite a difficult transition period, all the Russian-speaking faculty and students managed the switch to Ukrainian within a few months.

Latvian, like Russian, is in the Indo-European language family. Informants were divided on the costs of learning it for a Russian monolingual. On the one hand, in an interview with a Latvian administrator in charge of implementing the language law, we were told that because of the proximity of the languages, the burden on Russians of complying with the law would not be all that heavy. On the other hand, Pettai reports on widespread cynicism and cheating in Latvia as a result of sense of hopelessness in ever reaching competence in a language Russian speakers consider difficult to learn, even if not linguistically distant. One informant, married to a Russian-Latvian woman, had come to Latvia in the 1970s. Even so, he found the language exasperatingly difficult to learn and wound up buying a high-competence certificate on the black market.

Estonian, however, is a Finno-Ugric language. Russians understand well the costs of learning it. Leonid Gorobets at Narva Transport gamed this issue out carefully. He is a Ukrainian and his wife a Russian, who was looking for work in New York when I talked to him in 1992. He understands Estonian, but he doesn't speak it well enough to get citizenship. He was sympathetic to Estonian independence but saw no future in Estonia for himself. He wanted to get citizenship, but he figured that it would be easier to learn English in the United States than Estonian in Estonia, as Estonian is "more complicated." Leonid Guzhvin, a Russian who was posted to a defense plant in Tallinn in the 1970s, admitted that he should know the language, but stressed to Pettai that "Estonian is a Finno-Ugric language. It is not very easy."

It is possible to misjudge the costs of learning a language if one takes into account only proximity or distance. On the one hand, to the extent that the two languages are close (such as Russian and the mixed Russian-Ukrainian dialect called *surzhik*), there may be resistance to learning the proximate language because it is hard to take it seriously as a different language. Rein Taagepera suggested to me that Russians may find it easier to learn Estonian (because there is no doubt that it is foreign and requires serious study) than Ukrainian (because to Russians it sounds like a low-class dialect). In his analogy, demanding that Russians speak Ukrainian would be like demanding that a Columbia University professor speak Ebonics in order to retain her position there. The costs of learning a language too close to one's own might not be as low as a linear model of language distance would assume. On the other hand, language distance may not pose a great burden for potential learners if there is a will and need to learn it. In the United States, for example, language distance plays no role in explaining rates of intergenerational shift to English.[15] Nonetheless, all else being equal, proximity of languages (for example, with the availability of cognates) should lower learning costs.

The second calculation concerns the cost of courses in the language. This concern played heavily in the calculations of Russians in Estonia. For workers in Narva, many of whom were not receiving regular salaries, and whose unemployment benefits amounted to about 300 kroons per month, a tuition of 200 kroons for a course appeared outrageous. I talked to a worker at Baltic Energy in December 1992. He did not qualify for a company-sponsored program and felt that there was

[15] See the data in Joshua Fishman, ed., *Language Loyalty in the United States* (The Hague: Mouton, 1966).

no way to pay for a private course at his meager salary. He therefore decided to apply for Russian citizenship. Nadiia Sergeevna, assistant to the mayor of Narva, told me that in the past, with Narva's orientation toward St. Petersburg, there were no incentives to learn Estonian. Now, she said, "English is the fashion." But, she was quick to emphasize, if there were good courses, and the tuition were not so high, "of course" people in Narva would learn Estonian. She pointed out that the state had announced a program for learning Estonian but had not (at the time of the interview) funded it.

Even intergenerationally, if you cannot get your children in an environment where they can pick up the language naturally, the cost of learning will be high. In Narva, I was told, where the only Estonian-medium school has an average of between fifteen and twenty students per grade, the Estonian parents were worried that if they admitted Russian-speakers to the school, the effect would not be Russian children learning Estonian; rather it would be Estonian children speaking Russian in all play periods. The Estonian children would be overwhelmed by the numbers of Russian families wanting their children to get language competence for "free." Dave encountered the same problem in Kazakhstan. A Russian couple she interviewed in Almaty decided to send their child to a Kazakh kindergarten. But the authorities refused to accept the child, saying, "It is a Kazakh kindergarten. It is very difficult for us to teach Kazakh to a non-Kazakh. Besides the child will feel himself to be out of place."

A final consideration is that of probability of retention. In December 1992 in an interview with the manager of Baltiets, I was told that workers in the factory were studying Estonian but had no chance to use the language. Each lesson of Estonian, I was told "becomes like water into the sand." Although the factory paid for these courses, and they were free to the workers, motivation dissipated because there was little retention of the language.

Thus it is not that the costs of learning Ukrainian and Latvian are lower than those of learning Estonian and Kazakh, at least for Russian-speakers living in those republics. Rather the point is that under conditions less than ideal for reasoned analysis, our informants were weighing cost/benefit considerations as they pondered whether to move toward linguistic assimilation.

In-Group Status

Two in-group processes impact upon linguistic assimilation. The first is the pressure of "competitive assimilation," the pressure to learn the titular language before other members of your own community do in order to get first pick of the job and educational opportunities available to linguistically assimilated Russians. Competitive assimilation pressures favor rapid learning, and if those pressures are felt, they easily unleash cascades. This pressure, however, was only dimly felt by our informants. The second is the pressure of group solidarity, the fear of being seen as a traitor, which would discourage assimilation. This pressure, while more evident than the first among our informants, was also weakly exerted within Russian-speaking communities in the near abroad.

An important explanation for the lack of competition among Russian-speakers to learn the titular languages is a sense among them that their own language is of much greater status. In Kazakhstan, whatever the job possibilities involved, many Russians cannot take the study of the Kazakh language seriously. One Russian informed Dave that the Kazakhs don't really have a language; they merely have dialects. A somewhat more academic version of this negative view came from A. Zhovtis, who told Dave and me that "it is absurd to transform a spiritual folkloric language into a technical one." Zhovtis, who was strongly supportive of Kazakh independence, further told us that it is "not possible" for the Russian-speaking population to learn Kazakh, even if they wanted to. He considered the very idea absurd. Dave asked Maksim, the son of a nuclear physicist in Almaty, if he studies Kazakh at school. The very question made him grin and break into a laughter. When I asked my seventy-six-year-old landlady in Almaty, who considered herself a cosmopolitan intellectual, whether she spoke Kazakh, she blurted back incredulously, "but why?"

In the Baltics, the titular languages enjoy a much higher status than Kazakh does in the eyes of the Russian residents. But still, learning a language that lacks Russian's rich cultural and geographic scope appears to many Russians to be silly. For example, I was in the home of Sergei Nochenko, whose wife is Estonian, and whose children went to the Estonian school in Narva. Sergei himself had learned sufficient Estonian to pass the citizenship exam, which he took as a small thing to do in order to regularize himself to the country. When I came in, at 6:10 in the evening, the whole family was captivated by the (Mexican, but Russian dubbed) serial *Simply Maria* on Ostankino, the Russian TV station (now ORT). They were looking forward to (the American serial, again dubbed in Russian) *Santa Barbara* later in the evening. In between, they put on the Estonian station for a while, where there was a chef teaching a recipe, and then some traditional Estonian folk dances, which the two daughters did on the living room floor while watching. But the Estonian programs were of low quality and really captured no one's attention. There are many reasons for Russian youth to learn Estonian, but a desire to be on the cultural cutting edge is not one of them.

The language situation in Kiev is quite different from that in Kazakhstan or the Baltics. On the one hand, there is a Russian discourse of not taking Ukrainian seriously as a language. Here is a typical statement from Ukraine:[16]

> The Russian language is recognized in the whole world on a par with English, French, and Chinese as an international language and an official language of the UN. Thanks to the knowledge of Russian, the Ukrainian people have an opportunity not only to communicate with people from (the former republics) but also to have access to the most recent scientific publications, the majority of translations . . . being in Russian. To be against a broad state recognition of the Russian language, its knowledge by each citizen of Ukraine, means to impoverish the

[16] "Zaiava Prezydii Politrady Sotsialistychnoi partii Ukrainy z pryvodu propozytsii Prezydenta Ukrainy L. D. Kuchmy pro nadannia rosiis'koi movi statusu ofitsiinoi," *Tovarishch* (in Ukrainian), October 1994.

> spiritual potential of the people, to throw Ukraine into backwardness and narrow-minded provincialism.

Aleksandr Solzhenitsyn's similar view, expressed in an interview in *Forbes*, was quoted in the Ukrainian press. He had said that it would take more than a century for Ukrainian to rise to a true international level. This opiniion elicited a defensive response in the Ukrainian press, but it does reflect a popular Russian view.[17] One Ukrainian paper reported the following conversation on the street:[18]

> WOMAN: And why do these writers want to force us to speak Ukrainian?
>
> AUTHOR: What is your nationality?
>
> WOMAN: What does nationality have to do with it? Don't they understand that Russian is the language of the city [*chto russkii iazyk—eto gorodskoi iazyk*]?

Ukrainian sounds odd to many Russian-speakers when they hear it used in official contexts. Arel reports the views of his chauffeur, Leonid, on just this theme:

> Leonid may say that he has no problems with Ukrainian, but he is no partisan of the concrete manifestations of the linguistic revival in Ukraine. He often pointed out to me that the names of the streets and public places in Kiev should be in Russian only. When I asked him why, he said because "Ploshcha zhovtnevoi revolutsii" ["October Revolution Square" in Ukrainian; the Russian version is "Ploshchad oktiabr'skoi revoliutsii"] does not sound real.[19] In the same vein, in December 1995, during our short trip, he complained that foreign films are now dubbed in Ukrainian on TV and intimated that they sound ridiculous. What difference does it make whether they are dubbed in Russian or Ukrainian, I asked him? He said people are used to hear Russian used, while to have Ukrainian instead is not normal. Leonid grew up hearing only Russian used in public domains, which is his measure of normality. For him, Ukrainian does not appear to have the prestige to fulfill that function.

On the other hand, distinctions among Ukrainian speech forms need to be made. The mixed Russian-Ukrainian street dialect known as *surzhik* has universally low status. Arel's research assistant Olga is an ethnic Russian, born in Russia, but whose parents moved to eastern Ukraine when she was an infant. She was unwilling to use her Ukrainian in her job at the rural school in Zhytomyr oblast, not because she thought the language itself was low in status, but because she spoke a bastardized Ukrainian (*govorit griazno*) rather than a clean Ukrainian (*govorit chisto*). Even the peasant dialect from rural immigrants is not considered prestigious. Given the changed cultural environment in Kiev of the 1990s, however, Arel reports that she has overcome this psychological barrier and speaks Ukrainian without embarrassment.

17 "Ne vse harazd iz pravdy syloiu u gospodina Solzhenitsyna," *Ukrains'ka hazeta* (in Ukrainian), July 21, 1994.

18 Dmytro Mishchenko, "Shcho tse za natsiia," *Osvita* (in Ukrainian), March 2, 1994.

19 By September 1996 it had been changed again, to Maidan Nezalezhnosti.

The status of the western dialect of Ukrainian is quite different, and Iurii Petrus' feels this difference. Petrus' was born in L'viv Oblast, in western Ukraine, and came to Kiev at age twenty-six for training at the Higher Party School. Arel writes that many take Iurii for an expatriate, because he speaks Ukrainian in his work for a British company. What is interesting is that he can feel that the Kiev russophones (who form a vast majority in the business community) have no objection to hearing people like him use Ukrainian at an official level. What it instills in them is even more respect, a certain awe, the feeling they are really talking to someone important, who really knows Ukrainian. He says that this gives him a palpable sense of authority at first contact, probably because he is perceived as an expatriate from Canada or the United States. In a church, a young woman organist who heard him speak emphasized how charming he was! It appears that Iurii's command of "high" Ukrainian is part of his charm, or his commanding presence. Even Leonid, Arel's cynical informant, grudgingly agrees that he will willingly respond in Ukrainian if an "upper-class" Ukrainian speaks to him in "pure" (*chistii*) form. While expatriate Ukrainian, Estonian, and Latvian might get grudging respect from some Russians, the high status of these languages was not pushing them to learn it faster than their neighbors. The high status of Russian in all four republics constrained Russian-speakers from studying the titular languages too assiduously. Speaking it—or better, speaking it within earshot of fellow Russians, or studying it assiduously in the presence of peers—would lower your status among your own people.

We did not observe the "competitive" aspect of assimilation. In my visits to the Baltiets and Krenholm factories in December, 1992, I got an inkling of why this would be so. In both factories workers had little or nothing to do and were not being paid. They felt that they were all in a sinking ship together and that it made no sense to try to outdo one another. One Baltiets worker quipped that "Narva is the Siberia for the Estonian professorate. They'll never come here willingly to implement the language laws." To be sure, in my visit to the Narva special language school (where the Grigor'evs had enrolled their youngest child), which offered courses in English, French, German, and Estonian, there were six applicants for every place. Thus, to a certain extent Russians actually were competing with one another on the language market. And as we saw in the previous section, Russian-speakers, especially in the Baltics, were investing privately in language competence. But we saw practically no evidence of a fear that if they did not learn the titular language, they would be surpassed economically and socially by their neighbor who did.

In-group pressures to resist assimilation, at least in the early years of their linguistic reversal of fortunes, were more noticeable in the Russian-speaking communities that we lived in. Such pressures, to be sure, are not new to the region with the coming of the double cataclysm. The first published Latvian novel, *Mērnieku laiki* (Time of the Surveyors, published in 1879), was a stereotype of a prissy Latvian behaving and speaking as if he were a Baltic German, memorializing a move by Latvian nationalists to humiliate would-be assimilators.[20]

[20] Andrejs Plakans, *The Latvians* (Stanford, Calif.: Hoover Institution Press, 1995).

In today's Kazakhstan, Russian-speaking Kazakhs in the wake of the double cataclysm began to face strong in-group pressures to reverse the centuries-long russification process. Lida, one of Dave's informants, mentioned a Kazakh friend of hers who does not speak any Kazakh, and how all too often she gets asked questions in Kazakh—people ask for time or, for directions, obviously to test her. To protect herself, she has memorized certain sentences like "excuse me, but I am in a hurry," "I don't have a watch," and "I am sorry but I am new here." So far, she has managed to steer clear of problems. Russians have similar forms of group pressures to identify and humiliate potential assimilators. When Kazakhstan finally got rid of the old Soviet and Russian rubles, it introduced *ten'ga* and its coins, called *tiyin*. Most Russians can't (or don't want to?) pronounce these words, generally calling it instead *natsional'naia valiuta* (national currency) or saying, "Vot eti novyie den'gi" ("This is the new money"). Though the Russian word *den'gi* (money) came into Russian from one of the Turkic languages, Russians act as if the related word *ten'ga* came from Mars. It is clear that among Russians, correct pronunciation of the name of the currency would be a betrayal of the Russian community of Kazakhstan.

In Estonia, evidence of tension between those breaking Russian-speaking solidarity and those seeking to represent a united Russian front has already begun to appear. In Narva, N. Novak wrote an article in the local paper saying that an "overwhelming majority of my closest friends would choose citizenship in that country in which we live—Estonia. The obstacle—lack of knowledge of the state language." In a meeting in Narva with Novak, city council members, and Riigikogu deputies from the northeast, violence nearly broke out when Iurii Mishin (then a city councilor; a self-declared Russian citizen and permanent resident of Narva, who still demands full political rights in Estonia for Russian residents, whether citizens or not) tried to stop Novak from getting to the microphone. Novak represented the "assimilationist move" that was clearly a threat to the representation of Russians as a separate community that needed its own political institutions.[21]

Many of the resettlement organizations have faced similar tensions and get derogatory coverage in the Russian-language press. They are portrayed as opportunistic groups who promise people beautiful sites and cottages but then take their money and then send them off to swamps in the backwoods of Russia. There is the implication that these organizations are undermining the strength of the Russian-speaking community by legitimizing the Latvians' and Estonians' claim that people should return to their "ethnic homelands." This has led to much infighting between the groups and the press. When Lisa Trei (a freelance writer for the *Wall Street Journal*) and Pettai asked the deputy editor of *Molodezh' Estonii* about resettlement groups in Estonia, they were told, "We only deal with the people who want to stay here and live here!" And the editor abruptly ended the interview.

In a visit to School No. 11 in Narva, I spoke with the advanced students in English, and they asked me about my work. Through a lot of questions by Pavel (the

[21] N. Novak, "Esli khochesh' stat' grazhdaninom Estonii," *Narvskaia gazeta*, February 6, 1993; Iu. Mishin, "Vce eto bylo by smeshno, kogda by ne bylo tak grustno," *Narvskaia gazeta*, February 11, 1993.

student who had cultivated a friendship with an Estonian girl), I told them about my ideas of two different streams of Russian activity: protest by groups in favor of recognizing Russian, and subversion by individuals by learning Estonian. He came up to me afterward and said that he never put it into words, but it was his exact story. He told me of his ambitions to study at the University of Tartu law school, his fears that the Russians are discriminated against, by their names, their accents, or their looks, and his strategies to overcome his disadvantages, including his choice of girlfriend. But what was so intriguing to him, he said, was that many members of his family strongly opposed his doing this and said that he was merely playing into the hands of the national radicals. He said the criticism of him came close to being violent at times. He fears those friends who brag that they are storing weapons to fight the Estonian state when the opportunity arises. But he also fears their anger at him for his choices.

The tensions between assimilators and activists seem just below the surface. In April 1997, an international conference organized by the Russian Parties in Estonia and the Assembly of Russian Populations in the Baltic States (ARPBS) met in Tallinn, and represented the nonintegrated Russians. Russian Duma Deputy Dmitrii Rogozin articulated his disgust for the assimilators. "The assembly is not interested in those Russians who have decided to be more Estonian than the Estonians themselves," he declared, "but in the mass of Russians who are waiting for Russia to sometimes also say 'no' to these countries."[22]

Still, the tensions between the Russian assimilators and those seeking Russian solidarity in Estonia remain low. Aleksei Semionov reported to me that he faced little in-group pressure against his accommodating view toward Estonia. He was able to run for the Tallinn City Council because of the agreement between CSCE representative Max van der Stoel and Prime Minister Mart Laar that accelerated the naturalization process for moderates seeking office on local councils. He more or less met the criteria (knowing enough Estonian) and received his citizenship just before registration was closed. He told me that he faced no criticism from the Russian community for accepting citizenship in this way, because the Russians wanted "their leaders to represent them." He joked that his Russian-speaking colleagues remained quiet during council meetings, because they were incapable of speaking Estonian, which was required in the Tallinn (but not Narva) council meetings. He never faced within-community shame, he reported to me, for using his Estonian capabilities in speaking up at those council meetings.[23] Similarly, Vladimir Kuznetsov, a deputy of the Narva city council during the transition, who refused to take citizenship (although it was indicated that he could have it, by virtue of the van der Stoel/Laar agreement), told me in an interview on October 12, 1993, that he felt no anger at those who took citizenship and began learning Estonian. In Estonia (and

[22] Kristopher M. Rikken, "Alternatives to Integration," *Baltic Times*, April 10, 1997.

[23] Yet, after my field research, there is evidence of change. In an interview with Semionov on December 13, 1996, Pål Kolstø writes (in a personal communication): "If Aleksei told you that he did not feel any hostility from other Russians for being 'soft' on the Estonians, now he definitely feels this hostility in the form of a more or less organized smear campaign. The vigilantes are moving against the accommodators."

perhaps in Latvia), there is in the early years of nationalizing, only a limited degree of in-group policing by Russians against their assimilationist brethren. We have no evidence of such policing in Ukraine or Kazakhstan.

Out-Group Acceptance

Potential assimilators, according to the logic of the tipping game, need to assess the expected returns for learning the state language. This assessment must take into account not only the expected job returns minus the costs of learning but the probability that if they did learn the language, they would be accepted by members of the titular group as potentially one of them. Titulars may seek to police "boundary crossing," even if nontitulars develop facility in "their" language. Language learning is only one move in a larger assimilationist process. Signals sent by titulars about the value of assimilationist probes by outsiders play a crucial role in decisions whether to assimilate linguistically. Our data show that the titulars in all four republics, to different degrees, consciously sent signals that the payoffs to linguistic assimilants would be limited.

Common in popular titular discourse is a "primordial" or perhaps Stalinesque view of culture, one which sees assimilation as unnatural, and never really successful. Consider the view of Almas Almatov (thirty-nine), the head of the section on ethnomusicology in the music department at the Kyzyl-Orda Institute of Music and Art. He articulated a strong sense that groups should not assimilate, and that it isn't possible even if they wanted to. He talked disapprovingly of the "internationalism" of the Soviet years, which he noted, was still the official ideology behind the nationalities policy of the Kazakhstani government. He told Dave:

> Just because a Russian *akyn* [a Kazakh epic singer] sings in Kazakh, or even composes songs in Kazakh, it does not mean that such a person is rooted in Kazakh culture and tradition. After all, the Russian remains a Russian, because he or she can think and feel only like a Russian. There can be no real internationalism. For instance, when someone dies in a Russian family, they will put a cross on the dead person. A death in a Kazakh home, we put a crescent. When you have an international family, then you choose neither a cross, nor crescent, but some sort of a star [that is, the red star of communism, Dave notes] instead. Real internationalism does not exist, people should know their own cultures.

This very sentiment was articulated by a Ukrainian academician, M. Popova, to the effect that the nationality of the individual is inscribed in the DNA of his or her chromosomes. This "authority" therefore believes in genetic determination of nationality, transmitted by blood. A Russian commentator cited this paper and said that several scientists have proved that the blood group B is very rare among Ukrainians, whereas it predominates among Russians.[24]

[24] Popova, in *Molod' Ukrainy*, October 20, 1992. For a summary, see V. Barladianu-Byrladnik, "Likho i s kondachka," *Iug* (Odessa, in Russian), March 1, 1994.

One clear implication of such sentiments—nowadays often put in the less racist terms of the American political scientist Samuel Huntington, who refers to unbridgeable "civilizational" divides[25]—is a publicly stated wish by titulars, especially in the Baltics, that the Russians return to "their" homeland, where they really belong. In Estonia, the right-wing Estonian Progressive Party in April 1994 opened negotiations with Russian nationalists in Russia, saying that the aims of both parties were the same. Although this came from only a fringe movement, the notion that signals ought to be sent to Russians that it was natural for them to emigrate was widely shared in Estonia. Tiit Vähi, as I related in Chapter 5, told me in an interview that encouraging Russians to return to Russia voluntarily was widely favored by Estonian politicians. As Vello Pettai noted in his field observations, for many informants

> their method of distinguishing between "good" Russians and "bad" Russians was according to whether the Russian had a real ethnic identity as a Russian. . . . The prevalence of such an ethnically based worldview explains well the use by Estonians and Latvians of the term "ethnic homeland" in talking about repatriation. This is what repatriation means to many of them: the return of these people who should be living on their native ethnic soil and working for the good of their nation just as Estonians and Latvians do in theirs.

This feeling reaches an apotheosis in the polemic of Atis Skalbergs, a nationalist Latvian radio commentator, who scorned Russia for not even trying to help call its Russians back home. "Israel, Latvia, Estonia, Lithuania, Ukraine, are all calling on their conationals to return to their homeland, but Russia is doing everything to keep Russians from returning to theirs. . . . That's quite a love for your country—to do everything so as not to have to return there."[26] Potential assimilators in the Baltics are well aware that a considerable part of the titular population is motivated to police the boundaries separating Russians from titulars.

For those Russians who remain, anti-assimilationist titulars seek to give the impression that the returns for linguistic assimilation will be low. At the home of Igor, there was an intense argument about the insularity of the Kazakhs, and whether Russians could ever be accepted. Igor agreed that the Kazakhs were against Gennadii Kolbin (Gorbachev's appointee as first secretary) because he was sent from Russia. But, he argued, now so many have started complaining about Prime Minister Tereshenko, President Nazarbaev's appointee as prime minister in 1991. "They don't like him for he has a Ukrainian last name, or for what he looks like. They will remove him, for he is not a Kazakh, even though he speaks Kazakh." (Indeed, Nazarbaev removed him in 1994, shortly after this interview.)

These pressures are especially hard on the young. As one high school student told a TV reporter on the third anniversary of the Latvian referendum on independence,

[25] See his "Clash of Civilizations," *Foreign Affairs* 72, no. 3 (1993): 22–49. It is picked up favorably by the Estonian sociologist Marika Kirch, whom I quoted on this theme in Chapter 1.

[26] This broadcast was translated and published verbatim in Russian, in *Panorama Latvii*, March 11, 1994.

"We don't really feel very Russian, but we can't forget our nationality. . . . We're not allowed to forget it. If you try, you'll be reminded of it" (recorded by Pettai from Latvian Television, Channel 2, March 3, 1994). The student did not specify who would do the reminding—Russians or Latvians. But the interview took place with his school buddies around him. Pettai saw them all nodding, as if it were obvious that it was their Latvian schoolmates who were doing the policing.

This is felt in day-to-day living as well. Standards for attaining linguistic assimilation make potential assimilants feel like Alice on the Queen's chessboard. Lida, whose success in memorizing Kazakh phrases has, as I mentioned, saved her from embarrassment. "But," she complained to Dave, "these people deliberately ask such questions in Kazakh, and have no patience for Kazakh that isn't quite 'pure.' " Even for higher levels of linguistic facility, social acceptance by the titulars might not be forthcoming. In an interview with a Pskov resettler, Pettai was told that learning Estonian wouldn't be enough. This particular settler had already reached Category D, a level of moderate ability, and realized only that Russians will never be accepted, since the Estonians are a "closed nation." Another Pskov resettler, Anatolii, told Pettai that the language was easy, yet he still hadn't been able to get a job. But the Russians in Pskov, he was quick to point out, are friendly and have "open souls," unlike the Estonians. In Pettai's discussions with young Russian-speaking university students in Riga, members of the disaffected group of Russian Technical University students told him that they had friends who had sufficient Latvian ability to matriculate in Latvian University. But they were "treated as second rate there" anyway. From these reports, we begin to see that many Russians are beginning to feel that Estonians and Latvians do not really want them to learn the local language. As the authors of *SM-Segodniia* wrote: "The popular phrase 'we don't need you to know Latvian, we just need you to know your place!' crudely, but adequately explains to people who don't understand, what is demanded of them."[27]

Alice's chessboard may be insufficient to describe the feeling of Russian potential assimilators in Estonia. Not only did the criteria for full acceptance seem to get more distant, but new barriers were erected as well. On the legal front, with the passage of the Aliens Law in 1993, a whole new vocabulary to delegitimate Russians was put into service. The terms "immigrant," "colonizer," and "occupier" were part of social delegitimization on the popular level. But the legal terms "non-Estonian" (*muulane*), "noncitizen" (*mitte-kodanik*), and "alien" (*välismaalane*) were added. An exasperated Klara Hallik (from the Estonian Academy of Science; an Estonian with Russian roots of generations ago, who was a leader in the Popular Front period) commented to Pettai, "Who would have thought that the noncitizens' registration could now be interpreted [by Estonian authorities] as merely giving them the right to apply for a temporary residency permit in the Republic of Estonia?" New legal barriers to entry, no matter what Russians were trying to do, send clear signals lowering the expected payoffs for linguistic assimilation.

Perhaps worse than the letter of the law was its practice. Once in Pavel Grigor'ev's living room an Irish human rights activist was railing against the policies of

[27] "Kogda eti russkie zagovoriiat po-latyshski?" *SM-Segodniia*, November 1993.

the Estonian government. To defend the Estonian government position, I told them about the Estonian language exam for the retired people who want citizenship, which was administered in such a way in Narva so that there would be no failures. Tom, the activist, was incredulous, but Pavel helped clear things up. Although the law might be easy on one hand—and this was when the Kafkaesque image of Baltic policies came to my mind—their applications will be held up in bureaucratic processes until they die. Tom pointed out that the number of Narvans who have applied for and actually received citizenship (with proper papers) is in the hundreds, almost a drop in the bucket. Pavel agreed. Natasha, his daughter, had completed the application process and had been waiting for citizenship for almost two years. That reminded me of Pavel (the student in School No. 11) telling me that he had all his papers fully ready, and he got a call from the Passport Office that one paper wasn't really correct (his father's earnings and job) and therefore they were postponing his application for two months, even though he came the next day with the proper papers. Tom's wife, who is a Russian born in Estonia, said her application was denied because the passport agency had told her that key papers were "lost." She also told me that twice she had to resupply the agency with the same missing papers. She surmised that papers were being purposefully lost.[28] The Estonians, Tom argued, were "changing goal posts." Liuba added that the language exam had become more difficult over the years; level D was formerly the citizenship exam, but now it is easy compared to what they demand for citizenship. Even if they held the goal posts steady, Estonian authorities would not really allow many applications through, having already, as Pavel said, a "de facto quota." Since the Estonian government does not publish data on how many Russian residents who pass the citizenship exam actually receive citizenship, it is not possible to confirm whether such a quota actually exists.[29] Again, this is an example of how perceptions about the value of linguistic assimilation can be altered by the titular group. If they give no rewards to people who have invested in their language, they reduce the motivation to learn it.

A final "strategy" by titulars to lower the benefits of linguistic assimilation is to portray the society as one that has only "pure" Estonians and "fifth columnist" Russians. A good example was in the Estonian TV reporting before the October 1993 local elections. The story was on the fact that many Estonians when interviewed on the street did not know that the next day there was an election, or who was running. What was interesting here was that although in local elections all residents had the right to vote, not one Russian was interviewed on this program. It was as if loyal

[28] Notwithstanding my Kafkaesque leitmotif, a plausible explanation for these slights—though hardly one that would mollify the applicants—is that Estonia has created far more regulations concerning Russians than it is able to administer. For example, Estonia invalidated the Soviet "red passports" on May 15, 1997, but the vast amount of paperwork, and the imminent loss of all legal status by some 100,000 noncitizens, compelled the government to backtrack and return legal status to the red passports for emergency situations and for the receiving of pensions. See Lev Dorogyshin, "Net pasporta—net cheloveka," *Rossiiskaia gazeta*, May 20, 1997.

[29] As Vello Pettai explained it, in a personal communication, this is a two-edged sword. If the Estonian government (as is the practice in Latvia) published such data, it would be reifying Soviet nationality categories. If government ministries do not report cases of Russians becoming citizens of Estonia, it looks like they are hiding the de facto systematic denial of naturalization to Russians.

voters of a Russian background weren't part of the electorate, or even the society.[30] Similarly, Aleksei Semionov, on the Tallinn City Council, told me that Estonians seem not to realize how moderate the Russian community had become in the period from 1992 to 94. The political positions they take (even for full loyalty to Estonia), and the language decisions they make (even for learning the language) don't seem to alter Estonian views about what sort of people they are.

Out-Group Dropping Russian from Their Repertoires

Titulars can discourage linguistic assimilation by policing their group boundaries and by lowering the perceived rewards for learning the titular language. They can also abandon Russian altogether and make themselves deaf to Russian public discourse. To the extent the titulars move toward monolingualism (or bilingualism with a different world language), Russians living in the titular republics will feel a greater need to learn either the new international language or the titular language. In the Baltics, titulars have made a credible commitment to abjure Russian; in Kazakhstan, the commitment to the titular language is clear but not credible; and in Ukraine, with heavy policing by nationalists, there is a growing credibility of a tip toward Ukrainian as the principal language in Kiev, with broad implications for the entire country.

As early as 1991, according to the Saar Poll, 6.9 percent of Estonians agreed that there was no longer any need to know Russian. This was, of course, only an attitude, but that attitude has come to be reflected in behavior. In the Baltics, many young Estonians and Latvians have no facility, nor any desire to develop facility, in Russian. To be sure, children with access to Russian TV can become fluent in Russian behind, as it were, their parents' backs, as a leading linguist from Riga admitted to me in 1991 about his seven-year-old son. But Russian TV has been slowly forced from the public airways in much of the Baltics. In a visit to an Estonian family (where both parents, working in the Estonian Academy of Science, are fluent in Russian) in Lasnamäe, a predominantly Russian neighborhood in Tallinn, I chatted with Jüri, their school-aged son. He commutes to an all-Estonian school. He has few interactions with kids in the neighborhood "due to different values," according to his parents. I can communicate with Jüri in English, but he has no knowledge of Russian. His older brother, Oliver, was in the eleventh grade. In his room, there were many books and magazines in English and German but not one in Russian. He has a copy of Dostoyevsky's *Idiot* in Estonian (in the living room there is a beautiful version of *Anna Karenina* in Estonian), and a textbook on the greats of Russian literature, all in Estonian. He travels one hour each way to a school in Mustamäe, a predominantly Estonian neighborhood, so he gets his instruction entirely in Estonian, with a good program in English. Estonian parents, in fact, will go out of their way to help eliminate Russian from their children's repertoires. Pettai's interview with Inna Kustavus, mentioned earlier, demonstrates this same trend. In fact, examples of this sort abound, and the overall lesson is clear: monolingual Rus-

[30] I owe this observation to Martha Merritt.

sians will not be able to communicate effectively with the next generation of Estonia's leaders.[31]

The Õiger family language repertoire shows a loss of competence in Russian not only between generations but even within the present adult generation. Armilde, born in southern Estonia in 1914, was deported to Siberia in 1949. Her son, Karl, was brought up in Siberian exile, and his career was stunted by the stigma of being the son of a political criminal. He watches Russian TV news, intrigued by the alternative viewpoint, and many of the books in his personal library are in Russian. His son Peeter served in the Soviet army, where he learned not only Russian but also a deep hatred of Russia and Russians. His wife, although she doesn't speak much Russian herself, told Pettai that her children would speak even less. She felt this to be a problem, but Peeter did not and did all he could to ensure that their two children have virtually no exposure to Russian.

Perhaps a more stunning incident will make this point clearer. In the Tallinn Central Market in January 1994, Pettai observed two Estonian women in their thirties walking around the outdoor stalls and overheard one say to the other in a tone of mild surprise: "Imagine that! I've nearly forgotten all of my Russian! Now that's a problem!" This suggests that she was still willing to switch languages in order to communicate with Russian-speaking vendors, who once predominated in the market, but no longer is able to. And so, not only is the language being lost intergenerationally; the present generation is losing facility in it as well.

Combined with external signs that titulars are "losing" Russian, there is also evidence that those who use Russian publicly are being stigmatized. Among those planning to resettle in Pskov, Ivan Borblik, seventy-five years old, born in Ukraine, but a forty-year resident of Estonia, could take it no longer. He worked only with Russians and does not speak Estonian. Loss of free Russian TV may have been the last straw. But the everyday value of Russian was clearly declining. He felt that in Soviet times, there were no language problems, but now, "if you ask for something [in Russian, in the stores] they think you're stupid."

The creation of "Russian-free zones" has also had a stunning effect on the general perception of the future value of Russian monolingualism. As early as 1991, a conference at the Institute of History, was a good example of such a zone. Although all the delegates were fluent in Russian, they agreed to speak only in Estonian or (halting) English to one another. At the University of Tartu, the premier institution of higher learning in Estonia, where many of the children of my informants from Narva aspired to enroll, virtually all public signs were in Estonian and English. In this major university town, I had a hard time finding a single Russian-language newspaper. The only local Russian-language paper published in Tartu, the *Russkaia gazeta*, comes out rarely (on May 5, 1994, it published its thirty-seventh issue) and is of low quality. In the market, this was the first time that I had to rely solely on my

[31] Sheila Fitzpatrick, on reading an earlier draft of this chapter, gave personal testimony from Latvia in line with what I observed in Estonia. Her fluency in Russian does not serve her well in her efforts to communicate with the younger generation of her in-laws there. Not that they are "nationalists," she explains; they just don't like to speak Russian.

extremely rudimentary Estonian to conclude a purchase. The Tallinn City Council is another Russian-free zone. While 42 percent of the officials elected in 1994 had Slavic surnames, formal sessions are conducted solely in Estonian. No Russian living in Estonia could possibly miss the point that Estonians are systematically deskilling themselves in Russian. Latvia too has tried to create Russian-free zones. For example, authorities have removed all Russian-language books from their medical school library.[32] Throughout the two Baltic republics, clear signals are being sent that in many realms of life, the Russian language will be absent.

In Kazakhstan, despite great verve among committed nationalists, Kazakhs cannot demonstrate seriousness of purpose in their quest to reduce significantly the presence of Russian, even among Kazakhs. Thus Kazakh nationalists are unable to make credible the threat that Russian-speakers living in Kazakhstan will need to become fluent in Kazakh. They have, to be sure, tried. They have tried to give more power and status to residents in rural areas. For outside urban areas such as Almaty (except for the heavily russianized industrial areas in the northeast), Russian is not widely spoken. Kyzyl-Orda, halfway between Almaty and Tashkent, is, according to Dave,

> one of the poorest and most underdeveloped regions of the republic, which has the largest percentage share of Kazakhs. Kazakh is widely spoken in the city, and virtually no one spoke Russian in the villages and the *sovkhoz* that I visited. If I want to improve my Kazakh, I would have to spend a couple of months here and not in Almaty. The trip away from Almaty gave me the first real flavor of what it is to be in a predominantly Kazakh setting. The *sovkhoz* where I spent a couple of days has only Kazakhs.

On that trip, Dave met Ulzhan, a student of ethnomusicology whose father was a famous Kazakh singer. During her visit to Ulzhan's home she noticed that his mother (about fifty-five) appeared shy and distracted. She couldn't make a sense of Dave's Kazakh and constantly looked at Ulzhan. Asked if she spoke Russian, she looked embarrassed. Ulzhan pointed out that her Russian flows like water, without direction. The mother then switched to Russian. Despite all the mistakes and utter lack of regard for gender (Kazakh has no genders), it was perfectly understandable. But she was too embarrassed and then stopped speaking either Russian or Kazakh. The penetration of Russian here was quite limited.

Even in Almaty, certain ministries are seeking to initiate a linguistic sea change. Dave spoke about this with Aleksandra Dokuchaeva, president of the Slavic movement *Lad* (Harmony). At the State Television and Radio Office, the word of the minister [Sherkhan Murtaza—a well-known Kazakh writer, and a zealous proponent of Kazakh language], she complained, is the law.

> A Kazakh girl (Russian-speaking) left work just last week "of her own free will." We all know what it means. As I tell you again and again—remember—we have no rule

[32] Stanislav Govorukhin, "Nuzhny rossiiskie kul'turnye tsentry," *Rossiiskaia gazeta*, February 15, 1997.

of law. We may have the most democratic laws in written form, and the implementation may be very different. The law requires that all government offices have signs in both the languages. At the Ministry of Information and Press, there is not a single sign in Russian anywhere. . . . Last spring, beginning from Prospekt Al-Farabi, they changed all the road signs and street names into Kazakh and English. When we see this, we do get the message. All they want to prove is who's the boss now.

But, as we shall see, these moves are not credible.

In Lida Oskomov's Institute, we can see an excellent example of the extent of kazakhization by zealous nationalists. She is a teacher (*dotsent*—more or less an assistant professor) of organic chemistry at the zoological-veterinarian institute in Almaty. As Dave recounts:

After the language law was passed, all the faculty meetings were held in Kazakh. All her friends and colleagues (out of 11 teachers, she is the only Russian) who earlier used to speak Russian among themselves most of the time, and always spoke Russian when she was around, quickly switched over to Kazakh. Lida is not a touchy person, and moreover she knows generally what is being said, so she didn't pay much attention. "I don't mind asking them to explain it to me," she said. Soon the director of the Institute, who has spent several years studying and working in Moscow, started presenting his talks at the meetings in Kazakh, and all the general discussion shifted to Kazakh as well. "Generally such meetings are boring, and prolonged, so I don't really care. If anything important is being said, they [her colleagues] explain it to me in Russian, so I never miss anything that is important." However, she noticed that of late, the director seems to have run out of steam, and has again started using more and more Russian, "after all it is easier for him to speak Russian than Kazakh." Her friends and colleagues at work have also relaxed a little and speak more Russian than they did the year before [1992–early 1993]. "Though they do say more toasts in Kazakh now. Whenever it is my turn, I say it in Russian and there is no problem.

"Until a couple of years ago, there were no courses offered in the Kazakh language. Now you can choose to go either to the Kazakh or to the Russian section. The quality of students in the Kazakh-language section is, of course, far inferior to that of those in the Russian section. For instance, just after the sovereignty declaration, when there were still no provisions for teaching in Kazakh at the level of *vuzy* [college], all those students coming from the *aul* [village], who didn't study well, would often make excuses such as 'we don't understand Russian' or 'explain to us in Kazakh.' Now they have the choice to study in Kazakh, and their grades haven't improved. They still get a D. It is clear that they don't know the subject well."

I asked Lida if she knows what kind of textbooks are used for teaching in Kazakh, and what is the overall quality of teaching. She began describing to me how they are teaching upper-level courses in Kazakh, and developing vocabulary as well. [It appeared to me that she was trying to keep an open mind. She seemed to realize that something should be done to bring back the Kazakh language, and that people around her were making serious efforts]. I asked her again how her colleagues now teach in Kazakh, since all of them studied in Russian schools. She said

> "I will tell you how they teach" [there may have been a mild tinge of irony, or just a statement by her as an observer, who could no longer remain aloof] "take for instance the woman who now heads the Kazakh section of chemistry. She had studied in a Kazakh school in some *aul* or oblast in Chimkent. When she came to Almaty to study in the *vuz*, she found Russian very difficult, but she worked hard to master it. She says she never really forgot the [Kazakh] language, and it is all coming back now. The first several months she used to write her lectures in Russian, and then translated them into Kazakh with the help of dictionaries. Initially she simply read them out to the class, but now she seems to have gotten better, and can actually speak extemporaneously. Of course if they teach in Kazakh, they don't have to teach a full load, and they are given extra time for preparing the lectures."[33]

The impression Lida conveys is that at least at present, the linguistic nationalism that came with sovereignty is a train that has already lost some steam.

This view is largely confirmed when we examine our material on the intergenerational shift among Kazakhs in schooling. Occasionally Dave met committed nationalists who took the first step toward the intergenerational shift in language repertoires. One woman, Raushan, who is a russified Kazakh, proudly told Dave that she is sending her daughter to a Kazakh school. "We forgot our language," she complained. "They didn't let us study it. They wanted to turn us into Russians." But in most cases these commitments don't work out the way the parents hoped. In Kyzyl-Orda, where it is difficult even to hear much Russian, Dave interviewed Almas, a professor of ethnomusicology, who refused to speak to her in Russian. Because Dave's facility in Kazakh was still limited, she was unable to complete the interview. To remedy this, he called his eldest son, thirteen years old, who spoke very good Russian, and he was Dave's translator. Although Almas, who himself speaks adequate Russian, presented himself as someone who has no need for Russian, there was no way he would allow his son to be monolingual in Kazakh. In Almaty, Dave met Alia, who sends her child to a Kazakh kindergarten. The child knows no Russian, and Alia and her husband see no need for him to learn any. They visited their friend Madina, who has a child the same age. The children couldn't communicate with each other, and Alia's child was crying the whole time. Dave writes, "Madina didn't know how to tell them that the kid needs to communicate in Russian too, for it seems so obvious."

Parents like Raushan and Alia are rare in Kazakhstan; and even for them, it is hard to believe they will see through their intergenerational derussification program. There are three reasons for this. First, the degree of russification in urban Kazakhstan, and not only Almaty, is high. Second, the well-established russified Kazakhs (called *mankurty*) will not quietly give way. Third, even those russified Kazakhs who publicly agree with kazakhization (or derussification) privately subvert that goal through their own behavior.

[33] In the schools, instructors who teach in Russian have a teaching load of 900 hours; those who switch to Kazakh have their load reduced to 700 hours. Bhavna Dave, interview with Abduali Qaidarov, president of the Qazaq Tili (Kazakh-language) Society, January 10, 1994.

Russification of urban Kazakhs has been unremitting and powerful for well over a century. As a result, the Russian language has spread into every nook and cranny of urbanized and high-status Kazakh life. Ultai Zhunispeisova mentioned to Dave how Kazakh adaptation to russification sometimes reached absurd proportions. During the Soviet era, Kazakhs, she bemoaned, gave up their beautiful historical names for meaningless Soviet ones. One comes across names like Kolkhozbek, Traktorbek, Kosiurga (an abbreviation for Kosmonaut Iurii Gagarin—a name that abounded in the Baikanour cosmodrome region) even in the Kazakh *aul*.

In educated speech, Russian became widespread, and well taught. As A. Zhovtis explained to Dave:

> As a philologist I would certify that the Russian-speaking Kazakhs—especially those in cities—speak more correct Russian than many Russians themselves. They were lucky to be taught by the educated and cultured class of the former St. Petersburg gentry. This section of the Russian intelligentsia faced a great deal of persecution in those days. Many were banished to Siberia and Kazakhstan, where they ended up teaching in schools and universities. The Kazakhs who came to the cities for education were lucky to get such qualified teachers. . . . Of course, the Russian language is not a foreign language for Kazakhs. Chokan Valikhanov wrote only in Russian. . . . Look at Olzhas Suleimenov. His father died in 1937 during the purges. He comes from a family of the intelligentsia. His stepfather was a Kazakh as well. Olzhas was brought up in a Kazakh environment and he does know the language. Yet his education has been in Russian. He gave a speech in Kazakh at the World Kazakh Congress (Kurultai) in 1992. I did not hear the speech. But friends told me that it wasn't the same person. It lacked the richness and spontaneity that his Russian has.

Dave saw the same phenomenon at the celebrations for the second anniversary of Kazakhstan independence on December 16, 1993, where the keynote speaker was Chingiz Aitmatov, the famous Kirghiz author, whose novel *I dol'she veka dlit'sia den'* (The day lasts longer than a century) has become a symbol for nationalists who want the Central Asian republics to reinvigorate their cultures. In that novel, a *mankurt* is a zombie slave who has lost all memory of his past and culture. The term *mankurt* is now commonly used throughout the former Soviet Union to refer to the members of the sovietized and russified strata of non-Russian nationalities who have the traits of rootlessness and cultural amnesia. Aitmatov read from his prepared text in Kirghiz (a language closely related to Kazakh, and understood by most Kazakh speakers). Having finished his prepared text, he began speaking in Russian, and suddenly, Dave reports, his voice was authoritative and forceful. Ironically, Aitmatov is the ultimate *mankurt*.

Those who took advantage of *korenizatsiia* suffered for it. Nagima, a forty-year-old divorcee living with her fourteen-year-old son and her seventy-year-old mother in Almaty, told Dave that she was among the first to enter a Kazakh-medium school. After completing school, she tried to enter the Institute of Library Sciences in Sarkandy, in Jambul Oblast. She was denied admission on account of her relatively poor knowledge of Russian literature. At the exams, she was asked questions about specific (and relatively minor) works of Pushkin and other writers, some of whom she had never heard of. The Russian students, and the Kazakhs who had attended Russian-medium schools, looked down on people like Nagima with a sort of surprised condescension. She said there were times when she wondered if she was "bright enough."

Since her brother was such an "educated" person, she decided to share these anxieties with him. He explained to her at great length that the syllabus and teaching matter in Kazakh schools were deliberately devised to serve specific political purposes. It was in the interest of the Soviet regime that Kazakhs continued to work in the sphere of agriculture, farming, and petty labor, rather than becoming members of the urban working class. It was a lot easier to make milkmaids or kolkhoz workers out of the *chabany* (Kazakhs) than out of Russians or others. That is why, as the brother explained, the syllabi in Kazakh schools were designed to guide Kazakh students away from the prestigious *vuzy* and toward one of the *proftekhuchilische* [technical schools], or into study through correspondence courses, while continuing to work full time in the countryside. She clearly admired her brother for his ability to understand, criticize, and yet work within the system. She added quickly that since the early 1970s, after she had finished high school, things had begun to change. The subsequent school reforms have improved the standard of teaching in Kazakh schools.

But a century of marginalization is not reversed that quickly. Another informant, Galia, a math teacher of mixed descent (Russian mother and Kazakh father), observed the switch to Kazakh in the prestigious School No. 15 in Almaty. She summarized the situation to Dave:

> Beginning in the fall of 1994 they are going to switch to Kazakh as the medium of instruction in the first division. They have such a good foundation in Russian, but nobody wants to think about the long term. They have no clearly defined plan, program, or textbooks, nor do they have qualified teachers. Why destroy the solid base that we have? The children will only suffer. There are so many parents who sent their kids to Kazakh school under the influence of all this patriotism and propaganda—now they are regretting it and returning their children to the Russian-language schools. Many others are still afraid, and confused.

Because Russian is so deeply entrenched in Kazakhstan, the Russians there have no reason to fear a linguistic sea change.

To add insult to injury, the Kazakh *mankurty* are not disappearing from public sight, nor are they transforming themselves into Kazakh-speaking intellectuals. What's more, they defend their interests publicly. Nurbulat Masanov and Nurlan Amrekulov, in a subtle essay in *Karavan*, supported the country's privatization campaign. Though the authors do not mention it clearly in this article, their contention was that the promotion of Kazakh as the state language was a step in direction of ethnocracy in a multiethnic society, and they considered this policy a protectionist measure on the part of the nomenklatura, who are basically afraid of real market-like competition based on merit and efficiency.

Masanov is somewhat of a persona non grata among the nationalizing elite of Kazakhstan, though he is impervious to its criticisms. In an open cafe in Almaty (and inviting an angry response from a patron at the next table), he derided the language policies of the government as those which could only come, punning on "banana," from a *barani* (sheep-herding) republic. His wife Laura also remains indifferent to the frequent taunts from elders and nationalists that she does not speak Kazakh. She and Nurbulat are preparing to send their son to a Russian-medium school. So far, he speaks no Kazakh. "If he needs it, he'll learn it when the time comes," said Laura. For his part, Nurbulat is convinced that such a time will never come.

Like Masanov, Olzhas Suleimenov, whom Zhovtis referred to as a true Kazakh intellectual, has stood up for mankurtism. In an article in *Kazakhstanskaia pravda*, he highlighted a key period in eighteenth-century Kazakh history when Abul Khair and Ablai Khan cemented an alliance with Russia. Suppose, Suleimenov asked, they had chosen to seek protection from China? He answers his question by asserting that under those conditions, "the Kazakh *narod* would not have survived as an ethnos." After making this contentious point, he reiterates an earlier proposal to seek a new confederation with Russia.[34] This is hardly a signal that the *mankurty* are ready to lie low in a time of nationalist exuberance.

Consider further the professional situation of Murat Auezov. It would be a mistake to call Auezov a *mankurt*. His father, Mukhtar, was a famous Kazakh poet, and Murat himself has excellent Kazakh literary credentials. He is committed to the enhanced dignity of his nation; yet that goal unwittingly undermines the kazakhization of his country. In 1995 he was leading a quasi-state and inter-CIS television project called "Mir." He was committed to the development of TV programming from a Central Asian perspective free of Western or Russian biases. In order for this project to work, however, the programming had to be in Russian. About that, however, he had no regrets.

Kazakhization is equally undermined by those Kazakhs who subvert nationalization privately, whether or not they support it publicly. A premier example of this phenomenon are those ardent nationalists who vote to promote "their" language, yet send their children to more cosmopolitan schools, where the national language is given at best symbolic support. In Kazakhstan, Kazakhs vote for the nationalist program but work against it in their own language behaviors.

"Private subversion" has an element of deviousness to it, as we can see from Dave's interview with A. Dokuchaeva, a teacher at the Mathematics Institute of the Kazakh State University and the leader of the Slavic movement *Lad*. She wrote in *Mysl'*:

> It is necessary to mention that a large number of teachers, philologists, and scholars are now engaged in the work on revival of Kazakh language. Sincerely concerned by

[34] Nurbulat Masanov and Nurlan Amrekulov, "O dikom natsionalizme i podlinnom patriotizme," *Karavan*, January 14, 1994, pp. 10–11; Olzhas Suleimenov, "Chem opasny 'patrioty'?" *Kazakhstanskaia pravda*, August 7, 1993, pp. 1–2.

> its fate, these activists come to schools, to lecture halls and tell their fellow citizens about the beauty and the high culture of the Kazakh speech. But we also know that in the course of last three years since the Law [making Kazakh the state language] was passed, the state, implying its bureaucrats, the governmental institutions, are not all that excited about improving the state language or studying it. There is a lot of slyness [*lukavstvo*] beneath the taunts directed toward those "unwilling" to learn it.[35]

The slyness refers to the public display of Kazakhization with the private use of Russian.

One private subversion strategy is the acceptance of the notion that mastery of a few words in Kazakh fulfills the program. Dave met a couple, Farida and Yerik, both highly educated in technical fields, and self-described Kazakh-speaking Kazakhs. Yet as soon as Dave and Yerik had proved that they could maintain a conversation in Kazakh, Yerik switched to Russian, whereupon Farida joined in. Farida would occasionally say a sentence or two in Kazakh when Dave called, but she fumbled with the language. If titulars consider this to be an example of Kazakh-speaking, it sends a clear signal to Russians not to take kazakhization seriously. E. V. Kolomeets, the Russian physicist, would frequently spice his speech with phrases such as "it's all the same to me," "good," "excuse me," and "good bye" in Kazakh, perhaps to show his respect for the country where he works. But, he pointed out, full comprehension of the language is unnecessary: "They themselves never speak it."

Another private subversion tactic is rigid adherence to the accommodation norm—the rule that demands that you switch to Russian immediately when one interlocutor uses even a Russian phrase.[36] Dave reports no violations in her fieldwork in Kazakhstan. Nagima told Dave of how her father, who died in 1972, lived by this accommodation norm. He was the principal of a school in the village of Taras in Taldy Kurgan. He taught mathematics and was very interested in the sciences. He could read both the Arabic script and the Latin alphabet. He was very sociable and constantly entertained guests of all nationalities. As a mark of true Kazakh hospitality, the father laid down the rule that whenever they have a Russian (or Ukrainian) guest, all the members of the family should speak Russian, not Kazakh, out of respect.

This norm has remained in effect in Nagima's household. A number of Nagima's relatives visited when Dave was there. A niece of Nagima (Karlygash), who is about twenty-three and has lived in Almaty for five years, spoke only Kazakh with Nagima and Russian with Dave. She once dropped by to pick up something, and stayed for twenty minutes. They talked in Kazakh. As Dave explains in her field report,

> She was told that I know Kazakh, and I said a few things in Kazakh, but that was all the conversation we had. Karlygash said *sau boliniz* [good-bye in Kazakh] to Nagima and *do svidaniia* [now in Russian] to me, adding "nice to meet you" and

[35] A. Dokuchaeva, "O iazyke: ot emotsii—k zdravomu smyslu," *Mysl'* 5 (1993): 38–43.

[36] On the accommodation norm, see Kathryn Woolard, *Double Talk* (Stanford: Stanford University Press, 1989), pp. 69–73.

other pleasantries in Russian. She wasn't at all conscious of the change in her speech patterns. It was very natural and effortless for her to speak Kazakh in a Kazakh setting, and to switch to Russian if a non-Kazakh (or non-Kazakh-speaking Kazakh) is present.

The accommodation norm implies that in mixed settings, all interactions take place in Russian. In Dave's many visits to Igor (Russian) and Madina's (Kazakh) home, she found almost everything was in Russian, including a large number of translations from the world (including India) classics. Dave also observed that at meetings of the unified opposition, everyone used Russian, with no code mixing or switching. There are almost no examples in Dave's field notes of a committed language nationalist pushing the use of Kazakh with non-speakers of Kazakh present.

A third element to private subversion occurs when titulars accept the boundaries set by diglossia during the Soviet period. Diglossia, to recall from Chapter 1, is the language pattern that reserves one language for high functions (such as science) and another for low ones (such as expressing emotions).[37] Kazakhs that Dave interviewed never challenged the low status of Kazakh, which was reinforced through diglossic speech patterns. In the Lenin *sovkhoz*, Tsuimbev, a seventy-five-year-old epic singer, was Dave's host. He lived in an almost completely Kazakh environment. The interview was in Kazakh. Nevertheless, Dave reports, "whenever he had to impart an important message, like when our bus leaves . . . he switched to Russian, using it extremely parsimoniously."

A final element to private subversion is lack of any linguistic policing. In the Almas' Kazakh-speaking home, Dave reports that the TV was constantly on. The entire family—children, Mira, and guests—regularly watched serials like *Simply Maria* and *Santa Barbara*, as well as American thrillers and horror movies, all dubbed into Russian. Almost never did they watch a Kazakh program. And more important, no one attempted to use the TV to challenge Russian hegemony.

Dave also had occasion to interview Abduali Qaidarov, president of the Kazakh language society. During the interview, he received a phone call. He spoke Kazakh, while the interlocutor spoke Russian. After he hung up, Qaidarov commented, "See, you noticed too. I was speaking in Kazakh, but he kept answering in Russian all the same. Not that he cannot speak Kazakh. He knows it. It is just a matter of habit. What can we do?" While Qaidarov was obviously trying to push back the boundary of Russian dominance (and thus he was not accommodating here), his quiet resignation is remarkable, given the fact that he is the principal official in charge of promoting Kazakh.

On the lack of policing, consider Sheker, the head of the oblast department in charge of cultural activities. She is a self-appointed "vigilante" who publicly scorns assimilated Kazakhs. Yet in a visit to her home, Dave reports that her children speak Russian and were far more open to speaking Russian than Kazakh. Although she did not mention it in her formal interview, all her children studied in Russian schools. One day Dave dropped by her home. Sheker was out. Dave passed the time

[37] Charles Ferguson, "Diglossia," *Word* 15 (1959): 325–40.

waiting for her to return in conversation with one of her sons and his friend. Both of them were watching a video—some American movie—and conversing in Russian, with some Kazakh words and sentences thrown in. Dave had just returned from the celebrations of a festival called *saban toi* (harvest festival), an event that Sheker had helped organize. There were traditional Kazakh horse and camel races. Dave asked the boys if they had been to the festival to see the races. They laughed at the question, saying "who's interested in such stuff anyway?"

In Ukraine, the coin teeters on its edge. In the west, the use of Ukrainian is about as established as the use of Estonian is in Estonia. But in the east and the south, there is no evidence of movement away from Russian. In the center, Kiev can go either way. And which way Kiev goes will determine the future of Ukraine, and what kind of national state it will become.

Indeed we have seen signals of intergenerational shift. Iurii Petrus', Arel's informant who was born in L'viv, was taken aback by the fact that in Kiev he could barely hear any Ukrainian in the streets. He presumed that Ukrainians moving into a russified Kiev seek to integrate with the majority. Yet he found almost no awkwardness when he spoke Ukrainian. He now has a son, Vitia, who attends a special language school where instruction is in Ukrainian and he studies Arabic and English as his second and third languages. (His Arabic teacher doesn't know Ukrainian, and asks for translations in Russian, which Vitia can barely manage.) His parents only laughed casually at the thought that their son would not be able to speak Russian, probably assuming that even without formal instruction, Vitia will be able to communicate with Russians in the future, as his father did in the past. Unlike the child of the avid nationalist in Kazakhstan, Vitia does not seem to be paying a high social cost for his parents' linguistic values.

The commitment of Ukrainians to deemphasize Russian, or even to eliminate it as a state language, cannot be discounted completely. Leonid Kuchma, the president of Ukraine, campaigned in Russian, but has governed exclusively in Ukrainian. This is a powerful symbol of change, and the commitment of state authorities to bring it about.

And the signals are being picked up clearly. Marina Diatlova, the official of "Tovaristvo Rus'," noted to Arel and me that at least now Ukrainian is being taught properly in the schools, as opposed to the "joke" in her era, where everyone got an "A" for just fooling around. To be sure, Arel's ever cynical friend Leonid could not take the linguistic nationalists seriously. " 'The Lay of Igor's Host,' in the Middle Ages," he asserts, "was written in Old Russian, not in Old Ukrainian. . . . These [contemporary, nationalist] writers, where were they when Communists were in power? Where were their languages, their souls? They received their honoraria and sat silently. And now they have nothing to do. They can't publish because of a lack of demand." Yet Leonid was clearly agitated, in part because he believes that Kiev will tip toward Ukrainian, needlessly in his opinion, in the near future.

And he may be right. Oleksandra, a Ukrainian from the Left Bank (which is on the edge of a Russian-dominated region), reported that at her university, even after the language law was passed, teaching was done mostly in Russian. This was so because it became customary for professors to ask students during the first class which language the class ought to be conducted in. Suddenly, in her fifth year, three years after the decree, the students in her class asked that the lectures be given in Ukrainian. While between-class conversation remained in Russian, even among students from the west, there was a general consensus that formal communication be in Ukrainian. The commitment of Ukrainians to make Ukrainian the dominant language in Kiev is at least partially credible.

The most powerful signals of pending ukrainization in Kiev are being sent by the vigilantes. One such is Vitalii Karpenko, editor of *Vechirnii Kyiv*. He noticed that in the international treaty with Russia leading to the formation of the International Economic Committee (Mezhdunarodnyi Ekonomicheskii Komitet, or MEK) violated "the widespread international practice of signing any agreement in the languages of all the parties [*vysokikh storin*]" to ensure the mutual respect and equality of the parties. Yet this treaty said that it was completed in the city of Moscow, and that there would be only one original copy, and that one in Russian.[38]

Watchfulness by vigilantes is complemented with vigilante threats, for example concerning where russophone Ukrainians will wind up if they refuse to change their linguistic ways. Here is an example from *Molod' Ukrainy*:

> Should we exclude the russophone Ukrainians of today from the Ukrainian nation? Of course not! When you listen to their uneasy words, you get the impression that they sense that they are disadvantaged, since historical circumstances made them use Russian as their conversational language. Time will pass and these people will begin to speak the language of their ancestors. . . . with the exception of the trough-feeders [*korytnykiv*] and the Janissaries [*ianichariv*], for whom the motherland is associated with a tasty piece of sausage [*kolbasa*].

The implied threat here is that while today russophone Ukrainians can be forgiven, in the future they will be excluded from the nation. There follows a quotation from Mykola Ryabchuk, in a statement (of the Rada, the national-democratic faction in parliament) that a national language is not crucial for national consciousness. But Larisa Masenko answered him by saying that if the east and south don't ukrainize, there will be violence.[39]

And when the nationalists are not making threats, they are hurling insults at those Ukrainians who continue to speak Russian. P. Hrytsenko angrily writes that

> the previous experience of the functioning of Russian and languages of the autochthonous population has shown that the declared "harmonious bilingualism" is a philological fiction, which in practice has always led to a catastrophic shrinking of the sphere of use of the autochthonous languages. . . . The practice has shown that such "harmony" has spawned a generation of *mankurty* [here using the Kirghiz reference] on whom was grafted, not without results, the idea of *menshovartosti* [an

[38] Vitalii Karpenko, "MEKaiuchy, sunemo holovu v zashmorh," *Vechirnii Kyiv* (in Ukrainian), January 18, 1995.

[39] Oleh Hriniv, "Shcho my za narod?" *Molod' Ukrainy* (in Ukrainian), January 18, 1994.

inferiority complex, referring here to the popular notion of "Little Russians"] of all things maternal.[40]

Vigilante action instills shame and guilt in many russophone Ukrainians. Consider this confession published in *Samostiina Ukraina:*

> I was born in Kherson and after some time lived in a village in Mykolaiv, and in 1935 graduated from the Mykolaiv shipbuilding technicum where the majority of the disciplines were taught in Ukrainian, but when I got a job in the Donbas and wrote documents in Ukrainian, they forced me to rewrite them in Russian, since, they said, here it is not "that" Ukraine [*ta Ukraina*]. Eventually I was forcibly totally russified since I am writing this letter with the help of a dictionary, which is very *shameful* for me.[41]

In our examination of the Ukrainian press, we did not find russophone Ukrainians standing up against this vigilante tide. Between the vigilantes and the public perception that very few Ukrainian nationalists are privately subverting their own stated ideals, a tip toward Ukrainian (and loss of easy fluency in Russian) seems likely in Kiev. Those asserting this future as a nationalist commitment do so with some credibility. Less so than the Baltics, but far more so than Kazakhstan, Russians in western and central Ukraine should perceive a need, if they are to remain in their republic, to expand their repertoires.

Other Motivations

The way people think through issues of assimilation is inordinately complex. Not all calculations fit easily into the tripartite categorization of economic payoffs (and costs) and in- and out-group status. In fact, the credible threat of titulars to drop Russian is really a new element to the payoff function for potential assimilants that emerged from the field data. Yet even this new factor is not the whole story.

For example, Olga Guzhvina reported to Pettai that she feels a sense of "shame" (*stydno*) that although she has learned some Estonian, her husband doesn't speak a word of it. This shame reflects the "guilt trip" that Estonians laid on Russian-speakers for never making the effort to learn the language of the territory they had migrated to. Here "out-group" pressures pushed Olga (who might now be pushing her husband!) in the direction of learning the language rather than abjuring it, because without it, she could never really be accepted as an Estonian.

Another calculation has to do with property. Those who have property rights in Estonia might be willing to pay any cost to retain them. If noncitizens lose the right to own property, and citizenship requires facility in Estonian, many property-owning Russian speakers will do what they have to to acquire citizenship. Consider

[40] Pavlo Hrytsenko, "Deshcho pro movnu kontseptsiiu UT," *Kul'tura i zhittia* (in Ukrainian), May 7, 1994.

[41] Pani Yemel'ianova, of Kramators'k, quoted in Inna Dolzhenkova, "V us'omu sviti . . . ," *Samostiina Ukraina* (in Ukrainian), August 10, 1994 (my emphasis).

Pavel Grigor'ev. His cozy dacha was mentioned in Chapter 1. He built on the plot allocated to him, by himself, with his son Andreu, a two-story house that is at every point unique, and its garden provides fresh fruits and vegetables all summer as well as potatoes and canned goods (*konservy*) for the entire year. There is a bus to the dachas, but most people walk to their places and spend summers and weekends there. Virtually every garden in the neighborhood of Pavel's dacha was beautifully tended. One lovely day in October, overlooking his harvest, Pavel said to me, "This is why Russians don't want to leave Estonia!"

For those who do not reside in Estonia, the risks to their property are high. His next-door neighbor, an agronomist at a St. Petersburg agricultural institute hasn't been to his dacha since 1991; he has problems crossing the border, says Pavel. He has papers showing that he is the owner, but under current law, he owns only the dacha. He has a ninety-nine-year lease on the land. Returning to one's Russian homeland entails loss of property rights to one's dacha.

Liuba, Pavel's wife, was motivated to learn Estonian not by the fear that others would learn it first, as posited in the tipping game but by the fear that if she didn't learn Estonian quickly, she might be deported later. When I first began to live with the Grigor'evs, in September 1993, I explained to Liuba at breakfast my theory that many Russians would move to Tallinn to find jobs in the new industries that were cropping up there. She retorted that before that happened, many would go to Russia and homestead, more or less getting for free land formerly owned by large *sovkhozy* and *kolkhozy*, and planting potatoes, and living better off the land than it was then possible in the cities. I asked if she knew anyone from Narva who had already done this; she had no clear answer. I asked if Yeltsin's invitation for free settlement involved much paperwork. She said Russia is too big a country for Moscow to regulate, and this process would occur without paperwork, sort of like a populist squatter movement. Exit, she strongly believed, would trump assimilation.

But when I returned to Estonia in the spring of 1994, as I described, Liuba was singing a different tune. She had heard warnings not only about possible "repatriation" of noncitizens but also that Tallinn authorities were aghast at the high "pass" rate on examinations from the testing center in Narva. Rumor had it that testing was to be centralized. Liuba knew the local pass rate would drop if testing were centralized. She had decided to learn Estonian and pass the test as quickly as possible in order to secure citizenship and her future. Windows of opportunity are never seized so eagerly as when they seem to be closing.

Linguistic Assimilation: Is It Taking Place?

Soviet promotion of Russian as the "language of internationality communication" encouraged Russians living anywhere in the country to remain monolingual. With the double cataclysm, it is clear that there has been some strategic updating, and for many Russians the need to learn the language of the republic in which they live has moved from the realm of the absurd to the realm of the pressing. By the time of our field research, we were able to see some early results of a strategic shift in actual language behavior. Some of these linguistic practices go back to Soviet times, but many are in flux, suggesting that language behavior was indeed affected by the double cataclysm.

Consistent with the differences in state-building strategies, there are three distinct tracks of linguistic assimilation. In Ukraine, especially in Kiev, the two languages are fighting a border war through code mixing, code switching, mixed conversations, and changing functional domains for use. In some but not all areas, Ukrainian is encroaching upon Russian. Assimilation in Ukraine can be gauged by the degree to which Russian-dominant speakers rely on Ukrainian in an ever increasing set of speech domains. In the Baltics, the adult generation that faced the double cataclysm is making a serious effort to expand its language repertoires, but recognizes that their progress in the titular language can only be limited. Meanwhile, they are investing more heavily in expanding their children's repertoires. In Kazakhstan, the Russian-speaking titulars, are subverting the nationalist program through their linguistic practices, and their success so far has sustained their belief that learning Kazakh is unnecessary.

The Linguistic "War of Position" in Ukraine

Because Ukrainian and Russian are so closely related, even in Soviet times there was a great deal of code-mixing in Ukraine. It became normal for a Ukrainian native speaker to interject Ukrainian words and syntax in his/her attempt to speak Russian, and a Russian speaker would do the same in attempting to speak Ukrainian. The resulting mélange is called *surzhik*. There are different gradations of *surzhik*, and in one of Arel's field trips, he strove to establish the level of *surzhik* of his Ukrainian friends. Those from a western Ukrainian cultural background had very little *surzhik* (although the westerners' use of Polish words and expressions is considered a *surzhik* of a sort by easterners). One of the Russian-speaking drivers at the School for Ukrainian Studies used Ukrainian 10 percent of the time (for instance, systematically using the Ukrainian *nichoho nema*, as opposed to the Russian *nichego net*). The other driver, however, was using it more than 25 percent of the time: he would switch languages back and forth, more often than not in the same sentence. It is in Donets'k, however, that he witnessed the most remarkable display of *surzhik*, when the grandmother of a school teacher who had invited him for dinner with her friends showed up with her granddaughter. The grandmother lived in a village outside of Donets'k, and her *surzhik* was so intense that Arel could not determine whether she was speaking more in Ukrainian than in Russian!

His informants were often quite unaware of their mixing behavior. During his first visit, in 1990, he was talking to a maintenance employee who worked at the sanatorium where his school was located. His *surzhik* was of the order of only 20 percent Ukrainian, but he seemed convinced that he was speaking Ukrainian, not Russian! In Arel's research visits to two Kiev secondary schools, he found that the pupils in the Ukrainian school were systematically using Russian among themselves, although they claimed in the questionnaire he handed out to them to be using both when asked about their language behavior. And when they were asked why they were speaking Russian among themselves, they answered in Ukrainian!

The development of *surzhik* as an institutionalized speech form tends to subvert the nationalist program, which is one that sharply differentiates the languages in order to give preeminence to the national language. More consistent with the nationalist program are language practices that work toward slowly introducing the national language into new speech domains. Abundant evidence suggests that in Kiev, this linguistic "war of position," as Gramsci might have called it, has been in a stalemate, and therefore Russian hegemony has not as yet been undermined.

Under conditions of linguistic hegemony, speakers of the titular language develop the "accommodation norm," discussed earlier. The accommodation norm for Ukrainian-Russian bilinguals is easy to put into practice. The Ukrainian version of the common greeting "good day," *dobryi den*, differs from Russian. Russians, however, can rarely notice the difference, and if a Russian responds to a Ukrainian by using the Russian inflection, the Ukrainian speaker motivated by the accommodation norm will continue the conversation in Russian, without the Russian speaker ever knowing there was a strategic triggering.[42] Arel observed that most of his informants rely on the accommodation norm. Mykhailo Bilets'kyi, a journalist now in his sixties, is fluent in both Ukrainian and Russian, and he always chooses his languages depending on his interlocutors. His wife is a russophone, and with her he speaks only Russian. With his friends of "Ukrainian orientation," he speaks only Ukrainian, but there were very few of those. Iurii, too, Arel reports, quickly and almost unconsciously switches to the language of his interlocutor. "In the same room," Arel observed, "he can address different people in different languages."

Language switching[43] tends to follow clear rules, usually based on the status of the language, the status of the speaker, and how purely each language is being spoken. Here is the way Arel's chauffeur, Leonid, has deciphered these rules (now I'm quoting from Arel's field notes),:

> Leonid says that he uses Ukrainian in Kiev when people address him in Ukrainian. That does not happen very often, maybe ten minutes, maximum half an hour every day. Normally, it happens with people from the intelligentsia, who speak pure Ukrainian in their daily lives. It is true indeed that the first time Leonid had a conversation with Iurii [who speaks pure Ukrainian, from Leonid's vantage point] . . . he used Ukrainian. At the market, however, despite the presence of all these babushkas from the countryside, he will use Russian. He also told me that when he visits his wife's relatives in Cherkasy, they all use Ukrainian, while he sticks to Russian. It does not bother anybody, he adds. What appears to be important for

[42] Arel learned of this triggering from conversations with informants. In his survey research with Valeri Khmelko, they used this technique as an indicator of whether to begin the interview in Ukrainian or Russian. It turned out to be a valid unobtrusive measure of the language people were most comfortable speaking.

[43] Language switching (in which the speaker shifts from one language to another for at least an entire utterance) is distinct from mixing (as in *surzhik*); in mixing, the boundary separating the languages is eroded.

> Leonid is not the language spoken by his interlocutor, but the background of the interlocutor itself. When a lower-class person addresses him in Ukrainian, he will stick to Russian; but if the Ukrainian is emanating from an upper-class person, upper-class in prestige terms, then he will shift to Ukrainian. There is a linguistic element to it: Leonid was only one of many Ukrainians who told me that they do not mind using or hearing Ukrainian, as long as it is pure [*chistii*]. There is very little respect for *surzhik*.

Iurii, unlike Leonid, wants to build on western Ukraine's high status to alter somewhat the accommodation norm. He told Arel that he thinks that many Ukrainians have an inferiority complex and that this explains why they do not want to speak Ukrainian. Westerners like him do not have this complex and consider it normal to speak Ukrainian in the city. From the start, his linguistic strategy has been the following: if he knows that his interlocutor cannot use Ukrainian well, then he will use Russian "without prejudice." If he knows the person speaks Ukrainian, then he will use Ukrainian. This is one way to challenge the hegemony of Russian as the higher-status language.

Another strategy to challenge Russian language hegemony is that of maintaining bilingual conversations, in which the Ukrainian speaker, after hearing that his or her interlocutor is a Russian-speaker, continues to speak in Ukrainian, even if the Russian-speaker continues speaking Russian. (This strategy can only work—work in the sense of successfully transmitting messages—if each speaker has a high "passive" knowledge of the other's language, or if the languages are close enough that each speaker can figure out what the other is saying.) As an illustration of this communication norm, there was a vibrant public debate on whether or not Ukraine should have close relations with Russia in which one party (Malinkovich) spoke in Russian while the other (Zaiets') spoke in Ukrainian.[44]

Iurii follows the accommodation norm and consequently will rarely, if ever, get into these bilingual conversations. Iurii's wife, Natal'ka, however, does so all the time. Her strategy is basically to use Ukrainian all the time, unless the other person is not from Ukraine. She once told Arel, half-joking, that she was speaking only Ukrainian because she is a nationalist, but one could say that she does it because of her provincialism. She lived in the western town of Brody until the age of thirty and cried when she had to move to Kiev. By her own account, Brody is her world, and she would much rather live there than in Kiev. She obviously understands Russian well and watches both Ukrainian and Russian TV—the choices being so limited, the good programs are often on Russian channels—but her active Russian is not of high standard, and she mixes codes when trying to speak it. In Kiev, Natal'ka became very friendly with her neighbor, Khristina, a young Russian-speaker (it is not clear whether she is ethnically Russian or Ukrainian). In their conversations Khristina speaks Russian, and Natal'ka speaks Ukrainian. Apparently, it was the first time that Khristina had come into daily contact with such "pure" Ukrain-

[44] Vladimir Malinkovich and Ivan Zaiets', "Vladaiet li Dnepr v Volgu?" *Nezavisimost'*, March 26, 1993. The dialogue was taped and the editors of *Nezavisimost'* (a Russian-language paper) kept the original language used by the speakers.

ian. Natal'ka would prefer that Iurii speak Ukrainian to people like Khristina and others in the courtyard. She says Khristina could understand him. (By Natal'ka's account, Khristina did not understand everything at the beginning, since Natal'ka's "pure" Ukrainian in fact sounds heavily Galicianized to central Ukrainians.) For Iurii, however, the problem is not one of understanding. He wants his interlocutor to be able to communicate without any problems. He believes that his tolerance of Russian-speakers may be explained by his Poltava background, where there is a more accommodating view toward Russian than in his wife's home town.

Oleksandra, a Russian-speaking Ukrainian, has begun to find herself engaging in bilingual conversations. She rode with Arel to L'viv, and their driver (from Galicia) spoke only Ukrainian. Oleksandra responded in Ukrainian. When the conversation picked up, however, especially when they began to talk about the army—a topic on which she is well informed—she got impatient with her halting Ukrainian and switched to Russian. She even announced "that it will be easier if I speak Russian." The driver, Serhii, did not mind, but did not accommodate. He continued to use Ukrainian. Her switch to Russian is normal. The big change, and a sign of a successful language revival, is that the Ukrainian interlocutor, like Natal'ka, disregarded the accommodation norm.

Successful "wars of position" on the language front require not only the abandonment of the accommodation norm but the capture of new functional and territorial domains for the national language. In Kiev, there has been an inexorable shift since perestroika. During perestroika there was only an island of Ukrainian-speaking in downtown Kiev, near October Revolution Square (rebaptized Independence Square), in which there was a Hyde Park environment, with Ukrainian the language of debate. Elsewhere, Russian was hegemonic. But with rapid development of an independence movement, new political organizations in Ukraine (Rukh, Memorial, the Language Society, and then smaller parties—such as the Republican and Democratic) all emphasized the national revival and have been using exclusively Ukrainian in their public meetings. Demonstrations where Russian is heard are rare, although that surely happens when the Communists mobilize for Revolution and May Days. President Kuchma, who hardly spoke Ukrainian when he served as prime minister, surely was following this trend when after the 1994 presidential elections he began relying on Ukrainian in all public settings.

While it is still acceptable to speak Russian within ministries at all levels in Kiev, written documents are almost entirely in Ukrainian. As Arel writes:

> When interviewed by the author in the summer of 1993, a number of entrepreneurs all said that they are conducting their correspondence with the state in Ukrainian, since official papers (such as registration and tax forms) are now issued in Ukrainian only. Official acts emanating from the presidential office, the Cabinet of Ministers, or the parliament, such as decrees and laws, are also often published exclusively in Ukrainian, which is contrary to an article of the language law specifying that such documents must, as a rule, be made available in Russian. Documents sent from central organs to regional bodies are, it seems, exclusively in Ukrainian, when originating from parliament or the presidency. . . . When originating from Kiev-based

> ministries towards the regions, the documents are increasingly in Ukrainian. As for documents emanating from regional organs and enterprises, however, they are still written in Russian in eastern and southern Ukraine, but less and less so in central and western Ukraine. The pattern is thus one of the ukrainization of official correspondence between the center and the regions, but within the regions, ukrainization [has established itself] in the center and west only, while Russian persists in the east and south. As for the army, the sole use of Ukrainian in official documents was supposed to be introduced in the fall of 1993, but this policy was slowed down after the dismissal of Defense Minister Kostaintyn Morozov, who was perceived as too "nationalist." Real inroads, then, have been made for Ukrainian as a language of official documentation, but this is not to say that Ukrainian is now being used as the predominant language of oral communications in official organs and enterprises.[45]

In Donets'k, and presumably through much of eastern Ukraine, virtually all commercial signs are in Russian. During Arel's stay in Donets'k, he saw only two store signs—in a children's store and in a music store—in Ukrainian, and these dated from the 1950s. Official buildings and descriptions of paintings in the state museum, however, were in both Ukrainian and Russian. In L'viv the opposite is the case. The only sign Arel observed in Russian—"Pozhar" (fire)—was on an old street-corner fire alarm. In Kiev, and this may be the key to the future, he saw a linguistic tip taking place. Virtually all new official signs avoided Russian, being either only in Ukrainian or in Ukrainian and English. Some places (for example, at a kiosk-restuarant and the Andriivs'kyi Museum) held to pure Russian; but they were the exceptions.

Ukrainization has faced setbacks, however, in the media. For economic reasons, Ukrainian's standing in the newspaper and publishing industry has eroded since independence. With state subsidies diminishing, many Ukrainian-language periodicals and publishing houses are having great difficulties competing in emerging market conditions. The most symbolically significant victim of this economic reversal has been the weekly of the writers' union, *Literaturna Ukraina*, which had almost single-handedly championed the cause of the Ukrainian language in the early perestroika years. From its standard twelve pages, the paper has shrunk to four pages, and at times does not publish at all. It thus no longer affects public debate as forcefully as it once did. In eastern Ukraine, the Ukrainian press barely survives and the great majority of new papers are in Russian. In Kiev, a new Russian-language daily, *Kievskie vedomosti* is about the only Kiev paper that covers all aspects of life. It outsells its Ukrainian-language competitor, *Vechirnii Kyiv*, four to one in terms of circulation. Oleksandra's family, she told Arel, used to subscribe to *Vechirnii Kyiv*, when it was a mouthpiece for glasnost. But they canceled their subscription when it turned nationalist. The decline of the Ukrainian-language press—western Ukraine being, as always, an exception—does not mean, however, that the press from Russia is more widely available. Because of the increases in subscription costs, particularly severe for periodicals from Russia because of the unfavorable exchange rate be-

[45] From Arel, "Language Policies in Independent Ukraine," *Nationalities Papers* 23, no. 3 (1995): 597–622. This was written in May 1994.

tween the Ukrainian koupon [Ukraine's currency through August, 1996] and the Russian ruble, subscriptions to all newspapers have gone down precipitously. The Ukrainian Ministry of Communications in 1996 increased by five to ten times the price for newspapers and journals from the Russian Federation, and subscriptions again plummeted.[46]

In 1996 book stalls were still flooded with more Russian titles than ever, albeit the type of mass-market books one would find in a supermarket in the West. Serious works and scholarly books, which used to be hard to find in Ukrainian, are now harder to find in Russian as well, since distribution networks from Russia have been disrupted and libraries can no longer pay for them.

There is a similar story with film. Since cultural bureaucrats did not deem it necessary to develop an industry for dubbing Russian and foreign films in Ukrainian, and since most local films were actually shot in Russian, this meant that the great majority of films shown on Ukrainian TV have been in Russian, without translation. The same applied to films shown in theaters.[47]

For modern language movements, capturing TV audiences is the game with the deepest play. Unfortunately for the nationalists, they are making little headway in this crucial arena. Ukrainian TV (UT-1) is remarkably boring. The heavy dose of Ukrainian folk dancing and singing cannot capture contemporary audiences. Worse, as Arel's chauffeur pointed out, is the lack of professionalism, even in traditional dances. "They don't show us folklore of a world quality, from a troupe that tours the world all the time, but some ensemble from Transcarpathian Oblast that nobody has ever heard of." It seems that such shows remind him of Ukrainian's low prestige. And they show these political roundtables all the time. "Who needs it?" Leonid asks. "No one watches Parliament anymore. People come home tired, and they want to relax." He normally watched the two Russian channels from Russia (in 1996 only one was available). But Leonid admits that the Russian and Ukrainian news programs have their own points of view—for instance, on events surrounding the Black Sea fleet. When it gets too conflictual, he tries to catch the Ukrainian news, to compare it with the Russian version and make up his mind. But this rarely happens.

Oleksandra, also bilingual, expresses the same point: On Ukrainian TV, she relates, "they are dancing the *hopak* [a traditional Ukrainian dance] all the time. And they keep showing these debates on unintelligible themes." She does not know anyone who watches UT regularly. She watches the Russian channel, Ostankino, and Gravis, a local cable station. She complains that a lot of Galicianisms are used on Ukrainian TV. "Why use a western dialect not understood by the rest of the country?" she asks.

Sasha, a school assistant principal, offered an explanation. The relatively high quality of Ostankino, he hold Arel, is the result of all these decades of centralization, when everything was directed toward Moscow. Moscow got everything: better

[46] Nadezhda Azhgikhina, "Zhurnalisty vne zakona. Russkoiazychnoe informatsionnoe prostranstvo sokrashchaetsia," *Nezavisimaia gazeta*, September 26, 1996.

[47] This paragraph has been adapted from Arel, "Language Policies." Arel reports, in a personal communication, that change is rapid. In 1995–96, except for films from Russia, Ukrainian TV has begun showing an increasing number of foreign films dubbed in Ukrainian.

resources, and the best people. Many emigrated: if you wanted to make a career in the electronic media business, you had to go to Moscow. Incidentally, a lot of TV hosts and journalists from the republics working in Moscow decided to stay in Moscow after the breakup of the USSR, because they did not want to go back to small audiences, having been used to the big time.

Arel personally confirmed the consensus about the quality of Ukrainian public TV.

> I watched Ukrainian TV two Saturday nights in a row in July 1993, and each time it was dreadfully boring. The first time, in Donets'k, during prime time, there was a half-hour report showing [President] Kravchuk making empty-sounding speeches to various people in Vinnytsia, saying stuff such as "We've got to learn how to work. We are a country with great potential." Then they showed Prime Minister Kuchma and his retinue—all men, at least twenty of them—visiting a farm in Kiev oblast. Again, the same insipid speeches, going on and on and for close to half an hour. On prime time TV on a Saturday night! Who the hell would watch that? Pure Soviet-style.

There are signs of change. One of the local commercial channels, ITAR-Plus, functions mostly in Ukrainian. They broadcast CBS News every night without translation and then ITN News with a Ukrainian voice-over, plus their own local UTAR news in Ukrainian whose commentators are much more professional than those from the official Ukrainian channel UT-1. Even better, CNN news is now dubbed in Ukrainian on the cable channel ICTV, and many bilinguals seek access to cable to get this service. Since foreign news is not given much attention on the Russian channels, people may over time feel compelled to watch Ukrainian-language TV, especially the private cable offerings.

Russian-language media domination is clearly under attack. In 1997, a round table of Ukrainian organizations in Kiev made an appeal to the Cabinet that the dissemination of publications and transmissions in the "nonstate language" (meaning Russian) was "posing for national security of the country by its negative consequences a no lesser threat than the propaganda of rape and debauchery."[48]

In everyday life the linguistic war of position is being fought on every street corner. In Kiev in 1990, one hardly ever heard Ukrainian used in the street in normal settings. Three years later, there was clearly an improvement. Sometimes Ukrainian could be heard in shops, at the post office, or on the sidewalks, though not too often. By Arel's rough estimate, Ukrainian may have been used in 1994 about five to ten percent in day-to-day life, up from one percent in 1990. In L'viv, Ukrainian predominates, but Russian can still be heard, perhaps 20 to 25 percent of the time, reflecting the Russian minority of the city. Russian is no longer spoken in public offices, but it is significant that Russians do not fear speaking their language in the streets. (One of Arel's interlocutors, an ethnic Russian living in L'viv, prefers to hide her identity in public places and will use only Ukrainian.) In Donets'k, without ex-

[48] Tamara Logacheva, "Russkii iazyk vytesniaetsia s Ukrainy," *Nezavisimaia gazeta*, May 8, 1997.

aggeration, Ukrainian is never used in public, except when a small band of radical nationalists organize a demonstration.

In the retail trade, Ukrainian is winning. Kiev is obviously the swing city. Traditionally, only Russian was heard in state stores. Even as late as 1990, on those rare occasions when a customer used Ukrainian, the clerk answered in Russian. But by 1993, things were changing. At a bakery, Arel observed a few occasions when the saleswoman would switch to Ukrainian, without any tension or irritation. Although the great majority of customers still prefer to use Russian, the attitude toward Ukrainian seems to have changed: if you want to use Ukrainian, people will no longer look at you askance. In private stores, the customer is definitely king. Arel once made the rounds of computer and electronics shops with Iurii, his friend from western Ukraine. As a rule, Iurii used only Ukrainian and he was served in Ukrainian. "It's business," he observed. Only in the last store, actually an exhibition of imported goods, two young clerks, who did not look too serious, spoke entirely in Russian.

As an experiment in 1993, Arel tried to use exclusively Ukrainian in Kiev cabs. In early July, two drivers on the same day answered in Ukrainian, something that virtually never happened in 1991, weeks before independence. Arel remembers being astonished to hear a cab driver shout in Ukrainian "Pochekai, pochekai" ("Wait, wait") after he had motioned that he needed a ride. His first Ukrainian-speaking car driver said he speaks only Ukrainian with his father, a native of a small town from Kiev oblast. He himself went to Ukrainian school, but in fact Ukrainian was only used for Ukrainian language and literature; all the other subjects were in Russian! His wife speaks only Russian at home, although she is from Kiev oblast. He tries to speak Ukrainian with his daughter and wants to have her enrolled in a Ukrainian school. Considering that 90 percent of first-graders in Kiev were in Ukrainian classes in the fall of 1993, he probably did.

The battle for Ukrainian dominance in Kiev is thus in its early stages. As I. Dem'ianchuk has written, "Russophone Ukrainians are not a uniform mass. The majority consider, like [President] Kuchma, that their poor knowledge of the mother tongue is their misfortune. They do not want, when they become conscious of it, for Ukrainian to die in their generation. They feel they only need time, and they themselves and their children will begin to speak Ukrainian."[49] Thus there are self-conscious attempts by Ukrainians, at least in Kiev where a tip seems possible, to establish Ukrainian in domains where it had been marginalized. But because media are now subject to larger market forces, these attempts may be submerged by the demographic and (relative) economic power of Russian. The battle lines are drawn, however, and the war of position continues.

Intergenerational Shift in the Baltics

Unlike Ukraine, Estonia and Latvia are not linguistic environments that were conducive to code-mixing, code-shifting, and bilingual conversations. To be sure,

[49] I. Dem'ianchuk, "Buty chy ne buty ukrains'kii movi oznachaie buty chy ne buty ukrains'kii derzhavi," *Narodna hazeta* (in Ukrainian), October 1994.

Russian vocabulary infused both Latvian and Estonian in realms of cursing (where Russian may set the world standard!) and sport. In mixed environments, bilinguals will keep conversations going in both Russian and the titular language if that is conducive to efficient communication. And there is a small realm of code-mixing by Russians to demonstrate minimal solidarity with Estonians. For example, American consul Deborah Klepp reported that there were occasions when Russian petitioners in her office began their conversations in Estonian with "Kas tohib vene keeles?" ("May I speak in Russian?"). Here the petitioners want to appear as loyal residents and potential Estonian citizens. I have often heard the greeting in Narva *zdravstvuite, tere* ("hello" in Russian, "hello" in Estonian). This does not play the same sociolinguistic role as did the *dobryi den* greeting in Ukraine, because Russians who use this greeting are not prepared to continue the conversation in Estonian if their interlocutor answers *tere*. Yet it does signal a recognition of Estonian as the state language. Such linguistic practices are rare. It would be foolhardy to suggest (as I did with Ukrainian) that such practices could erode the boundaries separating the Baltic languages from Russian.

Nonetheless there are clear signals of early stages of assimilation—defined in Chapter 1 as "the process of adoption of the . . . cultural practices of dominant society"—of Russian-speakers into Estonian and Latvian, though this discussion will focus mainly on Estonia. First, there is an environment within the Russian-speaking community of acquiescence, not rejection. Second, the adult generation is making a good faith effort to reach government-set standards of linguistic achievement, both sides knowing that these standards will of necessity be low. Third, the young generation, still in school, has some, albeit limited, opportunity to develop fluency in Estonian. Many Russians in this generation, usually encouraged by their parents, are seeking such fluency. I predict that in the next generation a significant majority of Russian residents in Estonia will be as fluent in Estonian as Estonian adults are in Russian today.

Still, Estonian authorities think the Soviet flag flew too long on the roof of the Narva City Council building after Estonia's declaration of sovereignty; and Lenin's statue stood too long in Lenin (now Pushkin) Square after the collapse of socialism. These signs of Narva's defiance were not so powerful in the linguistic realm. The following incident occurred within the first few years of independence:

> On February 26, 1993, Mart Rannut, General Director of the State Department of Language of the Estonian Republic, dispatched a "Declaration of Invitation" to Vladimir Chuikin, Chairman of the Narva City Soviet, to appear before an administrative tribunal because, the letter stated, he "continually violated the demands . . . of the Law on Language." The letter was written in Estonian, a language Chuikin does not read, but it included an informal translation into Russian, prepared by Rannut who, like most Estonian officials, speaks fluent Russian. Rannut alleges in the letter that Chuikin had written official communications to a number of Estonians and Russians without using the official language of the state, and that he is liable based on a provision of the law on the Administrative Violation of the Law. When Mr. Chuikin showed me the letter, he laughed and called it nonsense. Why should

> he, a native Russian-speaker, not be able to communicate with others who are also fluent Russian-speakers, and even to monolingual Russians, in Russian?[50]

But this defiance was never public, and it quickly and quietly began to fade, turning into enthusiastic compliance, with Narva officials begging Tallinn for more money to administer their own language program. In my return visit to that same office in September 1993, still in the Chuikin era, I noticed that all the door signs were in Estonian, reflecting acquiescence to the new era. Later that fall, I interviewed the secretary to the mayor. She sat in an anteroom between the mayor's office and the prime minister's representative to Narva, Indrek Tarand, who was a member of the nationalist Isamaa coalition. I asked her how the mayor, who had served through much of the late communist era, and Tarand were getting along. She answered: "The mayor has changed. Years ago if someone came in talking Estonian he would look lost, wondering why. Now if this happens, he asks me to come in to translate, and treats it all very normally. In fact, the normality of using Estonian in the offices has happened quite quickly." In the post-Chuikin era, with the new mayor (as demanded by the election law) a fluent Estonian speaker, city council meetings continue to be held in Russian. But at the beginning of the meetings I attended, council members by voice vote agreed to a temporary suspension of the law requiring discussions to take place in Estonian. This was done to accommodate the members of council, not to defy the state. From the viewpoint of the Narva government—which was the slowest to accept the reality of Estonian rule—the nationalizing language program was a legitimate one.

An atmosphere of acquiescence pervaded Narva. In my fall 1993 lessons at the Narva Language Center, I was impressed by the furnishings and the technology but not by how empty those classrooms were for much of the day. But on my return in March 1994, there were hardly any open rooms, and the computer lab had queues of students. In the fall, I had volunteered to teach a small English class at the Center; by the spring, the director could not afford the space, as all rooms were filled with Estonian classes. There was a sign on the bulletin board in March to the effect that there would be no more places or class sign-ups until September 1994. In the course I took in the spring, with the unemployed workers, there were hardly any absentees throughout the course, and the students dressed as if they were going to jobs in high government offices. Learning Estonian represented for them the future. Perhaps the best sign of the social acceptability of learning Estonian was on the bus I took one morning into Narva from the village of Narva-Jõesuu. Two women with books open for all to see were studying Estonian.

Taking language examinations is another public display of acquiescence. In Estonia, in a report from the Ministry of Culture and Education, 56,000 people had passed some sort of language exam from 1991 through the end of 1993. From 1989 through mid-1993, about 43,000 had taken the citizenship exam, with about 20 percent reaching the level required for citizenship. *Estoniia* reported on one elderly

[50] David D. Laitin, "Language Planning in the Former Soviet Union: The Case of Estonia," *International Journal of the Sociology of Language* 118 (1996): 43.

lady, who on finishing the test, said, "Soon I will be an Estonian citizen and they will be able to bury me in the Tallinn cemetery." While there were no legal constraints about who could be buried in Tallinn, this quotation gives a flavor of a community that sees facility in Estonian as something that opens doors (or graves).[51]

The working-age population in the 1990s did not pretend that it would achieve the impossible and develop fluency in Estonian. My field notes are filled with examples of adults who nonetheless pushed themselves to their limits. Natal'ia, a Narva schoolteacher born in the old Russian city of Pskov, spouted Russian chauvinistic ideology to me during our first interview. In a later conversation, she surprised me when she said that she had taken two courses at the Narva Language Center and passed the citizenship exam. While she is committed to perfecting her English, she wants to speak enough Estonian to get full legal rights. Another Natal'ia, this one an activities coordinator in a Russian-language school in Tallinn, although eligible for citizenship through her husband, who is a citizen via his Estonian mother (yet hardly speaks any Estonian), nonetheless wanted to get *her* citizenship the proper way, and prepared six months for the language exam. In my language class with the unemployed workers, one day a policeman walked into the class with a message for the teacher. When he left, she smiled and told the class (in Russian!) that the guard was a former student, who passed his exam, and now could transact necessary business in Estonian. But this level was hardly close to fluency. In my earlier class in fall 1993, I noticed that there was no emphasis on diction. We did no phonetics, even though adult Russian-speakers cannot easily reproduce the multitudinous diphthongs in Estonian. The plan was clear: the adults would never sound like Estonians, or develop any fluency in that language. The goal was to make them capable of performing specific functions, and to break down the (Russian) societal consensus that speaking Estonian was unnecessary.

These are not considered adequate goals for the next generation. For them, greater fluency is expected. I interviewed Tat'iana, a teacher in a Russian school in Narva who passed the Estonian exam at the professional level and would be eligible for higher pay. I joked to her, "Now you can forget the language . . ." She responded, "No, I have to help tutor my daughter, who must also learn it." Again and again, I interviewed adults who saw little hope in acquiring Estonian, but put great stock in their children's acquisition of it. Pavel Grigor'ev's mother thought it absurd when I asked her whether she spoke any Estonian. Pavel's wife, however, studied day and night for six months to take (and pass) the citizenship exam. And Pavel's daughter is fluent in Estonian and is training to become a teacher of Estonian in Russian schools. I mentioned earlier about the baccalaureate students in Narva who made special studies of Estonian in order to get admission into Tartu University rather than take advantage of private arrangements in St. Petersburg. The Russian student who had made most progress in Estonian (through living with a farm family and finding an Estonian girl friend) proudly reported to me that his younger brother speaks Estonian even better than he does.

[51] *Estoniia*, February 17, 1994; *Estoniia*, October 20, 1993.

To be sure, many adults from Narva complain that their children have no access to Estonian, and they never hear it spoken. Indeed there will be large numbers left out during this generation's linguistic shift (toward Russian-Estonian bilingualism). But in significant numbers, even in the most Russian of all towns in Estonia, an intergenerational shift is observable.

In Latvia, the same trend of intergenerational shift is apparent as well. Pettai interviewed Sergei, a passport Estonian but a Russian-speaker, who considers himself a "Baltic Russian [who has] lost [his] nationality." Although he speaks some Estonian, Russian is his primary language. He is completely opposed to the latvianization of Riga, and he is bitter about how the bureaucracy is promoting Latvian. Yet his children, he reports, speak Latvian fluently. And the macro figures show that this is not an isolated case. According to the *Baltic Independent*, the Latvian Parliamentary Commission on Education announced that "students of Russian descent opting to attend Latvian schools has increased dramatically, leading to a figure of 58 percent taking the Latvian option." This has increased by 8 percent in one year alone. Janine Kusnere, an official at the commission, said that higher education is now conducted only in Latvian, and the language requirement for citizenship is the major imperative for linguistic assimilation. The big change, she said, is in the swing of children of mixed marriages, who now choose Latvian. To get into these schools, children must show a working knowledge of Latvian. But she said that some parents were prepared to allow their children to repeat a grade so that they could attend a Latvian school.[52]

Legal compliance for the present generation; greater fluency for the next. This is the trend in regard to language assimilation for Russian-speakers in Estonia and Latvia.

Kazakhstan—The Absurdity of Assimilation

In Soviet times, and in nearly all non-Russian republics, Russians thought the very idea of learning the titular languages absurd. This remains the popular conception today in Kazakhstan. Consider Olzhas, who is Kazakh, and a ninth-grade student in a Russian school. He talks to his grandmother in a mix of Russian and Kazakh, though mostly Russian. She answers in pure Kazakh. In almost no other interactions (including those with Dave, whose Kazakh he often said, in Russian, was admirable) did he use Kazakh. Most of his friends are Russians, he said, for Kazakhs are mean and spoiled, they are "not normal." Dave asked Olzhas if they are taught Kazakh at school. He laughed at the question and said, "We are required to go to those Kazakh classes . . . but who needs it? The students hate it, and nothing useful can ever come out of it." When Dave asked why that was so, he did not know what to say: the reasons seemed too obvious to him even to articulate. When she insisted on knowing the specific reasons, he pondered and said, "Well, it is everything. The teacher doesn't know what she is doing. She just asks us to translate those boring texts. The texts we read in Kazakh are of no interest to anyone. Everyone looks in the dictionary and mechanically translates. If you don't do those stupid

[52] "Russians opting for Latvian education," *Baltic Independent*, December 9, 1994.

translations, you get a 2 [a D] . . . I don't understand why Russians need to learn Kazakh," he continued. "Everyone knows Russian, why should they be forced to learn it? They are not learning it anyway. Who needs such village handicraft [*kustarnoe proizvodstvo*] at this juncture?"

Vera Nikolaevna works at the Institute of Railroad Transport as an accountant. At the Institute, they have a young Kazakh woman who teaches Kazakh to the workers. The Kazakhs who work at the Institute are too embarrassed to attend the course, thinking that they should be able to learn it spontaneously. The teacher hardly teaches, Vera told Dave; she is simply interested in fulfilling her "hours." She showed Dave her textbooks, and wondered how anyone could learn the language with such (paltry) materials.

Bad conditions; bad materials; bad teachers. But even more: active defiance by members of the Russian-speaking community against even gestures toward establishing Kazakh. Consider Ekaterina Ivanovna, who has been living with her daughter in Almaty for the last ten years. Before that she had lived in Astrakhan (a province in Russia near the Caspian Sea, with a large number of Kazakhs), which to her is "of course" Russia. She was very angry when Komsomol'skaia Street, where they live, was renamed Tole bi Koshesi. She could not say that name properly, while her daughter had at least learned that much. Ekaterina spent a lot of time watching TV, which began to have a heavier dose of Kazakh-language programs. The TV program listing in the newspaper has a section "Almaty station" with programs on Kazakh language, dombira music, and Kazakh culture. She usually took pen in hand and used it to strike off all the Kazakh programs in her weekly TV program guide.

Given the low prestige of the language, the minimal advantages of learning it, and the widespread subversion of Kazakh linguistic nationalism by titulars, Russian-speakers in Kazakhstan haven't really changed their views from the Soviet era, and still consider it absurd for any Russian to go out of his or her way to learn the titular language of Kazakhstan.

THE goal of this chapter was to put some flesh onto the skeletal tipping game. Once this is done, the neat categories—expected economic returns, in-group and out-group status—that were theoretically enumerated become a little messy. Calculations such as the threat of titulars abandoning Russian, and the fear that rising language standards would make certification more difficult in the future, were also part of the utility function "TT," the payoff for learning the titular language. Yet the overall assumption behind the game is largely confirmed. Despite the double cataclysm faced by Russian-speakers in the republics of the former Soviet Union, and despite the anger, fear, and dread that many of them felt, there was clearly an assimilationist calculus in their heads. Our informants were thinking about a variety of payoffs and comparing those payoffs with the costs of assimilating.

We have seen that the assimilationist logic has quite different consequences in Ukraine (where there is a "war of position" in the very heart of the country), in the Baltics (where formal compliance in the present generation is coupled with investments in intergenerational assimilation), and in Kazakhstan (where language assimilation remains an absurdity for Russians). But the assimilationist calculus, for Russian-speakers, was yet more complex, because there were other alternatives to be considered. They could emigrate back to their putative homeland; they could mobilize for greater minority rights within their republics of residence; or they could mobilize for more dangerous confrontations, of the sort we have observed in Transdniester and Nagorno-Karabakh. In the chapter that follows, relying still on ethnographic data, I explore how our informants calculated the value of those alternative options.

6

If Not Assimilation, Then What?

Assimilation is a strategy that nontitulars resident in a nationalizing state must consider. But nontitulars do not merely sit around and ask themselves whether or not to assimilate. There are a range of other strategies that can be pursued instead of, or simultaneously with, assimilation. First, they can seek merely to make the most minimal concessions to the national culture consistent with the attainment of citizenship. While this strategy is fully possible in Kazakhstan and Ukraine, the citizenship laws of Estonia and Latvia demand cultural concessions. Second, in another move that serves the purposes of the nationalizing elites, nontitulars can also return to their putative homelands. Facilitating this legally, the Russian Federation invited all former citizens of the USSR to take Russian citizenship and to resettle, if they wished, in Russia. Third, they can organize politically to seek recognition as an autonomous group within their state. Fourth, they can seek to exploit ethnic tensions through the instigation of violent confrontations. These strategies (deviating somewhat from Hirschman's formulation here) can be called, "loyalty," "exit," "voice," and "arms."[1] Finally, there is a move that doesn't fit well into the Hirschman framework, that of redefining Russian identity in a way that changes the ethnic calculus in the republic—in the cases at hand, in the invention of a "Russian-speaking protonationality." This chapter offers an ethnographic accounting of these five options.

Loyalty (Through Passive Integration and Citizenship)

Linguistic assimilation is not the only integrating process taking place in the post-Soviet republics. Russians are becoming more like titulars in other ways as well. This nonlinguistic integration process, especially when coupled with citizenship, is yielding a new form of national identity that blurs the divide between titulars and nontitulars, to the chagrin of the "purist" nationalizing elites.

[1] Albert Hirschman, *Exit, Voice, and Loyalty* (Cambridge: Harvard University Press, 1970).

Despite the image of "civilizational divides," there is abundant evidence that the Russians in the titular republics are taking on cultural characteristics once thought to be distinctive of the titulars. Young Russians in Latvia have started wearing the silver braided ring that Latvians wear as a national symbol. Russians in Kazakhstan are cooking more with rice and less with potatoes. In all the republics some Russians are making conspicuous efforts to show that they are different from the Russians in Russia. One informant in Almaty told Dave, "We are more rural, more family-oriented, more mixed in family, than Russians in Russia." In Ukraine, one of Arel's informants went out of his way (at least when he thought Ukrainian nationalists were around) to watch (unbearably boring) Ukrainian TV, and showed a special interest in Ukrainian songs, as a form of overcompensating for his Russianness. He may have been just acting to earn tolerance from the nationalists; but to the generation that follows, such activities can come to be seen as normal. In such a way, culture shifts.

In my field work in Estonia, I often came across the language of unbridgeable cultures—Russian and Estonian. I cited in Chapter 1 the vivid description by my collaborator, Marika Kirch, of "the civilizational border" that divides her homeland from Russia. In private conversations, Kirch elaborated on this comment. She told me that you can always tell a Russian household in Estonia because of the use of blue paint on the balcony. Estonians use only green or yellow. Russians, she observes, enjoy concentrated housing; Estonians yearn for a separated house. And Russian voices within housing complexes, she noted, are decibels louder than those of their Estonian neighbors. The leading Estonian pollster, Andrus Saar, in a private conversation, picked up on these subtle differences. Russians, he observed, do not understand "the Estonian sense of reserve, privacy, keeping one's personal distance. Estonians simply withdraw when they are in a group of Russians." From the Russian side, a mirror discourse is often heard. Nina Sepp, who is linguistically assimilated, holds that the Orthodox tradition lies deep, and thus she has "confidence in the unbreakability of the Russian soul, that can withstand the loss of religion and change in language."

Despite this discourse of difference, nonlinguistic assimilation by Russians into an Estonian world has been significant. I observed that the Russians in Narva interacted in public places far more like Estonians than like Russians in Moscow—they were quieter and they drank less beer and alcohol in public. Also, as data collected by Tuisk and others, using an "Identity Structure Analysis" shows, Russians in Estonia feel themselves closer in basic values to Estonians than to Russians in Russia. This experiment asks subjects to evaluate a range of items, and then to guess how the typical "Estonian," the typical "Russian in Russia," and the typical "Russian in Estonia" would evaluate the same item. The answers of Russian-Estonians about themselves were consistently closer to their guesses about "Estonians" than their guesses about "Russians in Russia."[2] In the data collected by Aksel Kirch, Marika

[2] Tarmo Tuisk, "Identity Structure Analysis in Estonia—An Interplay of National Allegiance or Ethnic Hostilities," in Marika Kirch, ed., *Changing Identities in Estonia: Sociological Facts and Commentaries* (Tallinn: Estonian Science Foundation, 1994).

Kirch, and Tarmo Tuisk on such items as orientation toward work, the longer the Russian-speakers were in Estonia, the more their answers are like those given by Estonians, and the further away from those given by recent immigrants from Russia.[3] And despite Marika Kirch's image of the two castles, and her observations about enduring cultural differences, she revealed to me in her home town of Pärnu that just by watching young couples walking, or mothers walking their children, she could not tell (without listening) whether they were Russian or Estonian. The (nonlinguistic) cultural divide separating Russians and Estonians is eroding perhaps faster than Kirch's sociological categories.

The slow cultural shift by Russians has been accompanied by a desire to become citizens of their republic of residence. While large numbers have taken Russian citizenship, since it is free for the asking, many Russians aspire to become citizens of the republic in which they were born, or in which they have spent a significant number of their most productive years. In Latvia, Pettai has recorded cases where informants have purchased language certificates, enabling them to get their citizenship without learning the language. This can be interpreted as defiance of the government in order to become a legal member of the state. In Estonia, in a 1992 survey, 60 percent of Russian respondents put positive value on Estonian citizenship.[4] Unlike Joseph K., Russians in the Baltics are pursuing a meaningful goal; but like him, they seem to be walking through bureaucratic mazes in order to get nowhere.

In Ukraine, especially in the center and east, there is among Russians a strong desire to become part of a reconstituted union, which would include Russia, Ukraine, and perhaps other former Soviet republics. Yet for most Russians in Ukraine, passively accepting Ukrainian citizenship and adapting to the realities of Ukrainian independence is the prudent course of action, despite the vitriolic xenophobia of the more extreme nationalists.

Even in Kazakhstan, Russians have some sense of membership in a Kazakhstani state. The term "Kazakhstani" is significant. Unlike "Kazakh" it refers to the political unit and not the ethnic/national group that claims a special right to rule over that unit. Volodia and Lida are clearly, in this sense, Kazakhstanis. When Dave asked them for the first time (in late November 1993) what citizenship they will choose or have already chosen, Volodia responded, "Where's the question of choosing," implying that they are unquestionable natives (*korennyie*) of Kazakhstan. The entire family, Volodia and Lida told her, immediately opted for Kazakhstani citizenship. They continued to maintain that "so far there is no problem. If some sort of nationalism breaks out in the distant future, Russia will accept all the ethnic Russians in the 'near abroad.' We aren't concerned, we feel well rooted in Kazakhstan." Somewhat later, in January 1994, Dave asked them how they felt on the citizenship issue. Volodia, having just heard that President Nazarbaev had ruled out dual citizenship as an option, said that had things been "normal" they wouldn't need dual citizenship. "But ours is not a normal system, and there is a lot of justification for

[3] Aksel Kirch, Marika Kirch, and Tarmo Tuisk, "Russians in the Baltic States: To Be or Not to Be," *Journal of Baltic Studies* 24, no. 2 (1993): 177.

[4] Ibid., p. 182.

dual citizenship in our absurd circumstances. I know that no 'normal' country has such legal provisions." Then Lida said, "For the time being of course we have chosen Kazakhstani citizenship." (Indeed I saw their passports in December 1995, and they had "citizens of Kazakhstan" stamped on the inside cover of their red passports, over the printed USSR insignia. That stamp was free, but it costs 1,000 tengi [64t = U.S. $1] to get a new Kazakhstani passport, and they did not need to spend this money.) Lida continued, "We still have time to rethink until [March] 1995 [the supposed deadline, since extended, for unencumbered Russian citizenship]. Of course all our ties, friends, relatives, are here. Thank God, the Kazakhs that we know and work with are more or less educated and cultured people, and they don't make us uncomfortable." Volodia interjected, "There are 'fools' all around, and enough at the top. I hope they don't get more numerous over there." The editor of *Kazakhstanskaiia pravda*, who came to Kazakhstan in 1954, from Ukraine, has a similar orientation. He considers himself a "Kazakhstani," a person who is a citizen of Kazakhstan, irrespective of national identity.

Noah Webster, through his dictionary project, sought to construct an "American" identity that would be different from "English."[5] To a certain extent, many Russians in the near abroad would be pleased to see a similar construction of national identities based somewhat on language but more on territory and common approaches to life. In these ways, significant assimilation is already taking place. These identities are sometimes referred to as "civic," but they have, as I've tried to show, a cultural element in them, and many Russians have assimilated along these lines. Along with this assimilation, there is willingness to commit to (even purchase!) citizenship. This option—with only minimal (if any) linguistic assimilation, still remains open. In a sense, it could be called (in a passive sense) "loyalty."

Exit

For most Russians, in three of our four republics (Estonia, Latvia, and Ukraine) emigration to Russia was not, in the aftermath of the double cataclysm, a feasible option. In Kazakhstan the double cataclysm combined with trends going back to the 1960s make exit seem the only feasible option. The reasons for this have little to do with degrees of unhappiness of the Russians, or the degrees to which Russians are welcomed by the titular elites, or the relative cost of emigration, or the economic conditions faced by Russians in their republics of residence. Our field data do not provide a clear answer to explain the vastly different orientation in Kazakhstan. There is a clear perception, discussed in Chapter 4, that while things are fine today, when Russians are no longer necessary to administer the economy, they will be "history." Another plausible inference from our data is that Russians cannot abide the status reversal of being ruled by a nationality group they had always considered subservient. And once a critical mass of Russians living in Kazakhstan packs its suitcases, there will be an emigration cascade.

[5] Brian Weinstein, "Language Strategists," *World Politics* 31, no. 3 (1979): 345–64.

Russians in all four republics manifest a thoroughly ambivalent reaction to Russia and Russians living in Russia. On the one hand, Russian informants resident in all four republics, but especially in Estonia and Ukraine, told us on many occasions that Russia was "chaotic" and Russians from Russia were "foreign" to them. Nina Sepp, the rector of the Narva Teachers Training College, who is a deeply religious Orthodox Russian, and who recruited many faculty for her school from St. Petersburg, felt she knew why there was so little emigration to Russia from Estonia. "Fear of chaos, or disorder," she told me in September 1993, "is far greater than the fear of loss of identity or dignity, that they face in Estonia." In the wake of Yeltsin's assault on the White House in October 1993, *Severnoe poberezh'e* (October 6) did man-on-the-street interviews in Narva. Vladimir, a taxi driver, responded diffidently: "I don't think that these events will harm us; we live in a foreign country, and we have sufficient worries of our own." In a conversation in the home at which I lived, Andreu Grigor'ev, eldest son of Pavel, mentioned to me that in his trips to Russia he learned that the "Russians hate us Russians from Estonia because we live so well, and that our thinking has changed. We think much more like people from the West, and they see us as different." He couldn't really give an example of this, however hard I pushed him, but he was sure that this was the case. Pettai talked similarly with Svetlana Kustavus, a Russian from Tver', who married a russianized Estonian and came to Tallinn on work assignment in the mid-1950s. By now, she says, she has few ties with Russia "and can't stand it when she visits." Natasha Bobrov, sixteen, from the Haabneeme kolkhoz, learned Estonian in kindergarten, since there was no Russian kindergarten in Haabneeme, and then later commuted to Russian-language schools to finish her education. She aspires to enroll at Tartu University, much to the chagrin of her friends. She told Pettai that she has "visited Russia only a few times and found it very different and unfamiliar." Marika Lugonova from Narva told me that her mother is now living alone (her father is working in the Tallinn electrical station), but would never think of returning to Russia, since she sees herself as being a Russian "from" Estonia. I received a similar answer from Volodia, the Russian-born husband of the secretary to Narva's mayor, whose father is Estonian and mother Russian. Volodia expected shortly to be laid off from his job at the textile factory. I inquired rather intensively about whether he planned to look for work outside Narva. He said that he would never think of looking in Russia, nor does anyone he talks with at work. "It is a mess there," he said, "and life in Estonia is much better." Leonid Guzhvin gave Pettai an answer in the same terms: "They're even more messed up there than we are."

Arel heard a similar refrain from Russians in Ukraine. Oleksandra is a left-bank Ukrainian, but with deep Russian roots; she is descended on her father's side, some ten generations ago, from a Russian serf named Ugarov who escaped to Ukraine. When she is in Russia, she no longer thinks that she is home. When there was a union, the whole union, she repeated the popular refrain, was her address. But it is absolutely clear to her that those times are over and that her address is now Ukraine. Arel asked her whether she feels closer to people who speak Russian than to ukrainophones, when she visits Galicia. The former is definitely the case. But if she were to find herself in Moscow with west Ukrainians, then she would feel closer to west Ukrainians, no matter what. Trying to make sense of this, a young scholar told Arel confidently that what unites Ukrainians, from east and west, is their mentality (*mental'nyi kharakter*). Oleksandra agreed with that point, although she was not able to define the features of this mentality. At her institute, they actually had a discussion on the topic. "Is it patriotism, the love of the land? You can't explain it, but to understand it intuitively," she adds, "you have to live here." She was sure that all who live in Ukraine distinguish themselves from the people who live in Russia, and look at things differently: "You can always distinguish a Ukrainian from a Russian. Even the Russians from Ukraine, at least those who have lived all their lives in Ukraine, distinguish themselves from the Russians 'over there.' " In Snezhanna's eyes, it has more a territorial than an ethnic connotation. This young Ukrainian, who could trace her origins back ten generations to a Russian serf who escaped and settled in the village in which she was born, is sick of these divisions between national minorities, and she does not like the word *natsiia* (nation).

The ethnic Russians from Kiev whom Arel knew best, Iaroslav and Lida, felt similarly. Despite his longing for Russia, Iaroslav never thought of moving there, since it is "simply not an option." Indeed, his entire family is in Russia but he has not been back to Samara (the town of his birth) in three or four years. If he had a nice job offer, with good conditions, perhaps he would consider it. But he does not think about it and says that he likes Kiev and is well settled. Considering her attachment to Ukraine, it is unclear whether Lida would agree to leave. Lida has no attraction to Russia, but she used to identify solely with the Soviet Union: "We lived in the Soviet Union. We did not feel that we lived in Ukraine. As in the popular Soviet song, my address was the Soviet Union." After the collapse of the Soviet Union, she did not transfer her sympathies to Russia. She believes, however, that Ukraine must maintain close economic links with Russia: "It is stupid to believe that Ukraine can live without an economic union with Russia." Arel asked her once how she would define herself, irrespective of her official passport nationality. She answered: "Ukrainian."

Arel's ever-complex friend Leonid has also lost his psychological attachment to Russia. He does not think Ukraine will survive, not because he is bothered by any "nationalizing" trend, but because any state must care for its people. There is no such care, he said, "we live like cattle." He therefore, as I indicated earlier, would happily vote for reunification with Russia. His longing, however, appears to be less, if at all, for a greater Slavic cultural-political world, than for a world (the Soviet Union) where things used to be more orderly, when "everything used to be linked." A realist, he believes that the USSR will probably not be resurrected, since it is not in the interests of those in power to do so. And for all his conviction that Ukraine should rejoin Russia, he cares little about what is going on in Russia. When Arel asked him about his opinion on the December 1995 parliamentary elections in Russia, he said he did not follow it and is mostly interested about what is happening in Ukraine! This feeling was not unique to Leonid. I took a taxi ride in Kiev on the day of those (exciting, to our research team) elections. I asked the driver, a russophone, if he had heard any early election returns. He responded (I think, making a point of his regard for Russia rather than his knowledge of current affairs) that he knew nothing about any election.

If on the one hand, our informants seemed to go out of their way to point to the chaos and foreignness of Russia, it should be remembered that excluded from our sample of respondents were those Russians who indeed did pack their suitcases and return. From surveys conducted with these populations, and consistent with the intergenerational tipping model, the plurality of respondents to these surveys reported that their principal motivation had to do with education and job opportunities for their children, with a heavy emphasis on the language demands that would be made upon them.[6]

Even the Russians who remained in the republics were not one-sidedly averse to Russia. Many referred to Russia as their "historic homeland" and center of their culture. The notion of Russia as "homeland" (*rodina*) reoccurs in everyday talk. Concerning the "cataclysm" that took place in October 1993 in Moscow, Narva politician, N. Kulikov, wrote in the local paper *Narvskaia gazeta* (October 5, 1993), "Russia—my historical homeland although I wasn't born there and have never lived there. But my father . . . I have a brother, sister, aunt, uncle there. . . . My soul hurts for them." More prosaically, in an overheard conversation in Riga, on problems of passport and money, a bitter young man said (and referring here to Ukraine), "You can't even travel anywhere. You can't even go to your homeland."

Because Russian television is still generally available, Russians in the near abroad often express great interest in Russian public affairs. During the tragic events of October 1993, word spread about the first killings in Moscow after the Yeltsin/White House confrontation. While Pavel Grigor'ev was harvesting apples at his dacha, one of his friends passed by his house with just a phrase telling him about the deaths. This was very much a sense of talking about their "local" news, and not of some foreign country. Roma, his youngest son, then in the sixth grade, reported the next day that most of the kids in his class supported Aleksandr Rutskoi, Yeltsin's vice-president and enemy, because he was a war hero. This was the first time I heard him discuss anything political at home, and certainly never anything about events taking place in Tallinn.

And so, despite their self-professed insouciance toward Russian politics, many Russian-speakers we visited were intensely interested. On New Year's eve of 1994, Dave was invited to Volodia and Lida's place to celebrate. Everyone was listening to Nazarbaev's address, but not that attentively. But at 3 A.M. (midnight in Moscow), they were very eager to know what Yeltsin had to say. The children were hushed, and the volume was turned up. On the eve of elections in Russia, Volodia and his colleague Boris were well abreast with what was going on and mentioned that they supported the Iabloko, Iavlinskii's party. But after elections were declared in Kazakhstan, Dave asked them if they were going to vote. Both Volodia and Lida said "of course." But they didn't know who the candidates were. Before the December 1995 elections in Russia, Dave and I were dining with Liudmila, the owner of the apartment where Dave was living. She had been calling up her friends and relatives in Russia advocating that they vote for the Communist candidate,

[6] E. I. Filippova, "Novaia russkaia diaspora," in M. Iu. Martynova, ed., *Novye slavianskie diaspory* (Moscow: RAN, 1996), p. 65.

Ziuganov. Obviously she was more engaged in Russian politics than in Kazakh public affairs.

Our Russian-speaking informants were also broadly engaged in Russian culture in its multifarious forms. For Olga Guzhvin from Estonia, it was the annual singing jamborees that took place on the shores of the Volga River. For Natal'ia Berezhkova, a teacher in Tallinn, it was the holiday celebrating the victory over the fascists, and waving flags on May 9th, with kids standing on guard at the Eternal Flame in downtown Tallinn. Also, she reminisced about the artistic and historical displays in the Lenin Room in her high school (as in all Soviet high schools). For Lydiia Kuzminitzna, from Narva, who is an artist, it is the "high" culture, such as Dostoyevsky and Tolstoy, that is quintessentially Russian. She criticized Estonians who speak Russian for not treasuring the ability to partake in this world-class artistic culture. For Dmytro Mishchenko from Crimea, Russia is also defined by its great literature. He wrote in *Osvita*: "We, Russian people, educated by the culture of Pushkin and Lermontov, are reduced [*tolkaiut s*] to the village culture of Ukraine."[7] For Lena, a Russian woman Pettai met while visiting a Latvian family, it is sports. She finds the Latvian Olympic team "pathetic," and identified only with the Russian team.

"Russia," it needs to be recalled, for most respondents implies the Imperial or Soviet boundaries. And this represents a special culture. Russians in the union republics felt like Ibn-Khaldûn, the fourteenth-century sociologist from Tunisia, who could travel through half the world speaking only Arabic. The Russian language and Soviet symbology served similar purposes. Pavel Grigor'ev explained that traveling from Samarkand to Tallinn using one language and one currency had given him a sense of mastery. Zheniia, aged sixty-one, is committed to staying in Latvia but says she misses "Russian culture," especially through TV. But Pettai's field notes say that she traveled extensively through Russia, for example to the Caucasus, and to Central Asia. She clearly thinks of "Russia" as having Soviet boundaries, and it is that expanse that is missed.

Thus we see two contradictory lines of thinking: Russia as "foreign" and Russia as "homeland." Sometimes the ambivalence comes out in a single person. In Almaty, Evgenii (Zheniia) Zhovtis is vice-president of the Independent Trade Union Center of the Republic of Kazakhstan. (In Soviet times, he was classified as a Jew by nationality.) In an interview with Dave, he insisted, "I have no ties with Russia—Russia is an alien country for me [*Rossiia mne chuzhaia*]." Yet, a few days later, Dave was walking home with Zheniia and a couple of others from the Dom Demokratii after attending a meeting of the political opposition to Nazarbaev. An acquaintance of Zheniia, who is a newspaper reporter, asked him about his recent trip to the United States. Zheniia mentioned the overall efficiency of capitalist countries, but felt that things are too efficient and rather cold there: "Americans aren't as emotional as we are . . . they are too businesslike." He went on: "Of course I could emigrate there, I have had offers, but I don't think I can survive in such a stiff environment. I'd rather live amidst this absurdity [*teatr absurdov*]." This was the popular

[7] "Shcho tse za natsiia," *Osvita* (in Ukrainian), March 2, 1994, p. 33.

Soviet characterization of life in the USSR. Zheniia is both "alien" to Russia and part of its essential culture. Russians in all four republics are more or less similarly ambivalent about Russia; so the vision of the homeland can hardly explain differences in the propensity to return.

The propensity to exit cannot be explained by signals by the titulars that the Russians are unwanted either. If that were the case, there wouldn't be any Russians to be found in post-Soviet Estonia. There, the titular rhetoric of "repatriation" is matched by the Russian rhetoric of "don't pack your suitcases."

Because of a commitment to join Europe shared by the entire Estonian elite, Estonian leaders never talk about "forced" repatriation. But they come quite close! In an interview in December 1992 with Endel Lippmaa, a well-regarded chemist at the Academy of Science and an active politician as well, he rhetorically asked me that if General Eisenhower could deport the Germans Hitler had resettled in Poland, why was it so undemocratic to contemplate sending Russians back to Russia? Although he insisted that this is not a recommendation, he surely raised the specter of forced remigration. When the Isamaa coalition formed the government, with Peter Olesk as minister of citizenship and migration, the specter reappeared. In April 1994, he was quoted to the effect that "I think that for a lot of people there is no place in this country."[8]

Estonian leaders, even before sovereignty was achieved, dreamed of easing the transition by helping Russians emigrate back to Russia in a peaceful, "voluntary" manner. This dream was unrealistic, and after independence, a heavy-handed attempt to rid the country of its Russians—through negotiations with Canada and Argentina, asking these countries to accept the Russians as immigrants—helped set a new frame for Russians in Estonia, that Estonians did not want them in their picture. This view that Russian-speakers in Estonia are not wanted by Estonians is articulated by Estonian leaders on all sides of the political spectrum. The fringe right-wing Estonian Progressive Party ignored local Russians in order to meet with "real Russians" in Russia to work on plans to resettle Estonia's Russian in Russia. Their "Central Decolonization Initiative" condemned the granting of citizenship for "service" to the state. On the respectable right, however, the position was not that different. Merle Krigul, a linguist and parliamentarian, insisted to me in an interview in July 1992 that Russians are not a minority but an "occupying force" or are "refugees" since they have no "historic roots" in Estonia. She is a member of the board of the "Estonian Foundation for Migration." This is a government-funded organization, and in 1993–94 had a budget of 10 million kroons. Its director was the then prime minister, and it had fourteen members (bankers, mayors, a deputy minister). They were trying to become a private foundation but had received almost no funds. While they did provide help to some Russian families who wanted to return but lacked sufficient resources, their principal effect has been to give the impression to Russians that they are not wanted. At the same time, in an interview with Marju Lauristin, who is considerably more liberal than Krigul, she told me that the government is willing to pay Russian residents, based on auctions, and time of resi-

8 "Ty vinovat uzh tem . . . ," *Molodezh' Estonii*, April 21, 1994.

dence, for their rental properties. But, she said (I think expectantly), "Many Russians are waiting till full privatization so that they can sell their apartments and return to Russia as millionaires." And even a critic of government policy, Andres Kolist, attacked the Law on Aliens, not for its intent, but for its unenforceability. "Who is responsible," he asked, "when a law is unrealistic and brings Estonia only political damage? That is, when it doesn't help solve the main thing—helping non-Estonians to really leave Estonia."

When prime minister, Tiit Vähi positioned himself in the absolute center of this narrow political spectrum on the nationality issue. Few Estonian politicians would diverge greatly from the views he expressed when running for his second term as prime minister:

> I had said very clearly, that I support remigration, but it has to be voluntary. And we found that remigration policy from the Estonian Republic has first to be the creation of a remigration fund, which gives support to these families, who want to go back to their home sites, but who don't have financial possibilities to do so. The second point was to negotiate with the mayor of Saint Petersburg and with the head of Leningrad oblast, that they should facilitate the creation of good living conditions for those who leave from Estonia into these areas. . . . And as for the third condition—we wanted seriously to resist a new immigration. These three points were the "cornerstones" of our nationality politics.

Russians in Estonia picked up these signals. In the Narva City Council, in February 1993, after voting to commit themselves to a constructive process of internationality peace, City Council members denounced the "Estonian decolonization fund." Although they [the Estonians] talk of the "velvet" application of international human rights norms with their "decolonization fund," one member said sardonically, if their goal is 80 percent Estonians, this will mean a "velvet expulsion." Or in the words of one Russian woman from Tallinn, born and bred in Estonia, and interviewed by Estonian TV: "It's as if they [the Estonians] are saying, 'I want you to leave, I want your kids to leave, there is no higher education for them.' They look down upon us from on high. . . . I didn't feel any problems or obstacles at first. I wasn't a Russian person. But later I began to feel it." She got the message quite clearly. It was hard to miss.

Almost in dialectical response to the Estonian chorus of "we wish you would voluntarily leave," leaders of the Russian-speaking population in Estonia have urged their fellow Russians to "unpack their suitcases." To be sure, those Russians who have left Estonia have also left the debate about whether to leave; but public discourse among Russians in Estonia is not over the question of when to leave, but on how to stay.

The most eloquent spokesman for remaining in Estonia is Sergei Sovetnikov. He was born in the Narva area, is fluent in both Estonian and Russian, and he and his wife are citizens of Estonia. Now, in retirement, though a member of the City Council, his entire existence (his everyday interactions, his reading, his TV watching) is in Russian. His daughter lives in Russia and he visits there regularly with his wife. He once told me in a visit in October 1993 that he is different from Pavel Grigor'ev in that Pavel thinks the future for Narva is in ties with the West, but he (Sergei) believes it must be with the East. Yet his articles in the Estonia's Russian-language press had a continuing theme: "Don't pack your bags. Stay in Estonia." In another article, he showed worry about the project of the "national radicals" and irritation that they were calling all Russians "foreigners." Yet he remained optimistic. He argued that with a decent budget for language instruction, eventually there will be many Russian votes in Estonia, who will be able to change things for the better. And then he went back to his leitmotif, urging readers not to pack their bags. Sovetnikov was also against any referendum for a Northeastern Secession from Estonia; such a move, he argued, would be nothing more than a repetition of the debacle in the Transdniester region, which he "categorically opposed." He has consistently argued that "we must get a handful of Russian-speaking Estonian Republic citizens to support our interests, and to work to increase our number of citizens." To help move this along, Sovetnikov has pressed for lower standards of Estonian language for citizenship tests in places where it is difficult to learn it. His work on the citizenship law, when he was a member of the Estonian Supreme Soviet, emphasized a lowering of barriers for those Russian-speakers who wanted it, rather than stiffening the requirements.

Considering himself someone who has always been and will always be a communist, Sovetnikov is hard to categorize as a moderate. Yet there are Russians in Estonia who are considered far more anti-Estonian than Sovetnikov. But they too, in general, advocate staying in Estonia. Consider the position of the Russian Society of Estonia, a group that remains nostalgic for the Soviet Union and for the Russian culture which dominated it. Yet in their journal *Obshchina: Russkii vestnik*, they write: "We are absolutely against the outmigration of Russians from the republics . . . as we consider ourselves as rooted residents as the Estonians are. Here is our land." And in Narva, the firebrand politico who asserts Russian rights is Iurii Mishin, the head of the organization "Russian Citizens of Narva." At a meeting in October 1993, Mishin said that his organization would support candidates for the Russian election who give support for "the rights of the Russian diaspora." What he was advocating was that Russian citizens with residency in Estonia should have full right both to Russian benefits (economic vouchers, voting in Russian elections) and Estonian benefits (unemployment insurance, voting rights) as well. He and his fellow members had no intention of returning to the land of their citizenship.

Parallel to Estonia's elite discourse is a popular discourse of the impracticality of exit. The obstacles to exit are many.

A difficult housing market—Russians seeking to resettle in Pskov told Pettai that they could not sell their apartments in Estonia because of their cooperatives' implicit requirement that sales can only be to Estonian citizens. But, they claim, few Estonian citizens are in the market for flats, especially in largely Russian neighborhoods. This problem is compounded by an unregulated moving industry. New firms have entered the market, charging exorbitant fees for organizing a resettlement. Yet once many of these firms have been paid, they disappear. One resettler told Pettai of being defrauded of 150,000 kroons by one such firm. Fear of high and unregulated transition costs holds back explorations of new possibilities in Russia. Similarly, Russians underemployed at an electronics factory in Narva told me that the market for flats situated near comparable factories is equally dry in Russia, so they can't take the risk of moving. To be sure, housing markets are liquefying rapidly in the post-Soviet world; but in Estonia, Russians tend to focus on the illiquidity and high transactions costs of the housing market.

Insufficient resources—One group of Russians from Narva had organized themselves to homestead in Russia. They heard of the resettlement funds available from Estonian organizations and sought to tap into those resources. L. Shliminov, a correspondent from the *Narvskaia gazeta*, interviewed them and found they were utterly disgusted that the actual funds available to them were paltry. They gave up their effort. Nikolai Vaganov, writing in *Estoniia* (April 8, 1994) reported that all of the examples of searching for help and money should prove to any potential settler that he is not needed by anyone. Klara Hallik confirmed to me that the repatriation organizations of Estonia had much spirit but almost no funds.

No real "homeland" to return to—Few Russians in Estonia could provide Pettai or me with a locality that is their home. For example, Natal'ia Berezhkova sees herself as "Russkaia," but couldn't say precisely where her homeland was. Or again, Olga Guzhvina claimed that she moved around so much that she couldn't really say where her homeland is. In the Estonian-language class that I participated in for the unemployed, an early dialogue required us to say (in Estonian) where we were from. More than half of the students who did not say "Estonia" reported places outside of the core Russian zone, such as Uzbekistan, Kazakhstan, Moldova, and Siberia. I surmised that many of them grew up in prison camps, yet like many Russians even today were unwilling to admit it. Virtually all lived in families where there was such fear of the state that information about parental roots was hidden from the child. For most Russians in Estonia whom we spoke to, there is no village, no neighborhood, no housing bloc in Russia, that represents their "real" home.[9]

Declining links to Russia—Russia has since 1991 slowly begun to fall beyond the horizon for Russians in Estonia. Ninety-five percent of Estonian trade was with Soviet states in 1991; only 26 percent in 1993.[10] Lena in Tallinn saw free access to Russian TV as her link to the homeland. "If they cut Ostankino," she told Pettai, "it will cut the last thread we have left to Russian culture. We all grew up on Ostankino and learned about culture through it. All our favorite actors and artists are there. We know them all. Now we will lose them."[11] Liuba Grigor'ev was affected in another way, living halfway between St. Petersburg and Tallinn. It used to be, she said, if

[9] In answering surveys in the 1970s, Russians in Russia pointed to place of residence as a uniting factor for the national self-consciousness two to three times as often as Russians in other republics. See Iu. V. Arutiunian et al., *Russkie: Etno-Sotsiologicheskie Ocherki* (Moscow: Nauka, 1992), p. 378.

[10] Republic of Estonia, *Estonian Economic Survey* (Tallinn: Ministry of Economic Affairs, 1994).

[11] Indeed, Estonia stopped the transmissions of St. Petersburg TV on May 1, 1993. Transmissions of Russia's Ostankino programs were stopped a year later because the Russian Company failed to pay its 2.5 million kroon debt to Estonian Telekom. The Latvian State TV and Radio Council cut off broadcasts of Russian state TV (then Ostankino) on August 29, 1996. See the *Baltic Independent*, May 5, 1993; the *Baltic Times*, September 5, 1996; and Radio Free Europe, "Russia's Ostankino TV Defaults on Payments: Broadcasts to Cease," March 28, 1994.

you needed to get your cat spayed, you would take it to St. Petersburg, as there is no such facility in Narva. But now the border is too slow, and it is better to do that kind of business in Tallinn. Russia is slowly disappearing from Russian-Estonian consciousness as their "exemplary center."[12]

Some, however, are hanging on. The headmistress of School No. 13, Tat'iana, was brought up in Siberia and received her higher education in Leningrad. We talked about the cultural connections with Russia that still exist, and she insisted that regular trips to St. Petersburg (for the museums, the theater, the exhibits) were still part of her school's regular schedule. Someone from the school goes to the Russian consulate and gets a "group" one-day visa for a class of students. And all is easy, she bragged, as there is rarely a check by officials on either side of the border. I started to really push this claim. It turns out that the students (they are now quite few) with Estonian passports run into trouble at the second border post at Kingisepp, beyond the free border zone. And coming back into Estonia, where the non-Estonian-citizens face troubles, they usually send out one Estonian-speaking person who tells the Estonian guards that all the students are from the Estonian school and very tired from a long day of travel, and the Estonian border guards so rarely hear Estonian, they usually let all the students through without checking their passports, not all of which are in order. During our conversation, I saw a stack of books on the divan in the headmistress's office, and was told they were prizes for students who won in this year's academic "olympiad." All were published in Moscow or St. Petersburg. I asked if they bought them in Russia. The answer was that they were bought in the local store, because it is difficult to get them through customs. I concluded from this interview that cultural trips for schools to Russia are still a reality, but the possibility to do this easily, without visa costs, and without all sorts of legal hassles, is quickly disappearing. The school cultural trips are being maintained by a visionary teacher, a cooperative Russian consulate, and a certain amount of cleverness when dealing with slack officialdom. It is a process that cannot be sustained indefinitely.

A tight job market in Russia—Just after independence, Andres Tarand (who was then a minister of environment, but was to become an interim prime minister) told me, many highly technical personnel, "the ones we least wanted to lose," emigrated to Russia. "But many are remigrating," he told me in December 1992, "and we make sure they can get their jobs back. They found nothing for themselves in Russia." The message that there is nothing in Russia was loudly heard by potential emigrants. There can be little doubt that had Russia's economy boomed after the collapse of the Soviet state, the emigration figures of Russians from the republics would have been significantly larger.

This catalog of obstacles to emigration is well known to Russians in Estonia. In spite of this, some emigrate anyway, and quickly, fearing that the opportunity to do so will soon vanish. Russian citizenship for Russians living in the near abroad had a deadline, and this motivated some in Estonia, as we saw in Kazakhstan, to

[12] This phrase, taken out of context, is from Clifford Geertz, *Negara* (Princeton: Princeton University Press, 1980).

act quickly. Russians living in Estonia realized that once they had Estonian passports they would need visas to visit Russia. Since Russian visas had become expensive and difficult to obtain, this was unacceptable in terms of keeping up family contacts. As Pskov-resettled Olga told Pettai, Estonian citizenship "will open doors to new countries, but not to Russia. For us the most important country is Russia." Some wanted to leave mostly due to severe economic distress, and still others to assure their children's formation in Russian, and these were the reasons most often given by those seeking Russian citizenship, according to the Russian consul in Narva. But the great majority of Russians in Estonia have no intention of leaving.

A vibrant Russian cultural life therefore remains *in* Estonia. The Russian Theater of Tallinn, for example, puts on a full repertory. On the evening I was there, the play was a modern work called *Oboroten'* about a young blind man whose mother intervenes in a romance between her son and his neighbor. The theater was about half full. The audience consisted of people of all ages. The Russians remaining in Estonia have a settled cultural life, and their suitcases are not packed. Despite the clear desire of the Estonians that they leave, the Russians in Estonia have resolutely decided to remain.

In Kazakhstan, however, a cascade is in the making. The official government position, reiterated time and again by the president, is that Kazakhstanis of all nationalities are welcome in Kazakhstan. Nazarbaev has said, "We are a multiethnic state, there is no distinction between Russian and non-Russian-speakers, since all our inhabitants are Russian-speaking ones [*russkoiazychnoe naselenie*]." Citizenship was open to all with legal residence in Kazakhstan. While there certainly have been anti-Russian incidents in the streets and in certain ministries, unlike in Estonia, there was no official drive to induce Russians to leave the republic.

The cascade will begin as soon as a critical number of Russians believe that a critical number of Russians believe that a critical number of Russians will leave. That is all it will take. Clearly, Kazakhstan is not Tajikistan of 1991–93, or Bosnia in 1996. Life is peaceful in Kazakhstan for Russians, and no immediate decisions are necessary. Still, Dave in 1994 asked Lida and Volodia, both highly trained scientists, if they thought the situation was alarming enough now, or could get worse soon. Both of them were very guarded in their responses. They had obviously given the issue some thought and were trying to stay as calm and collected as possible. Lida said, "Time will tell. We'll wait and see. What the hell . . . if they don't want us, we'll leave. One wants to live with some dignity, and lead a normal life. If we have to leave, it won't be the end of the world. We are still fit, capable of working. But Kazakhstan is our *rodina* [homeland] . . . we'll wait and see." At that point Volodia filled the glasses with the last drops of vodka and said a toast, "Chtoby durakov ne bylo" (Let's wish that fools don't prevail), echoing a poem by Vysotsky.

But not everyone is this guarded. A common expression among Russians, *chemodan nastroyennie* (which I gloss as "suitcase fever"), suggests that at every meal they ask, "Should I stay or leave," and keep their suitcases ready to go. Consider Galia. Galia's mother was Russian, her father Kazakh. Her husband's father is Kazakh and mother Tatar. She and her husband are both linguistically russified and hardly speak Kazakh. Their seventeen-year-old son knows no Kazakh. In discussions with Dave, Galia referred to how the number of Russians (with whom she identified) leaving has drastically increased. "Just look at all those ads in *Karavan* for selling apartments. They are selling apartments at rates much lower than the market rates. They have panicked so much, fearing that they may not be able to sell their property at all." Subsequently, Dave heard from an acquaintance of theirs that Galia's sister and her husband Oleg (Russian-Chechen background) had already succeeded in exchanging their Almaty apartment for one in Moscow. Galia is right that the ads for apartments for sale indicate that the buyers are few and the sellers many. Prices are falling. The common topics of conversation among Russians are who has already left, who is leaving, the growing instances of attempted and successful looting/burning of their dachas (very few Kazakhs have dachas), and the failure of the *militsiia* (which is mainly Kazakh) to take any action.[13]

And even the level-headed Volodia and Lida are affected by this sense of imminent cascade. On a hike in January 1993, Lida mentioned that Volodia's sister Liuba, who lives in the village Malovodnoe, was planning to move to Russia. "We had some serious discussions on issues during last week's visit. Unfortunately, things are no longer the same outside Almaty. The Kazakhs over there aren't very educated. Mother and Liuba hear all the time 'you colonizers . . . go back to your Russia . . . we don't need you . . . you have overstayed your welcome.' Perhaps Liuba can move to Almaty, but the economy is so bad, and so hard to find a job. Besides who knows what will happen here?"

One of the big sources of fear among Russians in Kazakhstan is their inability to procure dual citizenship.[14] To become Kazakhstani citizens, they must renounce Russian citizenship, with no promise that they will be able to attain it again. In an interview that Dave conducted with the editor of *Kazakhstanskaiia pravda*, he downplayed the exodus, arguing that there has been a constant in- and outmigration of Russians. Many Russians, he pointed out, are moving to the northern and eastern regions of Kazakhstan from places like Kyzyl-Orda and the war-ravaged Tajikistan.

But then he got to the issue of citizenship. Of course, he admitted, many Russians are leaving places like Mangyshlak and Shevchenko (Aktau) because they are anxious about the citizenship issue. Dual citizenship is very important to these Russians. Most of them were sent to Kazakhstan to work (*po napravleniiu*), without knowing how long they would be there. They have settled down and raised families and cannot easily relocate. If dual citizenship were granted—and he agreed that it is a rather absurd institution ("No civilized country has such a practice to my knowl-

[13] For a good journalistic account of the buyer's market for apartments, see Boris Giller and Viktor Shatskikh, "Opredelenie berega: russkoiazychnye v Kazakhstane," *Karavan*, December 12, 1993, pp. 1–3. They also point out that hundreds of three-to-five-ton containers labeled "to Russia" were leaving the capital.

[14] Since Dave's field research, Russia (in a treaty with Kazakhstan) has promised automatic change of citizenship to Russians when and if they immigrate. To the extent that this provision is credible, it will certainly reduce fears of non-Kazakhs that they will become people without a homeland should they feel the need to leave Kazakhstan.

edge, but then our country is replete with absurdities")—then they will feel more secure. They will at least know that they have some place to go back to.

In a conversation with Sergei, the Russian in Almaty who complained about being thrown around like a football by Kazakhstani officials (see Chapter 5), Dave asked if he were a rooted (*korennoi*) Kazakhstani. "How can I not be a *korennoi*? I was born and brought up here, I am a third-generation Kazakhstani Russian," he said. Yet, he sardonically added that still, anything can happen, because it is "their" country.

Kazakhstan is not Tajikistan. But nevertheless, the Russians there do not believe that they or their children have a future in Kazakhstan. Consider Igor's story—begun in Chapter 5—whose paternal grandfather emigrated from Ukraine and settled in a village called Bezlesnoe (literally, "without forest") on the southern border of the Kokchetav Oblast. He was one of those peasants "liberated" by the Stolypin reforms who came to the steppes in search of farmland. Igor's father, Fedor Alekseevich, was born in 1938 in the Kokchetav Oblast. They came to Almaty in 1964. Igor's father finished technical school in north Kazakhstan and worked as an accountant. Yet Igor and his Kazakh wife, Madina, are thinking of leaving. Where to? It is not yet clear. Dave remembered that during her very first meeting with Igor, he had said that he does not feel there is any "discrimination" against Russians, that Russians are generally treated well. A month and a half later, he no longer thought so. In fact, he was thinking about quitting his job to give himself time to look around, perhaps even in Russia. His parents were very upset the first time he mentioned his anxieties about his future, the future of their daughter Marina, and the general treatment of Russians as second-class citizens by the state. His father did not even talk to him for the whole week, saying, "If you leave, you are not my son anymore." But gradually the wider family has noted a steady deterioration of the ethnic situation and the elders say, "We will manage to live here somehow, after all we have eaten the bread of this land. But things have changed so much, you and your children have no future in this country." And Igor adds: "I am fourth-generation 'Russian' in Kazakhstan, yet I am *nekorennoi* [not indigenous]." He went on: "I don't want to be treated as a second-class citizen. I want to have the right to speak in a language that I prefer. I don't want them to dictate to me what school my child should go to. I don't want to be singled out based on what I look like." And Madina ruefully noted: "With a name like Marina Igor'evna Grib, our daughter has no future here. Heaven forbid, if things didn't work out between us and we would have to divorce, the stigma will still stay. If I kept Marina, I would still have to answer all the questions like why she looks the way she looks, why is she called Marina, and so on."

The assessment of the future has also affected Lida and Volodia. Lida said, "We've told Kostia [their son] to look around for options in Russia." He has been accepted at the graduate program at Tomsk University, but he still hadn't heard whether he would be receiving a fellowship. Under the circumstances, his parents felt, it was the best thing for him. "If things settle down here, he'll come back, if not, we will see. He is still young," his parents told Dave, "he doesn't have to decide now." And in my meeting with the family in December 1995, Kostia had won the fellowship, and the family was pretty sure he would settle in Russia, because there are no opportunities for "science" (they did not say "Russians") in Kazakhstan. E. V. Kolomeets, Volodia's dissertation adviser, is in a similar situation. His daughter and son-in-law got their masters degrees in physics from Syracuse University. Both are now working in New York. The son-in-law will get his green card soon. The father is very pleased to have them out of Kazakhstan.

Migration continues from Kazakhstan with 70,000 registered migrants in 1995 and 26,200 in the first six months of 1996. A report of Russian immigrants working in the Tutaev motor factory in the Iaroslavl region of Russia found that for the first six months of 1996 they received no pay, and this was because they were not considered by locals to be "our own." The reporter found that immigrant families were starving for months, with children sick with TB and a nervous illness. Many said that they wanted to return to Kazakhstan. In one survey, every fifth person who left Kazakhstan for Russia had returned, because of job and living conditions, and even for being refused local residence permits. President Nazarbaev bristled over allegations that Russians were unwelcome in Kazakhstan. "Regarding 'ousting,' " he said, "every day I sign decrees about the restoration of citizenship to those former Kazakhstanis who are returning from Russia." Yet the flood from Kazakhstan remained twice as high as any of the former union republics in the eighteen months since January 1995.[15]

In Kazakhstan, then, a cascade is being set in motion, not by present catastrophe, but by a subjective assessment of future possibilities, only partially ameliorated by the knowledge of long-term official welcome by Russia as citizens, which should reduce the temptation to do so now, and by the knowledge of the terrible circumstances that exist in places that earlier emigrants settled. Yet to the extent that Russians in Kazakhstan watch their neighbors exit because of negative assessments about Kazakhstan's future, the Russians who remain will feel even more isolated and even more fearful about the future.

What accounts for cascades of emigration? Clearly they cannot be explained by a strict accounting of costs and benefits. For Estonia, a glance at the data from the surveys of the sociological team of Kirch, Kirch, and Tuisk shows that where emigration would be least costly (Narva), it is least likely to be considered. They conclude from this and other examples that remigration was a theoretical but impractical issue for Russians in Estonia. From Iaroslav's comment in Kiev, that despite his longing for Russia, he never thought of moving there, since it is simply "not an option," we hear the same point. If the impracticality of emigration is widely believed, precise calculations about its costs and benefits are not made. Nor can the Kazakh cascade be explained by a lack of welcome in the republic, even though some of our informants emphasized this factor. In no case has the welcome mat been less visible than in Estonia; yet in Estonia, there is no movement toward a cascade. Finally, the cascade cannot easily be explained by economic hardship. To be sure, post-Soviet life has not been the fulfillment of an eco-

[15] Natal'ia Airapetova, "Bespredel s pomoshch'iu zakonov," *Nezavisimaia gazeta*, October 26, 1996. Also, Iurii Kirinitsiianov, "Pereselentsev ne zhdut," June 7, 1997; interview with Nazarbaev, in *Nezavisimaia gazeta*, November 11, 1996; and data from *Rossiiskaia gazeta*, November 2, 1996.

nomic dream for Russians in Kazakhstan, but life hasn't been easy for Russians in Russia either.

From our ethnographic data, there is no unequivocal answer to the question of why exit is not an option in Estonia (or in Latvia, or in the Ukraine), yet seems the only option in Kazakhstan. Perhaps the answers lies in the clear sense the Russians in the near abroad have of how their culture ranks against the cultures of the republics in which they are living. Learning a language from the West (Estonian, or Latvian) is not an indignity, if doing so is required for future social mobility in those republics. Learning another Slavic language (especially if it is a higher-status Ukrainian than *surzhik*) is a lateral move, but not a descent. But learning a Turkic language and assimilating *downward* in a status hierarchy is a psychological impossibility. Russians believe that Kazakhs must know the loss of in-group acceptance Russians would face by learning Kazakh, and it is therefore unrealistic to compel Russians to learn it. This is how I interpret Sergei's contemptuous tone when he says, " 'They' don't want us here."

In a similar vein, A. Zhovtis told Dave a revealing anecdote of an event that occurred over twenty years ago, when he was returning from the Medeu mountain resort, and thumbed a lift from a Russian. Moments later, Zhovtis reports, they saw a Kazakh standing on the street, trying to hitch a ride. The driver did not stop. Instead, he muttered, "It is not pleasant when such ugly fat-faced ones ride along. They're all the same." It is hard to conceive of a Russian making such a comment about a Balt or a Ukrainian. The ethnic slurs we heard in Ukraine—*moskali* (allied with Moscow) for Russian-speakers, and *banderovtsy* (Banderites, or followers of a Ukrainian leader with fascist sympathies) for western Ukrainians—do not imply ranking. Arel once heard Anatolii Pohrybnyi, vice-minister of education, refer ironically to the Russian put-down of Ukrainians as *khokhol* or *maloros* ("Little Russian"), but as we shall see, these very terms are also used by Ukrainians to refer to peasants (or Russian-speakers among Ukrainians).

Tales of ethnic slurs by high Russian officials suggesting ranked differences with Kazakhs are the stuff of urban folklore. One story concerns Brezhnev, who was then second secretary of the Communist Party of Kazakhstan. A studio director, Semenov, had an appointment with him, yet had to wait for a long time, and there was a Kazakh petitioner already in line ahead of him. The Kazakh said that he only needed a few minutes. He appeared very well educated. He was talking to Brezhnev very politely—though it appeared that they had some disagreement. Then the Kazakh left, and the studio director went into Brezhnev's office. Brezhnev immediately wanted to let off the steam, saying, "Opiat' eti kolbity negramotnye" ("Once again, these illiterate lice"). This particular slur, *kolbit*, or lice, dates back to Cossack times, and is a reference to what was then seen as the nomads' parasitic relationship to the land. More recently, the reckless and racialist V. Zhirinovskii has been quoted as saying, in reference to the president of Kazakhstan, "Just because Nazarbaev can wear shorts and play tennis, it doesn't mean he is civilized." The Russian image of Kazakhs as illiterate lice is evidence of a system of ranking deeply programmed into Russian consciousness.

Accommodating to some lower status "them" (that is, accepting Kazakh rule in Kazakhstan, without Russia's "overrule") implies a revolution in rank. It is something the Russian diaspora in Kazakhstan cannot abide. In the long term, most reckon, if Russians are compelled to integrate into a Turkic state, they will resist. It is better to leave now, or plan for your children to leave, rather than face the inevitable crisis later. This is one important source of the impending cascade.

Voice

Outside Moldova and Crimea (and the attempts to create autonomous republics for Russians outside the Russian Federation), the degree of political mobilization by Russians qua Russians has been quite low in all the republics of the former Soviet Union. Some have attributed this to television, which tends to keep Russians in their living rooms and off the streets.[16] Others have pointed to the scarce resources available to dispossessed Russians, thereby limiting effective political mobilization.[17]

These explanations are not convincing. In all four republics, social ties among Russians make the costs of organization quite low. In Estonia (as in the other republics) all towns have "Houses of Culture" built in Soviet times, with large meeting rooms and professional staff, also held over from Soviet times, to organize events. When the leaders of the Russian community of Narva want to have a meeting, they have access to these culture houses, and announcements of their meetings appear on every kiosk in town. During the early days of independence, there was an organization of moderate Russian-speaking deputies in the Supreme Soviet using the Estonian place name Virumaa to identify themselves. Russian-speakers had little organizational trouble in setting up referenda for autonomy in Narva and Sillamäe. They organized a representative assembly made up of a coalition of a host of previously existing organizations and elected delegates among noncitizen residents of Estonia.[18] In Ukraine, strikes by Donbas teachers and coal miners belie any notion that the Russian-speaking population lacks resources for political mobilization. In Latvia, there are several ethnically based organizations of Russians. There is a Russkaia Obshchina Latvii (Russian Community of Latvia), which was launched in 1992, with over 1,000 members. Its original purpose was to create business ventures to finance Russian culture and community life in Latvia. This idea failed, but its newspaper, *Russkii put'* (*The Russian Path*), has continued to publish and remains a vibrant weekly. There is also a Balto-Slavianskoe Obshchestvo (Balto-Slavic Soci-

[16] Maris Brants, "Kapec Latvija viss mierigi?" *Labrit*, March 10, 1994.

[17] Vello Pattai has recorded problems of mobilization caused by scarce resources in Latvia and Estonia. Dominique Arel, in a personal communication, reports on a Cossack leader who complained to him in an interview that Russian-speakers in Kazakhstan are prevented from mobilizing through denial of registration to certain associations, by the banning of demonstrations, and by arrests of potential fifth columnists.

[18] For a list of participating associations, see *Estoniia*, September 18, 1993, in an article translated from *Hommikuleht*.

ety), which seeks to organize Russians based on a common Orthodox heritage. There are also more secular organizations such as Equal Rights, and League of Stateless Persons active on the political scene. Pettai observed large demonstrations in Riga during his spring 1994 research trip there. One was a demonstration of the League of Stateless Persons and the Equal Rights Movement, with about 2,000 protesters. Another was a demonstration of noncitizens organized by the Association of Independent Trade Unions, and the League of Stateless Persons. The local Hare Krishna organization offered the protesters free stew. In Kazakhstan, Dave met with leaders of Lad (Harmony) and Birlesu (Unity), both organizations representing Russian interests. The most popular newspaper in Almaty is *Karavan*, which makes great profit through its matrimonial classifieds, its apartment-exchange bulletin board, and its soft pornography. Its editorial position is in support of Russians and Russian-speakers of Kazakhstan. The editor is Jewish by passport nationality, who has vowed to remain in Kazakhstan, "his homeland," and to stand up for the rights of Russian-speakers there.

In none of these republics is it reasonable to blame the low levels of mobilization on a lack of organizational resources. Nor can one reasonably assert that the payoffs for mobilizing are too low. Andrus Park, a distinguished Estonian sociologist, pointed out to me that the Russian-speakers, who made an international issue out of the Estonian Aliens' Law in July 1993, got President Meri to veto the first (and more obnoxious) version of the bill. By so organizing, and raising the specter of violence, the Russian-speaking Estonians got results.

Students of international relations are inclined to explain the low levels of mobilization of Russians qua Russians in the former union republics by the fact that they remain physically "secure," given the relative power of Russia compared to the states they live in. If the titular leaders were to threaten their safety, the Russian communities in the republics of the near abroad are confident that Russia would come to their aid. The Russian-speakers get security, as it were, for free.[19] This international relations explanation is powerful and helps explain the lack of violence. But it would be incorrect to hold that should the Russian-speaking communities in the near abroad feel threatened, they lack the organizational infrastructure for rapid mobilization. As of 1996, most strategies by Russians are—as in the assimilation game—individual. But this does not rule out future mobilization as Russians.

Arms

In all four republics, the Russian-speakers are angry and frustrated. They blame the titulars in general, and the nationalist leaders of their republics in particular, for the uncertainty they are currently facing. For many theorists of ethnic tension, this is the recipe for war.

[19] Barry Posen, "The Security Dilemma and Ethnic Conflict," *Survival* 35, no. 1 (1993): 27–47; James D. Fearon, "Ethnic War as a Commitment Problem," paper presented to the 1994 Annual Meetings of the American Political Science Association, New York, September 2–5, 1994.

Yet in these four republics violence has been largely contained. With the market for high-tech weapons open and free in places like Georgia, Azerbaijan, and Moldova, it is significant that none of us on the ethnographic research team encountered arms' markets in our countries of study. The lack of preparation for interethnic armed struggle requires explanation. In Chapter 12, I shall make a case for *why* violence is contained, but here I shall say something about *how* potential violence is contained.

In the Baltics, the principal mechanism holding back violent expression of internationality tensions is the institutionalization of what Karl Deutsch has called a "security community."[20] There has been violence in the Baltics, but spokespersons for both sides of the ethnic divide have consistently given this violence a nonethnic "spin." In Ukraine and Kazakhstan, the principal mechanisms holding back internationality tensions from erupting into violence are first the balance of power and, second, the preeminence of *intra*ethnic tensions within the titular community.

This is not to say that interethnic war clouds have not flown over the horizons of the four republics under study. In Estonia, the skies were darkening when Soviet collapse appeared imminent. Perhaps the growing tension had more to do with dual sovereignty than with ethnic conflict, but the issues overlapped. After the August 1991 coup in Moscow, Tiit Vähi traveled to the northeastern city of Kohtla-Järve, in the name of the self-declared independent republic of Estonia, to serve as the prime minister's representative for the northeastern region. (His job, a later incumbent told me, was halfway between a prefect and a foreign dignitary plenipotentiary.) In his first meeting with the press, martial law was discussed, and Vähi reported that local military organizations were already forming. On Vähi's visit to Narva, he called the situation one of "lawlessness." Narva deputies responded by saying that the Estonian Republic had no laws because the republic itself was illegal. Vähi was not merely seeing phantoms. Months later, in 1992, the parliamaentarian Vladimir Lebedev told me that he believed a Transdniester would occur if Estonians tried to stop the election for a parliament of noncitizens, which was then scheduled to take place on September 13. While he insisted he was a "moderate," he feared that extremists would carry the day. And he said to me pointblank: if there is any shooting against the Russians, he would join those Russians fighting for independence. Similarly, at the time of the Narva autonomy referendum of July 1993, which the Estonian government declared illegal, rumors abounded that armed thugs or Cossacks were waiting across the border for a call for help. It was said that if Prime Minister Laar had used police to close the polling, these thugs would have crossed the "Friendship Bridge" over the Narva River and intervened.

The tensions over the establishment of republican sovereignty led young men to think of taking up arms. I had a long conversation with Sasha, nineteen years old in October 1993. He had been married since he was seventeen and already had a two-year-old child. He was working at the Narva furniture factory for 240 kroons per month. He was planning to take off from work that current week to go to Tallinn to

[20] Karl Deutsch et al., *Political Community and the North Atlantic Area* (Princeton: Princeton University Press, 1957).

respond to a notice that Russian citizens could get two to three thousand kroons per month to join in some militia. My sense is that he was doing this out of shame at his low salary, especially in comparison to his wife's, who was a skilled seamstress and worked in one of the very few shops still operating in the Krenholm factory. He decided later not to go to Tallinn, after a lawyer advised him that if he went abroad as a fighter for Russia, he might never be able to reenter Estonia, or reinstate his permanent residence rights, and he feared permanent separation from his family. Nonetheless, he is the type that, if the conditions were right, would have joined an anti-Estonian militia.

I spoke to another young Russian man in Estonia in the unsettling months of fall 1993 who had been a cadet during perestroika and had come to believe that Gorbachev was a CIA agent out to destroy the Soviet Union. He hated Yeltsin and believed that he had sold Russia out to the Americans. He liked Vice-President Rutskoi, and he himself had wanted to serve under his command in Afghanistan. He was also unemployed. He knew that there were gangs of young people, his age, on the other side of the border, eager to recruit young Russian-Estonians to vandalize Narva in the name of Russia. He was tempted and felt that unless the economic situation improved, many young people like himself would yield to that temptation.

Extremist groups have brought areas of Ukraine to the brink of ethnic war. The most visible formation is the UNA-UNSO, which regularly denounces Russia for its "imperialist plundering" of Ukraine. More to the fringe, yet more ominous in its rhetoric, is the *Derzhavna samostiinist' Ukrainy* (DSU). In November 1993, Viktor Desiatnykov wrote of efforts by the DSU to bring *sanatsiia* (sanitizing; i.e., extermination of the enemy) to Ukraine. DSU, he wrote, is recruiting small detachments of nationalists, comprised of eight people each, to "take care of" anti-Ukrainian political parties and commercial banking structures.[21] DSU chairman Roman Koval' said that the most urgent task is to instill in the youth aggressiveness, a spirit of revenge, and a commitment to the inevitable punishment of the enemies of Ukraine. The slogan "Death to the Invaders!" is his. In December 1994, the radical nationalist Volodymyr Yavors'kyi, interviewed in *Molod' Ukrainy*, said that "we reject democracy and espouse force and struggle as the spiritual foundation of our union, while the . . . KUN (Congress of Ukrainian Nationalists [the direct descendants of the national liberation movement, the OUN, from the Second World War]) has adopted democracy and objects to a powerful struggle [*sylovu borot'bu*]. We think that it is a big mistake. . . . Our priority task is to fully force out from Ukraine Russian cultural-economic domination."[22]

There had been violence in the streets as well. The violence during the celebration of the 1944 liberation from Germany in Ivano-Frankovsk was probably instigated by UNA-UNSO activists. The UNA-UNSO was also behind a conflict involving

[21] Viktor Desiatnykov, "Zahony Sanatsi vyrushaiut' . . . ," *Demokratychna Ukraina* (in Ukrainian), December 11, 1993.

[22] Volodymyr Yavors'kyi, "My prahnemo ukrains'koi Ukrainy," *Molod' Ukrainy* (in Ukrainian), December 15, 1994.

the attempted liberation of the Kyiv-Patriarchate Church from its supposed subordination to the Moscow Patriarchate. In July 1995, Ukrainian nationalists demanded that the body of Patriarch Volodymyr, the formal head of the Kyiv Church, be buried at the St. Sophia complex in Kiev, an act that would have compelled the government to take sides on a religious issue, one that would set Russians against Ukrainians, something it did not want to do. During the funeral procession, UNA-UNSO paramilitary demonstrators broke through police lines to dig a symbolic grave in front of St. Sophia. They were brutally repelled by riot police. In L'viv, in an incident provoked by the KUN, Stepan Khmara, the son of a famous OUN patriot, was arrested after his parliamentary immunity was suspended for attacking an MVD (Interior Ministry) officer. At a later date, he organized a number of confrontations in order to provoke incidents between Russians and Ukrainians. For example, he recruited trainloads of followers to travel to Crimea in order to stand in visible opposition to secessionist tendencies there.[23] To be sure, ultranationalist Ukrainians do not have a monopoly on fighting words. In Crimea, Sergei Shuvainikov, often called "the Crimean Zhirinovskii," has been most provocative in his public outbursts. The point here is that in Ukraine, there are reasonable fears of ethnic war.[24]

In both Estonia and Ukraine, violence has been contained. In Estonia, notwithstanding Lebedev's provocative comments or the appeal of pan-Russian militias, there seems to be an implicit compact on both sides of the ethnic divide to define acts of violence as random or caused by other factors than ethnic ones. Consider Vähi's mission to the northeast in the wake of the 1991 putsch in Moscow. Although he described the situation as lawless, his meetings with the local councils took place without any personal attacks or threats to the peace. In an interview with me in October 1993, he recalled that period of service as being difficult, but not personally threatening.

The lack of a real threat to the peace is a recurrent theme among people who have actually dealt with interethnic affairs in Estonia. Artur Kuznetsov, the first minister of nationality affairs in the Popular Front coalition, confirmed this view. Although he was anything but hopeful for the future of his Russian community in Estonia, he emphasized to me in 1991 that "our situation is without violence between ethnic groups, without sharp confrontations with victims. . . . Now Estonia is the only republic in the Soviet Union without one person hurt in the ethnic violence, we have had no victims." In my first interview with Mart Rannut, the general director of the State Department of Language, I learned that he was treated brusquely by Russians in his professional role. But he lives in an apartment complex with mostly Russian families. The only interpersonal incident he could report that reflected tension was that his neighbors surreptitiously turned the TV antennas on top of his building to

[23] April 12, 1991: RFE/RE Report; for the train brigade, see "Kak uchili odessitov nen'ku-rodinu liubit'," *Izvestiia*, March 3, 1992.

[24] On nationalist fringe groups in Ukraine, see Dominique Arel, "Ukraine: Stability through Ambiguity," Minority Rights Group (London), 1995. It should be re-emphasized that these ultranationalist groups do not have wide popular support. Altogether there are no more than a dozen ultranationalist deputies in the Ukrainian parliament. But they are quite visible.

improve the reception of the Leningrad station.[25] During his campaign for the presidency of Estonia in 1992, Rein Taagepera attended meetings of Russian militants and stood face-to-face with a Russian paramilitary guard, and never felt himself to be in personal danger.[26] Estonian high school students from Narva have told me that when they go into Russian bars late at night, they don't feel like they are in any special danger because they are Estonians.

Even in my interviews with radicals who raised the possibility of a Moldova or Yugoslavia in Estonia, there was no evidence of preparation for or expectation of communal hostility.[27] Ahto Siig, an Estonian journalist living in Narva, was able to show me some cracks in a window of the Estonian secondary school in Narva, and blamed them on vandalism by Russian hooligans who were incited by the propaganda pamphlets dropped from Soviet aircraft in March 1988. But he had no evidence (or even heard any rumors) of trigger-happy youths ready to take advantage of a tense political situation by engaging in violent acts. And Dr. Vladimir Khomiakov, a pediatrician who became a radical self-appointed spokesman for the plight of the Russians in northeast Estonia, who told me that a "Yugoslavia" was imminent in Estonia, had to admit to me that there were no weapons caches in either community, and that the young generation of Russians is totally apolitical and unmotivated to fight against Estonian oppression.

In a security community there is no expectation of violence, and therefore no preparation for defense against it. Yet if violence does occur, under conditions of a security community, there must be a common interpretive framework on both sides of a cleavage to define that violence in terms that do not refer to that cleavage. This is certainly what has occurred in Estonia. In July 1992, Moscow TV reported on five incidents of Molotov cocktails thrown on the balcony of the Russian ambassador's residence (in Estonia, it is called Zhdanov's balcony). In that same month, Moscow TV reported that a local citizen shot through the tire of a Russian military vehicle in Estonia. Also, TV reports that a Narva-based group called Ours was organizing to fight in Transdniester. A soldier from that war was buried in Narva, and the Russian Intermovement was said to have organized the funeral. In the wake of these incidents, however, there was no rhetoric of expected escalation. Spokesmen on both sides of the nationality divide treated these as isolated incidents and did not even consider them as invitations for revenge.

Political developments in Estonia's northeast have been highly conflictual; but even there without raising the specter of violence. Consider the referenda in the northeast cities in summer 1993 that many feared would bring Estonia to the brink of war. Earlier that year the Riigikogu had passed a series of laws that Russian-speakers saw as discriminatory, culminating with a Law on Aliens that threatened their future ability even to reside in Estonia. In response, leaders of the Russian-speaking population organized local referenda seeking support for territorial autonomy. The Estonian government declared these referenda illegal on the grounds that

[25] Interview with author, June 20, 1991, Tallinn.

[26] Reported in *Estonian Independent*, May 9, 1991.

[27] Ahto Siig, Vladimir Khomiakov, interviews with author, May 24, 1993, Narva.

the constitution had already stipulated that Estonia was a unitary state. I have already mentioned the rumors about the armed bands poised to cross the border. As the date of the referenda approached, international journalists hovered over Narva like ravens, positioning themselves to capture the early battles in what was perhaps to be the next Transdniester.

"Hot" July turned out to be cool, however, and journalists left without a big story. One reason for the peaceful outcome was international pressure. U.S. support for a roundtable discussion (a rather effective use of a mere $15,000 of taxpayer money to get talks started), and wily diplomacy by Max van der Stoel of the Conference on Security and Cooperation in Europe (CSCE) helped work out a compromise in which the election would be held but in which the outcome would not matter.[28] But a stunning move by President Lennart Meri, mentioned earlier as an example of the power of Russian mobilization, was also of great consequence. He humiliated his own prime minister by refusing to sign the initial legislation for the Law on Aliens until it was reviewed by legal experts in the Council of Europe. These experts recommended some softening of registration requirements, and the Riigikogu was compelled to accept these changes. These changes helped defuse some of the rhetoric of those calling for autonomy. The Estonian government permitted the referenda to take place. The results were overwhelmingly positive, though the procedures were questionable. Months later, the Supreme Council of Estonia nullified the results. Autonomy was not granted. Despite the explosiveness of the situation, as I learned from many interviews, no one in Narva (Russian or Estonian) bought arms to protect themselves or their families. This suggests that no one in Estonia took the rumors of armed Cossacks on the other side of the border seriously.

In the year following hot July, there were moments when social order could have broken down, but given the peaceful resolutions of past conflicts between Russians and Estonians, no one expected interethnic violence to break out. The first local elections, scheduled for October 1993, was one such moment. The Estonian Constitution of 1992 stipulated that self-governing localities would have their own elections for city council and mayor, and that permanent residents who were not citizens would have voting rights. It was assumed at the time that voting rights meant the right to vote and be voted for, and Estonian government officials assured foreign observers worried about possible nationality conflicts that this was indeed the case. But when spring 1993 arrived and it was time for local elections, there was still no election law to guide the process. The press hinted that even middle-of-the-road Estonians were worried about the possibility of noncitizens getting positions of local power. Former prime minister Tiit Vähi, who lost out to the more nationalist Isamaa coalition, asked in March, "Can someone who isn't a citizen be held responsible for Estonia's state problems?"[29] And on May 19, with only fifteen votes opposed, the Riigikogu adopted the election law that denied noncitizens the right to run for office in the elections to be held on October 17. Most delegates in the

[28] In 1995 it was renamed the Organization for Security and Cooperation in Europe (OSCE).
[29] See the *Baltic Observer*, March 26, 1993.

Riigikogu knew that they were violating the spirit, if not the letter, of the constitution, but they felt it was more important to undermine the Russian-dominated city councils in the northeast. They also stipulated that mayors had to be not only citizens but also fully competent speakers of Estonian. Thus they hoped to remove or bar from power those Russian-speaking politicians who had received citizenship for service to the state, but who themselves could not have passed the citizenship examination.

The law severely diminished the autonomy of the majority populations in the northeastern towns. First, given the population in the northeastern cities, there was a critical lack of candidates eligible to run in these elections. Therefore, the Estonian government, by virtue of its ability to grant citizenship to Russian-speakers for "service to the state," had enormous power to co-opt leaders who would be eligible candidates. The government was thereby assured that only moderates would hold office. Second, given the incentives of the electoral formula—a modified d'Hondt system, where the total number of votes that a party list received would enhance the chances of any candidate on the list—candidates on long electoral lists had a better chance to win than those on a short list. Consequently, politicians who were best able to recruit ethnic Estonians onto their lists (and thereby lengthening them) were more likely to win themselves. This also brought power to those Russians and Estonians most willing to make cross-ethnic alliances. Third, given the linguistic job requirements for mayors (which almost no Russian-speakers in the northeast could meet) a semi-itinerant group of Estonians who had an interest in administration and some exposure to the region, placed themselves as candidates for mayor, often in more than one city. In the electoral concourse in Narva, where all candidates gave speeches and answered questions, I heard one Russian-speaker whisper that the citizens of Narva were voting for their colonial officer. Despite this set of humiliations, especially for the politicians of the old order, the towns of the northeast remained peaceful and participated in these elections at higher rates than did Estonians in Tallinn. Conflict and humiliation did not, in this case, lead to violence.[30]

In the subsequent months in Narva, there were a few well-publicized murders of prominent Russians. Never was there a finger pointed to any Estonian (qua Estonian); and in my interview with the secretary of the Narva Court, I found that there were no murders that reached the court in which one nationality member was accused of killing a member from another nationality. But in the era of the mafia, she told me, with high officials being in some way implicated, most murder cases do not reach the courts. In late 1995, the only Estonian secondary school in Narva was destroyed by arson. Everyone from Interior Minister Edgar Savisaar to the spokesmen for the Russian community interpreted this attack as an act by the Russian mafia against the police powers of the state. No ethnic retribution followed.

[30] Fuller details of both the referenda and the October 1993 elections are available in David D. Laitin, "The Russian-Speaking Nationality in Estonia: Two Quasi-Constitutional Elections," *East European Constitutional Review* 2, no. 4; 3, no. 1 (Fall 1993/ Winter 1994): 23–27.

Consider the following incident in Narva in May 1994. There was a session in one of the Houses of Culture with a delegation from Tallinn made up of high officials from the Ministry of Immigration. The meeting brought out all the hotheads in the Russian-speaking community, who were excoriating the ministers at every opportunity. The members of the delegation were dressed in expensive suits, and compared to the drab coats worn by the pensioners, the largest group at the meeting, their suits looked like imperial uniforms. The delegates refused to speak Russian and communicated to Narvans through interpreters, which only increased the sense of distance between rulers and ruled. Yet after the rather vitriolic session, as I saw the government ministers leave for their next meeting in a bus without police protection and without incident. Neither side expected violence or sought to provoke it.

In 1996 the Estonian government raised the language requirements for citizenship, which made it even more difficult for Russian-speaking candidates to run in local elections. In response, Iurii Mishin, the head of the Union of Russian Citizens in Narva, went to the streets in protest. Estonian state authorities threatened to try him on sedition charges. Yet the security community survived. Press reports revealed that all parties felt that the conflict would be resolved through negotiations, and neither side made any visible preparations for violent conflict.[31]

The key to the containment of interethnic violence in Estonia in the post-Soviet period is that no one expects it. When no one expects violence, no one prepares extensively for defense against it. When no one makes any preparations to defend themselves against interethnic violence, no one fears that defensive weapons might be used offensively. This sense of no expectation of violence is the essence of what Deutsch meant by the term "security community." A security community exists in the minds of strategic planners, or individuals who cross boundaries, and it is sometimes (but not always) recognized in institutional practice. In Estonia, the security community contains a self-fulfilling prediction that acts of violence between persons of different nationalities do not constitute internationality violence, and therefore do not call for ethnic retaliation. This expectation has been an important mechanism in containing violence in Estonia.

In neighboring Latvia, however, there are signs that the tensions between Russians and Latvians could lead to bloodshed. Indeed there are signs that Russians are growing indignant with Latvians *qua* Latvians. *Diena* reported on a member of the language inspectorate working in Liepaja who complained of impolite treatment and threatening letters and phone calls.[32] In fact, the director of the Latvian Language Bureau, Dzintra Hirsche, told Pettai and me that after Zhirinovskii's parliamentary success in 1993, many inspectors had been attacked, and that one received a broken jaw, and another was beaten into blindness. One inspector's apartment was bombed, she recounted to us in a tone of resigned indignation during an interview on April 25, 1994. But there is a broader anger that is evident in our observations. Leading Russians from the Popular Front (PF) period are angry about the capture

[31] See the *Baltic Times*, May 16–22, 1996.

[32] "Valodas inspektoriem Liepaja draud ar izrekinasanos," *Diena*, March 12, 1994.

of the movement by radical nationalists in the mid-1990s. An article by V. Bykov in the press takes the ditty from the PF era ("we are building a common home") and says that these songs no longer sound the same to the many Russians who signed the petitions demanding Latvian independence.[33] In my conversations with Alex Grigorievs, former journalist and PF activist, I heard the same theme of angry disillusionment. In my first meeting with him in the summer of 1991, he showed anger at Russians (from Russia) who took the best apartments in town, leaving Latvians (as he then considered himself, though of Russian nationality) in cold-water flats. But by 1995 (at a chance encounter, at the convention of the American Association for the Advancement of Slavic Studies), he was complaining to me that the Latvians were undermining all hopes for an open society. Or, as one student who feared the loss of university education in Russian put it: "Up till now, I didn't think anything bad about the Latvian government . . . but now it seems they've suddenly begun to push us toward confrontation." To be sure, there has been no mobilized violence between Latvians and Russians in Latvia. Nor are there any threats of a spiral of violence. Still, no one seems confident that there will always be peace between the two nationalities either. Thus, if violence does break out between gangs from the two nationalities, it will probably be difficult to contain.

Ukraine does not enjoy the interethnic security community that I observed in Estonia. Its potential for violence is more like Latvia's, though it comes from a different source. Ordinary citizens are not buying guns to protect their families; local ethnic entrepreneurs are not storing weapons against a day when internationality violence does erupt. But people are taking the provocations by the ardent Ukrainian nationalists and the equally provocative acts of the Russian Crimean leaders to gain autonomy for their peninsula very seriously. In 1994, Ukrainian troops were reported to have begun a march to Crimea to assure that no secession occurred.

The major mechanism holding back interethnic violence in Ukraine and Kazakhstan—identified earlier as the international relations viewpoint[34]—is the feeling by Russians in both of these republics that if they were ever terrorized (*qua* Russians) by the titulars, the Russian Federation would come to their aid. They did not therefore feel a need to fight for autonomy (as did the Serbs in Croatia) before the newly independent states gained sufficient power to suppress them. But another mechanism reducing the likelihood of interethnic violence in these two republics is the embarrassing fact (for both sides) that the boundaries of opposition are not at all clear. For example, the significant percentage of Russian-speaking Ukrainians in the east, south, and central Ukraine makes it virtually impossible for Ukrainian leaders to count on the support of all Ukrainians in an ethnic confrontation with Russians. Similarly, Russians cannot easily act *as* Russians against Ukrainians, because they share a common interest with Russian-speaking Ukrainians, whom they do not wish to antagonize.

[33] V. Bykov, "My postroim obshchii dom, ochen' druzhno zazhiviom . . . ," *SM-Segodnia*, March 10, 1994.

[34] This is the interpretation James Fearon presents in his paper "Ethnic War as a Commitment Problem."

One result of this *pas de trois* is that the greatest venom spewed in the Ukrainian political context is intra-ethnic, of "pure" Ukrainians against russianized Ukrainians. In everyday life, there was a kind of pejorative attitude from westerners about people from the east. The latter were called *skhidniaki* (easterners, but in a derogatory sense) in Ukrainian. In political debate they have been referred to as *bezbatchenkamy* ("those without a homeland"). "Degenerate" is another common trope. Russophones, claims Oleksa Novak, are "characterized by a disrespectful attitude toward everything Ukrainian. [They are] *comprised of Russians and national-degenerated [vyrodzheni] groups of Ukrainians* from the east and south. . . . These people do not believe in the renaissance of Ukraine, in its statehood."[35] In another context, Yosyp Bahlai held that those who applauded President Kuchma's call for granting Russian the status of an official language were "pro-imperial communo-chauvinists and degenerate 'Russian-speaking' Ukrainians with family names ending in 'enko' [which constitutes] the irrefutable [proof] of their Cossack descent."[36] In a similar vein, the national communist Vitalii Karpenko has written that "it is a myth that independence is responsible for the current critical state of our economy, state, and society. This fabrication is spread by people who are not at all patriots of Ukraine, but by people who have in their genes the instinct of a slave, people who are used to bend and serve with servility [*prysluzhuvaty*]—they simply do not know another life."[37] Arel's informant Oleksandra, a Ukrainian from Poltava, on the Left Bank, who speaks good eastern Ukrainian at home, gave Arel a vivid reminder of how these stereotypes create divides between peoples. She told him that at her Institute (of Foreign Languages, in Kiev), they were told, in Ukrainian, that someone who does not master his/her mother tongue [meaning here the mother tongue of their nationality] is not psychically normal. She is troubled by that. This intra-Ukrainian rhetoric is as hot as any rhetoric one would see between groups on the brink of interethnic violence.

Ukrainian analysis of the intra-Ukrainian divide suggests that it is the source of many of Ukraine's problems. One Ukrainian article argued that "we do not simply have a situation of bilingualism. What we have is a fissure [*rozkolyna*] at the very core of Ukrainian culture."[38] In another article, A. Marenych writes that "among residents of Ukraine there are many Russians and, which is so annoying, Ukrainians who . . . due to spiritual poverty of mind or intellectual laziness are evading the use of Ukrainian, although the great majority knows it. In this way they are not supporting Ukrainian independence, do not believe in it, and have some hope for a return of Ukraine to a new colonial slavery."[39] In this case it is the intra-Ukrainian divide which the author is sharpening. And so, Dmitrii Kornilov, leader of the

[35] Oleksa Novak, "Do pytannia pro natsional'ni menshyny Ukrainy," *Klyn* (in Ukrainian), no. 8, 1993; my emphasis.

[36] Yosyp Bahlai, "Ofitsiina chy derzhavna mova, abo Liapas Prezydenta Zakonovi pro movy v Ukraini," *Shliakh peremohy* (in Ukrainian), September 10, 1994.

[37] Vitalii Karpenko, "Peredvyborni mify," *Vechirnii Kyiv* (in Ukrainian), January 12, 1994.

[38] "Zaiava-protest," *Shliakh peremohy* (in Ukrainian), July 16, 1994.

[39] Anton Marenych, "Masky zniato, bud'mo pyl'nymy!" *Molod' Ukrainy* (in Ukrainian), October 11, 1994.

Intermovement of the Donbas, told Arel (and his collaborator Andrew Wilson) in an interview in July 1993,

> The real conflict is not between Ukraine and Russia, but within the Ukrainian ethnos. [The fight is between pure Ukrainians and] those Ukrainians who think that Ukraine is part of a general Russian [*obshcherusskoi, obshcherossiiskoi*] culture. They simultaneously think of themselves as "Little Russians" as distinct from the Great and White Russians, and, on a higher plane, part of the same nation [*edinaia natsiia*] and [stand apart from] the separatists [*samostiiniki,*] who think that Ukraine and Russia are absolutely distinct, that Ukraine never understood Russia, and vice versa. This struggle has been going on for two centuries.

It is the battle for the souls of the "degenerated" Ukrainians that helps keep internationality conflict between Russians and Ukrainians on a back burner.

In Kazakhstan, as in Ukraine, intra-Kazakh tensions, between the Kazakh russophones (the *mankurty*) and pure titulars, are quite evident in daily life. The cosmopolitan mankurty stereotype the Kazakh nationalists as uncultured. For example, Nurlan Amrekulov wrote, "It is this rural mass with its traditional reverence to the authority structure that is supporting the movement for a strong authoritarian state." His alternative is the small group of mankurty, as "it is this thin layer, acting in unison with the Russian democratic intelligentsia, that is capable of steering the country in a centrist position, and there is absolutely no other alternative to this position in Kazakhstan in the given conditions."[40]

The fissure between the mankurty and the so-called pure Kazakhs has deep roots. As far back as the 1940s, A. Zhovtis claims that he "could not help but notice the animosity between the Russian-speaking and Kazakh-speaking Kazakhs. The latter hated and envied their Russian-speaking brethren. There were all kinds of petty squabbles, intrigues and so on." And he sees evidence of all this today. "Just look at the new minister of science and technology. He is a highly qualified Russian-speaking Kazakh and now he is being swallowed by the nationalists." In an earlier interview, Zhovtis angrily pointed out:

> Just look at Nurkadilov [the infamous mayor of Almaty]. He is far worse than Ruslan Khasbulatov [the equally infamous parliamentary ally of Rutskoi]. All those rural migrants constitute his support base. Such people are responsible for this new polarization and segregation within the society. They simply cannot tolerate Russian-speaking Kazakhs. Russians think they are being persecuted. But they [Russians] simply do not understand what the hell is going on inside.

The irony here is that Nurkadilov and other populists who claim to represent the interests of the pure Kazakhs, are themselves russophones. Take for example a political meeting of all opposition groups that took place in Almaty's Dom Demokratii on November 3, 1993. All discussion was in Russian, and pure Russian at that.

[40] Nurlan Amrekulov, "Demokraticheskii potentsial kazakhskoi intelligentsii: ispytanie suverenitetom," *Panorama*, March 1993, p. 3.

There was no code-mixing or code-switching. Dave noticed Zhasaral Kuanishuli, the uncompromising nationalist, who in November 1992 had written an extremely virulent, angry polemic, published originally in a Kazakh newspaper and translated in *Vechernaia Alma-Ata* for the Russian-speaking Kazakhs. She was surprised to hear him speaking excellent, unaccented Russian at the meeting. This shows, as a practical matter, it is impossible to enter the Kazakhstan political arena without being a russophone. In this case, the fissure between the pure Kazakhs and the mankurty is not as raw as the parallel cleavage in Ukraine.

Meanwhile, the tensions between Russians and Kazakhs seem to dominate, at least when it comes to the production of ethnic vitriol. Consider the following episode: one evening, Almas (speaking in high Kazakh) was narrating a story to friends that had them laughing uproariously. It had several references to some (Russian) drunkard, implying that Kazakhs who spoke the pure language like he did would never drink vodka like that. Sheker, the head (*bastik*) of the oblast department in charge of cultural activities, had a related view of the Russians: "There are very few Russians in Kyzyl-Orda," she observed,

> because they are a shrewd people. They have taken over the best lands of the Kazakhs. They won't live where the soil isn't very good, where there is little water. After all, they need their dachas, with all the greeneries, berries, etc. They want to live in the midst of plenty, and won't tolerate any hardships. The Kazakhs, on the other hand, are very tolerant people who can put up with a great deal of hardship. They will never complain, or express displeasure, and they will never leave their native place [*tugan zheri*]. Russians have no such ties. If it gets hard to live at one place, they will simply pack and leave. No wonder they are all over.

Then she asked Dave to "look at Zhirinovskii. People like him have no roots, they are of obscure origins. That's why no land is enough for them." Mira, whom Dave met at a party, had strong anti-Russian feelings. In the following remarks, her tirade was aimed at Igor, the Russian husband in a Kazakh family:

> As soon as even a little step is taken to restore the prestige, culture, and self-respect of Kazakhs, many people are immediately offended. They simply don't understand. All these years there was unabashed russification. All the Kazakh schools were closed one after another. I came from a village in Jambul oblast to Almaty at the age of six, and knew no Russian whatsoever. My mother was a single parent. She came to Almaty in search for a job and some relatives helped her to get settled. There were no Kazakh schools. I was sent to a Russian school. My mother told me all the time that you have to learn Russian well, even better than Russians themselves, if you want to live like a human being. Stop crying and work hard. Thanks to my mother's insistence, and the fact that I had to give it back to those Russians who would look at us as if we are uncivilized, just because we did not speak Russian. Now I know Russian much better than they know it themselves. I finished the school with distinction, got the best "diploma" and medals, etc., and got admitted to the university on my own merit without any *blat*. We never said a word then. We couldn't . . . when they

> would not let us study in Kazakh. Now things are changing, though so slowly, just a little step is taken in the direction of reviving Kazakh, which was on the edge of extinction, and people start complaining about discrimination.

Discrimination against Russians, now popular, is a theme in everyday conversation. For example, Madina, a young Kazakh mother who is married to a Russian, mentioned to Dave that a neighbor had come to her apartment, collecting money for fixing a lock in the building. She gratuitously mentioned, believing Madina to be as pure Kazakh as she, how "nice it would be for us when these Russians leave. Then we won't have to live in such a faraway district [*mikroraion*]. . . . It will be so much easier to get jobs and so on."

Aziza Zhunispeisova, who was the only surviving child out of sixteen siblings and illiterate, although critical of Russians, was more ambivalent. "We will remain dependent on Russia for years and years to come," she told Dave.

> Russians, especially those who came here during the virgin lands campaign, are slovenly, and extremely limited. They sent all those criminals, drunkards, and idlers from villages in Russia and Siberia. The Russian village has often been in a terrible state, not much better than the Kazakh *aul*. They sent such swindlers and idlers from these villages to us, "to build factories and cities" and these became our urban citizens. Russian people wanted that we remain grateful to them all our life. True, Kazakhs did not know how to work in factories. But did these Russians know? At least those who came here in the 1920s and 1930s were different. They respected our culture, and our language. They all learned Kazakh. If they knew Kazakh, they got a raise in their salary.

Kazakh ethnic self-criticism is prominent in current discourse as well. Here is an analysis from Nellia, Madina's mother, who had in the course of a visit mentioned something about her dacha. Dave seemed surprised that a Kazakh would have a dacha. Nellia reported that this is not at all common, as nomads never really had to work the soil and don't know how to use it productively. But her family was exposed to agriculture a long time ago, and she loves growing her own vegetables and fruits and living far away from the city. Then she went on to say how most Kazakhs are lazy. In the past when "everything was easily available," she explained, there was no need for Kazakhs to grow their own vegetables or fruits. But now, in her opinion, things are so expensive that a person cannot survive without a garden. Now Kazakhs envy all the Russians for having the dachas, but in the past when they were given plots of land, they grazed sheep on it or neglected it. "Just by a look at the property," she sardonically advised, "you can tell who lives there. If you see flowers all around, very well-mowed grass, there is no doubt that it is a German family. When you see lots of berries and vegetables, it is surely owned by a Russian. And when you see an abandoned piece of land, some hungry dogs running around, you know what kind of an owner [*khoziain*] it is."

Russians, as we have seen, are not shy when it comes to stereotyping the Kazakhs. For example, talking about Islam and fundamentalism, Boris (a senior scientist in Almaty) mentioned how Kazakhs are far more *dikie narody* (savage people) than the Uighurs, Uzbeks, or Tadzhiks, who had some "civilization." Kazakhs, being "savage" in the sense of being uncivilized, are far more receptive to various influences, whether Baptists, Hare Krishnas, or Jehovah's Witnesses. "The party is dead, the *komsomol* is dead, and they have few traditions, but the need to believe in something is there nonetheless. So Baptists and other new sects serve a function." Then Boris referred to the psychology of dependence on Russia from which Kazakhs suffer. He pointed out a sign he read near a gas station "Out of gas; Russia didn't send any" ("Benzina net, Rossiia gaz ne daiot"). He laughed, saying that of course they mention nothing about Kazakhstan's unwillingness (or inability) to pay for it.

The cleavage pattern in Ukraine and Kazakstan has certain parallels, but with important distinctions. In neither country do the Russians feel the need to fight for autonomy. In both, the Russians feel that they can count on help from Russia, should violence break out. The titulars of both countries are also divided by a linguistic intranationality cleavage of some importance. The titular populations of both countries are also divided along regional (in Ukraine) or clan (in Kazakhstan) lines. In Ukraine the regional issue surpasses the ethnic as a source of political conflict, and in Kazakhstan, disputes among the three hordes dominates discussions about government distributions and jobs to a greater degree than any tension between the mankurty and the nationalists or the Russians and the Kazakhs. In both cases, these divisions have helped to prevent (or perhaps only delay) internationality violence.

For practical purposes, the security community that exists in Estonia and the expectation that Russia will come to the aid of the Russian-speakers in Kazakhstan and Ukraine if the need arises have the same result—interethnic peace. But if conditions change—if, for example, Russia becomes less able to project force in the near abroad—the two mechanisms will have somewhat different results. It is unlikely that either ethnic community would take advantage of a new power balance in Estonia; but in Ukraine and Kazakhstan, the nontitulars would react quickly, perhaps even arm themselves, to protect their security.

Reconfiguration of the Choice Set: Toward a Russian-Speaking Nationality

A principal theme of this book is that as Russians in the near abroad decide whether to assimilate, to organize politically as Russians, or to return to their putative homeland, the basic identity categories that guided them in the past become eroded. Russians in all four republics are, with varying degrees of self-consciousness, inventing new categories of identity to help them make sense of who they are. One self-description becoming pervasive in all four republics is that of a "Russian-speaking population" (*russkoiazychnoe naselenie*).[41] It is significant that experienced

[41] According to A. D. Dulichenko, *Russkii iazyk kontsa XX stoletiia* (Munich: O. Sagner, 1994), p. 205, the first time this term appears as a noun in a dictionary is in the twenty-ninth edition of the *Orphograpicheskii slovar'* (1991), where it is defined as the equivalent of *sovetskii* (Soviet).

observers of the Soviet scene seem to have overlooked this development. For example, one of my co-fieldworkers, who speaks Russian far more fluently than I, tended to ignore it, thinking of it more or less as a commonplace. As Dave wrote in her field notes after she interviewed the editor of *Kazakhstanskaia pravda*, "he almost always used the term 'Russian-speaking' [*russkoiazychnoe*]. I did not pay special attention to it then. Only after David's paper [Laitin, 1995, *Archives*] on the formation of a Russian-speaking nationality did I notice that my notes have the reference to *russkoiazychnoe naselenie*."[42] In the literature on post-Soviet nationalism, only Mark Beissinger has taken notice of the term, yet he found it to be of no great significance.[43] But in matters of identity, clichés are more significant than reasoned categories. They reflect popular understandings and are therefore crucial for understanding what sort of messages will catch popular imagination.

Our interviews demonstrate that "Russian" is by no means lost as a category for national identification for nearly all nontitulars in the former union republics. They further demonstrate that the tenacity of passport nationalities remains strong, and many of our informants see those categories, ultimately, as "really real," to use an expression of Clifford Geertz's.[44] Nonetheless, especially because "Soviet" is no longer a socially acceptable category (even if many of our informants still think that this is what they really are), the old categories have become inadequate for nontitulars, and there is a good deal of exploration for new categories of identity. Of these, "Russian-speaking population" appears to have a "naturalness" about it—the cliché quality I just mentioned—that gives it social power.

"Russian" as a conglomerate identity category is not at all inappropriate for the Russians (and many non-Russians) in the diaspora. As many interpreters of Russian nationalism have pointed out, there has never been a Russian nation-state, and a notion of "Russianness" as a nationality never had a state apparatus that consistently promoted it. Thus the commonly heard ditty throughout the Soviet Union: "My mother is Tatar, my father Greek, and I'm a Russian" ("Mama tatarka, otets grek, i ia russkii chelovek"). In the diaspora, especially in Kazakhstan, the label "Russian" is easily adopted by the nontitulars who are not Central Asians. Dave's informants Volodia and Sasha give a good sense of this view. They were talking about what kind of "Russians" they are. "The further away from Russia, the easier to be labeled [registered] Russian," said Sasha. In fact they were talking about all the "Russians" in the physics department where Volodia works. One of them, Kolomeets (Volodia's colleague and former dissertation adviser), is of course Ukrainian ("A last name like Kolomeets can only be Ukrainian," said Volodia), but he passes for (and is registered in his red passport as) a Russian. (On another occasion Volodia said, in reference to Kolomeets, "a peasant-Ukrainian last

[42] To be sure, another of my co-fieldworkers, Dominique Arel, has been quite sensitive to the existence of "russophones" as a social formation in Ukraine. See his "Language and the Politics of Ethnicity" (Ph.D. diss., University of Illinois, Urbana-Champaign, 1994).

[43] Mark R. Beissinger, "The Persisting Ambiguity of Empire," *Post-Soviet Affairs* 11, no. 2 (1995): 169–72.

[44] Clifford Geertz, "Religion as a Cultural System," in *Interpretation of Cultures* (New York: Basic Books, 1973), pp. 87–125.

name, but he is regarded as Russian.") Another colleague—"a Jew—is of course a Russian," said Volodia with a twist of irony. The third person is of mixed Kalmyk-Chuvash ("like Lenin") descent, and "pure Russian, like Lenin"—both of them noted. Dave heard expressions of this sort from her landlady, who in responding to her questions about nationality, would say, "What sort of Russians are they? . . . There are no pure Russians. . . . Now we are all Russians." "Russian" is apparently such an ambiguous category that nontitulars in the diaspora adopt it readily.

Furthermore, Stalin's tradition of reifying national identities on passports, along with memories of primordial attachments that cram most people's brains in the modern era, has assured the continued vibrancy of separate national identities among the nontitular populations in the near abroad. In Kazakhstan, the national museum in Almaty has a window celebrating each of the nationalities in Kazakhstan, archaeologizing Ukrainian, Belarusan, Orthodox, Korean, Uzbek, and Kazakh national traditions. Typical display items in the windows were dictionaries, national clothing, and documents attesting to their immigration to Kazakhstan.

In Almaty, in the famous Dom Demokratii, where all opposition parties have offices, there are offices for the various nationality groups as well: the Korean Center, the Ukrainian Cultural Center, and the Slavic movement *Lad*. In a long interview with Feliks Rytkov, vice-president of the Ukrainian Society of Kazakhstan, Dave was told that both the Ukrainians and the Kazakhs were victims of Russian chauvinism. His society, he claims, seeks Ukrainian-language education for Ukrainians in Kazakhstan and helps to resettle Ukrainians back to their homeland. While the activities of national cultural organizations are almost invisible outside of their offices, they remain places where the separate organs of a Russian-speaking population are given nationalist nourishment.

Indeed, these nationalities are alive in people's self-images. Dave talked with Valentina Mateevna, who is about seventy years old. She considers Kazakhstan to be her homeland now, but she remains intensely interested in the moves of her fellow "Germans" from Issyk, many of whom left for Germany, and considers herself "really" German. And Volodia, whose mother is German, keeps his options open for future emigration by assembling and storing official papers that would allow him to retire in Germany. In this era of national revival, nontitulars in Kazakhstan are quite conscious of their supposedly (and often externally imposed) "real" roots and have reconnected with them.

The same is the case in the other republics we have studied. In Ukraine, Arel traveled to L'viv with Oleksandra, an eastern Ukrainian. Oleksandra stayed with a local woman who spoke perfect Ukrainian and Russian. Arel asked Oleksandra how she perceived the woman, and was told (correctly) "Jewish." He then asked the local Russian woman with whom he was staying about Oleksandra's host, and that woman quickly guessed "Jewish" as well. Indeed, despite (and maybe because of) three-quarters of a century of "internationalism," the instincts of knowing others' real nationalities has not eroded at all. In Estonia, I learned that the Israeli government is offering retirement packages to Russian-speaking Jews that are far more attractive than those offered by the Estonian government to its own retirees. Israel is making them an offer, one of my informants told me as we sat on beach chairs overlooking the Baltic Sea, that they could not resist. The married couple with whom I talked would receive from Estonia about 1,000 kroons (about $80) per month, with 350 kroons going for rent. The Israeli government would pay them a full pension of about 1,400 shekels (about $450) per month, plus housing and basic furnishings for their flat. This package has helped to separate the Estonian Jews from other elements of the Russian-speaking population, because on a fundamental issue, social security, the Jews do not need to organize. The Estonian government as well, with its (quite limited) funding of a "Union of Nationalities in Estonia," has helped separate some non-Russian Russian-speakers from joining in a conglomerate Russian-speaking identity group. In Latvia, too, the Popular Front helped to initiate eighteen national cultural associations as a way to erode any support the anti-independence Interfront movement might have had among Russians.[45] In the local press, *SM-Segodnia* wrote critically against the government's requirement that in Russian-language schools, internal memoranda must be written in the state language. The journalist asks, in a rare breakdown of the conglomerate identity that has become a cliché in this newspaper, "So when can we remember that we are Russians, Ukrainians, Poles, or Lithuanians?"[46]

Despite the usefulness and simplicity of "Russian," and the primordial memories supporting passport designations, in all four republics there has been significant exploration to find a better category to fit that set of residents who were derailed by the double cataclysm. Aleksandr Niklass captured the problem nicely in an article published in *Baltiiskaia gazeta*. Niklass claimed that he has no nationality, but in today's Latvia, this isn't so easy, since citizenship is tied to nationality. Thus he feels frustrated because he can't just be himself. He wrote: "One thing worries me: while one part of the population is off finding its national distinctiveness and other interesting things, what is the other part supposed to do . . . those people who aren't concerned by all of this? And what should be done with the nationality listed in the passports of these people who 'aren't doing the right thing'?"[47]

An article in *Karavan* (Kazakhstan) from 1993 picks up on this issue and gives a sense of the movement from passport nationality to "the unrooted" (*nekorennyie*, a new category) to Russians, and finally to a tentative use of "Russian-speaking."[48]

> Shall we conclude . . . that in recent years there has occurred a significant erosion in the intellectual potential and professional aptitudes among Russians, Ukrainians, Tatars, Koreans, Uighurs, Jews, Germans, living in Kazakhstan? . . . Incidentally, among the adult and working population of the country, the percentage of

[45] Nils Muiznieks, "Latvia: Origins, Evolution and Triumph," in Ian Bremmer and Ray Taras, eds., *Nations and Politics in the Soviet Successor States* (Cambridge: Cambridge University Press, 1993), p. 197.

[46] Ol'ga Novikevich, "Prikazano zabyt' russkii," *SM-Segodnia*, December 2, 1993.

[47] Aleksandr Niklass, "V poiskakh national'nosti," *Baltiiskaia gazeta*, February 18, 1994. In Latvia, the reification of passport identities has persisted. In Estonia it has been abolished. In Kazakhstan, plans have been announced to permit voluntary marking of nationality on the passport, without any constraint on personal choice. The effects of these different policies remain to be investigated.

[48] Giller and Shatskikh, "Opredelenie berega," pp. 1–3.

> the unrooted is even greater. The growth of the birth rate in a Kazakh family is 4.5 percent, for Russians it is just 1.1 percent. By these calculations, almost 70 percent of the adult working population of the country consist of the unrooted. . . . Russians would have packed their bags even earlier, if only the Russian-speaking reader had been able to read some of the publications in the Kazakh-language press.

In Ukraine, the Communists come equally close to giving official designation to a Russian-speaking identity group that has collectively faced the indignities of national chauvinism. They write: "The extremist attacks against the official status of the Russian language are filled with an open disrespect and gross violation of the rights of Russians, and citizens of other nationalities, who consider Russian as their mother tongue."[49]

A range of designations for the group that suffered from the double cataclysm has been attempted. In 1986, a survey by Kaarel Haav found 78 percent of the Russian population in Estonia saw themselves as "Soviets." If the project to create the "Soviet" nationality (which, in many regards, is comparable to an "American" one) was successful anywhere, it was in the non-Russian union republics. Yet "Soviet" has lost its luster, and it is an identity rarely evoked nowadays in popular rhetoric. On Latvian TV, Jelena Berotsova saw the problem in a perceptive way. "We need to look for traditions and find a feeling for them," she said. "We have no traditions now. People lack traditions. The Latvians have traditions. They are a small nation. That has helped them preserve these traditions. We are many and we have lost all of this. We have no heroes. We were Soviets. Now who are we? Russia is still far away. There is also some sense of collective guilt, a sense of shame for the people."[50]

The term "the unrooted" has become a standard reference, although it is more negative than a vendor of group identity might like. In Kazakhstan, Dave heard the expression "Europeans" in reference to those who Nazarbaev most trusted to provide him personal security in his Kazakhstani presidential guard. This term wouldn't work very well in the other three republics in distinguishing potential members of a Russian-speaking nationality from titulars, but it has a certain power in Central Asia. An alternative is the promotion of a "Slavic" identity. E. V. Kolomeets, for example, has been active in the founding of a Slavic University in Bishkek, after Nazarbaev turned down the opportunity to have it in Kazakhstan.[51] In Estonia, too, the "Russian Society of Estonia" has been active in promoting the idea of a common "Slavic" identity in many of its articles. Finally, in the Baltics, there are numerous references to a "Baltic Russian" identity. In a 1991 interview with Vladimir Lebedev, he told me that Russians living in Estonia are not "pure" Russians but "Baltic Russians." "When they go to Russia," he insisted, "they are not at home." He

[49] "Ni—movnii dyskryminatsii i fundamentalizmu! Zaiava Prezydii Tsentral'noho Komitetu KPU," *Komunist* (in Ukrainian), no. 25, September 1994. *Komunist* is a bilingual paper, the organ of the Communist Party of Ukraine, although most of its political articles are in Russian.

[50] Recorded by Vello Pettai from Latvian Television, February 22, 1994.

[51] Paul Kolstoe, *Russians in the Former Soviet Republics* (Bloomington: Indiana University Press, 1995), p. 241, emphasizes that the Slavic card is not played here. In the by-laws, the need to cater to the ethnically Kyrgyz part of the population is stipulated.

felt that Baltic Russians should be treated in Estonia the same as Baltic Germans (as aristocrats!) were in a previous era.

In an environment of search, "Russian-speaking population" has begun to emerge as the default option to describe those in the union republics who were struck hardest (and commonly) by especially the first of the cataclysms, that is, the new language laws. At first, as already noted, it was a term of opprobrium designating those Russians who still had a Soviet consciousness. Russians in Russia today, a point I develop in Chapter 10, use it in a derogatory manner to refer to unwanted foreigners. But in the countries of the near abroad, this identity category began to take on a positive value by people who adopted it as a core aspect of their social identities.[52]

In Kazakhstan, for example, in the interview in which Dave noted that she first recognized the power of the term, the editor of *Kazakhstanskaiia pravda* told her:

> The atomic plants in the [Mangyshlak] oblast had attracted the most qualified defense cadres from all over the Soviet Union. These form our best personnel and almost all of them are Russian-speaking. The city of Shevchenko—inhabited by the Russian-speakers in western Kazakhstan, is located in the midst of desert. The city was literally built on rocks. It was constructed in the late fifties, and water had to be brought in because it is in arid heartland. Look at Karaganda—it too stands on bare rocks. . . . Actually right from the Caspian to the Aral Sea the land is arid, rocky, dry, and totally devoid of water. The only viable means of livelihood in Mangyshlak is sheep breeding. It has the lowest population density in Kazakhstan. The Russian-speakers did not come to these regions of their own free will. In fact, the highly qualified cadres are leaving because they are very much in demand, and they feel they can do better in Russia. If these Russian-speakers leave, the few Kazakhs [working there] will leave it as well, for who would man all these industrial plants?

Again, in a debate on nationality, Faizulla Iskakov wrote: "In terms of their behavioral stereotypes and psychological temperament, the Russian-speaking people in Central Asia differ fundamentally from the Russians of Russia, Belarus', Ukraine, etc."[53] In December 1995, my first conversation with my landlady in Almaty left me in little doubt that this category was a common one. She used the term "Russian-speaking population" regularly, to refer to those who had lost all dignity in the face of the nationalism pervading Kazakhstan at that time. The Russian-speaking population's role in building Kazakhstan had not been, in her acidic judgment, given its due.[54]

[52] Isabelle Kreindler, in a private communication, informs me that in the rightwing *Literaturnaia Rossiia*, the term "Russian-speaking population" continues in 1996 to be a regular term of opprobrium. Kolstoe, *Russians in the Former Soviet Republics*, p. 110, reports on its use, with a strong negative valence in Riga. The data in Chapter 10 demonstrate the change toward a positive valence of the term in the Russian and republican press, when reference is to ethnic issues in the near abroad.

[53] Faizulla Iskakov, "My pochti vse esche v odnoi lodke," *Azia*, December 14(?), 1993, p. 7.

[54] Pål Kolstø, personal communication, points out that in Kazakh discourse "the Russians" is a common term for all non-Westerners and non-Muslims. Since physiognomic differences are so noticeable, there is no need for "-speaking" to differentiate "us" from "them." I analyze these and related issues in Chapter 10.

In Ukraine, "Russian-speaking population" is an ambiguous term. In Arel's discussions with Iurii and Lida, Arel asked how many of Iurii's colleagues are ethnic Russians. He said about half, but his wife objected, saying that only two were Russian according to passport (*po pasportu*). Iurii corrected himself, recognizing the mixed nature of the families in his circle of acquaintance, and said he meant about half were from "Russian-speaking" environments. This term can take a vitriolic turn in Ukraine, as one ultranationalist wrote that "the government, which administers the productive life of Ukraine, is not only Russian-speaking, but totally Russian-statist-in-thinking [*rosiis'komysliachyi*]."[55]

In Estonia, the Narva City Council resolved in 1991 to oppose Yeltsin's policies that went against "the interests of the rooted Russian-speaking peoples." The *Narvskaia gazeta*, some time later, reported the political effort to create a united group for the "Russian-speaking residents of Estonia." In *Estoniia* there was an appeal against cutting off the Russian TV network, Ostankino, from free transmissions to Estonia. "Cutting Ostankino means cutting the last thread of contact . . . [for] the Russian-speaking people."[56]

To sum up this section on the "Russian-speaking population," Russians living in the near abroad were not only calculating their opportunities *qua* Russians in the newly independent republics; they were also, consciously and semi-consciously, trying on different identities, to represent themselves in different ways on their new political stage. Not only do we observe in the post-Soviet republics identities in confrontation; we observe as well identities in formation.[57]

THE 1989 language laws threatened the security of the monolingual language repertoires of the Russian-speaking populations of the near abroad; the 1991 collapse of the Soviet Union threatened their political rights and undermined their secure identities as Soviet internationalists.

Despite the great anxieties and fears faced by the Russian-speaking diaspora in response to this double cataclysm, they were able (indeed, were compelled) to calculate the individual costs and benefits of a variety of courses of action, especially in regard to their (and their children's) future language repertoires. The people we interviewed, or whose commentaries we read in the press, were sensitive to the expected economic returns of learning the titular language. They observed the degree of compliance to those laws, especially of the titulars themselves, as a signal indicating to them the probability that the titular language would establish itself as hegemonic within the republic. They assessed the costs of learning the language and

55 Mykhailo Kosiv, "Kolonizatsiia shliakhom asymiliatsii?" *Prosvita* (L'viv, in Ukrainian), no. 30, December 1993.

56 *Narvskaia gazeta*, January 19, 1991, and January 28, 1993; *Estoniia*, March 17, 1994.

57 This phenomenon is not unprecedented. The closest analogy, as Jeremy King explained to me, is the creation of a German-speaking identity after World War I in Bohemia, Moravia, and the former Austrian Silesia. Hitler obliterated this identity project by incorporating its members into an integral German nationality. I concede that a force as great as Hitler's could do the same for the "Russian-speaking population," but this is not to deny that the "Russian-speaking population" has some staying power as an identity group, a point I develop in Chapter 10.

were sensitive to the levels of status gains and losses they would experience should they learn the language.

The simple tipping game, based on whether to add the titular language to your (or your children's) language repertoire, was not the only show in town. Our informants had to assess the expected returns of emigration, of political mobilization *qua* Russians, of quiet incorporation into the republic without much cultural change, and of violent confrontation with titular authorities. These alternative strategies were also highly constrained by questions of cost, questions of the likely choices made by other Russians, and questions of future returns. To be sure, our informants considered certain choices to be unthinkable or impractical and not subject to choice, yet the realm of calculation is wide indeed. Therefore a choice model is quite appropriate for the study of alternatives to assimilation.

There were similarities in all four republics in the relevance of the choice model of cultural shift. Yet the different calculations made in the various republics were also based on the differences in historical context—specifically, the three models of state incorporation—from republic to republic. Thus the "micro" choice models of the tipping game are heavily influenced by "macro" historical factors.

In Kazakhstan, where a colonial model of incorporation was dominant, the national revival has tended to be subverted by cosmopolitan forces from within the titular group. Picking up on these signals, and with their own sense of status superiority, Russian-speakers cannot themselves take the idea of assimilation seriously and have not therefore paid the cost of expanding their language repertoires. Since postcolonial nationalism in Kazakhstan is more about job protection for nationals than cultural shift, many young Russians fear that they won't be needed when they are sixty-four. They see exit as the only reasonable response to secure their future.

In the Baltics, where the Soviets relied on an integralist model of state incorporation, the nationalizing project of the titulars is not in doubt. The Kafkesque *Trial* that the Baltic States put Russians through, even to maintain residency status, only works to convince Russians of the inexorability of the nationalizing project. The Russians who remain in these republics are making clear plans to comply with present regulations in regard to language and to invest in their children's fluency in the titular languages.

In Ukraine, as a most-favored-lord republic, there is a deep ambivalence toward Russia, as both the same and different. And thus the "Dr. Jekyll and Mr. Hyde" approach to Russians. Because the two languages are so similar, the boundary between Russian and Ukrainian is constantly tested, with code-mixing, code-switching, and bilingual conversations being part of everyday speech, especially in Kiev, the republican center. The nationalists in Ukraine are committed to keeping the boundary between the two languages distinct, and in Kiev (the central battleground) we have detected a war of position between the two languages fought on a variety of fronts.

The Russians in the near abroad are also exploring new identity categories. For most of our informants during the ancien régime, a "Soviet" identity was quite useful and adequate. It downplayed any chauvinism that might have been associated with their Russianness. Although many held that their "real" identities were the ones written on their passports and joined cultural associations to nurture those primordial attachments, these associations have not, up till now, excited many imaginations in the diaspora. The "Soviet" identity had allowed Russians, Ukrainians, Belarusans, and Jews, when out of their national homelands, to become part of a common culture—Russian in language and socialist in appearance. Among our informants, this common cultural group suffered equally both cataclysmic blows, and there was little incentive to break down into constituent national elements. After the second cataclysm, many who saw themselves as Soviets groped for a new category, as "Russian" may have sounded too chauvinist for their brand of internationalism. In Kazakhstan, "European" began to describe non–Central Asians and served the interests of those with some German roots. In Estonia and Latvia, a "Baltic Russian" identity has attracted attention. In all the republics, "Orthodox" and "Slavic" have become code words to house substantial parts of the diaspora as well. But no category has served better than that of the "Russian-speaking population," a term that is hardly a decade old but already commonplace in all four republics. This term, as far as I can see, has emerged almost unconsciously from a need by members of the diaspora to talk about their plight in a coherent way. It has crept into the everyday vocabulary of elites and ordinary people in all four republics. It would be a grave error to think about identity politics in the post-Soviet republics as a bipolar conflict between titulars and Russians. When categories of identity change, the old labels are no longer relevant.

PART THREE

THE RUSSIAN RESPONSE: ASSIMILATION

7

Assimilation: Survey Results

Part III deals principally with the question of assimilation. I ask the question that brought cynical laughter from specialists in the early 1990s: Can the Russians become titulars? Or in the just-so language of Gellner: Can Megalomanians become Ruritanians? The answer is that in the two integral republics (Estonia and Latvia), despite the cultural distance and the lack of a warm welcome by the titular governments, the pressures for intergenerational assimilation are very powerful, and they are already being felt. In the most-favored-lord republic, the pressures are lower than would be expected from a theory of cultural distance. Russians are not rapidly redefining themselves as Ukrainian and remain, at least compared to their beached compatriots in the Baltics, more hostile to the idea of their children becoming titulars. In the colonial republic, as would be predicted by models of cultural distance as well as by the models developed in this book, Russian-speakers feel few incentives to assimilate into titular culture.

Correlating openness to assimilation with patterns of state incorporation tells us little about the mechanisms that give people incentives to assimilate. In the tipping model—and supplemented by the ethnographies—I have elucidated three mechanisms that translate the macro patterns into micro-incentives. The first was expected economic returns; the second was in-group status; and the third was out-group acceptance. In Part III, I present quantitative data on each of these dimensions to help explain the relative degree of openness to assimilation by the Russian-speaking populations in the four republics.

Over the course of this and the next two chapters, I provide survey data to rank the Russian-speaking population in the four republics on the dependent variable—openness to assimilation. I also use sociolinguistic data (Chapter 8) to explore the relative importance of each of the mechanisms associated with the tipping calculus in explaining the variation on openness to assimilation. I show how the perceived status of speakers of a language, in key contexts more important than expected economic returns, plays a powerful role in calculations about linguistic assimilation. In Chapter 9, the final chapter of Part III, I combine the survey and sociolinguistic data (but with an interpretive frame developed from ethnography) to outline a more comprehensive theory than Gellner was able to provide on the conditions under which assimilation takes place.

The Assimilation Index

Openness to assimilation is an index that reflects the degree to which Russians living in the republics of the near abroad have assimilated culturally, accepted the cultural rationalization measures of their countries of residence, and agreed to suggestions for furthering such a national project. A high score on this index reflects "openness to assimilation"; a low score reflects a propensity for Russian national mobilization against the cultural rationalizing policies of their country of residence.

The openness to assimilation index is constructed from answers to twelve questions in the survey, and a summary of the possible answers to each component question is provided in Table 7.1.[1] A perusal of the index mean for each republic, and the frequencies on each component of the index to these questions—provided in Table 7.2—suggests one very stunning finding at the outset. Despite the cataclysms described in earlier chapters and the pictures of antinational feelings among Russians presented in many accounts of post-Soviet rule, Russians in the titular republics are sensitive to the goals of the nationalists. An average of 93.4 percent of the Russian respondents had a positive or intermediate score in support of a requirement that the titular language become a required school subject in all republican schools; 86.9 percent answered that the titular language ought to be on street signs in their cities; and 91.7 percent of the respondents had either positive or intermediate answers in regard to the usefulness of learning the titular language. Only 13.9 percent of the Russian respondents answered that the future for Russians in their republic was best fulfilled by mobilizing politically as Russians; and 42.5 percent of the respondents were strongly opposed to territorial autonomy for Russians in their republics. Although there are variations within the populations surveyed, it is crucial to point out at first that the heavy balance at the time of the survey was toward acceptance by Russians living in the near abroad of the nationalizing programs set by their new republican governments.

The Social Bases of Assimilationist Attitudes

Within each republic, the differential social background of the survey respondents (or their "socioeconomic status"—SES), as would be expected, helps explain variation on individual scores on the index of assimilation. But the amount of the variation these social conditions can explain is not great. An initial perusal at the

[1] The significant covariation among all the variables (with an Alpha statistic of .81) of this index gives confidence that the index is measuring a single propensity. I analyze the reliability of the openness to assimilation in the appendix.

Table 7.1. Assimilation index: Questions and coding

Question	Kazakhstan	Estonia	Latvia	Ukraine
A & B: Attitude to marriage with member of another nationality (son & daughter)	0 = Undesirable 1 = Unimportant if spouse respects traditions 1 = Prefer same nationality, but would not protest 2 = Nationality is insignificant in marriage	0 = Undesirable 1 = Unimportant if spouse respects traditions 1 = Prefer same nationality, but would not protest 2 = Nationality is insignificant in marriage	0 = Undesirable 1 = Unimportant if spouse respects traditions 1 = Prefer same nationality, but would not protest 2 = Nationality is insignificant in marriage	0 = Completely approve 1 = Somewhat approve 1 = Indifferent 1 = Somewhat disapprove 2 = Categorically disapprove
C: How well do you know the [titular] language?	0 = I don't speak it at all 1 = I speak it with great difficulty 2 = I speak it with difficulty 3 = I speak it fluently 4 = I think in it	0 = I don't speak it at all 1 = I speak it with great difficulty 2 = I speak it with difficulty 3 = I speak it fluently 4 = I think in it	0 = I don't speak it at all 1 = I speak it with great difficulty 2 = I speak it with difficulty 3 = I speak it fluently 4 = I think in it	0 = I don't speak it at all 1 = I speak it with great difficulty 2 = I speak it with difficulty 3 = I speak it fluently 4 = I think in it
D: Would knowledge of the [titular] language be economically beneficial to your children?	0 = Completely disagree 1 = Partially disagree 2 = Partially agree 3 = Completely agree	0 = Not very useful 1 = Somewhat useful 2 = Very useful	0 = Completely disagree 1 = Partially disagree 2 = Partially agree 3 = Completely agree	0 = Completely disagree 1 = Partially disagree 2 = Partially agree 3 = Completely agree
E: Do you agree that Russians in [republic] should have the right to territorial autonomy?	0 = Completely agree 1 = Partially agree 2 = Partially disagree 3 = Completely disagree	0 = Completely agree 1 = Partially agree 2 = Don't agree 3 = Completely disagree	0 = Completely agree 1 = Partially agree 2 = Partially disagree 3 = Completely disagree	0 = Completely agree 1 = Partially agree 2 = Partially disagree 3 = Completely disagree
F: How do you envision the future for Russians living in [republic]?	0 = Leave republic 0 = Organize to separate territory 1 = Remain with cultural rights 1 = Strive to join Eurasian Union 2 = Learn language, become brethren to titulars	0 = Return to Russia 0 = Organize to separate territory 1 = Remain with cultural rights 2 = Assimilate	0 = Leave republic 0 = Organize to separate territory 1 = Remain with cultural rights 2 = Learn language, become brethren to titulars	0 = Leave republic 0 = Organize to separate territory 1 = Remain with cultural rights 2 = Learn language, become brethren to titulars

Table 7.1. Assimilation index: Questions and coding, *continued*

Question	Kazakhstan	Estonia	Latvia	Ukraine
G: If a government employee asks you a question in [titular], in what language do you reply?	0 = Russian 1 = mix (if high language ability) 2 = mix (if medium language ability) 3 = mix (if low language ability) 4 = titular	0 = Russian 1 = mix (if high language ability) 2 = mix (if medium language ability) 3 = mix (if low language ability) 4 = titular	0 = Russian 1 = mix (if high language ability) 2 = mix (if medium language ability) 3 = mix (if low language ability) 4 = titular	0 = Russian 1 = mix (if high language ability) 2 = mix (if medium language ability) 3 = mix (if low language ability) 4 = titular
H: In your opinion, in what language should street signs be written in your city?	0 = Russian 1 = mix (if high language ability) 2 = mix (if medium language ability) 3 = mix (if low language ability) 4 = titular	0 = Russian 1 = mix (if high language ability) 2 = mix (if medium language ability) 3 = mix (if low language ability) 4 = titular	0 = Russian 1 = mix (if high language ability) 2 = mix (if medium language ability) 3 = mix (if low language ability) 4 = titular	0 = Russian 1 = mix (if high language ability) 2 = mix (if medium language ability) 3 = mix (if low language ability) 4 = titular
I: In what language would you like your children to be taught in school (now or in the future)?	0 = Russian 1 = mix 2 = titular	0 = Russian 1 = mix 2 = titular	0 = Russian 1 = mix 2 = titular	0 = Russian 1 = mix 2 = titular
J: Do you agree that [titular] should be the only official/state language in [republic]?	0 = Completely disagree 1 = Partially disagree 2 = Partially agree 3 = Completely agree	0 = Completely don't support 1 = Don't support 2 = Partially support, partially don't support 3 = Support 4 = Fully support	0 = Completely disagree 1 = Partially disagree 2 = Partially agree 3 = Completely agree	0 = Completely disagree 1 = Partially disagree 2 = Partially agree 3 = Completely agree
K: Do you think that all permanent residents of [republic] should speak the [titular] language fluently?	0 = No 1 = Yes	0 = No 1 = Yes	0 = No 1 = Yes	0 = No 1 = Yes
L: Do you agree that the [titular] language should be a required school subject in all schools in [republic]?	0 = Completely disagree 1 = Partially disagree 2 = Partially agree 3 = Completely agree	0 = Completely disagree 1 = Partially disagree 2 = Don't disagree 3 = Completely agree	0 = Completely disagree 1 = Partially disagree 2 = Partially agree 3 = Completely agree	0 = Completely disagree 1 = Partially disagree 2 = Partially agree 3 = Completely agree

Note: All variables are standardized to the unit interval. Thus, to obtain the scale for any given cell in the table, divide each value by the highest value in that cell.

Table 7.2. Descriptive statistics of index of openness to assimilation

Elements of index	Kazakhstan	Estonia	Latvia	Ukraine	Total
Openness to assimilation					
Mean	.38*	.63*	.72*	.51*	.52
Standard deviation	.16	.14	.14	.16	.20
Minimum/maximum	.00/.78	.10/1.0	.16/1.0	.11/.97	0.00/1.00
Valid *n*	1,147	665	552	584	2,948
Marriage of a child to someone of a different nationality (percent)					
A: Son: positive/intermediate	31.3/44.9	72.6/24.6	72.0/25.8	67.4/32.1	54.6/34.7
B: Daughter: positive/intermediate	29.6/43.0	71.6/25.7	70.4/27.3	64.6/34.4	52.5/35.0
C: Ability in titular language (high = fluent): standardized mean	0.12	0.25	0.43	0.42	0.26
D: Titular language beneficial (percent): positive/intermediate	27.2/59.5	73.3/24.2	59.4/37.0	21.6/66.9	44.4/47.3
E: Territorial autonomy for Russians: percent strongly opposed	27.0	58.0	63.3	35.5	42.5
F: Future for Russians: percent mobilizing response	29.6	5.3	2.6	3.8	13.9
G: Answer to a government official who asks question in titular language (percent): in titular/in titular-Russian mix	4.6/8.6	16.0/29.0	43.1/23.3	24.7/7.3	18.6/15.8
H: Language of street signs (percent): titular/titular-Russian mix	1.5/84.7	27.4/69.6	56.2/43.6	16.8/48.0	20.1/66.8
I: Language of education (percent) titular/Russian	0.2/61.9	14.0/75.5	9.6/73.7	6.6 / 57.7	8.0/66.2
J: Titular as state language (percent): positive/intermediate	1.8/26.7	6.0/76.1	27.2/57.9	7.3/22.7	8.4/42.3
K: Agree that all permanent residents should have facility in titular language (percent)	28.3	72.2	82.7	39.5	50.4
L: Titular language should be a required subject in school (percent): positive/intermediate	33.2/53.2	78.0/21.5	87.3/11.6	61.4/32.8	59.4/34.0

*A difference of mean from each of the other four republics that is significantly different from zero at the 5% level (LSD and Tukey-HSD tests).

best specification we were able to achieve relying only on social background conditions—presented in Table 7.3—yields an R^2 of only 9 percent in Latvia, going up to 38 percent in Ukraine.[2] Although there are some important findings based on these regressions, the really interesting differences between the republics are not captured by an analysis of the social bases of national orientation within any one republic.

Estimates of the effects of several social-structural regressors on the assimilation index done separately for each republic—shown in Table 7.3—reveals that the only regressor that predicts the index well across cases is the size of the titular population in the respondents' city of residence. The coefficient is significant at the 1 percent level for all four republics. Further, this variable exhibits a quadratic relationship with the index; the squared transformation of the original variable is also significant at the 1 percent level for all four cases, but with a negative sign. This suggests that ethnic Russian respondents appear to have a more positive attitude toward assimilation when they constitute a smaller percentage of the population of their city of residence. The small negative coefficients on the squared term suggest that this positive relationship flattens out somewhat at higher percentages of titular residents.[3] Furthermore, this relationship must be judged quite significant in substantive terms. On average, for every additional percentage point of titular population, the value of the assimilation index increases by anywhere from roughly 0.4 percent (Estonia) to 1.6 percent (Latvia) of its total value.[4] In substantive terms, this effect is impressive.[5]

[2] Brian Silver, in his "Political Beliefs of the Soviet Citizen: Sources of Support for Regime Norms," in James A. Millar, ed., *Politics, Work, and Daily Life in the USSR* (Cambridge: Cambridge University Press, 1987), pp. 100–141, has shown that with great ingenuity, it is possible to explain more of the variation in Soviet citizen attitudes with SES variables than standard models would have allowed. Using Silver's techniques, further analysis of the survey data might yield improvements, but I leave that for scholars who have a theory about how to respecify the model. I should add here, though, that the gender of the respondents is not included in the tables presented herein because I have been unable to reject the null hypothesis of no gender effect on assimilation in all of the republics and for all model specifications.

[3] An interpretation of the quadratic relationship between assimilation and percentage of the titular population is provided in the appendix.

[4] I express the marginal effects of individual regressors as percentages because the metrics of the various measures are substantially different. The range of variation of the independent variables should also be taken into consideration in assessing the size of their effects. For instance, the regression coefficient for an independent variable with a 5-level scale that yields a 1 percent change in the index per unit change in that independent variable should not be considered as significant as a 1 percent change per unit change for an independent variable on a scale from 20 to 80 (as in the case of age). In the latter case, the difference between low and high values on the independent variable could cover as much as 60 percent of the value of the index, while in the former case, the difference between the highest and lowest values would cover only 5 percent of the value of the index.

[5] Despite the strong performance of this variable, the result must be interpreted with caution, since the samples were drawn from a small number of cities—and because only two cities are represented in the data from Ukraine. Moreover, although a fairly representative degree of variation is present for each of the republics surveyed, the cities in the sample were not chosen randomly within republics. Finally, I have not considered here other specific characteristics of the cities in the sample which might be related to ethnic attitudes—for example distance from the homeland, which would be highly correlated with percentage of Russians in the city. Nevertheless, the pattern of higher assimilation values for respondents from cities with a higher percentage of titular population is persistent throughout the samples.

Table 7.3. Social bases of Russian assimilation: Linear regression analysis (OLS)

Social basis	Kazakhstan	Estonia	Latvia	Ukraine
(Intercept)	0.0088	0.50[a]	0.16	0.19[a]
	(0.040)	(0.044)	(0.17)	(0.046)
Population of birthplace (0–4, 4 = most urban)	0.035[b]	0.0061	−0.036	−0.025
	(0.016)	(0.021)	(0.026)	(0.026)
Population of birthplace (squared)	−0.0054[b]	−0.0025	0.0058[c]	0.0041
	(0.0026)	(0.0034)	(0.0044)	(0.0041)
Attitude to religion (0–4, 4 = most religious)	0.0021	−0.0085	−0.011[c]	−0.017[a]
	(0.0046)	(0.0052)	(0.0057)	(0.0053)
Educational attainment (0–5, 5 = beyond B.A.)	0.0063	0.0065	0.022[a]	0.0032
	(0.0062)	(0.0065)	(0.0073)	(0.0075)
Occupation (0–9, 9 = most prestigious)	−0.0001	0.0093[a]	−0.0021	0.0053
	(0.0023)	(0.0027)	(0.003)	(0.0035)
Age (in years)	0.0003	−0.0015[a]	−0.001[c]	−0.0009
	(0.0005)	(0.0006)	(0.0006)	(0.0006)
Residence in republic (in years)	0.0001	0.0022[a]	0.0017[a]	0.0014[a]
	(0.0005)	(0.0006)	(0.0006)	(0.0005)
Percentage of titulars in city of residence	0.011[a]	0.0037[a]	0.016[a]	0.0061[a]
	(0.0012)	(0.0007)	(0.0059)	(0.0004)
Percentage of titulars in city of residence (squared)	−8.4e–5[a]	−2.0e–5[a]	−1.0e–4[b]	
	(1.2e–5)	(9.1e–6)	(4.7e–5)	
Sigma:	0.15	0.12	0.13	0.12
R^2:	0.15	0.28	0.09	0.38
n:	998	498	451	454

Note: Parameters estimated by using OLS. Standard errors for parameter estimates appear in parentheses below the estimates.

[a] $p < .01$.

[b] $p < .05$.

[c] $p < .10$.

The regression analysis also shows that the number of years a respondent has resided in his or her republic is positively related to openness to assimilation. Long-term residents appear to be less inclined toward ethnic mobilization and more comfortable with assimilation. The regression coefficients are significant at the 1 percent level for Estonia, Latvia, and Ukraine; however, the null hypothesis cannot be rejected in the case of Kazakhstan. For the three cases with statistically significant coefficients on this regressor, a unit change in years of residence yields a change of between 0.14 percent and 0.22 percent. In relative terms, this effect is rather substantial: the difference between a newcomer to the republic and a forty-year resident covers, on average, 10 percent of the value of the assimilation index.

Although other regressors show statistical significance in some republics, none of them performs well across all four. In several cases, the coefficients have opposite signs in different republics.

In Kazakhstan, urbanization (the size of the respondent's place of birth) appears to have a strongly positive, though nonlinear, relationship with an assimilationist attitude of its Russian population: every unit change in the five-level ordinal measure of urbanization corresponds to a change of 3.5 percent in the assimilation score of the respondent. The square of the urbanization measure, on the other hand, has a strongly negative relationship with the index: every unit change in the square of urbanization yields a negative change of 0.5 percent in the index of assimilation. These results suggest that in Kazakhstan, on average Russian individuals from more urban backgrounds tend to have a more positive attitude toward assimilation, though this tendency becomes less pronounced at higher levels of urbanization. Nevertheless, urbanization fails to predict attitudes toward assimilation in the other three republics.

Occupational status is statistically significant at the 1 percent level and positively related with the assimilation index in Estonia but does poorly in the other republics. A unit change in the ten-point occupational status variable predicts nearly a 1 percent positive change in the value of the assimilation index. In Estonia, but not in the other three republics, Russians in high-status occupations appear to be more assimilationist.

Age also appears to be a factor in determining attitudes toward assimilation in Estonia. The regression coefficient on age is significant at the 1 percent level, and a unit change in the age of the respondent predicts a 0.15 percent change in the value of the assimilationist index. Latvia and Ukraine may exhibit somewhat smaller effects as well, but the null hypothesis in these cases can only be rejected at the 10 percent level of confidence.

The degree of religious attachment of Russian respondents appears to be an important factor impeding assimilation in Ukraine, but nowhere else. In Ukraine, the estimated effect is about half as strong as that of urbanization. A unit change in the five-level religiosity variable predicts a 1.7 percent change in the value of the index, which amounts to an 8.5 percent change in the value of the index between the least and most religious respondents. The model predicts that religious Russians are somewhat less likely to assimilate in Ukraine than nonreligious Russians. This may reflect the social reality in central and southern Ukraine, where the survey was conducted, where a great many Ukrainians rely normally on the Russian language for communication. Ethnic difference in this context may—as in the case of Ireland, where language differences have been largely erased—be conceived of as primarily religious.

Differential Russian Responses in the Four Republics

As was clear from Table 7.2, the overall performance of the social structural model differs dramatically among the republics. I should emphasize that the divergence from 9 percent of the variance explained in Latvia to the 38 percent explained in Ukraine cannot be explained by differences of simple variation in either the dependent or independent variables. Table 7.3 shows clearly that the variance of the assimilation index is consistent across republics, and summary statistics on the independent variables (shown in Table 7.4), show similar levels of spread between the best- and worst-performing republics in the multiple regression analysis. Nor is the difference in performance explained by sample sizes, given that the model performs poorly for Kazakhstan, with a sample size twice as large as the next largest sample. These initial findings highlight the likelihood that there are significant structural differences between the determinants of assimilation in the various republics, a fact that can be taken into account through pooling the data.

To check whether social structural variables are important in explaining interrepublican variation, I therefore conducted a separate multiple regression analysis of pooled data from all four post-Soviet republics. This analysis has two stages, discussed in the appendix. The results of the first step of the analysis are summarized in Table 7.5. The results show that the size of the titular population and its squared

Table 7.4. Descriptive statistics on the independent variables, by republic

Variable	Mean	Standard deviation	Minimum	Maximum	*n*
Kazakhstan					
Urban	3.05	1.48	1	5	1,202
Religion	2.75	1.05	1	5	1,134
Occupation	3.42	1.40	0	6	998
Education	3.65	1.05	1	6	1,202
Years resident	34.88	14.86	0	88	1,202
Percent titular	38.47	17.46	22.61	91.34	1,202
Age	39.36	15.41	16	88	1,202
Estonia					
Urban	3.02	1.53	1	5	687
Religion	3.03	1.10	1	5	669
Occupation	3.30	1.76	0	6	498
Education	3.58	1.11	1	6	684
Years resident	28.27	12.58	0	76	678
Percent titular	38.47	25.21	4.70	88.20	687
Age	40.26	14.25	15	84	686
Latvia					
Urban	3.04	1.55	1	5	562
Religion	2.63	1.14	1	5	549
Occupation	2.83	1.63	0	6	451
Education	3.46	1.18	1	6	562
Years resident	31.96	14.35	0	77	562
Percent titular	54.07	10.03	41.75	81.38	562
Age	41.86	16.02	15	82	562
Ukraine					
Urban	3.47	1.71	1	5	560
Religion	2.65	1.13	1	5	596
Occupation	3.47	1.22	0	6	454
Education	3.57	1.29	1	6	597
Years resident	32.34	15.78	0	68	597
Percent titular	55.76	15.07	46.40	80.00	597
Age	46.28	17.26	16	89	596

Table 7.5. Openness to assimilation: Country-by-country pairings

	Estonia & Kazakhstan	Estonia & Latvia	Estonia & Ukraine	Kazakhstan & Latvia	Kazakhstan & Ukraine	Latvia & Ukraine
Intercept (of 1st country)	0.50[a] (0.051)	0.50[a] (0.047)	0.50[a] (0.045)	0.0088 (0.039)	0.0088 (0.038)	0.16 (0.17)
Population of birthplace (0–4, 4 = most urban)	0.0061 (0.024)	0.0061 (0.022)	0.0061 (0.021)	0.035[b] (0.016)	0.035[b] (0.016)	−0.036 (0.025)
Population of birthplace (squared)	−0.0025 (0.0039)	−0.0025 (0.0036)	−0.0025 (0.0034)	−0.0054[b] (0.0026)	−0.0054[b] (0.0025)	0.0058 (0.0043)
Attitude to religion (0–4, 4 = most religious)	−0.0085 (0.0059)	−0.0085 (0.0055)	−0.0085 (0.0053)	0.0021 (0.0045)	0.0021 (0.0044)	−0.011[b] (0.0055)
Educational attainment (0–5, 5 = beyond B.A.)	0.0065 (0.0074)	0.0065 (0.0068)	0.0065 (0.0066)	0.0063 (0.0061)	0.0063 (0.0059)	0.022[a] (0.0071)
Occupation (0 – 9, 9 = most prestigious)	0.0093[a] (0.0031)	0.0093[a] (0.0028)	0.0093[a] (0.0027)	−0.0001 (0.0023)	−0.0001 (0.0022)	−0.0021 (0.0029)
Age (in years)	−0.0015[a] (0.0006)	−0.0015[b] (0.0006)	−0.0015[a] (0.0006)	0.0003 (0.0005)	0.0003 (0.0005)	−0.001[c] (0.0005)
Residence in republic (in years)	0.0022[a] (0.0006)	0.0022[a] (0.0006)	0.0022[a] (0.0006)	0.0001 (0.0005)	0.0001 (0.0005)	0.0017[a] (0.0006)
Percent of titulars in city of residence	0.0037[a] (0.0008)	0.0037[a] (0.0007)	0.0037[a] (0.0007)	0.011[a] (0.0012)	0.011[a] (0.0012)	0.016[a] (0.0057)
Percent of titulars in city of residence (squared)	−2.0e–5[c] (1.1e–5)	−2.0e–5[b] (9.7e–6)	−2.0e–2[b] (9.3e–6)	−8.4e–5[a] (1.2e–5)	−8.4e–5[a] (1.2e–5)	−1.0e–4[b] (4.5e–5)
Intercept shift (for 2d country)	−0.49[a] (0.063)	−0.34[b] (0.17)	−0.38[a] (0.072)	0.16 (0.19)	−0.13[c] (0.066)	−.36[a] (0.076)
Δ slope: birthplace (for 2d country)	0.029 (0.028)	−0.042 (0.033)	−0.031 (0.033)	−0.071[b] (0.032)	−0.059[c] (0.032)	0.011 (0.037)
Δ slope: birthplace (squared) (for 2d country)	−0.0029 (0.0046)	0.0083[c] (0.0055)	0.0066 (0.0053)	0.011[b] (0.0053)	0.0094[c] (0.0053)	−0.0017 (0.0061)
Δ slope: religiosity (for 2d country)	0.011[c] (0.0073)	−0.0023 (0.0077)	−0.0086 (0.0074)	−0.013[c] (0.0075)	−0.019[a] (0.0074)	−0.0063 (0.0078)
Δ slope: education (for 2d country)	−0.0003 (0.0094)	0.015[c] (0.0097)	−0.0033 (0.0098)	0.016 (0.0098)	−0.0031 (0.010)	−0.019[c] (0.011)

Table 7.5. Openness to assimilation: Country-by-country pairings, *continued*

	Estonia & Kazakhstan	Estonia & Latvia	Estonia & Ukraine	Kazakhstan & Latvia	Kazakhstan & Ukraine	Latvia & Ukraine
Δ slope: occupation (for 2d country)	−0.0093[b] (0.0038)	−0.011[a] (0.0041)	−0.004 (0.0044)	−0.0021 (0.0039)	0.0053 (0.0045)	0.0074 (0.0047)
Δ slope: age (for 2d country)	0.0018[a] (0.0008)	0.0006 (0.0008)	0.0007 (0.0008)	−0.0013 (0.0008)	−0.0012 (0.0008)	0.0001 (0.0008)
Δ slope: residence (for 2d country)	−0.0021[b] (0.0008)	−0.0005 (0.0008)	−0.0008 (0.0008)	0.0015[c] (0.0008)	0.0013 (0.0008)	−0.0002 (0.0008)
Δ slope: % titular (for 2d country)	0.0074[a] (0.0014)	0.012[b] (0.0056)	0.0049[a] (0.0007)	0.0046 (0.0063)	0.0055[a] (0.0006)	0.0034[a] (0.0008)
Δ slope: % titular (squared) (for 2d country)	−6.4e–5[a] (1.6e–5)	−8.4e–5[c] (4.5e–5)		−2.0e–5 (5.1e–5)		
Sigma:	0.14	0.13	0.12	0.14	0.14	0.13
R^2:	0.50	0.25	0.44	0.58	0.32	0.50
N:	1,496	949	952	1,449	1,452	905

Note: Parameters estimated using OLS on pooled data from two countries in column heading. Standard errors and significance levels as in Table 7.3. Slope change (Δ slope) is estimated with an interaction term between a dummy variable for country (1 = country that appears second in column heading) and the independent variable noted.

[a] $p < .01$.

[b] $p < .05$.

[c] $p < .10$.

transformation continue to be both statistically and substantively significant across cases. Length of residence continues to be significant across four of the six paired comparisons; the Kazakhstan/Latvia and Kazakhstan/Ukraine pooled models are the exceptions. The latter is not surprising, considering that length of residence appears to have no effect on the assimilation index in the Kazakhstan-only model. Age and occupational status are both significant in all the paired comparisons including Estonia, reflecting the powerful effect of these variables in the Estonia-only analysis. Urbanization and its squared transformation are significant in the comparisons of Kazakhstan with Ukraine and Latvia, once again presumably reflecting the powerful effect of urbanization on the index seen in the Kazakhstan-only model. Religion is significant in the Latvia/Ukraine comparison, reflecting the strong effect found for religion in Ukraine in the single country model. All of this serves as background for a specific analysis of the sources and degree of country effects.

Country Effects on the Assimilation Index

A structural break across cases can be assessed by considering the effects of the country dummy variables and their interactions with the social-structural variables in the analysis. Three of the six country dummies are statistically significant at the 1 percent level, and one is significant at the 5 percent level. Under the usual interpretation of nominal-level variables in regression analysis, the coefficient of a dummy variable represents the change in the value of the intercept between the portions of the sample coded zero and one. That is, the coefficients of our country dummies suggest a large difference in attitudes toward assimilation between republican subsamples when all the social-structural variables in the model are held constant at zero.

The four statistically significant country coefficients are extremely significant in substantive terms, yielding an average change of 39 percent of the value of the index. The country effects are extremely significant in substantive terms in the comparisons of Estonia with both Kazakhstan (which would be expected) and, somewhat surprisingly, with Latvia. From the descriptive statistics on the dependent variable (Table 7.2), it is clear that the Latvian sample has a higher average score on the assimilation index than does the Estonian. Yet in the country comparisons, the Latvia dummy has a large negative slope. That is, it appears that after controlling carefully for social-structural variation between the two republics, the independent, residual effect of living in Estonia has a positive relationship with the assimilation index relative to living in Latvia, exactly the opposite of what was expected given the analysis of the means. The likely explanation for this result is that, all other things being equal, ethnic Russians living in Estonia are more likely to assimilate than those living in Latvia. The original examination of the descriptive statistics, if broken down by republic, can therefore be thought of as a one-variable model that suffers from an omitted-variable bias. By failing to control adequately for social-structural variation, the estimate of the effect of different republics is biased. The regressor that accounts best for this intercept shift is titular population percentage. Reanalysis of the pooled Latvia/Estonia sample, minus the slope-shift term for titular population, leads the positive intercept shift for Estonia to disappear. When we controlled for this social-structural variable, the apparently higher level of assimilationist attitudes in Latvia turned out to be a statistical mirage.[6] The country effects between Estonia/Ukraine and Latvia/Ukraine are also large and negative, as would be expected knowing the differences in mean values on the index. The negative coefficient for Ukraine vis-à-vis Kazakhstan is also anomalous and unexpected.[7]

The overall insight gained from looking at the individual country effects is that the social-structural variables in the analysis leave a great deal of residual variation

[6] It is possible that this outcome is merely an artifact of the relatively poor fit our model exhibits with the Latvia sample. The titular population variable "varies" far less in the Latvia sample than in the other three samples, while it varies the most within the Estonia sample. This anomaly in data collection may have biased the estimate of the slope-shift in the titular population regressor between the Estonian and Latvian samples, as well has having biased the intercept-shift parameter. The limitations of the current data set preclude any definitive discrimination between this possibility and the possibility that, controlling for social structure, Estonians are actually significantly more likely to assimilate than Latvians.

[7] The 5 percent confidence interval, however, covers zero in this case, rendering this estimate suspect.

between individual republics still unexplained. The country effects, or intercept-shift terms, capture these residual differences.

Four-Republic Pooled Analysis on the Index of Assimilation

To capture the "republic effect" independent of the social structural variables, I compare three regression models with the pooled four-republic data (Table 7.6). The first model is a regression of the social structural variables used in the within-country analyses on the assimilation index, excluding the country variables. The second model is the same as the within-country model, but adds the nominal-level country variables to test for intercept shifts. The third model is the same as the second, but adds selected multiplicative interactions between country variables and social-structural variables.

The idea behind the third model is that there are substantial, statistically significant differences in the size of the effects of key social structural variables between republics, even in the one case (percentage of Russians in the city of residence) where the relationship is significant in all republics. Thus the need to add interaction terms. For example, the degree of urbanization of the respondent's background is positively related to assimilation, but only for Kazakhstan. The two-country pooled analyses (Table 7.5) suggest that, indeed, the relationship between this variable and the assimilation index may be quite different for respondents from Kazakhstan. Thus I include a multiplicative interaction between the Kazakhstan dummy variable and urbanization in the four-sample pooled analysis.

The interactions of occupational status with the country variables in the comparisons of Estonia/Kazakhstan and Estonia/Latvia are negative and statistically significant at the 1 percent level of confidence, suggesting that the effect of occupational status on attitudes toward assimilation is higher in Estonia than in either of these other two republics.

In the comparison of Estonia with Kazakhstan, two additional interaction terms showed up as statistically significant. The country interaction with age is significant and positive, suggesting that the effect of age on attitude toward assimilation is about zero for Kazakhstan. The interaction with years of residence in the republic is also significant, but negative, indicating that the effect of living in Kazakhstan on the likelihood of assimilation is lower than for Russians living in Estonia.

An overall comparison of the three models is a startling portrayal of the independent effect of country of residence to predict the respondent's openness to assimilation. From model 1 in Table 7.6 to model 2, the R^2 value increases from 0.17 to 0.53. That is, model 2 appears to explain over 35 percent more of the sample variance than model 1 does.[8] This overall comparison of fit tends to confirm the results

[8] The F-statistic on the linear restriction is F is approximately equal to 625.70 on 3, 2388 d.f. (pr [F > 625.70] < .01). A further improvement of fit follows the introduction of the interaction terms in model 3. The R^2 improves to approximately 0.56, and the F-statistic on the linear restriction (model 2 vs. model 3) is F is approximately equal to 14.42 on 9, 2379 d.f. (pr [F > 14.42] < .01). In other words, our final model specification can be demonstrated to be a dramatic improvement in statistical terms over the more parsimonious models 1 and 2.

Table 7.6. Pooled data: Four countries in a single model

	Original model	Intercept shifts	Slope shifts
Intercept (of first country)	0.29[a]	0.43[a]	0.34[a]
	(0.031)	(0.025)	(0.038)
Population of birthplace	0.015	0.017	−0.008
	(0.014)	(0.011)	(0.014)
Population of birthplace (squared)	−0.002	−0.0025	0.001
	(0.0023)	(0.0017)	(0.002)
Attitude toward religion	−0.0036	−0.0063[b]	−0.004[a]
	(0.0035)	(0.0027)	(0.003)
Educational attainment	0.018[a]	0.011[a]	0.01[a]
	(0.0047)	(0.0035)	(0.003)
Occupation	−0.0082[a]	0.0026[c]	0.0003
	(0.0019)	(0.0014)	(0.002)
Age	0.0014[a]	−0.0003	−0.0006[b]
	(0.0004)	(0.0003)	(0.0003)
Residence in republic	−0.0015[a]	0.001[a]	0.001[a]
	(0.0004)	(0.0003)	(0.0003)
Percent titular in city of residence	0.0041[a]	0.0038[a]	0.01[a]
	(0.0007)	(0.0005)	(0.001)
Percent titular (squared)	−1.3e−6	−7.9e−6	−7.5e−5[a]
	(7.0e−6)	(5.4e−6)	(1.03e−5)
Intercept shift: Latvia/Estonia[d]		−0.029[a]	0.13[a]
		(0.0081)	(0.040)
Intercept shift: Kazakhstan		−0.27[a]	−0.30[a]
		(0.0098)	(0.033)
Intercept shift: Ukraine		−0.22[a]	−0.46[a]
		(0.0099)	(0.036)
Δ slope: birthplace (Kazakhstan)			0.04[b]
			(0.020)
Δ slope: birthplace (squared) (Kazakhstan)			−0.006[c]
			(0.003)
Δ slope: occupation (Estonia)			0.007[a]
			(0.003)
Δ slope: age (Kazakhstan)			0.0003
			(0.0005)
Δ slope: residence (Kazakhstan)			−0.001
			(0.0004)
Δ slope: percent titular (Estonia)			−0.007[a]
			(0.001)
Δ slope: percent titular (squared) (Estonia)			5.0e−5[a]
			(1.5e−5)
Δ slope: percent titular (Ukraine)			0.005[a]
			(0.0006)
Δ slope: religion (Ukraine)			−0.012[b]
			(0.006)
Sigma:	0.18	0.14	0.14
R^2:	0.17	0.53	0.56
N:	2,401	2,401	2,401

Note: Parameters estimated by using OLS on pooled data from all four countries. Standard errors and significance levels as in Table 7.3. Slope change (Δ slope) is estimated with an interaction term between a dummy variable for country (1 = country that appears in parentheses) and the independent variable noted.

[a] $p < .01$.

[b] $p < .05$.

[c] $p < .10$.

[d] In the second column, this term represents Latvia, while the intercept represents Estonia. In the third column, the order is reversed.

of the previous one- and two-sample analyses: namely, that significant residual variation between the republics remains unexplained by the social-structural regressors that have been considered.

THE survey data presented in this chapter lead to three general conclusions. First, standard sociological variables have modest effects on propensities toward assimilation and mobilization among the Russians in the republics of the near abroad. These Russians are more likely to assimilate when they live in cities with a higher percentage of ethnically titular residents. But as the titular population percentage becomes larger, the assimilation effect diminishes and, in some cases (Latvia and Kazakhstan), even reverses itself at very high percentages of titular residents. Titular population percentage must be considered by far the most significant structural predictor of assimilation we have managed to identify.

The four-sample pooled models demonstrate modest effects for other structural regressors as well. The degree of religiousness of the respondents bears a negative relationship to assimilation, but only in Ukraine. Education has a positive and statistically significant relationship to assimilation in all four samples. Occupational status is a statistically significant predictor of assimilation, but only for Estonians. The number of years the respondent has resided in the republic of the survey bears a positive and statistically significant relationship to assimilation.

Second, overall there is not a polarized view of Russians against the titulars. In the index of openness to assimilation, the majority of Russians in the republics of the near abroad largely accept the nationalist framework constructed by the titulars. A bipolar titular/Russian consciousness is certainly not evident from the data collected in 1992–94.

Third, despite our best efforts to explain interrepublic variation through social-structural variation, coefficients on our republic indicators remain large and statistically significant (at the one percent level of confidence). Russians are 13 percent more likely to assimilate to Estonian culture and society that they are in the Latvian context, when social structure is held constant.[9] Russians in Kazakhstan and Ukraine are dramatically less likely (30 percent for the former, 46 percent for the latter) to assimilate than they are in Latvia. As was the case for the Latvia/Estonia comparison, Ukrainians are less likely to assimilate than Kazakhs, holding structure constant, despite the fact that they are more likely to assimilate in absolute terms.

These interrepublican differences are strong in spite of (but perhaps caused by) the extraordinary lack of linguistic accommodation attitudes—as demonstrated in Figure 3.5—by the titulars in the Baltics. This suggests that there is some contextual factor associated with each republic that accounts for these differences. I have already suggested that the mode of state incorporation into these republics—that of the most favored lord (Ukraine), the colonial model (Kazakhstan), and the integralist model (the Baltics)—is the basis for the different contexts.

[9] Note well that, in absolute terms, the simple descriptive statistics tell more about who will assimilate than the regression results. That is, the measurements tell us that in absolute terms, Russians in Latvia are more likely to assimilate than Russians in Estonia. But that greater likelihood is explained not by the Latvian context per se, but by generic features of the social structure.

In the most-favored-lord republic, we would expect a sufficient number of Ukrainians who operate freely in Russian, and who remain interested in maintaining the hegemony of Russian. Given the division among the titulars, Russians remain uncertain whether the nationalist project in Ukraine will fail or succeed. Given the mixed signals from the dominant nationality group, Russians, even if they speak some Ukrainian, tend to dismiss it. Under these conditions, their ability to assimilate (which is high) is tempered by the low expected payoffs from assimilating. In the colonial republic, where cultural differences are great, the cost of assimilating for Russians is much higher than in Ukraine. Therefore, they are least likely—given the mixed signals from the titulars and high costs for assimilating—to accept assimilation or be very accommodating linguistically. Interestingly, however, they are more willing to accept symbolic titularization (street signs in both languages, as shown in Figure 3.5) than the Russians in Ukraine, who see these symbolic moves as a waste of time.

In the integralist republics, where Estonian and Latvian were more consistently used at high places than in Ukraine and Kazakhstan, and where a state bureaucracy operated in the titular language a generation ago, the titular claim of restoration of their languages as the primary language of state business is taken very seriously by Russians. Knowing this, they have accepted the reality before them. The lack of linguistic accommodation by the titulars therefore is seen not as lack of mutual accommodation, but rather as an unchanging fact of life, compelling Russians to adjust or lose out in the status, job, and education markets of the future. The different models of state incorporation help make sense of, although they cannot fully explain, the interrepublican differences in assimilation propensities.

8

Calculating Linguistic Status: An Experiment

Survey data show that there is an unusually strong incentive for Russians in the Baltics to assimilate linguistically. I say unusual because these languages are quite distant from Russian, because they have so few speakers worldwide, and because of the so-called imperial mentality of Russians in regard to the national groups in the Russian periphery. The survey data were consistent with what was portrayed in the ethnographies—namely, that the resoluteness of the titulars to abjure Russian, the economic returns for learning the Baltic languages, and the lack of any strong status constraints all favored linguistic assimilation for Russians living in the Baltics. But neither the ethnographic nor the survey data could sort out these factors to provide a well-specified theory of intergenerational linguistic shift. It is only when we examine experimental data from all four republics that progress in this direction becomes possible.

History of the Matched-Guise Test

The matched-guise test,[1] developed by Wallace Lambert, was created to examine interethnic or intercultural group attitudes by measuring how people form perceptions of others after hearing only their speech. Lambert doubted that direct reports by individuals revealed their true attitudes and developed a new technique in an attempt to elicit concealed or unconscious assumptions that people make about others when they hear them speaking. The innovative feature of this experiment was its attempt "to minimize the effects of both the voice of the speaker and his message by employing bilingual speakers reading the same message in two languages,"[2] and to

[1] The matched-guise test is first described in W. E. Lambert, R. C. Hodgson, R. C. Gardner, and S. Fillenbaum, "Evaluational Reactions to Spoken Languages," *Journal of Abnormal and Social Psychology* 60, no. 1 (1960): 44–51.

[2] Ibid., p. 44.

have respondents judge attributes of these speakers without knowing that they were being asked to give separate scores for the same "speaker" in two different "guises." In analyzing the data, the researcher can then "match" the two "guises" and determine whether—with (nearly) all other variables controlled for—one guise is ranked more highly than the other. If so, the analyst would be able to claim that the speech style with the higher scores has greater prestige or status in the place where the experiment was conducted.

In the founding experiment, Lambert and his associates recorded the reactions of French and English Canadian college students who had listened to tape-recorded samples of a spoken text in French and English. Four bilingual speakers read the text in both guises. Lambert expected that the test subjects would evaluate the personality traits of members of their own linguistic groups more favorably, confirming theories of in-group prejudice. He found, however, that both English Canadians *and* French Canadians rated the English guises more highly than the same speakers in their French guises. In fact, French-speaking respondents gave the English guises higher scores on more personality traits than did the English-speaking respondents. Lambert and associates interpreted these surprising results as evidence that French-speakers in Canada had internalized negative stereotypes concerning the social inferiority of their community.

Since Lambert's pioneering work, the matched-guise technique has been used to examine how group stereotypes inform attitudes toward different dialect and accent communities, as well as distinct language groups. Initial studies generally confirmed Lambert's overall conclusion that speech serves as a social identifier, and his more specific finding that both standard and nonstandard language, dialect, and accent speakers rate the guises using the standard speech form higher than those using the nonstandard form. For example, high school students from southwest England and South Wales ranked the guise of R.P. English (received pronunciation, or "BBC English") as more prestigious than the guises of twelve regional accents.[3] In a U.S. study, G. Richard Tucker and Lambert found that college students from a northern white and a southern black college all evaluated "Network English" more favorably than five other dialects.[4] Studies comparing classical with colloquial Arabic and Canadian French with Parisian French reported similar results.[5]

Investigators who applied the matched-guise technique in other regions noted a more subtle trend: some minority or standard speech groups evaluated their own

[3] Howard Giles, "Evaluative Reactions to Accents," *Educational Review* 22, no. 3 (1970): 211–27. In this experiment, Giles found a single speaker who could perform in thirteen different guises! Respondents did not rank traits as with Lambert's experiment; rather, they were asked to rank the prestige of the speaker.

[4] G. Richard Tucker and Wallace E. Lambert, "White and Negro Listeners' Reactions to Various American-English Dialects," *Social Forces* 47 (1969): 463–68.

[5] Linda El-Dash and G. Richard Tucker, "Subjective Reactions to Various Speech Styles in Egypt," *International Journal of the Sociology of Language* 6 (1975): 33–54; Alison D'Anglejan and G. Richard Tucker, "Sociolinguistic Correlates of Speech Style in Quebec," in R. Shuy and R. Fasold, eds., *Language Attitudes: Current Trends and Prospects* (Washington, D.C.: Georgetown University Press, 1973), pp. 1–27.

speech style *more* favorably than the standard on traits possessing an affective or emotive value. Thus W. Wolck's study of Spanish and Quechua in Peru found that although student respondents rated the speakers in their Spanish guises as more educated and as belonging to a higher class than the same speakers in their Quechuan guises, the Quechuan guises were rated as stronger, more sincere, and less arrogant. Wolck concluded that the upgrading of Quechua on affective traits demonstrated a loyalty to Quechua, despite the superior status of Spanish.[6] Likewise, W. Cheyne found similar in-group cohesiveness by Scots respondents who rated Scots guises as friendlier and more generous than the same speakers in their English guises, whom they nevertheless considered to possess higher status.[7] Carranza and Ryan formalized the analytical constructs of solidarity and status by using factor analysis to distinguish these two clusters of traits from adjective scales evaluating Anglo and Mexican-American dialects. Results showed that while all respondents rated the Anglo dialect higher on both status and solidarity, Mexican-American speech received higher scores (from Mexican-American respondents) on solidarity than status.[8] These studies do not disconfirm Lambert; rather they show two separate factors at work. On the status factor, the Lambert effect seems strong; but on the solidarity factor, the effect is minimal, and sometimes negative. Speakers of low-status languages may lose societal respect for maintaining their speech forms, but they gain in-group solidarity and cohesiveness. In the tests I performed, I employed confirmatory factor analysis (described in the appendix) to delineate and to weigh these two factors, which I call "respect" and "friendship."

Typical of all the early studies, social class divisions reinforced linguistic cleavages, suggesting that listeners were reacting both to perceptions of the speakers' class affiliation and to preconceptions about their language style, and it was hard to separate language status from the economic status usually associated with speakers of that language. Several more recent studies, however, have tackled this problem of collinearity. Dominic Abrams and Michael Hogg attempted to control for social class by comparing two middle-class Scots' accents with RP English. The respondents, Scots teenagers from Dundee, demonstrated high in-group loyalty on both the solidarity and the status dimensions, preferring a Dundee accent to both a Glasgow accent and to RP English. Thus the investigators concluded that in the absence of status differentials, language loyalty shifts to the language of in-group membership, and that the Dundee Scots' secure middle-class position within Scotland influenced their upgrading of their own group vis-à-vis other groups located both inside and outside their regions.[9]

[6] Wolfgang Wolck, "Spanish and Quechua in Bilingual Peru," in Shuy and Fasold, *Language Attitudes*, pp. 129–47.

[7] W. Cheyne, "Stereotyped Reactions to Speakers with Scottish and English Regional Accents," *British Journal of Social and Clinical Psychology* 9 (1970): 77–79.

[8] Michael Carranza and Ellen B. Ryan, "Evaluative Reactions of Bilingual Anglo and Mexican American Adolescents toward Speakers of English and Spanish," *International Journal of the Sociology of Language* 6 (1975): 83–104.

[9] Dominic Abrams and Michael A. Hogg, "Language Attitudes, Frames of Reference, and Social Identity: A Scottish Dimension," *Journal of Language and Social Psychology* 6 (1987): 201–13.

Kathryn Woolard challenged the assumption that all language communities in a given society perceive the official, standard speech form as possessing the most prestige. She examined Catalonia, where the language used in official contexts and generally considered to represent the "standard"—namely, Castilian Spanish—differs from the language spoken by the economic elite. Matched-guise results show that both Catalan-speaking and Castilian-speaking respondents (all from Barcelona, the capital of Catalonia) favored the in-group on solidarity traits, while Catalan received higher status ratings from respondents in both language communities. Woolard concludes that in her case, Catalan's prestige came from Catalan-speakers' domination in the socioeconomic order rather than their politico-legal status.[10]

The nationalizing states of the near abroad, where Russian-speakers are facing a cataclysmic shift in political status, offered an unusual opportunity to replicate the Lambert technique. Students in the republics of the former Soviet Union know that the status of Russian is under assault by the nationalizing elites. Monolingual Russian-speakers must decide whether or not to adopt the titular language of the republic in which they live. Perhaps they will base that decision on their perceptions of the prestige of the titular language and their degree of solidarity with other Russian-speakers. If we were to ask respondents about the prestige of a language they do not know, their reports might reflect what they think they ought to say. The Lambert technique offered us the opportunity to collect data on the prestige of a language without contaminating the results with respondent dissimulation.

Application of the Test to the Four Post-Soviet Republics

In July 1993 the ethnographic research team met in Chicago to design a matched-guise experiment appropriate for the nationalizing republics of the former Soviet Union. The goal was to make the procedures as similar as possible in the four republics without losing sight of the particular situation of each. We agreed that to save time we would have only two bilingual speakers accounting for four voices, along with a single voice in the titular language to introduce the procedure.

Choice of Passage

We agreed to use the same passage Woolard used in her test in Catalonia—an explanation of the development of Euclidian geometry. We translated the text into and back out of Russian until we were confident that it read well. We decided to translate the text into the republican languages, choose the speakers, and record the voices once we were in the field. In Estonia, Latvia, and Ukraine, this was no problem. But in Kazakhstan, getting an acceptable translation for a technical subject proved exasperating. Bhavna Dave, who conducted the research in Kazakhstan, could not even find a textbook with a Kazakh and Russian version. The only places

[10] Kathryn A. Woolard, *Double Talk* (Stanford: Stanford University Press, 1989).

where there were precise translations were in a political journal (and we wanted to avoid political subjects) and the Bible. Eventually she found a text on planetary movements and the invention of calendars that proved suitable.

Choice of Qualities to Be Ranked

We needed qualities on which each voice would be ranked that the students acting as our experimental subjects would see as positive. Certain of the qualities used in the Catalan study: ambition, a sense of humor, progressiveness, and generosity—had no clearly positive Russian equivalents. These we had to omit. We eventually chose the following attributes: educated (*obrazovannyi*), cultured (*kul'turnyi*), reliable (*nadezhnyi*), witty (*ostroumnyi*), open (*otkrytyi*), self-confident (*uverenniu v sebe*), magnanimous (*velikodushnyi*), pleasant (*priiatnyi*), attractive (*vneshne privlekatel'nyi*), spiritual (*dukhovnyi*), intellectual (*intelligentnyi*), proud (*gordyi*), having leadership qualities (*kachestva rukovoditelia*), diligent (*trudoliubivyi*), and amusing (*zabavnyi*).

In three of the four republics (Estonia, Latvia, and Ukraine) we found ready titular-language equivalents for these qualities. Again in Kazakhstan, there were problems. As Dave explains it in her field report:

> Finding a suitable translation of the fifteen personal attributes in Kazakh was not that easy either. There are no suitable one-word equivalents of terms like "having leadership qualities," "generous," "self-confident," and "reliable." . . . Again, I asked five different people to provide me with the equivalents, and each person gave me different adjectives. Each of them seemed dissatisfied with the Kazakh version I had, saying "that is incorrect!" Eventually with the help of the graduate student who translated the Russian version (and whose knowledge I found more reliable than others), we picked what seemed the most appropriate terms. I picked "hospitable" as the Kazakh equivalent of "generous," since hospitality is considered a very specific national trait of Kazakhs. The equivalent of "having leadership qualities" is "organized"—a word with a definitely sovietized connotation; however, the Kazakh word for "having leadership qualities" has a negative connotation (of bossiness).

Eventually six of the adjectives—pleasant, attractive, spiritual, proud, intellectual, and amusing—were dropped. Five additions were made: honest (*chestnyi*), kind (*simpatichnyi*), nice (*dobryi*), cheerful (*veselyi*), and erudite (*erudirovannyi*).

Choice of Speakers

The choice of speakers involved a set of difficult decisions. First, there was the issue of nationality of the speaker. The ideal was to have one Russian national who was capable in the titular language and one titular national who was capable in Russian. It was very difficult to find Russian nationals who felt comfortable reading formally a titular-language text. The results, as will become apparent, were not ideal.

Furthermore, Dave could not find a Russian national who would read a Kazakh passage about astronomy on a tape. As Dave explains:

> Once I had selected the suitable text, I began looking for the suitable voices. Since virtually no Russians speak Kazakh—with or without an accent—there was no point seeking to find this rare human being. [I may note that in my entire stay in Kazakhstan, I personally know only one Russian—a pensioner—who speaks Kazakh without any accent.] Two Kazakh women with proficiency in both the languages did not really pass the audition test. A few others were too shy to read the Kazakh passage. I mentioned this problem to an acquaintance, who is the head of the Kazakh-language section of the faculty of television and media in the school of journalism. He offered to provide me with "professional" voices, since his students are trained in media-related skills, and he has a professional recording device. When I arrived at the time we had set up, none of the "professionals" were around. Instead I was told that there was a small get-together at the department, and I was taken to a room with twenty other people, plenty of food on the table, and enough vodka, whiskey, gin, and rum at 1 P.M. Needless to add, the workday was over at that point. I had to reschedule the meeting for the next day. None of the "professionals" arrived, for it was exam [*zachyot*] time. Furthermore, all the telephones were out of order. Sensing my growing impatience, my acquaintance Kaldibai said he will find me the kind of voices that I need if I waited a bit longer. He began looking for his *qizdar* ["girls," but here referring to his students].

Eventually Dave chose two speakers, both of them Kazakhs. For the purposes of the data analysis, I call the one who speaks high Kazakh the "Kazakh-speaker" and the one who had minimal facility in Kazakh the "Russian-speaker."

Second, there was the related issue of language skill. In Lambert's original experiment, each speaker (though with a detectable accent) was fully bilingual. This turned out not to be feasible under the conditions in which we were working. In light of our compromises in regard to equality of competence among our bilingual speakers, we thought it best to give the reader, where relevant, a linguistic biography of each speaker, which will provide extra interpretive information, though not of a quantifiable sort. For example, Vello Pettai, who administered the test in Riga and Tallinn, and who speaks Russian, Estonian, and Latvian, made the following useful observation:

> On the whole the two main speakers were much more equal in quality [on the Latvian tape] than on the Estonian tape. That is, the Latvian woman read the Russian text fairly cleanly, while the Russian also read the Latvian quite well. The gap between each reader's knowledge of the other language was not as great as that between the Estonian and Russian readers in Tallinn in which the Russian clearly could not read the Estonian as well as the Estonian could the Russian. The reason for the fairly clean Latvian Russian voice was partly after two previous failures to get half-decent Russians to read the text. Two other women kept on making mistakes and finally the Latvian woman whose voice I used saw my dilemma and in-

vited a Russian coworker to read it with her and this woman turned out to be quite bilingual.

Third, there is the issue of the sex of the speakers. In one replication of the Lambert experiment, the sex of the speaker did not have a significant influence on the outcome.[11] For practical reasons, we decided to settle for all female voices.

The Voices

Kazakhstan Kazakh-speaker—Indira. She is a fifth-year student in a radio and television department. She was fluently bilingual, though it was very clear that Kazakh is her first language. Her Russian had a well-marked Kazakh accent, visibly not the kind of Russian spoken by Kazakhs in Almaty or other russified settings. She is also a native of the city of Kyzyl-Orda. Indira went over the Kazakh text a couple of times, did not seem very pleased with the structure of a couple of sentences, then read the Russian version, and appeared to be satisfied—however, she suggested a Kazakh equivalent for the word *kalendar'* (Dave's translator either did not know or had not considered it necessary to use the Kazakh term.)

Russian-speaker—Roza. She is a fifth-year student in a journalism school. She is a russified Almaty-based Kazakh, who speaks little or no Kazakh. She refused to read Kazakh at first ("I am ashamed of my Kazakh, I can't read Kazakh"). Indira urged her to try, and so did Dave, who was getting tired of this never-ending search. She attempted to read the text at Indira and Dave's behest, though there were at least a couple of words in every sentence that she simply could not enunciate well. It took almost forty minutes to coach her and get the pronunciation right. At one point she was on the verge of giving up, telling Dave, "Why don't you read instead, you can read like any other Kazakh, they ["My advisers or the students?" Dave wondered] will never find out!" Dave had to assure her that her pronunciation was perfect, "You can do it better than me, after all it is your native language!" It certainly had an effect. Eventually she did manage to read more or less correctly, though it was rather obvious from the intonation that she had little clue about what the text meant. She pronounced the syllables that are normally silent in the speech of a native speaker. Her Russian had a very slight Kazakh accent. She told me that she never had to prepare so hard for any Kazakh exams!

Estonia Estonian-speaker—Marju. She is an Estonian who went to Russian schools, but at home speaks Estonian with her mother. Her father's side is German/Jewish, and she speaks to her father in Estonian and Russian. She is a professional interpreter and is fully bilingual.

Russian-speaker—Olga. She is a Russian by nationality. She was born in Narva. She speaks Estonian but with a strong Russian accent. Her reading of the Estonian

[11] Michael A. Hogg, Nicholas Joyce, and Dominic Abrams, "Diglossia in Switzerland? A Social Identity Analysis of Speaker Evaluations," *Journal of Language and Social Psychology* 3, no. 3 (1984): 185–95.

passage was quite slow, almost tedious, and with considerable stammering. In the Estonian school in Narva, when she began speaking in her Estonian guise, the students broke out in laughter by the second word. She is a university graduate in Russian philology.

Latvia Russian-speaker—Lidiia. She is a Russian by nationality, about forty-five years old, and is a secretary in the main government building, with a university education. Speaking Russian, she had a clear voice of authority. She read the Latvian passage without any hesitations, giving the impression of someone who is a well-educated person, but definitely Russian.

Latvian-speaker—Tamara. She is a Latvian in her late thirties. She serves as an archivist at the Cabinet of Ministers in the government. She has a university education. Her Russian is clear and clean, but with a detectable Latvian accent.

Ukraine Russian-speaker—Ekaterina. She works at the International School of Ukrainian Studies and the experts there say she sounds typically Russian when she speaks Ukrainian. Arel's ears, however, could not pick up the differences, though when he interviewed the respondents after administering the tests, they said they knew that the last (her) guise in Ukrainian was from a Russian woman whose Ukrainian had a slight rural twang. Ekaterina speaks Russia at home, but uses mostly Ukrainian at work, which is not typical for Kiev.

Ukrainian-speaker—Nina. She is a ukrainophone-educated woman who is perfectly fluent in Russian.

Administration of the Test

After getting permission from the school directors, asking to have a full class period with students from the upper three forms in their schools for the test, we entered the room with the answer sheets and cassette recorders. We made the following introduction to the students in the language that was normally used in that class for instruction.

> We are here to perform an experiment to see how people develop impressions about other people only by hearing their voices, as we often need to do when listening to radio or hearing a new voice on the phone. In the field of psychology we are learning how people can build an entire picture of a stranger only by hearing his or her voice. This experiment is being funded by the United States' National Science Foundation, and it will be carried out in many of the republics of the former Soviet Union. The same experiment has been done earlier in Canada, Spain, and Norway and we are trying to get a larger sample of countries by including [this country].
>
> You will be asked today to give your impressions of five different people, all from [this country], and all reading exactly the same passage about mathematics. They did not write this passage. They are only reading it. From hearing their voices, you will be asked what their whole personality is like and what kind of work they do. Some of you will not understand this passage, but it doesn't matter. We want you to think about what kind of person is reading those words.

Any questions? [The students got the questionnaires earlier, and they were able to ask about what they had in front of them]. Before we hear the first voice, I want to say that you should not put your names on the answer sheets. We are not testing you or identifying you, but we are only interested in how students from [this country] form general impressions of others.

Now please let us listen to the first voice. [After the voice, we took the students through each characteristic, and explained the meaning of the 1 through 6 scale. This was not necessary for voices 2–5].

The Experiment in Estonia I prepared the tapes for the Estonian test in Tallinn at the Academy of Sciences and supervised the tests in Narva. My research assistant, Tarmo Tuisk, introduced and administered the tests in the classrooms, while I observed. Estonian is his first language. He learned Russian in the Soviet army, and is not fully fluent. This did not apparently bother any of the students in the Russian-medium school. In Tallinn, Pettai used the same tape as we used in Narva and administered the test in schools there.

In Narva, there were only thirty Estonian students in the upper three forms. We had to invite a few students from a lower form to reach our forty student quota. The atmosphere in the social hall was of liberal informality, as the students straddled into the hall in small groups, extinguishing their cigarettes and joking around. Jokes abounded throughout the rankings of the first voice (which was not counted in the results), but by the second voice, the students got into the exercise and took it quite seriously, except for the giggling mentioned above. In the Russian school, we were in a large science lab, and all fifty-nine students, in a cacophonous moment of freedom before we arrived, immediately fell quiet and stood up when Tuisk and I entered the room. The acoustics were bad, but the students leaned forward better to hear the voices.

Pettai administered the Estonian test in four schools in Tallinn, choosing from a Russian-dominated neighborhood (Lasnamäe) and an Estonian-dominated neighborhood (Mustamäe), choosing a Russian-medium and Estonian-medium school in each district. Of the four republics, only in Estonia do we have data from both the capital and a Russian-dominated city. To our amazement, there were absolutely no differences that could be explained by city![12] The status of the four guises remained the same, whether the rankings were done in Tallinn or Narva.

The Experiment in Kazakhstan Here it is best to quote directly from Dave's field observations, which I have substantially cut and slightly edited. First person singular in this section, though, refers to Dave.

> When I called up the school principal [experiment one in a Kazakh school (No. 12)], asking for permission to conduct the experiment, she was extremely delighted and suggested right away that I . . . teach English to the higher classes. After I politely

[12] I therefore combined all the Estonian responses into a common file and analyzed them as I did the data from the other republics. Analysis of inter-city similarity goes beyond the scope of this book.

turned down the request, saying I was leaving in ten days (the principal felt I could teach for ten days at least!), there was some dampening of interest. When I arrived at the school, the principal wasn't present, and I had to walk through the entire school to find the teacher who was supposed to receive me. The teacher appeared to be extremely tired (she complained of headaches) and unhappy with her job.

I was introduced to the class, but the kids were paying no attention to their teacher whatsoever. Finally I decided to take over, introduce myself, and read out my introduction, written in Kazakh. I had spent enough time getting it translated in plain and effective Kazakh, and practiced speaking with the right intonation. But my preparation didn't seem to have impressed them much. The boys kept yelling, "Speak English, we all understand English. . . . Don't you speak English?" Not a single kid desired to know where, why, and how I learnt Kazakh, nor were they amused/impressed at the way I spoke.

I felt the experiment was a total disaster, and that I would have to do it again in more favorable surroundings. The tape recorder in the class was so bad that all voices sounded alike. The pupils were unruly, the corridor was unmanageably noisy (other kids found out about my presence, and were trying to have a peek inside; the door couldn't be closed so I had to stand and hold it), the teacher lacked any authority whatsoever. Rather than helping me to control the class, or distribute the sheets, she simply absconded. She miraculously returned after the show was over, expressing a desire to write a *doklad* [paper] containing my critical observations for the board meeting of the school. She was constantly complaining of a headache. I just happened to have some aspirin for her. Teaching in schools is extremely hard, and low paying. As a result no one wants to stay in the job. I asked if Russian schools are better or different, and her answer was a reluctant "yes." She herself recently switched from a music school (mixed) to the Kazakh school (all Kazakhs) and found a very marked deterioration in discipline and behavior of students in the Kazakh school. According to her, mixed schools are more conducive to bringing out "human qualities" of kids, while "national schools seem to bring out a lot of aggressive behavior." She wants to quit the job, for she couldn't take the daily stress any more.

Over half the kids filled out the Russian answer sheet, a few began filling the Kazakh sheet, found it rather cumbersome, and switched to the Russian one. Roza's voice, with the well-marked accent in Kazakh, escaped the kids' notice; nor do I think that a well-functioning tape recorder would have helped them notice it. At the end of the test, about five out of the fifty kids felt that probably I was reading the text in Kazakh, while others unanimously mentioned that no—after all, the taped voices had no accent. When at the end I explained the purpose of the test, they appeared to be far from impressed. One kid asserted that everyone knows that now Kazakh is the most prestigious language (implying the question as to why it is necessary to conduct such experiments!), as from the year 1995 all the official business in Almaty [was to be] conducted in Kazakh, and those who don't know it won't find jobs. Others echoed this opinion. Thus the "prestige" of Kazakh is brought out by the carrot and stick in the hands of the state apparatchiks and *chinovniky* [officials].

After the test, I spent some thirty minutes answering various questions, beginning with the language situation. . . . I overheard conversations among kids, some of which were presented to me as their remarks and observations: "Russians are the worst lot," "Jews are an extremely sly race—as soon as Kazakh schools opened up, they immediately transferred their kids from Russian to Kazakh schools, even before we did—they change so quickly with the changing wind," "There won't be any Russian schools, if Russians don't like it, they can leave." I had to constantly request them to be quiet during the test, for many of them (boys on the whole, for the girls were shy and quiet) found the questionnaire silly. Later, another clever kid suggested that if I really wanted the class to remain quiet, I should have simply said "shut up" in English, for they all understand that. Many of them said "hi" to me when I was distributing the questionnaire. They said it in a tone that clearly aped some of the worst of Hollywood movies shown on the TV, and was certainly out of place, and I could not but help reporting later to the teacher that I found the class to be extremely uncultured [*nekul'turny*]. The experiment was such a disaster that I counted it as a field experience, and sought four other schools.

[At this first Kazakh school], all of the students without exception asked their questions in Russian (though some attempted to do so in English). I had begun my introduction in Kazakh, but every time the teacher needed to say something to me, she would do it in Russian, and the kids quickly noted that my Kazakh was nowhere as good. Loitering around in the school yard and corridor, I noticed that most of the conversation among kids was in Russian, and they spoke Russian, and a mix of Russian-Kazakh with the teachers. Code-mixing was so common, and done as a matter of habit.

This first Kazakh school that I visited has the reputation of being the best Kazakh school in town. It was the only Kazakh school that survived all through the Khrushchev-Brezhnev years, when all other Kazakh schools closed down. I was told that the kids of the city intelligentsia were educated in this school. However, a lot of kids in the 10th and 11th grades transferred from Russian schools over the course of last 4–5 years. To my mind, as a rule, their Russian is far better than their Kazakh.

Later, during conversation with another pupil at the school—a girl in the 11th grade (who was not in the experimental group, I simply happen to know her family, and was visiting them), reported to me that the new school principal is very strict and a "nationalist." She wants the school to have a clear Kazakh profile, a bastion of Kazakh culture, and has prohibited girls from wearing short skirts, etc. She has also waged a battle against smoking and drinking among kids (all this "lack of culture" (*beskul'tur'e*) according to the principal is a result of their having studied in Russian schools earlier).

Experiment 2 was conducted in a Russian school, No. 15, also in Almaty. The English-language teacher, who seemed to have an effective control over her students, introduced me to the class. Students were well behaved though noisy—a sign of liveliness and not unruly behavior. The class was ethnically very mixed: a majority of Russians, and quite a few mixed faces. I had probably failed to mention to them that the first voice would be in Kazakh—it appears natural to assume that they expected to hear Russian. They had already asked me if the text was going to be in English, and I said no. As soon as the kids heard the first voice (Kazakh), they spontaneously broke into laughter. I heard voices amidst laughter "Kazakh radio," "*govorit* Almaty," "the first [radio/TV] channel." [This in part explains why quite a few put down the profession of the first girl—a radio announcer, or translator or something pertaining to Kazakh language rather than another "independent" profession.]

Many kids wanted to know if I work for the CIA or something as a translator, jokingly asking if I were on a "secret mission." When I explained the real purpose of the test, a boy in the front row said, "Oh, again nationality and language divisions, why do Americans need all this?" Another kid supported him: "Why can't they leave nationality alone?"

While filling out the question sheet, one boy said that he does not know his nationality, and could he not simply leave it blank. He appeared to be of Russian/Tatar/Kazakh mix. I said put down whatever you consider yourself to be. The boy sitting next to him giggled, "Write Russian—what difference does it make?" (*Zapishis' russkim, kakaia raznitsa?*). Another pupil, who was fourteen, told me that they choose a nationality only at sixteen, when they get a passport. So he did not know what to write. I said whatever—it does not matter. "Can I leave it blank?" he asked. I don't know what he finally wrote.

The English-language teacher was urging them all to speak in English. The students seemed a bit shy. One boy, who was urged by her to ask in English, when he had begun his question in Russian, retorted to the teacher, "If she speaks Russian so fluently, why should we use our English? After all we understand each other perfectly." Another pupil also spoke out: "We don't get to hear foreigners visiting us and speaking Russian so well." I might have mentioned that I speak some Kazakh too, but there was no appropriate context, so I said nothing. When I asked them if they understand Kazakh [many laughed, appeared amused]—someone said, "Well, we're learning it" [*Nu izuchaem*]. They have been studying Kazakh for three to four years. Basically my question went unheeded.

I had requested to have a class of about fifty students, but there were at least a dozen more. A number arrived after the introduction was over. I did not have more copies of the Russian questionnaire, but all the Kazakh questionnaires, which no one had used, were intact. I told the latecomers that they could fill out the Kazakh *anketa*, if they wished. Most of them smiled and exited immediately. Three Kazakh girls—they looked like a team—stayed, sitting together, and filled out the whole thing through cooperative effort. [Their answers were in Russian.]

Experiment 3 was performed in a Russian school, No. 25. Like the other Russian school, it must rank fairly high on discipline. The kids were a lively lot. The principal (a Russian) was a very energetic and efficient person. She is actively pursuing all kinds of exchange programs with kids abroad.

I was accompanied by Karlygash, the daughter of the famous and respected Kazakh historian Bekmakhanov (deceased now for a long time). Karlygash teaches psychology at a professional training institute. She studied in this school and knows the principal well. So it was very easy to make all the practical arrangements. The test went very smoothly. Pupils were excited to participate in such an experiment, they listened to what I said and did not ask many questions. Then another teacher, who also teaches English, came in and urged them to ask me questions in English. Somehow the entire class remained quiet, rather subdued and eager to hear something from me. They appeared dumbfounded when Karlygash said that I speak Kazakh, but no one asked me any questions about it. When I told them what the real purpose of the experiment was, they did not appear to be that excited, nor did it make much sense to them. When I asked them if they could guess which was the Russian voice (I had not yet told them that the same person spoke more than once, and that they were all Kazakhs), they hesitated. There was a general consensus that all the voices had some sort of a Kazakh accent, but a few believed it could well have been a Russian voice. Then one boy asked me who were these people in real life. Someone yelled from the back, "The last one was a *kolkhoznitsa* [collective farmer]!" [obviously referring to the Kazakh voice with a clear Kazakh accent] and there was laughter. Someone else said a "radio announcer" [implying Kazakh radio], others said "philologists/student of ZhenPI (Women's Pedagogical Institute, whose students come mainly from rural areas).

I asked the principal about Kazakh-language teaching. She mentioned that three years ago they had no Kazakh teacher. Of course Kazakh was one of the subjects, but as a norm, it was taught in a most formal fashion. Now they have hired the best teachers, have all the textbooks, yet somehow the results are nearly invisible. A very good teacher left after her first child was born, and many other women who know Kazakh well do not really want to teach in schools, she said. They would rather stay home and bring up children. "I don't know why, we are doing our best, the teachers are doing their best, yet it seems so hard to make much progress." Then she mentioned how some students from the school were sent to Canada on high school exchange—some more to England—three to the United States—they are negotiating to send some students to Germany and France as well. She was far more excited reporting these activities than answering questions on the state of Kazakh-language teaching. She also mentioned that they were lucky to have a young American man who was teaching English and geography for very little money, and the pupils had made very good progress in English.

The principal left her office to attend to other matters. The Kazakh-language teacher—a woman in her late fifties—entered. Karlygash suggested that I ask her all questions and she began talking to her in a mix of Kazakh and Russian [Karlygash by and large speaks Russian]. Karlygash took it upon herself to do the interview on my behalf. In response to her rather tactless question "Is there any progress?" the teacher retorted, "How can there not be progress, they are all learning it. . . . Earlier they knew nothing, now they recite poems and converse. We have textbooks, and a very well worked-out program. We are teaching them from an early age, and you can see the difference." She herself had retired a couple of years ago, but decided to plunge into the language-revival work. "How could I remain on the side when my country needs my services? I know my language, and never have forgotten it. Now I can do something very useful with it." I asked her what textbooks they use. Suddenly she got very defensive, asking, "Why do you want to know all this?" I told her what kind of research I was doing. To be fair, she had not been told who I was and why I was there. The principal had been too busy to introduce me, and Karlygash had never thought of it. All through the interview, I sensed a certain hostility and defensiveness in her tone. Maybe this was because she was still at a loss about why I was there. But I think otherwise. I've talked to far too many language vigilantes to know what to expect when they sense an unsympathetic ear. I thanked her and left soon thereafter.

Experiment 4 was conducted in a Kazakh school (No. 41), "Shkola internat." This school draws a fairly large number of pupils from rural areas as well as other oblasts. Traditionally such schools were geared to answer needs of orphans and families with a large number of children living on *kolkhoz/sovkhoz* where secondary schools are not available. Galina Bekmakhanova (widow of the well-known Kazakh historian Ermukhan Bekmakhanov) told me about this school when she heard about my experience at School No. 12. Her granddaughter studied at No. 12, and now she is in Byron, California, on a high school exchange, thanks to a Baptist organization. Bekmakhanova said that the Kazakh School No. 12 has all the spoiled rich children kids of the high-placed functionaries—the school was far better when her granddaughter studied there. This "Shkola internat," she said, will give me a chance to compare the rather boisterous city kids with the more modest and really intelligent ones from the provinces. Now they are trying to make English a major focus too.

The class teacher introduced me and Bekmakhanova (she is seventy) to the students. All the school pupils know the name of Bekmakhanov—he wrote their history textbook. Moreover, he was sent to labor camps in Siberia for presenting an apologia for "feudalism" in Kazakhstan. He was released after five years, when he revised his version of history under duress—though the charges were also relaxed. Bekmakhanov is a very respected figure, and Khalima Adamovna is very proud of her deceased husband. Thus there was little doubt that I was in a very "prestigious" company.

The experiment went very smoothly, and the pupils took everything seriously, too seriously. Besides, every time they appeared a little spontaneous or laughed, the teacher, as well as Bekmakhanova said, "Shh . . . *tikho* . . ." So I could not really sense what was happening beneath the surface. After the experiment was over, I asked them to guess what the real purpose was. They were thinking hard. None came close to guessing. Then I asked them to say something about the nature of Kazakh/Russian accent of the voices. Most of them guessed correctly that one of them did not really know Kazakh well, though she was Kazakh. The pupils of the other Kazakh school had failed to observe this. The very first voice, they all noted almost unanimously and correctly, reflected very good knowledge of Kazakh.

When I did spill the beans, they were surprised. They were also pleased that they had made the correct guesses about which speaker knew Kazakh and which one did not.

I observed the principal's cabin and the signs in the corridors. Unlike the Kazakh school (No. 12) where most signs were in Kazakh, this school had a number of posters, announcements, and material on the wallpaper in Russian, Kazakh, and English. The principal's cabin had a picture of Pushkin, as well as of the Kazakh poet Abai.

The Experiment in Ukraine We administered the matched-guise test in two Kiev schools: first at Ukrainian-language School No. 155, with seventy-seven respondents, then at Russian-language School No. 79, with seventy-nine respondents. School No. 155 is located near L'viv Square, approximately twenty minutes by bus from the main downtown street, Khreshchatyk. It was founded in 1937 and used to offer both Ukrainian and Russian as primary languages of instruction. Now it has only Ukrainian as the primary language, but specializes in the teaching of English in higher grades. There are 546 pupils in the entire school, in twenty classes, from grades 1 through 11. Most pupils have been at that school since grade 1. In their answers, most of the students claimed to use both languages with their friends, but they spoke Russian among themselves only during class breaks when Arel was there. Arel suspected that many of them answered "as they should," as opposed to "as it is." Most also indicated they speak both languages at home, but Arel had his doubts about that as well.

Russian-language School No. 79 is located downtown, near the Respublikans'kyi football stadium, a few blocks from Khreshchatyk. Before the 1930s, it used to be a Jewish school. Hebrew is now offered, by a private firm, in the afternoon. Approximately 600 pupils are enrolled in twenty-four classes, also in grades 1 through 11.

In his field report on the administration of the tests, Arel wrote:

> The Ukrainian school which we visited yesterday could not accommodate a hundred students in a large room, so we had to do the test in three consecutive classes, which was quite tiring. I took care of everything in the first class, making all the explanations in Ukrainian, but the students were quite unruly, and I was not really pleased with the whole experience. For the second class, I asked Olga, my RA, to explain the test and read your introductory text, after I had introduced them to the *anketa*, on the assumption that Olga might project a more authoritative aura, having been a teacher herself. It worked beautifully for the second, as well as the third group, who were really attentive and quiet. It seems that what Olga was really projecting was familiarity: the students were more at ease to ask questions about the test. I was really upbeat when we left the school, although quite tired, and was hoping that I could have it both ways today, when we were scheduled to go to the Russian-medium school, i.e. a quiet and attentive group, but in a large auditorium, so that we would not have to do it three times in a row. (A shortage of tape recorders—we had to bring our own—was preventing us from running two or three tests simultaneously). Well, I got eighty of them in one room, but quiet and attentive they were not. In addition, the acoustics were not very good, since we kept hearing the vibrations of a nearby metro line, and we were all freezing in this unheated assembly hall [*aktovyi zal*]. We barely got through in the forty minutes allowed to us (each class lasts only forty minutes, and the students then move to another room). Yesterday, we managed to complete the test for the second and third class in thirty-five minutes, which gave us a few minutes to ask the students about their reactions. Although I was dreaming the day before of administering the test to everybody at once, I realized this morning that it is much better to do it in a regular classroom with a regular group. You had asked us to test approximately one hundred students per school, and this is what we had requested, but because quite a few pupils were sick (critical conditions nowadays in Ukraine), we fell short of that target in both schools, with seventy-seven answers for the Ukrainian school, and eighty for the Russian school. I did not want to abuse the hospitality of our hosts yesterday (I had naively told them that the tests would last twenty minutes, but we ended up taking—three times in a row—the whole time allocated to a class).

Administration in Latvia In Riga, Pettai attempted to vary the schools between Latvian- and Russian-dominated districts of the city. But in Riga, the differences between such districts, Pettai observed, are not as stark as they are in Tallinn, where he was able to make such distinctions. Latvians are only 35 percent of the population in Riga; thus the segregation is much less pronounced. Nonetheless, he chose two schools in the Plavnieki district and two in the Teika district, one Latvian dominant and one Russian dominant in each district.

I accompanied Pettai as he administered the test in one of the Russian schools. The school was extremely orderly and well run, and the experiment was conducted without a hitch, as the students were inquisitive and engaged. As I sat in back of the tenth form classroom, I thumbed through the class's literature text, which was published in Riga in 1992 and designed for Russian students in Latvia. There was a major section of the text that had Russian translations of Latvian national literature. This was not a postindependence phenomenon, as there was also a fourth form literature text on the shelves, published in 1980, and it had mostly Latvian folk tales translated into Russian.

The Respondents

Table 8.1 gives basic data on the respondents in the four republics. Four points from the data on this table merit emphasis. First, the question of the language used on the answer sheet, which we computed just by examining the language that was actually used in responding to the questions or circling the attribute scores, plays a key role in my analysis. I use it as the principal indicator of the primary language of the student. We know that students do not report accurately what languages they use in particular functional domains, so I was reluctant to use their self-reports to divide the respondent population into titular-speakers and Russian-speakers. I was also unwilling to use a question that asks for their nationality, so as not to alert the students to the purpose of the test. In Estonia and Latvia, the correspondence between language of answer sheet and language used with father or mother is quite close, with less than a handful in either sample speaking a language with either parent that was different from the language of the answer sheet. In Ukraine, the family situations reported by the students were so complex that a clear distinction between a Ukrainian-speaker and a Russian-speaker cannot be made. Only 16 of the 156 respondents reported speaking Ukrainian to both their parents; 69 reported speaking Russian to both their parents; 61 reported speaking a mixed language to either parent; and 6 reported speaking Russian with one parent and Ukrainian with the other. In Kazakhstan, the number of Kazakhs who used the Kazakh answer sheet was quite low (less than 30 percent) although half the respondents were in Kazakh medium of instruction schools. As Dave pointed out in her field notes, many Kazakh students began filling in the questionnaire in Kazakh and gave up because it was too hard, and switched to a Russian answer sheet. In all republics, the only dichotomous indicator of language preference is the language students used on their answer sheets. This imperfectly correlates with language of home life; but it accurately represents the language that students felt comfortable using in a schoollike situation. In our

Table 8.1. Matched-guise testing: Characteristics of subjects

Characteristic	Kazakhstan	Estonia	Latvia	Ukraine
Number of subjects	232	370	326	165
Male/female	53.7/46.3	38.9/61.1	35.9/64.1	42.2/57.8
Mean age	15.294	15.642	16.21	14.693
Answer sheet:				
Percent Russian	73.3	44.4	51.2	48.7
Percent titular	26.7	55.6	48.8	42.3
Percent mixed				9.0
Language with friends:				
Percent Russian	55.7	39.7	39.3	56.5
Percent titular	9.1	43.8	31.0	1.3
Percent mixed	33.9	15.4	29.7	42.2
Language with mother:				
Percent Russian	41.7	42.7	43.2	51.9
Percent titular	29.8	50.8	47.9	16.0
Percent mixed	26.3	6.5	8.9	32.1
Language with father:				
Percent Russian	38.1	40.2	42.1	60.3
Percent titular	33.5	46.5	48.4	17.9
Percent mixed	27.5	8.9	9.2	21.8
Percent other			0.3	
School language: primary level				
Percent Russian	56.7	41.3	47.2	89.5
Percent titular	22.9	51.5	44.1	3.9
Percent mixed	18.6	7.2	8.4	6.5
Percent other	1.7		0.3	(n.b. Kindergarten)
School language: lower middle	(NA)			
Percent Russian		37.9	44.9	61.5
Percent titular		51.3	43.0	22.4
Percent mixed		10.0	12.1	16.0
				[n.b. Primary level]
School language: upper middle				
Percent Russian	33.6	36.3	43.0	43.1
Percent titular	29.7	50.4	44.6	41.1
Percent mixed	35.8	12.5	12.4	15.7
Percent other	0.9			[n.b. Current school]
Russian bilingualism*	11.681	9.375	10.504	7.647
Titular bilingualism*	6.0	9.694	6.84	6.947

*Respondents rated their abilities to speak, write, understand, and read on a four-point scale, from 1 = fluent to 4 = not at all. The minimum score is 4, reflecting perfect fluency; the maximum is 16, reflecting no abilities at all. "Bilingualism" in this table refers to the Russian-speakers' abilities in the titular language and the titular-speakers' abilities in Russian.

analysis, those who used the Russian answer sheet were coded as "Russian-speaking"; those who used the titular answer sheet were coded as "titular-speaking."

Second, on the question of language used with friends, the answer of the Kiev students merits consideration, reflecting, accurately Arel believes, the social reality. Almost no Kievans can get by in a public institution without reliance on Russian. Only 1.3 percent of the respondents claimed they did so; but even here, one might surmise a little forgetting of talk in the school yard, on the football field, on the dance floor, when Russian was used. Far more Latvian and Estonian students lived in a world without code-switching or -mixing.

Third, and again pointing to Kiev, the language of school instruction changes toward Ukrainian for the cohort then finishing secondary school. This trend predated the collapse of the Soviet Union. While only 3.9 percent of the Kiev respondents went to a Ukrainian-medium kindergarten, 22.4 percent matriculated in a Ukrainian-medium primary school, and 41.1 percent were currently enrolled in a Ukrainian-medium high school. In the other three republics, the general rule that the medium of instruction in your first school determines your future path seems to hold.

Finally, there is the question of student bilingualism. The data on Table 8.1 show that bilingualism was rather symmetric in Estonia and Ukraine, with just about the same rates of Russian students claiming facility in the titular language as titular students claiming facility in Russian. In Latvia and Kazakhstan, however, the reported bilingualism is asymmetric, with far more titulars claiming facility in Russian than vice versa.

Analysis of the Data

Loss of In-Group Status for Speaking the Titular Language

In all four republics (as indicated on Tables 8.2 and 8.3) the Russian-speaker lost respect among Russian respondents when in her titular guise. This finding is significant at $p < .01$ in all four republics. In Kazakhstan, the Russian-speaker loses the greatest amount of respect in her titular guise among Russian respondents, followed by the Russian-speaker in Estonia, and the Russian-speaker in Latvia. The Russian-speaker in Ukraine loses least respect in her titular guise, but it is still a strong and significant relationship.

Russian-speakers in all four republics also lose points in in-group friendship when in their titular guise. This relationship is significant in Estonia (where the loss is greatest), in Kazakhstan (where the loss is second greatest), and in Latvia (where the loss is third greatest). In Ukraine, the loss is least, and it is not statistically significant.

Gain in Out-Group Status for Speaking the Titular Language

The titular respondents did not reward Russian-speakers for their efforts at linguistic assimilation. On the respect factor, Russian-speakers in all four republics lost

Table 8.2. Scores of all guises on friendship and respect

Respondents	FTT	FTR	FRT	FRR	RTT	RTR	RRT	RRR
Kazakhstan								
All	3.50	3.68	3.77	4.10	2.11	2.50	2.92	3.40
Russians	3.39	3.63	3.69	4.06	2.04	2.46	2.86	3.35
Titulars	3.81	3.85	4.00	4.21	2.31	2.62	3.08	3.53
Estonia								
All	4.07	3.67	3.57	3.96	2.89	2.49	2.57	2.94
Russians	4.18	3.96	3.76	4.28	2.95	2.69	2.69	3.10
Titulars	3.98	3.45	3.43	3.71	2.84	2.35	2.47	2.81
Latvia								
All	3.81	3.53	3.59	3.93	2.98	2.81	2.92	3.23
Russians	3.79	3.31	3.67	4.10	2.95	2.81	3.03	3.37
Titulars	3.84	3.40	3.50	3.76	3.01	2.81	2.81	3.10
Ukraine								
All	3.73	3.58	3.11	3.42	2.48	2.65	2.23	2.60
Russians	3.70	3.69	3.41	3.66	2.45	2.73	2.46	2.81
Titulars	3.74	3.53	2.84	3.17	2.50	2.62	2.03	2.38

Note: These data are based on confirmatory factor analysis that separated respect from friendship as underlying variables. A best-of-fit model was employed that constrained estimated factor loadings and the overall factor pattern to invariance across each matched pair.

Key: FTT = mean friendship score for titular speaker in her titular guise.
FTR = mean friendship score for titular speaker in her Russian guise.
FRT = mean friendship score for Russian speaker in her titular guise.
FRR = mean friendship score for Russian speaker in her Russian guise.
RTT = mean respect score for titular speaker in her titular guise.
RTR = mean respect score for titular speaker in her Russian guise.
RRT = mean respect score for Russian speaker in her titular guise.
RRR = mean respect score for Russian speaker in her Russian guise.

Table 8.3. Values of *t* for significance of differences: Evaluations of titular and Russian speakers

	Russian speakers		Titular speakers	
Respondents	FRT-FRR	RRT-RRR	FTT-FTR	RTT-RTR
Titular				
Kazakhstan	−2.20*	−5.76†	−.57	−6.16†
Estonia	−3.93†	−6.46†	8.04†	11.09†
Latvia	−3.86†	−5.22†	8.83†	4.77†
Ukraine	−1.70	−2.32*	2.07*	−1.04
Russian				
Kazakhstan	−5.27†	−8.98†	−3.66†	−10.07†
Estonia	−6.63†	−7.08†	3.29†	5.70†
Latvia	−6.56†	−6.06†	9.10†	3.22†
Ukraine	−1.31	−3.00†	.17	−3.34†

Note: A positive *t* score represents a higher score for the titular guise.

*$p < .05$.

†$p < .01$.

respect points from titular-speaking respondents in their titular guises, and all at the $p < .01$ level. The most powerful loss was the Russian-speaker speaking Estonian, followed by the Russian-speaker speaking Kazakh. Third and fourth were the Russian-speaker speaking Latvian and the Russian-speaker speaking Ukrainian. On the friendship factor, again the Russian-speaker in her titular guise lost points in all four republics, but the relationship was not a significant one in Ukraine. The loss was greatest in Estonia, followed by Latvia, and then Kazakhstan, among the republics where the difference was below the .01 level of significance.

It is remarkable and true that the Russian-speakers lost in-group respect and friendship from Russian respondents *and from titular respondents as well* when in their titular guises. From the perspective of the utility function in the tipping game, there seems to be no status incentive for Russians to assimilate linguistically. Yet, as we will see in Chapter 9, we can pose the question in a different way—where do Russians face the lowest status *dis*incentives to assimilate? With this question in mind, the matched-guise data help tell part of the story of comparative openness to assimilation.

Status of the Titular Language for Russians When Spoken by a Native Speaker

In the measures of in- and out-group status of a language in which the Russian-speaker was evaluated in her two different guises, respondents were sensitive not only to the language that was spoken but also to how it was spoken. With this in mind, the consistently better scores received by the Russian-speaker in Latvia (who spoke very good Latvian) than the Russian-speaker in Estonia (who spoke only halting Estonian) may be a function of their linguistic abilities rather than any status factor for the language.

One way of partially separating these two factors (the language itself; and the competence of the speaker) is to examine the prestige accorded to the titular-speaker in her two guises, as evaluated by Russians. On Tables 8.2 and 8.3, we see that in both Latvia and Estonia the rankings of respect and friendship by Russian respondents for the titular-speaker in the titular guise are significantly higher than the titular-speaker in her Russian guise, even though in both cases the speakers were quite fluent (although with titular accents) in Russian. In Kazakhstan, the relationship is strongly negative on both the friendship and respect factors; in Ukraine, the relationship is strongly negative on only the respect factor. But in both Baltic cases, we can conclude that the status of the titular languages is high.

Expected Job Returns for Russians Speaking the Titular Language

As indicated on Tables 8.4 and 8.5, Russian respondents do not surmise that Russian-speakers who speak the titular language have more prestigious jobs than Russian-speakers (without information about whether they speak the titular language). In Latvia, Estonia, and Ukraine, the Russian respondents gave, on the average, more prestigious jobs to Russian-speakers in the Russian guises than they did to Russian-speakers in their titular guises, though only in Latvia and Estonia is this

Table 8.4. Job status for all guises

Respondents	Titular-speaker in her titular guise	Titular-speaker in her Russian guise	Russian-speaker in her titular guise	Russian-speaker in her Russian guise
Kazakhstan				
All	4.869	4.569	4.443	4.668
Russians	4.897	4.530	4.406	4.634
Titulars	4.789	4.678	4.554	4.768
Estonia				
All	4.028	4.228	4.549	3.898
Russians	4.065	4.365	4.380	3.894
Titulars	4.000	4.117	4.682	3.901
Latvia				
All	3.812	4.137	4.173	3.441
Russians	3.986	4.171	3.858	3.383
Titulars	3.639	4.099	4.525	3.503
Ukraine				
All	3.542	3.647	5.259	4.310
Russians	3.485	3.641	4.730	4.262
Titulars	3.476	3.339	5.721	4.524

Note: The data in this table reflect the mean rankings of respondents for each guise. The lower the score, the greater the prestige of the job.

1 = jobs in the higher intelligentsia.
2 = middle-level specialists.
3 = entrepreneurial role in commerce or business.
4 = white-collar professional work.
5 = skilled labor (and students).
6 = unskilled services.
7 = unskilled labor.
8 = farm work.
9 = some indication of deviancy.
10 = unemployed.

Table 8.5. Loss of status for Russian guise (*t*-scores comparing job statuses by same speaker in different guises)

Respondent	JRT-JRR	JTT-JTR
Titular		
Kazakhstan	.77	−.82
Estonia	−4.21†	.72
Latvia	−4.27†	2.47*
Ukraine	−3.01†	−.22
Russian		
Kazakhstan	1.44	−2.60†
Estonia	−2.26*	1.94
Latvia	−2.64†	.54
Ukraine	−.98	.46

*Significance level of $p < .05$.

†Significance level of $p < .01$.

Key: JRT = mean job status for the Russian-speaker in her titular guise.
JRR = mean job status for Russian-speaker in her Russian guise.
JTT = mean job status for titular-speaker in her titular guise.
JTR = mean job status of titular-speaker in her Russian guise.

relationship significant. In Kazakhstan, this relationship is reversed, but only weakly so, and it is not statistically significant. The strong negative relationship between the Russian-speaker in her Latvian guise and the status of the job ascribed to her by the Russian respondents is in marked contrast to the relatively high levels of respect given to that same guise by the same respondents, suggesting that characteristics like leadership, intelligence, and education (which weigh heavily in the status factor) are not well associated in the Latvian context with higher-status jobs.

Does a Colonial Mentality Persist?

As Table 8.6 demonstrates, only in Kazakhstan could it be said that a "colonial mentality" persists. There, and in none of the other three republics, titular-speaking respondents attributed much higher levels of respect to the Russian-speaker in her Russian guise than they did to the titular-speaker in her titular guise. This reflects a view that a "pure" Russian voice merits more respect than a "pure" indigenous voice. In Ukraine, there was a strong and significant negative relationship, as Ukrainian-speaking respondents ranked the Ukrainian-speaker in her primary language as meriting more respect than the Russian-speaker in her primary language. Somewhat surprising is that lack of disrespect for the Russian-speaker in her own guise in the Baltics. While the titular-speaking respondents in the Baltics gave slightly higher scores to the titular-speaker in her titular guise than they did to the Russian-speaker in her Russian guise, the differences were trivial and insignificant.

Costs of Mankurtism

Mankurtism—especially in the Baltics, but not in Kazakhstan—can be costly indeed! A clear way to show this is to examine the scores by the titular-speaking respondents on friendship and respect (see Table 8.7). Here I compare the mean scores for fellow titular-speakers who are reading the passage in Russian and fellow titular-speakers who are reading the passage in the titular language. In the Baltics, the *t*-scores on both the respect and friendship dimensions (see Table 8.3) are significant at the $p < .01$ level, in favor of the titular guise. The punishment for mankur-

Table 8.6. Persistence of a colonial mentality: Rankings by titular-speaking respondents

Republic	RRR	RTT	RRR-RTT	*t*-score
Kazakhstan	3.196	2.714	0.482	8.00†
Estonia	2.773	2.79	−0.017	−.17
Latvia	3.065	3.089	−0.024	−.49
Ukraine	2.319	2.724	−0.405	−2.70†

Note: The respect and friendship scores are means taken from a confirmatory factor analysis that was a best-of-fit model performed by constraining factor loadings and factor patterns to invariance between all four of the samples from each republic.

†Significance level in a two-tailed test of $p < .01$.

Table 8.7. Cost of mankurtism: Rankings of titular-speaking respondents

Republic	FTT-FTR	RTT-RTR
Kazakhstan	−.04	−.31
Estonia	.53	.49
Latvia	.44	.20
Ukraine	.21	−.12

Note: The scores are taken from the means of a confirmatory factor analysis that was a best-of-fit model by constraining estimated factor loadings and the overall factor pattern to invariance across each matched pair. The column FTT-FTR reflects the difference in the mean friendship score for the titular-speaker in her titular guise and in her Russian guise. The column RTT-RTR reflects the difference in the mean respect score for the titular-speaker in her titular guise and in her Russian guise.

tism is therefore strong. In Ukraine, the loss of friendship for mankurtism was significant; on respect, there was some gain, but not at a significant level. Mankurtism in Ukraine evokes at best an ambivalent reaction among titular-speakers. You might be a more important person if you are a Ukrainian who is speaking Russian, in the calculation of titular respondents, but you are not a friend. In Kazakhstan, great respect is earned for mankurtism, but on the friendship dimension, the results, as with Ukraine, are neutral. The in-group policing in the Baltics against mankurtism is strong indeed; the policing against mankurtism in Ukraine is at best weak, and in Kazakhstan, there are, as of now, only positive payoffs in respect among the indigenous in-group for mankurtism.

Primordial Solidarities Are Strong

People who speak their own language merit higher rankings than those speaking a language foreign to them. This can be called the primordial principle. Table 8.8 shows this in a simple way. In the Baltics on both dimensions of friendship and respect, both sets of respondents always ranked the Russian-speaker higher in her Russian guise than in her titular guise. And the titular-speaker is, again by both sets of respondents, always ranked higher in her titular guise than in her Russian guise. In Ukraine, both titular and Russian respondents rank the titular-speaker in her Russian guise, in terms of respect, higher than that same speaker in her titular guise. On all other categories, the primordial principle holds in Ukraine. In Kazakhstan, both groups of respondents favored the titular-speaker in terms of friendship in her Russian guise over that same speaker in her titular guise; both groups also gave greater respect to the titular-speaker speaking Russian than that same speaker speaking Kazakh. Indeed, in all thirty-two comparisons, both respondent groups agreed on the voice to be favored. There seems to be a general preference

Table 8.8. Respondents' primordial sentiments

Respondent	FTT > FTR?	FRR > FRT?	RTT > RTR?	RRR > RRT?
Kazakhstan				
Russians	No	Yes	No	Yes
Titulars	No	Yes	No	Yes
Estonia				
Russians	Yes	Yes	Yes	Yes
Titulars	Yes	Yes	Yes	Yes
Latvia				
Russians	Yes	Yes	Yes	Yes
Titulars	Yes	Yes	Yes	Yes
Ukraine				
Russians	Yes	Yes	No	Yes
Titulars	Yes	Yes	No	Yes

Note: The answers in the cells reflect data in Table 8.1.

for hearing people speak their own language than hearing them speaking in a non-native way a language foreign to them.[13]

Bilingualism of Respondents and Influence on Matched-Guise Values

The respondents' level of bilingualism often has a significant effect on how they value Russian-speakers in their titular guises. Table 8.9 reports the results. (Note that because the bilingualism score is inverted, with 4 being "most bilingual" and 16 being "least bilingual," a negative slope reflects a positive relationship.) In all four republics (but only significantly in Estonia and Kazakhstan), the more bilingual the titular respondent, the less highly they rank the Russian-speaker in her titular guise. Familiarity with Russian by titular-speakers breeds contempt for Russians who are attempting to assimilate. Or another way to put it is that titular respondents who had best assimilated to Russian are least supportive of Russians moving toward assimilation into the titular language. The implications of this for out-group status are somewhat hopeful. As the titular nationality loses facility in Russian, this could mean greater accommodation to and respect for Russians seeking to assimilate linguistically into the titular language.

Meanwhile, although the relationship is never significant, in all four republics the Russians who have greater facility in the titular language give higher rankings to the Russian-speakers in their titular guises. This has implications for long-term projection of in-group status. It suggests that as more Russians become bilingual in the titular language, the greater will be the mean in-group value of Russians who publicly employ the titular voice.

THIS chapter has presented the results of an experiment that seeks to find the value that both Russians and titulars give to speakers of the two languages, controlling

[13] Woolard, *Double Talk*, p. 115, found a similar phenomenon in Catalonia.

Table 8.9. Bilingualism and value of assimilation (How degree of bilingualism of respondent affects evaluations of speakers)

Respondents	FRT	RRT
Kazakhstan		
Russians	−1.243	−1.029
Titulars	3.391*	3.574*
Estonia		
Russians	−.873	−.798
Titulars	3.911*	3.381*
Latvia		
Russians	−.872	−.897
Titulars	.541	.746
Ukraine		
Russians	−.801	−.726
Titulars	.542	.516

Note: A negative *t*-value reflects that less bilingualism yields more positive rankings. These are *t*-values of a regression equation in which FRT (friendship of the Russian-speaker in her titular guise) and RRT (respect for the Russian-speaker in her titular guise) are dependent variables. Here the factor loadings are based on the same criteria as in Table 8.2. The bilingualism score (knowledge by titular of Russian and vice versa) is the independent variable in both equations.

*Significant at $p < .05$.

for other attributes of the speaker that normally influence our evaluations of people. This experiment was not run in a scientific laboratory where all environmental effects could be erased but in precisely the environments where language mattered and where the respondents did not feel constrained to do as the scientists wanted. From our descriptions of the test situations, the most important difference between the tests in the four republics was in the quality of the Russian-speakers' rendition of the text in her titular guise. I have reminded the reader of this difference in the analysis of the results, but I cannot weigh its importance from the data available from the experiments themselves.

The principal finding, for purposes of this book, is that there are no in-group or out-group gains to be had for Russian-speakers to speak the titular language. This is so for two separate factors: a factor of respect and a factor of solidarity. Rewards from the Russian-speaking in-group are not to be found for demonstrating a move toward assimilation; moreover, costs from the out-group are to be paid for Russian-speakers who use a marked dialect of the titular language. Furthermore, Russian-speakers who are heard using the titular language are not "coded" by Russians or titulars to have captured better jobs. In fact, in Latvia, where the Russian-speaker speaking Latvian earned considerable relative respect, the job ascription to this guise was relatively low status. These are not auspicious signs for an easy route toward assimilation.

A few other findings merit summary. First, only in Kazakhstan did we find evidence of a "colonial mentality," where titular respondents would give greater respect to a Russian-speaker speaking Russian than to a titular-speaker speaking the titular language. In the other three republics, each group held the "authentic" voice of their own language to be more valued than the "authentic" voice of the Russian. Second, only in Estonia and Latvia did titular-speaking respondents give strongly negative rankings to titular-speakers in their Russian guises. This phenomenon of titulars speaking Russian as their normal language of everyday use has been called "mankurtism" in Central Asia, but the phenomenon, and the negative reactions it evokes among titulars, is evident in all the republics. The data here show that mankurtism is valued in Kazakhstan, faced ambivalent reactions in Ukraine, and is scorned in the Baltics. This is consistent with the ethnographic finding that in the Baltics, Russians were cognizant that the titulars were serious in their nationalizing project, and therefore Russian parents upgraded the probability that their children would need to become proficient in the titular language. Third, all other things being equal, respondents normally ranked voices in their authentic guise more highly than in their second-language guise. This suggests a generalized value that it is better to be who you are, and that assimilation is suspicious. Finally, data on the degree of bilingualism among respondents shows that in general, the more bilingual the titular-speaking respondents are, the less tolerant they are toward Russians speaking in the titular language. To the extent that titular-speaking bilingualism (titular/Russian) is on the decline, this bodes well for lowering the out-group costs of assimilation in the succeeding generation.

9

Turning Megalomanians into Ruritanians

Ernest Gellner, in his classic work *Nations and Nationalism*, addressed the question of whether the rural, semiliterate, and socially inert immigrants from the mythical backwater of Ruritania living in the modernizing and exciting mythical state of Megalomania would themselves become (through assimilation) Megalomanians, or whether they would become disaffected with chances for social mobility and return home, now socially mobilized and literate, as Ruritanian nationalists, ready to transform a rural dialect into a world-class literary language.[1] In the Soviet period, asking whether Kazakhs, or Yakuts, or any other non-Russian nationality would become, through exposure to Russia's modernization, russified is a question central to the domain of Gellner's theory. As for the situation of a "beached" diaspora, Gellner never theorized about a change in the tide, in which Megalomanians would have to decide whether or not to become Ruritanians.

Gellner's Theory of Assimilation

The most important contribution of Gellner's work on nationalism has been its unrelenting insistence that the existence of a "nation" is not a sufficient condition for the emergence of nationalism; rather, nationalism is the result of the uneven diffusion of industrialization. The theory is evocatively explicated in Gellner's robust "just-so" story, related in *Thought and Change*, about two territories, A and B,

An earlier version of this chapter was presented at what was to be a celebration of Gellner's work at the Central European University in Prague, in December 1995. He tragically died weeks before the conference, and consequently, this critical discussion of his work lacks any reference to what I am sure would have been a spirited and devastating counterattack. The conference version of this paper is published as "Nationalism and Language: A Post-Soviet Perspective," in John A. Hall, ed., *Ernest Gellner and the Theory of Nationalism* (Cambridge: Cambridge University Press, 1998).

[1] Ernest Gellner, *Nations and Nationalism* (Ithaca: Cornell University Press, 1983), pp. 58–70.

which are parts of an overarching empire. Modernization hits the world "in a devastating but untidy flood," coming first through A, and only later to B. This means that as A finally plows through the misery and dislocation of early modernization, B will still be mired in it. Impoverished and hopeless youth in B will consequently seek to better their lives by emigrating to A. From this situation, different sorts of nationalism will arise. If Bs can blend into A without being noticed, and if B's intellectuals get elite positions in A, then there will emerge a wider A-&-B society, on the road to becoming a nation. Nationalism will be the doctrine of the A-&-B elites seeking to naturalize state power inside the boundaries of A-&-B, through the standardization of a national culture.[2] But if Bs cannot blend in—that is, when Bs are radically differentiated from As by race, skin color, or religion, what Gellner later calls "entropy-resistant" classifications[3]—the discontent caused by this inability to achieve social mobility in A will express itself in a form of separatist nationalism, of an A vs. B type. In both the A-&-B and A vs. B cases, nationalism was impelled, not by culture, but rather by the uneven development of modernization.

Language is not an entropy-resistant classification. Full citizenship in a modern society requires literacy; and practical necessity demands that from clerks to those in more specialized occupations, citizens of a modern society must be able to communicate efficiently with each other in a single language. Small communities with their own languages cannot produce the range of specialists needed to run a modern society; therefore, the nation-state is the minimal territorial unit in the modern world. And the nation-state will impose a standard dialect or language within its boundaries, one more associated with scholastic high culture than with the folk cultures of the peasants—demonstrating that the claim by nationalists that they represent the "folk" is a sham—and this new standard language will become the distinguishing mark of the nation. This theory, however, does not predict a universal industrial culture, or a universal language of industrial society, mainly because uneven development will assure breakaway nationalisms (from those places where assimilation is blocked by a jealous working class focusing on cultural difference in order to discriminate against immigrants) whose leaders will consecrate some dialect or a language that differentiates it from its neighbor.[4]

The motivating factor in this model—quite parallel to the most-favored-lord model I proposed in Chapter 3—is the opportunity for bureaucratic and other literacy-demanding jobs that impels rural folk to learn the elite language of the cities to which they have migrated. If mobility prospects are blocked, these migrants will sense higher expected economic returns for having their own nation-state, where the elite dialect of their language would be the standard. These frustrated job seek-

[2] Ernest Gellner, *Thought and Change* (Chicago: University of Chicago Press, 1964), pp. 166–68.

[3] Gellner, *Nations and Nationalism*, chap. 6.

[4] See Gellner, *Thought and Change*, pp. 158–63. In *Nations and Nationalism* Gellner writes about "assimilation" without defining it formally. Because many citizens throughout the globe are fully incorporated into political life without having assimilated, it seems unduly provocative, as Alfred Stepan pointed out at the Prague presentation of this chapter, to hold this to be the criterion of ultimate loyalty to a nation-state. Nonetheless, any theory of the nation needs to have a criterion of culture shift in line with a national standard, for which the term "assimilation," as I defined it in Chapter 1, is perfectly appropriate, and I believe consistent with Gellner's use of the term.

ers would then become recruits for a nationalist movement, whose victory would make them highly paid clerks. To be sure, Gellner shied away from this bald economism and claimed that his theory had been "travestied" by others who held that nationalism was based on calculation. This formulation, he protests, is a misrepresentation. He points to the real experience of rural migrants in a city ruled by bureaucrats who speak a language absolutely foreign to them. "This very concrete experience," Gellner imagines, helps them learn "the difference between dealing with a co-national, one understanding and sympathizing with their culture, and someone hostile to it." From this experience, a sort of "love" can emerge for their culture, "without any conscious calculation of advantages and prospects of social mobility." Nonetheless, Gellner admits, "*had* there been such calculation (which there was not) it would, in quite a number of cases . . . have been a very sound one [to become nationalists]."[5] And so, even though his peasant migrants never calculated, they more or less acted as if they had!

It is an intellectual treat to read Gellner's clear, acerbic, and powerful prose, whether he is battling Kedourie, one-upping Hroch, or elaborating his alternative vision. Yet Gellner's work, as is especially apparent today when modernization theory has faced generations of critics, is deeply flawed. Its functionalism runs mad. Its reifications deny human agency. And when the theory does include agents, these agents are portrayed in caricature.[6]

In functionalist logic, the identification of a "need" is used to explain an outcome, ignoring the historical reality that many needs go unfulfilled, to the detriment of organizations and individuals. The need itself, it should be apparent, can hardly explain its fulfillment, though Gellner often writes as if it can. In *Nations and Nationalism*, for example, Gellner summarizes his explanation of why centralized states monopolize culture within their boundaries. This kind of state, he tells us,[7]

> must be so. Its economy depends on mobility and communication between individuals, at a level which can only be achieved if those individuals have been socialized into a high culture, and indeed into the same high culture. . . . Also, the economic tasks set these individuals do not allow them to be both soldiers and citizens of local petty communities. . . . So the economy needs both the new type of central

[5] Gellner, *Nations and Nationalism*, p. 61.

[6] Gellner's core argument, in what he refers to as the LSE debate on nationalism, in *Encounters with Nationalism* (Oxford: Blackwell, 1994), p. 61, is that the motivating factor in inducing nationalism is industrial society. In my judgment, especially when he considers sub-Saharan Africa, he uses fancy footwork to ignore disconfirming evidence. African nationalism clearly was not motivated by industrialization. So Gellner makes the dubious assertion that nationalism developed in Africa because Europeans there were intent on setting up an "eventually industrial type of society." Gellner, *Nations and Nationalism*, p. 82. Intentions (such as they were) to set up an industrial society are quite a different matter from industrialization itself. This chapter is not concerned with the causes of nationalism, and I will not enter into the LSE debate. Rather, this chapter is concerned mainly with the elaboration of the mechanisms that translate the macro forces (whether they are from industrialization, modernity, or ideas) into micro incentives for people to assimilate into a cosmopolitan culture or to seek fulfillment as a member of a separate nation, built on cultural materials recognizable from their rural roots.

[7] Gellner, *Nations and Nationalism*, pp. 140–42.

> culture and the central state; the culture needs the state; and the state probably needs the homogeneous cultural branding of its flock. . . . So the culture needs to be sustained *as* a culture, and not as the carrier or scarcely noticed accompaniment of a faith.

Some more examples follow. "The state [under conditions of industrialization]," Gellner asserts, "is charged with the maintenance and supervision of an enormous social infrastructure." "In the industrial world high cultures prevail, but they need a state not a church, and they need a state *each*," we are told. "That is one way of summing up the emergence of the nationalist age." And in his subtle and clever posthumous manuscript *Nationalism Observed*, Gellner retains his functionalist view of social causation. "Egalitarianism beats out stratification in industrial societies," he writes, "because it helps to reduce friction." "In the second zone," Gellner writes with his focus on Germany and Italy, "nationalism *could* be benign and liberal, it had no inherent need to go nasty (even if in the end it did)." Here "needs" could not explain fascism. But for Gellner, that is an anomaly. Usually, needs create fulfilling outcomes.[8]

Like many functionalist accounts, Gellner's relies on a technique of reification, giving human attributes to unspecified globs of humanity or territory. "Mankind is irreversibly committed to industrial society," Gellner preaches. How precisely one can feel, or see, or measure this commitment, or find precisely where it resides, is left to the readers' imaginations. "Cultural minorities," we are told, "refrain from developing an effective nationalism because they have no hope of success." How do groups of people, most of whom don't know each other, "refrain" from doing anything? Elsewhere: "advanced lands do not have any interest in sharing their prosperity with the ill-trained latest arrivals." How can we attribute "interests" to lands?[9]

Reifications come from all corners of his work. In his chapter "What is a Nation?" in *Nations and Nationalism*, he affirms that "polities then will to extend their boundaries to the limits of their cultures"; that "nationalism uses the preexisting, historically inherited proliferation of cultures . . . and most often transforms them radically"; that "the cultures [nationalism] claims to defend and revive are often its own inventions"; that "societies worship themselves brazenly and openly . . . in a nationalist age"; that "nationalism has its own amnesias . . . which . . . can be profoundly distorting"; and that "modern . . . society . . . believes itself to be perpetuating . . . a folk culture." And in his posthumous manuscript, he writes that in his second zone, that of Prussia and Italy, "A nation wanted its own state in addition to its own Main Poet." In these snippets, polities, nationalism, and societies are personified and given intentions and goals. Revealing is his argument with Hroch. In it, Gellner points out that Hroch "faces one of the most persistent and deep issues in this field: is it nations, or is it classes, which are the real and principal actors in history?" Gellner never even suggests that it may be "people."[10]

[8] See ibid., p. 63, and pp. 72–73; and "Nationalism Observed," unpublished book manuscript, 1995, p. 16.

[9] See Gellner, *Nations and Nationalism*, p. 39, and *Thought and Change*, pp. 174 and 167.

[10] See Gellner, *Nations and Nationalism*, pp. 55, 56, 58, and *Encounters with Nationalism*, p. 194.

To be sure, actors are not entirely absent from Gellner's writings. In his posthumous manuscript, *Nationalism Observed*, Gellner introduces more fully the goals and aspirations of the "nationalist," thereby overcoming some of his functionalism and reification. But his view of nationalists is quite caricatured. Nationalists "are in fact aware, with bitterness" that their nations did not always exist.[11] Perhaps, though, some were aware with a sense of irony, or maybe were not aware because of a self-imposed amnesia that their nation did not always exist.[12] And immediately following, Gellner writes, "The nationalist squares the assumption of the universality of nationalism with its widespread absence . . . by claiming that it was there . . . but . . . asleep." "Reawakening" is indeed a common trope by nationalists; but the presentation of this line hardly captures the complex set of reasons that motivates real nationalists. A caricatured vision of actors is an inadequate improvement upon a functionalist logic that has no actors at all.

Gellner's use of functionalism, reification, and caricature, in my judgment, were for him a shorthand, to elide the issue of mechanisms, in order to get at the basic structure of nationalism. In that regard—where nationalism is firmly placed into a social calculus—I am in thorough debt to Gellner's work. From Chapter 1 of this book, through the exposition of the tipping model, I have tried to develop a more plausible micro component to the study of assimilation as a complement to—not as a contradiction of—Gellner's macro theory.

One way to do this, as I have shown in both the tipping model and the ethnographies, is to assume that *people* are oftentimes the principal actors in history. Don't misunderstand; I'm not a radical methodological individualist. By no means am I opposed to macro-theorizing in analyzing the structural effects of industrialization, of state construction, and of interstate conflicts of interest. My most-favored-lord model, presented in Chapter 3, is after all a macro theory heavily indebted to Gellner's formulations. Rather, I believe that our macro stories must be made consistent with parallel stories told on a micro level. That is to say, the predictions of the macro and micro stories need to be calibrated. It may be the case, for example, from a macro perspective, that cultural minorities "refrain" from nationalism because they believe success unlikely. Nonetheless, a convincing theory would need to show that for all (or most) members of that set, there would be no *individual* interest in developing a nationalist program and insufficient resources to "sell" it to the putative members of that nation. To be sure, Gellner often reconciles the micro and macro stories, especially when writing about the role of the intelligentsia in the forging of nationalism.[13] But his typical story line has macrohistorical forces (industrialization and modernization) impelling unspecified actors (minorities, states, lands, classes) into nationalist movements. This requires revision.

I propose that we subordinate Gellner's functionalist logic to a model that also takes real individual incentives—and not just the economic ones that Gellner

[11] Gellner, "Nationalism Observed," p. 5.

[12] See, for example, Juan Díez Medrano, *Divided Nations: Class, Politics, and Nationalism in the Basque Country and Catalonia* (Ithaca: Cornell University Press, 1995), on Sabino de Arana in Basque country.

[13] See Gellner, *Thought and Change*, pp. 169–70.

concentrated his analysis on—into account. The data, once examined on a micro level, allow me to complement Gellner's theory with a nonfunctionalist microcalculus, a calculus that does not require a pure job-mobility motivation that Gellner knew to be inadequate.

In this chapter, the spotlight will be on ordinary people, like the ones who were introduced in the ethnographic discussions in Part II of this book. In the wings, of course, there are the intellectuals, those people often referred to as the "ethnic entrepreneurs," who have an interest in altering the payoffs for individual identity choices. These entrepreneurs will be introduced in the discourse analysis in Chapter 10, and they will be spotlighted in Chapter 12 when I consider the issue of interethnic violence. But ethnic entrepreneurs cannot create ethnic solidarities from nothing. They must, if they are to succeed, be attuned to the micro incentives that real people face.

National Revivals and the Tipping Game

It is now apt to reconsider Figure 1.2. It should be recalled that the x-axis represents the percentage of Russians who speak the titular language. (Alternatively, and as a much better indicator of assimilation, it could represent the percentage of Russian-speakers who send their children to titular-medium schools. The number of Russian parents who have done so is so low as of this writing that the model does not have much interest; however, it is possible that at a certain point along the x-axis—say at around the 50 percent level—a second tipping game, one involving sending their children to a titular-medium school, will be triggered. Meanwhile, the y-axis portrays the average payoff (less learning costs) for a Russian-speaker in the population who acquires facility in the titular language (or who sends her child to a titular-medium school). The utility function RR represents the payoff for maintaining a monolingual Russian repertoire; and TT represents the payoff for developing a Russian/titular bilingual repertoire (in the medium-of-instruction tipping game, RR would represent Russian-language dominance and TT would represent titular-language dominance).

The structure of this game makes for a powerful story about language shift. For one, there are only two stable equilibria, at 0 percent speaking the titular language or 100 percent. Anywhere to the left of *k*, the tipping point, the average payoff for learning the titular language is less than maintaining monolingualism in Russian. Those who speak the titular language will have little incentive to maintain facility in it or to pass it on to their children. The long-term consequence of this situation is for the society to return to a 0 percent equilibrium. Anywhere to the right of *k*, however, the incentives are reversed. And any Russian speaker who is monolingual will anticipate a higher payoff for facility in the titular language. If all remaining Russian monolinguals make the same calculation (which would be rational for all those facing more or less average costs and payoffs), the trend would be toward 100 percent facility in the titular language, the other stable equilibrium.

A second crucial element of the tipping-game plot is that the difference between the average payoff for R at 0 percent and the average payoff for T at 100 percent plays almost no role in individual choice. Suppose the average individual payoffs for Russian-speakers at 100 percent along the x-axis were much higher than the average individual payoffs for Russian-speakers at 0 percent along the x-axis. Here, we might say that there were strong macro (economic, political, or social) incentives for assimilation. But if the status quo were at 0 percent, there would be no incentive for a particular individual to shift her language repertoire. In this case, and contra Gellner's functionalist formulations, the "needs" of the society would not be met by the actions of its members.

Each of the utility functions has an unusual shape, and this merits some comment about two assumptions hidden in those curves. My first assumption is that at 0 percent along the x-axis, there will be extremely high rewards for a few Russian-speaking individuals to serve as what Abram de Swaan calls "monopoly mediators" between the elites of the nationalizing state and the cultural minority.[14] These mediators serve as translators of the laws and regulations of the polity to their community and as spokespersons to the state apparatus on behalf of members of their community who need special services from the state. If there are virtually no bilinguals, and if bilingual titulars abjure playing such a role (or are not trusted by the minority community), the returns for learning the titular language (for some Russians) would be great, raising the average payoff, making it come close to the payoff for RR at 0 percent on the x-axis. This is why TT drops at first before rising as more and more Russian-speakers become fluent in the titular language.

My second assumption is that as more and more of the once monolingual Russian-speakers (and their children) become fluent in the titular language, many people in that community will feel a sense of wistfulness that their culture is disappearing as a viable aspect of the society in which they live. (This is especially the case in the second game, in which the choice is whether to send your child to a Russian or titular medium-of-instruction school.) Yet despite a general nostalgia for the days when the culture of the immigrant community was intact, only a few individuals will have an incentive to maintain monolingualism in Russian. Those who do, especially those who can demonstrate that they have "pure" Russian roots, and under conditions when most other members of the Russian-speaking community have become either bilinguals or monolinguals in the titular language, will become cultural heroes. They will pine for the day when interests change, and the payoffs favoring a Russian-language revival increase.[15] These culture heroes would become the vanguard of such a revival. But with no revival in sight, they will get honor and respect from members of the assimilated community who remember their roots, and perhaps receive professorships in Russian culture in the national university, and their payoffs at RR will begin to rise as the society moves toward the right-hand equilibrium.

Economists (and Gellner, in some of his formulations) would have little trouble calculating the payoff functions RR and TT. They would be the expected economic

[14] Abram de Swaan, *In Care of the State* (New York: Oxford University Press, 1988), chap. 3. Of course, the Russian-speaking titulars had long played the mediation role and could under this reversal of the tide continue to do so. But I assume here that with a reversal of the tide, people who consider themselves "pure" Russians will want mediators from their own group.

[15] David Laitin, "Language Games," *Comparative Politics* 20, no. 3 (1988): 293.

returns for each language repertoire depending on how many other people of the Russian-speaking community had the same repertoire or a different one. If, for example, Russian-speakers project that as the society moves toward its tipping point, it would be impossible to get a job as a sales clerk, as a customs official, as a production manager, or as a teacher unless one spoke the titular language, they would set their expected economic returns for speaking the titular language as significantly higher.

Utility functions for language-related issues, as should be quite apparent from the ethnographies, and from the matched-guise experiments, are not so simple. People will be reluctant to reposition (or better, re-present) themselves culturally—say by assimilating—if they know people who share their background will taunt or ostracize them or their children. They will be equally reluctant if they know that assimilation is like being an Alice on the Queen's chessboard. The closer they get, the more the fashion leaders of the high culture change their styles in order to create a moving target. Gellner hinted at these factors but never specified them in his just-so stories.

In light of these considerations, and in line with the data collected for the matched-guise experiment, I postulated two other variables that help constitute the language-utility function, both of which have more to do with status than income.[16] First, there is the value of in-group status. Suppose Russian-speakers who attempt to learn the titular language (through seeking social relations, or even relations of affection) suffer ridicule, ostracism, or even bodily harm from members of their own community. To the extent that vigilantes within the migrant society can impose costs on potential assimilators into the titular culture, the payoff for TT will be reduced. Second, there is the value of out-group acceptance. Suppose Russian-speakers who learn the titular language are easily identified by titulars and are barred from enjoying the fruits of assimilation. Titular clubs, social groups, and spouses remain out of bounds for assimilators, or nouveaux titulars. Under such conditions (even if they could get decent employment that requires knowing the titular language), the returns for TT, compared with RR, will be lowered.

A number of important questions relating to this model and its predictions will remain unanswered: first, how and with what weight are the three elements of the language-utility function to be combined; second, how are the opportunities and constraints set by the policies of the nationalizing state to be included in the model. It makes a big difference if the state subsidizes language instruction for its minorities, or whether the governments refuse even to sponsor the publication of textbooks oriented to teaching the outside group how to speak the national language. There may be precious little "choice" involved if there are no opportunities to learn the titular language; third, there are a range of other realms in which assimilation can take place—in dress, in surnames, in diet. The relationship of language assimilation to these other forms, and how they play into one another, awaits specification.

[16] These considerations were raised in Chapter 2. I am indebted to Roger Petersen, whose work on this three-pronged utility function informs mine. See Roger Petersen, "Rationality, Ethnicity, and Military Enlistment," *Social Science Information* 28, no. 3 (1989): 563–98.

Despite these theoretical lacunae, the data from Chapters 7 and 8, reassembled in the section that follows, demonstrate that expected economic returns cannot tell the whole story of assimilation, at least at the early stages of language rationalization in the newly nationalizing states of the former Soviet Union, but that concerns of in- and out-group status can be made part of a rational calculus in questions of assimilation and nationalism.

Russians in the Post-Soviet Diaspora

The 25 million Russians living in the now-independent states that were formerly union republics of the Soviet Union find themselves somewhat like "Bs" in Gellner's just-so story of nationalism. The question of the fate of this "beached diaspora" remains a central concern of this book.

An economistic interpretation would have us look at the relative modernization of the nationalizing state and Russia. According to this model, the diaspora will remain in the titular republics that are developmentally ahead of Russia (e.g., Estonia and Latvia) and leave those that are behind Russia (e.g. Kazakhstan) in search of the better things in life associated with advanced modernization. In the former case, where the Russians remain, the theory then demands that we look to social mobility prospects within the nationalizing state for Russians. If they are more or less equal to that of the titulars (and this would happen where the working class cannot easily distinguish titulars from Russians, for example in Ukraine), the theory predicts assimilation by Russian-speakers into the standard language of the titular republic. If the Russians face discrimination through easy detection (e.g., in Estonia or Latvia), the theory predicts a counter nationalism led by the Russian-speaking disaffected intelligentsia living in the titular republic.

To test these predictions—but with more of a focus on individual incentives than Gellner's formulations demand—I propose to consolidate the data analyzed from the large-*n* surveys and from the matched-guise experiments. The relevant data from the surveys, from the matched-guise tests, and from a few other sources of published data, are presented in Table 9.1. The dependent variable of consequence for a test of Gellner's theory is the reaction of the diasporic population to the nationalizing projects of their new states in which they are now citizens. Consequently, I shall focus here on the openness of Russian-speakers to assimilation into titular society, an index that was described and analyzed in Chapter 7. As row 1 on Table 9.1 shows, on the dependent variable "openness to assimilation" Latvia's Russians are by far the most open, followed by Estonia's, then Ukraine's, and finally Kazakhstan's.

The tipping model, if presented as a monotonic process in which positive attitudes toward assimilation increase to the extent that other members of your group have already assimilated, requires some revision in light of these data. If the point on the x-axis of the tipping model is coded based on the percentage of Russians who speak the titular language (row 2), one would expect Ukrainian Russians to be most open to assimilation, with Latvian Russians in second, Estonian Russians in

Table 9.1. Accounting for Russian assimilation

Variables	Kazakhstan	Estonia	Latvia	Ukraine
Dependent variable: openness to assimilation				
1. Index of openness to assimilation	.31	.53	.67	.49
Demographic background variables				
2. Percentage who speak titular language: 1989 census/survey (those who think in it or speak it freely; question C in Table 7.1)	.86 3.5	13.8 6.4	21 20.1	33.3 26.4
3. Religious distance of titulars from Orthodoxy	High	Medium	Medium	Low
4. Linguistic difference of titular language from Russian	High	High	Medium	Low
5. Percent of Russians in capital city: 1897/1970/1989	58/70/59	16/35/42	16/43/47	54/23/21
6. Percent of Russians in republic	37.8	30.3	34.0	22.1
Economic returns for assimilation				
7. Regression analysis: job status explained on basis of knowing titular language (B/SEB), from survey	−.0043/ .0588	.4313/ .0826	−.237/ .0988	.3456/ .0539
8. Economically useful to learn titular language (percent agreed from survey)	51.6	72.2	49.5	59.2
9. Mean quality of job for Russian in Russian guise less quality of job for Russian in titular guise (matched guise)	.225	−.349	.268	.949
10. Percentage of Russians in unskilled labor/ratio of percent of Russians in unskilled labor to percent of all respondents in survey	9.4/ 1.54	26.0/ 1.42	10.1/ 1.07	5.2/ 1.08
Status variables				
11. Loss of in-group status in friendship for speaking titular language	.37	.52	.43	.25
12. Loss of in-group status in respect for speaking titular language (matched guise)	.49	.41	.34	.35
13. Gain in out-group status in friendship for speaking titular language (matched guise)	−.21	−.28	−.26	−.33
14. Gain in out-group status in respect for speaking titular language (matched guise)	−.45	−.34	−.29	−.49

Table 9.1. Accounting for Russian assimilation, *continued*

Variables	Kazakhstan	Estonia	Latvia	Ukraine
Titular accommodation to Russians				
15. Percent of titular respondents who fully accept internationality marriage of son/daughter (survey)	14.3/12.4	14.5/13.9	24.7/23.0	52.8/50.8
16. Citizen/job rights for Russian monolinguals	High/few limitations	Low/ restricted	Low/ restricted	High/high

Notes: Specifications of the survey and matched-guise test are provided in Chapters 7 and 8, as well as in the Methodological Appendix. The research team that made judgments for rows 3, 4, and 16 were the author (Estonia), Dominique Arel (Ukraine), Bhavna Dave (Kazakhstan), and Vello Pettai (Estonia and Latvia). The source for row 5 is Chauncy D. Harris, "The New Russian Minorities: A Statistical Overview," *Post-Soviet Geography* 34, no. 1 (1993): 18–19.

most open to assimilation, with Latvian Russians in second, Estonian Russians in third, and Kazakhstani Russians in fourth.

What then explains the point on the x-axis for each republic at the time of the survey, shortly after the Soviet collapse? From the data on Table 9.1, the answer seems clear: social distance. The proximity of religious doctrine (row 3) and language group (row 4) accounts for Ukraine's Russians (with a Slavic language and Orthodox religion), who are on the point farthest toward assimilation, followed by Latvia (an Indo-European language and Christian in religion), then by Estonia (a non–Indo-European language but Christian), and finally Kazakhstan (a non–Indo-European language and Islamic). Furthermore, consider the 1989 figures for percentage of Russians in the capital city (row 5) and in the entire republican population (row 6). The lower the number, a demographic perspective would assume, the higher the probability of language assimilation, as the probability of interacting with a non-Russian would be higher. Again, these data are nearly consistent with each republic's point on the x-axis (with Estonia and Latvia reversed).

Does this mean that a choice model is not useful for studying assimilation? If cultural distance and demographics can explain placement on the x-axis, where do calculations about economic returns and social status come into play? The answer is that under Soviet rule, the payoffs in status and economic returns for speaking the titular language for Russians hovered around zero; those who learned it did so passively, and the closer you are to native speakers (in terms of cultural or geographic distance), the more likely you will pick up the language at virtually no cost.

In the post-Soviet period, because the language policies of the nationalizing states have raised the expected returns for speaking the titular language, Russian-speakers need to calculate more consciously the potential payoffs for learning the titular language. Therefore, while a choice model would not have explained bilingual repertoires among Russians living in titular republics during the Soviet era (although it would have explained Russian-learning behavior among titulars!), such a model has a great deal of explanatory power in the present era. In fact, the ordering of the four republics in terms of where they stand on the x-axis and where they stand regarding openness to assimilation in the survey suggest that the incentives to learn the titular language have changed in the post-Soviet era. For Russians in the Soviet successor states, as demonstrated by the different rankings on the x-axis and on the openness to assimilation variable, there is a new prospective market in language learning; that is to say, it is now a long-term human capital investment worthy of consideration. Let us now examine the utility functions of Russians in their new states (based on survey data) to tease out criteria of their early decisions.

If the tipping model relied solely on expected economic returns and probabilities for occupational mobility, these data present an insurmountable challenge. The data show that the economic returns for speaking the titular language are highest in Estonia, second highest in Ukraine, neutral in Kazakhstan, and negative in Latvia. Job prospects and occupational mobility cannot therefore be the principal motor for assimilation. In the four surveys, I regressed job status of respondent on his/her knowing of the titular language (row 7). In Estonia, for each level of increase in knowledge of Estonian, Russian respondents' job status category went up nearly a half; in Ukraine, it went up by about a third; in Kazakhstan it was neutral; but in Latvia, it went down by nearly a quarter level! This is reflected in respondent attitudes (row 8); over 70 percent of Russians in Estonia agreed that it was economically useful to learn the titular language; 59 percent of Ukrainian Russians similarly agreed; and again Latvian Russians, of the four republics, agreed in lowest numbers.

The same results are partially confirmed in the matched-guise test (row 9). To be sure, only in Estonia was the job attributed to the Russian-speaker in her titular guise higher in status than in her Russian guise. In the other three republics, the job status of the Russian-speaker in her titular guise was lower than in her Russian guise. But the relative standing is what is of interest. Here respondents in Ukraine had the highest bias in favor of the Russian in her Russian guise. Students in Ukraine envisioned the Russian voice speaking the titular language as having a far worse job than that same person speaking Russian. Latvia and Kazakhstan stand in the middle, where the Russian-speaker in her Russian guise is clearly seen to have a better job, but not overwhelmingly so. Finally, an examination of respondents' actual jobs (row 10)—with the notion that a high percentage in unskilled labor would give the greatest incentive to assimilate, as clerical jobs are the next step up for the children of unskilled laborers—suggests that opportunities for social mobility through learning the titular language should be highest in Estonia, which comes in second in openness to assimilation. Openness to assimilation, *pace* the predictions of a pure job-mobility theory, cannot be explained by jobs associated with speaking the titular language and the opportunities in the titular republics for occupational mobility.

The status variables, however, can help account for variations in openness to assimilation that are missed by models, such as Gellner's, that rely primarily on expected economic returns. To be sure, Gellner's writings do not ignore status. In his preface to *Encounters with Nationalism*, he writes:[17]

[17] See Gellner, *Encounters with Nationalism*, pp. vii–viii.

> Modern man enjoys, or suffers from, no . . . rigid and reinforced ascribed status. He *makes* his own position, not by a single contract, but by a vast multiplicity of minor contracts with his fellows. In order to negotiate and articulate these contracts, he must speak in the same idiom as his numerous partners. A large, anonymous and mobile mass of individuals, negotiating countless contracts with each other, is obliged to share a culture. They must learn to follow the same rules in articulating their terms. Cultural nuance no longer symbolizes status, for the status is no longer given: but a shared, standardized culture indicates the eligibility and ability of participants to take part in this open market of negotiable, specific statuses, to be effective members of the same collectivity.

But for Gellner, in modern society there is no value in sharing, for its own sake, outside the requirements of the macro-economy, a set of customs, or a language. In contrast to this view, the status variables that I elucidated in the discussion of the tipping game, which are captured by the matched-guise test, stand independently from economic rewards or occupational standing. And they play some role in individual decisions about whether assimilation is desirable.

In-group status—the degree to which respondents of the minority group accept as friends those conationals seeking to assimilate—is coded here by the relative scores on friendship and respect measures given to the Russian-speaker in her Russian and her titular guises. The higher the former score in relationship to the latter, the lower the value of in-group respect for potential assimilators. In all four republics, the mean score (for both Russian and titular respondents) for the Russian-speaker in her Russian guise was more positive (on both friendship and respect dimensions) than for the Russian-speaker in her titular guise. None of the speakers gained points for speaking the titular language for the Russian students making their evaluations. Yet the relative status loss was different in each republic. As Table 9.1 shows (row 11), the Russian-speaker in Ukraine lost least on the friendship dimension in her titular guise; the Russian-speaker in Estonia lost most. On the respect dimension (row 12), the Russian-speaker in Latvia lost least in her titular guise, while the Russian-speaker in Kazakhstan lost most. The Russian-speaker in Ukraine had the lowest cumulative loss, followed by the Russian-speaker in Latvia. The Russian-speaker in Kazakhstan had the third lowest cumulative loss, and in Estonia the fourth.

As for out-group status—measured here by the degree to which respondents in the titular group accept in friendship and respect members of the Russian-speaking community who seek to assimilate—I have coded that based on the differential score for titular respondents between the Russian-speaker in her Russian guise and in her titular guise. It is curious—and this was analyzed in Chapter 8—that in all four republics, Russian-speakers suffered a status *loss* among titulars for speaking in their titular guise! The question here, as with in-group status, is that of relative losses between republics. On the friendship dimension (row 13), the Russian-speaker in Kazakhstan lost least in her titular guise; the Russian-speaker in Ukraine lost most. On the respect dimension (row 14), the Russian-speaker in Latvia lost least and the Russian-speaker in Ukraine lost most. On the cumulative score, the

Russian-speaker in Latvia lost least, the one in Estonia second least, the one in Kazakhstan third least, and the one in Ukraine lost most. The relative contempt Ukrainian respondents showed for the Russian-speaker in her Ukrainian guise reflects the hostile face of Ukrainian nationalism I discussed in Chapter 4. This helps explain why Ukrainian Russians, so far along the x-axis in 1991, have the next-to-lowest score for openness to assimilation.

Two other measures of out-group acceptance supplement the data from the matched-guise test. From material in the survey, but also in actual political life, I sought data on whether Russians were accepted as potentially equal to titulars in the social and political domains. The more accepted, the higher the "out-group status" score, the greater the likelihood of assimilation. First, in the survey, we asked respondents what they thought of a marriage of their son (and then their daughter) to a person of another nationality.[18] Of the titular group who responded to this question (row 15), Ukrainian respondents were most willing to accept non-Ukrainians as members of their family, while Kazakh respondents were least willing to do so, with the Estonian respondents quite close to the Kazakhs. Second, in an examination of citizenship and language laws (row 16), I sought to rank the four republics based on the degree to which Russians were accepted immediately and without question as citizens and as eligible for sensitive government jobs (these jobs I consider measures of status, and not so much for expected income). These would be tests of the degree to which there were restrictions put on Russian-speaking permanent residents of the republics in the immediate post-Soviet period. The greater the restrictions, the lower the out-group status. As Table 9.1 indicates, Ukraine was the most accommodating of the four republics; Latvia second (it is far in front of Kazakhstan on the first and weakly behind in the second), Kazakhstan third, and Estonia fourth. In an average on the four indicators of out-group acceptance, Ukrainians are most accommodating, Latvians a close second, Kazakhs third, and Estonians last.

How best to understand the layout of the dependent variable, openness to assimilation? The high assimilationist attitudes of Russians in Latvia (despite low economic returns) and the low assimilationist attitudes of Russians in Estonia (despite high economic returns) are worthy of special comment. Russians in Latvia, based on calculations of economic returns for learning Latvian, should all remain monolingual and have little interest in assimilating. Yet in our survey they show a greater willingness than respondents in the other four republics for doing so. An examination of status returns provides a clue. While in no cases were there positive status incentives for assimilating, as I pointed out in Chapter 8, in Latvia the status disincentives were far lower than in Estonia. The matched-guise data show that Russians in Latvia do not scorn fellow Russians who are seen to be speaking Latvian as much as Russians in two of the other republics, coming quite close to Ukraine's score; and that Latvians do not scorn assimilationist efforts by Russian-speakers as much as the titulars in all three other republics. Concern for friendship and respect, of one's own

[18] Note well that this question is a component of the index of openness to assimilation for Russian respondents. Here the answers from titular respondents form part of the explanation. I am not, then, using information on the dependent variable as one of the independent variables.

in-group, and a sense of acceptance of assimilationist moves by members of the out-group, irrespective of occupational returns, play an important role in calculations about assimilation. Similarly, Estonia's high score for economic returns for assimilating is counteracted by the low (in-group and out-group) status scores received by Russians who speak Estonian. This helps explain why Estonia's score was lower than Latvia's on the dependent variable.

These findings fit in with data differentiating the two republics that have never been adequately analyzed. The long periods of political cooperation between Russians and Latvians may help explain the feelings of mutual respect shown in the matched guise. In the 1890s there were "new currents" (known in Latvian as the "jaunā strāva") that challenged nationalist ideas. Some of these were Marxists or other forms of socialists. The 1905 revolution brought strikes and violence in Riga instigated by the Latvian Social Democratic Workers Party, mostly against Baltic German landowner power. By 1897, some 115,000 Latvians had taken up residence within the empire outside the Baltic provinces, mostly in European Russia. By World War I, the figure was about 220,000, about 12 percent of all Latvians, mostly as factory workers. Some went to Russia for higher education. In the first and second dumas, six and then seven Latvian delegates were Kadets. This included Jānis Čakste, who would become the first president of independent Latvia. These Latvians were not anti-Russian; rather they sought reforms within Russia. As World War I broke out, many in the Latvian intelligentsia supported the Russians. Estonians do not have a similar history of mutual cooperation.

More recently, the greater neighborhood mixing of Russians in Riga, as compared to Russians in Tallinn, mostly because of the relative size of the groups, has also brought Russians and Latvians closer than Russians and Estonians. This is clearly reflected in the higher rates of Russian-titular intermarriage in Riga than in Tallinn. In 1988, 33.1 percent of the married Russian population in Riga were married to someone of a different nationality; in Tallinn the figure was 16.1 percent. That Russians who speak Latvian in public lose less status among titulars than Russians in Estonia do is not entirely surprising, given these factors, even if speaking it is not a sign of economic success.[19]

Historic connections between Latvians and Russia have not all been cut. Consider Viktors Alksnis. He was born in Siberia but with nationality roots in Latvia, and was a Soviet military officer and pro-Soviet Interfront leader in Latvia. He left Latvia in 1996 and emigrated to Russia. He then became deputy chairman of the Russian All-Peoples Union. His dream, he told the Latvian press in an interview, is a reincorporation of Latvia into the Russian Federation.[20]

[19] Terry Martin, in a personal communication, suggested to me the importance of the prerevolutionary connections between Latvians and Russians. The material on the "new currents" and subsequent alliances is from Andrejs Plakans, *The Latvians* (Stanford, Calif.: Hoover Institution Press, 1995), chap. 6. Vello Pettai has noted to me the greater neighborhood mixing of Russians in Riga. See also Jerry F. Hough, "Data on Ethnic Intermarriages," *Journal of Soviet Nationalities* 1, no. 2 (1990): 160–71, for the data on internationality marriages in the capital cities of the union republics. He analyzes those data in chap. 6 of his *Democratization and Revolution* (Washington, D.C.: Brookings Institution, 1997).

[20] See the interview with Alksnis published in *Panorama Latvii*, March 8, 1997.

Further research, applying the model to cases that were not used to fine tune the theory, is obviously necessary to work out the precise weighting of the components of the tipping model. But it should be clear already that status concerns, by both in-group and out-group, motivate orientations to assimilate or to sustain cultural difference. And while a simple occupational mobility calculus is clearly inadequate, a theory of nationalism based on calculations of economic and status concerns does not do injustice to social reality. The ethnographic materials in Chapters 4–6 give added support to the social reality of language calculations.

Exit as a Strategy

Consistent with the tipping model, but ignored in my earlier formulations of actor utility functions, are calculations concerning the possibility of return to one's homeland through emigration. Here the data help make further sense of why Ukrainian Russians are far less open to assimilation than the position on the x-axis would have predicted.[21] It also helps make sense of why Estonian Russians, who are closer to Kazakhstan's Russians on the x-axis, and rebuffed strongly by Estonian policies, are more open to assimilation than are Ukraine's Russians. As can be seen from Table 9.2, in the 1991–93 period, a lower percentage of Russians from Ukraine migrated to Russia than in any of the other three republics included in this study. Yet of the four republics in between the two cataclysms, more Russians in western Ukraine claimed they wanted to migrate, and more claimed they thought it likely they would migrate than those from the other republics.

What this suggests is that Russians in (western) Ukraine in the Soviet period were passively picking up Ukrainian, without giving it much political or economic significance. Once Ukraine became independent, they feared that assimilation would be at the expense of their Russianness and developed anti-assimilationist attitudes. Few have left because there has been little pressure on them to ukrainize; but they know it will be easy (compared with other republics) to emigrate if necessary. The high expectation along with the low realization of migration suggests a community that will resist coercive assimilation (which has not been attempted, but only suggested, despite the ultranationalist rhetoric) by emigrating. Data show that since 1992 there has been significant emigration of Russians from western Ukraine to the eastern and southern oblasts of Ukraine (where the ultranationalists are weaker), but not so much to Russia.[22]

Estonia, on the other hand, has had relatively the highest emigration of Russian-speakers, along with the second highest score for Russians wanting to emigrate. This suggests that the Russians who remained were those most accepting of Estonian society. Even though in the 1989 census less than a quarter as many Russians in

[21] Perhaps it is not the perceived ease of exit but rather the quasi-utopian belief in an eventual *Anschluss* that weakens these Russians' incentive to learn Ukrainian. This possibility was drawn to my attention by Valeri Khmelko, whose data show the strength of desire for reunion with Russia among Russians in eastern Ukraine.

[22] S. S. Savoskul, "Ukraina i Belorussiia," in M. Iu. Martynova, ed., *Novye slavianskie diaspory* (Moscow: Institut etnologii i antropologii, RAN, 1996), p. 129.

Table 9.2. Russian emigration to Russian Federation, 1989–1993

Emigrants	Kazakhstan	Estonia	Latvia	Ukraine
1989				
Number	95,084	4,877	7,362	147,343
Percent of Russian population	1.5	1.0	0.8	1.3
1990				
Number	97,325	5,316*	9,398†	136,445
Percent of Russian population	1.6	1.1	1.0	1.2
1991				
Number	84,063	4,924	10,415	112,284
Percent of Russian population	1.3	1.0	1.1	0.9
1992				
Number	132,529	20,685	22,507	124,645
Percent of Russian population	3.1	4.4	2.5	1.1
1993				
Number	144,837	8,276*	11,840†	119,341
Percent of Russian population	2.3	1.7	1.3	1.1
1989–93				
Number	614,838	44,082	61,522	640,058
Percent of Russian population	9.9	9.2	6.8	5.6
Percent of Russians desiring to emigrate to Russia in 1990	20	23	16	26‡
Percent of Russians expecting to emigrate to Russia	24	28	31	41‡

Sources: V. Tishkov, *Migratsii i novye diaspory* (Moscow: Institute of Ethnology and Anthropology, 1996), pp. 72, 114, 203. The items marked * come from the *Statistical Yearbook of Estonia, 1996* (Tallinn: Statistical Office of Estonia, 1996), p. 78. These data are listed for all migrants to Russia, and to make them commensurate with the Tishkov data (done through interpolation based on years with common data), I reduced the figure by a factor of .723. The items marked † come from the *Reference Book of Population Statistics, 1995* (Tallinn: Statistical Office of Estonia, 1995), p. 61. These data reflect all external migrants. To make them commensurate with the Tishkov series, I multiplied these figures by .370. The data on Russians desiring and expecting (those who answer "likely" or "fairly likely") to emigrate is from a 1990 survey conducted by *Moscow News* and reported in RFE/RL, November 15, 1991. The items marked ‡ indicate that the Ukrainian data of this survey are from only the western oblasts.

Estonia than Russians in Ukraine claimed to speak the titular language—in the survey the figure was less than a half as many, suggesting that most of those who left were those who knew no Estonian—Russian respondents in Estonia on the dependent variable of this study were more open to assimilation than those in Ukraine. Not only the economic returns help explain the closing of the incentive gap, but the possibilities and actualities of exit also played an important role.

More work needs to be done in conceptualizing the role of exit for assimilation. On the one hand, high levels of exit might lower incentives for assimilation. Because foreign residents can say that if things get tough, they can always leave, the possibility of exit should lower the incentive to assimilate. On the other hand, high levels of exit might indicate that the antititulars are all leaving, with only those willing to assimilate remaining. With a lower percentage of Russians in the republic, because of high exit, it might also make the chances for a binational republic (the Belgian model) seem more remote, thus adding incentives to assimilate. This is why

I have not yet included emigration figures, or the cost of emigration, into the tipping calculus. But the three variables—economic returns, in-group status, and out-group acceptance—have given us an excellent first cut into the issue of the possibilities for A-&-B national states in the former republics of the Soviet Union.

The true test of the tipping model, at least in these four republics, will not be available for many years. The model predicts that in cases where the expected returns for assimilation begin to appear positive for a few social or demographic groups of Russians in the post-Soviet republics, this will alter the payoffs for closely related social or demographic groups. There should then be a slow but steady growth of potential assimilators. But at some point in this process, there should be a rapid acceleration, when all Russians come to believe that assimilation is inevitable. As we near the tipping point, the incentives for Russian political entrepreneurs, whose status is based on representing the Russian-speaking population as Russians, would be strong to attempt to induce fellow Russians to resist assimilation, and to return to "their" culture. In republics where growth is slow and few Russians expect positive returns for assimilation, the model predicts stagnation or negative growth intergenerationally in assimilators. In this case, Russian political entrepreneurs will maintain their representative monopolies to speak for the Russian-speaking population, and they will probably bargain for regional autonomy, as the Flemish nationalists have done in Belgium. Obviously, the data in the early moments of nationality politics in the Soviet successor states, which provide only a snapshot, cannot pick up these trends. But future research can and should.

Megalomanians can become Ruritanians. And the process can be analyzed with considerable power from a game-theoretic perspective. But as is clear from the ethnographies in Chapters 4–6 and the survey and matched-guise data summarized in this chapter, the reversal of assimilationist tides is not a simple process on the micro or game-theoretic level. It is clear that reasonably high expected economic returns for linguistic assimilation is not in itself powerful enough to induce Megalomanians to a tip toward Ruritanian fluency, which would be a significant step in the road toward Ruritanian assimilation. It is also clear that language status—standing independently of economic returns—plays an important role in assimilationist calculations. Methodologically, incorporating status variables into a rational-choice framework will enrich that framework, enabling researchers to theorize more realistically about social and cultural change. Substantively, the finding that the likelihood of a linguistic tip in Kazakhstan is nil will surprise few readers. But that Russians (at least intergenerationally) are moving toward an assimilationist tip in the Baltics, while their compatriots are at the same time resisting such a tip in Ukraine, is important news. And the future of interethnic relations, as well as the future of the national components of the post-Soviet states will be in large part a function of the assimilationist trends uncovered in this chapter.

PART FOUR

NATIONALISM AND IDENTITY SHIFT

10

The Russian-Speaking Nationality in Formation

Extending Hirschman's categorization of individual opportunities under conditions of organizational decline (in Chapter 6), I examined the strategies of loyalty, exit, voice, and arms. One possibility that Hirschman did not consider, a point I discussed at the end of Chapter 6, was *redefinition of identity*. Strategic redefinition of identity makes possible not only assimilation (identification with the dominant group) but becoming part of a conglomerate identity (joining forces with other nondominant identity groups) as well.

Historically, redefinition into a conglomerate identity is quite common. In benign form, we see it with Hispanics and Asian-Americans in the United States. Another well-known case is that of the *pieds noirs* in Algeria, who were made up of French, Greeks, Portuguese, Italians, and Jews, all of whom assumed a common colonial identity. In far less benign form, we see it with Palestinians in the Middle East, which in a generation turned from a population category that was defined almost solely by reference to a political catastrophe (the creation of Israel and the evacuation of the diverse non-Jewish populations from it into resettlement camps during the 1947–48 war) to a nationality that has tenaciously—and at enormous cost for all parties involved—claimed a right to its own state.

Without getting into the issue of whether it is benign or not, this chapter will address the emergence of a conglomerate identity category in formation (though in different ways) in all four republics under consideration. This identity category is that of the "Russian-speaking population." Identification as a member of this population is in some way an alternative to assimilation (as titulars), and mobilization (as Russians). While our findings demonstrate the emergence of a rather unconscious—and certainly not manipulated—identity category, ethnic entrepreneurs play a far greater role in defining the discourse categories here than they did in my portrayal of the tipping game. The ethnic entrepreneurs who engaged in the discourse described here had no easy task. If it was nearly impossible in the late Soviet period, as Roman Szporluk has observed, for Russian nationalists in Russia to find commonly agreed symbols to stand behind,[1] it was much more difficult for Russians in the near abroad. The data do not show a fully worked out identity project—which would mean the infusion of symbols into a shared collective memory—but the early makings of a new category, built from the detritus of the collapsed Soviet identity, that form only the raw materials for a future social identity.[2]

Nonetheless, in the few years since the double cataclysm, "Russian-speaking population," a term basically invented in 1989, has already become a cliché, though one used less often now than in the years immediately following the first—the language—cataclysm.[3] The term "Russian-speaking population," has clearer boundaries and is a more powerful identification in the Baltic states than it is in Ukraine or Kazakhstan. In the former cases, it could well evolve into a new form of national identification, in competition with assimilation. In the latter cases, it is more likely to emerge, as will be emphasized more fully in Chapter 12, as a fulcrum for intratitular conflict. In all four republics, however, the term has become deeply interwoven in the fabric of identity discourse.

The Choice Set of Identity Categories

Before 1989, it was rare to see any public identification of Russians living in the union republics outside the Russian Federation. The Soviet Union, according to the official line, had solved its nationality problem and become a "family" of nations. To be sure, Russians were sometimes described as the "elder brothers" of this family, but Lenin's excoriation of "Great Russian chauvinism" made that term politically incorrect. Among the titular populations, many of whom resented the presence of outsiders in "their" republics, the diverse set of postwar immigrants and soldiers were called "Russians," and these Russians were called many things besides "elder brother" by angry titulars eager to see them return to their homelands.[4] Nationality "talk," to the extent that it was permissible, existed within the confines of the vocabulary on the fifth line of the Soviet passport.

During the period of publicity (glasnost), nationality talk mushroomed, though most of it concerned titular rights, in which the Stalinesque categorization of identity categories was completely accepted. But with the double cataclysm, a new form

[1] Roman Szporluk, "Dilemmas of Russian Nationalism," *Problems of Communism* 38 (1989): 27.

[2] See John Gillis, *The Politics of National Identity* (Princeton: Princeton University Press, 1994), and Mustafa Emirbayer and Jeff Goodwin, "Network Analysis, Culture, and the Problem of Agency," *American Journal of Sociology* 99, no. 6 (1994): 1411–54, for fuller statements on what is required culturally and structurally for a cogent national identity project. The "Russian-speaking" identity elucidated in this chapter shows at best only the early markings of such a project.

[3] I do not claim that there was no social foundation for this invention. Data from the Soviet period show high rates of Russian, Belarusan, and Ukrainian intermarriage in the non-Russian republics. See O. D. Komarova, "Ethnically Mixed Marriages in the Soviet Union," *GeoJournal*, Supplementary Issue 1 (1980): 31–34.

[4] Rasma Karklins, *Ethnic Relations in the USSR* (Boston: Allen & Unwin, 1986), pp. 29, 52.

of discourse arose—one that tried to categorize, or stigmatize, the beached diaspora of the Soviet Union.

Simply calling the diaspora "Russians" had great appeal, especially for the titulars. From the point of view of nationalist-minded Estonians, Latvians, and Kazakhs the subtle differences between Russians, Ukrainians, Belarusans, and Jews were not very important. They were all Soviet agents and the Soviet Union was—in their mind—just another euphemism for the Russian empire. Of all the terms that referred to the diaspora, only "Russian" (*russkii*) could serve as an adjective modifying "nationality" (*natsiia* or *natsional'nost'*).

But "Russian" was an uncomfortable label for many participating in nationalist discourse in the wake of the double cataclysm. The terms used in the Russian-language press both from Russia and the republics to describe the diaspora as an identity category were diverse. In coding these terms, I broke them down into the following categories:

1. *Russian-speaking population (russkoiazychnoe naselenie).* There are many variations on this theme. At first, it was common to use "the Russian-speaking *part* of the population." Later, the "part" was dropped in most uses of the term. Before "Russian-speaking population" became the cliché, there were other circumlocutions, such as "those for whom Russian is their native language" ("tekh, dlia kotorykh russkii iazyk iavliaetsia rodnym") or "the population whose native language is the language of internationality communication" ("naselenie rodnym iazykom kotorogo iavliaetsia iazyk mezhnatsional'nogo obshcheniia") or "those who think in Russian" ("te kto dumaet na russkom iazyke"). *Russkoiazychnoe* (literally "Russian-tongued," in the sense of "languaged") indeed became the preferred usage, but *russkogovoriashchie* (also to be glossed as "Russian-speaking," but coming from the verb *govoriat'*, "to speak," "to say") is still used as a synonym. The "Russian-speakers" are often referred to as persons (*liudi*) or as a community (*obshchestvo*), but they are never, as suggested above, referred to as a nationality (*national'nost'*), and very rarely as a people (*narod*). To the extent that I have identified a new identity formation around the concept of Russian-speakingness, it should be underlined that the designations of "population" (*naselenie*), "persons" (*liudi*), and "community" (*obshchestvo*) suggest that the term "Russian-speakingness" does not now refer to a national project.

2. *Negations.* After the double cataclysm, the characteristic most widely shared among the diaspora was that they were not titulars. They were categorized in a variety of ways in terms of what they were not. They were called "the unrooted" (*nekorennye*), "people without a country" (*apatridy*), "foreigners" (*inorodtsy* or *inostrantsy*), "foreign speakers" (*inoiazychni*), "the denationalized groups" (*denatsionalizirovannye gruppy*), "noncitizens" (*negrazhdane* or *nepoddanstvo*), "people with undefined citizenship" (*neopredelivshiesia c grazhdanstvom*), "nontitulars" (*netitul'noe naselenie*), "not-from-Russia Russians" (*nerossiiskie russkie*), "illegals" (*nelegal'nye emigranty*), "residents of other nationalities" (*zhiteli drugikh natsional'nostei*), "nonspeakers of the titular language" (e.g., "grazhdane Estonii, ne vladeiushchie Estonskim

iazykom"), nonnatives (*inozemtsy*), "unwanted residents" (*nezhelatelnye zhiteli*), "those without rights" (*bezpravnye*), and "voiceless" (*bezgolosie*).

3. *Slavs.* To the extent that the diaspora could be differentiated from Asians (in Kazakhstan) or Europeans (in the Baltics), a unifying aspect of the diasporic population was that they were Slavs.

4. *Members of the Russian state (rossiiskii or rossiiane).* In Russian, there is a clear differentiation between Russian as an ethnic category (*russkie*) and Russian as a political category (*rossiiskii* or *rossiiane*). It was perfectly understandable in the context of post-Soviet politics to refer to a range of nationality groups of the diaspora as *rossiiskii* or *rossiane* to demonstrate their political identification with the Russian Federation. This is especially the case in reference to members of the Russian army or veterans, and they were referred to as "Rossiiskie voennye," indicating loyalty to Russia rather than ethnic identification as Russians.

5. *Colonists or occupiers.* References to the diaspora as either colonial settlers (*kolonisty*) or the occupying forces of the Soviet state (*okkupanty*) became so common in the early nationalist rebirth of the 1980s that Russians would commonly refer to themselves in this manner, although sarcastically.

6. *Co-fatherlanders or compatriots (sootechestvenniki).* This term leaves ambiguous the identity of the fatherland, whether it is Russia or the Soviet Union. In either case, identification as a co-fatherlander suggests a close identity link between the diaspora and the dominant identity group of the Russian Federation, however that is defined. In fact, the State Duma of the Russian Federation has a Committee for CIS [Community of Independent States] and Links to Compatriots.[5] A reference to *Kazakhstanskie soplemenniki* ("fellow countryman" in this context of Russians in Kazakhstan) is analagous to co-fatherlanders. Also similar is "co-citizens" (*sograzhdane*), those who are Russian citizens living in countries not of their will but as "a result of the liquidation of their country."[6]

7. *Soviets.* "Soviet" had become a protonationality in Soviet official discourse by the 1950s, with the hope that the nationalities would merge. Designating a population as "Soviet" referred to this identity project. Sometimes the word is used in a more neutral way, as in "citizens of the former Soviet Union" (*grazhdane byvshego SSSR*), or the humorous *eks-grazhdan SSSR* (ex-Soviet citizens). In Crimea, Soviets are referred to as those who carry "sickled" (*serpastye*) passports.

8. *Migrants.* There is a range of distinctions for migrants. *Migranti* is the most common term, but "movers" (*pereselentsy*) and "leavers" (*vykhodtsi*) are synonyms. Sometimes "fresh" (*svezhie*), "fresh migrant" (*svezhii migrant*), or "newcomers" (*priezzhie*) are used to differentiate Soviet-era newcomers from the pre-Soviet Russians (*starorusskie*). Those who came under stress, especially after the war, are sometimes referred to as refugees (*bezhentsy*) or "postwar people" (*poslevoennye*). Those who came to the titular republics under state supervision are called "transfers" (*peremeshennye litsa*). Finally, those who are preparing to return or who have already returned are called "repatriates" (*repatrianty*).

[5] E. I. Filippova, "Novaia russkaia diaspora," *Novy slavianskie diaspory* (Moscow: RAN, 1996), p. 58.
[6] Ibid., p. 60.

9. *Residents*. The diaspora is often thought of as "residing" in the republic without really belonging to it. "Permanent residents" (*postoiannye zhiteli*) is a way of describing the social fact of the group's existence without legitimating them as members of the emerging national society in the titular republic.

10. *Minorities*. The diaspora (or particular national subsets of it) is often referred to as a "national minority" (*natsional'noe men'shistvo*).

11. *Cossacks*. Cossacks were historically an ethnically and racially mixed set of frontiersmen who entered state service in defense of the Russian borderlands. They have taken on a kind of separate nationality, and Yeltsin has formally recognized them as a *kul'turno-etnicheskaia obshchnost'* (cultural-ethnic social formation). In fact, one of the leaders of the Cossack Union declared, "We are the only national group in Russia that does not want to break off from Russia. We stand strongly for the territorial integrity of Russia."[7] In the near abroad, "Cossack" is now a term to refer to a subset of the population that are descendents of the Cossack armies, which in Ukraine includes titulars but in Kazakhstan tends to exclude them. In the Baltics, there was no Cossack tradition at all. But "Cossack" picked up added semantic baggage after the double cataclysm and often refers to those who have an interest in the restoration of the Soviet Union.

12. *Epithets*. A range of expressions that are less than cordial pepper nationalist discourse in the near abroad. In the perestroika period, a combination of *pokupat'* (to buy) and *okkupant* (occupier) produced *pokupanty* to refer to Russians who came into the Baltics merely to buy goods. In Ukraine, Russians are often called *moskali* (Muscovites), but in a sense of being from the filthy political center. There is an occasional reference to the hibernating foreign force that will one day arise to confront the new titular nation, the "Bear" (*medved'*). In Estonia, these foreigners were referred to as "envoys" of Russia, Belarus', Ukraine, and other Soviet republics (*poslantsev Rossii*, etc.). One Estonian correspondent referred to those envoys ironically as the "guardians of the peace" (*strazhi mira*). Occasionally they were referred to merely as "enemies" (*vragi*). In the Baltics, nontitulars sometimes ironically describe themselves—making gallows humor out of the state classifications of nontitulars—as "citizens of the second sort" (*grazhdane vtorogo sorta*), or up to the tenth sort. The Russian term *chuzhaki* (aliens) is a typical epithet. Less typical is "Ivan i Petr" to refer to Russians as imperialists all. In Latvia, a bitter joke in the editorial office of *Emigratsiia* shortened "noncitizen" (*negrazhdanin*) to *negr* (which the English-speaking staff pronounced as "nigger"). This term caught on as a popular epithet. Russians used the term sardonically, as in "belye negry," calling themselves the "white niggers" of the near abroad.[8] Newspapers now use street expressions such as "damned Russians" (*prokliatye russkie*) and "Russian shit" (*Russkoe govno*).

[7] Barbara Skinner, "Identity Formation in the Russian Cossack Revival," *Europe-Asia Studies* 46, no. 6 (1994): 1017–37.

[8] Dominique Arel, an authority on Ukrainian nationalism with a deep knowledge of Quebec, informs me that this rhetorical move has antecedents in Canada. See Pierre Vallières, *Nègres blancs d'Amérique* (Montréal: Parti Pris, 1968).

13. *Mixed categories*. Interlocutors in nationalist discourse were not imprisoned by these categories, and often mixed them up within a single paragraph. Previously unknown combinations took on new meaning. One common expression was *etnicheskie rossiiane*, which is a contradiction in terms, but easily understood.[9] Often there were interesting mixes with one category serving as adjective, the other as noun. Already mentioned are "illegal immigrant" (a negation and a migrant) and *nezhelatelnye zhiteli* (unwanted residents), but there were others: *nekorennye russkie* (unrooted Russians), *russkoiazychnye negrazhdane* (Russian-tongued noncitizens), *inostrantsy negrazhdane* (foreign noncitizens), and *moskal' velikoross* (Muscovite Great Russian). The choice set for describing the beached diaspora had almost no boundaries.

Discourse Analysis in the Russian-Language Press

In order to demonstrate the range of identity terms used to describe the beached Soviet diaspora, and to evaluate the claim that the "Russian-speaking population" is an emergent nationality category, I conducted a "discourse analysis" on a large collection of Russian-language newspaper articles, provided by a Moscow-based clipping service, on issues of inter-nationality relations.[10] My first concern was to get a raw sense of how often the different identity terms were used. This is often called content analysis. Then I studied how they were used in context.[11]

Content Analysis

Table 10.1 provides a ready outline of the overall sample. There were from 73 (Ukraine) to 88 (Estonia) articles from each country, with a total of 2,197 identity terms coded, with a low of 376 in Ukraine and a high of 711 in Estonia. I tried to get one half of the articles from the press based in the Russian Federation and one half from newspapers published in the republics, but this proved impossible. Because the sample (and my ability to code reliably) included only Russian-language press, the "voices" of the titulars were not fully heard. Nonetheless, because I used either quotations from titulars, articles by titulars translated into the Russian press, or articles by titulars in Russian, from 19 percent (in Kazakhstan) to 29 percent (in Ukraine) of the coded voices (of only the first ten uses in each article) were those of

[9] Neil Melvin, *Russians beyond Russia* (London: Royal Institute of International Affairs, 1995), p. 16, and p. 144 n. 49, explains: "This term [which he glosses as "ethnically citizens of Russia"] means more than simply ethnic Russians. Slavs and heavily Russified ethnic groups within the settler populations are also considered to be *etnicheskie Rossiiane*. Abdullah Mikitaev [*Rossiiskie Vesti*, August 16, 1994], the head of the Presidential Committee on Citizenship, has identified more than 30 million *etnicheskie Rossiiane*, 25 million of whom are ethnic Russians."

[10] Details about the criteria of article selection for this discourse analysis are in the appendix.

[11] For a justification of this combination of approaches, see David D. Laitin and Guadalupe Rodríguez, "Language, Ideology and the Press in Catalonia," *American Anthropologist* 94, no. 1 (1992): 9–30.

Table 10.1. Discourse analysis of identity terms in the press: Nature of the sample

Attribute	Kazakhstan	Estonia	Latvia	Ukraine
Total number of identity terms	417	711	693	376
Total number of articles	77	88	80	73
Articles in RF press	48	30	34	35
Liberal	27	19	20	18
Old guard	21	11	13	17
Not classified	0	0	1	0
Articles in republican press	29	58	46	38
Russian slant	5	53	33	9
Titular slant	1	5	9	7
Not classified	23	0	4	22
Voices in first 10 uses	375	566	550	324
Russian voices				
Number	281	436	390	216
Percent of total voices	75	77	71	67
Journalists	220	275	261	152
Officials	44	151	113	58
Ordinary people quoted or in letters to editor	17	10	16	6
Titular voices				
Number	70	127	129	94
Percent of total voices	19	22	23	29
Journalists	12	38	43	47
Officials	39	88	74	28
Ordinary people quoted or in letters to editor	19	1	12	19

titulars. It would be imprudent to claim that these articles were truly representative of anything; yet it would be reasonable to judge that the selection casts a wide net on nationalist discourse in the post-Soviet republics.

In discussions about the nationality question in the near abroad, the overwhelming referent is to "Russians." Of the 1,815 coded references to identity categories, 719 (40 percent) referred to Russians as an ethnic category (see Table 10.2). Coming in second, with about half that number of references, are the myriad expressions of negation. But third, in a category that did not exist a decade ago, "Russian-speaking population" garnered 314, or 17 percent, of the references. The variants of "Russian-speaking population" had nearly four times as many uses as "Russian-political," the next most frequent category. "Slavs" and "Soviets," two categories that have long traditions in nationality discourse in Russia and the Soviet Union, were comparatively scarce in contemporary nationality discussions.

Another way that I assessed the prevalence of the term "Russian-speaking population" was by creating a ratio of all uses in an article of "Russian-speaking population" to the total number of identity terms used in that article, with as many uses of categories as the article had. The all-republic mean is .1829, which reveals that the term is used on average about one-fifth of the time for all 308 articles. The republican means, shown in Figure 10.1 range from .1459 in Ukraine to .2452 in Estonia.

Table 10.2. Content analysis of terms to identify the diaspora (for first ten uses in all articles)

Term	Number of uses	Percent
Russian-ethnic	719	40
Negations	362	20
Russian-speaking population	314	17
Russian-political	84	5
Migrants	56	3
Slavs	49	3
Colonists and occupiers	40	2
Residents	37	2
Cossacks	25	1
Soviets	21	1
Co-fatherlanders	19	1
Minorities	12	1
Other (including epithets)	67	4

The term "Russian-speaking population" and its variants were used (as can be seen in Table 10.3) by Russians and titulars alike, though slightly more frequently by Russians. The data show that 73 percent of the coded identity terms were terms used by Russians, 81 percent (200 out of 247) of the uses of "Russian-speaking population" were by Russians themselves; however, the emotional valence of the term was quite different. In all four republics, Russians used the term in a positive way, whereas Russians in Russia, like the titulars in the republics, use it as a pejorative.

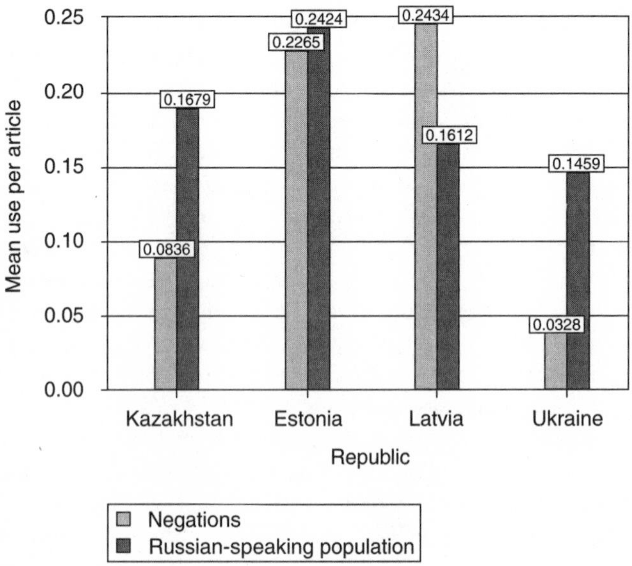

Figure 10.1. Mean use of "Russian-speaking population" and negations in the four republics

Table 10.3. Valence in use of "Russian-speaking population"

Speaker	Positive	Negative	Neutral	Sum (+ less −)
All Russians	134	7	59	
Percent of total	67	3	30	+64
All titulars	12	19	16	
Percent of total	26	40	34	−14
Kazakhstan				
Russians	21	1	18	+20
Titulars	2	2	6	0
Estonia				
Russians	69	3	22	+66
Titulars	6	5	6	1
Latvia				
Russians	34	2	22	+32
Titulars	2	2	6	0
Ukraine				
Russians	10	1	6	9
Titulars	2	10	1	−8

Note: Valence for the all-republic sample is the percentage positive less the percentage negative. For each republic (where numbers are insufficiently high to use percentages), the valence is the absolute positive less the absolute negative.

"Russian-speaking population" appeared in newspapers of all types, as can be seen from Table 10.4. Perhaps most interesting in this table is the high incidence of the term in the newspapers that I have coded as "Russian-liberal," a category that includes *Nezavisimaia gazeta*, *Argumenty i fakty*, and *Segodnia*, offspring of the glasnost era, as well as *Izvestiia* and *Literaturnaia gazeta*, older papers that have taken a reformist bent. Although reported in an old-guard Russian newspaper (*Krasnaia zvezda* June 26, 1993), Russian president Boris Yeltsin used the term freely in his critique of Estonia's policies. "The leadership of Russia," he declared, "will take all necessary measures to defend our national interests and to protect the Russian-speaking population from political, social and police arbitrariness." His forcefulness was old guard; but the use of "Russian-speaking population" made it seem more liberal, less chauvinist, than if he had sought to defend only "Russians." My explanation for the liberal penchant for "Russian-speaking population"—though I haven't tested the accuracy of this assertion—is that Russian-liberals in Russia are strongly antinationalist. Therefore, their spokesmen do not wish to overemphasize the ethnic frictions in the near abroad. Thus they refer to a population category (Russian-speakers) rather than a nationality (Russians) in order to reduce the neoimperialist connotations of expressions of solidarity with their conationals in the near abroad. In second place, among newspaper types in the use of "Russian-speaking population," after the Russian-liberal press, comes the republican newspapers with a Russian bent. Here, the purpose is most likely not to tone down nationalism, but to find a meaningful term to refer to their natural readership, that set of people most affected by the double cataclysm.

Use of "Russian-speaking" has declined since the cataclysms (though the null hypothesis that there has been no secular decline cannot be rejected), as I show in

Table 10.4. Mean use of "Russian-speaking population," by newspaper type

Newspaper type	All	Kazakhstan	Estonia	Latvia	Ukraine
Titular					
Russian dominant	.1914	.1000	.2209	.1639	.1250
Republican emphasis	.1856	.3000	.2600	.1759	.1286
Other	.1504	.2233	—	.0417	.0913
Russian Federation					
Liberal	.2134	.1792	.2592	.1539	.2846
Old guard	.1548	.1029	.3013	.1975	.0915
Other	.0909	—	—	.0909	—

Note: Each article represents a distinct observation. I took for each observation the ratio of uses of "Russian-speaking population" to all identity terms. The figures represent the mean of the ratios of all observations.

Table 10.5. When all attention was on the language laws of 1989, the Russian-speakingness of the Russian population was of considerable importance. Now that the problems of adjusting economically and socially to life in postsocialist nationalizing states have come to the fore, the focus on the diaspora as a linguistic community under stress has weakened. If the term is used less often, it has taken on more of a cliché quality, as the subsequent discussion will make clear.

Comparing the four republics, as in Figures 10.1 and 10.2 (and here using only the first ten uses for each article), we again see (as I first proposed in Chapter 2) a marked difference between the Baltic states and Ukraine and Kazakhstan. In the Baltics, the mean use of negations approaches one-fourth of all identity category usages, compared to negligible use of such terms in Kazakhstan and Ukraine. This is largely because in the Baltics, the diaspora was denied citizenship because they lacked historical roots in those republics. Their lack of legal rights became central to their identifications. In Ukraine and Kazakhstan, the diaspora lost no legal rights after independence, and so they had no brief to refer to themselves as negations. Meanwhile "Russian" was used twice as often in Kazakhstan and Ukraine as in Estonia and Latvia, and "Slav" was used over 6 percent of the time in Kazakhstan and Ukraine, but almost never in Estonia or Latvia. In Kazakhstan, "Slav" was a way to

Table 10.5. Mean use of "Russian-speaking population," 1990–1996

Republic	1990–1992	1993	1994–1996
All republics	.2178	.1840	.1416
Kazakhstan	.2273	.1544	.1302
Estonia	.3225	.2471	.1608
Latvia	.1921	.1560	.1159
Ukraine	.1475	.1452	.1782

Note: Because of the low number of cases in 1990, 1991, 1995, and 1996, I collapsed the sample into three categories for this table. In a regression analysis, the years were not collapsed. The regression equation: mean use of RSP $= f(\text{year})$ yielded a $b = -.025562$, SE $(b) = .014497$, with $p = .0788$.

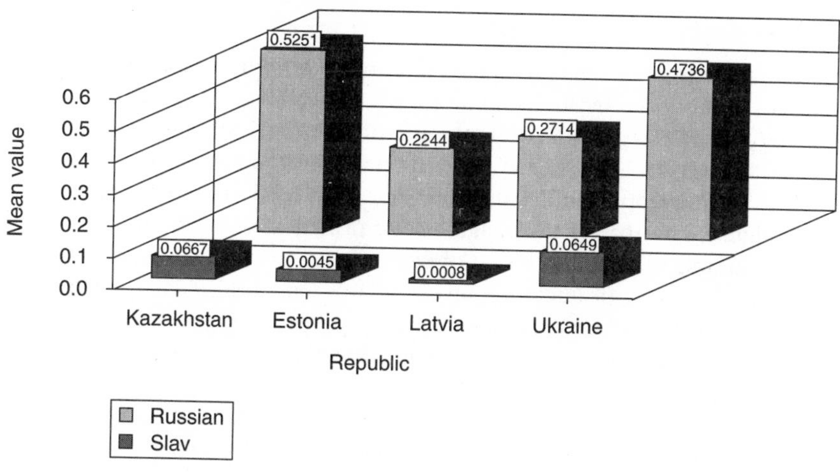

Figure 10.2. Mean use of "Russian" and "Slav" in the four republics

identify Russians and Ukrainians as a common category, clearly excluding all Kazakhs. Russian-speakingness, as we shall see, did not necessarily exclude Kazakhs and was therefore not useful to those authors who wanted to draw clear lines between Europeans and Asians. In Ukraine, "Slav" was used mainly to show the historic unity between the titulars and the Russians and was usually used by Russians who wished to delegitimate the Ukrainian national project that sought to differentiate Ukrainians and Russians as entirely separate nations.

Only the category "Russian-speaking" fails to fit into a Baltic versus Kazakhstan/Ukraine bifurcation. In Estonia, it is used the most, and Ukraine the least, but in Latvia and Kazakhstan its mean appearance is about the same. Among the four republics, the between-republic analysis of variance is not statistically significant ($F = 2.1912$; $p < .0891$). While there are major interrepublican differences in other identity terms in use to describe the population affected most by the double cataclysm in the near abroad, the term "Russian-speaking" has taken root in all four republics, and while losing ground to other terms over time, it has been the third most used category in nationality discourse to identify that social group that was left stranded by the Soviet Union in the countries of the near abroad.

Context Analysis

Now that we have a sense of its categories and the prevalence of those categories in the discourse, we can put identity discourse into context. Each republic has its own story in regard to identity categories.[12]

[12] The data base for this contextual analysis comes not only from those articles used in the content analysis but from my perusal of the entire set of articles from which the data were sampled, along with articles collected by me and my research team as part of our fieldwork.

Estonia

The term "Russian-speaking population" appears with greatest frequency in Estonia. To be sure, the mean use of the term per article declined from .3225 in 1990–92 to .1608 in 1994–96, while the use of "Russian" increased in that same period, from .1719 to .3547. Yet in the entire sample of identity terms in Estonia, "Russian-speaking population" is the most frequently used. Its mean use per article is .241, higher than that of the conglomerate of negations (.226) and "Russian" (.224). An examination of the context of its use in newspaper writing demonstrates a powerful confluence of interests—involving Russians, titulars, and members of other nationalities—to reify the category of "Russian-speakingness." And so, by sort of a rhetorical consensus, a "Russian-speaking" social identity is in an early stage of formation in post-Soviet Estonia.

Despite a free rhetorical market in post-Soviet Estonia, Russian nationalist symbology is not being liberally produced. Residents in Estonia tracing their roots to Russia almost never rely on symbols of Russia's historical past. To be sure, veterans and schoolteachers refer regularly to the "Great Fatherland War" (World War II), but the fatherland referred to is Soviet not Russian. In a systematic review of the Russian-language press in Estonia (but mostly Narva) from 1988–94, I came across practically no examples of Russian chauvinism. When the Estonian government passed the "law on foreigners," L. Shlimonov, a correspondent for the *Narvskaia gazeta* (January 14, 1993), wrote a philosophical essay on the "greatness" of "the Russian people," who were "humbled" to be called "foreigners." But this symbolism is mixed, as Shlimonov refers to Russians inhabiting a variety of republics in "the common *Soviet* [my emphasis] home." This is similar to the view expressed by N. Kulikov (see Chapter 6) in the wake of the October 1993 events in Moscow. In that passage, Kulikov both identifies himself with Russia (*my* historical homeland) and separates himself from Russians (my soul hurts for *them*).[13] One schoolteacher emphasized to me in an interview (May 11, 1994) the depth and richness of her Russian culture. This, however, was more of a wistful memory of teaching great literature during the Soviet era than it was a current category of national membership. But even vague references like this to a period of Russian cultural greatness are quite rare among Estonian Russians. Thus, of the four republics, the very term "Russian" is least used to identify the diaspora.

This cannot be explained by the raw figures of national diversity. In the 1989 census, Russians constituted 30 percent of the population in the Estonian Republic, with Ukrainians 3 percent, Belarusans 2 percent, and others, including Poles, Jews, and Finns, 3 percent. This is somewhat less diverse than Kazakhstan, for example, where Russians constitute 38 percent of the population to 5 percent for Ukrainians.[14] Yet there is a firm perception among nontitulars of the diversity of the nonti-

[13] A content analysis of the Russian-language press in the 1970s and 1980s in Russia proper that was quite similar in method to the approach taken in this chapter found that Russians in Russia were referred to as "we," but that Russians in the former Union republics were referred to as "they." See Iu. V. Arutiunian, *Russkie: Etno-sotsiologicheskie ocherki* (Moscow: Nauka, 1992), p. 389.

[14] That is, in Estonia the ratio of Russians to Ukrainians is 10:1; in Kazakhstan it is 7.6:1.

tular population. An article in *Molodezh' Estonii* (March 1, 1994) called "Who Are These Other Peoples and Why Do They Fight Each Other?" complains about infighting among organizations seeking monopoly rights to represent "the unrooted," "the noncitizens," the "Russian diaspora," who make up the "non-Estonian part of the population." The author sadly concedes that the battles between these organizations are caused by the "Babel-like diversity of local Russians" (*"babilinskii" sostav mestnykh russkikh*) and adds that the only hope is for the creation of a single organization capable of representing all the "Russian-speaking" structures. The perception of diversity, and the lack of coordination among nontitular groups, was the impetus for the invention of a "Russian-speaking" society.

The route toward a clear alternative to "Russian" to encompass the not quite Russian identity has not been smooth, however, and nontitulars from Estonia have experimented with a variety of terms. From the Estonian sample nontitulars were referred to (in *Rossiiskie vesti*, September 19, 1992) as *bezgolosye* (without voice) and "envoys [*poslantsy*] of Russia, Belarus', Ukraine, and other Soviet Republics." An organization in Narva (reported in *Estoniia*, May 4, 1993) appropriated the Estonian word *taotleya* (applicants) as its name, with its purpose to help those nontitulars who were seeking legal recognition of their Estonianness.

Yet "Russian-speakingness" quickly began to emerge as the normal referent. An early formulation was in a response to the draft of the Estonian Republic's language law in late 1988, and what this would mean for the "Russian-speaking part of the population" (*russkoiazychnoi chasti naseleniia*) (Iu. Mishin, *Narvskaia gazeta*, November 17, 1988). Later on, as I noted earlier, the "part" was dropped. As the data show, in the early independence years, it became the predominant form of reference.

Still, the rhetorical value of referring to the Soviet diaspora as Russians remains high, especially for Estonian politicians seeking to link this population to Soviet totalitarian rule. In a symposium on the future of "Non-Estonians in Estonia" (*Molodezh' Estonii*, February 17, 1994), the single Russian interlocutor wrote that we should not expect the "Russians [Russian-tongued, Russian-speakers] to leave the country." Meanwhile, the two Estonians relied on terms such as "migrants" and "non-Estonians" and of course "Russian." "Russian" in these contexts is often a synonym for "occupier," "foreigner," and "KGB." Peter Olesk, then serving as minister of nationalities, said in an interview with *Narvskaia gazeta* (February 19, 1994) that "I never said Russians presented a danger to Estonia. The danger will come with a much greater quantity of Russian citizens. Let it be one-third of those who live in Estonia, not more." In an interview in *Molodezh' Estonii* (April 21, 1994), Olesk was asked if it is true that "Estonians don't want to invite the Russian-speaking inhabitants to integrate." In his answer, Olesk changes the identity term and speaks about the desire of "Russians" to integrate economically. In an ironic statement to the Estonian parliament on the ambiguities of the Law on Foreigners, and how the Russians had misinformed the world of its contents, one deputy mused: "We Estonians don't know how to write laws, but the Russians don't know how to read them" (*Den' za dnem*, July 1, 1993).

The Estonian fear that the Russian-speaking population might become a Russian-speaking *nationality* is shared by some Russians. One Russian from Estonia (writing in the RF newspaper *Narodnaia pravda*, March 28, 1993) refers to himself as "Russian by family," and derisively refers to potential Estonian assimilants as "Russian-speaking juniper Estonians" (*russkoiazychnye mozhzhevelovye Estontsy*). In a rare example of a chauvinistic nationalist expression, a correspondent for *Estoniia* (February 2, 1993) reported that during the effort to mobilize activists for the Representative Assembly of Russian-speakers, flyers were hung on mailboxes one evening urging "genuine Russians" (*istinnye russkie*) to attend this meeting to assure themselves that "Zionists . . . who are ready to plunge a knife into the back of the Russian people [*russkii narod*]" will not hold sway.

Despite the variety of names attached to this new identity and the attempts to stigmatize (or promote) all noncitizens as "Russians," the prevalence of *russkoiazychnoe naselenie* (Russian-speaking population) among every sector of Estonian political life cannot be denied. Its popularity is due to the reality that however unfortunate the category is for many people in Estonia, it has its conveniences for actors at all points on the Estonian political spectrum. Russian politicians in the former Soviet republics may be the only remaining fervent Soviet internationalists in the world. They see themselves as historically beyond attachment to nationality (*natsional'nost'*). Many therefore bristle at the idea of organizing themselves as "Russians." But there is no doubt among the internationalist Russian-speakers, even if they are not a nationality but merely a population, that they have a grievance in Estonia. Organizing their aggrieved members (as a conglomerate Russian-speaking population) to stand against the policies of what they see as a linguistically discriminatory state has no chauvinistic overtones. In the analysis of Nelli Kuznetsova, spokesperson for the United People's Party of Estonia, Russian nationalism only serves the interests of the (Estonian) "national-radicals," who have already "brought so many troubles to the unrooted population." She refers to her group as "Russian-speaking" to eliminate any implication that "we" (the Russians) are as chauvinistic as they (the Estonians).

Meanwhile, Estonian leaders, who face international criticism for policies that look too nationalistic, have an interest in showing that they have nothing against Russians *qua* Russians. Their laws, they insist, put pressures only on illegal immigrants and those Russian-speakers who have not yet adjusted to the language requirements of the state. For Estonian nationalists, then, using the term "Russian-speaking population" allows them to set de facto national criteria for membership in the society without naming a particular nation.

In regard to the non-Russian minorities, there are cross pressures. For those Estonian authorities engaged in internal politics and not external legitimization there is an interest in dividing the Russian-speaking population into its constituent parts, so that there will be no unified minority of non-Estonians. Thus with its Law on Cultural Minorities, the state finances the development of small nationality groups. As for these minority groups themselves—the Ukrainians, Belarusans, Poles, and Jews, all of them minuscule in numbers, and all Russian-speaking—their members have an interest in uniting with Russians to further their language and citizenship goals. One purpose of the law was to prevent the emergence of a united nontitular front on the Estonian political stage. As the author of the law, Ants-Enno Lõhmus, told the press (reported in *Estoniia*, January 10, 1993), the adoption of the law will demonstrate that the term "Russian-speaking nationality" is inadequate—"really just an updated version of *Homo sovieticus*." The Estonian government has given the non-Russian members of the Russian-speaking population resources to develop organizations representing their own ethnic groups. But because they are few in number and fully integrated into the world of the Russians, they are not very interested in establishing national organizations. Thus their leaders, for the most part, have claimed to be representing parts of the "Russian-speaking population," which includes them along with Russians. Thus Nikolai Aksinin, a Ukrainian, and a spokesman for the Union of Estonian Veterans, objects (in *Estoniia*, January 22, 1993) to the notion of a "Russian community" in Estonia as a "simplified notion." "Ethnic principles," he insists, "do not play a role. The Russian-speaking population," he writes, "these are the Ukrainians, and Belarusans, and Jews, and Tatars." "We all," he concludes, "Russian-speakers . . . have been put into the same politico-social circumstances."

In light of a confluence of interests in using "Russian-speaking" as if it were a social category, it has become a cliché in Estonian popular speech and writing. I have recorded its use by the Estonian State Minister in Charge of Negotiations with the Russian Federation, J. Luik (Protocol, Narva City Council, June 30, 1993, p. 2); a leading politician of Isaama coalition, I. Hallaste (Protocol, Narva City Council, April 14, 1992); the leader of Estonia's first Popular Front Government, E. Savisaar (*Narvskii rabochii*, June 30, 1990); the Secretary of the Estonian Community Party, M. Titma (*Narvskii rabochii*, June 6, 1989); the leader of the Center Coalition and twice prime minister of Estonia, T. Vähi (*Narvskaia gazeta*, September 14, 1991); and many others. There is even a reference by the then prime minister, Mart Laar, to his electoral tactics in regard to the "Russian-speaking" voters (interview in *Molodezh' Estonii*, November 4, 1993).

Of vital importance on this issue is the creation of an assembly of those noncitizens who were not represented in the Estonian parliament. The leaders of the various organizations that met to form such an assembly recognized that the term "Russian" was too exclusionary, since there were many non-Russians who were sinking politically in the same boat. An assembly of "noncitizens" would not do either. This label implicitly accepted as a fact a status category that many of the leaders sought to contest—they believed that they were rightfully citizens of the Estonian Republic as they had been citizens of the Estonian Soviet Socialist Republic. Eventually, leaders agreed on calling themselves the "Representative Assembly of the Russian-Speaking Population of Estonia."

Legally, this is a social organization called merely the Representative Assembly. It was formally registered with state authorities on July 6, 1993. It could not be registered as a party, because noncitizens are not legally permitted to join political parties in Estonia. And the tag-on "Russian-speaking population" was deleted from official registration documents, since the organizers doubted that the Estonian government would permit a legal organization that named itself after an aggrieved and potentially revolutionary segment of the population.

Despite legal niceties, this organization is connected in the public mind with an inchoate group called the "Russian-speaking population." In the Estonian press, in its Russian-language and Estonian-language variants (see *Estoniia*, September 18, 1993, with translations from the Estonian press), as well as in everyday references to the organization, the Representative Assembly is seen as representing the "Russian-speaking population" of Estonia. For example, A. Semionov, a leading figure in the Representative Assembly, gave an interview to the Estonian-language press (reported in *Narvskaia gazeta*, April 23, 1994) in which he spoke movingly about the psychological problems faced by the Russians, who had not been fully prepared for Estonia's sudden independence. In his attempt to downplay the significance of the more ethnically based Russki Sobor, he emphasized to the press that mobilizing politically based on national criteria was alien for this "Russian-speaking population." He therefore claimed that his leadership in the Representative Assembly has allayed some of the fears faced by Russian-speakers and helped keep nationality politics off of the streets.

The term goes beyond those Russians seeking to integrate themselves into Estonian political structures. In December 1995 the First Congress of Russian Citizens living in Estonia met in Tallinn with 190 delegates. Its deputy chairman Petr Rozhok (an official in Vladimir Zhirinovskii's Liberal Democratic Party in Russia) told the press (and reported through the Baltic News Service, December 12, 1995) that the goal of the newly formed Estonian Republican Union of Russian Citizens was to "indicate to Russian-speakers in Estonia which candidates they should vote for in [Russian] elections." Even a leader of the most "Russian" of organizations in Estonia found himself referring to his constituency as "Russian-speakers."

To be sure, the validity of this term is occasionally questioned. L. Vahtre, a deputy of the Estonian State Assembly, referred to non-Estonians as members of the "Russian-speaking nationality" when addressing a scientific seminar. A leader of the Jewish Society of Estonia questioned him on this term, and Vahtre, a bit defensive, said that the expression went back to "Soviet times," and that since Russian-speakers use it themselves, he felt that he could without offending anyone.[15] Earlier, I had asked my principal collaborator in Estonia about the citizenship situation for the "Russian-speaking population." Livid, he responded to me that there was no such category and, therefore, there could be no official figures on it.[16] Be that as it may, the term has become so widely accepted, from such a wide range of ideological and institutional positions, that it has become a tradition.[17] In Estonia, then, a "Russian-speaking" identity has become, in Durkheim's phrase, a "social fact."

Latvia

Non-Letts in independent Latvia are referred to by a variety of euphemisms and unflattering terms. The content analysis reveals that negations are used more regu-

[15] Friedrich-Naumann-Stiftung, "Kodanikud ja Mittekodanikud-Õiguslikud ja Sotsioloogiliset Probleemid Taastuvas Eesti Rahvusriigis," May 31, 1994.

[16] Thus, in an interview Kirch gave to the pro-Russian newspaper *Molodezh' Estonii* (July 7, 1993), all his references to nontitulars were negatives: "non-Estonian minority," "illegal immigrants," etc.

[17] Eric Hobsbawm and Terence Ranger, eds., *The Invention of Tradition* (Cambridge: Cambridge University Press, 1983).

larly (a mean of .3222 per article) than in the other republics, far more often than "Russian" (.2032), with "Russian-speaking" coming in a distant third (.1539). Nonetheless, the context analysis will show why the term has become such a powerful descriptive category—and perhaps even an emergent national one—in Latvia.

The range of negations to identify non-Letts is great. They have been referred to as "people born in Latvia whose parents did not have Latvian citizenship" and "unwanted residents" in a single article (*Izvestiia*, November 16, 1993); and the "denationalized group" (*Kommersant*, December 3, 1990). A correspondent for *Izvestiia* (August 28, 1993), in criticizing Latvian policies, relied on Latvian identity categories. "Already twice this century," he wrote, "Latvia has lost its most entrepreneurial and hardworking citizens among the nonindigenous nationalities [*nekorennye natsional'nosti*]: in 1939 50,000 Germans left who still haven't returned to Latvia; and during the German occupation a genocide of Latvian Jews took place." The author fears for the "Russian-speakers" today, whom he also refers to as nonindigenous. In a witty ideological spin, Nikolai Gudanets, in a letter to *SM-Segodnia* (December 28, 1993), pleads to be legally identified as a noncitizen (*negrazhdanin*). He promises that if the present "psychological pressure" that noncitizens now live under is removed, he will carry the title of "Latvian noncitizen with honor." Perhaps totally imbued in the spirit of Latvian discourse, a U.S. Department of State statement on the nationality situation pointed out that although Latvia's constitution guarantees that all of its residents are equal before the law, "non-ethnic Letts [*neetnicheskie latviisty*] cannot participate in civic life."

Latvian political discourse is noted for its lack of directness. A Latvian law dealing with a housing shortage was titled "On the temporary residence of those people finding themselves in Latvia due to the temporary dislocation of the Russian Armed Forces in Latvia" (reported in *Diena* April 23, 1993). In a *Komsomol'skaia pravda* (February 10, 1994) report, the leader of one Latvian party invented the term *vol'nostrantsy* (self-made foreigners) to attack a group he seemed to be incapable of naming any other way.

In this mode, Latvian nationalists try to differentiate the bad non-Letts from the good ones by referring to the former as "newcomers" and the latter as "historical minorities." In *Diena* (November 1, 1993) an article contrasts Jews, Estonians, and Gypsies, which are "historical minorities" with the high percentage of Latvian citizens from Ukraine and Russia, who are considered "occupiers" or "new arrivals." Russians in Latvia, bothered by this sort of rhetoric, have fought back. A pamphlet "Russians in Latvia: History and Present" builds up a case that Russians and Latvians had close personal and territorial relations going back to the twelfth century. One chapter of the pamphlet closes with the assertion that "Russians inhabited and settled the territory of Latvia and lived in peace with the indigenous [*korennoe*] population, the Latvians. Over the course of 700 years, they [the Russians] were a loyal minority."[18]

The notion of "rootedness" comes up constantly in articles concerning ethnic relations. An article in *Pravda* (November 5, 1993) recounts tales of woe for

[18] *Russkie v Latvii: Istoriia i sovremennost'* (Riga: LAD, 1992), p. 38.

"non-Letts" in Latvia. One group of retired women sought official help for housing repair. Seeing that they had filled out the application in Russian, the official "rebuked the retirees for their nonindigenous origins and communist past." Another story is of a Russian journalist born in Latvia who was upbraided by the president-elect for referring to Latvia as his homeland (*rodina*). "Why do you think you have the right to call Latvia your homeland just because you were born here? For that, he says, you need to have deep hereditary roots [*korni*] in the country." In an article in *Rossiiskaia gazeta* (November 3, 1993), there is a report on the radical nationalist Movement for National Independence in Latvia and its new citizenship bill (wittily called by its opponents the "Law of Eternal Refusal"). Here the newspaper refers to those affected by the law as the "nonindigenous residents" (and in another context, as the "Russian-speakers"). To a great extent accepting the Latvian nationalist view that Russians haven't sunk roots in Latvia, a group of Russians in Latvia who intend to return to Russia actually calls itself "Roots" (*Korni*). In an interview with the *Baltiiskoe vremiia* (Riga) (September 1992), its leader Viacheslav Tikhomirov admits that while the Latvian government seems enthusiastic about the project, it hasn't provided any funding; however, he has received some support from former Russian vice-president Aleksandr Rutskoi.

"Nonrooted" seems to be all the explanation the Latvian government needs for refusing to grant automatic citizenship to its "newcomers," and this negation has taken on the properties of an identity in Latvian discourse. Even though 39.1 percent of Russian nationals in Latvia were automatically granted citizenship, the term "noncitizens" (*negrazhdane*) is often used as a generic reference to non-Letts. A related term that is commonly used in the same context is "stateless" (*apatridy*). Many Latvians wish the Russians living within their border were indeed wards of the international community. Nationalist Latvian politicians delayed passage of the naturalization law as long as possible in hopes of creating a de facto zero quota. In one sardonic article in *Emigratsiia* (January 3, 1994), noted earlier, Vladimir Steshenko, editor of *SM* and director of the Nationalities Question in the first Latvian Popular Front government, related that in his newsroom, noncitizens (*negrazhdane*) are called by the first four letters, suggesting that among Latvians they are thought of as "niggers." The article's title refers to Latvia's "soft ethnic cleansing." This "joke" got so well circulated that a serious jurisprudential column in *Panorama Latvii* (May 17, 1995) was headlined "Legalized Niggers" (*Negry v zakone*). Russians have organized politically around this issue. There is a Noncitizens' League (reported in *Diena*, March 9, 1994, and also in *Literaturnaia gazeta*, January 26, 1994) that works to remedy some of the inequities that noncitizens face in Latvia (in taxation, in ownership of property, in rights to vote in local elections). *Literaturnaia gazeta*, in the same article, suggested that Latvian nationalists consider this Noncitizens' League a security threat.

Latvians use the term "Russian" without hesitation. In an article in *Diena* (January 14, 1994) titled "Unemployed Russians in Latvia," the author insists that because they are newcomers (*priezzhie*), all unemployed Russians are potential supporters of Zhirinovskii and can easily become tools of neoimperialist Russian chauvinists in Russia. Not only does this author use the notion of "newcomer" to differentiate

"Russians" from "historical minorities," he uses the term "Russian" as a catch-all to refer to Ukrainians, Poles, and Belarusans as well as Russians. In *Novoe vremia* (1992, no. 29) an article titled "Russians without Russia" treats a similar theme from the opposite point of view. The author complains that the very Latvians who once stood as democrats against Soviet power are now treating the Russian people (*russkie liudi*) who are newcomers (*priezzhie*) and immigrants (*migranty*) as second-class people. The post-Soviet film *Russian Exodus*, directed by Andrei Nikishin, portrays Russians coping with Latvian nationalist hostility by taking refuge in unrealizable escapist fantasies of flight abroad and drinking. Nikishin uses *Russian* stereotypes to portray Russians and non-Russians alike. In these examples, especially in the headlines, we see how normal it still is to label the non-Latvian population merely as "Russians."

Negations (however prevalent) rarely stick as identity categories.[19] And, for reasons made clear in the Estonia section, "Russian" is not fully satisfactory to Russian political entrepreneurs because it excludes people whom they want to include, and because it marks them as "national chauvinists," a charge they prefer to see leveled against the titulars, not themselves. Thus the reliance, albeit less prominently than in Estonia, on the notion of "Russian-speakers," a term that can serve most interests. The first reference to this term I found in a Latvian-related context is in a summary of the 1989 political scene in Latvia by Iu. G. Prichozhaev, who writes, in reference to the Popular Front, "One of the sharpest and nerve-wracking problems in Latvian political life appears to be the granting of citizenship to the Russian-speaking part of the population."

The "part" was dropped in the course of regular reference to this part of the population as a natural group. An article by William Schmidt for the *New York Times* (translated in *Diena*, March 9, 1994) describes the interethnic scene in great detail, dividing the population between Latvians and the "Russian-speaking minority" or merely the "Russian-speakers." In the black-humored article about "niggers" reported earlier, the newspaper *Emigratsiia* in a routine way tells the reader the article is about the "Russian-speaking residents" of the Baltics. In an article in *Moskovskie novosti* (October 4, 1992), Uldis Augstkalns, the deputy chair of the Latvian National Liberation Movement (LNNK), promises a fair citizenship law. His idea of fair sounds ominous to those who will be affected by the law. "Those Russian-speakers who wish to take Latvian citizenship and pass the language exam will become citizens," he assures the reader. "The rest can expect a normal, civilized departure." In a touching letter to *Pravda* (March 2, 1994) a woman who describes herself as a "Russian-speaking citizen of Latvia" tells of her visa problems, because she has a sister in Belarus' and another in Russia. Her anger is directed mostly against the Russian government; but her self-description demonstrates that the conglomerate identity "Russian-speaking" has become normalized in everyday speech. In an ominous political commentary "There Is No Time to Lose!" (*Vremia ne terpit!*, *Diena*, February 20, 1991), Vladimir Lukashuk writes that "the number of convulsively

[19] The word for "German" in Russian, *nemets*, is a negative: one who cannot speak. I do not believe, though, that Germans refer to themselves in this way when they are speaking Russian.

created societies that supposedly could unite the Russians, are already close to ten. . . . They wouldn't be created if the Russian-speaking Latvians felt that they were common citizens of a common democratic republic." To be sure, as in Estonia, some Russians express doubts about the term. For example, Vladimir Sorochin, general secretary of the Russian Citizens of Latvia Party, told an interviewer (*SM-Segodnia*, April 29, 1995) that his party is "currently emphasizing the word '*Russian*' in 'Russian-speaking,' because for a Russian [in Latvia] to be [just] a Russian-*speaker* is no good at all." But, as in all the other republics, Russians rarely criticize the notion of "Russian-speaking" as an identity category.

The situation for Letts is quite different, although they also use the term routinely. In *Vek* (December 17, 1993), the Latvian Consul to Russia was quoted as saying that "Russian-speakers do not take seriously the law on languages and have not started to study Latvian." Somewhat more sympathetic, K. Bikshe, the director of Latvian-language courses, told an interviewer from *SM-Segodnia* (November 10, 1993) that "you cannot request that Russian-speakers immediately speak Latvian without any mistakes." Another Lett, Visvaldis Latsis of the Latvian Committee, wrote (in *SM-Segodnia*, September 11, 1991) that the "Russian people" should recognize that the Russian empire subjugated many nations, and that is why all nations (e.g. Tatars, Bashkirs) "try to separate from the Russians." The idea of a unified nontitular identity that is not dominated by Russians is looked upon with great skepticism. Indeed, the Riga-based correspondent for the RF newspaper *Trud* (November 3, 1993) understood clearly the pragmatics of "Russian-speakingness" for most Letts. "It is not rare for Russians to be identified with Communists," he reported. "The term 'Russian-speakers' is widely used as a designation of a mass hostile to the Latvian mass."

A major reason for the focus on the "Russian-speaking" aspect of their identity for Russians is that in principle, a person's lack of fluency in Latvian (and very few Russians have such fluency) exposes him or her to severe material hardships, including the loss of job. While there are only a few examples of people actually claiming to have lost a job because of the activities of the so-called language police, what is taking place is the gradual destruction of the Russian-speaking milieu in which non-Letts lived for fifty years. Fewer and fewer Letts now study Russian; more now study English. Russian is gradually losing its position as the language of inter-nationality communication in Latvia.[20]

Meanwhile, Latvian is being systematically promoted and its use in a broad variety of settings is encouraged, or even required by law. To be a Russian-speaker in today's Latvia marks one as the member of an out-group. In a fascinating sociological survey of readers of *SM* (November 3–5, 9–12, 1993) a team of sociologists (Natal'ia Sevidova, Larisa Persikova, and Iuliia Aleksandrova) tried to find out "why Russian-speakers [*russkogovoriashchie*] up to this time have not become Latvian-speakers en masse." While the articles focus on many of the difficult administrative problems in learning Latvian, they capture how Latvia's Russian-speaking popula-

[20] On this point, see Angelita Kamenska, "The State Language in Latvia: Achievements, Problems, and Prospects" (Latvian Center for Human Rights and Ethnic Studies, 1995).

tion feels about Latvian attitudes. The respondents intuit that Latvians feel that "if they [the Russian-speakers] don't speak it [Latvian], they don't respect us." While this belief is not supported by the findings of the matched-guise test, it is perfectly plausible that Letts criticize publicly people who do not use Latvian and despise privately those who do. In any event, each time Russian-speakers open their mouths in front of Latvians, they now feel humiliated, a complete reversal in status since 1988.

A particularly good example of the power of status reversal is in the government's insistence that science teachers in Russian-medium schools pass the Latvian-language exam. Some teachers complained, and asked why a biology teacher needs to know Latvian. The official answer was that "teachers represent the intelligentsia . . . they are not only specialists in their subject but educators in the broadest sense."[21] No one is to be esteemed as an intellectual, or so they seem to be implying, without fluency in Latvian.[22] Given such pressures, it becomes clear how non-Letts can coalesce around an identity that reflects their common linguistic plight.

Indeed, the category "Russian-speakers" has already had practical implications. An article in *Izvestiia* (November 16, 1993) tells of the deportation of Igor Zaretskii to Russia from Latvia, a place he considered his homeland. He told a reporter, "My father is Belarusan, and my mother also has no connection with Russia. Are they sending me to Russia because I speak Russian?" The journalist remarks that the Latvian Department of Citizenship and Immigration, by performing these deportations in a routine way, makes Latvia "the only country in the former USSR which continues to recognize, in a fashion, the existence of the now-disappeared state."

In Latvia, the "Russian-speaking population" is a term in common use among foreigners observing the ethnic scene, among nationalist Latvians (who see nonnatives as a homologous mass), and Russians, Ukrainians, and Belarusans (who see the language law as one of the great threats to their future in Latvia, and feel that they all suffer from this common fate). The term is far less frequently used than a set of garden-variety negations and epithets, and less used than "Russian" as well. But negations and "Russians" won't serve in the long term, while "Russian-speaking" is valued by Russians and useful for Letts—despite its decline.

Kazakhstan

The notion of a Russian ethnos is alive and well in Kazakhstan's nationalist discourse. Indeed, the mean use of "Russian" is greater than half, and the highest of the four republics for this study. One major reason for this is the fact that in Kazakhstan, people who are both non-Muslim and non-Kazakh have rapidly assimilated a "Russian" social identity. When "Russian" is used in many contexts in Kazakhstan, what is usually meant is "Russians, Ukrainians, Belarusans, and Jews." In popular speech in Kazakhstan, "Russian" casts even a wider net. A respondent revealed to an interviewer that "in our class there are three Russians: Volodia, Vania,

[21] Ibid.

[22] This reasoning hits hard for people brought up in a Russian tradition, where intellectuals are considered *chest' i sobest' nashego obshchestva* ("the honor and conscience of our society").

and Kim." Although Kim is an ethnic Korean, this reference to her as a "Russian" makes perfect sense in Almaty.[23] Another reason for the prevalence of the term "Russian" in Kazakhstani political discourse is the massive in- and out-migration of Russians to and from northern Kazakhstan. In 1993, for instance, 250,000 Russians emigrated from, while from 100,000 to 150,000 migrated to, Kazakhstan. There is hardly any other way to refer to these migrants than as Russians (*russkie*). This issue gets preeminence in RF press concerning Kazakhstan, and the mean use of "Russian" is .5618 in RF press stories about Kazakhstan. In one article (in *Emigratsiia*, March, 1994), for example, even the Ukrainians who were visiting or returning from, or leaving to their homeland were referred to as Russians! And in a typical letter to the press, here to the newspaper *Sel'skaia zhizn'* (January 18, 1994), a forty-three-year-old farmer wrote that the "Russians [*russkie*] in Kazakhstan are at fault simply for not knowing Kazakh." He concluded that there is no future here for their children, since Kazakhstan doesn't want or need Russians. There is some evidence to support him in the RF press. An extremist Kazakh nationalist was reported in *Rossiiskaia gazeta* (August 5, 1992) to be chanting at the capital center, "Go to Russia! If you do not go, we will beat all Russians."

Meanwhile the mean use of "Russian" in the Kazakhstan Republican press on inter-nationality issues is only .4656. But this figure is still very high. For example, in an interview in *Kazakhstanskaia pravda* (November 24, 1992), Iurii Bunakov, leader of the *Russkaia Obshchina Kazakhstana*, said his "group plans to create national Russian schools on the foundation of the Russian *gymnasii*, to organize a Russian, not Russian-speaking, university," and to achieve dual citizenship. And to open the category "Russian" to all comers, N. Svetova in *Russkii vestnik* (August 5, 1992) reports that "any human being who considers himself a Russian can be a member of the Russian Community of Kazakhstan."

As with Ukraine, in Kazakhstan the notion of a Slav identity holds some rhetorical advantages over Russian. This category would include the 6,255,983 Russians as well as the 823,156 Ukrainians residing in Kazakhstan at the time of the 1989 census, who face a common fate in regard to the nationalizing state policies. But unlike in Ukraine, in Kazakhstan a Slav identity excludes those Russian-speakers who are members of the titular nationality. Thus Slavism in Kazakhstan has a civilizational—or perhaps racial—intonation missing from Ukrainian discourse. Nonetheless, Slavic self-identifications cross the political spectrum among non-Kazakhs. On the one hand there are those who wish to create a permanent Slav presence. For example, Viktor Mikhailov, as is reported in *Kazakhstanskaia pravda* (March 5, 1994), leads a movement called Lad (Harmony), which by May 1993 had sixteen regional organizations and more than 8,000 activists. "Unfortunately," he told a reporter, "the collapse of the USSR shook the confidence of Kazakh Slavs in living a life with full rights in this land. . . . We will try to open a Slavic university in Kazakhstan." On the other hand there are those who see the handwriting on the wall for Slavs. A

[23] Olga Vasil'eva, "Novaia natsiia? Russkie v SSSR kak natsional'noe men'shinstvo," *XX vek i mir*, no. 7 (1991): 15–19, cited in Pål Kolstø et al., "Integration and Nation-Building in Bifurcated Post-Soviet Societies: The Cases of Latvia and Kazakhstan" (unpublished manuscript, 1996 draft).

Russian living in Kazakhstan wrote to *Vek* (January 28, 1994) that "we can confirm that the Slavic population [*slavianskoe naselenie*] is leaving and the process is speeding up. All classes of society have 'suitcase fever.' " A survey reports that 3.2 million, or 33.4 percent, of the "Russian-speaking population" intend to leave. The majority of those leaving are Ukrainian and Belarusan.

This last reference mixes the Slavic imagery with the category of a Russian-speaking nationality, which is far more common than "Slavic" in Kazakhstan's political discourse. As with the case of "Slavic," the "Russian-speaking" category is most often used to unite Russians and Ukrainians against Kazakhs.[24] The alliance between Russians and Ukrainians in the context of Kazakhstan has historically been seen as natural, with nearly all Ukrainians becoming Russian-speaking monolinguals. Yet in today's nationalist environment, Ukrainians don't easily fit into the category "Russian." When Nazarbaev visited Moscow in March 1994, the Kazakh embassy, reported in *Moskovskii komsomolets* (March 29, 1994) was surrounded by pickets from a group calling itself "Russian Societies and Cossack Communes" (*Russkii obshchiny i kazach'e zemliachestvo*), somewhat of a cumbersome title for an alliance. That same month, in *Izvestiia* (no date indicated), there was an announcement of the founding of a union of "Russia's and Kazakhstan's Siberian Cossacks" to defend the citizenship rights of the Russian-speaking population living in Kazakhstan." "Russian-speaking" was a convenient way to refer to Russians, Ukrainians, and Cossacks without making a long list. Within Kazakhstan as well, *Kazakhstanskaia pravda* (January 15, 1994) reports on a meeting of the "Conference of the Society for Agreement and Assistance" to discuss issues concerning the "Russian-speaking population."

President Nazarbaev has sought to dampen the threat of a united Russian-speaking population standing against Kazakhs. In an interview with *Kazakhstanskaia pravda* (January 15, 1994) he was asked whether Kazakhstan would respect the rights of the Russian-speakers. He responded testily:

> First of all, I don't use the term "Russian-speaking nationality." In Kazakhstan, practically all the residents are Russian-speaking, including, of course, Kazakhs. Only rarely do you find a person who does not command Russian. . . . Regarding nationality issues . . . I think that before a politician . . . seizes upon this delicate theme, he should first carefully consider whether he possesses all of the necessary arguments. Even after this, he should consider seven times over whether such a theme will incite the formation of a people [*narod*], and bring tension to society.

In short, too much talk about a threat to a population (*naselenie*) can turn it into a people (*narod*).

The official line in Nazarbaev-led Kazakhstan is that Kazakhstan is the home for many separate nationalities, with Kazakhs being the first among equals. Rhetorically,

[24] As of this writing, I have found only one reference to a Russian-speaking population in which the referent was non-Kazakh and non-Russian. *Pravda* (March 1994) writes that "the most important question for millions of Russians [*russkiye*] and Russian-speakers [*russkoiazychnye*] in Kazakhstan is citizenship."

this ideology leads to the listing of all relevant nationalities, without any conglomerates. In a Forum of the Nations of Kazakhstan (reported in *Kazakhstanskaia pravda*, December 15, 1992), chairman of the Kazakhstan parliament Serikbolsyn Abeldin declared, "We all should create our future—Kazakhs, Russians, Ukrainians, Germans, Uzbeks—the representatives of many nationalities." President Nazarbaev followed: "Many Russian, Ukrainian, Belarusan, and Polish settlers came to Kazakhstan due to Stolypin's reforms."

Keeping with official ideology, in an article in *Iuzhnyi Kazakhstan* (December 15, 1992), which starts off in a cosmopolitan way ("we internationalists"), the nationalities are listed separately, as the author reports that he met with "Russians, Kazakhs, Germans, Tatars, Ukrainians, Jews, Belarusans, and Azerbaijanis." In his native village, he nostalgically mentions, all these groups "lived as a happy family." In *Rabochaia tribuna* (May 17, 1994) Valerii Kuklin, the correspondent in Kazakhstan, writes that non-Kazakhs (*litsa nekazakhskoi natsional'nosti*) cannot have a successful army career now in Kazakhstan, "and therefore, young Ukrainians are moving to Ukraine, Russians to Russia, Belarusans to Belarus', and even Tatars to Tatarstan." In an article in *Sovety Kazakhstana* (April 22, 1993) the demographer Makash Tatimov reports on family size. The categories are Stalinist in precision: "The demographic situation of the Ukrainians, Germans, Belarusans, Polish, Mordvinians, and Jews," he concludes, "are similar to the demographic situation of the Russians." The Russian paper *Emigratsiia* has adopted the Kazakh practice of enumerating nationality groups individually: "Many Russians, Kazakhs, Germans, Ukrainians, Letts, and representatives of other nations have been living in Kazakhstan" (in a story that appeared March 1, 1994). Even the leader of the Russian Society (Russkaia Obshchina) in Almaty, Iurii Bunakov, repeats, like a mantra, the list of nationalities in Kazakhstan, and the special suffering of Russians. "We feel bitter and offended," he complained to an interviewer for *Rossiiskaia gazeta* (January 12, 1993).

> In Almaty there are the Korean community, the Chinese community, the Jewish community, the Greek community, the German community, the Uighur community—all but a Russian community. And each of them receives support from their countries. But it's as if we don't exist for Russia. . . . We are Russian people who can help Russia here. . . . If we create . . . a Russian bank, if Russia gives us privileged credits, we'll be able to guarantee the observance of the interests of the Russian population in Kazakhstan.

Because of nationality enumeration as standard practice in Kazakhstani nationalist discourse, the prevalence of "Russian" in the content analysis is widespread.[25]

Despite efforts by President Nazarbaev and his acolytes, both the Kazakh and Russian governments collude in reifying the "Russian-speaking" population category. In an article from *Novoe vremia* (March 1994), a correspondent writes that

25 Melvin, *Russians Beyond Russia*, p. 116, reports in Kazakhstan a "weaker development of a Ukrainian ethnic identity, though this generally merges into the overall settler identity." The first conference of Ukrainians in Kazakhstan took place in May 1993, but it is not considered an important political force.

"Moscow has conveyed the idea that the only republics of the former USSR that can count on economic support from Moscow are those which recognize the rights of the Russian-speaking population on an equal level with the indigenous population." The article goes on to quote a leader of a Russian society, who said that "only fear, which is sitting in the genes of the Russian-speakers in Kazakhstan . . . is saving Nazarbaev from the enormous displeasure of the people in northern Kazakhstan." Correspondingly, an article in *Pravda* (March 1994) mentions that Nazarbaev, in a speech to the Russian society of Petropavlovsk, tried to allay fears of the "Russian-speaking population" that a massive emigration from Kazakhstan is taking place. Lumping Russians, Ukrainians, and Belarusans into a simple "Russian-speaking population" is a standard post-Soviet reference in Kazakhstan. To demonstrate its cliché quality, consider this letter from a Russian woman living in Kazakhstan, sent to the RF newspaper *Rabochaia tribuna* (December 28, 1993). In it, she complains how Russians are now treated by Kazakhs. She says that "the largest part of the populace is, as it is now fashionable to say [*seichas priniato govorit'*] Russian-speaking. . . . Yes, we no longer have a nationality; we are merely the Russian-speaking population."

The principal challenge to the notion of a Russian-speaking population consisting of Russians and Ukrainians against the titular Kazakhs is that of a Russian-speaking population that includes Russians, Ukrainians, and russified Kazakhs. Of the sixty-five uses of "Russian-speaking population" in the Kazakhstan data set, seven clearly included russified Kazakhs, and in two, only the russified Kazakhs were the referent. These russified Kazakhs, as we saw in Chapter 5, are often referred to as *mankurty*. "*Mankurt*," writes Bhavna Dave, "has become an apt metaphor for the 'modernized' members of uprooted nomadic cultures, forced to part with their cultural roots in the process of adaptation and survival."[26] Although in the 1989 census 97 percent of Kazakh nationals reported that Kazakh is their native or first language—making the idea of forgetting your "own" language seem beside the point—it is widely believed that this claim was wildly inflated, and was more of a symbolic gesture rather than an accurate representation of their language history. The number of *mankurty* is surely higher than the 2.2 percent of urban Kazakhs who report Russian to be their first language, as reported by Robert Kaiser. Indeed, referring to Brian Silver's work, Kaiser admits this: "Clearly," Kaiser points out, "the designation of first language in the censuses was not necessarily a choice made on the basis of fluency level alone, and also reflected attitudes toward the native and Russian languages."[27]

[26] Bhavna Dave, "Becoming *Mankurty*: Russification, Progress, and Social Mobility among Urban Kazakhs" (paper prepared for the Annual Meeting of the American Political Science Association, New York, 1994), p. 2.

[27] See Robert J. Kaiser, *The Geography of Nationalism in Russia and the USSR* (Princeton: Princeton University Press, 1994), table 6.4. He is referring to Brian Silver's articles "Language Policy and the Linguistic Russification of Soviet Nationalities," in Jeremy Azrael, ed., *Soviet Nationality Policies and Practices* (New York: Praeger, 1978), pp. 250–306, and "The Ethnic and Language Dimensions in Russian and Soviet Censuses," in Ralph Clem, ed., *Research Guide to the Russian and Soviet Censuses* (Ithaca: Cornell University Press, 1986), pp. 70–97. The quotation from Kaiser is from p. 283.

The widespread existence of mankurtism in Kazakhstan is palpable in everyday urban life. (It is no coincidence that the cities of Kazakhstan were all initially populated as cities by Russians.) Virtually all government meetings, public announcements, and directives throughout the Soviet era in Kazakhstan were in Russian. Popular stereotypes in Central Asia further suggest that the Kazakhs have massively underreported their linguistic assimilation. Dave reports an popular refrain in Uzbekistan: "If you want to become a Russian, first become a Kazakh."[28] This view has some official recognition, as Kazakh ambassador to Russia, Tair Mansurov, told a *Pravda* correspondent (March 26, 1994) that "in Kazakhstan, the whole population is Russian-speaking" ("V Kazakhstane vse naselenie russkoiazychnoe"). In 1989, 62.8 percent of Kazakhs reported speaking Russian as a second language, the second highest (next to Latvians) of reported Russian proficiency among titulars of the former union republics.[29] The percentage of *mankurty* falls somewhere between 2.2 and 62.8 percent, but it is significantly closer to the higher figure than the census reports would lead us to believe.

The key question for national identity formation in Kazakhstan is whether Kazakh nationalists will be able—as their L'viv counterparts have already begun—to forestall a conglomerate identity that conjoins all the Russian-speaking populations, including the *mankurty*. In the newspaper *Kuranty* (February 18, 1994), Mikhail Schipanov points out that not only many Russians, but "some Kazakhs" aim to receive dual citizenship. This is a subtle message that the *mankurty*, like the cosmopolitan Algerians, are planning their resettlement into Russia if nationalists get too powerful at "home." In an article in *Delovoi mir* (February 17, 1995) there was reference to a letter written by ten well-known Kazakh businessmen who encouraged Russians to remain in the country. The article reports on a Kazakh group called Azat that has organized a demonstration in order to "stigmatize" these "apostates," presumably referring to Russian-speaking Kazakhs. Apostasy and betrayal are the charges nationalists will make against those Kazakhs who see themselves as part of a Russian-speaking population. While "Russian" far outpaces "Russian-speaking" in the nationalist discourse of Kazakhstan, social reality helps keep the "Russian-speaking" identity category alive; its vague boundaries help keep that identity category contested.

Ukraine

Ukraine, of the four cases, has the lowest mean use of the identity term "Russian-speaking population," yet it is the only republic where the use of the term has increased over time, so that its mean use in 1994–96 became the highest of the four republics in the sample. And to a greater extent than any of the four republics, largely because nearly all eastern, southern, and central ethnic Ukrainians (constituting 86.8 percent of the entire ethnic Ukrainian population living in Ukraine) are them-

[28] Dave, "Becoming *Mankurty*," pp. 18–19.
[29] Kaiser, *Geography of Nationalism*, table 6.8.

selves conversant in Russian, the meaning of the term is the most highly varied.[30] Of the forty-one uses of "Russian-speaking population" in the Ukrainian data set, only ten were references only to nontitulars; twenty-four included Russian-speaking titulars along with other Russian-speakers; and seven excluded Russian altogether from membership in the Russian-speaking category. Identity talk of Russians and Slavs (but almost no negations) is normal in Ukrainian nationalist discourse; but as with the other three republics, in Ukraine the category of "Russian-speaking population" has become a new and powerful social reality.

The notion of a Russian ethnos whose members live as a new minority remains a vibrant discourse in Ukraine, with a mean use of .4736, second only to Kazakhstan. A sharp distinction between "Russians" and "Ukrainians" serves many interests, though for different reasons. Radical Ukrainian nationalists, especially from western Ukraine, seek to purify Ukrainian from all traces of Russian influence. One ultranationalist organization, Derzhavna Samostiinist' Ukrainy (DSU, State Independence of Ukraine), sends out propaganda in support of a pure Ukrainian nation, and this propaganda is filled with anti-Russian invective (*Den'*, June 26, 1993). As one deputy in the Crimean Supreme Soviet put it to a correspondent, "I can't turn on my radio without a shower of humiliations against Russians on every program: Russians are imperialists, Russians are chauvinists, Russians made the Ukraine so unhappy . . ." (*Pravda Ukrainy* September 4, 1992). Indeed, at a meeting in Crimea led by the mayor of L'viv and the son of a famous figure in the OUN, a prominent sign was held up: "Kravchuk, leave the CIS, and don't step in shit" (*Svobodnyi Krym*, July, 1992).

Ukrainian moderates take a line closer to Nazarbaev's, in trying to picture Ukraine as a home for all (separate) nations, with Ukrainians having a somewhat special role. In his inaugural address of 1991, quoted earlier, the newly elected president, Leonid Kravchuk, a centrist ukrainophone who had been ideological secretary of the Central Committee of the Ukrainian Communist Party, set a very moderate tone. The well-known Ukrainian writer Ivan Drach had taken a similar line (in *Literaturnaia gazeta*, April 11, 1990), mocking the radical nationalists. The term *moskal' velikoros* (Muscovite Great Russian, here transliterated in Ukrainian), he analyzed, shows anger not only with the *moskali* but with the implication that Ukrainians are *malorosy* (Little Russians). This vocabulary, he maintained, takes on a life of its own. The Ukrainian knitted shirt became known in Ukraine as the *antisemtka* (anti-Semite) and has become associated with the Ukrainians as *malorosy*. Drach ended his piece with the hope that all "nations," including Jews, Russians, and Poles, would freely embrace Ukraine as their fatherland [*rodinoi*]."[31]

Russians in Ukraine—especially those Russians in Crimea and Galicia, neither of which was part of Ukraine before the Second World War—have responded to

[30] This figure, derived from the 1989 Soviet census, counts only Galicia (L'viv, Ivano-Frankivs'k, and Ternopil' oblasts) as "western" Ukraine. A more liberal accounting that includes Rivne, Volyn', Zakarpattia, and Chernivtsi would bring the figure down to 76.8 percent. Dominique Arel kindly supplied me with these data.

[31] This is the pre-independence "Dr. Jekyll" face of Drach. An example of his later, "Mr. Hyde" side is in Chapter 4.

Ukrainian nationalism with a vibrant self-identification as Russians. Sometimes the reactions are benign and open to compromise. An article in *Svobodnyi Krym* (July 1992) reports on a L'viv demonstration condemning Crimean "chauvinism," with the mayor reported as saying that these chauvinists seek to ruin Ukraine. The author of the article objects, and says that the "simple Russian people [*prostye russkie liudi*] in Crimea consider that it is better to live in rich Ukraine than in starving Russia." More often, however, the tone is defensive. A Russian author in L'viv writing for *Rossiia* (June 2, 1992) was angered by Ukrainian attacks on the premises of the Pushkin Society, making life, he confessed, "for Russians safer in Russia than in Ukraine." And in counterattack, he accuses Ukrainian nationalists of bringing the word *zhyd* (Yid) back into service as well as *kosoglazye* (slant-eyed) and the derogatory *moskali* for Russians. In *Vybor* (June 8, 1991) Sergei Grigor'ev excoriates Ukrainians for "trying to foster animosity toward the *moskali-okkupanty*." In waxing eloquent about Kievan Rus' as "the second part of their Ukrainian souls," he insists that "Great Russians within the Union's diaspora [*Velikorossy vnutrisoiuznoi diaspory*] will never abandon Ukrainian Rus'."

But Russian self-expressions of Russianness are not only reactive. Nationalist rhetoric in the name of Russianness is a powerful independent force in Ukraine. In Crimea, a "Russian Society" is quite active (see, e.g., *Pravda Ukrainy*, September 16, 1992, and *Nezavisimaia gazeta*, January 12, 1993). Its goal is to "unite the Russian people [*russkikh liudei*] in a foundational social organization . . . reflecting the Russian idea [*russkaia ideia*]." Its leader A. Los', was questioned by a reporter from *Nezavisimaia gazeta* about the role of the "non-Russian nationalities" in Crimea. He answered that "we are all Russians, we all speak Russian freely . . . producing a new ethnos, the Rossians [*rossiiskii narod*]."[32] In *Russkaia pravda Shuvainikova* (the publication of the Russian Party of Crimea, on September 10, 1994) there is an appeal by V. Katorgin of the organization "Rus'" to create a "Russian revival," and in the meantime, to discredit any attempt to make the boundaries between the national groups ambiguous. "Only if we revive Russian cultural and historical traditions and realize ourselves as a Russian nation, as Russian people," he insisted, "will we be able to defend ourselves, our families, and our future, not only in the Crimea, but in all the lands that belonged to Russia, where Russians turned out to be foreigners, second-class citizens, and a faceless, Russian-speaking population [*bezlikoe russkoiazychnoe naselenie*]."

Even those people who have an apparent interest in blurring ethnic boundaries get caught up into the Russian/Ukrainian boundary project. A well-known professor of history at Kiev University told a newspaper reporter that Russians should either love Ukraine or leave it. He then revealed, "By blood, I'm Russian [*ia russkii*], and of course I wish good fortune to my native people [*rodnomu narodu*]" (interview with Igor Losev, *Ostrov Krym*, no. 11, n.d.).

If it weren't for the devastating conflict between (to outsiders) indistinguishable cultural groups such as Serbs and Croats, the heroic attempts to mark boundaries

[32] The notion of an eastern Slavic identity, going back to Kievan Rus', is the best gloss on this term *Rossian*.

between Russians and Ukrainians in Ukraine would seem comical. Much of it has to do with the question of who is more impure. In the newspaper *Put'* (August 31, 1991), a Ukrainian writer, in a well-known Ukrainian nationalist move, denies any common Slavic identity.[33] He refers to "Russian despotism," "Russian cruelty," and "Russian chauvinism," and this can only be explained by the fact that the Muscovite elite descended from the Tatars. This battle has a linguistic element. In *Donetskii Kriazh* (June 18, 1993), a Russian ideologue pointed to the common Slavic roots of Russian and Ukrainian, but then points out that the latter is different because it has incorporated Turkish words, including *rukh* ("movement," and the name of the Ukrainian independence movement of the 1980s). A few days later, the DSU in one of its luscious outpourings of bile, derisively pointed to Pushkin's notion of "the great and mighty Russian language," and reveals to its readers that it "is really the 'Mongol-Tatar' language" (*Den'*, June 26, 1993). Language purity issues are seized upon for great satiric effect. In one humorous but factual report, Ukrainian nationalists were humiliated that they could not find the Ukrainian word to describe the color blue on the Ukrainian flag and had to rely on "Russian-speaking sources" for the term (*Izvestiia*, September 14, 1991).

A clear alternative to "Russian" as a category of identification (suggested by the use of "Rossian") and one that would build a closer union between Russians and Ukrainians, is "Slavic." Indeed this rhetorical move is common in nationality discourse in Ukraine. In a typical article in the Russian-language press in Ukraine, the author reveals that he took Russian citizenship but plans to remain working in Ukraine. To resolve this apparent contradiction, he seeks the "integration of all Slavs" and perhaps other peoples as well (*Pravda Ukrainy*). In a similar tone, *Pravda Ukrainy* (May 26, 1993) printed a letter from Crimea in which the author emphasized the Slavic (*slavianskaia*) identity of the peninsula that unites Russians and Ukrainians. Indeed, the *Rossiiskaia gazeta* (November 11, 1993) reported a new Party of Slavic Unity, as a counter to the anti-Rossian (*anti-rossiiskii*) propaganda in the western oblasts. V. Parenko, party leader, said that he "mourned" the collapse of the Soviet Union, which harmed the "spiritual" culture of the Slavs. I. Komov, the leader of Democratic Crimea, in an interview (*Izvestiia* October 16, 1991), wistfully noted that already there is an "intra-Slavic" (*mezhslavianskii*) conflict. Ukrainians, too, have appealed to this common Slavic bond. An officer in the Ukrainian army wrote to *Pravda Ukrainy* (September 15, 1992) very understandingly about Russians, pointing out that Iurii Meshkov (the secessionist leader in Crimea) isn't a typical Russian, and shouldn't be seen that way. The correspondent concluded by saying that he did not want anything to come between the "Slavic" nations.

Mixed Russian-Ukrainians would have the greatest interest in promoting a Slavic identity. The noted poet Borys Oliinyk (whose father was a passport Russian, his mother a Ukrainian) has written extensively on the theme of a "Slavic core" (*Slavianskoe iadru*). He writes (citation not available) of a common basis of Russian

[33] This is the claim of Mikhail Hrushevsky in the nationalist bible, *History of Ukraine-Rus'*. An abridged English-language version is available: *A History of the Ukraine* (New Haven: Yale University Press, 1941).

identity in Ukraine's history—"up till now we called ourselves just Russian—children from a single pre-Mongolian Russian womb, with similar rights of inheritance," and is appalled that Russian is being "driven out" of the parliament. This, he says, shows disregard for the "Russian-speaking population." Here we see that Oleinik moves to the less incendiary, more comfortable label—"Russian-speaking population"—to give boundaries to the group that is suffering from what he considers to be an unnatural Ukrainian nationalism.

But the "Slavic" card faces constraints reflected in its limited use. For one, during the Soviet period, "Slavic" wasn't an official category, and it has no institutions that speak for its population. The Commonwealth of Independent States (CIS) was first intended as a union of Slavic states, that is before President Nursultan Nazarbaev of Kazakhstan insisted on being included. There was hardly a way to exclude him, since neither Yeltsin nor his liberal comrades were willing to reveal publicly the reality of an exclusionary (and racialist) "Slavic" bond. Partly for this reason, the rhetorical space of "Slavism" has been occupied by extremists, and even fascists. The leader of the Slavic Union in Kiev was arrested for selling newspapers in a metro underpass. In an interview with a correspondent from *Russkii vestnik* (no. 1, 1993), he could not hold himself back from gratuitous anti-Semitic remarks, such as pointing out that three of the members of the Slavic Union were mysteriously attacked on the Jewish holiday of Purim. Probably for these reasons, in the data set, the term "Slav" occurs only 6.5 percent of the time.

"Slavic" is therefore far outpaced by "Russian-speaking" as an identity category. The notion of a Russian-speaking population as a social/cultural category in Ukraine has several distinct—and somewhat contradictory—bases. First, it is a common category for those who wish to unite the 11.4 million ethnic Russians with an even larger group of self-identifying Ukrainians mainly from the east and the south who do not normally speak Ukrainian (but rather Russian) at home. Of the forty-one uses of "Russian-speaking" in the data set, twenty-four referred to that set of people (Russian and Ukrainian) who were most comfortable speaking in Russian. To the extent that they form a united block, the major cultural division in Ukraine would suddenly be erased, to be replaced by a geographic, east/west division. Indeed, this set of Russian-speakers is the electoral bloc that overwhelmingly supported presidential candidate Leonid Kuchma (a russophone Ukrainian) over incumbent Kravchuk in the 1994 election. In that election, as Arel demonstrates, a "Russian-speaking population" voting bloc was clearly evident in the eastern and southern oblasts.[34] Many eastern Ukrainians identify closely with the Russian language and see themselves as part of a greater Russian-speaking world. In *Emigratsiia* (March 1993), a Ukrainian correspondent evoked the name of Vladimir Korolenko, a writer who wrote about the Ukrainian countryside in Russian. The article raised concerns that the diminishing of the teaching of Russian would deprive "Russian-speakers" (including Ukrainians) of the ability to read his great works.

[34] Dominique Arel and Valeri Khmelko, "The Russian Factor and Territorial Polarization in Ukraine," *Harriman Review* 9, no. 1–2 (1996): 81–91.

In Crimea, this notion of a Russian-speaking population consisting of Russians and russophone Ukrainians is common, in this case with the intent of maintaining cultural/political solidarity in the face of Tatar claims to ownership of the peninsula. The Tatars, returning to their home area after a generation of exile, are still few; yet their claim to be the sole nationality rooted in Crimea threatens the Russians and Ukrainians, who constitute an overwhelming majority of the peninsula's residents. To be sure, the Russian press often refers to the non-Tatars merely as "Russians." The Institute of National Problems in Education, in a report summarized in *Rossiiskaia gazeta* (date obscured), referred to the Russian population of Crimea ("Russkoe naselenie Kryma") as having been in formation for two centuries. *Literaturnaia Rossiia* (June 25, 1993) described Sevastopol' as a Russian city (*russkii gorod*) within a Russian Crimea (*russkogo Kryma*).

But categories are in flux in Crimea. *Pravda* (January 28, 1993) routinely cited that among Crimeans "85 percent are Russian-speakers." In 1993, a Russian-Speaking Movement (*Russkoiazychnoe dvizhenie Kryma*) organized to push for closer ties with Russia (reported in *Nezavisimaia gazeta*, April 2, 1993). This strong potential alliance was not lost on the Tatars. In *Krymskie izvestiia* (September 9, 1992) a Tatar, complaining about the slow pace of restitution of property, wrote "At this time, there are many who are called the Russian-speakers (by the way, I up till now did not know there was such a nationality [*natsiia*]), who have two, or even three, dwellings." In Crimea the term "Russian-speakers" serves not only the interests of Russians who want a united Crimea, in the face of the Ukrainian nationalizing state; it serves as well the interests of Tatars, to expose a united threat against their interests. The term, therefore, appears widely in discussions of nationality issues in Crimea.

In the rest of Ukraine, however, the "Russian-speaking population" is more often used to refer specifically to Russian-speaking Ukrainians in the east and south, as distinct from Russians. S. S. Savoskul claims that the Russian-speaking Ukrainian culture (*russkoiazychnoi Ukrainskoi kul'tury*) was produced by ambitious titular parents who wanted to maximize their children's opportunities during the Soviet era.[35] In my newspaper sample, seven of the uses of "Russian-speaking population" in Ukraine used the term in this way. In *Russkii vestnik* (April 29, 1992), in a critique of Ukrainian nationalism, one author complains that "when the Russians and Russian-speaking people say the slightest word in their own defense, the champions of the great and indivisible Ukraine immediately become very angry." In a story in *Moskovskie novosti* (November 20, 1991), Vladimir Grinev, the deputy chairman of the Ukrainian Supreme Soviet, was described as "popular among his Russian and Russian-speaking co-citizens." In a letter from a Donetsk mining collective to a fascist paper in the Russian Federation (*Den'*, June 20–26, 1993), the writers complain that "in Ukraine live 12 million Russians [*russkikh*] and 2–3 million Russian-speaking people [*russkoiazychnykh narodov*], and in the government of Ukraine there isn't a single Russian [*russkogo*]. Is this not discrimination?!" In a letter from the

[35] S. S. Savoskul, "Russkie v slavianskoi srede: Ukraina i Belorussiia," in M. Iu. Martynova, ed., *Novye slavianskie diaspory* (Moscow: RAN, 1996), p. 95.

Odessa organization Rus' printed in *Vecherniaia Odessa* (September 18, 1992), officials complain of a "humiliating" division of the "people of Ukraine" (*naroda Ukraini*) into natives (*korennaia natsia*) and national minorities (*natsional'nye men'shinstva*). They agree that many in the south and east feel personal ties with the motherland (*Rodina-mat'*). Yet, they argue, half of the people in this zone are non-russified Russian-speakers (*russkoiazichnye ne russifitsirovanye*) who are still natives (*korennye zhiteli*). The Russian weekly *Argumenty i fakty* (December 1991) reported on a survey of 5,000 Kievans, more than 80 percent of whom had never encountered discrimination against Russians (*russkie*) or against the Russian-speaking population (*russkoiazychnoe naselenie*) at work or in everyday activities. In these examples, Russian-speakers are that set of Ukrainians who normally speak Russian, not the set of ethnic Russians who live in Ukraine.

Ukrainian nationalists pick up on this notion of a Ukrainian Russian-speaking population and speak of these people as potential fifth columnists who haven't yet been weaned from imperial subjugation. As Arel points out:

> Ukrainian nationalists . . . treat Russophone Ukrainians as "victims" of Russian-Soviet policy at best. Increasingly, however, the Russophone Ukrainians are being referred to as "denationalized" beings who do not know who they are, or as "Little Russians" (the pre-revolutionary name for Ukrainians) who like to defer to and be dominated by the "elder brother," the Great Russians. Nationalists are convinced that their "Russified" brethren will "re-acquire" their national consciousness only through the Ukrainian language.[36]

In an incendiary article in *Iug* (January, 1993), a pro-Ukrainian candidate in science accused the Russian-speakers of Ukraine of intimidating the population at large, pushing Ukrainians toward bloodshed, which would destroy Ukraine. These were the activities, he suggested, of fifth columnists. In an even more incendiary polemic in *Holos Ukrainy* (Kiev, date obscured) an eastern Ukrainian sarcastically describes a rally in Simferopol, where protesters demanded, "Stop the peasant Ukrainians [*khokhly*] who deprive the Russian-speaking population of its native language." Here the colloquial epithet for untutored Ukrainians implies those from the west who are pushing a radical nationalist program. The writer sees this so-called Russian-speaking population as a threat to the continued ukrainization of Ukraine. For Ukrainian nationalists, especially from Galicia (and those from Galicia who serve in Kiev ministries), the threat of the Russian-speaking Ukrainians is the principal threat to the nationalizing project. "Russian-speakers," for them, is a code word for denationalized, threatening, yet potentially recoverable, conationals.

In Ukraine, the category of "Russian-speaking population," as we have seen, serves multifaceted interests. Authorities from the Russian Federation and Russian ethnics in Ukraine can refer to this population without obvious national chauvinist overtones. Ethnic Russians, furthermore, can use the term to build an alliance with

36 Dominique Arel, "Ukraine: The Temptation of the Nationalizing State," in Vladimir Tismaneanu, ed., *Political Culture and Civil Society in the Former Soviet Union* (Armonk, N.Y.: M. E. Sharpe, 1995), pp. 157–88.

Russian-speaking Ukrainians, who themselves use the term because it suggests that they may speak Russian but they are still Ukrainians. Tatars and Ukrainian nationalists use the term to point to a potential threat to their national projects.

There is some evidence that the Russian-speaking label has very little power to frame identities in Ukraine.[37] In response to an earlier formulation of my thesis, Lowell Barrington shows that on an index of love for the Ukrainian homeland, Ukrainians are distinct from Russians, with the implication that a Russian-speaking identity is no different from a Russian one. Second, he shows that the Russian members of the Russian-speaking population are distinct from non-Russian members of the Russian-speaking population, and from that he argues that there is no evidence of a conglomerate Russian-speaking identity. While these are important findings, Barrington incorrectly derived from my model (which included Estonia and Bashkortostan, but claimed that there would be similar formations in all republics) the thesis that the Russian-speaking population would have the same group boundaries in all republics. For him, "Russian-speaking" includes all nontitulars who rely principally on Russian. My present formulation, however, explicitly encourages the inclusion of Ukrainian Russian-speakers in the Russian-speaking population, as popularly conceived, and the exclusion of groups such as Romanians and Hungarians, who are not considered members of the Russian-speaking population in Ukrainian popular discourse. Barrington might have found—confirming Dominique Arel and Valeri Khmelko—that the divide between the population that normally uses Russian at home and those who do not is a principal political cleavage in Ukraine.[38] With this notion of a Russian-speaking population in Ukraine, my thesis should receive stronger support from Barrington's data.

But I reiterate that the notion of a Russian-speaking population that includes all those Russians and Ukrainians who rely principally on Russian is only one of a set of possible configurations of this identity group. Because it is an identity still in formation, which interest in Ukraine will capture the term as theirs remains uncertain.

Toward a Russian-Speaking *Nationality*?

The data from Estonia, Latvia, Kazakhstan, and Ukraine show only that the Russian-speaking population is a commonly used identity category in the post-Soviet republics. Furthermore, as the data clearly show, the category has different content in the various republics, making the formation of a transrepublican "Russian-speaking population of the near abroad" highly unlikely at best. Adding to this diversity, in the Russian Federation itself, the "Russian-speaking population" has become a code to identify non-Russians who are living illegally in Russia, and it

[37] Lowell Barrington, "Russians in the Near Abroad: Identity, Loyalty, and Homeland" (paper presented at the Annual Meeting of the American Association for the Advancement of Slavic Studies, Washington, D.C., 1995). Barrington was reacting to my formulation of a Russian-speaking population in a prepublication version of my "Identity in Formation," *Archives européennes de sociologie* 36 (1995): 281–316.

[38] Arel and Khmelko, "Russian Factor."

is a term of derision. This use of the term is well understood among the Russian-speaking populations in the near abroad, and it does not give any pride to the term.[39]

For a Russian-speaking population to transmogrify into a Russian-speaking *nationality* would require far more than the trends shown in this chapter. Ronald Suny claims that for such a development there have to be emergent claims to group autonomy, to cultural nationhood, and eventually to the right of statehood. Perhaps the Russian-speaking identity is part of a longing, he suggests, for the "lost transnational cosmopolitan space in which they lived," being able to move easily between Moscow center professionally and their republic culturally. The Russian-speakers, he pointed out, may want symbolically to preserve this cosmopolitan identity. While these feelings may be strong, he concludes, this is only one identity that is competing for people's imaginings. And because it lacks claims for ultimate statehood, it is not likely to emerge as a bona fide national identity.[40]

Alternatively, the Russian-speakers might well be considered not as a vague transnational diaspora but rather as a standard interest group. Under quasi-democratic conditions, in which the government has passed language and citizenship laws that put hardships in the way of certain segments of the population, it is perfectly reasonable for those segments to coalesce into a movement that seeks to alter those laws, or to ameliorate the difficulties that the target population faces because of them. Once these issues move off of the political agenda, we should expect other groups to form, with the Russian-speaking coalition breaking up into other political formations. Why, it can be asked of my perspective, should an interest group formation be considered an emergent nationality?[41]

As I emphasized in Chapter 1, simply naming the Russian-speaking population as a diaspora, or an interest group, or a conglomerate identity, or an emergent nationality serves no analytic purpose. The question at hand is whether those who now represent themselves as Russian-speakers will sharpen the boundaries that separate them from others, and make claims for political/territorial autonomy based on the cultural distinctiveness of the group within those boundaries. There is no evidence that such efforts are now taking place, but there are reasons for holding that the groundwork has been laid for such a project.

A primary consideration here is that the Russian-speaking population, like the Palestinians a half century ago, was formed amidst a political cataclysm. The shock of national independence of the titular republics for Russians was sudden. Many young men were serving in the Soviet army, and suddenly found—to their utter disbelief—that they and their officers were suddenly from different countries. They returned to their homes in what they incorrectly considered their homelands. Workers in All-Union factories, facing unemployment and loss of the safety net they assumed would carry them for life, were astonished that Moscow had no obligation

[39] E. I. Filippova, "Latviia, Estoniia," in V. Tishkov, ed., *Migratsii i novye diaspory b postsovetskikh gosudarstvakh* (Moscow: Institut etnologii i antropologii, 1996), p. 118.

[40] These comments were delivered at the American Association for the Advancement of Slavic Studies, Washington, D.C., October 26, 1995.

[41] This was the principal criticism that an earlier version of this paper faced at a seminar organized by Robert Price at the University of California, Berkeley, November 13, 1995.

to hear their claims. These cataclysmic shocks created a new form of diaspora that could not easily accept that they were living "abroad." Standard forms of diasporic analysis therefore do not fully apply to this case.

Closely related to this point is the intensity of the nationalist rhetoric in the titular republics that accompanied the breakup of the Soviet Union. This rhetoric went even further toward convincing Russian-speakers that they would likely be deported, or lose all rights to pensions and medical care. They were called, especially by the loudest voices, "occupiers" and "colonizers." The cataclysmic breakup and the salience of the nationalizing rhetoric both worked to increase the salience of the category into which nontitulars were lumped. Russian-speakingness became a central component of this population's imaginings. High salience of the category as an identity marker, I am assuming, gives it greater meaning than merely an ephemeral interest group.[42]

A third consideration is that significant numbers of the Russian-speaking populations in the near abroad received property rights in the Soviet period that give them meaningful ties to the land. There is more here than squatter's rights to Soviet apartments in large industrial cities. Many Russian-speakers, as part of their compensation packages at work, received plots of land, on which they constructed dachas. On this property, vast numbers of Soviet citizens planted potatoes, apple trees, and vegetables that feed their families throughout the year. Their psychological attachment to these properties gives the Russian-speaking property owners a sense of rootedness in territory that is a core component to the organization of nationalist claims. That is to say, these communities of property owners are areas for which young men will fight to defend what is historically theirs; here we see the possibility of the territorialization of cultural identities, a core element of nationality formation.[43]

A final consideration is that although the term "Soviet" has been discredited by history (as can be seen by its appearance in only 1 percent of the observations in the data set)—the Russian-speaking populations in the near abroad share many Soviet symbols—the songs, the holidays, the memory of the Great Fatherland War in which fascism was defeated, the jokes, and the sense that they were part of a truly internationalist society. Thus there are more symbolic threads than merely language-sharing that can form the basis of a national imagining. Surely it will take a great deal of imaginative effort—in a process Lévi-Strauss has called "bricolage"[44]—to turn a population category into a nationality group, but some of the raw materials are there.

In a judicious treatment of the issue of the identities of Russians in the near abroad, Neil Melvin is emphatic that "there was no 'objective' Russian diaspora simply waiting to be recognized by Russian politicians" but that an identity had to

[42] I owe this point to a line of questioning from Donal Cruise O'Brien, who kindly invited me to deliver an earlier version of this chapter to his seminar at the School of Oriental and African Studies, University of London, December 1, 1995.

[43] I owe this point to a suggestion by Lee Schwartz, made at the meetings of the American Association for the Advancement of Slavic Studies, Washington, D.C., October 26, 1995.

[44] Claude Lévi-Strauss, *The Savage Mind* (Chicago: University of Chicago Press, 1966).

be constructed. From his examination of the rhetoric, quite contrary to the thesis advanced here, he finds that, "the eventual redefinition of the settler communities as a Russian diaspora [*Rossiiskaia diaspora*] marked a victory for the political ideas of one particular elite." The precise identity of this elite is not specified, but it is implied that it was the project of Russian state builders after the Soviet collapse.

Despite this claim of victory, Melvin is hardly consistent about which term became dominant. He writes, for example, that "from the beginning of 1993, the Ministry of Foreign Affairs and other government departments . . . began to employ the terms *sootechestvenniki* (co-fatherlanders) . . . , *Rossiiane* (Russians by citizenship) . . . , *etnicheskie Rossiiane* (ethnically citizens of Russia), and *vykhodtsy* (emigrants)." Meanwhile, in many places in the book, Melvin uses "Russian-speaking" as the easiest way to describe his subject group, as he says, it serves a "neutral" purpose. For example, he writes that, "the Russian-speaking populations of the Baltics were ill prepared for the dissolution of the USSR." And elsewhere: "The Russian-speaking activists within the Popular Fronts were quickly marginalized and support for Russian cultural organizations ceased." Once again: "As in the Baltic states of Estonia and Latvia, the Russian-speaking settler community became central to the development of Moldova from the late 1980s." And later on, Melvin writes that in the settler communities "Russian ethnicity has begun to be viewed primarily in cultural-linguistic (Russian-speaking) rather than simply genealogical terms."

Yet in his conclusions, he reinforces his unsubstantiated thesis. "At least in part through the efforts of politicians and activists in Russia," he judges, "Russians, Russian-speakers and others with some link to Russia or Russian civilization have been bound together conceptually and linked by Russian foreign policy to form the 'Russian diaspora.' As a result, large sections of the Russian-speaking settler communities have, for the first time, begun to think of themselves as members of the Russian nation and of the Russian Federation as their homeland." The quantitative data in my analysis show, however, that the "diaspora" project was less successful than Melvin suggests; and that his term of convenience, "Russian-speaking," is actually the more accurate term for the social reality he was studying.[45]

For the wider purposes of this book, it should be reiterated that the construction of a conglomerate identity is clearly an alternative strategy to that of assimilation (to the titular nationality), voice (to protect the rights and preserve the privileges of Russians), violent confrontation, and exit (to return to one's putative homeland). In this chapter, I have dissected one arena of nationalist discourse to explore the role that the conglomerate identity referred to as the "Russian-speaking population" has played in the nationality issue. I found that the data do not demonstrate that this conglomerate identity has replaced that of "Russian" as the core identity of the so-called beached diaspora; in fact, the data show that after playing a large role in consolidating those who suffered most poignantly from the double cataclysm,

[45] Melvin, *Russians beyond Russia*, pp. 15–16, 22–24, 37, 76, 126–27. I should emphasize that although I use the term "diaspora" throughout my analysis, and it is common in the analyses of expert commentators both in Russian and in the West, it is a term that had virtually no resonance in the discourse analysis itself.

the term is less often invoked today. Yet the data also show that a "Russian-speaking" identity is far more prevalent than some identities available from the historical past, such as "Slav" and "Soviet." It is far more prevalent than "diaspora" as well. Although less prevalent than a catchall category of negations, unlike negations (except in the ironic tone discussed earlier) the "Russian-speaking population" is a more positive portrayal that an activist can stand behind. That is to say, it has nonnegligible mobilizational potential. It is not now, in any of the republics, a banner for nationalist claims, but its very use does help lay the rhetorical foundation for such claims in the future.

11

Russian Nationalism in Russia and the Near Abroad

A recurrent theme in this book is that the "Russian-speaking population" in the near abroad is developing a new corporate identity that has within it the possibility of evolving into a national group. If this is correct, then we should be able to observe trends in Russian nationalism in Russia that are distinct from the trends of nationalism in the near abroad. Survey data based on interviews with Russians in Russia and in the near abroad do not, however, capture these differences. From the point of view of mass attitudes—as opposed to elite discourse of nationalist themes—we cannot reject the claim that there is no difference in Russian nationalism in Russia and the near abroad. This may be because it takes longer for differences I hypothesize to appear in public attitudes. If this is the case, the data presented here can serve as an excellent baseline of attitudes in the early 1990s. Or it may be because the survey instrument was too blunt to capture the proposed differences, in which case a better-controlled and better-constructed survey would be indicated. In either case, it is the challenge for future research to determine whether my theory about difference is correct.

What Is the Russian "Nationalist" Tradition?

Nationalism—the doctrine that the justification for the boundaries of a state lies in its encompassing a nation—is a modern phenomenon. But as Anthony Smith has insisted, the roots of nationalist myths go back to much earlier times.[1] A search for the roots of Russian nationalism—whether in legitimations for the state or the church—yields, however, very few rewards. Russian tsars, it is often pointed out, rarely relied

[1] On the modernity of nationalism, see Elie Kedorie, *Nationalism* (London: Hutchinson, 1960). On the ancient roots of nationalist myths, see Anthony Smith, *The Ethnic Origins of Nations* (Oxford: Blackwell, 1986).

on notions of a Russian people to legitimate their rule. Peter the Great founded the modern Russian state and created a myth justifying his rule based on "conquest and power." Patriotism for him and his successors in the eighteenth century therefore became "state patriotism."[2] Similarly with the Orthodox Church. It was imbued with the Greek tradition that the church should be submissive to civil power. It became a "state" church rather than one that represented a people, or a nation.[3]

Students of nationalism, seeking a comparative tradition in Russia, often portray the Slavophile/Westernizer debate in Russia as the principal nationalist discourse. Roman Szporluk argues, for example, that "there is a large and growing body of writings on Russian nationalism. . . . Under the Romanov empire, there were Slavophiles, Westernizers, and adherents of 'Official Nationality,' as well as *pochven-n'iky* [ideologues of a 'return to the soil'], Pan-Slavs, liberal nationalists, and integral nationalists." [4]

But a historian's reading of those debates, examined on their own terms, came to a much different conclusion. Consider the standard reference on the Slavophile/Westernizer debate, that of Andrzej Walicki, who hardly mentions nationalism in his treatment of this extensive literature. For him, Slavophilism is not a nationalist but rather a conservative worldview, a style of thought antagonistic to bourgeois liberalism and the rationalistic-individualistic philosophy of the Enlightenment. In Slavophile doctrines, one might have expected an electoral affinity with rationalist and romantic defenders of the nation. Yet Slavophiles rejected Hegel's conceptions of the state and nation, which they saw as inimical to a way of life where "truly Christian" and unrationalized forms of social bonds still prevailed. The Slavophiles were closer to Herder in rejecting the Eurocentric premise of the Hegelians; but they rejected as well the relativist (i.e. nationalist) aspect of Herder. Not every nation, in Slavophile thinking, had its own particular contribution. They sought a "truly Christian" universalism and believed in "absolute truth," which they saw as incarnated in the Russian people. In Walicki's judgment, "the Slavophile/Westernizer controversy . . . had certain distinctive features of its own. . . . The quarrel between the conservative romantics (including the Slavophiles) and the Hegelians was essentially a dispute over rationalism, whereas the conflict between the Slavophiles and Westernizers was largely about the concept of personality." Neither debate was about nationalism. Slavophilism, Walicki concludes, is best seen as a "backward-looking utopia[nism]."[5]

[2] Richard Wortman, *Scenarios of Power: Myth and Ceremony in Russian Monarchy*, vol. 1, *From Peter the Great to the Death of Nicholas I* (Princeton: Princeton University Press, 1995). But Hans Rogger, cited by Ronald Suny in his lecture "Russia, the Soviet Union, and Theories of Empires" (Center for International Security and Arms Control, Stanford University, 1996), points out that in the reign of Anna, Russian nobles bitterly resented the high positions in court that were held by German barons, and Peter I was being remembered as an "authentic Russian."

[3] On Peter I, see Wortman, *Scenarios of Power*, vol. 1. On the Orthodox Church, this is my summary of the position taken by John Shelton Curtiss, *The Russian Church and the Soviet State, 1917–1950* (Boston: Little, Brown, 1953).

[4] Roman Szporluk, "Dilemmas of Russian Nationalism," *Problems of Communism* 38 (July–August 1989): 15.

[5] Andrzej Walicki, *The Slavophile Controversy: History of a Conservative Utopia in Nineteenth-Century Russian Thought*, trans. Hilda Andrews-Rusiecka (Oxford: Clarendon, 1975), pp. 3, 330, 333, 336, 601. Peter Bushkovitch confirms this view in his unpublished paper "What Is Russia? Russian

In the nineteenth and early twentieth centuries, nationalist traditions were hardly resonant in Russia. To be sure, nationalist doctrines appeared in intellectual circles. The conservative nationalists, such as Mikhail Katkov (1818–87) in his newspaper *Moskovskie vedomosti*, conceived Russian identity as state-centered and called for the russification of society. But his arguments, Peter Bushkovitch points out, had little popular appeal. Later on, the so-called *Landmarks* group associated with Nikolai Berdiaev constructed a nationalist doctrine to respond to the growth of Marxism that "called for a return to religious, aesthetic, and spiritual values" of Russia. But this call had as little resonance in Russian society as Katkov's articles had had. Pavel Miliukov, the author of a three-volume work on Russian culture, responded to Berdiaev by arguing that nationalism in Russia was weak, and he attributed this to a lack of well-defined Russian symbols. He wrote that the Landmarks group's attempt to create a Russian nationalism was at best "artificial." Indeed, Berdiaev understood the constraints he faced, as he himself noted that reactionary tsarist rule had deformed the national identity of the adherents of the liberation movement, producing a revulsion against the very idea of a "nation." Similarly, Nikolai Bukharin, despite his antiliberal philosophy, agreed with Miliukov on the fact of a weak nationalism "among the Russian masses," and said that they had "not yet awakened to patriotism." In a sensitive summary, Ronald Suny concludes: "Though tsarist Russia succeeded in building a state, it succeeded too well in building an empire and failed to create a 'Russian nation' within that empire."[6]

Historical sociology has ventured where standard historiography will not tread. There is no major historical work on the theme of the sources of Russian nationalism largely because there is no such history on its own terms. This is not to say that there have been no nationalist sentiments in Russia, or sociological phenomena functionally equivalent to nationalism. But it is the historical sociologists who are not themselves specialists in Russia who have analyzed these phenomena in terms of a nationalist discourse.[7]

One Tradition or Many?

Tracing the historical roots of nationalist sentiments, even where there are strong traditions of nationalist discourse, carries with it thorny methodological

---

National Consciousness and the State, 1500–1917," p. 12. "The Slavophiles," he writes, "failed to fully establish a tradition of ethnic, rather than statist, identity for Russia."

[6] On Katkov, see Bushkovitch, "What Is Russia?" p. 12. On Berdiaev, Miliukov, and Bukharin, see Frederick C. Barghoorn, *Soviet Russian Nationalism* (New York: Oxford University Press, 1956). The judgment about Berdiaev's views is from Victor Zaslavsky, "The Evolution of Separatism in Soviet Society under Gorbachev," in Gail W. Lapidus et al., eds., *From Union to Commonwealth: Nationalism and Separatism in the Soviet Republics* (New York: Cambridge University Press, 1992), p. 86. The quotation is from Suny, "Russia, the Soviet Union, and Theories of Empires."

[7] I rely principally on the work of two sociologists, Reinhard Bendix and Liah Greenfeld, both of whom write about Russian nationalism in a comparative context. See Reinhard Bendix, *Kings or People* (Berkeley: University of California Press, 1978); Liah Greenfeld, "The Formation of the Russian National Identity: The Role of Status Insecurity and *Ressentiment*," *Comparative Studies in Society and History* 32, no. 3 (1990): 549–91.

problems. There is a tendency to paint a still portrait of a national culture as it currently exists, search out strands in that country's past that can plausibly be linked to the present, and announce the discovery of a nationalist tradition. Consider this portrayal of the Russian tradition by Andrei Sinyavsky. He begins with a quotation from the memoirs of Grand Duke Aleksandr Mikhailovich, recalling a moment in his youth, in 1885. "My spiritual apparatus was burdened," Mikhailovich wrote, "with a strange excess of hate. . . . It was not my fault that I hated Jews, Poles, Swedes, Germans, the English, and the French. I blame the Orthodox Church and the doctrine of official patriotism that was drummed into my head during twelve years of study."

Sinyavsky uses evidence of this sort to claim that Russian great-power xenophobia led directly to Soviet communism. The Russian "national character," he argues, required mixing "Russian patriotism" with mysticism. For him, the diverse references to "poor Russia," to "great, powerful Rus'," to "the might of the Soviets," all convey this same patriotic idea, drenched with messianic mysticism. Russian patriotism is inevitably xenophobic, and Sinyavsky demonstrates this by saying that Russian thinking separates everything into "ours" and "the other" (*svoi* and *chuzhoi*). Thus the long tradition of calling foreigners "mute" (*nemoi*) and Tatars the "damned." Xenophobia even became part of the internationalist ideology of Soviet rule, leading to such absurdities as "We Russians are better than everyone else because we live worse than everyone else." Thus hatred is combined with envy. After the invasion of Czechoslovakia in 1968, Sinyavsky remembers hearing Russians saying, "They were right to do it! What did those Czechs lack? They lived better than us Russians. Nothing's enough for them!" Even in the period of perestroika, Sinyavsky saw the rise of nationalism as having fascist connotations. This is because in his Russia, there is a single nationalist tradition, which can only feed anti-Semitism and xenophobia.[8]

Sinyavsky's diatribe lacks nuance, but the attempt to explain the present by portraying a coherent picture of the past is a common methodological error. Consider Reinhard Bendix's masterful *Kings or People*. In this work, the value on the dependent variable—the nature of political authority—for each country he considered was well known. England, for example, was a democratic state of long standing with vibrant local institutions, whereas Russia was (at the time of the writing) an autocratic state with no civil society. The task of tracing the historical bases of the nature of political authority is inevitably biased by one's knowledge of those outcomes. Bendix's leitmotif for premodern England is "balance" between king and barons; his leitmotif for premodern Russia is patrimonial rule that supersedes all local authority. One can't help wondering whether, if the outcomes in the twentieth century had been reversed, historical sociologists would trace different branches from the historical roots (of English authoritarianism and Russian democracy) to find equally compelling narratives linking the past to the present.

[8] Andrei Sinyavsky, "Russian Nationalism," *Radio Liberty Research Bulletin*, December 19, 1988, pp. 25–35.

One way to avoid this methodological problem is to recognize the complex root system that underlies all national cultures, allowing for a variety of culturally supported presents.[9] Just as present-day sociologists can appropriate different aspects of a cultural tradition to make a link between the past and the present, present-day nationalists can pick and choose from their own traditions to support different sorts of political programs. In light of this point, I propose to trace two strands of Russian nationalism, with quite different emphases. One of those strands—with its focus on the Russian soul—appears natural and appropriate for Russians now living in Russia, while the other—with its focus on Russian internationalism—rings true for Russians in the near abroad. Both are equally "authentic," yet each supports a distinct political program.[10]

Historical Trends in Russian Nationalism

Both of the strands that I shall trace travel a route from Orthodoxy and geography to a particular form of authority that Bendix calls "plebiscitarian domination." I shall begin with Orthodoxy. Its legacy was a system of unquestioned authority that gave unswerving support to the tsars. Since the major doctrinal disputes in Europe had ended by the time Byzantine missionaries came to Kiev Rus' in the ninth century, Russia got Christianity in an uncontested form. Emphasis therefore was on ritual rather than on belief or theological exegesis. Indeed, many of the clergy were practically illiterate. The Church, unquestioned in its own realm, gave its full support to autocratic rule in Russia. Thus Russia's rulers derived their authority from God and did not require further support to legitimate their domination. With the fall of the Byzantine empire, the heads of the Russian Church were elected by a synod of Russian bishops, and their election was confirmed by the grand prince of Moscow, further tying together unquestioned orthodoxy and unquestioned autocracy.[11] The automatic equation of Orthodoxy and Russianness—

[9] I address this problem in David Laitin and Guadalupe Rodríguez, "Language, Ideology, and the Press in Catalonia," *American Anthropologist* 94, no. 1 (1992): 25. This article shows that it is currently of use to Catalan nationalists to emphasize the cultural tradition of *seny* (feet-on-the-ground practicality) and to deemphasize the equally available tradition of *rauxa* (impulsiveness, and quickness to anger and revenge). Historians are increasingly aware of the necessity of elucidating cultural roots that have fallen (perhaps only temporarily) into disuse. For an exemplary treatment of these themes, see Prasenjit Duara, *Rescuing History from the Nation* (Chicago: University of Chicago Press, 1995).

[10] I do not claim to be the only interpreter of the multiple strands of Russian nationalist thinking. Although Frederick Barghoorn, in *Soviet Russian Nationalism*, refers to "traditional" Russian nationalism as if it were a coherent doctrine, his analysis of that tradition leads him to see several distinct strands. See chap. 6, especially pp. 149–50. Since Dunlop's treatment of the nationalist tradition is different from the standard line of Sinyavsky, multiple strands can be woven by juxtaposing the two interpretations. See John Dunlop, *The Faces of Contemporary Russian Nationalism* (Princeton: Princeton University Press, 1983). For the only systematic attempt to compare national self-consciusness in Russia as compared to the Union republics, see Iu. V. Arutiunian et al., *Russkie: Etno-sotsiologicheskie ocherki* (Moscow: Nauka, 1992), chap. 7.

[11] Bendix, *Kings or People*, pp. 94–106.

such that Feodor Dostoyevsky could write that "he who is not Orthodox cannot be Russian"[12]—undoubtedly goes back to the time when Orthodoxy itself was unquestioned in Russia.

Geography had a parallel legacy. Russia's vast steppes exposed it to marauding raiders from the east and organized armies from the west. This susceptibility to foreign invasions—in which local villages were thoroughly indefensible—led to near total reliance on state authority for protection, and therefore the concentration of Muscovite authority, which was able to neglect local government and estate managers. Tsars were able to extract service from the aristocrats in return for state recognition of their ranks. With local authority decimated by the fifteenth century, Ivan IV in the sixteenth century deported and resettled landed nobles as he pleased, thus destroying any remaining vestiges of local independence.[13]

The system of authority that emerges from this orthodox and centralized tradition Bendix calls "plebiscitarian domination." This is his term for "modern, one-party dictatorships in which governments typically rule in the name of the people." "The extension of this term to nineteenth-century Russia," he admits, "may be awkward, since the tsars ruled over the people in the name of God; but the patriarchal claim of being the father of his people implies quasi-plebiscitarianism in the sense that the tsars periodically appealed to the people for declarations of loyalty by acclamation."[14]

Plebiscitarian domination as a system of rule, exemplified in the reign of Nicholas I, ensured social order at the expense of economic and social development. Nicholas's "Official Nationality" proclamation declared Orthodoxy, Autocracy, and Nationality as the three principles of his governing doctrine.[15] This doctrine could hold at bay the successors to the Decembrists, who threatened the monarchy after the death of Nicholas's elder brother, Alexander I, in 1825. Order was restored for nearly a century, but the doctrine of Official Nationality could not yield reform or economic development, which required local initiative and freedom of movement. Consequently Russia fell further behind Western Europe. Russian nationalism emerged under the trying conditions of plebiscitarian domination and economic backwardness.

It is here that the two strands of Russian nationalism relevant to my concerns begin to diverge. The dominant strand focuses on the political and psychological

[12] Quoted in Natalia Dinello, "Religious Attitudes of Russian Minorities and National Identity," in Vladimir Shlapentokh, Munir Sendich, and Emil Payin, eds., *The New Russian Diaspora* (Armonk, N.Y.: M. E. Sharpe, 1994), p. 198.

[13] Bendix, *Kings or People*, pp. 107, 114, 125.

[14] Ibid., p. 524.

[15] The term *narodnost'* is usually glossed as "nationality" when the reference is to Nicholas's 1833 proclamation. "Russianness" was not the reference; rather it was the people's acclamation for a regime built on principles of orthodoxy and autocracy. See Nicholas V. Riasanovsky, *A History of Russia* (New York: Oxford University Press, 1984), p. 324. To be sure, Nicholas's "Official Nationality" had as part of its program the use of Russian in the court, and Russian language and history became required subjects at the university. See Suny, "Russia, the Soviet Union, and Theories of Empires," p. 14. But this requirement was intended more to keep out Western (especially liberal French) ideas than to promote a sense of a Russian nation.

problems facing "late developers"[16] as their leaders seek to maintain national integrity under conditions of near total emulation of the economic front-runners. Russia is perhaps the classic case of this phenomenon. In their first encounters with the West, Russian nobles admired and copied much of what they saw. Throughout Peter I's reign, in the late eighteenth century, an optimistic belief that Russia would copy, equal, and then surpass the West forestalled any sense of inferiority—for a time. In Liah Greenfeld's interpretation, this slow recognition of inferiority led to both shame and denial. For example, in a letter to Voltaire in 1769, Catherine claimed that there was no hunger in Russia; rather, she wrote, Russian peasants are overfed with chickens. Denials, Greenfeld asserts, were psychologically unfulfilling, because the speakers knew them to be lies.

The next step, Greenfeld reasons, was to present equality with the West as undesirable or unsuitable. This trend began around the end of the eighteenth century. N. Karamzin, for example, wrote that there ought to be a better history of Russia than the French one written by Levesque. He hoped for a substitute written by a Russian (in Greenfeld's gloss) "which would emphasize the uniqueness of Russia and show its equality to Europe not because it is like it, but because there is a distinctively Russian parallel to everything European of note."

But there was no solace in equality, for there was no equality, and so this last attitude gave way to *ressentiment*, a term Greenfeld borrows from Nietzsche that refers to "a psychological state resulting from suppressed feelings of envy and hatred (existential envy) and the impossibility to satisfy these feelings (to get revenge or act them out)." If the costs of catching up with the model are so high, Russian nobles reasoned, given low local resources for cultural and material development, the best course is to hate the model and reject it as evil. Those who admired the West were dubbed people of "self-contempt," and foreigners living in Russia were equally held in contempt.

This ressentiment made its subjects feel good, but it did not solve their problems. Still needed was "the construction of an identity with which one could live." A transvaluation of values—that is, a change in the value scale so that the supreme values in the original scale are denigrated, while formerly nonexistent or unimportant values are elevated to the status of new supreme values—made possible a new image of Russia. The West became the antimodel, and for each of its vices there was a hidden Russian virtue. Because rationality required liberty and equality, and Russia did not have liberty or equality, its intellectuals now rejected rationality altogether; and instead they glorified the life of feeling, the hyperbolic.

Thus, to handle the problem of backwardness, Russian patriots argued that Russia had been spared the curse of too much civilization. For their discourse they invented the concept of the "people." Fixation on the "soul," which was held to have derived from "blood and soil," led these patriots, through a kind of deductive logic,

[16] The classic statement of Russian "late development" is that of Alexander Gerschenkron, *Economic Backwardness in Historical Perspective* (Cambridge: Harvard University Press, 1962). For the relationship of late development to ideologies of nationalism, see Ernst Haas, "Nationalism: An Instrumental Social Construction," *Millennium* 22, no. 3 (1993): 505–46.

to the peasants. After all, the peasants had nothing but blood and soil. Their soul—and consequently their expression of Russian nationality—was Russia at its purest.

This enigmatic Slavic soul was useful, Greenfeld reasons, because "nobody could deny the Russian nation a superiority which expressed itself in the world beyond the apparent." It is thus the convoluted logic of ressentiment, and not sympathy for the peasantry, that made the peasant a symbol of the Russian nation. If the spirit of the nation resided in the "people," it was nonetheless revealed through the medium of the educated elite, which, apparently, had the ability to divine it. The special individuals who knew what the people wanted naturally had the right to dictate to the masses, who, while pure, could not know what to do.[17] In the resulting mélange of nationalist ideologies, with all participants in bitter contest with the Westernizers, orthodoxy and populism were somehow combined (by the so-called Slavophiles, who, as we saw, were fighting different battles) to represent a Slavic alternative. This might not lead to development but it was guaranteed to provide redemption.

There is a second strand of nationalism that also flows from Russia's late development. As I pointed out in Chapter 2, late political development in Russia had consequences for the assimilation of peripheral nationalities into Russian culture. States that developed first were able to rationalize language—requiring use of the court's language in all official domains—before the state's activities entered into the daily lives of the nonelite populations. When mass education was introduced as a state function, it was institutionally preordained that the state language would be the common medium of instruction. Later developers, however, in order to perform functions that were considered normal for states, had to provide public education before language in their states had been fully rationalized. Under these conditions, local elites and parents could be quickly mobilized against what they perceived as linguistic imposition. Late developers therefore faced great pressure to provide education through the medium of local or regional languages.[18]

In the nineteenth century, the Russian state was not directly involved in providing free and universal primary education. In a Ministry of Education conference in 1911, in which the widespread development of pubic education was the topic, state authorities were compelled to recognize the linguistic diversity of the realm and to offer instruction in the languages of the peoples of the various *gubernii*.[19] Rationalization of Russian, then, remained incomplete. Unlike France, Russia was to

[17] Greenfeld, "Formation." One need not accept Greenfeld's full psychological story—as I do not—to accept her overall analysis that the conditions of backwardness lead to ambivalences about the culture of the leading states and a search for a countermodel of catch-up. Bendix's account emphasizes the "bad conscience" that troubles all privileged elites in backward environments, provoking among them a populism and glorification of the people.

[18] This is the argument in David D. Laitin, *Language Repertoires and State Construction in Africa* (New York: Cambridge University Press, 1992). It is applied to Russia in David D. Laitin, Roger Petersen, and John Slocum, "Language and the State: Russia and the Soviet Union in Comparative Perspective," in Alexander Motyl, ed., *Thinking Theoretically about Soviet Nationalities* (New York: Columbia University Press, 1992), pp. 129–68.

[19] John Slocum, "The Boundaries of National Identity: Religion, Language, and Nationality in Late Tsarist Russia" (Ph.D. diss., University of Chicago, 1993).

consolidate itself as a multinationality state. Thus late nineteenth- and early twentieth-century state development in Russia compelled a distinction between a Russian as a subject of a political entity (*Rossiia*), which was itself a vast multinational state, and as a person of the nationality (*russkii*) that was at the core of the Russian state, but not the sole nationality of that state. A dual or ambiguous national identity emerged: Russians were both ethnic Russians and subjects of a state that was Russia, in which Russians were "elder brothers" to a wide variety of nationality groups that were not *russkie*, but only *rossiiskie*.

This identity as an "elder brother" within a continental Russian state is nearly placeless. The continental citizen knows no locality. I was shocked at first to discover that virtually none of my Russian-speaking informants in Estonia could relate to a specific place as their family home. Later I learned that this is a commonplace among people with a Russian identity. With the medieval destruction of local institutions and identities, few Russians in Russia identify with a particular locale (as a totally assimilated Frenchman might relate to Gascony or the Midi).[20] There is then a strand of Russian nationalism that sees nearly the entire Eurasian continent as its natural home. Russians, in this frame, are part of an internationalist nationality.

This internationality character of Russia—often phrased in terms of empire-consciousness—forms the basis of a second strand of Russian nationalism. It helps explain the rather uncomplicated cover of a "Soviet" nationality after the Bolshevik Revolution. To most Russians, it seemed natural that each of the "other" republics would have its own Communist Party, its own Academy of Sciences, and its own capital city, but Russians would have the Soviet or all-Union variants. In many surveys in the final years of the Soviet Union, over 70 percent of Russians, no matter where they lived, claimed that the Soviet Union (not Russia) was their "motherland."[21]

Russian Nationalism in Russia and the Near Abroad after 1987

These two strands of Russian nationalism coexisted, albeit with tension, throughout the Soviet period and continue today. Frederick Barghoorn portrays the issue as a juxtaposition of "Russian" and "Soviet" elements, leading to confusion that "reflects an insoluble contradiction of Soviet ideology derived from the fact that one national culture, interpreted by a single government, is arbitrarily combined with Marxist universalism."[22] Lenin represented the side of Marxist universalism, unequivocally expressed in his tract "On the National Pride of the Great

[20] Sheila Fitzpatrick, in a personal communication, informs me that though her observations generally corroborate this point, Russians in both Moscow and St. Petersburg identify rather strongly with their cities. Perhaps in Siberia and the Urals as well there are strong regional identifications.

[21] Leokadia Drobizheva, "Perestroika and the Ethnic Consciousness of Russians," in Lapidus et al., *From Union to Commonwealth,* pp. 101, 103.

[22] Barghoorn, *Soviet Russian Nationalism*, pp. 231–33, and see more generally chap. 8, "Soviet Chauvinism and Messianism."

Russians." This strand was indelibly sewn into the social fabric in the adoption of the "Internationale" as the anthem of the Communist Party of the Soviet Union.

But Russian messianism did not disappear. During the Second World War especially there was a revival of Russian themes. "The Russian component of Soviet messianism," Barghoorn explains, "places particular emphasis upon the claim that a Russian, Lenin, rendered unique . . . service to humanity by his application of . . . Marxism. . . . Russia is the chosen nation . . . duty bound to bring light and truth to the 'toilers' of those parts of the world who have not yet been saved from 'capitalist slavery.'" In order to justify the appropriation of Lenin as a Russian nationalist, chauvinists dug deep into his works. A *Red Star* article of 1943 reports that in exile, Lenin once reproached Gorky for having "forgotten Russia." Lenin was also reported to have said that "our" fishermen work more boldly than those in Capri. During the war, the state anthem, adopted in 1943, refers to "Great Rus'" as the source of the "unbreakable union of free republics."[23]

Throughout the Soviet period the "Russian" and "internationalist" traditions each waxed and waned. In the debates at the Tenth Party Congress in 1921, for example, Barghoorn found the terms "Russia" and its variants used 183 times; yet a post-1945 examination of the press showed a highly restricted use of the term "Russia" and its cognates. The editorials published in *Pravda* in February 1953, for example used "Stalin" 191 times, "Party" 37 times, and "American imperialist" 17 times, but "Russian" not even once.[24]

In more explicit debates about nationalism in the late Soviet period, the two strands are alternately separated and intertwined. Zaslavsky, in a commentary that divides the nationalist tradition in a way quite close to the line drawn herein, contrasts the *Novyi mir* group with the groups associated with *Molodaia gvardiia* and *Nash sovremennik*, which took up the banner of Russian patriotism, with a "contradictory complex of ideas . . . combining their genuine anguish for the destruction of Russian culture and the peasantry, the Russian Orthodox Church, and Russian traditions with a defense of a Stalinism which was seen as the legitimate continuation of Russian imperial traditions."[25] Thus within the two patriotic groups, both strands of nationalism and imperialism are intertwined, and both of them distinct from the *Novyi mir* tradition, which represents the Westernizer branch of the Slavophile debate.

Roman Szporluk has portrayed the late Soviet nationalist debate as one between the "empire savers" and the "nation-builders." The former includes right-wingers (Russian chauvinists) and left-wingers (Marxist internationalists). The nation-builders did not all agree on the boundaries of the Russian nation, but all saw it as distinct from the empire. In terms quite close to the ones guiding the analysis in this book, Szporluk suggests that the Russians in the Baltics are like the Germans in Bohemia, Slovenia, and other regions of the Habsburg empire before 1918, where indigenous nationalist movements were a threat to the Germans not simply

[23] Ibid., pp. 41, 236–37.
[24] Ibid., pp. 29–30, 59.
[25] Zaslavsky, "Evolution of Separatism," pp. 80–81.

as Germans—that is, as one of the many ethnic groups—but also as representatives of imperial authority. These Russians in the Baltics, Szporluk suggests, demonstrate a sentiment not Russian but (in the words of Sergey Grigoryants) "unquestionably Soviet," living not only in a country different from Russia but in a "potentially rebellious province." While one might want to discount Szporluk's evaluation of the Baltic variation as "abnormal," he has clearly separated the two strands of nationalism that can be traced back to Russia's traditions.[26]

One hypothesis that follows from this historical discussion is that there should be links between the Russian traditions and nationalism in the post-Soviet period, but the way the traditions are appropriated should depend on the context. As Szporluk suggests, Russian nationalism in Russia itself should differ from the Russian nationalism of the near abroad.

Religion and Language

Throughout this book, I have demonstrated that the double cataclysm in the near abroad brought to preeminence the linguistic aspect of the political identities of the Russian populations that live in the former union republics. In Russia itself, leaving aside the former ASSRs, language is not an issue. To be sure, the status of Russian in Russia was historically quite low. This is best exemplified by the use of French among the nobility through much of the nineteenth century, despite the heroic efforts of M. V. Lomonosov. Lomonosov, in the mid–eighteenth century, passionately argued that as a great world language, Russian should supplant German as the language of scholarly work in the Russian Academy of Sciences. Lomonosov's panegyrics were reprinted time and again in the mid-1930s, along with repeated references to the supposed fact that Marx himself had begun to study Russian. By 1944, the Central Committee of the Communist Party of the Soviet Union, still seeking to establish the status of Russian, published a book by a noted philologist called *The Mighty Russian Language*.[27] But by the 1980s, Russian was the unquestioned language of inter-nationality communication and scientific advance in Russia. Language therefore has played virtually no role in the reassertion of Russian nationalism within Russia.

Yet the Orthodox aspect of Russian identities, quite marginalized for seventy-five years, has taken on a new and powerful meaning. After 1987, with Marxism-Leninism in decline in Russia, John Dunlop observed, "Russian conservatives found themselves increasingly looking to the Russian Orthodox Church as an institution that might potentially play a helpful role in propping up the unity of the Soviet state." In 1990, Ivan Polozkov, a Russian Communist Party leader, termed the Church "a natural ally of the CPSU in the struggle for moral values and against interethnic conflicts." Walter Laqueur has noted how strange this alliance was between Russian nationalists (who despise Lenin, as déraciné) and neo-Stalinists (who would not be

[26] Szporluk, "Dilemmas of Russian Nationalism," pp. 15–35. Szporluk quotes from Sergey Grigoryants, "The Russian National Movement," *Russkaia mysl'*, May 12, 1989, p. 6.

[27] Barghoorn, *Soviet Russian Nationalism*, pp. 252–53, 256.

caught dead in a church). But because of a common desire to save the state, Orthodox imagery has become quite popular, even fashionable, in Russian society, in groups as far apart as conservative communists and radical nationalists.[28] Kathy Rousselet points out that even President Yeltsin in his liberal period mixed with religious officials in order to garner political legitimacy.[29]

The neo-Orthodox move in Russian nationalism was hardly preordained, for a number of reasons. First, few Russians practice Orthodoxy. Second, the Church is not very "Russian." In 1988, 4,000 of the Church's registered parishes were in Ukraine—most of them in western Ukraine!—and only about 2,000 in Russia proper. Aleksei, who became patriarch of the Church in 1990, is equally foreign. He is the son of a russified Baltic German father and a Russian mother and was brought up in Estonia. He is fluent in German and Estonian—hardly a symbol of Russian purity. And to make matters even more foreign, there is a vibrant movement in Russia to ally with the Russian Orthodox Church Abroad (whose metropolitan lives in New York). The Orthodox Church today can at best be considered quasi-Russian. Third, the Church since 1990 has become egregiously out of touch with on-the-ground realities in Russia. Aleksei more or less supported the military assault on Lithuania and allied himself in a public statement with the activists in the August 1991 putsch. Despite these negatives, the Church gets vital support from right-wing nationalists in Russia, and its imagery gets appropriated by liberals as well.[30]

It would be incorrect, furthermore, as the survey data will show, to argue that these feelings that Orthodoxy equals Russianness are absent from Russians in the near abroad. In data analyzed by Natalia Dinello, Russian minorities in surveys conducted in 1991 in the Baltics, Ukraine, and Central Asia have more trust in the Russian Orthodox Church than in any other institution, with complete trust claimed by 45.3 percent of respondents in the Baltics, 44.4 percent in Ukraine, and 43.8 percent in Central Asia. These figures are higher than those Americans accord their religious institutions.[31]

Yet because Russians, at least in the Baltics and Kazakhstan, have been thrown into the same boat with Ukrainians, Jews, and Poles (many of whom are not Orthodox), it is politically inconvenient to rely on religious symbols (no matter how strongly they resonate) for purposes of consolidating new political identities. Thus, in the fieldwork reported in Chapters 4–6, we saw very little evidence of the political use of Orthodox symbolic material.

Ukraine is somewhat of an exception, given the incident reported in Chapter 6 regarding the "burial" of Patriarch Volodymyr at the St. Sophia complex in Kyiv. Data collected by Vicki Hesli and her colleagues show that religious identification

[28] This alliance is discussed and Laqueur quoted in John B. Dunlop, *The Rise of Russia and the Fall of the Soviet Empire* (Princeton: Princeton University Press, 1993), pp. 158, 129.

[29] Kathy Rousselet, "Anomie, recherche identitaire et religion en Russie," *Social Compass* 41, no. 1 (1994): 140.

[30] The material on the foreignness of the Church and on Aleksei is from Dunlop, *Rise of Russia*, pp. 159–62.

[31] Dinello, "Religious Attitudes," p. 195.

in Ukraine (Russian Orthodox, Greek Catholic, Ukrainian Autocephalous, nonbelievers, and atheists) can explain a variety of political values (party identification, relations with Russia, and willingness to use Ukrainian troops to maintain stability abroad), and these relationships hold up even if you control for language, region, age, gender, and income. Given the associations between Autocephalous membership and Ukrainianism and between Russian Orthodox membership with desire for reintegration, it is easy to imagine how religion could supplant language as the fulcrum for the national purification of Ukraine. Yet the extremely large number of respondents in this survey who claim to be nonbelievers makes the notion of an all-encompassing, religiously defined mobilization not fully plausible.[32]

Although taken from surveys done in the near abroad, two of Dinello's findings speak directly to the issue of Russian nationalism in Russia and its relation to Orthodoxy. Using regression analysis, she found that the choice of Orthodoxy as a criterion of Russianness increases the odds of agreeing with the statement "The fact that I am Russian is of primary value to me" by 80 percent, and the preference for Russian over Soviet citizenship by 23 percent. Furthermore, in another regression analysis, those who saw Russianness as a cultural category favored both Soviet and Russian identities; but those who saw it as religious "unequivocally" had a Russian identity.[33] Thus Orthodoxy is strongly associated with a Russian (and much less so with a Soviet) identity. To be sure, the percentage of Russians who identify themselves as Orthodox had decreased even between 1990 and 1991. Furthermore, the percentage of Russians (around 9 percent) who desire an official state church is small. Yet, as Kathy Rousselet shows, Orthodox imagery is experiencing a renaissance in Russia. Vladimir Osipov's political party "for the spiritual and biological health of Russia" and more generally the prevalence of its symbols in a "federating" ideology (i.e., in reintegrating the former Union)—make religion a ubiquitous element in post-Soviet Russian identity projects.[34] Orthodoxy has become a linchpin of nationalist expression in Russia. It might—though I think it unlikely—even supplant language and region as the principal basis for social identities in Ukraine, but will continue to play a minor role (next to language) among nontitulars in the three other states of the near abroad.

Inclusive (Soviet) and Exclusive (Russian) Nationalist Imagery

Russian nationalism has a strong exclusivist strain in Russia, while in the near abroad it has a more inclusive (or maybe nationalist-subsuming) strain. This has a lot to do with the context of state collapse. As Michael Urban has pointed out, reconstruction of identities has been more difficult in Russia than in Eastern Europe or the former Union republics. This is because in the dual aspect of reconstruction—the positive expression of nation and the negative expression of rooting out

[32] Vicki L. Hesli et al., "The National Nexus: Religion, Language and Political Values in Ukraine" (paper prepared for the Annual Meeting of the American Political Science Association, San Francisco, 1996).

[33] Dinello, "Religious Attitudes," pp. 200–203.

[34] Rousselet, "Anomie," pp. 140, 144.

that which is alien—Russia lacked easy reference to the latter, while the other republics all had "Russians as communists" to serve them well in developing a common reconstructed identity.[35] Russian nationalists in Russia had to rely more heavily, then, on finding cultural traditions than on distinguishing themselves from outsiders. This is surely one source of the strong post-Soviet trend of nationalist exclusivity in Russian nationalist expressions. It helps explain why President Yeltsin moved to establish the two-headed eagle, the symbol of the tsarist empire, as the new state emblem.[36]

The difference between the exclusivist and internationalist strands comes out clearly in the debate between Andranik Migranyan (an Armenian who served in Yeltsin's Presidential Council) and Aleksandr Tsipko, working for the Gorbachev Foundation. Migranyan published an article in *Znamiia* saying that

> very soon it would be possible to rule out the concept of the Russian [*rossiiskaia*] idea and say the Russian [*russkaia*] idea . . . because—no matter how odd it might look—if we consider the national composition of our republics, after Armenia and Belarus', Russia is the third of the fifteen republics where the indigenous population amounts to 83 percent. Look at Georgia: they claim to be a national Georgian state with only about 70 percent Georgians living there. . . . And why should 83 percent of the Russians in the RSFSR be the Russian [*rossiiskoe*] state but not the Russian [*russkoe*] state.

Tsipko, appalled by Migranyan's exclusivist analysis, responded that

> the Russians preserved the state—by losing their national traditions and national memory. . . . It is not accidental that "Russian" is an adjective that denotes belonging to a particular culture, history and . . . state, rather than to an ethnos. The present-day Russian language and the present-day Russian culture present a product of the last 200 years, a product of the empire. Therefore, they rightly belong by right to all the ethnic groups inhabiting it.[37]

This debate—often framed in terms of a civic versus an ethnic definition of the nation—remains a hot one in Russia today. On the civic side are such figures as Valery Tishkov, once Yeltsin's minister of nationalities and currently director of the Institute of Ethnology and Anthropology of the Russian Academy of Sciences. He insists that "Russia is not a 'national state' of ethnic Russians." Rather, he proposes, "Rossia" is the real name of the country, and it is inhabited by "Rossians" (i.e.,

[35] Michael Urban, "The Politics of Identity in Russia's Postcommunist Transition: The Nation against Itself," *Slavic Review* 53, no. 3 (1994): 733.

[36] Mark Beissinger, "Demise of an Empire-State: Identity, Legitimacy, and the Deconstruction of Soviet Politics," in Crawford Young, ed., *The Rising Tide of Cultural Pluralism* (Madison: University of Wisconsin Press, 1993), p. 111. Gannadii Burbulis reports that Yeltsin insisted that "the eagle not look very evil."

[37] Andranik Migranyan, "In What Country Shall We Live?" *Znamiia*, no. 1 (1992). Tsipko quotes and rebuts Migranyan in "A New Russian Identity or Old Russia's Reintegration?" *Security Dialogue* 25, no. 4 (1994): 451–52.

citizens of Russia). Ethnic Russians, he insists, have no special claim to the country. On the ethnic side is Vladimir Lakshin, who is a literary critic and was a staunch liberal with the *Novyi mir* group in the 1960s, supporting the publication of Solzhenitsyn's work. In a series of articles in the 1990s, however, he wrote of the "funeral" procession for Russian culture and blames it on people who define themselves as *rossiiskii* (comparable to Rossian) rather than *russkii*. "And while we are ashamed of the word 'Russian,' " Lakshin ironically notes, "Americans use it to denote the Russian inhabitants of Brighton Beach." The question whether Russians are *russkie* or *rossiiskie* remains vital in Russia today.[38]

This debate has vast implications for the issue of inclusion of outsiders. Already in the late Soviet period, it was possible to discern the political divide among Russians on the exclusivist and internationalist dimension. Within the All-Union Congress of People's Deputies there was a voting bloc known as Soiuz (Union). Many of its leaders, such as Evgenii Kogan from Estonia and Anatolii Chekhoev, were not themselves Russians. Their message was internationalist, saving the Union. The comparable bloc in the RSFSR parliament was known as Rossiia, and it represented a far more purist "Russian" theme, with the stated goal of saving Russia.[39]

The exclusive strain of Russian nationalism manifested itself in multitudinous ways in the late Soviet period as well as in contemporary Russia. As early as 1964, underground groups such as the All-Russian Social-Christian Union for the Liberation of the People, using *Molodaia gvardiia* as its unofficial organ, spewed out anti-Semitic themes.[40] Russian nationalists in this pre-perestroika period were already strongly opposed to russification, as they saw ethnic merging (the ideology of the Brezhnev state) to be the route toward national impurity.[41] In the perestroika period, loud noises were made by the fringe organization Pamiat', with equally exclusivist anti-Semitic themes. Open expressions of Russian chauvinism became normal by this time. Vladislav Krasnov reports that in a Moscow art exhibition of the work of Il'ia Glazunov, there was a samizdat of visitor comments: "Here is the Russian spirit, here one senses the true Rus' "; "For the first time I felt proud to be a Russian"; "After 60 years of kike power [*zhidovskoe zasilie*], finally, one begins to smell Rus'! Long live the Russian state!"[42] Elsewhere, Leokadia Drobizheva reports that in the 1989 meetings of the All-Union Congress of People's Deputies, voices often blurted out, "Vote for *X*—he is a Russian."[43] This change in Russian imagery has

[38] Valery A. Tishkov, "What Is Rossia?" *Security Dialogue* 26, no. 1 (1995): 41–51; Vladimir Lakshin, "Rossiia i Russkie na svoikh pokhoronakh," *Nezavisimaia gazeta*, March 17, 1993. Eleanor Gilburd brought to my attention the recent papers of Lakshin.

[39] Dunlop, *Rise of Russia*, pp. 146ff.

[40] Dina Rome Spechler, "Russian Nationalism and Soviet Politics," in Lubomyr Hajda and Mark Beissinger, eds., *The Nationalities Factor in Soviet Politics and Society* (Boulder, Colo.: Westview, 1990), pp. 281–83. Enumerations of Russian nationalist groups formed in the 1980s are available in Dunlop, *Rise of Russia*, and Drobizheva, "Perestroika," p. 105.

[41] John B. Dunlop, "Language, Culture, Religion, and National Awareness," in Robert Conquest, ed., *The Last Empire: Nationality and the Soviet Future* (Stanford, Calif.: Hoover Institution Press, 1986), p. 271.

[42] Vladislav Krasnov, "Russian National Feeling: An Informal Poll," in Conquest, *Last Empire*, pp. 117–21.

[43] Drobizheva, "Perestroika," p. 104.

been quantitatively established. A content analysis of *Sovetskaia rossiia* shows that the frequency of the use of the term "Russian patriotism" increased fivefold from 1957–58 to the end of the 1980s, and the frequency of the use of old Russian folklore terms rose fourfold.[44]

Equally exclusivist were the reactions coming from Russians concerning refugees from the near abroad. In southern and central Russia especially, "Russian-speaking population" refers to non-Russians and nontitulars who were evacuated from dangerous zones in newly independent union republics. As was discussed in Chapter 10, in Russia, as opposed to the near abroad, "Russian-speaking population" is a derogatory term, and "pure" Russians use it only to refer to ethnic others.[45] These "Russian-speaking" immigrants were considered unwanted foreigners by the local populations.[46] Thus Russian nationalist concern is merely a theoretical one for the "Russians" suffering in the near abroad rather than an actual desire to bring them material relief or to reclaim the territories that they inhabit, or to give any aid to their local allies, the non-Russian, nontitular Russian-speakers. In 1991, when Moldova rejected a federalist structure and when the Baltic leaders withheld citizenship from Russians, Russians across the political spectrum in Russia were quick to point to these issues as cases of persecution of Russian minorities. These issues became a cause célèbre among nationalist politicians; throughout 1992 nationalist groups made ritual marches on the Moldovan and Baltic consulates in Moscow.[47] Popular nationalism in early 1990s Russia marked both the russianization (but not russification, as this term connotes an attempt to assimilate non-Russians) and, in Szporluk's words, the "de-Sovietization of Russia."[48]

Indeed, in the late communist period in Russia, a Soviet identification was used mostly in an ironic tone. A special derogatory term for those who were considered lazy, inert, well housed, and ideologically attached to the regime's pronouncements was *sovki*. But after the collapse of the Soviet Union, according to Igor Kon, the term "Soviet"—in Russian political discourse—became "meaningless."[49]

In contrast to the inward nationalism of Russians (or at least the more openly nationalist Russians) in Russia for whom "Soviet" no longer has meaning, the nationalism of Russians in the near abroad reflects internationalist imagery and a repackaging of the Soviet identity in a more positive light. In January 1989 in Latvia, John Dunlop records, the International Front's leader, Anatolii Balaichuk, said, "The

[44] Ibid., p. 107.

[45] This point was emphasized to me by Nikolai Rudensky, in a personal communication. Elise Giuliano, "Nationality and Russian Federal Integrity," qualifying paper, University of Chicago, 1996, quotes a Russian deputy in the Tatar parliament complaining about the draft constitution: "They are trying to make me not a Russian Federation citizen or a Tatar Republic citizen but a nonindigenous person, a member of the so-called Russian-speaking population. It is bad enough that this is downright insulting" (Vladimir Morokin, reported in *Rossiiskaia gazeta*, February 7, 1992).

[46] For examples, see Vladimir Mukomel, "Demographic Problems of Russian Adaptation in the Republics of the Former Soviet Union," in Shlapentokh et al., *New Russian Diaspora*, pp. 155–68; and Aleksandr Susokolov, "Russian Refugees and Migrants in Russia," ibid., pp. 183–94.

[47] Mark Beissinger, "The Persisting Ambiguity of Empire," *Post-Soviet Affairs* 11, no. 2 (1995): 165.

[48] Quoted in Beissinger, "Demise of an Empire-State," p. 97.

[49] Igor Kon, "Identity Crisis and Postcommunist Psychology," *Symbolic Interaction* 16, no. 4 (1993): 400.

Latvian Interfront differs from the Latvian Popular Front in its assessment of the leading role of the Communist Party of the Soviet Union in society and in its defense of the principle of internationalism." In an epigraph Dunlop records the voice of "a heavy-set [Russian, who] was recounting how he had ended up in Latvia. And he kept repeating: 'I did not move to Latvia, I went to the Soviet Union.'" Later on, Dunlop quotes from a variety of Interfront leaders of Estonia. Evgenii Kogan, the leading spokesman for the Estonian Intermovement, fervently spoke about "Soviet man." "One hears voices," he said, "which claim that there is no such concept as the Soviet people (*narod*)! But I can produce as much evidence as you want to prove that such a people does exist." Dunlop points out that there is truth to Kogan's claim. *Sovetskaia Rossiia* published a poll in Estonia in which 78 percent of the Russians and Russian-speakers considered themselves to be "in the first place Soviet people." Or in the words of Mikhail Lysenko, chairman of the Council of Strike Committees in Estonia, "I consider myself to be a citizen of the Soviet Union."[50] There are no traces of anti-Semitism (indeed, Kogan is Jewish) or antititular prejudices in these high-minded expressions.

Perhaps in too strongly distinguishing these two strands of Russian nationalism, I have neglected their overlap, possibly most articulately exemplified in the career of Vladimir Zhirinovskii. Zhirinovskii had a Soiuz-type profile with his Jewish roots and his upbringing in Kazakhstan. In April 1991, when forty-four delegates of the LDP nominated him for the RSFSR presidency, many of the delegates came from Ukraine, Belarus', Lithuania, Latvia, and Uzbekistan. The irony of a candidate for the Russian presidency being nominated by residents of foreign countries has often been noted. Yet his nationalist message was of the most inward type. On TV he said, in one of his early addresses, "Russians today are the most insulted, disgraced, and abused nation."[51] What this suggests is that it is the *context* of the nationalist message (coming from within Russia or from the near abroad) rather than the deep feelings of the spokesman that determines which nationalist strain is cultivated. It further suggests that as internationalist Russians migrate to Russia from the near abroad, they will be more xenophobic than the Russians who have never left Russia.[52]

Russia as a Great Power

National political cultures are best understood not as sets of values that all members must uphold but rather as "points of concern" over which members think it most worthwhile to debate.[53] Seen in this light, Russian nationalism in Russia can be seen as being consumed by the debate over Russia's future role as a great power. Meanwhile, Russian nationalism in the near abroad can be thought of as being consumed by the debate over what category of minority they belong to.

[50] Dunlop, *Rise of Russia*, pp. 123, 139, 137–38.

[51] Quoted ibid., pp. 155–56.

[52] This point is suggested by Lev Gudkov, "The Structure and Character of Migration of Russians from the Former Republics of the USSR," in Shlapentokh et al., *New Russian Diaspora*, p. 180.

[53] This term is borrowed from Thomas Metzger, and I develop it in David D. Laitin, *Hegemony and Culture* (Chicago: University of Chicago Press, 1986).

While Russians in the near abroad speculate and argue about the need for the reintegration of the Soviet Union, this is not the debate that encapsulates their primary concerns. More important to them is the question of what sort of minority they constitute. Are they a people without a country (with passports from a defunct state), a legitimate minority within an equally legitimate nationalizing state, or a beached diaspora, awaiting high tide? In Mark Beissinger's terms, are they part of a *russkoiazychnoe* population united among themselves by linguistic marginalization, or are they *sootechestvenniky* (co-fatherlanders), which of course "begs the question of which fatherland is being referred to here: the new Russia, the old Russia, or the former Soviet Union?"[54] The question of the proper social/cultural identity group in which they are members, under conditions of radical uncertainty, drives debates about nationalism among the Russians in the near abroad.

In Russia itself, the identity not of the group but of the state drives national debates.[55] The idea that the Russian state has a historic role as a superpower still lives. In September 1994, *Nezavisimaia gazeta* noted that "the creation of a new state on the territory of the former Soviet Union" is "a historically ordained necessity" and is, according to the author, "quietly understood as that" among former republics.[56] Furthermore, many think that such a reintegration would be painless. As one Gorbachev ally wrote in 1994,

> There are no serious obstacles for a political reintegration of a considerable part of the post-Soviet territory or for a formation of a new state in the place of the USSR. . . . Today life in most of the former Soviet republics, especially in Tadzhikistan, Georgia, Armenia, Moldova, and Belarus', fully depends on aid from Moscow. The population of these republics, exhausted by poverty and often also by civil war, would deem it right to form a tighter alliance than the present CIS.

He further points out that in Ukraine after Kuchma's election, in Sevastopol, the Donbass, and Odessa, there are strong positive feelings about reintegration. In fact, he continues, in reference to most of the borders, the structures (railroad network, TV, frontier guards) are operating more or less as before.[57]

Despite these neo-Soviet assurances, there is no agreement at all in Russia about reintegration. Liberals want to drop all pretenses to "empire" and seek to build a new identity in line with "normal" or "civilized" countries.[58] Aleksandr Solzhenitsyn advocates only partial reintegration, in areas of historical Russian settlement. David Remnick quotes him as saying:

[54] Beissinger, "Persisting Ambiguity," p. 170.

[55] See Ted Hopf, "Identity and Russian Foreign Policy" (unpublished manuscript, University of Michigan, 1994), who announces a research program on the relationship of state identity and foreign policy in post-Soviet Russia.

[56] Beissinger, "Persisting Ambiguity," pp. 167–68.

[57] Alexander Tsipko, "A New Russian Identity or Old Russia's Reintegration?" *Security Dialogue* 25, no. 4 (1994): 447.

[58] Urban, "Politics of Identity," p. 741.

> [Yeltsin] simply said, "I accept all the borders," and let it go at that. It was Lenin who established these false borders—borders that did not correspond to the ethnic borders. They were set up in a way as to undermine the central Russian nation—as conscious punishment. The Donetsk and Lugansk regions supported the Cossacks in their fight with the Bolsheviks, and so Lenin cut those regions off from the Don as punishment. Southern Siberia rose up massively against the Bolsheviks, so he gave the region to Kazakhstan. . . . As far as Ukraine is concerned . . . [i]f you want to be separate, by all means, go ahead, please. But within the borders of the true Ukraine. The historical Ukraine, the place where Ukrainians really live. . . . So it has turned out that twenty-five million Russians all of a sudden live outside Russia. This is the biggest diaspora in the world. The leaderships of Ukraine and Kazakhstan are both extremely shortsighted. They have taken upon themselves a task that culturally cannot be worked out. For example, in Kazakhstan they will have to turn those Russians into Kazakhs.[59]

Yeltsin's position on this issue, nicely put by Alexander and Gregory Guroff, is like that of Talleyrand, who had to abandon Napoleon's dream. He wrote: "To be great again, France must cease to be colossal."[60] Russia will play a telling role in international affairs, in Yeltsin's mind, only if it ceases to see itself as a transcontinental superpower.

How great and how big Russia must be in order for its pride as a state to be restored is clearly the subject of wide-ranging debate within Russia, and it is at the heart of debates about the proper state for the Russian nation. The agreement within Russia, among all participants, is that this is the point of concern for anyone thinking about the future of the Russian nation. It is a debate lively and vibrant within Russian nationalist discourse in Russia; but is a rather foreign debate among Russians in the near abroad.

Survey Data

If the trends identified in this chapter are correct, Russians in Russia should already be expressing values concerning religion, concerning Russia, and concerning the former Soviet Union that are distinct from those of Russians in the near abroad. Fortunately, my co-principal investigator for the surveys in this project, Jerry Hough, was conducting pre-election surveys in the Russian oblasts and in the Russian republics at about the same time that the surveys for this study were being administered. If the "internationalist" strain had been strongest in the former union republics, at medium strength in the Russian republics (where Russians are not tit-

[59] David Remnick, "The Exile Returns," *New Yorker*, February 14, 1994. This position is fully worked out in Solzhenitsyn's "Kak nam obustroit' Rossiiu?" *Komsomol'skaia pravda*, September 1990, and available in English as ***Rebuilding Russia: Reflections and Tentative Proposals*** (New York: Farrar, Straus & Giroux, 1991).

[60] Gregory Guroff and Alexander Guroff, "The Paradox of Russian National Identity," in Roman Szporluk, ed., *National Identity and Ethnicity in Russia and the New States of Eurasia* (Armonk, N.Y.: M. E. Sharpe, 1994), p. 95.

ulars, but have representation in the Russian State Duma), and weakest in the Russian oblasts (which are almost exclusively Russian)—and vice versa for the "exclusivist" strain—the historical tracings of this chapter would have received strong confirmation. The data presented on Table 11.1 do not provide such support. But they are worth examining, if only to provide a general picture of Russian attitudes toward homeland, toward religion, and toward the former Soviet Union in six different contexts.

Concerning religion, there is no evidence of greater attachment to Orthodoxy in Russia than in the near abroad. In fact, the largest proportions of reports of religious practice among Russians are from Latvia and Ukraine. Nor is there any evidence of a stronger rejection of religion in the near abroad, with perhaps only

Table 11.1. Russians in Russia and the near abroad: Attitudes toward religion and their native lands

	Russia					
	Oblasts	Republics	Kazakhstan	Estonia	Latvia	Ukraine
Religious involvement						
Believer/practices	9.6	9.9	10.4	7.9	18.0	17.1
Believer/doesn't practice	31.9	32.5	34.8	30.3	33.1	35.2
Nonbeliever, but respects believers	37.9	35.8	29.9	41.5	31.5	33.4
Religion is bad	0.9	1.1	0.9	3.7	0.9	0.7
Native land						
USSR	29.8	25.8	48.8		9.1	
Russia	58.0	41.3	10.9		15.8	
Republic	8.2	29.3	32.2		61.9	
End of USSR						
Extremely useful	8.3	6.8	6.1		13.7	
Extremely harmful	49.4	45.8	49.6		20.8	
Russians gave help to all people of USSR						
Unqualified yes	79.9	76.6	77.5	46.0	45.0	72.2
More harm than help	1.4	1.0	0.9	2.5	2.1	1.0
Strong CIS is desirable						
Yes	81.9	82.3	60.9	53.1	74.0	67.9
No	4.7	3.5	14.0	27.0	3.7	19.5
Strong Russia is desirable						
Yes			49.8	45.7	26.5	
No			27.2	36.6	46.8	

Note: For the Russian surveys, Hough included a number of questions asked in the Laitin/Hough survey. Where questions were not asked in a particular survey, the corresponding cell in the table is left empty.

Sources: The data for the Russian oblasts and for the Russian republics are from the "Predvybornaia Situatsiia v Rossii" surveys conducted under the auspices of the Tsentr Sotsiologicheskikh Issledovanii Obshchestvennogo Mneniia Moskovskogo Gosudarstvennogo Universiteta im. M. V. Lomonosova and the Tsentr po izucheniiu mezhnatsional'nykh Otnoshenii Instituta etnologii i antropologii im. N. N. Miklukho-Maklaia, Rossiiskaia Akademiia Nauk, both conducted in spring 1993. The principal investigators of the project were Jerry Hough and Timothy Colton from the United States and Mikhail Guboglo and Sergei Tumanov from Russia. The data from the four independent republics are from the Laitin/Hough surveys.

Russians in Estonia—with about four times the mean rejection rate of the five other samples—having an orientation toward religion more in the direction that I had hypothesized. The most interesting difference—and one I cannot explain in the context of this research design—is that between the Russians in Estonia and those in Latvia, with the latter being far more observant in relatively similar environments. It needs to be emphasized that the hypothesized mobilization of religion in Russia does not require strong adherence to religious doctrines or regular attendance at religious ceremonies—therefore, the observation that there is an appropriation of religious symbology in Russia and that such appropriation is relatively absent from the Russian political arena in the near abroad is not disconfirmed by these data. Nonetheless, the data do not support the notion of a religious awakening in Russia that is distinct from what is occurring in the near abroad.

The attachment of Russians in Russia to a "Russian" identity and the attachment of the Russians in the near abroad to a "Soviet" identity is weakly supported by the survey data. Russians in Kazakhstan more strongly than elsewhere identified the USSR as their native land. Furthermore, identification with Russia as one's native land was far lower in the two republics of the near abroad where that question was asked than in the Russian oblasts (where it is strongest) and in the Russian republics (where it is less strong). But on the question whether the breakup of the Soviet Union was harmful or helpful, Russian respondents in Kazakhstan lined up with the Russians in Russia to emphasize great harm, and Latvia's Russians gave twice as much support for the usefulness of the collapse as did Russian respondents in the Russian republics or in Kazakhstan. Again, on the question whether "Russians [*russkie*] gave great help in the development of other peoples in the former Soviet Union," the great difference is between the Baltic Russians (who gave many fewer unqualified yeses and twice as many negatives as the mean of the other sets of respondents) and the Russians in the other four surveys.

The responses that support the notion that a reconstituted Soviet identity has meaning in the near abroad were those to the questions on whether respondents favor a strong CIS (which is often considered the old USSR in lamb's clothing) and whether they favor a strong Russia. While Russians in all four republics are far less enthusiastic about a strong CIS than are the Russians in Russia, the Russians in the near abroad are much happier with a strong CIS than with a strong Russia. At most, the data allow me to say that there is a clear poverty in identification with Russia among Russians in the near abroad but no consistent evidence of a strong attachment to a Soviet identity.

NATIONALIST movements draw on, appropriate, and even invent national traditions. The traditions themselves are invariably complex and multivocal and can therefore support a wide range of representations. In the post-Soviet world, it might be thought that the task for those who purport to become Russian nationalist leaders has been formidable. After all, Russia never was a nation-state, and there are no Russian (as opposed to Orthodox or Slav or Soviet) patriots whose writings and biographies bespeak a Russian nation in search of a state. Yet this has not deterred a vibrant contemporary nationalist discourse.

In fact, this chapter has identified two contemporary Russian nationalist discourses, depending upon political context. The nationalist discourse in Russia has appropriated the Orthodox tradition, and on its fringes it singles out the pure Russian who manifests the soul of the nation. Across the political spectrum, the point of concern of Russian national discourse is how great the Russian state must be as a representation of the Russian people. Meanwhile, the nationalist discourse in the near abroad has focused on the Russian language as the essential element of Russianness, and thereby has been more inclusive. Its point of concern is how to define themselves as a group—as a diaspora, as people without a country, or as normal minorities within legitimate nation-states.

Survey data were used to see if Russian respondents in Russia differed from Russian respondents in the near abroad in a manner consistent with these two nationalist strands. The data that I collected, however, do not capture these differences very well. I cannot reject the possibility that there is no difference between Russians in the near abroad and in Russia on questions of religious adherence or on naming (and evaluating) their homeland. There is clearly a low recognition of "Russia" as an identifying symbol for Russians in the near abroad, especially in the Baltics. There is also greater relative support for a strong CIS than for a strong Russia in the near abroad. These data are consistent with my narrative in this chapter, but not strongly so.

Even if mass attitudes do not distinguish the Russians of Russia from those in the near abroad according to the separate strands of Russian nationalism, this chapter has shown that the appropriation of Russia's national culture has a quite distinct focus in Russia as compared with the near abroad. This difference should, in the course of a generation, frame distinct Russian identities depending on whether they were fashioned in Russia or in one of the now-independent republics of the former Soviet Union. If it does, the core theme of Part IV of this book will be confirmed—that a clear alternative to assimilation is the reconfiguration of identity categories in the direction of a new national identity.

PART FIVE

EXTENSIONS OF THE ANALYSIS

12

Identity and Ethnic Violence

Ethnic violence—whether in former Yugoslavia, Somalia, Rwanda, Liberia, Georgia, Azerbaijan, Moldova, or Sri Lanka—has been particularly gruesome in recent years. The sources of this violence and its apparent intensity have been of great concern to scholars, public officials with the power to mobilize an international gendarmerie, and populations throughout the world now accustomed to seeing the worst excesses of this violence on TV. This study is not perfectly set up to provide a compelling answer to the question of what motivates this violence. The principal dependent variable of this study has been cultural identity shift, both from Russian to titular, and Russian to Russian-speaking. Furthermore, the selection of cases (Kazakhstan, Ukraine, Estonia, and Latvia) all have the same value (virtually nonexistent) on the dependent variable (level of inter-nationality violence), and it would be in consequence impossible from the data collected for this project to nail down an explanation on the causes of ethnic conflict. Nonetheless, the analyses contained in this book have some contribution to make toward the development of a theory of ethnic violence.

The Postindependence Peace

Consider Estonia. Consistent with the ethnographic material (in Chapter 6) demonstrating the existence of an interethnic security community in Estonia, my survey data show very low expectations of ethnic violence among both Russians and titulars. On a four-point scale on whether respondents thought that there might be civil war in Estonia (1 reflecting a strong possibility, and 4 being a feeling that there never has been such a possibility), the mean for Narva—considered by many to be the tinderbox for an Estonian ethnic conflagration—was 2.74 (close to 3, which reflects the position that there may have been a danger earlier, but not when the survey was taken, in June 1993). And on a question about the level of inter-nationality tension they feel in their home area, with 1 reflecting no tension and 5 a high level, Narva respondents' mean answer was 1.75 between "no tension" and "a little tension." This is hardly an attitude set of one nationality group seeking revenge against or protection from the other. These data help buttress the story that between Russians and Estonians in Estonia there exists a security community, in which the lack of expectation of violent resolution of conflict leads to lack of preparation for it, thereby precluding it as an option when conflicts do arise.

Compelling evidence, however, tells us that peaceful past relations, attitudes in favor of ethnic accommodation, and even high rates of interethnic marriage—while not the case in Estonia, it was the case between Serbs and Croats in former Yugoslavia—are not good predictors of ethnic peace. Even under the special conditions of a security community the expectation of peace can disappear in a moment. The reason for this, as both Timur Kuran and Russell Hardin show, using models quite similar to the language-tipping games that I used to analyze assimilation, is that an equilibrium of peace can quickly and unexpectedly be replaced by an equilibrium of war.[1]

Kuran uses a tipping model to explain the failure of social science to predict the East European revolutions of 1991. His principal insight is that under conditions of oppression, people systematically engage in "preference falsification," in which they publicly reveal their support for the regime, or at least their apathy to politics. They lie not only to survey researchers but to their neighbors as well. If friends and neighbors each decide to conceal their true hatred for a regime unless it is safe to do otherwise—and consider safety to be only in large numbers—there can be long periods of quiet under conditions of profound enmity. Unpredictable events—in this case Gorbachev's signal that Soviet troops would not be used to support the East European communist regimes—can bring enough people (those who are willing to reveal their true preferences if only a small number of compatriots do so as well) into the streets to set off a cascade of protest. In May there was order in Eastern Europe with no expectation whatsoever of imminent revolution; but by October all the East European satellite regimes had fallen.

In a similar fashion, and again from a tipping perspective, Hardin explains the violent collapse of Yugoslavia, the murderous anarchy of Somalia, and the continued terrorist assaults in Northern Ireland. Suppose (in the case of the IRA) a revolutionary cell is formed with the intention of undermining British rule in Northern Ireland. A terrorist act succeeds. This leads other Irish nationalists, who had been afraid of challenging British rule, to consider the possibility of forming a cell for themselves. It also leads Protestant Unionists to consider vengeance for the initial terrorism. Each successful act draws new people (who had much higher thresholds of resistance to political action) into the arena. As Hardin reasons, "If the first few cells had been stopped, there might not have been twenty-five years of such violence."[2] But once there was success, there was a tip, and formerly peaceful citizens became ethnic warriors.

[1] See Timur Kuran, "Now out of Never: The Element of Surprise in the East European Revolution of 1989," *World Politics* 44, no. 1 (1991): 7–48, and Russell Hardin, *One for All* (Princeton: Princeton University Press, 1995), chap. 6.

[2] Hardin, *One for All*, p. 146.

Now, let us reconsider the Narva local elections of 1993 and subsequent events that were described in Chapter 6. Russian-speakers knew that in the formative period of their republic, when foundational laws were being passed, they remained without a vote in national elections and without a chance to be candidates in local contests. They were treated by the new Estonian leaders, at least in the eyes of many of their spokesmen, like colonial subjects. By 2001, however, virtually all Russians who remain in Estonia will be eligible for citizenship. New political entrepreneurs will have little trouble exploiting the feelings of humiliation that are now being shaped into memories and will seek basic changes in the framework of Estonian politics. Fears of becoming a minority in their "own" homeland could lead to a hostile Estonian response to such a challenge. And so, while the 1993 elections were peaceful and successful from the point of view of the Estonian state, and while strong evidence of a security community, in attitudes and expectations, is observable, darker clouds remain on the horizon. After all, an equilibrium in a tipping game has only the feel of permanence. Therefore, the existence of a security community is not sufficient to project future harmony between nationalities. We need to examine possible sources for change.

The sources of change, however, are often found within societies. This point is often missed by students of international relations who have examined the ethnic scene in the post-Soviet world. I shall therefore make a detour in my line of argument in order to explore the discoveries and problems of international relations theory as its experts have begun to explore the sources of ethnic violence.

Ethnic Violence in International Relations Theories

The contemporary study of international relations, following the seminal work of Kenneth Waltz, has been built on a core insight that wars cannot be explained by ancient hatreds or popular attitudes. Rather, the situation of "anarchy" (where no Leviathan can bring order) induces all states to prepare heavily for their own defense. If all states do that, no matter how the people feel about each other, war is invariably imminent. A new generation of scholars, influenced by Waltz, has turned its attention—turning Waltz's insight into a premise—to intrastate "ethnic" wars.[3]

These international relations scholars saw in the collapse of the Soviet and Yugoslav states a situation approaching the anarchy that exemplifies the international state system. With this analogy in mind, they have identified a few mechanisms under which that anarchy sets the stage for communal conflict. First, at the time of (Soviet) state collapse, it is very difficult for leaders trying to rule from the decaying

[3] Kenneth N. Waltz, *Man, the State, and War* (New York: Columbia University Press, 1959); Barry Posen, "The Security Dilemma and Ethnic Conflict," *Survival* 35, no. 1 (1993): 27–47; and James D. Fearon, "Ethnic War as a Commitment Problem" (paper presented to the 1994 Annual Meetings of the American Political Science Association, New York, September 2–5). The offense/defense balance and window of opportunity arguments are Posen's; the credible commitment argument is Fearon's. The insight about mixed signals coming from the national homeland is from Pieter van Houten, "The Role of the Homeland in Ethnic Relations" (paper presented at the Midwest Political Science Association, Chicago, March 1996).

center, or leaders of ethnically distinct regions within the state (e.g. Estonia), to properly calculate the balance of power between center and region. Bad calculations on both sides (especially if they exaggerate the weakness of their adversaries) may yield the expected probabilities of victory by planners on each side to be greater than .5, a situation that might lead both parties to calculate positive returns to war.

Second, leaders of a weak region may see the collapse of a state as only temporary and therefore as a "window of opportunity" to press for claims (full sovereignty) that were unimaginable earlier. If the region succeeds, minorities (in this case, Russians) within the region, especially if they are ethnically related to the group that controlled the former central state, will probably fear for their future security. The window of opportunity again motivates ethnic mobilization. Even if the leaders of the newly independent region wanted to assure their new minorities that their security would be protected, there is no way, under conditions of anarchy, for them to commit credibly to that policy. The minority within the region would certainly fear that once the regional government, police, and army were consolidated in power, the leaders of the region would conveniently forget their commitments. Minority leaders (as with the case of Croatian Serbs, to apply this analysis to former Yugoslavia) might well press for war before the regional government got strong enough to effectively suppress their community.

Third, international relations scholars have shown that when defensive weapons predominate in an anarchic environment over offensive ones, the probability of attack goes down. Suppose, for example, that it is three times as expensive to launch a successful attack as it is to sustain a viable defense. This means that by spending merely what your opponent spends, even if your opponent occasionally goes on a military spending spree, you are secure. But if it takes only 1.1 times the expenditure for a successful attack, any small deviation in expenditures could bring a spiral of arms purchases, and an expectation of imminent war. In this sense, a strong nationalist ideology, with potential recruits willing to walk into danger in the name of the nation, provides the possibility of added offensive power. The fact that the United Nations usually pushes for cease-fires after ethnic skirmishes is another booster to offensive power. Leaders of a group can press militarily for territorial gain. If they get it, and the UN immediately calls for a cease-fire, their forces will be protected by the international gendarmerie. Thus the UN rewards quick and clean captures of territory in civil wars.

Finally, international relations scholars have never lost sight of the role of outside states, as either deterrents or fomenters of civil wars. Consider the situation of a "national homeland" (such as Russia) neighboring a newly independent "nationalizing state" (such as Estonia) in which live a significant proportion of a "national minority" (Russians) who are linked by nationality to the dominant nation of the national homeland.[4] If the national homeland is powerful enough, it might provide sufficient security to the national minority that the minority would not deem it nec-

[4] This "triadic" relationship has been brilliantly analyzed by Rogers Brubaker, "National Minorities, Nationalizing States, and the External National Homelands in the New Europe," *Daedalus* 124, no. 2 (1995): 107–32.

essary to rush into conflict before the window of opportunity closed. Leaders of the minority would likely reason that their group would always be protected, even if the commitments of the nationalizing state turned out to be ephemeral, by the armies of the national homeland.

A more strategic analysis of this complex triadic field points out that if the government of the national homeland shows too great an interest in the national minority, it will give that minority an incentive to initiate violence, in order to produce martyrs, and thereby drawing in the armies of the national homeland to reincorporate their territory. Yet if the national homeland shows too little an interest in the national minority, it would be giving the leaders of the nationalizing state the courage to renege on their security commitments to that minority. This could heighten tensions and raise the probability of ethnic war. Consequently, if the government of the national homeland takes a middle path between solid support and complete indifference to their ethnic brethren now living in nationalizing states, it has, according to this logic, done its best to guarantee peace.

The probabilities of a homeland invading a nationalizing state are also affected by the demographics of the national minority population. In three of the republics in this study (Estonia, Ukraine, and Kazakhstan), there are high concentrations of Russians in relatively self-contained regions across the border from the Russian Federation. This is not the case in Latvia. To the extent that the homeland's army can easily enter and cleanly delineate a territory populated by their national brethren, a military threat is more credible. Yet in all four republics, as recorded in Table 4.1, there are significant percentages of Russians living in the capital cities of these nationalizing states. Were Russia to capture the Russian-populated regions only, it would be abandoning its co-fatherlanders to the vengeance of the titulars. This demographic fact, from an international-relations perspective, lowers the expected payoff to Russia of an invasion.

These theories help make sense of ethnic conflict in the post-Soviet world. First, journalistic tales of ancient hatreds erupting as soon as central authority disappeared can be ignored. These journalists never look for ancient hatreds between dyads that are today at peace (Welsh and English, Bashkirs and Russians); and since there are invariably some available narratives of ancient wrongs between any ethnic dyad, once war breaks out, those narratives in some way become explanatory. As I emphasized in Chapter 4, there is a xenophobic face to Ukrainian nationalism. The vitriolic anti-Russian narratives tend to be ignored by the Western press. But if ethnic war were to break out, these narratives would be "discovered" and used as evidence to explain the violence. This won't do. Nonetheless, these sorts of explanations have persisted. The international relations school has provided a clear (and superior) alternative: under conditions of state collapse, with windows of opportunity and the difficulty of new incumbents to make credible commitments to the security of new minorities, there are strong incentives for ethnic leaders to press for war.

Second, we can now explain why the Russian minorities in thirteen of the fourteen former union republics have not been engaged in ethnic war. This can be explained by Russia's power and its mixed signals to the nationalist leaders in the near abroad (both titular and Russian) about their probable reactions if ethnic war broke out in a former union republic. Within those new republics, neither titulars nor Russians had sufficient surety (about Russia's probable reaction) to aggress upon the other. Thus, when the Ministry of Foreign Affairs under Andrei Kozyrev took a moderate line in regard to Russian minorities in the near abroad in summer 1992, "the publication of the draft new Russian military doctrine indicated that the Ministry of Defense was planning to use protection of Russians abroad as a basic justification for future external military action." The two power ministries were giving contradictory signals.[5] As a corollary, we can see how among the Armenians in Azerbaijan and the Abkhazians in Georgia such disincentives to interethnic war were lacking.[6] Or, on the other side, as in Bosnia-Herzegovina and Croatia, when the national homeland took an inordinate interest in their brethren in the near abroad, it gave incentive for the national minorities in these republics to take full advantage of their windows of opportunity.

The only exception to the absence of ethnic conflict directed at Russians in the union republics is Moldova, where war broke out in November 1990, in the wake of a declaration of an Transdniester Republic by ethnic Russians who feared that they would be incorporated into a union of Moldova and Rumania, a country in which they feared they would be an excluded minority. Although Gorbachev tried to conciliate, the Dniestrians relied on the support of the commander of the 14th Soviet Army, General Gennadii Iakovlev, who agreed to serve as minister of defense of the Transdniester Republic. His successor claimed neutrality, but there was a de facto "revolving door" in which members of the Russian 14th Army put on the uniforms of the Republican Guard whenever they were needed, and made their weapons available to the Transdniester soldiers.[7] In this case, under conditions of a short window of opportunity while Moldova was still weak, the Transdniestrians' expectation of support from Russia (or one of its armies) permitted grievances to escalate into armed conflict.

Compare this to the situation in northern Kazakhstan, also a predominantly Russian zone within a non-Russian former union republic. Boris Supruniuk, the leader

[5] The quotation is from *Voennaia mysl'* (special edition), no. 4–5 (1992), and cited in Neil Melvin, *Russians beyond Russia* (London: Royal Institute of International Affairs, 1995), p. 13. In this light, Aleksandr Lebed's threatening statements in regard to Latvia's 1996 education law, which he claimed is a "programme for the forced assimilation of Russians," was not necessarily provoking violence, even if Lebed is a former general and was at that time in charge of Russian Federation national security issues. As long as some voices from Russia declare disinterest while others monitor the situation threateningly, neither titulars nor Russians in the Baltics can predict how Russia will respond to outbreaks of ethnic violence. On Lebed's comments, see Dmitry Polikarpov, "Lebed Watches Baltics," *Baltic Times*, July 25–31, 1996.

[6] On ethnic war in the Transcaucasus, see Ronald Grigor Suny, "Elite Transformation in Late-Soviet and Post-Soviet Transcaucasia; or, What Happens When the Ruling Class Can't Rule," in Timothy J. Colton and Robert C. Tucker, eds., *Patterns in Post-Soviet Leadership* (Boulder, Colo.: Westview, 1995), pp. 141–67. In Transcaucasia, the higher the percentage of non-Russian minorities, the heavier the post-Soviet ethnic violence. This is consistent with the international relations predictions.

[7] I rely on the summary of Pål Kolstø and Andrei Edemsky, with Natalya Kalashnikova, "The Dniester Conflict: Between Irredentism and Separatism," *Europe-Asia Studies* 45, no. 6 (1993): 973–1000.

of the northern Kazakhstan section of the "Russian Community," a settler organization officially registered in 1992, was arrested in 1994 on charges of promoting ethnic hatred in his newspaper *Glas*. The organization's registration was thereby revoked and their candidates were barred from participating in the February 1994 elections. This was no aberration. The 1994 local elections in Kazakhstan have been widely condemned for being undemocratic. Of the 690 candidates registered for 135 constituencies, 566 were Kazakhs. Supruniuk was released in May 1994, after the elections, and he has become a hero among Russian nationalists. Yet for all the conflicts and provocations, there has been no interethnic violence.[8]

To some extent, the international relations perspective, by showing the low expected value for ethnic war in most post-Soviet republics, helps explain the containment of ethnic conflict, with only limited violence. But one problem with this perspective is that it has little to say about ethnic conflict and violence after states have consolidated power. After the first five years of Soviet collapse, whatever window of opportunity was opened, had closed. The military and police apparatuses of the new states have become institutionalized. Minorities that did not take advantage of the weakness of the new nationalizing states by 1992 have little incentive now to press violently for independence in the final years of the century. Yet this doesn't mean that ethnic violence is no longer possible. Far from it. What it does mean is that the mechanisms that drive ethnic conflict in anarchy's wake are no longer relevant. Of moment now are the internal mechanisms that prevent or provoke conflict over state power. And it is concerning these that the analyses in this book provide some perspective.

International relations theory, while appropriate for analyzing the situation of anarchy in immediate post-collapse situations, does not provide an appropriate model for ethnic conflict within more or less consolidated states. Those international relations scholars who have tried to analyze interethnic conflict within consolidated states as if it were a form of interstate conflict, have made counterproductive policy recommendations. They assume an isomorphy between states and nations, and that is their error. While it is useful and often powerful to assume that *states* are unitary actors; it is equally powerful but misleading to assume that *nations* (or putative nations) are. Thus analyses based on this error, that states and nations are isomorphic, can lead to policy recommendations that promote not ethnic peace but violent conflict.

Liberal Ethnic Cleansing

Standard international relations accounts of ethnic violence reflect what Ronald Suny calls the "Sleeping Beauty" view of nationalism—a dormant ethnic group is awakened with the kiss of freedom, and it returns to the world it lived in centuries ago, when it was put to sleep by socialism or totalitarianism. Those who hold this view have ignored the findings of thirty-five years of research in the field of ethnic

[8] Melvin, *Russians beyond Russia*, pp. 113–14 and 165n.

relations.[9] This would not be so bad if the Sleeping Beauty account were only a fairy tale told by wistful nationalists to their children. But this view is beginning to drive policies of the international gendarmerie as it intervenes in many messy nationality conflicts in the post-Soviet world. One might call the policy implications of one strand of this type of thinking "Wilson redux." I prefer "ethnic cleansing, liberal style."

My attempt to discredit this view should be seen as a cautionary footnote to the brilliant analysis of this issue presented by Stephen Van Evera, who assumes the validity of the Sleeping Beauty account of nations.[10] Much of the structure of his argument is cogent and solid, but it is undermined at its foundations by its uncritical acceptance of an outmoded view of the nation. It overlooks the work done by scholars in the late 1950s, who began to notice the situational and constructed aspect of nationality. They developed what Suny calls the "Bride of Frankenstein" approach to ethnicity. Van Evera's policy analysis would have been quite different if he had assumed that the Son of Frankenstein, to mix a metaphor, had trumped Sleeping Beauty.

Van Evera's paper, nonetheless, is seminal, in that it sets up an inventory of current knowledge about the international implications of nationalist politics and seeks help from others to build up that inventory. He writes that since "our stock of hypotheses on the consequences of nationalism is meager[,] our first order of business should be to expand it, to set the stage for empirical inquiry by others."[11] In this spirit, I shall here add to his inventory by making two simple points. First, Van Evera's hypothesis that the probability of war increases in direct proportion to the ratio of nationalisms and states[12] both ignores the social, economic, and political factors that alter the value of the numerator (that is, the number of nationalisms) and underestimates as well the often peaceful outcomes where the ratio is high. Second, the policies that follow from Van Evera's analysis, if looked upon from a micro perspective, provide incentives for political entrepreneurs to increase the value of the ratio, thereby undermining the recommended palliatives. After making these two points, relying on selected historical cases (admittedly ones that support my argument), I shall outline a new policy alternative.

If the Ratio of Nationalisms to States Rises, So Does the Probability of War

This is a core claim in Van Evera's inventory. He leaves the issue of the origins of nationalism "unexplored" and takes Anthony Smith's notion of an *ethnie* as a proxy

[9] This section is adapted from David Laitin, "Ethnic Cleansing Liberal Style" (paper delivered to the Weyland Collegium, Brown University, October 12, 1995). It was presented as well to the Harvard/MIT MacArthur colloquium, in November 1995, where it was distributed as a working paper of the colloquium. Ronald Suny, *Revenge of the Past* (Stanford: Stanford University Press, 1993), pp. 3–4.

[10] Stephen Van Evera, "Nationalism and the Causes of War," in Charles A. Kupchan, ed., *Nationalism and Nationalities in the New Europe* (Ithaca: Cornell University Press, 1995).

[11] Ibid., p. 137.

[12] Ibid., p. 138.

for nation. He thereby becomes an unreconstructed "Sleeping Beauty" theorist and defines nationalism, inter alia, "as a political movement [in which] individual members give their primary loyalty to *their own* ethnic or *national community*."[13] Since the number of nations varies directly with the number of potential nationalisms, he hypothesizes that "the more closely the boundaries of emerging nation-states follow ethnic boundaries, the smaller the risk of war." These statements imply that nations (or ethnic groups) are fixed, but only in a subset of them will its members become sufficiently mobilized for them to accept a nationalist agenda. But if nationalisms can emerge only from nations without states, it follows that if the ratio of nations to states approaches unity, a necessary condition for the nonarousal of state-seeking nationalisms has been met, and thereby the probability of nationalist war has been reduced.

In response to the assumption that nations are fixed communities and the claim that we would reduce tensions worldwide if each nation had its own state, I make three counterclaims. First, nations are not fixed entities. Second, there is evidence that a higher nation/state ratio, under some conditions, has tension-reducing characteristics. Third, there is a flaw in a chain of reasoning that supports Van Evera's argument, although he does not use it, that nation-states are more likely to be democratic; that democratic states are less likely to provoke war against other democracies; and that therefore a world of nation-states (where all nationalisms are fulfilled) would be a more peaceful world. These three counterclaims do not speak to Van Evera's argument directly; however, they do support a line of reasoning that does.

The historical literature on nationalism has provided many examples of the number of "nations" in a territory being altered without any changing of boundaries. In *Peasants into Frenchmen*, Eugen Weber took the example of the most "real" nation state in the Western world, France, and showed that until the final third of the nineteenth century, the boundaries of the French state did not surround a French nation. At the time of the Revolution, startled primordialists have read, only a tiny percentage of the residents in Marseille could have understood the words of the "Marseillaise"! In the 1850s, there were a plethora of nations within the hexagon; by the end of the century, there was only one.[14] For our purposes, the key implication of Weber's study is that the number of potential nationalisms within the French hexagon has changed radically in the last 150 years. How is it possible to preempt nationalisms, one can ask, if nations themselves come and go, or get reconfigured with changing subsets of populations included in them? This finding was reproduced almost everywhere by other historians, culminating in Eric Hobsbawm and Terence Ranger's classic collection, *The Invention of Tradition*.[15] Here we see that few national myths and practices are genuinely ancient. National traditions require architects and builders; the raw materials can be mined from a variety of quarries.

[13] Ibid., p. 136; my emphasis.

[14] Eugen Weber, *Peasants into Frenchmen* (Stanford: Stanford University Press, 1976).

[15] Eric Hobsbawm and Terence Ranger, eds., *The Invention of Tradition* (Cambridge: Cambridge University Press, 1983).

Much of the research on ethnic groups in social science support this new historiography. Crawford Young's classic analysis of the Bangala "tribe" in the Congo demonstrated that this group did not exist as a group until the Belgians reorganized local boundaries. Yet they made ethnic demands to their Belgian rulers almost simultaneously with the emergence in their self-understanding that they constituted a "tribe."[16] The Igbos and Yorubas did not exist as tribes until the ancestors of those people who now call themselves by these names lived under British rule in Nigeria. Yet the Igbos in 1967–70 fought (and lost) a bloody war for independence from the rest of Nigeria.

My research in Somalia (which was considered, like France and Japan, one of the few "real" nation-states in the world) over a number of years took me on the long road from primordialism to a more constructed view of nations. In my first book, *Politics, Language and Thought: The Somali Experience*, I saw the movement to make official the Somali language for the Somali people in a near-Hegelian way, as the fulfillment of a nationalist potential.[17] In that book, there were seeds of doubt, which I saw as ironic rather than symptomatic. A particularly good example (cited in my book) comes from colonial Kenya, when the British denied Africans the right to engage in petty trade, thereby giving monopoly rights in certain sectors to "Asians." The small but vibrant Somali community in Mombasa immediately began to attend mosque with Muslim Indians and re-presented themselves to British officers as Asians.[18] Nearly a century later, when the Organization of Petroleum Exporting Countries (OPEC) caused tremors through the industrial world, countries with Arab populations were recipients of munificent gifts skimmed from the inflated prices of oil. Somali ideology was quick to react, and the foreign minister announced that Somalia was an Arab state and joined the Arab League. Arabic became a semiofficial state language, and poets as well as ministers began heralding Somalia's natural place as part of the Arab nation. Again, I wrote about this in an ironic tone.

It was only after conducting research for an article in a book on ethnicity that I saw the full flowering of those seeds.[19] In examining the near chaos in the wake of the Somali irredentist war of 1977–78, I began to see the possibility of a variety of different "nations," with different boundaries, that could be configured, with "Somali" being only one of them. There was the possibility of a breakup into a set of clan families, with separate Dàrood, Isaaq, and Dir nations. Already at the time of the writing, Isaaq politicians were beginning to construct a narrative of the unique characteristics of Isaaq, which merited a separate political entity. (In the 1990s, this narrative became common, in light of the secession of the Isaaq-dominated former British colony from the rest of the carcass of Somalia.) But there were other possi-

16 M. Crawford Young, *Politics in the Congo* (Princeton: Princeton University Press, 1965).

17 David Laitin, *Politics, Language, and Thought* (Chicago: University of Chicago Press, 1977).

18 E. R. Turton, "Somali Resistance to Colonial Rule and the Development of Somali Political Activity in Kenya, 1893–1960," *Journal of African History* 13, no. 1 (1972).

19 David Laitin, "The Ogaadeen Question and Changes in Somali Identity," in Donald Rothchild and Victor Olorunsola, eds., *State vs. Ethnic Claims: African Policy Dilemmas* (Boulder, Colo.: Westview, 1983).

bilities. Since Somalia claimed a national right to the Ogaden desert, it was rather an embarrassment to its leaders when officials from the United Nations High Commission on Refugees began to find significant numbers of Oromos as refugees into the Somali camps. The Somali government and many strong nationalists sought to suppress this knowledge. When they found this impossible, they began to suggest that Oromos (because they, like Somalis, were Cushitic speakers) were really brothers, and quite distinct from the hated Amharas, who currently ruled the Ogaden. The emergence of a supra-Somali Cushitic nationality was yet another possible reconfiguration.

My Somali research taught me the following lesson: theories predicting when nationalism will arise provide only a minor subplot of nationalism. The important part of the story is how the boundaries get drawn and membership determined of the newly mobilized nations. These were the priors I took into my post-Soviet research, and they helped prepare me for the findings of the emergence of a potential Russian-speaking nationality.

My claim is that you cannot just count the number of potential nationalisms in any state, for the number of potential nationalisms is endogenous to the processes set in motion to ameliorate their effects. This claim does not really require exotic evidence from Congo, Nigeria, or Somalia. One need only ask to code Germany for the number of potential nationalisms it contains. Consider the cultural differences between East and West, the permanent communities of Turks who feel little connection with Turkey, and the mid-1990s rumblings about the possibilities of a Bavarian or Saxon nation. One needs to know a good deal about the context of German politics, and of Germany in Europe, before one can assess the number of potential nationalisms there. Or what about the United States? Are American "Hispanics" a single nation, or many (Cubans, Puerto Ricans, Mexicans, Guatemalans, etc.), or are they an integral part of the American nation? Nations, my point is, are not "out there" to be counted; they are a function of social, political, and economic processes.

Let us now assume for the moment that it is possible to count nations. Is it clear that as the ratio of nations to states decreases, grievances decrease, thereby lowering societal tensions? Van Evera holds to this view. "Borders," he writes, "may bisect nationalities, or may follow national demographic divides. Nation-bisecting borders are more troublesome, because they have the same effect as demographic intermingling: they entrap parts of nations within the boundaries of states dominated by other ethnic groups, giving rise to expansionism by the truncated nation."[20]

An alternate view would point to the phenomenon that having brethren on the other side of the border is a safety valve and can reduce social and political tensions. Consider Somalia once more. In the 1970s, under the dictatorship of Siad Barre, there was a deep societal consensus within Somalia that the redemption of all Somali lands by the Somali state was desirable; however, the existence of a rooted Somali community in northeastern Kenya served the interests of Somalis from

[20] Van Evera, "Nationalism," pp. 146–47. Anthony Asiwaju, in *Partitioned Africans* (New York: St. Martin's Press, 1985), makes this claim in regard to African borders.

Somalia who were opponents of the regime. Many of them surreptitiously crossed the border to Kenya, bribed a sheik to sign a statement that they were born in Kenya, and received Kenyan passports. Perhaps interclan war would have broken out earlier if the Somali border surrounded all Somalis? One might argue that civil war in Mexico (perhaps with a regional, protonational flavor) would have occurred if there were not the safety valve of the United States, where illegal immigrants can successfully hide behind a boundary that does not reflect the true division between the Hispanic and Anglo colonial societies.

My argument here coincides with the message that Salman Rushdie has been sending to the world since his quasi-incarceration caused by the Ayatollah Khomeini's infamous *fatwa* in 1989. Rushdie has argued that transnational diasporas are a liberating force that enhance human freedom. Without them, there would be ever growing numbers of discontented artists, intellectuals and dissidents who would have little choice but to organize (perhaps on ethnic or national criteria) groups of friends and neighbors with the hope of toppling (or seceding from) the hated regime in which they lived. The higher the ratio of nations to states, the easier it becomes to support transnational diasporas.[21]

Van Evera, in support of his claim that nation-bisecting boundaries have war-provoking possibilities, cites Hungary and its neighbors, and the Russian-Ukrainian boundary. He does not code all world boundaries in all eras on the basis of whether or not they bisect nations and then determine the probability of war based on these two types of boundaries. In light of my theoretical criticism (that the national definition of border groups is not easily coded, because its members have a variety of options on how to code themselves nationally), coding all boundaries is not a straightforward empirical test. As Peter Sahlins has shown, the national composition of border communities is especially ambiguous.[22] But even if such a coding were possible, I am not convinced (despite the riveting example of Hitler) that the proposition would get much support. The greatest number of nation-bisecting boundaries is in Africa; yet the number of interstate wars has been few. Julius Nyerere, the founding president of Tanzania is reported to have mused that the borders of African states are so absurd, there is no choice but to consider them sacrosanct. But even in cases in the industrial world (Spain and Portugal, where Galicia is Portuguese-speaking; the significant Swedish communities in Finland; Canada and the United States, where the English-speaking communities of North America are separated), nation-bisecting boundaries do not have an ominous quality that Van Evera suggests is inherent in them. I invite Van Evera's supporters to put his hypothesis on bisecting boundaries and violence to statistical test.

A second tack (not taken by Van Evera) linking the "nation/state" ratio to war relies on two theoretical traditions. The first is that ethnically homogeneous societies are more likely to have stable democracies. This idea was initially proposed by John

[21] David Lipscomb, "Caught in a Strange Middle Ground: Contesting History in Salman Rushdie's *Midnight's Children*," *Diaspora: A Journal of Transnational Studies* 1, no. 2 (1991): 163–89.

[22] Peter Sahlins, *Boundaries* (Berkeley: University of California Press, 1989).

Stuart Mill and introduced into American political science by Robert Dahl.[23] The second is the phenomenon of the "democratic peace" identified by Kant and reintroduced into current debates by Michael Doyle.[24] The combined chain of reasoning is as follows: as the expression "nation/state" approaches unity for all states, the probability of a democratic world goes up; since democracies do not attack other democracies, in this world, the probability of war approaches zero.

There are two problems with this chain of reasoning: one empirical, the other theoretical. Empirically, as Arend Lijphart and numerous empirically minded political scientists in his wake have shown, the probability of democracy (broadly understood) under conditions of ethnic heterogeneity is much higher than Dahl originally hypothesized. Consociational democracies (and quasi-consociational forms) are quite common (Switzerland, Netherlands, Belgium, and Canada are the principal examples), and are able to accommodate wide ranges of cultural difference. While many scholars point to the fragility of Belgian cabinets when confronted by ethnic issues, and others to the secessionist movement in Quebec, the remarkable feature about these movements is that they are not threats to democracies; nor are they producing systematic inter-nationality violence.[25]

There is a theoretical problem with the "homogeneity leads to democracy leads to peace" chain of reasoning as well, and this has much to do with the Sleeping Beauty view of nations that pervades discussion of these issues. I suggest that those who claim that ethnic homogeneity leads to a higher probability of democracy are committing the error of endogeneity. Perhaps it would be more accurate to say that democracy leads to a perception of common nationality. Consider the following. Why is it that Americans consider Black English in Louisiana (which I was not able to understand after living in such a community for a few months) a dialect while Serbs and Croats consider themselves (now) to speak different languages? Or suppose it were shown that the linguistic distance between Black English and American Standard were greater than that between Kievan Ukrainian and Moscow Russian. Could it be that in an open (democratic) society, where social and geographic mobility are widespread, people tend to emphasize what unites them with their fellow citizens rather than what separates them? If this is the case, the empirical association between homogeneity and democracy would hold, but the line of causation would go in the opposite direction from what J. S. Mill and R. Dahl envisaged.

Inadvertently Increasing the Nation/State Ratio

Liberal ethnic cleansers propose that groups whose leaders can make credible claims to being a nation be rewarded with plebiscites, recognition, and aid packages to help the process of state consolidation. To be sure, Van Evera is a cautious proponent of such a set of rewards. Before nationalist movements receive any rewards

[23] Adam Przeworski et al., *Sustainable Democracy* (Cambridge: Cambridge University Press, 1995), chap. 1. (I was the principal author of that chapter.)

[24] Michael Doyle, "Kant, Liberal Legacies, and Foreign Affairs," *Philosophy and Public Affairs* 12 (1983): 205–35, 323–53.

[25] Arend Lijphart, *Democracy in Plural Societies* (New Haven: Yale University Press, 1977).

from international gendarmes, their leaders would have to prove that they are nice, and inter alia, that they "renounce the use of force."[26] Even under Van Evera's policy, however, political entrepreneurs who can demonstrate that they are leaders of mobilized nations can earn a seat in the United Nations.

If I have successfully discredited the Sleeping Beauty view of the nation, the implications of this reward system should be clear. A policy of liberal ethnic cleansing (i.e., rewarding nations with states) will raise the "nationalism/state" ratio that Van Evera seeks to reduce. By examining how new nationalisms can arise, we should notice the perverse incentives of policy interventions seeking to reduce the "nationalism/state" ratio.

Abram de Swann's "floral" model of language acquisition can help clarify the microdynamics of nation creation.[27] Think of a state-building nationality group as the stamen of a flower (for example, the French of Ile-de-France), with all monolingual Frenchmen bounded by that stamen. Connected to the stamen are a set of petals which do not touch each other representing linguistic groups within the state's boundaries (in this case, the Bretons, the Catalans, the Alsatians, the Corsicans, the Languedocians). In early periods of state construction, the petals touch the stamen only at the point of attachment. That is to say, most people in the petals are monolingual in the regional language. Those people in the union of the stamen and petal are bilinguals, and they receive rents as "monopoly mediators" between center and region. These mediators have an interest in keeping "their" own people monolingual, so that they can continue to profit from representing them to the political center. De Swaan uses this theory to explain why bilingual cosmopolitans have a greater interest in nurturing the nation than do the peasants in the periphery, who have an interest in assimilation into the center's culture. This model helps us see as well that as the return for monopoly mediation goes up, cultural and political entrepreneurs have an interest in expanding the number of petals, through differentiation within previously existing petals.

Examples of the de Swaan model abound. In colonial Ghana, for example, the system of "indirect rule" reproduced the floral pattern perfectly. Local leaders who could demonstrate that they represented a separate nation received higher salaries, distinct textbooks, and a regional capital with high-quality infrastructure. Linguists recognized that over the course of a century, the many Akan dialects that had been mutually intelligible before colonialism grew in linguistic distance. Today, Fanti and Twi (both of which, under different incentives, might have been seen today as dialects of Akan) are considered separate languages representing different nations. The Fanti and Twi leaders received higher returns for differentiating themselves from each other than they would have received for emphasizing their cultural similarities.

In post–civil-war Nigeria, this phenomenon has reached absurd proportions. During the war, President Gowon, who felt that a Nigeria of three regions would always lead to a two-vs.-one coalition, thereby leading the "one" into a secessionist mode, proposed twelve states, based on the major national boundaries. Each state

[26] Van Evera, "Nationalism," p. 155.

[27] Abram De Swaan, *In Care of the State* (New York: Oxford University Press, 1988).

received funds for its capital city, a governor, a legislature, a branch of the national university, and transfer payments from international oil revenues. These gifts for being regarded as a national formation were too generous and induced a politics of national differentiation. The number of states began to expand, and the figure in 1996 stands at thirty-one. And "new" nations are on the horizon still—as of late 1996, the government was considering twenty-two new applications for statehood, all based upon claims of national awakening.

Soviet rule gave similar rewards for establishing your group as a nation. As we know from the work of Barbara Anderson and Brian Silver, the higher the status of your nation in the Soviet institutional hierarchy, the greater the payoffs in jobs and status for the monopoly mediators.[28] In the early period of Soviet rule, the Maris were given autonomous status as a nation. But by invoking a minute difference between the mountain and valley dialects, as I mentioned in Chapter 3, the mountain Maris successfully created a new nationality. The Abkhazis used similar tactics in Georgia to receive autonomy, and the Georgian attempt to deny those differences in the post-Soviet period has led to violence.

This approach to nationalism also helps account for the variety of repackaged Native American nations that emerged in the 1970s, when generous land packages (and the right to flaunt state betting laws!) induced people who saw themselves as "Americans" into ethnic identities connected to indigenous nationalities.[29] Or on another continent: to the horror of state officials in India, affirmative action programs led large numbers of people to register as members of the "scheduled" (the euphemism for untouchables) castes.

The de Swaan model is fully consistent with Donald Horowitz's "law" of group identity: "As the importance of a given political unit increases, so does the importance of the highest available level of identification immediately *beneath* the level of that unit, for that is the level at which judgments of likeness are made and contrasts take hold."[30] Changing boundaries (e.g. by giving territorial autonomy to a successful nationalism) will unleash national differentiation politics at a lower level.

To conclude this section: if you raise the rewards for being considered a nation, the value of the expression "nationalisms/states" will rise, thereby undermining the goals of the liberal ethnic cleansing project.

Ethnic Conflict within National Revival Movements

The international relations perspective on ethnic conflict, as has been argued up to now, has missed a key element to nationality politics—the more you appease

[28] Barbara Anderson and Brian Silver, "Some Factors in the Linguistic and Ethnic Russification of Soviet Nationalities: Is Everyone Becoming Russian?" in L. Hajda and M. Beissinger, eds., *The Nationalities Factor in Soviet Politics and Society* (Boulder, Colo.: Westview, 1990).

[29] James Clifford, "Identity in Mashpee," in his *Predicament of Culture* (Cambridge: Harvard University Press, 1988).

[30] Donald Horowitz, "Ethnic Identity," in Nathan Glazer and Daniel P. Moynihan, eds., *Ethnicity: Theory and Experience* (Cambridge: Harvard University Press, 1975), p. 137.

nationality groups making claims for political recognition, the more actors appear making national claims. While the number of states in the international system can also change based upon incentives for conquest or amalgamation of units, international relations theorists have found it useful to ignore these potential changes in the size and number of states because of their interest in observing the actions of the (more stable) great powers. It is dangerous to ignore this factor for nations, because the costs of entry into the game of national revival are much lower. Nowadays a group no longer needs to demonstrate effective control over territory to make legitimate national claims.

There is a second disanalogy—of even greater consequence—between the study of interstate and inter-nationality relations. The boundaries of states are territorially defined, and despite border wars, remain fixed over time. Classic theories of international relations assume fixed boundaries. But the boundaries of nations are defined by the cultural stocks of people, and these boundaries are forever ambiguous. This point provides a clue to a major source of inter-nationality violence. When ethnic entrepreneurs feel they are losing mediation rights over a nationality group they claim to represent, they have an incentive to punish ethnic brethren defined as apostates as well as ethnic others with whom those apostates are beginning to identify. Any careful examination of the targets within conflicts that are popularly described as interethnic (Africans vs. Afrikaners in South Africa; Basques vs. Spaniards in Spain; Blacks vs. Whites in urban America) will reveal that much of the violence is *intra-ethnic*. International relations models—holding to an isomorphy between state and nation—cannot account for intra-ethnic violence as part of interethnic war. Projections of the nationality scene in the four republics of the former Soviet Union that have constituted the empirical foundation of this book will demonstrate how a tipping model can provide a coherent account of intranationality violence in the context of national revival movements.[31]

In a national revival movement, leaders need to do more than convince those people in whose name the movement is being organized that they would all be better off if their nation, or ethnic group, had greater political autonomy. It must convince people (of their purported nationality) to hook their wagons to the national movement (to change their language repertoires, to send their children to schools with different media of instruction, to become regular churchgoers, to change friendship networks, to ostracize members of a different group who are members of one's wider family). And they must convince people to do these things before there is a critical mass of supposed ethnic/national brethren who have already done so. The expected payoffs for sending your child to a Ruritanian-medium school, to use Gellner's somewhat dismissive label for a revival movement in a low-status cultural zone, is certainly low if the parent is not confident that other Ruritanians will do the same.

As is well known in the collective-action literature, leaders in such a situation consider offering "selective incentives" for early movers. They can be called "heroes

[31] I first developed these ideas from a double comparison: of the violent Basque country and peaceful Catalonia in the wake of Franco's death in Spain; and of violent Georgia and peaceful Ukraine in the wake of the Soviet collapse. See David D. Laitin, "National Revivals and Violence," *Archives européennes de sociologie* 36, no. 1 (1995): 3–43.

of the nation" or be given important honorific titles within the national movement. Writers can be subsidized heavily if they publish their works in Ruritanian, giving them an incentive to do so. Also, the more books on the shelves in Ruritanian, the higher the probability people will assign to the achievement of the goal of the Ruritanianization of culture, and the more likely they will try to learn the language. Slowly, as evidence mounts that others are accepting the new national culture, more and more people will begin to alter their cultural self-representations. This describes the movement toward the "tip," after which change in favor of the national revival should look like a cascade.

Suppose, however, there is a drop in the utility function for accepting the national program somewhat before the tip is reached, say at about 20 percent of the members of the new national group. (See Figure 1.1.) The reason might be that at some point, there is no added honor for switching repertoires (enough have done so to make it ordinary), but the great mass of people still see the costs of operating in a new cultural world as high. If this occurs, then the difference between the expected returns for the status quo and the expected returns for switching suddenly gets larger, inhibiting the next potential switcher from making such a move. From the point of view of the leaders (and the strong believers, those 20 percent who have already moved) this is a disaster. If it became common knowledge that it was irrational for the next potential mover to do so, it would signal failure for the revival movement, giving incentives for those who had switched to the side of the revival to switch back to the side of the status quo ante.

There are a number of tactics possible at this point, and they are carried out by a set of actors whom I have called "vigilantes"—those people for whom the rewards of the revival are so great that they are willing to sacrifice time and their own security to hasten its arrival. Vigilantes can humiliate non-switchers, calling them "traitors" to the nation, as we saw in Ukraine; they can mobilize popular demonstrations in favor of the national revival to give the impression that the tip is imminent; and they can harass nonmembers of the putative nation (and their children) in such a way as to induce them to leave the region, thereby enhancing the demographic argument that their region is ethnically distinct.

If these harassment tactics yield low returns, the "moment" arrives when a strategy of violence seems rational, or at least the only chance left for national recovery. By terrorizing prominent regional actors of their own nationality (or kidnapping their children), vigilantes raise the status costs of not switching. By provoking the police forces of the political center, the vigilantes hope for massive reprisals, the creation of martyrs, and the sense that all Ruritanians are in danger of state-induced violence. To the extent that vigilantes can provoke the center, they can cogently claim to their reluctant fellow nationals that the benefits of the status quo are rapidly declining.[32] Terrorism, then, is a viable tactic in the national revival tipping

[32] Not deduction from any game-theoretic law, but rather reading about the Basque terrorist organization ETA, taught me about the rationality of the action-repression-action cycle as a strategy of building terrorist strength. See Fernando Reinares, "Sociogénesis y evolución del terrorismo en España," in Salvador Giner, ed., *España: Sociedad y política* (Madrid: España Calpe, 1995).

game for vigilantes when the differences in payoffs from identifying with the center and those for identifying with the region begin to increase in a direction unfavorable to the national cause. This analysis suggests that it is the weakness of revival projects rather than their strength that motivates violence.

What are the implications of this analysis for the republics that have consumed my attention in this book? In the four post-Soviet republics under examination here—as has been suggested by the differential successes of the national revival movements—there are two distinct intranational sources for inter-nationality violence—one more likely in the Baltics; the other more likely in Ukraine and Kazakhstan.

In the two Baltic states, the national revival of the titulars tipped even before independence. Those few titulars who maintained Russian/Soviet cultural repertoires disappeared from public view quite rapidly, and most re-presented themselves as long-term nationalists or quickly (and surreptitiously) emigrated to Russia or to the West. With the enormous solidarity among titulars, the incentives for Russian-speakers to assimilate are considerable, and this incentive threatens the mediating position of leaders of Russian (and Russian-speaking) political movements who claim to speak in the name of all Russians (or Russian-speakers) living in each of these republics. Thus, with the tipping game pictured in Figure 1.1 resolved on the right-hand equilibrium in the Baltics, the unresolved tipping game portrayed in Figure 1.2 will be the dynamic source of tension. Aware of the potential assimilationist tip, Russian-speaking leaders will surely try to construct cultural boundaries around their republic's Russian-speakers and seek remedy for the threatening consequences of the double cataclysm. To build these boundaries, they will need to inaugurate a Russian-speaking national revival and to win support from their supposed national brethren. But if the payoffs for assimilation become increasingly attractive, these leaders will need to raise the payoffs for asserting Russian-speakingness, or to lower the expected returns for titular assimilation. Honoring cultural heroes and ostracizing apostates are first-order (nonviolent) tactics. As I reported in Chapter 5, the Tallinn city councilman Aleksei Semionov has already been the object of such a campaign. I predict that Russian-speaking nationalist entrepreneurs will soon begin to spin narratives of loss and blame connected to the events of 1989–93, reminding their brethren the humiliations they (or their ancestors) faced in the dark past. I also expect them to develop a move to give ideological substance and cultural meaning (and perhaps a new name for) the "Russian-speaking population." Under these conditions, a label can become a category invested with meaning. Once the group has cultural meaning, apostasy is not like quitting a club; it is more like abandoning a family.

But if these tactics fail, physically punishing defectors (or their children) and provoking titular police to attack Russian-speaking communities become obvious substitutes. In both cases, the rhetoric will be that of interethnic tensions; yet in both cases, the reality will be that of violence in the attempt to forge intra-ethnic solidarity motivated by fear of a tip toward titular assimilation within the Russian-speaking population.

In Kazakhstan and Ukraine, the outcome of the national revival game (Figure 1.1) among the titulars remains in doubt. The probability that all ethnic Kazakhs will in the next generation consider Kazakh to be the principal language of their scientific, cultural, family, and administrative life seems, in the late 1990s, remote. The probability that all ethnic Ukrainians will in the next generation consider Ukrainian to be the principal language of their scientific, cultural, family, and administrative life seems moderately high, but not assured. Under these conditions, it is the vigilantes among the titulars (not among the Russians or Russian-speakers) who are in tactical charge of changing the tipping calculus. Suppose humiliation of being called *mankurty*, or "Little Russians" is insufficient to motivate the titulars to switch to a titular cultural frame. Suppose the expected returns of maintaining Russian as the principal language of business and professional life remain higher than the titular language, with no real status loss for Russian-speaking titulars. Nationalist vigilantes under these conditions might begin to calculate the payoffs of resorting to violence. Kidnapping the children of Russian-speaking titulars, burning the houses of titulars who join political parties seeking to reinvigorate the union through the promotion of the Commonwealth of Independent States (CIS), and provoking the Russian government in such a way that it might consider sending troops to the republic to protect the physical security of Russians so that martyrs could be manufactured—these tactics can all help alter the expected returns for maintaining a Russian-dominant cultural repertoire. As with the scenario I portrayed for the Baltics, the ensuing violence would be popularly seen as inter-national. Yet the motivation for the violence would have been to alter the calculations of switching the cultural repertoires of members of one's own group.

These scenarios are, to be sure, only projections of current trends based on a tipping model of ethnic violence. But they are not pure fantasies. In Estonia, for example, politicians such as Iurii Mishin, the head of the Union of Russian Citizens in Narva, is most probably hoping that the Estonian police will attack members of his protesting cadres. Should that happen, he knows that he would get support from many Russian-speakers who have been keeping their distance. Mishin's only hope for winning over Russian "moderates" (i.e., those who accept integration, and who watch as their children move toward assimilation) is through the production of viable martyrs. In Ukraine, national activists from Galicia, such as Stefan Khmara, have already tried to foment violence in order to bring "Little Russians" over to the side of true Ukrainians. One of his tactics has been to send trainloads of vigilantes to eastern and southern Ukraine and to provoke Russians into ethnic combat. I assume he wants to create the impression that there are only two possible "sides" to be on: either you are a Ukrainian (and a true nationalist) or you are a foreigner. If interethnic violence were to become self-sustaining, this impression would become a social reality. Under such conditions, the costs to Russian-speaking Ukrainians of remaining a middle category would become prohibitively high. The expected returns of Ukrainizing themselves would, relative to remaining Russian-speaking Ukrainians, increase.

The Estonian and Ukrainian scenarios I have just outlined are but two examples of incipient violence that cannot be ruled out. I cannot assess their likelihood. But I can say that this is one important route toward interethnic violence that has been largely absent from previous analyses of the phenomenon.

Policy Recommendations

Those who accept the Sleeping Beauty view of national revival, as did Woodrow Wilson and V. I. Lenin, support the preemptive recognition of nations by giving them states, whether or not they revealed a desire for states through nationalist mobilization. After all, the peaceful redrawing of boundaries in order to lower the value of the expression "nations/states" would reduce the probability of war. This is the policy of liberal ethnic cleansing, and it was a key component of President Wilson's Fourteen Points as well as the policy preference of many equally well-meaning people today. All they needed to do, according to Wilson, was to register their desire in a plebiscite. But Horowitz argues against partition and secession, as his "law" predicts that such a policy would create new nationalisms at lower levels.[33] Although Van Evera shies away from Wilsonian ethnic cleansing, he nonetheless prescribes that national minorities be given a legal right to secession, and that national borders be (under stringent conditions) subject to renegotiation, in light of patterns of national settlement.[34] Here, I think, Van Evera does not have the incentives right.

An alternative policy, in light of a more flexible theory of the "nations/states" ratio presented here, would require that we demand that countries do more than "recognize" minority rights, for the recognition of such rights (as Van Evera's "robust guarantees for the rights of national minorities, to include, under some stringent conditions, a legal right to secession") might give incentives for cultural entrepreneurs to create new minorities![35]

A key component of an alternative (or better, supplementary) approach relies on an orientation to minority elites that I have called in Chapter 2 the "most favored lord." The basic idea behind this orientation is that for elites who could identify with a regional culture as their "nation" (de Swaan's monopoly mediators), the expected returns for mobility in the center must be greater than the expected returns for a position of high authority in an independent periphery. This means that minority rights (which might satisfy the mediators) are not enough. There must be opportunities for these elites, or aspiring subelites in the cultural periphery, at the center with higher expected returns than they would receive as regional "lords." This involves more than economic advancement. The out-group acceptance of assimilants needs to be promoted. This may require state policies to assure social as well as occupational mobility. Under such conditions, the incentives of elites to engage in ethnic outbidding (demanding ever higher levels of autonomy, and eventually secession) would be reduced, as aspirants for wealth and power in the region would be reluctant to lose the possibility for higher rewards at the political center.

A second policy, in addition to assuring a route to social mobility for minorities at the center, would be a set of policies to reduce the incentives for nationalist bifurcations within regional minorities, as has occurred in Nigeria. First, there ought

[33] Horowitz, "Ethnic Identity," p. 139.
[34] Van Evera, "Nationalism," p. 155.
[35] Ibid., p. 155, but see his qualifications in his note 64.

to be, as in India, a strict system with high bureaucratic hurdles for determining whether a minority within a minority region has a right to secession. Second, the center could negotiate with its autonomous regions a system of transfer payments that increased per capita with the size of the group. Such a policy would give leaders of protected minority groups an incentive to reward leaders of potential spin-off groups for holding back their nationalist aspirations.

Implied from the intra-national tipping game, a final component of a minorities policy should protect people who are of the minority group but have no interest in being classified as a member of that minority.[36] These people may want education for their children in a school where the center's language is the medium of instruction. They may want to join a political party (say on the left–right continuum) that happens to have an anti-autonomy platform. Others may vote for the regional "nationalism" but nonetheless wish to subvert its program privately. As I have pointed out, nationalist "vigilantes" may terrorize such people and this intra-national violence could easily become, as it did in Basque country, the basis for inter-nationality violence.

Reducing potential intra-national vigilante terror—especially when vigilantes have an incentive to provoke state police to incarcerate, or even shoot at them, as a way to create an "us vs. them" type of conflict—may be the most difficult aspect of handling nationality issues. It seems to me that the regional police force must be well paid and made up of people recruited from the region, but rotated back and forth from center to region. Furthermore, vigilantes who have disappeared into the underground must be given well-constructed safe-return offers to help them return to normal life, or else they can become a permanent thorn in society, even if they see the futility of their cause.

The hoped-for result of these minority policies that go beyond protection is the emergence in the society of an ethnic layering. Juan Linz found such a layering in Spain, as Catalans in his surveys felt equally strongly that they were Spaniards as well as Catalans.[37] In the Spanish case, the value of the expression "nations/state" is impossibly hard to code. The number of "nations" is a function of the policies used to contain or promote them; however, as "nations" and their "nationalisms" become cosmopolitan and internally heterogeneous, and when ethnic entrepreneurs know that the rewards for layering are far higher than sustaining hard boundaries, the probability of nationalist warfare will be reduced, no matter what the number of nations.

The search for "real" nations living within "real" boundaries, as has been shown throughout this book, is a chimera. It is a chimera that used to haunt romantic nationalists. It would be foolhardy for liberals to ignore the social reality of nations in search of that very same chimera.

[36] This is the key element in Will Kymlicka's view of liberal recognition of cultural groups in *Multicultural Citizenship* (Oxford: Clarendon, 1995).

[37] Juan Linz and Alfred Stepan, "Political Identities and Electoral Sequences: Spain, the Soviet Union and Yugoslavia," *Daedalus* 121 (1992): 123–39.

13

Future Trajectories of Nation and State

Plato's panegyric on the polis was an unintended postmortem on that institutional form; the glorification of the nation-state by leading elites in the republics of the former Soviet Union may be equally anachronistic. The ideal of the nation-state—where the boundaries of the nation coincide perfectly with those of the state—is being exposed throughout the globe as unrealistic. Yet in the new republics of the postcommunist world, this ideal has maintained its compelling force. Given the identity changes outlined in this book, are approximations of idealized nation-states in the offing? And if not, what alternatives are most likely?

A cogent analysis of nation-state formation requires an understanding of the goals and strategies of state actors as well as those of the members and leaders of all nationality groups that live within state borders. This book has focused more sharply on the attitudes and behaviors of Russian-speakers than on those of the state governments and titular populations. Still, if we supplement the materials presented in this book with findings on the nation-state that I have published elsewhere,[1] we should be able to project the contours of nation and state in the republics of the near abroad.

State and Nation in Historical Perspective

The classic nation-states were hardly natural. State boundaries were the results of wars, dynastic marriages, and contracts between sovereigns. The populations within state boundaries were rarely homogeneous in language, in religion, or in other forms of culture. Still, in eighteenth-century France, the *myth* that all those legitimately living within the hexagon were of the same French nation had explosive

[1] David D. Laitin, *Language Repertoires and State Formation in Africa* (Cambridge: Cambridge University Press, 1992).

implications, in the revolution's ability to legitimize a postmonarchical order and the Bonapartist government's ability to conscript an army cheaply. The mythic formula of nation being the legitimating foundation of a state was easily and powerfully transferred to other places—like a module, it could prosper in virtually any environment—and it became within a century the fundamental state form. State elites sought within their boundaries to forge nations; and nationalist entrepreneurs whose populations lived within specific regions of states sought states of their own. In either case, to use Max Weber's term, culture was standardized or "rationalized" within state boundaries to make possible efficient rule. By the mid–twentieth century, only futurists envisioned a world "beyond the nation-state."[2]

In the very period in which political analysts were assuming that the nation-state was the ideal form of governance, the powerful dynamics that permitted France to assimilate its minorities, China to hide them, and America to subsume them into a new historical community gave way to social and political processes that made rationalization (at least of language) far more costly.[3] In the postcolonial states of India and Africa, regionally based language communities appear to be tenacious, and suggestions that one indigenous language ought to be the official language of all state business—say Hindi in India or Amharic in Ethiopia—are met with anger and derision among minority populations. Early analyses of the failure of postcolonial states to "build" nations focused on the arbitrary boundaries of these states. These analysts were blind to the historical reality that today's nation-states were forged from boundaries equally arbitrary.

An examination of the contemporary period of state consolidation, however, does provide a clue to why twentieth-century postcolonial states have not been on the route toward cultural rationalization. For one thing, colonial rulers established formal bureaucracies in their colonies that operated in the language of the metropole. Indigenous entrants into these bureaucracies developed access to power and influence mainly through their competitive competence in the metropolitan language. Throughout the anticolonial struggles in these states, colonial civil servants lived in privilege and were alone capable of administering the hoped-for postcolonial state. These civil servants were invaluable to the political elites who ran for elective office in the late colonial period; and the politicians could hardly propose a policy to develop an indigenous official language without threatening the capital investment of those who would be entrusted with the administration of the state

[2] Reinhard Bendix, *Kings or People?* (Berkeley: University of California Press, 1978), sets the historical stage for the transition of legitimacy from the monarch to the nation. Benedict Anderson, *Imagined Communities* (London: Verso, 1983), emphasizes the "modular" quality of nation-states. Eugen Weber, *Peasants into Frenchmen* (Stanford: Stanford University Press, 1976), discusses the late development of a French nation living within the French state. For Max Weber on rationalization, see his *Economy and Society* (Berkeley: University of California Press, 1968), pp. 71, 655, 809–38, 1108. Ernst Haas, *Beyond the Nation-State* (Stanford: Stanford University Press, 1964), is one of those visionaries who saw beyond the era of the nation-state, though he recognized that the shift would be slow.

[3] For a creative examination of the emergence of national (demographic) cultures that parallels language rationalization, see Susan Watkins, *From Provinces into Nations* (Princeton: Princeton University Press, 1991).

they were about to inherit. The ultimate acceptance of the metropolitan language as the language of administration and education meant that bilingualism in an indigenous language along with the metropolitan language would remain adequate for most people who wished for mobility in their home region as well as the national center.

A second reason why state consolidation in the twentieth century differs from that of earlier periods is that the set of normal state functions has expanded since the eighteenth century. In the twentieth century, states have played a central role in the provision of education and social welfare. These functions have required ease of communication between a new set of state actors (such as teachers and doctors) and the general population. The announcement in the sixteenth century that all official documents handled by the king of France would be in French, or the decree in the eighteenth century that all court materials in the Spanish king's audience would be in Spanish, caused no popular uproar. But when Haile Selassie tried to do the same, announcing that Amharic would be the language of Ethiopian state documents, there were protests from all over the country, especially from parents who wanted their children to receive education in either a European or their local language.

The institutionalization of an indigenous state language in postcolonial states therefore faces two barriers. First, bureaucrats (and ambitious parents) have an interest in maintaining the official role of an international language. Second, parents and citizens have an interest in maintaining some official role for local languages. An indigenous state language is only one of three (sometimes four) languages competing in each region of a state for dominant status. For example, in India a citizen wishing to have a range of mobility prospects needs to develop facility in at least 3 ± 1 languages: English (the language of interregional communication) and Hindi (the national language, and the language of popular culture) are both essential. Each of the federal states has its own official language as well. Hindi speakers living in states where Hindi is the state language (such as Uttar Pradesh) need to know only 3 – 1 languages, but those living in states where English or Hindi is not the state language need to learn a third. Finally, minorities within states (for example, Marathi speakers in Karnataka) have the right to an education in their mother tongues, but still need to know Marathi, Kannada (the state language of Karnataka), Hindi, and English. For them, four languages (3 + 1) are important.[4] A "constellation" of languages and cultures is getting institutionalized in states that have consolidated in this century rather than a single language representing a dominant nation.[5]

This wisdom—that the twentieth century is not a propitious era in which to construct classically conceived nation-states—has not been lost on those living on the rubble of the collapsed Soviet Union. For example, an article in *Kazakhstanskaia*

[4] A similar exercise is possible to delineate the language repertoire that will likely develop within an emergent Europe, where a constellation of multilingual repertoires rather than a single national language is already becoming institutionalized. See David D. Laitin, "The Cultural Identities of a European State," *Politics & Society* 25, no. 3 (1997): 277–302.

[5] In *Language Repertoires*, I formalize this outcome as a 3 ± 1 language repertoire. The notion of an institutionalized "constellation" is from Abram de Swaan, "The Evolving European Language System: A Theory of Communication Potential and Language Competition," *International Political Science Review* 14, no. 3 (1993): 252.

pravda in 1994 advocated the development of a civic state (*grazhdanskoe gosudarstvo*), because "to construct a national state at the end of the twentieth century when the whole world is sick to death of nationalism and affirms the priority of human worth, can only result in the construction of a multinational country."[6] The implication of this historical understanding for the republics of the former Soviet Union is to expect a language constellation similar to the situation in India in each of the newly independent states. Titular nationals will have an interest in fulfilling the dreams of the 1989 language laws and promoting the titular languages as official. Some strategically placed civil servants, however, will have an interest in maintaining an official role for Russian, even as Russian administrators from the CPSU return to their homeland. Civil servants and other highly educated personnel from the republics will seek to consolidate a grasp on "their" titular language, but they will make it very difficult for other titulars to remain monolingual and have access to all scientific and management roles. This is not all. Given the mixtures of populations, and the prevalence of minority groups in each of the republics, it will be difficult indeed for the leaders of the newly independent states to compel the children of these minority groups to adopt the titular language as the medium of instruction. Since state functions come so close to everyday life, the post-Soviet states will more likely accommodate the desires of minority leaders and provide state services in all minority languages. If this occurs, all citizens desiring a broad range of mobility prospects would need to develop competence in up to three languages (Russian and titular for Russians and titulars; minority language, Russian, and titular for minorities).

Despite this prediction based on a historical sociology of the state, the political trends analyzed in this chapter show a renewal in possibilities for the rationalized nation-state in the post-Soviet republics. For Estonia and Latvia, high levels of titular unity of purpose for rationalization, combined with strong incentives for Russians to assimilate into titular culture, are leading to strong pressures in favor of language rationalization and with it the emergence of Estonian and Latvian nation-states. For Kazakhstan, division within the titulars provokes mostly uncertainty and fear among the non-Kazakh Russian-speakers, many of whose children will eventually emigrate to Russia, Ukraine, Germany, and elsewhere. This will isolate the Russian-speaking Kazakhs, who will feel a similar pressure to emigrate to Russia or accept the long-term reality of a Kazakh nation-state. Of our four cases, only Ukraine is likely to institutionalize a multilingual constellation within a consociational framework.

The implications of these trends are important for the consolidation of "Russian-speaking populations" as ethnic or national formations. The present boundaries of this social formation will give us clues to the nature of internationality conflict and how it might have an impact on the outbreak of violence in the near future. In the Baltics, the analysis suggests that a Russian-speaking minority (mostly bilingual) will long remain a thorn pricking internationality relations. Although they are likely

[6] "Politicheskii tupik dvoinogo grazhdanstvo" (The Political Deadlock of Dual Citizenship), *Kazakhstanskaia pravda*, January 21, 1994.

to remain an active ethnic minority rather than become a national force, there is a small possibility that they could emerge, in another generation, much as the Palestinians did, as a nation seeking a sovereign state. Furthermore, the analysis in this chapter suggests that unlike the Russian-speaking populations in Latvia and Estonia, the Russian-speakers of Kazakhstan are not likely to persist as a group, as most non-Kazakh Russian-speakers or their children, like the *pieds noirs* in Algeria, will disappear and live in their reinvented homelands (primarily Russia). In Ukraine, it is especially hard to project the future of Russian-speakers as an identity group. There is a likelihood that Ukrainian and Russian Russian-speakers in the east and south will consolidate as a consociational pillar and see themselves as part of a Russian-speaking identity group in the context of a Ukrainian state.

State and Nation—A Strategic Analysis

In 1991, as the authority of the Soviet Union receded from the shores of its Union republics, the titular elites who inherited the state apparatuses had a historical opportunity to set the national agenda. They had the power of initiative, to call referenda, to pass new laws, and to make treaties with foreign countries. They could, in the course of their founding activities, attempt to realize states that were not only national in form but also national in content. Meanwhile, the Russian-speaking populations had no organizational resources to take any such initiatives, and they could only respond to the situations the republican leaders fashioned for them.

And so, in this strategic confrontation, each of the nationalizing governments could move first. Their leaders could have pressed for a vigorous nationalist agenda in which membership in the nation would have been carefully controlled by racial, linguistic, or religious criteria (a set of policies I shall loosely combine as "cultural"), or they could have defined national membership based primarily on "civic" (territory, work, loyalty) criteria. In response, members of the Russian-speaking population had a complementary choice. They could have accepted the regime as structuring their opportunities or they could have rejected it. If they rejected it, they could have exited from the republic or sought to pressure the government to recognize the national distinctiveness of their group.

Each of the four end points—illustrated in Figure 13.1—is the outcome of the choices made by a government led by titulars and by members of a minority group. And each end point evokes a somewhat distinct political trajectory with its own strategic dynamics. The outcomes in this tree should not then be considered final but rather new fields in which the game of ethnic politics will be played. Here I will give a capsule summary of the dynamics that are unleashed by the confluence of choices within Figure 13.1.

If the government presses a culturalist agenda and the minority population accepts the regime, *rationalization* will be set in motion. Rationalization, as I outlined earlier, is the process by which a ruler, in order to make ruling more efficient, prescribes a set of practices that become standard for the entire population. Under conditions of rationalization, a significant part of the Russian-speaking population will

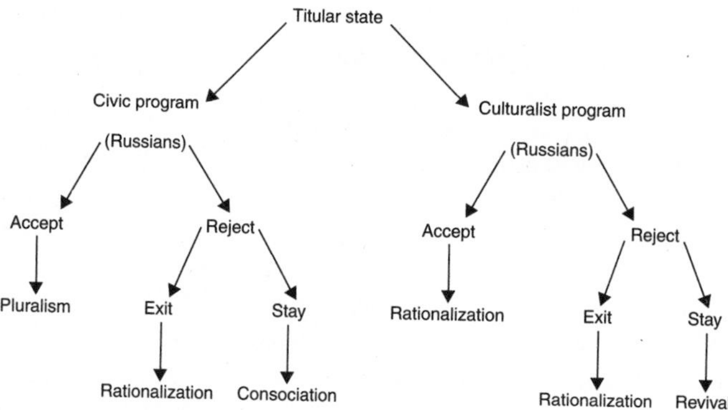

Figure 13.1. Political contexts and national trends

slowly (intergenerationally) become titular in a way that Alsatians became French and Scots British. If the dominant elements of the Russian-speaking population reject the culturalist agenda and refuse to assimilate, they can "return" to Russia or whatever their imagined homeland. In this case, rationalization will also occur, for there will be very few minorities remaining in the republic to assert a subnational program. If either of these trends are dominant, within a few generations, these post-Soviet republics will be ideal-typical nation-states in which a single nation is encompassed within the boundaries of a state.

If the titular republics press a culturalist agenda and the Russian-speaking minorities pressure the government for the right to their own national programs, *regional revivals* will be set into motion. A regional revival is a political movement headed by self-appointed leaders of a nationally distinct minority living within a distinct area of a state who assert their group's "historic" right to autonomy based on cultural distinctiveness. Regional revival movements in Flanders, Quebec, Catalonia, Basque country, and Piedmont have been constant reminders to Europeans and North Americans about the unsettledness of the ideal-typical nation-states. Regional revivals in the former Soviet Union in the late 1980s were reminders to all of the power of cultural entrepreneurs to upset state domination through appeals to common national membership. If this trend becomes dominant in any of the republics we have analyzed, we will observe a politics in which the state reluctantly grants minimal levels of autonomy to a quasi-autonomous Russian-speaking territory within the state while the leaders of the newly recognized Russian-speaking autonomous community press for ever higher levels of such autonomy.

If the titular governments downplay their national agendas (choosing the "civic" course) while the Russian-speaking populations nonetheless organize themselves as political communities within these republics, *consociations* will be in the making. A consociation is a form of government in which there are distinct cultural pillars. Each pillar has a considerable degree of autonomy on a range of political functions (especially in education and cultural affairs), and policy at the center is made through bargains among the leaders of the pillars. Each group has the right to a veto over any policy, and proportionality becomes the basis for political representation, bureaucratic position, and distribution of government funds.[7] Consociational systems have helped bring stable democracy to culturally (quasi)-heterogeneous states such as Netherlands, Belgium, and Austria. Should this be the trend in any post-Soviet state, there would be reserved positions for Russian-speakers in the parliament, in the Cabinet, in the police force, in the army, and in the bureaucracy; and all central policy will be the result of intergroup bargains, with Russian-speaking leaders able to veto any policy they find anathema to their group's interests. If a titular government downplays its national agenda and if the great majority of the Russian-speaking population ignores the opportunity and exits the country, the result will be not consociation but rationalization.

If the titular government downplays its national agenda and the Russian-speaking population does not organize itself (as Russians or Russian-speakers) against the titular majority, *pluralism* will be the political trend. Pluralism, as defined by Dahl, is a political system "dominated by many different sets of leaders, each having access to a different combination of political resources."[8] Under pluralism, political coalitions are distinct for each policy domain, and the political elites in any issue domain are usually nonelites in other issue domains. In the United States, the politics of Italian, Irish, Jewish, German, and Japanese Americans have a pluralist element. Each forms to a limited degree a voting bloc, but cleavages are so cross-cutting that cultural membership is only a limited element of an individual's political identity. (For African Americans, the situation is quite different.) Under pluralism, a *process*, in R. A. Schermerhorn's classic definition, "whereby units or elements of a society are brought into an active and coordinated compliance with the ongoing activities and objectives of the dominant group in that society,"[9] complete assimilation strategies are not essential; many citizens can retain distinct cultural repertoires as long as they integrate into the new society. This corresponds to the strategy of loyalty (through passive integration and citizenship) outlined in Chapter 6.[10] In a post-Soviet republic, under conditions of pluralism, for some issues Russian-speakers might coalesce against the interests of titular-speakers (say on educational policy), but on other issues, the population might be divided by class, by region, or by associations with the past regime. If Russian and titular cleavages in a republic are noncumulative, we can say that the cultural divide in that republic is real but has only limited salience, and in only a few issue domains.

[7] Arend Lijphart, *Democracy in Plural Societies* (New Haven: Yale University Press, 1977), p. 25.

[8] Robert Dahl, *Who Governs?* (New Haven: Yale University Press, 1961), p. 86.

[9] R. A. Schermerhorn, *Comparative Ethnic Relations* (Chicago: University of Chicago Press, 1970), p. 14. Consistent with the definitions associated with the tipping model, integration means that individuals adopt only a limited number of cultural practices of the dominant society, without wishing to cross the fluid cultural boundaries separating them from dominant society. It thus has a moderate value on the assimilation scale. By treating the first steps toward learning the language of the dominant nationality as evidence on the "assimilation" dimension—as opposed to integration—I have altered my conceptualization of the relationship of assimilation and integration from an earlier formulation in David Laitin, "Introduction," in *Post-Soviet Affairs* 12 (January–March 1996).

[10] This is the vision upheld by Alfred Stepan, then dean of the Central European University, in a critique of a version of Chapter 9 of this book.

Concerning the possibilities laid out in Figure 13.1, the four cases that I have examined fall into two distinct patterns. In Estonia and Latvia, hegemony of the titulars in capturing the post-Soviet state has made it possible for the nationalizing governments to set a strong and unequivocal "culturalist" course for their states. Meanwhile, in both Ukraine and Kazakhstan, radical nationalists could not achieve hegemony and have had to play minor roles in the state apparatuses with leaders who have been setting civic courses for their states.

State and Nation—An Empirical Summary

The Baltics

In the Baltics the titular populations were quick to commit to a regime in which the titular language would be predominant. The explanation, suggested in Chapter 2, is that Estonia and Latvia both experienced an "integralist" pattern of Russian and Soviet state expansion. In this model, indigenous elites had great mobility prospects within their republics. Given the relative economic dynamism compared to the political center, the fact that their mobility prospects in Russia itself were quite limited did not pose much of a career problem for ambitious young people in the arts, the sciences, or in management. While Soviet elites did not fully trust Estonians and Latvians who were born in those republics, and who had experienced independent statehood, they entrusted these republics to Russian-born Balts who had participated in the Revolution. These russified Balts hardly spoke the language of their ancestors; but after years of service in their titular homelands, many of them developed fluency in Latvian and Estonian. Although the Russian language was crucial for occupational mobility in the Soviet period, Estonian and Latvian, although less so, remained languages that were often heard in the corridors of republican power. In the wake of the 1989 language laws, very few Balts were threatened by the prospect of having to operate in a language that was "theirs" but which they did not speak fluently. In the national revival tipping game, with virtually all Balts fluent in the titular language, and with Russian thoroughly discredited as an alternative, the cascade to 100 percent compliance with the titular language regime (for the titular population) was instantaneous.

For the Baltic states the collapse of the USSR meant the restoration of the interwar republics rather than the independence of the Soviet-created Union republics. This too had important implications. It meant that Russian-speakers who immigrated in the Soviet period could be denied the right to vote, on the grounds that they were illegal immigrants who had never been naturalized under republican law. Therefore, nationalist candidates in post-Soviet elections would not have to worry about a Russian vote that would undermine the culturalist program. The titulars were therefore determiners of their own fate. In reference to Figure 13.1, the titulars moved first and chose to promote a culturalist program.

Facing the double cataclysm, the leaders of the Russian-speaking population sought desperately to cut their losses. Although nearly all Russian-speakers considered the idea of an Estonian or a Latvian nation-state to be anathema, only a limited percentage seriously considered leaving. To be sure, many thousands of Baltic Russian-speakers returned to their homelands, and they were very much encouraged to do so by the nationalist titulars. Despite this, the overall percentage, as reckoned in Chapter 9, has been low. Because the political and economic systems in the Baltics were far more stable than in Russia or Ukraine, most Russian-speakers had no interest in leaving. Furthermore, their respect for the Balts as Europeans, as having a window on Europe and the Western world, gave Russian-speakers a strong disincentive to pack their suitcases.

Without an incentive to exit, the goal for most of the leaders who remained was to have a consociational system, in which there would be autonomy for Russian-speaking zones, and in which Russian-medium education would remain the norm. While the Russian-speaking leaders recognized the need for facility in the titular language for those whose work demanded interaction with titulars, they felt that in most circumstances, if local government were in the hands of locals, a Russian-speaking lifestyle would be consistent with Baltic republican sovereignty. If members of the Russian-speaking population could have been assured representation in the counsels of state and the power to veto legislation that went clearly against their interest—two vital aspects of a consociational arrangement—the losses incurred from the double cataclysm would surely be recoverable.

But consociation was not a plausible alternative. As can be seen from Figure 13.1, that alternative was ruled out once the titulars were able to commit to the culturalist program. In 1993, as I described in Chapter 6, the leaders of the Russian-speaking population in northeastern Estonia organized referenda for local autonomy. The Estonian government rejected all attempts to seek local autonomy as unconstitutional. Even after the radical nationalist Isamaa Party was voted out of office, with a more moderate coalition governing Estonia in the late 1990s, the government has remained hardheaded in its rationalization program. First, there is the education law. In 1996, the Russian faction leader in the Estonian parliament, Sergei Issakov, led an unsuccessful attempt to amend the 1993 education law that projected the phasing out of Russian-medium secondary schools by the year 2000, and this despite the fact that all agree there won't be sufficient teachers fluent in Estonian to carry out the law as planned. Second, there is the language legislation. A language law requires that all TV broadcasts not in Estonian must be subtitled. For four years this was not enforced, but in early 1997 the government began issuing fines to TV stations for noncompliance. The Estonian TV director Hagi Shein speculates that the enforcement is due to fear that a private Russian-language station was in the offing, and this would capture a large portion of the advertising market. Enforcement of the law would substantially deter the emergence of such a station, by raising the costs of transmission. Thus, even if commercially viable, Russian-language TV will be kept off the airwaves. Third, there is the administration of the immigration law. On July 22, 1997, an Estonian commission led by Foreign Minister Toomas Ilves denied residency to eight former officers of the Soviet army. All eight of them have Estonian wives. One, Evgeni Zobnin, with Estonian children, was deported, but international pressure led the Estonian authorities to allow him back in. The Estonian government fears that demobilized soldiers who are still young may not really be demobilized. Zobnin's father-in-law, Vello Ruusna, an Estonian, said that immigration officials told him, "There is no place for Russians in Estonia. . . . They are nobodies."[11]

In Latvia, where the region of Latgale has been predominantly Russian for generations—with an urban center, Daugavpils, having only 13.8 percent Latvians—there has not even been an organized movement pressing for consociation. At best, at some time in the future, leaders of the Russian-speaking population could seed a national revival and mobilize for regional autonomy, or even sovereignty. But they could not bargain for it within the post-Soviet constitutional frame, thus ruling out consociation.

Consociation was ruled out because the titulars, by moving first and decisively, successfully negated that opportunity. But a Russian-speaking revival was ruled out because Russian-speakers themselves, despite all expert predictions to the contrary, began to accommodate themselves privately to the new cultural order.

Consider Latvia. Juris Dreifelds, a knowledgeable and fair-minded observer of the ethnic scene, raises the possibility of Russian assimilation but sees too many forces countering it. First, he notes that russification in the Soviet period was far more brutal and successful in Latvia than in the other Baltic republics. He writes that

> in Latvia the government, the local party and the KGB formed a cozy seamless web of Russian-speaking camaraderie, reinforced by periodic drinking and hunting parties and other bonding practices, and by the widespread illegal appropriation of dachas and other desired objects. . . . In Estonia and Lithuania natives were much more prominent in the hierarchy of power and the KGB had to contend with structures which provided a counterforce to its optimal programs of repression.[12]

The level of Russian knowledge by Latvians was therefore quite high, providing disincentives for Russians to assimilate linguistically. The second reason is demographic. In 1994, Latvians constituted only 54 percent of the population, had less than 50 percent in the economically powerful 19–44 age group, and 67.3 percent of those aged 75 or older.[13] If Russians know they will have full voting rights within a decade and can then change the language law, and even the immigration law which presently restricts immigration from the east, they should have no incentive to assimilate, but rather to wait for the demographic edge. Third, unlike Estonia, which has in Tartu a city that has a rich cultural and intellectual tradition and in which Estonian is the language of everyday life, Latvia does not have a major center that is unquestionably Latvian in language and culture. This dampens the chance for a

[11] James Carrol, "Russian School Debate Heats Up," *Baltic Times*, November 21, 1996; Kristopher M. Rikken, "Language Law to Be Fully Enforced," ibid., March 27, 1997, and "Estonia Concerned about Fifth Column," ibid., July 31, 1997; Aleksandr Shinkin, "Gospodin Lennart Meri!" *Rossiiskaia gazeta*, June 19, 1997.

[12] Juris Dreifelds, *Latvia in Transition* (Cambridge: Cambridge University Press, 1996), p. 49.

[13] Ibid., pp. 143, 150–51.

dynamic flowering of the Latvian language in an autonomous and free environment.[14] Finally, the Latgale region, with its urban center of Daugavpils, was russified in the pre-Soviet period. There, Latvian language regulations are ignored with impunity. With such a heavy concentration of Russians, it is hard to imagine a cascade toward Latvian. If Latgale remains Russian in language and culture, there is all the more reason for Russians in Riga and in other cities to resist assimilation. Latvians, Dreifelds suggests, have every reason to fear "demographic suicide."[15]

Yet the trends identified in the survey and sociolinguistic data presented in this book are on the margin different from these expectations. Russians in Latvia have shown themselves to be willing and even expecting to assimilate. They seem to have more faith in the ability of the Latvians to construct a viable Latvian nation-state than the Latvians themselves do. Dreifelds's subtle understanding of the political scene suggests that the process of assimilation of Russian-speakers into a Latvian nationality is by no means assured and will face many counterpressures. But the logic of the tipping game suggests that what look like heavy constraints today can easily—if a cascade looks probable—wash away. To the extent that the assimilationist trends continue, as Figure 13.1 illustrates, rationalization of an Estonian and a Latvian nation-state rather than a revival of a Russian (or Russian-speaking) cultural zone within Estonia or Latvia is the more likely outcome.

Despite the trend toward rationalization, the Russian-speaking populations in the Baltics will not fall into the dustbins of history. In the short term, as I have argued in Chapter 12, its present leaders will view as a threat those members of this population who make moves toward assimilation. Not only leaders, but many Russian-speakers in all walks of life, will see assimilators as defectors and will seek to police such behavior through strategies of humiliation or ostracism. This is a potential source of violence as well. In the longer term, as the tipping model presented in Chapter 1 identifies, there will remain a small coterie of Russian speakers who will derive utility from not assimilating. These are the people who will keep alive the memories of past humiliations (such as the denial of the right to vote for so-called "occupiers," or laws of "aliens" directed against them, of having to pass exams in Latvian in order to teach biology to Russians, of being called "niggers" by the press, of having to answer to the investigators working at a linguistic inspectorate), and await the time when a rising social class, with an interest in regional autonomy, will ally with them in the name of a Russian-speaking nation.

A complete strategic analysis of the nation-state dynamic that I am describing would require that I consider the possibility that the titular elites, recognizing the possibility of a future Russian-speaking revival, would preemptively act to split up the Russian-speakers into their Soviet-era national groups. In Latvia, this strategic move would not seem to require much effort. In the late Soviet period, as is well-known, Latvians were overrepresented in the Popular Front (LPF) and underrepresented in the Communist Party of Latvia, and the reverse was true for Russians. But

[14] Ibid., p. 148.
[15] Ibid., p. 143.

Poles, Jews, and other minorities were overrepresented among the LPF candidates.[16] The situation of the Jews is especially interesting. During the Second World War, Jews were stereotyped as communists who helped undermine the republic and deport thousands of Latvians. From the Jewish perspective, Latvians were eager to participate in the Holocaust. Yet in the Soviet period, Latvian-Jewish relations were normalized with little visible tension. This is partly due to the fact that the Jews who had suffered were either dead, in Israel, or in other Soviet republics. The majority of postwar Jews in Latvia came from other republics and they fit right into a secular sovietized Russian-speaking community. Yet a greater majority of Jews came out in favor of Latvian independence than Russians living in Latvia, especially in early 1991 when the voices of Russians in Latvia were much more sympathetic to Moscow.[17]

Nonetheless, the political framework for the creation of a solid identity group of Russian-speakers is currently being constructed. The Supreme Council passed on October 15, 1991, a regulation that the Latvian electorate would be restricted to those who could prove citizenship ties to preoccupation Latvia. In the Saeima elections of June 1993, therefore, 78.8 percent of the voters were of Latvian origin. Only 61.7 percent of the Poles, 45.4 percent of the Jews, 39.1 percent of the Russians, 20.1 percent of the Belarusans, and 6.3 percent of the Ukrainians were eligible voters.[18] No wonder that Plakans concludes: "Notwithstanding the fact that ethnic Russians made up only about 34 percent of the country's population (with Belarusans constituting 4.5 percent, Ukrainians 3.5 percent, Poles 2.3 percent, and Lithuanians 1.3 percent), the public disputes over this and related issues tended to be cased in terms of Latvians and Russians."[19]

In Estonia, in October 1993, the Riigikogu passed the Law on Cultural Autonomy of National Minorities. Specifically named in the law were Germans, Russians, Swedes, and Jews, but any other minority with a membership of greater than 3,000 was invited to apply for national minority status. The law grants these minority groups special rights, for example to publish ethnic language material, to organize mother-tongue education, and to elect a cultural counsel that would be recognized (and partially financed) by the state.[20] One effect of this law—and one of its drafters told me in confidence that this was intentional—will be to divide the Russian-speaking minorities into separate political forces, thereby diminishing their overall impact in opposition to the Estonian culturalist program. There are certainly incentives for minute nationality groups to "go it alone" and get recognition by the state. Yet in the few years since the passage of this law, there has been no mobilization of

[16] Rasma Karklins, *Ethnopolitics and Transition to Democracy* (Baltimore: Johns Hopkins University Press, 1994), p. 100.

[17] Dreifelds, *Latvia in Transition*, p. 40.

[18] Ibid., p. 86.

[19] Andrejs Plakans, *The Latvians* (Stanford: Hoover Institution Press, 1995), p. 189. Dreifelds, in *Latvia in Transition*, puts this more correctly as not Russians but "Russian-speakers."

[20] *Legal Acts of Estonia*, no. 7 (November 30, 1993), pp. 177–83 (unofficial translation from "Riigi Teataja").

non-Russian cultural societies to differentiate themselves from Russians. While it is true that Russian-speakers remain a group "as such" rather than "for such"—to use a Marxian turn of phrase—there is little evidence that the potential concretization of Russian-speakers will be dissolved by the separate mobilizations of Ukrainians, Poles, Belarusans, and Jews.[21]

In the longer term, then, a rising social class with an interest in pushing a Russian-speaking regional revival is not hard to imagine. Consider Estonia. In the mid-1990s there was an economic boom in the region around Tallinn, the national capital. Unemployment was near zero. Meanwhile in the Russian-speaking cities in the northeast, unemployment hovered around 40 percent. The only thing holding back massive immigration of Russian-speakers from the northeast into the Tallinn region was the illiquid housing market, which severely restricted regional mobility. Should the housing market liquefy, and assuming the heavy constraints against international immigration into Estonia stay in force, the incentives for Russian-speakers to pour into the Tallinn area would be enormous. Even though about half the population in the Tallinn region are presently Russian-speakers, the fact that the local government and all government enterprises operate entirely in Estonian would mean that assimilation would accelerate. But suppose the government puts constraints on such mobility, and Russian capital (say second-generation mafia profits) gets invested in the northeast, and it becomes a conduit for trade from northwestern Russia to Europe. Under such circumstances, one would expect periods in which the economic interests of the northeast would diverge from those of the Tallinn region. Should political leadership in the northeast find itself regularly losing out in such conflicts, its interest in a regional revival—allying with the semidormant cultural category of Russian-speakers—could be sparked.

In Latvia, this possibility is equally easy to imagine. A regional revival of Russian-speakers in Latgale, with its center in Daugavpils, could become quite popular if Russian-speakers there feel that their development is being held back, perhaps by a Latvian-dominant government that is more attentive to the needs of the rural population (which is predominantly Lett) than the urban. If the Latvian government quickly changed its strategy, accepting a civic agenda, and thereby agreed to a Belgium-like compromise (with Riga, like Brussels, becoming a binational city), a consociation is not out of the question. More likely there would be resistance from a united Lett front, compelling the Russian-speakers to fight for their regional revival in the streets.

In other words, there now exists a basis for the transformation of a Russian-speaking population into a Russian-speaking nationalist movement. The cultural elements are in place; the historical memories are available for narration; but the economic incentives are only dormant. In the Baltics then, the Russian-speaking *population* is presently an ethnic thorn pricking a successful rationalization program. But the Russian-speaking *nationality* is a potential counterhegemony, which could

[21] Indeed, Petr Rozhok, the spirited chairman of the Estonian Republican Union of Russian Citizens, whose pro-Russian activities were mentioned in Chapter 10, is himself a Ukrainian. See Viktor Cherepakhin, "Aparteid po-pribalitiiski," *Nezavisimaia gazeta*, January 10, 1997.

become activated if conditions ripen. My analysis points to the powerful incentives for the fulfillment, through the cumulative assimilation of Russian-speakers into Balts, of both an Estonian and a Latvian nation-state; but it also points to the long-term possibility of a revival pushed by those who claim to represent a Russian-speaking "nationality."

Kazakhstan

In Kazakhstan, the likely outcome is rationalization, but the play of the game has been and will be quite different from what is occurring in the Baltics. As suggested in Chapter 2, the analogy with Algeria should be kept in mind as the route toward rationalization is mapped. In the wake of the 1989–91 cataclysms, the non-Kazakh Russian-speakers committed themselves to noncompliance with a culturalist program. They had a myth of the impossibility of ever learning Kazakh and a threat that they would exit (or their children would) if a culturalist program ever got seriously under way.

Unlike the Letts and the Estonians, the titulars in Kazakhstan have been divided on the issue of whether to press for a culturalist or a civic program. Because Russian dominated all official realms in the Soviet period, it was utopian, or visionary, to hope for immediate success of a program that would rationalize Kazakh as the language of Kazakhstani politics, administration, education, and business. The "prudent" nationalists, such as Kazakhstan's first president, Nursultan Nazarbaev, pressed for a civic agenda, with the hope that Russians would accede to this vision, with a pluralist outcome. The Kazakh language would play important roles in some domains, and Russian would remain important in others. Both languages would have official roles.

If the Russian-speakers felt that Nazarbaev's government's choice was stable, they might have organized themselves in such a way as to bargain for consociation. The Russian zones are geographically distinct, and a few places, such as Almaty, would require binational charters, such as Brussels has in Belgium's consociational framework. But little effort has gone into such a move, largely because the non-Kazakh Russian-speakers fear that Nazarbaev's civic agenda has no long-term credibility.

The reason for this is that while Nazarbaev has been able to marginalize the radical nationalists, he hasn't been able to silence them. Their voices and programs are daily threats to the Russian-speakers, both Kazakh and non-Kazakh. By the mid-1990s, although the threat of a total Kazakh-speaking administration is not credible, the enormous investment in new mosques gives the impression of an Islamic revival, perhaps even more threatening to Russian-speakers both Slavic and Kazakh than a linguistic revival.[22] Russian-speakers clearly recognize that time is short for them, and nearly all have contingency plans for exit, should a culturalist agenda

[22] Data on mosque construction in independent Kazakhstan in presented in L. F. Kolesnikov and A. I. Artem'ev, "Sovremennaia religioznaia situatsiia v Respublike Kazakhstan," in Rossiiskii Institut Strategicheskikh Issledovanii, *Kazakhstan: Realii i perspektivy nezavisimogo razvitiia* (Moscow: Rossiiskii institut strategicheskikh issledovanii, 1995), pp. 295–314.

become dominant. As Russian-speakers exit, and here I include at least some of the ethnic-Kazakh Russian-speakers, support for the civic agenda will decrease relative to the support for the culturalist agenda. The deepening conflict between the Kazakh nationalists and the "mankurty" will help make the fears of the Russian-speakers into self-fulfilling prophecies. As the threat of the radical nationalists taking control of the state increases, the pace of the Russian-speaking exit from Kazakhstan to Germany, to Ukraine, and to Russia should increase as well. Through the process of the cumulative exit of non-Kazakhs and Kazakh "mankurty" from Kazakhstan, the rationalization of a Kazakh Kazakhstan will result. The Russian-speaking population of Kazakhstan will, if this scenario is correct, likely live for generations—as the Algerians and *pieds noirs* did in France—as a partially assimilable disaffected community in immigrant pockets throughout Russia. Many will remain in Kazakhstan as well, in the wings, as it were, to serve as a future cosmopolitan elite. I have no theory, however, how this cosmopolitan elite might reestablish itself as contenders for the cultural core of a denationalizing Kazakhstani state, but as a social formation, this "Russian-speaking population" will likely consolidate as an energetic, well-educated, but politically marginalized counterhegemony.

Ukraine

In Ukraine, rationalization is not likely. Here I predict consociation.[23]

As in Kazakhstan, the titulars in Ukraine have been divided on the question of whether to pursue a civic or a culturalist national program. The radical nationalists in the west have not been able to undermine the electoral weight of the civic nationalists in the east. But the radical nationalists have been able, because of the low cost of learning Ukrainian for Russian-speaking Ukrainians, to humiliate Ukrainians who do not learn to use Ukrainian in public. Therefore, unlike the situation in Kazakhstan, the prospect of a successful national revival, in which all those who identify as Ukrainians become dominant speakers of Ukrainian, is plausible in the short term. Already in Kiev, in *raion* by *raion*, schools are moving toward Ukrainian as the medium of instruction. Ukrainian parents who might prefer Russian are too embarrassed to announce this publicly, and the capital city—at least in regard to educational medium of instruction—is inexorably becoming a Ukrainian-dominant zone.

Furthermore, the Russian-speakers, unlike those in Kazakhstan, have not committed themselves to rejection of the ukrainization of the society. There is no myth of the impossibility of learning Ukrainian. Russians who do not speak it have little trouble, after a while, understanding it. There is therefore no immediate threat of exit, or turmoil, in response to ukrainization. The costs of a culturalist program are low for all nationalities, with the result that the Russian-speakers in Ukraine are not as worried about the future as the Russian-speakers in Kazakhstan.

[23] For a sophisticated plea for the promotion of a Ukrainian consociational solution—Switzerland being the model—in which "the reality of the cultural linguistic community of people . . . of Russian-speaking culture" is recognized, see V. Gorodianenko, "Ne golos krovi, a obshchii interes," *Rabochaia gazeta* (Kiev), January 13, 1993. Pål Kolstø kindly supplied me with this reference.

With civic nationalists in power in Kiev, eventually the problem of Russian-speaking dominance in the east and the south will have to be addressed. Tensions were mounting on this issue in 1997 in the Russian-dominant city of Khar'kov, in southeastern Ukraine. When the Ukrainian Committee of the Regional Administration of Education developed a plan according to which, as of September 1, 1997, bilingual kindergartens and grade schools would become Ukrainian, Vladimir Komladze, the (Georgian!) spokesman for Rus' in Khar'kov, protested, pointing out that if the plan were to be carried out, only 20 percent of children from Russian-speaking families would be able to attend Russian-medium schools.[24] Because of these potential protests, a bargain—cultural autonomy for republican loyalty—is an obvious solution. Russians in the east and south will be able to work and study in their regions while remaining monolingual in Russian; if they want power or influence in their republic, they will need to learn Ukrainian as well. Ukrainians living in Russian-speaking oblasts will surely feel pressure to develop full facility in Ukrainian, but to live a normal life in their home areas, they will probably continue to rely on Russian as the principal language of school and business life. To the extent to which Kiev (or a western nationalist group ruling in Kiev) presses for rationalization, the ethnic-Russian and ethnic-Ukrainian Russian-speakers living in the Russian-speaking oblasts will continue to act collectively in order to press for their common interests in a consociational bargain.

Why the Renewed Vibrancy of the Nation-State?

In an era of transnational populations and multicultural states, the nation-state is alive and well in the post-Soviet world. Within a generation or two, it will be possible for citizens in Estonia, Latvia, and Kazakhstan to prepare themselves for a range of intra-republican mobility prospects while speaking only the national language of their states. While I believe that a mastery of English will become essential for a wider range of mobility prospects that takes them beyond the boundaries of their state, I am projecting that for many ambitious young people in these three states, a monolingual repertoire will carry them far. And in Ukraine, Ukrainians and Russians will be able to remain monolingual and still achieve social mobility in a wide range of occupational domains.

To explain this outcome, it is necessary to go back to the failure of the nineteenth-century Russian state to go beyond linguistic rationalization, to get the peoples of the periphery to become Russian-dominant speakers. It is equally important to go back to the language principles and practices of Soviet rule, and the success of the Stalinist project to reify titular groups, thereby legitimating their efforts in the post-Soviet period to pursue culturalist programs of state building. Titular elites during the Soviet period had great legitimacy—they were believed to represent "their" people; they lacked only authority to rule. The collapse of the Soviet Union

[24] Aleksandr Chepalov, "Ukraina: Takie raznye novosti. Kuda podat'sia pervoklassniku?" *Reklama* (Chicago), August 27, 1997.

inadvertently gave them that authority, and thereby gave new life to the nation-state in our era.

The historical model of nation-state formation presented at the opening of this chapter identified two factors that made the forging of nations within the boundaries of states especially difficult in the twentieth century. First, formal bureaucracies operated in a cosmopolitan language and its incumbents had a strong interest and powerful resources to maintain the linguistic status quo ante. In the Baltics, because of what I have called the "integralist" model of state expansion, the post-Soviet republican administration quickly moved to Estonian and Latvian. In Ukraine, the Russian-speaking administration in Kiev is much stronger but has been effectively challenged by administrative elites recruited from the west, who are creating pockets of Ukrainian dominance throughout the government. The ideological power of ukrainization—made possible by the formal recognition of Ukrainian by Soviet authorities, especially in the *korenizatsiia* period—suggests victory in Kiev, and in central ministries, within a generation. In Kazakhstan, which had more of a classical "colonial" system of rule, the administration remains largely Russian-speaking, and incumbents have a strong interest in maintaining this norm. But like in Algeria, the logic of an anticosmopolitan revolution, supported by democratic election—but only after a substantial number of non-Kazakh Russian-speakers have exited—is compelling. In the Baltics, the route countering bureaucratic inertia has been easy; but in all four republics, in large part because of the nature of Russian and then Soviet rule, a transformation of bureaucratic linguistic norms is likely.

A second reason militating against the rationalized nation-state emerging in the twentieth century has to do with the provision of government services to minority populations. Indeed, even in Estonia, as I just reported, minorities will be accorded all the linguistic protections that are enshrined in contemporary ideas of human rights. Yet the myth that the titulars "own" their republics and represent the core area of their nation in the world legitimizes policies that require all citizens who want occupational mobility to learn the titular language.[25] The minority language groups in India, Kenya, and Ethiopia do not accord Hindi, Kikuyu, or Amharic similar legitimacy. The notion that one must come to linguistic terms with the post-Soviet titular culture or leave the republic is a powerful one. This myth of titular ownership—which seems to be accepted by both titulars and minorities—will not lead to the rapid abandonment of minority languages; but it will allow for the intergenerational assimilation of the hegemonic national culture.

Assimilation will hardly be rapid; nor can we expect it to remain peaceful. The Russian-speaking populations will give support to interest groups that seek to reduce the strains of the double cataclysm on their constituents. The representatives of this conglomerate social identity will have difficulties protecting the boundaries of their groups through the exaction of penalties for defection. Therefore, assimilation cannot be systematically punished and the mobilization for group rights will

[25] Rogers Brubaker develops the idea of national groups' "owning" their states in his "National Minorities, Nationalizing States, and the External National Homelands in the New Europe," *Daedalus* 124, no. 2 (1995): 107–32.

be hard to sustain. But as a diasporic social identity, its representatives will have an impressive cultural reservoir to rebuild a national myth.

In the Baltics, the Russian-speaking population is both a conglomerate and diasporic social identity. Diasporic memories of a Russian-speaking Soviet world will help bind peoples with quite different roots. But even if Russian-speaking leaders become attracted to vigilante action as many of those whom they purport to represent defect, their task will be hard to sustain. Given the status gains that can be achieved intergenerationally in the Baltics, the trend will be for sustained assimilation into the Latvian and Estonian cultures. But the route to assimilation will not be a velvet one—and to the extent that defection to Baltic identities grows, the incentives of representatives of a Russian-speaking diasporic/conglomerate identity to nurture a nationalist symbolic message—as Russian-speakers—will increase.

In Kazakhstan and Ukraine, given the large presence of titulars in the Russian-speaking identity group—or at least in some versions of it—the population is a conglomerate but not unequivocally diasporic. Thus, even more so than in the Baltics, boundary policing will be harder for its representatives. In Kazakhstan, should the radical nationalists gain power, most of the nontitular Russian-speakers are likely to emigrate, to become an angry but impotent presence in Russia. There should remain in Kazakhstan, however, a cosmopolitan minority of Russian-speakers (mostly Kazakhs) seeking to recapture power in the name of a civic or Western-oriented state. These ethnic-Kazakh Russian-speakers (in alliance with the few Russian, Ukrainian, Belarusan, and Jewish Russian-speakers who remain) will pose a cosmopolitan threat to the nationalizing elites—and remain, as I suggested, a marginalized counterhegemony waiting in history's wings.

In Ukraine, if Ukrainians cascade toward Ukrainian-language dominance, the Russian-speaking population will split into two: Ukrainian nationals and Russian-Ukrainians. The former group could then assert a culturalist agenda. The latter group would become a strong diasporic presence, but it would be a "Russian" and not a "Russian-speaking" identity that draws them together. It would thus be a diasporic but not conglomerate identity. In this case, the notion of a Russian-speaking identity could well become a historical artifact. Politically, the Russians will probably not accept rationalization but instead press, when resources and opportunities permitted, for revival.

But if the cascade toward ukrainization does not spread east, and the country's language situation remains unresolved, Russian-speakers (made up of all nationality groups) will continue to exert pressure on the government as a major political force, and could quite plausibly make claims to be recognized as a consociational pillar. If they achieve this, they will have the institutional resources for policing defection, and a Russian-speaking nationality could be in the making.

It is most likely in the Baltics, but also possible in Ukraine, that a Russian-speaking population will have the memories, the interests, and the possibility of emerging as a new *national* form. But in all four republics, the social formation of "Russian-speakingness"—an identity group forged from the double cataclysm—will continue to play an important political role as titular leaders in the post-Soviet republics seek to fashion, within their republican boundaries, nation-states.

Methodological Appendix

Science advances despite, or perhaps because of, error. I take solace in this banal claim, because in this project I invited error at every step. A student of Africa, I did not begin to study Russian until 1988, when I decided that a student of political linguistics could not ignore Soviet policies. I reached a moderate level of speaking and reading proficiency in the course of my fieldwork, in which I lived with a monolingual Russian family for seven months. During those seven months I also studied Estonian but never gained any proficiency in it or in any other language spoken in the region (save English).

For this project, I relied on large-*n* surveys in four republics, although I had never organized a large survey or even studied statistics before, and as a result, I constructed indexes and ran regressions with an amateur's verve but without a professional's wisdom. To make matters even more difficult, the politics of the region never stabilized long enough to permit the easy establishment of baseline facts. If I were deterred by potential error, I would never have begun.

Science may be tolerant of error. But the scientific community demands that the researcher report all deviations from standard scientific practice in such a way that the reader will be able to estimate their potential impact on the reported results. Some readers will reject my results because of the admissions made in this appendix; others might want to replicate the tests under proper controls to check if the findings hold up in a more rigorous testing environment; others may be satisfied that I have done about as well as possible under the circumstances and accept my results in a provisional way. The goal of this appendix is to help the scientific community assess the quality of the findings presented here, and to prevent others from building their interpretations on what might prove to be an inadequate foundation.

Methodological Preliminaries

There are three general issues that have implications for all future work on questions of nationalism and social identity: the relevance of rationality to a theory of culture; the compatibility of macro-historical and micro-contemporary approaches within a single study; and the validity of focusing on language as a proxy for culture. I address them here in a skeletal way; my hope is that the proof of the methods has been in the doing.

Rationality versus Culture

For years there has been an unquestioned division of labor in the social sciences. Economics has required theories of rationality; the study of culture has required theories of affect and feeling. We have assumed that culture, because it is part of the unquestioned reality in which all people live, is not a realm of maximization, or even of calculation. To a certain extent, this division makes sense. Normal behavior in my society demands that I use English to greet my children, pass a person coming toward me on the sidewalk on the right, and stand for the national anthem. These norms are the result not of calculation but of enculturation. They can be interpreted but not subjected to maximization equations.

Yet there are two important reasons why we cannot justify this division of intellectual labor. First, much of my *economic* activity is the product of habit, not calculation. I no more calculate the expected returns from purchasing the *New York Times* rather than the *National Enquirer* than I do the expected returns of greeting my children in English rather than French. Second, if the costs of one of my customary cultural behaviors were to rise quickly, I would begin to calculate whether these costs had begun to exceed the expected returns. Indeed, Liuba Grigor'ev, one of my principal informants, never questioned her Russian monolingualism until the collapse of the Soviet Union. Suddenly she was willing to forgo good gossip in Russian for free practice in Estonian—that is, she used her time with her neighbor (who is an ethnic Estonian) to practice rudimentary phrases, which convey little information, rather than to pick up on the latest community events. The expected returns for maintaining Russian monolingualism dropped precipitously among Russians in Estonia; as a consequence, calculation of its value based on rational assessments of the future—albeit clouded with uncertainty—became normal.

Throughout this book—and guided by the rational choice framework of the tipping game—I present an approach toward culture that includes rational calculation. I should reemphasize, however, that "rational" is not synonymous with "material." Status and honor are integral to choices about identity; and people calculate about the maximization of status and honor in much the way that they calculate about the maximization of wealth. If this book is successful, it will have legitimated the use of rational choice theory to answer important questions concerning shifts in cultural identity.

Micro versus Macro

I acknowledge at the outset that although microanalysis—that is, the focus on individual choice as a source of social change—can explain how and why individuals shift their identities, or even organize members of their own group to confront ethnic others, it has usually been blind to the broad historical forces that brought nationalism into the modern world.

These concerns have been the long-term preserve of macrotheorists, who focus not on individual choice but rather on how individuals are swept up in the economic and historical forces that drive social change. Ernest Gellner emphasizes uneven industrial development as the motor for nationalist expression. Benedict Anderson has delineated how the introduction of "print capitalism" contributed to the decline of religious solidarity and the rise of national solidarity. Ernst Haas, similarly, has traced the effects of particular forms of "modernization breakdown" on patterns of national arousal. Ideologies linking nationalism and imperialism, he has argued, are far more attractive under conditions of late development than under conditions of early development.[1]

In this book I seek to bridge the micro and macro divide. To be sure, as I showed in Chapter 9, Ernest Gellner's work is pioneering in this direction. Yet Gellner too often portrays individuals as if they were poor players, unable to take advantage of situations that may be driving them and their neighbors into oblivion. I bridge the macro–micro divide in a way that more fully integrates broad historical patterns with an insistence on future-oriented individual choice. It was not enough for me to show that the forces of industrialization drove individuals into assimilation with those cultural groups living in areas of rapid growth; I wanted also to demonstrate that real individuals had incentives to assimilate.

Macro and micro have been mutually informing throughout this book. In Chapter 3 I presented a macro theory of Russian state expansion and showed how it differentially affected the republics analyzed in later chapters. But then in Chapters 4–6 I moved to the micro level, to see how those historical forces affected individuals such as the Grigor'evs, and how individuals developed strategies to cope with the constraints imposed and the opportunities presented by those great forces of history. A compelling theory in the social sciences is one in which the predictions from the macro and micro levels are calibrated. The macro forces of history delimit individual choice, but they do not determine it. Both the identity choices of an age and the relative costs of those choices must be analyzed in a coherent fashion. Bridging this divide, as well as the divide between rationality and culture, has been my methodological ambition in this project.

Language and Culture

In the 1950s an ugly debate in Russia led to attacks on the philologist N. Y. Marr. Stalin, it is said, was enraged at Marr for suggesting that language was (like all of culture) part of superstructure and would change as the Soviet Union moved to full socialism. The idea then current in ruling circles, contra Marr, was that the Russian language stood apart from culture in general and would remain the vehicle for the expression and expansion of socialism.

[1] Ernest Gellner, *Nations and Nationalism* (Ithaca: Cornell University Press, 1983); Benedict Anderson, *Imagined Communities* (London: Verso, 1983); Ernst Haas, *The Rise and Decline of Nationalism*, vol. 1, *Nationalism, Liberalism and Progress* (Ithaca: Cornell University Press, 1997).

It is not my intention to take a side in this historical debate; nonetheless, in this book I treat language as a proxy for culture and linguistic assimilation as an indicator of cultural assimilation. This seems wildly unrealistic, at first cut. Surely, one can learn a language—as an Indian rickshaw driver might learn some English in order to attract fares—without any implications for assimilation. The Irish and Scots rely on English, but they will have you know that they have not become English! Furthermore, assimilation requires a range of readjustments of one's cultural repertoire—in dress, in manners, in religion, in food, and in artistic taste—far beyond the acquisition of language.

Despite these cogent points, I focus here on language as a proxy for culture for two reasons. First, there is the methodological point that the wider the scope of a topic, the harder it is to pin down the details. By taking up a single aspect of culture (under the assumption that language, religion, dress, cuisine, and family patterns are all interrelated), we can see rates and degrees of assimilatory behavior. Under conditions of language rationalization people may remain monolingual in their native language. They may learn enough of a second language to perform minor tasks (unassimilated bilingualism); they may develop full facility in that second language (assimilated bilingualism); finally, their children (or grandchildren) may speak only the language of the rationalizing state, without developing any facility in their ancestral tongue.[2] Each of these stages of assimilation can be monitored and measured. Language, because it is relatively easy to monitor and measure, is particularly kind to social scientists seeking a window on identity shift. This is not to say that I have presented a complete theory of cultural change; rather I have presented an analysis of one aspect of cultural change, one that will need to be calibrated (for a general theory of assimilation) with other cultural realms.

There is a second reason for the focus here on language, as I emphasized in Chapter 4. When the Soviet Union broke up, the language issue was at the forefront of the political challenge to Moscow center. In the late 1980s, the republics of the Soviet Union made their principal challenge to Soviet rule through the passage of language laws that promoted the republican languages above Russian in status. After 1991, with full independence, it was the threat of the enforcement of those language laws that most Russians considered the principal challenge of integrating into republican life. Because language was the most salient cultural issue surrounding the breakup of the Soviet Union, a focus on its dynamics gives us a compelling picture of the overall problem of cultural shift in the post-Soviet world.

Case Selection

Sociolinguistic research has demonstrated that people are notoriously bad reporters of their linguistic repertoires and behaviors. Census and survey reports on language abilities and language use are egregiously untrustworthy. Add to this the problem that

[2] Brian Silver, "Methods of Deriving Data on Bilingualism from the 1970 Soviet Census," *Soviet Studies* 27, no. 4 (1975): 574–97.

in the former Soviet Union—as elsewhere—people had strategic reasons to misrepresent their language patterns. My project required accurate data on language use, language repertoires, and language investments. While I did not want to give up on the high-*n* possibilities of surveys, I wanted to get a clear sense of how those data might be biased, in what direction, and for which subsets of the populations being studied.

The innovative feature of the research design for this project—one that was highly praised by NSF peer reviewers—was to complement large-*n* surveys with ethnographic investigations. These ethnographic studies are quite distinct from those of standard anthropological practice, where a lone ethnographer chooses a unique combination of tools from a large toolbox of standard techniques. In my project, to ensure, or at least increase the likelihood of, comparable data, I applied a common research design for all republics. This approach ruled out a methodology that would yield a random stratified sample throughout the former Soviet Union. Resources permitted only four studies, and thus I had to select cases from the total set of fourteen non-Russian former Soviet republics.[3] This selection had to be done to meet at least two criteria. First, the logic of the comparative method required me to get controlled variation on my proposed independent variable in order to avoid a bias in selection. Second, the practical realities of a project of this sort required ethnographers capable in both Russian and the republican languages to conduct the prescribed field research. The very need for field data posed an additional constraint. I could not in good conscience include republics in the midst of civil war, such as Georgia, Moldova, Tajikistan, and Azerbaijan. Concern for the personal safety of people working on my research project weighed heavily on me. Therefore, discussion of the sources of ethnic violence—analyzed in Chapter 12—had to proceed in only a provisional way because of a lack of variation on the dependent variable. Of the republics at peace, four were the most my budget would permit. I insisted from the beginning of the project—perhaps with the deathly boring geographer in Saint-Exupéry's *Petit Prince* in mind—that I could not sit in Chicago waiting for my ethnographers to bring me their field data. I had to be one of the ethnographers as well as the group supervisor. I had already invested time and effort in the study of Estonia, largely because it served as a perfect comparison with Catalonia, the country I was studying when I decided to drop everything and learn Russian.[4] I therefore planned to conduct one ethnographic study in Estonia. Three

[3] In fact, resources permitted six surveys and four ethnographies. Two surveys were done in republics from within the Russian Federation. I relied on one of these surveys (Bashkortostan) and one from the former union republics (Estonia) to explore some of the issues that went into this book. See David D. Laitin, "Identity in Formation: The Russian-Speaking Nationality in the Post-Soviet Diaspora," *Archives européennes de sociologie* 36 (1995): 281–316.

[4] The key to the comparison is that both Estonia and Catalonia are small regions with movements to promote languages spoken nowhere else in the world. Both had significant twentieth-century immigration from the poorer regions of the central state that ruled over them. These immigrants never learned the local language, given their sense that they spoke the language of central rule. Normalization of Catalan succeeded, in large part because of the presence of a Catalonian industrial bourgeoisie. I posed the question whether Estonia, without such a bourgeoisie, could have similar success in assimilating its immigrants. See David D. Laitin, "Language Normalization in Estonia and Catalonia," *Journal of Baltic Studies* 23, no. 2 (1992): 149–66.

other republics had to be chosen. The exceptional talent of Dominique Arel, Vello Pettai, and Bhavna Dave—far more qualified linguistically and astute anthropologically than any of the other applicants—was the principal reason I chose Ukraine, Latvia, and Kazakhstan as the other cases for intensive analysis. All three ethnographers were advanced graduate students at or near dissertation stage when I hired them. My grant paid for six months of fieldwork; all of them were able to conduct research for their dissertations while gathering data for our joint project. We met in Chicago to coordinate our research programs before we went out in the field, and regular communication by electronic mail enabled us to make simultaneous adjustments in our research techniques in the field.[5] The potential payoff of a long-term collaboration with Arel, Pettai, and Dave was certainly a motive for choosing the republics they were qualified to work in. Therefore, the scientific justification for the selection of cases, which I shall make presently, is admittedly somewhat ex post facto.

Another, powerful justification for selecting these particular republics for study was their variation on a key hypothesized independent variable that might explain differential patterns of interethnic relations and assimilation—the degree to which titulars had occupational mobility in Russia itself both in the nineteenth century and in the Soviet era. This I call the "elite-incorporation" model of state development, with high scores earning their regions the label "most-favored-lord republics."[6] On this dimension, Kazakhstan was low, the Baltic states were medium, and Ukraine was high. My sample therefore looks like a scientifically acceptable selection based on variation on the independent variable. In Chapters 3 and 7 I make inferences from the data collected in these four republics about all the former Soviet republics based on the curvilinear pattern of outcomes explained by the degree of elite incorporation.

But there are problems with such inferences, as Lawrence Robertson has demonstrated.[7] Robertson codes all fifteen former Soviet republics on the basis of a fifteen-indicator variable called "secession"; this is the dependent variable of his analysis. He then codes these republics on the basis of whether they were most-favored-lord republics, on a three-step scale. He also finds that Ukraine is a most-favored-lord republic, Kazakhstan is not, and Estonia and Latvia are in an intermediate category. He then plots the fifteen republics on a scattergram on the basis of their scores on these two variables.

That scattergram captures part of the reality that I outline in Chapter 3. Ukraine, a most-favored-lord republic, has a low score for secession, explained by the elites' interest in the job opportunities afforded them at the center. Kazakhstan, which fits the colonial model, also has a low score, explained by the interest of traditional

[5] Articles by all four team members in a special issue of *Post-Soviet Affairs* (1996) 12 (January–March) give some of the flavor of the separate field experiences. Thus our collaboration went far beyond the common collection of data and deposit of those data in my coffers.

[6] This hypothesis is first offered in David D. Laitin, "The National Uprisings in the Soviet Union," *World Politics* 44, no. 1 (October 1991): 139–77.

[7] Lawrence Rutherford Robertson, "The Political Economy of Ethnonationalism: Separatism and Secession from the Soviet Union and the Russian Federation" (Ph.D. diss., UCLA, 1995).

elites in protecting their investments in the language of the center and their fear that they would be superseded by nonrussianized indigenous elites in the event of a powerful independence movement. In the Baltic republics, the high score for independence reflects moderate to low opportunities at the center for Baltic elites and the fact that few Baltic elites had constructed their careers on their knowledge of Russian.

The problem for my theory, according to Robertson's analysis, is that there are a few cases of intermediate codings on the most-favored-lord dimension (Belarus', Georgia) that have low scores on secession. His analysis suggests that my study suffers from selection bias. If I had chosen Belarus' instead of Latvia, I would have a high and low case of secession in the intermediate category, and the curvilinear relationship found in my analysis would disappear. Thus, for Robertson, who looks at the entire range of cases, there is no relationship, either linear or curvilinear, between most-favored-lord status and orientation to secession.

I have two problems with this analysis as a test of my model. First, there is a problem of the coding of states. If Moldova were "moved" to the intermediate category from the non-most-favored-lord, and if Belarus' joined Ukraine in the most-favored-lord category, the curvilinear relationship discussed in Chapter 3 would look much stronger. I maintain that with the exception of Belarus', the other republics in the intermediate category (Georgia, Lithuania, and Armenia) show (and further research should show) qualities similar to the ones I identify in Chapter 3 for Estonia and Latvia.

Second, and more important, I think Robertson's analysis misses the longer-term dynamics that my model identifies. It seems increasingly clear that in the most-favored-lord republics (Russia, Ukraine, and Belarus') feelings run strong among both Russians and titulars for a restoration of the old Soviet Union. In the non-most-favored-lord republics, cadres of old elites are fighting against time to preserve and institutionalize close relations with the old Soviet structures, but they will not be able to overcome social forces that are slowly working towards a complete break with the past. In the intermediate cases, the break with the Soviet Union was rapid, and the forces seeking reintegration, at least among the titulars, are much weaker than in the other two categories.

I therefore alert the reader to Robertson's critique and admit that a slight change in the codings of states on the independent variable and a different choice of cases for one of the categories, could have erased the results reported in Chapter 3. Since the codings on the independent variable were based on historical judgment rather than a clear inference from reliable data, readers need to be alerted to the possible bias in my selection of cases.

One other issue of selection bias needs to be addressed. In the NSF proposal justifying the methodology, I presented a game theoretical approach to explain the conditions, inter alia, under which Russians would feel pressure to adopt the language of the titulars.[8] This was the micro component of my theory, and I see it as

[8] Those models were first published in David D. Laitin, "The Four Nationality Games and Soviet Politics," *Journal of Soviet Nationalities* 2, no. 1 (1991): 1–37.

complementary to the macro theory focusing on the incorporation of elites. The tipping game, presented in Chapter 1, captures the essence of the earlier models. Game models describe equilibria; they don't provide causal theories. If the tipping model provides a theory of assimilation, how can that be reconciled with standard methodological appeals to base one's choice of cases on variation on the independent variable? Since I opportunistically based my choice of cases on the availability of ethnographers, I decided to leave this problem for others to solve. I only report the problem here.

The Surveys

Original protocol statement (before surveys were administered): This survey will be administered in six republics of the former Soviet Union: Estonia, Latvia, Ukraine, Kazakhstan, Tatarstan, and Bashkortostan. The number of respondents and the methods of constructing a sample will be decided at a later date.

This survey will be translated into Russian (L1), the official language of the republic in which it is being administered (L2), and the majority language of the region within the republic in which it is being administered (L3). The interviewer will address the respondent in any language that is convenient but make available the survey for self-administration in L1, L2, and where relevant, L3. The interviewer should help the respondent interpret any question should there be a problem.

In the surveys, we will use not the designations L1, L2, and L3 but the actual names of the relevant languages. I use the L1 . . . designations only to present a general survey that can be given in all republics.

Introduction [INTERVIEWER TO RESPONDENT]: I am administering a survey on the problems of multilingualism in this republic. The survey was designed by researchers in the United States and six of the former Soviet republics. Your answers to these questions will help us understand the problems real people are facing in regard to language. We therefore urge you to let your voice be heard on this important problem. We will not ask your name or identify you in any way. There is no way that you can be personally identified as a respondent to this survey. We can therefore hope to get truthful answers. The survey can be administered in [NAME LANGUAGE YOU ARE USING] or in [OFFER THE ALTERNATIVES]. Which language would you like to conduct the survey in?

History of the Survey

I drafted a survey document in October 1992 and distributed it for comment to a survey researcher (Henry Brady at the University of California), an expert on language issues (Jonathan Pool), and experts on the republics (Dominique Arel and William Crowther) for comment and correction. In December 1992, I visited ISEPP (Institute for Social and Economic Problems of Population) in Moscow, directed by N. M. Rimashevskaia, to consult on issues pertaining to jobs and social status. In February 1993 I met with Jerry Hough, Michael Guboglo of the Institute of

Ethnography and Anthropology in the Russian Academy of Sciences, and N. M. Rimashevskaia in Chicago to rework the questionnaire. In March 1993 I met with Hough, Guboglo, and Susan Lehmann of Columbia University in Moscow. Technical help at the Institute of Ethnology and Anthropology was provided by I. A. Subbotina, of the Center for the Study of Internationality Relations. The work continued in Ufa, Bashkortostan, where the American research team met with Guboglo and local researchers, and there put together a final document, which would be run first in Bashkortostan. A major addition to the questionnaire at this time consisted of questions about the changes in the economy (for Hough) and demography (for Lehmann) that were not part of the original proposal. Since Hough and Lehmann could piggyback this work onto other grants they administered, we were able to conduct our survey in six republics rather than the four we originally planned on.

Subsequent to the trip to Ufa, I traveled to Tallinn, Estonia, with a copy of the completed questionnaire for Bashkortostan. I worked with the sociological team of Aksel Kirch, Marika Kirch, and Tarmo Tuisk to draft an Estonian version of the questionnaire. It became apparent that many of the changes we made in the original to make the questionnaire meaningful for the Bashkortostan survey were inappropriate for the Estonian environment. I therefore decided that changes in questionnaire wording, answer set, or questions themselves were permissible if the local environment demanded it. All differences in the questionnaires, down to the specifics of wording, are reported in the codebook, available at the University of Michigan archive, where all data from the surveys are available for other researchers.

In all surveys, a "local" sociological team vetted the questionnaire, and members of that team were permitted to add questions to the survey that would be of use to their own research. The principal investigators felt that there would be more local surveillance of the administration of the survey if the local team had an interest for its own research in the validity of the survey. The local team received the data at the same time the principal investigators did, and in most of the cases, the initial publication of the data of the surveys was in Russia or the republics in which the survey was conducted.

The principal investigators did not monitor the administration of the surveys directly. They did no spot checks on the actual interviewing. They relied solely on the reports of the local sociological team for information on the progress of the surveys.

Survey Procedures

Table A.1 gives basic demographic data of the respondents in each of the four surveys.

Estonia

Date of Survey: May 1993.

Administration of survey: The local team of Aksel Kirch, Marika Kirch, and Tarmo Tuisk consulted with me about final editing of the survey. They took responsibility for the translation of the survey from Russian into Estonian. They contracted

Table A.1. Republican surveys: Basic demographic frequencies

Respondents	Kazakhstan	Estonia	Latvia	Ukraine
Total in survey	2,327	1,482	1,146	1,949
Titulars (percent)	48.3	49.2	50.4	57.2
Russians (percent)	51.7	46.7	49.0	30.7
Others (percent)	0.0	6.2	0.5	12.1
Mean age	36.063	40.398	42.456	44.671
Minimum/maximum	16/90	15/84	15/92	16/89
Female (percent)	54.1	54.6	55.9	58.7
City 1	Almaty	Tallinn	Riga	Kiev
Titulars (percent)	40.88	51.6	52.71	80.0
Russian Rs	362	348	356	166
Titular Rs	303	548	252	677
Russian Rs (percent)	30.1	50.7	63.3	27.9
Titular *Rs* (percent)	26.9	78.0	43.6	60.9
City 2	Talgar	Narva	Daugavpils	Donetsk
Titulars (percent)	36.16	4.70	41.75	46.40
Russian Rs	102	227	102	430
Titular Rs	82	10	46	434
Russians Rs (percent)	8.5	33.0	18.1	72.1
Titular Rs (percent)	7.3	1.4	8.0	39.1
City 3	Gur'ev	Jõhvi	Valmiera	
Titulars (percent)	69.28	53.4	81.38	
Russian Rs	31	71	51	
Titular Rs	78	67	212	
Russians Rs (percent)	2.6	10.3	9.1	
Titular Rs (percent)	6.9	9.5	36.7	
City 4	Balykshi	Võru	Ventspils	
Titulars (percent)	76.23	88.2	60.64	
Russian Rs	30	41	53	
Titular Rs	160	78	68	
Russians Rs (percent)	2.5	6.0	9.4	
Titular Rs (percent)	14.2	11.1	11.8	
City 5	Turkestan			
Titulars (percent)	91.34			
Russian Rs	46			
Titular Rs	136			
Russians Rs (percent)	3.8			
Titular Rs (percent)	12.1			
City 6	Chimkent			
Titulars (percent)	57.91			
Russian Rs	126			
Titular Rs	167			
Russians Rs (percent)	10.5			

Table A.1. Republican surveys: Basic demographic frequencies, *continued*

Respondents	Kazakhstan	Estonia	Latvia	Ukraine
Titular Rs (percent)	14.8			
City 7	Petropavlovsk			
Titulars (percent)	22.61			
Russian Rs	308			
Titular Rs	79			
Russians Rs (percent)	25.6			
Titular Rs (percent)	7.0			
City 8	Mamlytka			
Titulars (percent)	24.64			
Russian Rs	197			
Titular Rs	120			
Russians Rs (percent)	16.4			
Titular Rs (percent)	10.7			

Ariko, a private survey firm, to conduct the actual surveys. They subcontracted with a government agency to get the residential data that served for sample selection.

Choice of cities: We chose the capital city (Tallinn), one large city that was predominantly Russian (Narva), one moderately sized city with a mixed Russian/Estonian population (Jõhvi), and one southern city that has had very little Russian migration and represents a "purer" Estonian environment (Võru).

According to 1992 currency lists of adult residents, Tallinn had 120,942 Russians and 129,153 Estonians; Narva, 39,601 Russians and 1,941 Estonians; Jõhvi, 7,000 Russians and 8,000 Estonians; and Võru, 1,128 Russians and 8,451 Estonians.

We thereby had a capital city (Tallinn), two large cities (Tallinn and Narva), two small cities (Jõhvi and Võru), one predominantly Estonian city (Võru), one predominantly Russian city (Narva), and two cities with mixed population (Tallinn and Jõhvi).

Target number of respondents in each city: The method we used is a model to attain 1,300 respondents based on the percentage of the four city populations. (Ariko was contracted to fulfill the goal of 1,600. Their official report on why they failed to meet this goal testified to, among other things, the fear of surveys that was still widespread in the population. I discuss other reasons in the section on sources of bias.) Then we added 50 respondents to each of the six population groups outside Tallinn (to get a sufficiently large sample for each group in cities where they are not well represented).Thus:

Total Russian population in the four cities: 168,671
Percentage of total Russian population in Narva: 23.47%
Russian Rs targeted for Narva: 152 + 50 = 202

Percentage of total Russian population in Tallinn: 71%
Russian respondents targeted for Tallinn: 462 + 0 = 462
Percentage of total Russian population in Jõhvi: 4.15%
Russian respondents targeted for Jõhvi: 27 + 50 = 77
Percentage of total Russian population in Võru: 0.7%
Russian respondents targeted for Võru: 5 + 50 = 55
Total Estonian population in four cities: 147,545
Percentage of total Estonian population in Narva: 1.3%
Estonian respondents targeted for Narva: 8 + 50 = 58
Percentage of total Estonian population in Tallinn: 87.5%
Estonian respondents targeted for Tallinn: 569 + 0 = 569
Percentage of total Estonian population in Jõhvi: 5.4%
Estonian respondents targeted for Jõhvi: 35 + 50 = 85
Percentage of total Estonian population in Võru: 5.7%
Estonian respondents targeted for Võru: 37 + 50 = 87.

Sample procedure:

(a) Currency lists as source of population information. These lists were constructed in 1992, for the purposes of issuing the newly minted Estonian kroons to all residents. It was the best list of the voting age population available, since the local research team deemed the electoral lists of 1990 to be of questionable accuracy.
(b) The survey team chose 25 percent of the voting precincts at random from each city chosen.
(c) The survey team chose three lists at random from the currency lists, with names and addresses. Each list had enough names to cover the entire target sample.
(d) If a potential respondent was neither Russian nor Estonian by nationality, the name was crossed off, and the name with the corresponding number on the second list was put on the first list.
(e) The surveyor had to tell the respondent that the survey could be administered in Russian or Estonian, no matter what the surveyor thought the respondent would prefer.
(f) The surveyor had to return to a house three times before crossing the name off the list and inserting a new name, unless of course the surveyor learned that the person had died or moved away; in that case, the name was crossed off immediately.
(g) If a surveyor needed a new name for the list, a name was provided from the second randomly selected list of residents of the same precinct.
(h) If currency lists included children (no birth dates were provided), a surveyor who contacted a child under 18 questioned the mother if the child was a girl, the father if it was a boy. We wanted respondents in the survey between the ages of 18 and 70, but in fact, the range turned out to be from 15 to 84.

Latvia

Date of survey: February 1995.

Administration of survey: The entire administration of the survey was subcontracted to M. N. Guboglo, of the Institute of Ethnography and Anthropology, Russian Academy of Sciences. The data entry and all checks for data errors were performed by T. Guboglo. The Latvian contact for this survey was M. Ustinov of the Institute of Ethnography. Vello Pettai of Columbia University checked the translation into Latvian and the appropriateness of questions for the Latvian context.

Choice of cities: The criteria for choice of cities were ethnic composition, population, and situation as regards the geographic and ethnographic zone.

All Latvian cities can be coded in one of the following categories: (a) primarily Lett (greater than 55 percent Lett); (b) Latvian-Russian (both ethnic groups from 35 to 45%, with Latvians having the greater population); (c) Russian-Lett (both ethnic groups from 35 to 45%, with Russians having the greater population); and (d) primarily Russian (more than 55 percent Russian but 10–20 percent Lett).

For the population of the city, there are four categories: (a) capital; (b) large city (more than 100,000 people); (c) mid-sized city (50,000 to 100,000 people); and (d) small city (fewer than 50,000 people).

The goal was to choose four cities representing the four ethnic situations and population groups. For this reason, we chose Riga (capital, Russian-Lett), Daugavpils (large city, primarily Russian), Ventspils (mid-sized city, Lett-Russian), and Valmiera (small city, primarily Lett). Riga is in north-central Latvia, Ventspils in the northwest, Daugavpils in the southeast, and Valmiera in the northeast.

Target number of respondents in each city: We chose respondents of each nationality proportional to its population in each city and adjusted to the aggregate role of that situation for the entire country. In Latvia, the capital had 43.9 percent of the country's Letts, and therefore that percentage (352 of 800) of proposed Lett respondents. It had 62.2 percent of the total Russian population in Latvia, and therefore 498 of 800 proposed Russian respondents.

Large cities (other than the capital) had 8 percent of the Letts in the country and therefore Daugavpils got a proposed 64 Lett respondents; large cities had 17.6 percent of the total Russian population, and therefore in Daugavpils there were a proposed 141 Russian respondents.

Mid-sized cities had 11.3 percent of the total Lett population in Latvia and therefore Ventspils got 90 proposed respondents; such cities had 10.3 percent of the total Russian population in Latvia and a proposed 82 respondents.

Small cities had 36.8 percent of the total Lett population in Latvia and therefore Valmiera received 294 of the proposed Lett respondents; small cities had only 9.9 percent of the Russian population in Latvia, and received 79 (of 800) proposed respondents.

Sample procedure: Only in Riga did we choose particular raions of the city. We established the following criteria: population of the raion, ethnic composition, existence of industrial or cultural institutions, and predominant types of living units.

For each raion of the city, we chose 25 percent of the voting districts, each with its full list of voters.

The next step of the selection was the choice of respondents. From the set of streets, alleys, homes, and apartments, we chose every second (tenth, twentieth) house, each even (odd) entryway, each even (odd) floor, and each even (odd) apartment, until we reached the number of respondents planned for the survey. We had rules for variation in sex and age, and those variables colored the selection of respondents at each apartment.

KAZAKHSTAN

Date of survey: December 1994.

Administration of survey: The entire administration of the survey was subcontracted to M. N. Gubolgo, of the Institute of Ethnography and Anthropology, Russian Academy of Sciences. The data entry and all checks for data errors were performed by T. Guboglo.

Choice of cities: There was a multilayered stratified sample. At the first level, Kazakhstan was divided into two types of features: the ethnic component of the city population and the geographic zone of the city within the republic. All seventeen oblasts yielded four general ethnic environments: (a) Kazakh (two oblasts), where Kazakhs made up greater than 56 percent of the urban population; (b) Russian (six oblasts), where Russian made up from 55 to 80 percent of the population and Kazakhs 9 to 17%; (c) Kazakkh-Russian (four oblasts), where both Russian and Kazakh populations were close to 30–40 percent of the population; and (d) Russian-mixed (five oblasts), where Russians accounted for more than 50 percent, and Kazakhs 20–30%. We chose one oblast of each of these four types to ensure that all four geographic regions—north (Severo-Kazakhstanskaia), south (Alma-Atinskaia), center (Chimkentskaia), and west (Gur'evskaia)—were represented.

The second step was to choose cities from the selected oblasts to ensure that we would have examples of each of the following types: (*a*) capital city (more than 500,000); (*b*) large city (100,000–500,000); (*c*) mid-sized city (50,000–100,000); and (*d*) small city (fewer than 50,000).We chose eight cities to represent the four ethnic environments and all four population categories: Almaty (660,522 Russians, 251,336 Kazakhs), Talgar (23,554 Russians, 6,831 Kazakhs), Gur'ev (45,229 Russians, 87,523 Kazakhs), Balykshi (5,310 Russians, 16,812 Kazakhs), Turkestan (5,666 Russians, 34,009 Kazakhs), Chimkent (164,638 Russians, 114,146 Kazakhs), Petropavlovsk (185,429 Russians, 20,375 Kazakhs), and Mamlytka (8,018 Russians, 448 Kazakhs).

Target number of respondents in each city: To choose targets, we took census reports from each of the four types of oblasts. We then computed the percentage of each nationality in each. The target number of respondents for each oblast was the absolute number of that ethnic group's population in the oblast divided by its population in the entire republic, multiplied by 1,000. By this reckoning, in the Kazakh oblast, 250 Kazakhs and 50 Russians were to be interviewed; in the Kazakh/Russian oblast, 290 Kazakhs and 150 Russians were to be interviewed; in the Russian-mixed oblast, 260 Kazakhs and 310 Russians were to be interviewed; and in the Russian oblast, 200 Kazakhs and 490 Russians were to be interviewed.

Sample procedure: The first step in choosing the sample for the survey, once the cities were chosen, was to select raions in each city—a step that was practicable only in Almaty. The choice of raions was based on getting variation on the following criteria: size of population, ethnic composition, presence of industrial and/or cultural institutions, and predominant types of living units.

The second step was to select electoral districts. In each raion of the city we chose 25 percent of the electoral districts.

The third step was the choice of respondents. Here we used the same procedure as in Latvia.

Ukraine

Date of survey: Spring 1994.

Administration of survey: Dominique Arel, in association with the Kiev International Institute of Sociology (KIIS), was the principal contact between the principal investigators (PIs) and the field administration in Ukraine. He assumed full responsibility for the administration of the survey in Ukraine. The Ukrainian team took the basic survey developed for Bashkortostan and revised it to conform to local conditions. The final version incorporated suggestions by the KIIS sociologists Leonid Finkel, Vladimir Paniotto, and Roman Lenchovs'kyi. Several of the changes were based on the results of a pretest administered in Kiev in early March 1994. Survey administration coincided with the Ukrainian parliamentary elections (the first round of the vote took place on March 27, followed two weeks later by the second round) and therefore included many political questions (in addition to the standard survey) on parties, candidates, and issues. KIIS, a private Ukrainian-American research joint venture that works with the Kiev-Mohyla Academy, is headed by Valeri Khmelko, chairman of the Department of Sociology at that university. The institute has a network of twenty interviewers' groups, assigned to cover Ukraine's twenty-four oblasts and the Crimean Republic. Since its foundation in 1991, the institute has conducted several representative all-Ukrainian surveys for organizations such as the United States Information Agency (USIA), the Radio Free Europe/Radio Liberty (RFE/RL) Research Institute (since 1995, the Open Media Research Institute [OMRI]), and the British Broadcasting Corporation (BBC).

Choice of cities: Kiev was chosen because it is the capital of Ukraine and all the republican surveys of the Hough-Laitin NSF project included capitals. Donetsk was chosen as the second city because it has the highest concentration of Russians among the five largest cities of Ukraine (i.e., cities of more than a million inhabitants) and has emerged as the center of counternationalist mobilization since independence.

Target number of respondents in each city: There were no nationality targets in the Ukraine survey: 69 percent of the respondents identified themselves as Ukrainian and Russian; 13 percent responded to the nationality question with "Hard to say"; 2.8 percent were Jews; 0.9 percent were Belarusans; and 4.2 percent answered "Other."

Sample procedure: Because voting lists are not reliable and Ukraine has no central registry of the population, KIIS has developed a sampling method based on post office lists, made possible by the fact that Ukraine is divided into more than a thousand post offices, serving approximately the same number of addressees. To build a sample, random numbers were generated by the mathematical technique of basic numbers. If an interviewer was given, say, the number 5 and was assigned to a particular district, he then selected the fifth post office in the district. (In Soviet administrative practice, these offices were given numbers.) If, however, there were only three post offices in the district, the interviewer then selected the second one (1, 2, 3, 1, 2). At the post office the interviewer selected the fifth street and the fifth house or apartment building on that street. The interviewer then constructed a numbered list of all inhabitants living in each apartment, always listing the women first, by descending order of age. Thus, if five people lived in the first apartment, then the oldest woman in the next one was given the number 6, and so forth. The potential respondents were determined randomly (every third, or fifth, or ninth, say, in the building).

If a potential respondent was not home, the interviewer had to come back twice. After three unsuccessful attempts, or if the respondent refused to answer, the interviewer did not interview the next person on the list; instead, she was reassigned a random number and had to begin the whole process anew. If, however, the interviewer ran out of potential respondents in a given housing unit (say she had to interview the fifteenth person on the list and there were only fourteen people living in the building), she then extended the list by including the residents of the next building (the first person of the next building was counted as the fifteenth person of the first building). If there were no more housing units on the street, the interviewer selected the first house on the next street. What was randomly selected, then, was not a given housing complex but a "chain" (*tsep'*) of addresses, whose inhabitants were rank-ordered according to the technique described above.

Interviews were conducted face to face at the respondent's place of residence. The interviewer read each question aloud and, when required to do so, showed it to the respondent. Questionnaires were prepared in Ukrainian and Russian, and the respondent chose the language of the interview, after hearing an introductory statement in both languages by the interviewer. Each interviewer received general training (four-day classes and the study of an interviewer textbook prepared by KIIS) and was briefed by instructors before each survey on the peculiarities of each research project. Ten to 20 percent of sample addresses were revisited by inspectors to check the work of interviewers. In both Kiev and Donetsk 1,000 respondents were randomly selected and interviewed in two districts. The response rate was more than 95 percent. KIIS coded the data on SPSS files.

Index Creation and Data Analysis

The construction of index variables:[9] The constructed variables consist for the most part of "indexes" designed to capture certain attributes or propensities of the re-

[9] I relied on the research assistance of Eytan Meyers, Andrew Kydd, Matthew Kocher, Meredith Rolfe, and Ari Zentner for the construction of the indexes.

spondent. Typically each index is constructed from several related questions in the survey. The index of cosmopolitanism, for instance, is designed to capture how many of a respondent's immediate circle are of a different nationality. Thus it groups together questions about the nationality of the respondent's parents, spouse, and best friend. The indexes are scaled from 0 to 1, where 0 represents the minimum and 1 the maximum of the attributes being measured. We constructed the indexes by assigning points to the various possible responses to each of the related questions, adding up the points each respondent received, and then dividing by the total possible points that could be given. In the cosmopolitanism index, a respondent received 1 point if his or her father was of another nationality, 1 point if his or her mother was of another nationality, and so forth for his or her spouse and best friend. In more complicated indexes, 2 or more points could be added for certain responses to a question. Dividing the sum by the maximum possible points ensured that the index was on a scale of 0 to 1. If one of the questions was coded as missing for a particular respondent, the raw score was divided by a number equal to the total number of questions minus 1, because no points could have been assigned for a question that was not answered. The index itself was coded as missing if more than a certain number of questions were coded as missing for a respondent.

In the specifications below, Estonia serves as the paradigm; changes in the values for other republics are provided at the end of each section. If the only change is the actual number of the response, it is not indicated here. The precise questions and numbers are in the codebook deposited in the University of Michigan archive. I leave the question and answer numbers given here, so readers will be able to calibrate them with those in the codebook, should they download it from the archive. Throughout, *R* refers to the respondent to the survey. The index of openness to assimilation, because it is the core dependent variable of this book, is described in Chapter 7.

Index of cosmopolitanism

This index is designed to reflect how many people in the respondent's immediate circle are not of the respondent's nationality. It is constructed from the following four variables:

e14 father's nationality
e15 mother's nationality
e16 spouse's nationality
e17 best friend's nationality

The raw score increases by an increment of 1 for each of the following:

R's father is not of *R*'s nationality (e14 $\geq$ 2 for Estonians; e14 $\neq$ 2 for Russians),
R's mother is not of *R*'s nationality (e15 $\geq$ 2 for Estonians; e15 $\neq$ 2 for Russians),
R's present spouse is not of *R*'s nationality (e16 $\geq$2 for Estonians; e16 $\neq$ 2 for Russians), and
R's best friend is not of *R*'s nationality (e17 $\geq$2 for Estonians; e17 $\neq$ 2 for Russians).

Ukraine: The cosmopolitanism raw score also increases by 1 if the respondent identifies him- or herself as "Russian and Ukrainian," a choice not available in the other surveys.

Index of Russian-Estonian mix

This index is designed to reflect how many people in the respondent's immediate circle are of the other main nationality: if the respondent is Estonian, how many are Russian, if Russian, how many are Estonian. It is constructed from the following four variables:

e14 father's nationality
e15 mother's nationality
e16 spouse's nationality
e17 best friend's nationality

For Estonian respondents, the raw score increases by 1 for each of the following:

R's father is Russian (e14 = 2)
R's mother is Russian (e15 = 2)
R's present spouse is Russian (e16 = 2)
R's best friend is Russian (e17 = 2)

For Russian respondents, replace "Russian" with "Estonian" (e14–e17 = 1).

Ukraine: A Ukrainian *R*'s answer of either 2 (= Russian) or 3 (= Ukrainian and Russian) is counted as a "mix"; a Russian *R*'s answer of either 1 (= Ukrainian) or 3 (= Ukrainian and Russian) is counted similarly.

Index of linguistic homogeneity of family

This index is designed to reflect the extent to which the members of the respondent's family speak the same language. It is constructed from the following three variables:

e81 mother's first language
e82 father's first language
e83 first spouse's first language

The raw score increases by 1 under each of these three conditions:

R's mother speaks same language as *R* (for Estonians e81 = 1; for Russians e81 = 2)
R's father's first language is same as *R*'s (for Estonians e82 = 1; for Russians e82 = 2)
R's first spouse's first language is same as *R*'s (for Estonians e83 = 1; for Russians e83 = 2)

Ukraine: *R* gets 2 points if person speaks same language; *R* gets 1 point if person answers 3 ("Ukrainian and Russian") or 4 ("mixed Ukrainian-Russian").

Index of homogeneity of language use

This index is designed to reflect the extent to which the respondent speaks his or her native language with family members, at work, and with his or her best friend. It is constructed from the following eleven variables:

e80 *R*'s native language
e84 language used at home with father
e85 language used at home with mother
e86 language used with paternal grandmother
e87 language used with maternal grandmother
e88 language used with present spouse
e89 language used with preschool children
e90 language used with oldest child
e91 language used at home with closest friend
e92 language used with colleagues at work
e93 language used with superior at work

The raw score increases by 1 if *R* speaks *R*'s native language with each of the people designated in e84 through e91 (i.e., a response of 1 for Estonians and 3 for Russians).

Note: A response of 5 ("Difficult to say or NA") to any of the questions is counted as representing a language different from *R*'s.

Index of language mixing

This index is designed to reflect the extent to which the respondent mixes language with family members, at work, and with his or her best friend. It is constructed from the following eleven variables:

e80 *R*'s native language
e84 language used at home with father
e85 language used at home with mother
e86 language used with paternal grandmother
e87 language used with maternal grandmother
e88 language used with present spouse
e89 language used with preschool children
e90 language used with oldest child
e91 language used at home with closest friend
e92 language used with colleagues at work
e93 language used with superior at work

The raw score increases by 1 if:

R uses Estonian and Russian at home with father (e84 = 2)
R uses Estonian and Russian at home with mother (e85 = 2)
R uses Estonian and Russian with paternal grandmother (e86 = 2)
R uses Estonian and Russian with maternal grandmother (e87 = 2)

R uses Estonian and Russian with present spouse (e88 = 2)
R uses Estonian and Russian with preschool children (e89 = 2)
R uses Estonian and Russian with oldest child (e90 = 2)
R uses Estonian and Russian with colleagues at work (e92 = 2)
R uses Estonian and Russian with superior at work (e93 = 2)
R uses Estonian and Russian at home with closest friend (e91 = 2)

Note: A response of 5 to any of these questions ("Difficult to say or NA") is counted as representing another language.

Ukraine: the answers 3 ("Ukrainian and Russian") and 4 ("Mixed Ukrainian and Russian") will each give *R* 1 point.

Language used in respondents' schools and in their children's schools

Several indexes were constructed to summarize the relationship between the language used in the school the respondent attended and the language used at the school that his or her children attend. These indexes are all coded according to the following matrix:

		Child's school	
		Estonian	Russian
R's school	Estonian	1	2
	Russian	3	4

They were constructed from the following variables:

e95 language used at child's kindergarten
e96 language used at child's elementary school
e97 language used at child's high school
e98 language used at child's university
e110 language used at respondent's kindergarten
e111 language used at respondent's elementary school.
e112 language used at respondent's high school
e113 language used at respondent's university

Ukraine: A response of "mixed Ukrainian-Russian" was coded as no response.

Index of language and national accommodation

The index of language accommodation was constructed in the following manner. We chose agreeing to have street signs in the other language as a reflection of accommodation and measured accommodation as varying inversely with the number of speakers of the other language residing in *R*'s locale and with *R*'s proficiency in the other language.

Table A.2. Coding for index of language accommodation: Response to question H (language of street signs)

Composition of city	Only in respondent's language	In both languages (or hard to say)	Only in other language
More than 67% of one's own group			
R fluent in other language	0.00	0.3	0.6
R speaks it with difficulty	0.03	0.4	0.7
R doesn't speak it	0.05	0.5	0.8
Between 33% and 67% of one's own group			
R fluent in other language	0.03	0.6	0.7
R speaks it with difficulty	0.05	0.7	0.8
R doesn't speak it	0.07	0.8	0.9
Fewer than 33% of one's own group			
R fluent in other language	0.05	0.7	0.8
R speaks it with difficulty	0.07	0.8	0.9
R doesn't speak it	0.09	0.9	1.0

Index of bilingualism

This index was constructed from the following variables:

e80 native language
e101 fluency in Estonian
e103 fluency in Russian
e110—e113 language used in schooling
e114 language of newspapers read by *R*
e115 language of television shows watched by *R*
e116 language of artistic literature read by *R*

Russian speakers who were unsure how fluent they were in Estonian and Estonian speakers who were unsure how fluent they were in Russian were coded as having given no response.

For Russians, the raw score increases by:

4 if *R* thinks in Estonian (e101 = 1)
3 if *R* speaks Estonian freely (e101 = 2)
2 if *R* speaks Estonian with some difficulty (e101 = 3)
1 if *R* speaks Estonian with great difficulty (e101 = 4)
1 if the language of *R*'s kindergarten was Estonian (e110 = 1)
1 if the language of *R*'s elementary school was Estonian (e111 = 1)
1 if the language of *R*'s high school was Estonian (e112 = 1)
1 if the language of *R*'s university was Estonian (e113 = 1)

2 if *R* reads Estonian newspapers only (e114 = 1)
1 if *R* reads Estonian and Russian newspapers (e114 = 3)
2 if *R* watches Estonian television only (e115 = 1)
1 if *R* watches Estonian and Russian television (e115 = 3)
2 if *R* reads Estonian artistic literature only (e116 = 1)
1 if *R* reads both Estonian and Russian artistic literature (e116 = 3)

For Estonians, a corresponding index is constructed with languages switched.

4 if *R* thinks in Russian (e103 = 1)
3 if *R* speaks Russian fluently (e103 = 2)
2 if *R* speaks Russian with difficulty (e103 = 3)
1 if *R* speaks Russian with great difficulty (e103 = 4)
1 if the language of kindergarten was Russian (e110 = 2)
1 if the language of *R*'s elementary school was Russian (e111 = 2)
1 if the language of *R*'s high school was Russian (e112 = 2)
1 if the language of *R*'s university was Russian (e113 = 2)
2 if *R* reads Russian press only (e114 = 2)
1 if *R* reads Russian and Estonian press (e114 = 3)
2 if *R* watches only Russian television (e115 = 2)
1 if *R* watches Russian and Estonian television (e115 = 3)
2 if *R* reads fiction only in Russian (e116 = 2)
1 if *R* reads fiction in both Russian and Estonian (e116 = 3)

Kazakhstan: Same except for k115. For Russians: 2 points if *R* watches Almaty TV in Kazakh (k115 = 2); 1 point if *R* watches Almaty TV in Russian (k115 = 3). For Kazakhs: 2 points if *R* watches Ostankino (k115 = 1); 1 point if *R* watches Almaty TV in Russian (k115 = 3).

Ukraine: For u110–u113, *R* gets 2 points for having as a medium of instruction the other language; and 1 point for answering "Ukrainian and Russian" (response 3) to questions u110–u113. *R*s get more credit for choosing the other language as the medium of instruction in Ukraine than elsewhere. Since they have a choice between the other language and mixed media of instruction, I assume saying "the other language" is a more powerful statement of use of the other language.

Index of cultural conservatism

This index was constructed from the following variables:

e9 relationship to religion
e43 value of economic transition
e46 preferred workplace
e74 son marrying other nationality
e75 daughter marrying other nationality
e71 parental permission for marriage

The raw score increases by the following values:

2 if *R* is a practicing believer (e9 = 1)
1 if *R* is a nonpracticing believer (e9 = 2)
2 if *R* thinks a market economy is unacceptable (e43 = 3)
1 if *R* would prefer to work for a state enterprise (e46 = 1)
2 if *R* would consider it undesirable for his or her son to marry outside his nationality (e74 = 1)
1 if *R* would prefer his or her son to marry within his nationality (e74 = 3)
2 if *R* would consider it undesirable for his or her daughter to marry outside her nationality (e75 = 1)
1 if *R* would prefer his or her daughter to marry within her nationality (e75 = 3)
2 if *R* needed his or her parents' permission to marry (e71 = 1)
1 if *R* could get permission but thinks it unnecessary (e71 = 2)

Ukraine: An answer of "completely disagree" (5) to variables 74 and 76 gets 2 points; "disagree" (4) gets 1 point.

Index of national exclusiveness

This index was constructed from the following variables:

e45 small entrepreneurs are welcome or not
e74 son marrying outside nationality
e75 daughter marrying outside nationality
e178 criteria for national membership

The raw score increases by the following values:

2 if *R* says entrepreneurs are absolutely not welcome (e45 = 4)
1 if *R* is alarmed by entrepreneurs (e45 = 3)
2 if *R* answers 1, "I would not desire such a marriage" (e74 = 1)
1 if *R* answers 2 or 3, "If spouse understands traditions" or "I would not protest" (e74)
2 if *R* answers 1, "I would not desire such a marriage" (e75 = 1)
1 if *R* answers 2 or 3, "If spouse understands traditions" or "I would not protest" (e75)
2 if *R* sees 1, "Culture and language," as criterion of national membership (e178)
1 if *R* sees 4 or 5, "Nationality of mother or father," as criterion of national membership (e178)

Variables 74 and 75, for Ukraine, only answer 2, "Somewhat approve," gets 1 point; answer 1 is "completely approve."

Variable 178:

Ukraine: 2 points for 178a = 1 (language); 1 point for 178d = 1 (parents)
Latvia: 2 points for 178a = 1 (language and culture); 1 point for 178d or e = 1 (parents)
Kazakhstan: 2 points for 178a or b = 1 (language and culture); 1 point for 178d = 1 (parents)

Coding:[10] The construction of the index of openness to assimilation is described fully in Chapter 7. Because of the centrality of this index for this book, I discuss here several technical details concerning its use and changes in it from earlier publications. The variables in this index have been substantially recoded in a number of instances for three principal reasons. First, the survey was conducted by different researchers in the four republics represented in the data set. Although an effort was made to standardize the survey texts, significant differences in the wording of questions remain. Question J (in Table 7.1), for example, asks the respondent to give his or her opinion on whether or not the titular language should be the sole official language of the given republic. In the Latvia, Kazakhstan, and Ukraine surveys, respondents are offered four choices; in Estonia, five. The use of the term "partially" for the intermediate categories of the three similar surveys suggests those questionnaires may be taking substantially different cuts than the Estonia survey on what I assume to be a naturally continuous range of opinion. Therefore, I coded the Estonian range on a 5-point scale, and the other three republics on a 4-point scale, all normalized from 0 to 1. The reader is invited to examine other such choices in recoding. Coding rules were never manipulated with an eye on the dependent variable; but I did base some judgments on the goal of getting normal distributions of values on the scale for each republic.

Second, in some cases I tried to extract additional ordinal variation from a given variable by using values on other variables to stratify existing categories. For instance, when the ethnic Russian respondent is asked to state his or her opinion on the language in which street signs should be written (question H), I further stratified assimilationist responses (as I did in on the index of language accommodation) by considering the respondent's level of skill in the titular language.

Third, in at least one case it is not clear that the survey responses adequately represent variation on a single axis. Among the respondent's choices for question F, assessing the probable future for ethnic Russians, were "leave [republic]" and "organize politically to separate territory from [republic]." Both of these responses are anti-assimilationist, so for this index I coded them identically.

[10] Matthew Kocher, Meredith Rolfe, and Ari Zentner performed the reliability tests, analyzed the data, and drafted this section. Readers who have read earlier versions of this manuscript or preliminary published papers that rely on this index should be aware that the index of openness to assimilation was reconstituted for the preparation of this book. Essentially, two former indexes—assimilation and mobilization—were combined into one. This maneuver enabled me to avoid using the same questions for different indexes. Also, I was able to get a high covariance score for the components of the index, which added to my confidence that I was measuring values along a single dimension. This point is developed in the next section of the appendix.

Convergent validity and reliability analysis: I had a theoretical justification for combining the variables in the assimilation index and for claiming that the resultant index indicates the respondent's propensity to assimilate (or, at the other end of the dimension, to mobilize). My argument is that while each of the components separately might be unreliable as the sole indicator of the propensity to assimilate—as local factors might skew one element away from the overall mean propensity—together they leave less chance for bias. Yet this strategy works only if there is significant covariation among all the variables in the index. The convergent validity of the indicators, because it suggests all the indicators are picking up on the same basic structure, would provide compelling justification for the index.

The reliability index (Table A.3) gives Pearson's correlation coefficients on each pair of variables included in the index. If the form in which I have constructed the index is valid, then we would expect to see entirely positive correlations. Of the 66 coefficients, only one has an unanticipated negative sign, and the average correlation is .28. The alpha statistic, a summary measure of the degree of covariance between a set of variables, is .81. Statisticians consider values greater than .7 to indicate an appropriate index construction. Thus, at the very least, there is strong evidence that the twelve variables that I have selected indicate a common underlying structure. Thus, the reliability analysis supports my theoretical prior belief that all of these variables reflect the propensity of Russians either to assimilate or to mobilize.

I am aware that a more sophisticated measurement model could have been constructed by factor-analytic methods similar to the one I used for the matched-guise experiment. In particular, the procedure I used gives identical weight to all of the variables in the index as measures of assimilation, though it makes sense to suspect that some of those variables pick up the "structure" better than others. Since I have no strong precedents to suggest which of the variables in the index are in fact better indicators, however, factor analysis would have been an atheoretic enterprise. Future scholars, with a theory about weighing, are invited to reconstruct the index.

An interpretation of the quadratic relationship between assimilation and percentage of the titular population in the city of respondent's residence: As I noted in Chapter 7, by far the strongest predictor of assimilationist attitudes among the social-structural regressors is the percentage of titular population in the respondent's city and its squared transformation. This fact holds across the three pooled models that I tested, but the more careful specification of Model 3 increases the size of the coefficients substantially. For Model 3, a one-unit increase in the percentage of titular population yields a 1 percent increase in the value of the assimilation index, while a 100-unit increase in the square of the percentage of titular population decreases the value of the assimilation index 0.75 percent.

However, the effect of the percentage of titular population on attitude toward assimilation varies considerably by republic. Using the pooled two-sample analysis as a guide, I incorporated interactions of the percentage of titular population with both the Estonia and Ukraine indicators, plus an interaction of Estonia with the squared transformation. All three interaction terms are statistically significant at the 1 percent level of confidence. There appears to be a stronger positive relationship between percentage of titular population and attitude toward assimilation in

Table A.3. Reliability analysis of elements of the assimilation index

	A	B	C	D	E	F	G	H	I	J	K	L
A	1.00											
B	0.92	1.00										
C	0.26	0.29	1.00									
D	0.16	0.17	0.11	1.00								
E	0.22	0.22	0.13	0.17	1.00							
F	0.29	0.30	0.29	0.27	0.25	1.00						
G	0.19	0.20	0.56	0.20	0.15	0.31	1.00					
H	0.05	0.06	(0.10)	0.29	0.15	0.27	0.21	1.00				
I	0.22	0.23	0.24	0.34	0.20	0.35	0.31	0.41	1.00			
J	0.17	0.19	0.28	0.30	0.22	0.39	0.39	0.40	0.40	1.00		
K	0.21	0.20	0.25	0.35	0.14	0.39	0.35	0.32	0.37	0.40	1.00	
L	0.32	0.32	0.26	0.41	0.31	0.35	0.24	0.25	0.38	0.32	0.40	1.00

Note: See Table 7.1 for a key to the variable names.

Ukraine than in the other samples. (This finding must be viewed with extreme caution in view of the fact that all of the observations in our Ukraine sample were drawn from only two cities.) For Estonia, the interaction with the percentage of titular population has a negative slope, while the coefficient on the squared term is positive. This finding suggests that the effect of the percentage of titular population is neither as strongly positive for smaller values on the independent variable nor as strongly negative for larger ones, as is the case for the other samples.

A linear prediction of Model 3 using all terms that incorporate the percentage of titular population in the respondent's home city shows that the absolute size of the effect is most strongly positive for relatively low values of the independent variable. The size of the effect flattens out at approximately the 60 percent titular range, then turns gently downward at approximately the 80 percent titular level. The size of effect appears to be substantially larger for Ukraine, but that finding cannot be considered reliable. The size of effect is considerably smaller for Estonia, and though the slope of the graph does flatten out at higher levels of titular percentage, it does not turn downward in the range of sample values.[11]

Potential Sources of Bias

The full truth on potential sources of bias, I fear, would make this section longer than the rest of the book. I will limit myself to some of the highlights.

Wording and order of questions: In each republic, I authorized the survey team to make changes if they felt the wording of the original questions and answers would

[11] On the question whether the nonmonotonicity in the effect of the percentage of titular population on assimilation is significant, I relied on the technique of restricted least squares, as described in Damodar N. Gujarati, *Basic Econometrics*, 3d ed. (New York: McGraw-Hill, 1995), pp. 256–62. The procedure shows that in Models 1 and 2 the null hypothesis that the relationship between percentage of titular population and assimilation is monotonic cannot be rejected. In Model 3, however, the null hypothesis can be rejected at a high level of statistical confidence.

be misinterpreted or considered inappropriate in their republic. In Estonia, for example, we could not ask whether respondents thought it would be good if the titular language were the sole language of official business, as we did in Kazakhstan, because Estonian was already the sole official language. We had to ask whether respondents agreed that it was a good policy to require that all official business be conducted in Estonian. Throughout the questionnaire, changes were made in the wording and order of questions and in the wording of the possible answers. I eliminated some of those questions from indexes when I felt that the bias would be too strong. But when the differences were small, I accepted the questions as equivalent. A master file (in English) that is a systematic comparison of the six surveys is deposited at the University of Michigan archive. It lists all differences in nuance in the wording of questions and answers.

Timing of the questionnaire: The first survey, in Estonia, was completed in 1993. The final survey, in Latvia, was completed in 1995. The potential bias here is quite obvious. The Russians living in Latvia had higher scores on the index of assimilation than those in any other republic. This outcome played an important role in my analysis of the sources for assimilation. Yet it could be argued that over time, as Russians got more accustomed to the reality of living outside of their homeland, they gradually accepted the necessity of assimilation. The timing of the survey, rather than the status and economic variables that I theorized about, could well have been producing the results. While I cannot rule out this hypothesis, I can suggest that if this were the case, then the index of assimilation would have been lowest in Estonia, where the survey was done first. Furthermore, as the costs of assimilation become more apparent with time, one might expect hardened anti-assimilationist views in the later surveys. I am not prepared to agree that the timing of the survey was consequential for outcomes; but readers should be aware of this potential source of bias.

Country teams, local teams: In the intrarepublican regression analyses, the one variable that remains powerfully significant is city of interview. In the Anova tests between republics, the differences between republics are significant again. I explain the intrarepublican differences as a consequence of the percentage of Russians in each city; I explain the interrepublican differences on the basis of the macro variables of the elite-incorporation model and the micro factors of the tipping model. Yet perhaps it should be acknowledged that the survey teams subcontracted with other interviewers in each city and republic. Therefore, the cues emanating from each interview team (on the city level) could have biased the overall results in a direction compatible with the ideology of the interviewing group. Subtle differences in the way a question is asked can have a large impact on the range of plausible or favored answers. I cannot rule out this effect; future intrarepublican and interrepublican testing should control for this possibility better than we did.

Compromises in the administration of the survey: Compromises between feasibility and optimality were everyday occurrences as the NSF team collaborated on the testing instrument. Grave errors were made. In the game models presented in the project proposal, for example, distinct dynamics of assimilation were proposed for urban migrants in the republic and agricultural settlers. The questionnaire was written to capture the hypothesized differences. Yet in our desire to increase the number of respondents to a level that would enable us to divide our respondent population into a variety of demographic subcategories, we reluctantly agreed to limit ourselves to urban samples, which are far cheaper to administer. I agreed to this strategy, not realizing at the time that I would then have almost no agricultural settlers in the samples. Future research will have to test this aspect of the theory, as the data collected in the surveys were inadequate to allow for the proposed tests.

Negotiations over approval of the final questionnaire for each republic were often protracted. In two of the republics, the printed version of the questionnaire differed from the final approved manuscript version, with key questions omitted. This is one reason why key indexes developed for the study, and used in the published Bashkortostan/Estonia article,[12] were substantially revised for this four-republic study.

Another compromise concerned Ukraine. I agreed to the proposal that allowed for a substantial increase in the number of respondents by limiting the survey to two cities, Donetsk and Kiev. I should have been aware that all the other surveys purposely included small towns that were dominated by the titular nationality. The statistical data reveal a curvilinear relationship between percentage of Russians in the city and, inter alia, the propensity for assimilation in three republics. This relationship could not be tested in Ukraine because there were only two cities in the survey.

Conditions prevalent in the near abroad presented problems far beyond those faced by surveyors in Western Europe and North America. In Kazakhstan, for example, local authorities expelled three of the interviewers from Kustanai and confiscated their box of half-completed questionnaires. New copies had to be printed, a city demographically similar to Kustanai had to be chosen (this is Petropavlovsk), and a new interviewing team had to be trained, at an unexpected cost of $1,100. In Estonia, the local team in Narva had trouble meeting its quota for Estonians. Instead of creating new lists until the quota was met, the team decided that they would seek no more Estonians and sent in their questionnaires without reporting the deficiency. Furthermore, the principal contractors lost a number of surveys and then reported technical difficulties in meeting the sample size. In neither case were valid substitutes provided. Such difficulties are endemic to field research in unstable environments without well-institutionalized survey organizations.

The Matched-Guise Tests

I describe the methodological considerations and present the data of the matched-guise test in Chapter 8. I describe the sources of potential bias there as

[12] Laitin, "Identity in Formation." That article was reprinted in the Studies in Public Policy series, no. 249, Center for the Study of Public Policy, University of Strathclyde. In that version, the original indexes (before they were revised for this book) are specified in the appendix, pp. 43–56.

well. Here, I shall only discuss the multisample "confirmatory" factor analysis that went into the two dimensions of evaluation, those of "friendship" and "respect."[13]

Previous research based on this technique, a theory about the underlying components of social status, and an initial analysis of each sample led me to conclude that there was sufficient warrant to accept a two-factor, single factorial-complexity measurement model of status factors, that of "respect" and "friendship." Before going on, I tested this two-factor model against a variety of other models, and the two-factor model came out the best. It did require the elimination of two variables, "pride" and "physical attractiveness," which varied negatively with both factors. I then tested this model against twelve individual samples, four each from Estonia, Latvia, and Ukraine. In each case the samples included (1) a titular-speaker in her Russian guise (TR); (2) a titular-speaker in her titular guise (TT); (3) a Russian-speaker in her titular guise (RT); and (4) a Russian-speaker in her Russian guise (RR). In each case, a two-factor, single factorial-complexity model performed reasonably well and significantly better than other models tested. Consequently, I decided to perform a multisample analysis that would allow me to estimate values for the hypothesized underlying factors in such a way that those values would be comparable for the samples within each republic.

The basic idea was to constrain a small set of variables either to 0 or to 1; for example, "educated" in our final model was a constrained parameter at 1 for the respect factor; "nice" was constrained at 1 for the friendship factor. Meanwhile "nice" was constrained at 0 for the respect factor, as well as "open," "magnanimous," and "spiritual." I was able to adjust the parameter constraints in order to maximize the adjusted goodness of fit index (AGFI).

Using first listwise and then pairwise deletion of missing data in LISREL, I calculated the four samples in all the republics. The results for Estonia, Latvia, and Ukraine were quite promising, with six of the twelve AGFI scores above .8 and none falling below .748. The AGFI was much weaker in Kazakhstan (although the X^2/d.f. is far below 10, which is favorable), with two of the scores falling below .7. I cannot be sure why this is so. As I pointed out in Chapter 8, there are some differences in the names of the variables in Kazakhstan, the administration of the test had special difficulties, and Kazakhstan was the only place where someone who was of the titular nationality assumed the role of the "Russian."

Despite the less than satisfactory results of the single-sample analysis for Kazakhstan, I attempted a multisample analysis for all four republics. This procedure involves recalculating all the parameters estimated in the single-sample analysis while constraining selected parameters to invariance among the four samples. I performed two multisample analyses. The first constrained estimated factor loadings and the overall factor pattern to invariance across each matched pair. Thus, for instance, I tested the hypothesis that factor loadings are invariant between the sample generated by an Estonian in her Estonian guise and the sample generated by the same person in her Russian guise. The second analysis constrained factor loadings

[13] This review of the factor analysis is based on technical reports prepared by Matthew Kocher, who served as a research assistant for this project.

and factor patterns to invariance between all four of the samples from a given republic. The difference between these models is not huge, and the factor loadings are quite close. The AGFIs and the X^2/d.f. are about the same as in the single-sample analyses. Furthermore, *t* values are significant at the 99 percent level for all parameters and all samples, save for the variable "amusing" in Ukraine. For the analysis in Chapter 8, when I compared a speaker in her two guises, I relied on the factor loadings that held invariant the factor loadings for each matched pair; when I compared overall republics, I relied on the factor loadings that held invariant the factor loadings for the four samples within each republic.

Tables of factor score regressions were used for the actual index constructions. These parameters estimate the multivariate regression of all the observed indicators on the hypothesized underlying variables. Thus, for each observation, the index value is the linear combination of all the observed indicators, weighted by the factor scores regression parameters. From the resulting regression tables, I calculated for each respondent his or her scores in each guise for each of the two factors on each of the two models (holding factor scores invariant within each pair; holding factor scores invariant within each republic).

Ethnographic Studies

The material that follows is based on the agenda (modified in accord with subsequent agreements) for meetings held in Chicago in the summer of 1993 in preparation for the ethnographic field research. The ethnographic team coordinated their field exercises in a way that made possible the comparative study presented in Chapters 4–6. (Coordination for the matched-guise testing was also completed at these meetings. The data from that exercise are reported in Chapter 8.) It should be noted that the ethnographic team met two times subsequently, and members were in regular touch with one another in the field (and at their home universities for their own write-ups of the material later on) through electronic mail communication.

Family Histories

We agreed that data on five families should be collected over a series of interviews with at least three members of the family of at least two different generations and at least two distinct households. This information would be far richer than the data we were then gathering through the mass surveys.

1. Information on the following people from each family: An "ego" should be chosen from each family, either male or female, with at least one child of school age. Information should be provided on:
   a. Ego
   b. All ego's siblings
   c. Ego's spouse, spouse's siblings, and spouse's parents

d. Ego's parents and grandparents
e. Siblings of ego's parents (uncles and aunts)
f. Ego's children and their spouses
g. Two friends or work partners of ego

2. Information about the following for each person:
   a. "Language repertoire"
   b. Places lived and school/work experiences at those places
   c. Passport nationality
   d. Sense of "unofficial" nationality or identity
   e. Sense of "native" place, if any
   f. Jobs and work before 1991 and "now" (anthropological present)
3. Information about households:
   a. Patterns of language use when researcher isn't intervening
   b. Description of family library and reading habits
   c. Radio and television patterns
   d. Newspapers brought home
   e. Language used in telephone conversations
   f. Recreational patterns (vacations, leisure activities)
   g. Nature of political talk not induced by researcher (partisanship; support for reform; support for democracy; alienation)
   h. Gratuitous comments on other nationality groups as part of everyday conversation
4. Choice of the five egos were to be based on access and chance, but as wide a range of residences, ages, and political viewpoints as possible should be sought, given the constraints of a low-*n* instrument.

Public Accounts of Language and Nationality Issues

We agreed that each researcher should collect, read, and summarize articles from newspapers, political pamphlets, cultural events (theater, street entertainment, art shows) that deal with issues of nation, nationality, other nationalities, and "Russia" in the anthropological present. The content would be summarized, with extensive use of quotations (in their original language and in translation).

Sociolinguistic Patterns

1. Where?
   a. Markets (especially open flea markets) and shops
   b. Schoolyards during recess
   c. Political meetings/electoral campaigns
   d. Bus queues
   e. Government offices
2. What?
   a. Common language of use
   b. Examples of language mixing

c. Examples of language switching
d. Examples of accommodation norms
e. Status indicators

Self-Reflexive Statement by Field Researcher

We agreed that field notes should be kept (and made available to the PI) about how the field researcher was perceived by the people being investigated. What language(s) did the field researcher use in what contexts? How was the field researcher perceived by the respondents? Did this perception have anything to do with the nationality/language ability/gender of the researcher? How was the field researcher accepted in homes? Did the reception vary among nationality groups? Did the researcher face resistance to the research? By whom? How was it overcome, if at all? These notes were to be in a diary.

Whose Data?

Rights of the principal investigator (PI): We agreed that the PI should get disks or a notebook that provided the information after completion of the field research. He would have the right to publish the results of these investigations as if the data were his. (As the reader surely recognizes, I have noted the source of all data and acknowledged the work of the researchers.)

Rights of field researchers: We agreed that field researchers could (in fact, we encouraged them to) carry out field investigations of their own during the period they were under NSF contract, and that these results did not have to be sent to the PI. These investigations, we agreed, could rely on the same contacts made for fulfillment of the NSF contract. The field researchers would have the same rights to the data collected for the NSF project as the PI, as long as they acknowledged the NSF contract and the PI as the funding source for the data. Field researchers would also get preferred access (before it was sent to the NSF) to the macrosurveys (in which Jerry Hough was the PI) done in the republic in which they worked.

Collaboration: Researchers were under no obligation to collaborate with the PI or with one another. (Collaboration became an agenda item when we met in Philadelphia in 1994 after field research was concluded and we decided to collaborate on a special issue of a journal.)[14]

Citation and Storage of Data

Within the field of comparative politics, as reflected in debates published in the *Comparative Politics Newsletter* of the Comparative Politics Section of the American Political Science Association, there is considerable disagreement over questions of citation and replication.[15] For this book, I have decided to omit all references to the

[14] In *Post-Soviet Affairs* 12 (1996): 2–3, we each give an account of our ethnographic experience, and I describe the reasons for the collaboration.

[15] See the articles of Gary King, Miriam Golden, David Laitin, and Ian Lustick printed in the following issues: *APSA-CP* 6, no. 1 (1995); 6, no. 2 (1995); and 7, no. 1 (1996).

precise dates of interviews, where they took place, and where the records of such interviews can be found in my data archives. I did this because such references appear cumbersome and distracting. I have, however, kept a version of the text with the full references, which can be made available to interested scholars. I have also decided to keep all interview data in my private archive, without depositing it publicly, because those notes contain much sensitive material, including the real names of informants for whom we provided pseudonyms to ensure their privacy. Interested scholars will be given access to all materials related to their research.

The Discourse Analysis

The purpose of the discourse analysis (presented in Chapter 10) was to evaluate the range and power of the "Russian-speaking population" as an identity category in the post-Soviet diaspora. The reason for having done it, however, is bad planning. In the original proposal for the NSF, Hough and I envisioned that the fieldwork would precede the mass surveys. Only then could the insights developed in the field be incorporated into the survey instrument, for confirmation. Unfortunately, shortly after we received the grant, the expected cost of the surveys began to rise so rapidly that it was about to exceed our budget. We decided to begin the surveys immediately, well before the field team was chosen. Because my concern was with Russians in the near abroad, in the group discussions concerning the sample I ruled that we should interview only titulars, Russians, and (in some republics) a third nationality. But during my fieldwork in Narva, well after two of the surveys were completed, I became acutely aware of the existence of a social (but not official) category of people—"Russian-speakers." I intuited their political significance from watching the rhetorical strategies of nontitulars seeking to organize a representative assembly of noncitizens. The activists were intent on finding a term that would put the set of people they hoped to represent in a more positive light. Although non-Russian Russian-speakers were not numerous, their existence in Estonia played into the hands of the antichauvinist Russian activists. The methodological problem I faced was that the mass survey could not tap into this insight, so I was unable to get cogent data to demonstrate the importance of this phenomenon.

A clear alternative was to engage in a discourse analysis of identity categories in the post-Soviet press. I took advantage of a huge collection of clippings that Pål Kolstø made available to me. Because he had collected these articles to obtain a full account of political events, he paid no attention to the rhetorical representations of identity. Thus there was no bias in the selection of articles.

My goal was to analyze about eighty articles for each republic, looking only at articles that contained at least three identity terms. We separated the articles first by republic, then by whether the newspaper was from the Russian Federation or from the republic. We then separated them by year of publication, one pile for articles through 1993, another pile for articles after 1993. We separated the articles from the Russian Federation again according to whether the newspaper was old guard or liberal. We separated the articles from the republics according to whether they were letters, news reports, opinion pieces, or interviews. We hoped to obtain ten articles in each of our categories from Russian publications and five in each category from republican publications. From each pile we then randomly selected articles until we met our quotas, though if we found a possibility of exchanging articles within a pile in order to increase the range of newspapers, we would do so. In fact, we could not meet our quotas for many of the categories and regularly had to use articles from another pile to serve as proxies. Proxies, however, were coded truthfully. Another problem was that the distinction between news reports and opinion pieces and even between opinion pieces and letters was difficult to apply in practice. Even interviews were usually embedded in news and opinion articles. The goal, however, was not to meet the quotas but to build in as much variation in the discourse as the data set would allow.

It was particularly difficult to code the Russian press on a liberal–old-guard dimension, especially with a focus on the nationality issue. We relied initially on codings developed by Joel Ostrow, who was writing his dissertation at Berkeley on the 1993 elections. He based his codings on the support newspapers gave to the candidates, which he ranked on a liberal/old-guard dimension, mostly from the point of view of political and economic reform. We supplemented Ostrow's codings with a parallel project provided by the Foreign Broadcast Information Service.[16] In general, *Rossiiskaia gazeta*, *Izvestiia*, *Novoe vremia*, *Kommersant*, *Literaturnaia gazeta*, *Segodnia*, *Argumenty i fakty*, and *Emigratsiia* were coded as liberal. *Pravda*, *Rabochaia tribuna*, *Den'*, *Trud*, and *Krasnaia zvezda* were coded as old guard. Throughout this coding exercise, June Farris of the University of Chicago Library and Molly Molloy of the Hoover Institution Library provided invaluable analysis of the newspaper collection. Again, making perfect judgments was less important for this exercise than maximizing the range of viewpoints.

The articles were coded by a team of four research assistants, two of them native speakers of Russian. They listed every use of an identity term, translated it in a wider context, and gave a valence on how the term was evaluated by the "speaker." In an article by a Russian, in which a titular is quoted, for example, the "voice" that was recorded was that of the titular, and his or her valence was evaluated by the context. Over a five-month period, this team, led by Elise Giuliano, met weekly to coordinate coding criteria. These data are not well documented, and therefore are not appropriate for public deposit. Scholars with an interest in replication of the data analysis are welcome to contact the author.

Readers will need to make their own judgment about sources of potential bias in this data set. One source is the lack of titular-language press.[17] But this drawback

[16] See Joel Ostrow, "The Press and the Campaign: Comprehensive but Fragmented Coverage," in Timothy Colton and Jerry Hough, eds., *Growing Pains: Russian Democracy and the Election of 1993* (Washington, D.C.: Brookings Institution, forthcoming), for his presentation of the coding scheme. The FBIS codings are published as FBIS-SOV-95-233-S, Tuesday, December 5, 1995, "Daily Report, Supplement, Central Eurasia, Pre-Election Survey of Major Russian Media, A Reference Aid."

[17] In much of my past work, for example, David D. Laitin, *Politics, Language, and Thought* (Chicago: University of Chicago Press, 1977), and David D. Laitin and Guadalupe Rodríguez, "Language, Ideology and the Press in Catalonia," *American Anthropologist* 94, no. 1 (1992): 9–30, I have found that the language used in political discourse in multilingual settings influences the con-

was partially remedied by the large number of reported references to titulars in the news articles. Another source of bias is the inevitable difference between newspaper discourse and the discourses of radio, TV, the street, and business. Yet I believe that the data set analyzed in Chapter 10 is remarkable for its ability to capture the range of nationalist expression in the post-Soviet period. Readers who disagree are invited to construct comparable data sets to see if they get different results. Finally, it could be argued that newspaper discourse (even in the republican press) is quite Moscow-centric, as most correspondents sharpened their professional claws in Moscow. There is some truth to this charge; but it should be noted that the communications center of the region ought to be heavily represented in a data set that seeks to capture the communication of nationalist categories.

Perhaps the most compelling argument for the lack of bias in the discourse data is the finding that the use of "Russian-speaking" as a social category has been declining over time. If there was any place in all the data-collection activities for this book where my expectations went directly against what the data revealed, this is the case.

WITH this appendix and accompanying documents in the University of Michigan archive, readers who wish to replicate our experiments and surveys will be able to do so. Science, because it is always built on imperfect experiments, demands replication of the work reported here.

---

tent of the message. I therefore would recommend a replication of Chapter 10 with reliance on the republican-language press. Even if such a replication produced different results, the findings of Chapter 10, that Russian-speakers have internalized a Russian-speaking identity, would not be undermined.

Authorities Consulted

Subject Index

The Wilder House Series in Politics, History and Culture

Language and Power: Exploring Political Cultures in Indonesia
by Benedict R. O'G. Anderson
Bandits and Bureaucrats: The Ottoman Route to State Centralization
by Karen Barkey
Making the Fascist Self: The Political Culture of Interwar Italy
by Mabel Berezin
Reclaiming the Sacred: Lay Region and Popular Politics in Revolutionary France
by Suzanne Desan
Manufacturing Inequality: Gender Division in the French and British Metalworking Industries
by Laura Lee Downs
State and Society in Medieval Europe: Gwynedd and Languedoc under Outside Rule
by James B. Given
New Voices in the Nation: Women and the Greek Resistance, 1941–1964
by Janet Hart
The Rise of Christian Democracy in Europe
by Stathis N. Kalyvas
The Presence of the Past: Chronicles, Politics, and Culture in Sinhala Life
by Steven Kemper
Identity in Formation: The Russian-Speaking Populations in the Near Abroad
by David D. Laitin
True France: The Wars over Cultural Identity, 1900–1945
by Herman Lebovics
Unsettled States, Disputed Lands: Britain and Ireland, France and Algeria, Israel and the West Bank–Gaza
by Ian S. Lustick
Communities of Grain: Rural Rebellion in Comparative Perspective
by Victor V. Magagna
Divided Nations: Class, Politics, and Nationalism in the Basque Country and Catalonia
by Juan Diez Medrano
Hausaland Divided: Colonialism and Independence in Nigeria and Niger
by William F. S. Miles
Moral Aspects of Economic Growth and Other Essays
by Barrington Moore, Jr.
Democracy in Translation: Understanding Politics in an Unfamiliar Culture
by Frederic C. Schaffer
Democracy, Revolution, and History
edited by Theda Skocpol
"We Ask for British Justice": Workers and Racial Difference in Late Imperial Britain
by Laura Tabili
Gifts, Favors, and Banquets: The Art of Social Relationships in China
by Mayfair Mei-hui Yang